Yale Language Series

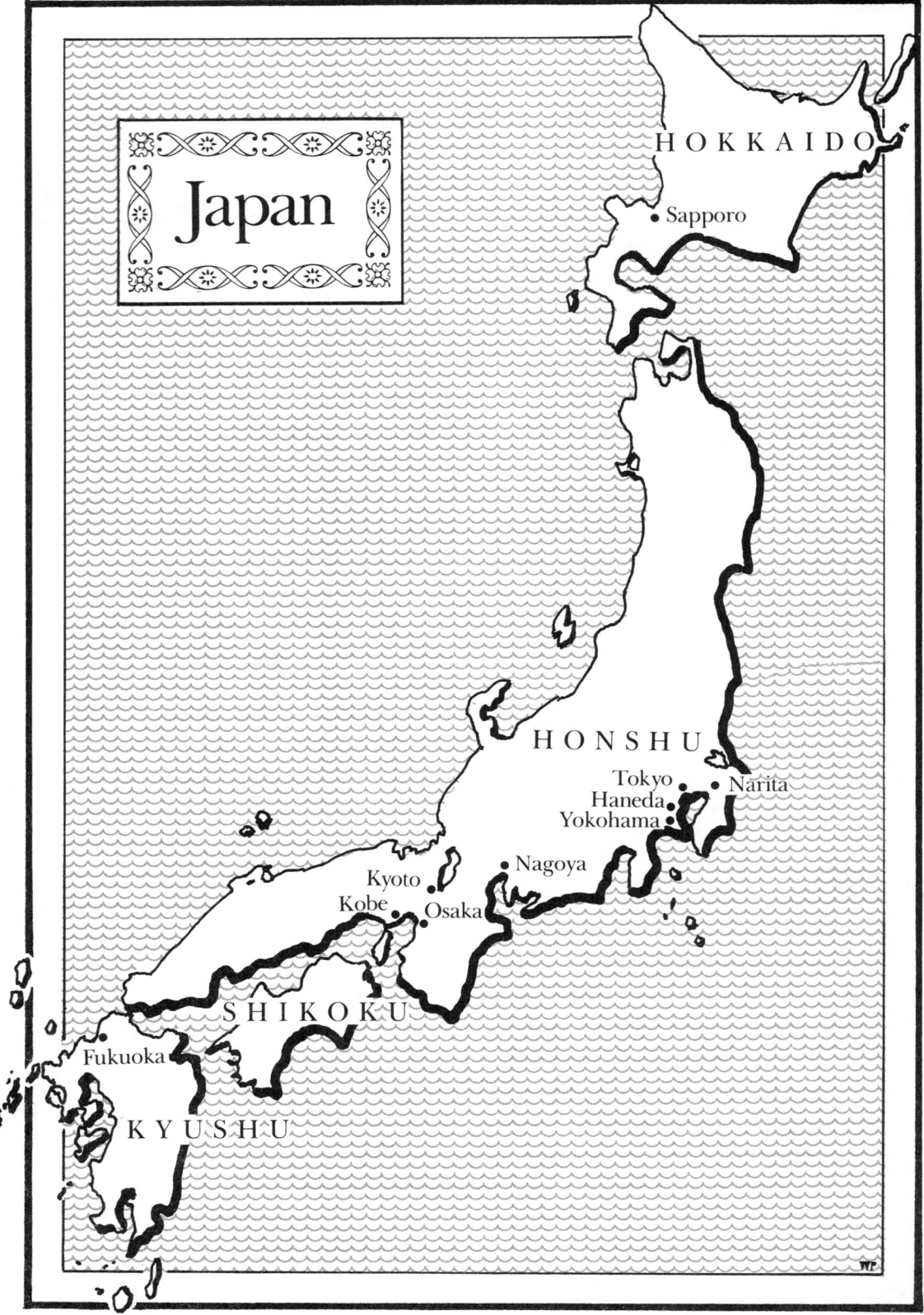

Japanese: The Spoken Language

PART 2

Eleanor Harz Jorden
with Mari Noda

Yale University Press
New Haven and London

For the preparation of parts of the manuscript of
this volume, special thanks are owed to Donna Chenail,
Shirley Busika, and Peggy Bryant of Williams College,
for their careful work and enthusiastic cooperation.

Copyright © 1988 by Yale University.
All rights reserved.
This book may not be reproduced, in whole
or in part, in any form (beyond that
copying permitted by Sections 107 and 108
of the U.S. Copyright Law and except by
reviewers for the public press), without
written permission from the publishers.

Designed by Sally Harris
and set in Baskerville type by
Brevis Press, Bethany, Connecticut.
Printed in the United States of America by
Murray Printing Co., Westford, Mass.

Library of Congress Cataloging-in-Publication Data
(Revised for vol. 2)
Jorden, Eleanor Harz.
   Japanese, the spoken language, 2.

     (Yale language series)
   Includes index.
   1. Japanese language—Text-books for foreign
speakers—English. 2. Japanese language—Spoken
Japanese. I. Noda, Mari. II. Title. III. Series.
PL539.3.J58 1987   495.6′83421   86–15890
ISBN 0–300–03831–3 (v. 1 : alk. paper)
ISBN 0–300–03834–8 (pbk. : v. 1 : alk. paper)
ISBN 0–300–04186–1 (v. 2 : alk. paper)
ISBN 0–300–04188–8 (pbk. : v. 2 : alk. paper)
ISBN 0–300–04189–6 (v. 3 : alk. paper)
ISBN 0–300–04191–8 (pbk. : v. 3 : alk. paper)

The paper in this book meets the guidelines for
permanence and durability of the Committee on
Production Guidelines for Book Longevity
of the Council on Library Resources.

10   9   8   7

To
The Japanese FALCons of Cornell University
Classes I–XV
with admiration and affection

NOTE

This volume is a continuation of
JAPANESE: THE SPOKEN LANGUAGE, Part 1.
A description of romanization, special symbols, procedures, etc.
appears in the introduction to that volume.

Contents

Lesson 13 — 1
  SECTION A — 1
    Structural Patterns — 5
      1. /Interrogative + **mo**/: **dare mo** — 5
      2. /**kâ mo sirenai**/ — 7
      3. Gerund of the Adjectival — 7
      4. Compounds — 8
  SECTION B — 14
    Structural Patterns — 19
      1. **no de** — 19
      2. **tikâi uti** — 20
      3. |**desu nê(e)**| — 20
  SECTION C — 26

Lesson 14 — 30
  SECTION A — 30
    Structural Patterns — 34
      1. /**môo** + Affirmative Predicate/; /**mâda** + Negative Predicate/ — 34
      2. More on Questions without **ka**: **Tabémàsita?** — 36
      3. /Nominal + **ni** + **suru**/ — 36
      4. Food and Drink — 37
  SECTION B — 43
    Structural Patterns — 48
      1. **keńkoo ni ìi** — 48
      2. /**mâda** + Affirmative Predicate/; /**môo** + Negative Predicate/ — 48
      3. Sentence-Final Gerund in Informal Requests — 49
  SECTION C — 53

Lesson 15 — 57
  SECTION A — 57
    Structural Patterns — 61
      1. Comparison of Two Items: **yòri** and **hodo** — 61
      2. More on Affective Predicates — 62
      3. Compounds in **-suḡìru** — 63

- 4. /(o)miyaḡe ni kau/ — 63
- 5. Phrase-Particle **ya** — 64

SECTION B — 69
- Structural Patterns — 72
  - 1. Verbals of Eating and Drinking — 72
  - 2. Comparing Three or More Items: **uti ~ nâka**; **itibañ** — 73
  - 3. Verbal Gerund + **ôru** — 74
  - 4. **narubeku** — 74

SECTION C — 79

Lesson 16 — 83

SECTION A — 83
- Structural Patterns — 87
  - 1. Verbal Pairs: Transitive/Intransitive — 87
  - 2. /Transitive Verbal Gerund + **âru**/ — 88
  - 3. /Operational Verbal Gerund + **oku**/ — 89

SECTION B — 93
- Structural Patterns — 98
  - 1. /Verbal Gerund + **simau**/ — 98
  - 2. /Verbal Gerund + **kara**/ — 98
  - 3. Expressing Purpose — 99

SECTION C — 104

Lesson 17 — 108

SECTION A — 108
- Structural Patterns — 111
  - 1. Verbals of Giving — 111
  - 2. /Gerund + Verbal of Giving/ — 113
  - 3. Additional Request Patterns — 114

SECTION B — 120
- Structural Patterns — 125
  - 1. Verbals of Receiving — 125
  - 2. /Gerund + Verbal of Receiving/ — 126
  - 3. **oyasui** — 127
  - 4. **kimeru/kimaru** — 127

SECTION C — 133

Lesson 18 — 138

SECTION A — 138
- Structural Patterns — 142
  - 1. Polite Requests: **oáḡari-kudasài** — 142
  - 2. Special Polite Adjectival Forms: **aríḡatài > arîḡatoo** — 142
  - 3. Embedded Alternate Questions — 143
  - 4. **Okámai nàku.** — 144

SECTION B	148
Structural Patterns	152
1. /**X to ~ (t)te iu**/	152
2. Embedded Information Questions	154
SECTION C	160

Lesson 19   164

SECTION A	164
Structural Patterns	169
1. Sentence Modifiers with Verbal and Adjectival Final Predicates	169
2. Anticipatory **no**	171
3. **dêru mâe**	172
4. /Verbal Gerund + **mîru**/	172
SECTION B	177
Structural Patterns	182
1. Sentence Modifiers with /Nominal + Copula/ Final Predicates	182
2. Sentence Modifiers as Partitive Descriptors	184
3. Onomatopoeia	185
4. **dête simátta àto de**	186
5. Spoken Narrative Style	186
SECTION C	191

Lesson 20   196

SECTION A	196
Structural Patterns	200
1. **ikû no ni wa**	200
2. Comparison of Activities	200
3. **deńwa ìp-poń de**	202
4. **tumori**	203
5. Approximate Numbers	203
6. The Direct-Style Consultative	204
SECTION B	212
Structural Patterns	216
1. **hazu**	216
2. More on **tumori**	217
SECTION C	223

Lesson 21   228

SECTION A	228
Structural Patterns	233
1. **kimátta monò**	233
2. Phrase-Particle **sika**	233
3. /Predicate + **sôo da**/	234
4. **kotô**	235

x • Contents

SECTION B	240
Structural Patterns	245
1. /Gerund + **mo**/	245
2. Permission	246
3. Interrogatives with /Gerund + **mo**/ Sequences	246
SECTION C	252

Lesson 22 — 257

SECTION A	257
Structural Patterns	261
1. /Negative Gerund + **mo**/; Negative Permission	261
2. /**X ni yoru to**/; /**X ni yotte**/	262
3. **hârete kuru**	263
SECTION B	269
Structural Patterns	273
1. /Gerund + **wa**/	273
2. Necessity and Prohibition	274
3. **-kata ~ -yoo**	275
4. Self-Correction	276
SECTION C	281

Lesson 23 — 286

SECTION A	286
Structural Patterns	291
1. /**o-** + Verbal Stem + **dà**/	291
2. **tamê**	291
3. Particle **si**	292
4. **pâat(e)ii de mo**	293
SECTION B	299
Structural Patterns	303
1. Alternate Negative Stem in **-(a)zu**	303
2. Uses of **-(a)zu ni/-(a)nai de**	304
3. **kan̄g̀aeta dakê**	306
SECTION C	311

Lesson 24 — 316

SECTION A	316
Structural Patterns	321
1. /—— **kotô ni suru**/; /—— **kotô ni nâru**/	321
2. /Interrogative + **ka**/	322
3. **-mìtai**	322
4. **yôo**	323
SECTION B	330
Structural Patterns	335
1. **-sa**	335

2. **-soo**	336
3. **-rasìi**	337
SECTION C	343
Japanese–English Glossary	349
English–Japanese Glossary	376
Index	395

Lesson 13

SECTION A

Core Conversations

1(N)a. **Morímoto-sañ no otaku dèsu ka⤴**
   b. **A, sitûree-simasita.**

(J) **Ie, tiğáimàsu.**

2(N)a. **Daré mo demaseñ nêe.**

(J)a. **Okásìi desu nêe. Tyôtto mâe made wa hanási-tyuu dàtta ñ desu kedo nêe.**
   b. **Kosyóo kà mo siremaseñ nêe.**
   b. **Dôo mo hêñ desu nêe.**

3(N)a. **Kotira wa, Nyuúyooku-dàiğaku no Sûmisu desu ğa, ohíma na tokì ni odêñwa kudasai.**
   b. **Ññ⤴ Îma no wa rusúbañ-dèñwa.**

(J) **Tuuzita?**

4(N)a. **A. Sono deñwa, kosyóo-sitè**[1] **(i)ru ñ desu.**

(J)a. **Komâtta nâa. Taísetu na yoozi nà ñ da kedo ..**

   b. **Zyâa, tonári nò o tukátte kudasài.**
   b. **Kamáwànai?**
   c. **Êe. Daré mo tukatte (i)nai to omoimàsu kara ..**

5(J)a. **Môsimosi. Tâkano desu ğa ..**

(N)a. **Môsimosi. Tyôtto deñwa ğa toòkute, kikóenikùi ñ desu kedo ..**
   b. **Môsimosi. Môsimosi.**
   b. **Sumímaseñ. Moó sukòsi ôoki na kôe de hanâsite kudasaimaseñ ka⤴**
   c. **Môsimosi. Kikóemàsu ka⤴**
   c. **|Anoo| Kakénaosimàsu kara ne! Ití-do kìtte kudasai.**

English Equivalents

1(N)a. Is this the Morimoto residence?   (J) No, you've got the wrong number.

---

1. Accented **kosyóo-sitè** occurs provided the (i) of (i)ru is deleted.

1

b.	Oh, I'm sorry.	(J)a.	That's funny, isn't it! Until a little while ago the line was busy, but . . . (now, nobody answers).
2(N)a.	Nobody answers.		
b.	Maybe it's out of order.	b.	It's really strange, isn't it.
3(N)a.	[Speaking on the telephone] This is [John] Smith of New York University; please give me a call when you're free.		
		(J)	Did you get through?
b.	Uh-uh. The thing [just] now [was] an answering machine.		
4(N)a.	Oh, that telephone is out of order.	(J)a.	Damn! (The fact is) it's an important matter [I must attend to] but . . . (what will I do?)
b.	Then use the one next door.	b.	Is it all right?
c.	Yes, I believe that no one is using it, so . . . (I'm sure it's all right).		
5(J)a.	Hello. This is Takano, but . . . (who's calling?)	(N)a.	Hello. You sound far away (*lit.* the telephone is far) and it's difficult to hear, but . . . (can you do something about it?)
b.	Hello. Hello.	b.	I'm sorry. Would you be kind enough to speak in a little louder voice?
c.	Hello. Can you hear?	c.	Uh . . . I'll call again so—O.K.?—hang up for a minute (*lit.* once).

BREAKDOWNS
(AND SUPPLEMENTARY VOCABULARY)

1. **Morimoto**   (family name)
   sitûree-simasita   excuse me (for what I have done)
2. **dare mo** /+ negative/ (SP1)   nobody
   deṅwa ni dèru   answer the telephone
   okásìi /-katta/   is funny; is strange
   hanásì   talking; talk
   (o)hanasi-tyuu   [in] the midst of talk; 'the line is busy'
   kosyoo   out of order
   kosyoo kâ mo sirenai (SP2)   maybe it's out of order
   dôo mo   in every way, in many ways, somehow or other
   heñ /na/   strange
3. **Nyuúyooku-dàigaku**   New York University
   (o)hima /na/   free time

tokî	occasion, time
(o)híma na tokì ni	at a time when you are free
tuuziru /-ru; tuuzita/	make oneself understood; get through
rusubañ	a caretaker
rusúbañ-dèñwa	telephone answering machine
4. **kosyoo-suru**	break down
nâa	/confirming sentence-particle/
taisetu /na/	important
5. **Tâkano**	(family name)
tooi /-katta/	is far
deñwa ḡa tooi	sound far away (on the telephone)
toôkute (SP3)	being far
kikoeru /ru; kikoeta/	can hear; be audible
kikóenikùi /-katta/ (SP4)	is difficult to hear
+**kikóeyasùi /-katta/**	is easy to hear
kôe	voice
ôoki na kôe	loud voice
+**tîisa na kôe**	low voice
+**naôsu /-u; naôsita/**	fix, repair
deñwa o kakenaosu /-u; kakenaosita/	telephone again
kîru /-u; kîtta/	cut; cut off; hang up (the telephone)

MISCELLANEOUS NOTES

1. In CC1, (N) makes a phone call and gets a wrong number. (CC1 picks up the conversation after the hellos.)
    (N)a. The honorific-polite equivalent of **otáku dèsu** is **otáku de (i)rassyaimàsu**.
    (N)b. **Sitûree-simasita**, *lit.* 'I committed a "rudeness,"' is an apology for something the speaker has already done. Following the appropriate time expression, it often occurs upon meeting a person again after previous interaction at the time mentioned: **Yuúbè wa sitûree-simasita**. *lit.* 'Last night I committed a rudeness' might have as its *situational* English equivalents 'It was good to see you last night'; 'I had a wonderful time last night'; 'Thanks for talking with me last night'; etc. The Japanese, in contrast with these English equivalents, focuses on the **sitûree** that would have been committed: imposing on someone's hospitality, interrupting someone's regular routine, etc.
    2. In CC2, two colleagues are commenting on a strange situation involving a telephone call. The style is careful, with distal predicates throughout. On the accompanying tape, the participants are Mr. Yamada and Deborah Miller, business associates at the Oriental Trade Company.
    (J)a. **Okásìi**, like 'funny' in English, can refer to something either amusing or strange: context, intonation, and facial expression distinguish the two meanings.
Tyôtto mâe made wa 'until a little while ago' contrasts with the present time.
-**Tyuu** is attached to nominals that refer to activity, to form unaccented compound nominals

indicating activity currently under way: '[in] the middle of ——.' Examples: **(o)hanasi-tyuu, (o)deñwa-tyuu, (o)siḡoto-tyuu, zyuḡyoo-tyuu, kaiḡi-tyuu, (o)yasumi-tyuu**. The forms with **o-** are used in polite reference to the out-group. The extended predicate construction in 2(J)a provides the explanation for why the situation is funny.

Compounded with a time word, **-tyuu** (or **-zyuu**) indicates duration of the interval (examples: **iti-niti-zyuu** 'all day long,' **kotosi-zyuu** 'all this year'). When followed by **ni**, such compounds indicate a point in time within the period specified (example: **kotosi-zyuu ni** 'within this year'). Note also /place + **-zyuu**/: **gakkoo-zyuu** 'throughout the school.'

Nê(e) is different from other sentence-particles in that it has no restrictions on the forms it can follow. Here it follows a fragment ending in **kedo** with its usual meaning of reflection, mutual understanding, agreement, and nonconfrontation. Note that every utterance in this CC ends in **nêe**.

(J)b. **Okásìi**, when it refers to strangeness, overlaps with **heñ**, but they belong to different word classes: **heñ na hito** but **okásìi hito**; **heñ ni natta** but **okâsîku natta**; **heñ zya nâi** but **okâsîku nâi**.

3. After leaving a message on a telephone answering machine, using careful-style, (N) switches to casual-style in speaking with a friend (J). On the accompanying videotape, (N) and (J) are male students who originally used careful-style in speaking with each other, but who now have established a closer, more relaxed relationship.

(N)a. **Tokî** is a nominal referring to times or occasions. It belongs to the group of time words that may or may not take particle **ni** when indicating the time at which something happens. It occurs in such combinations as **kodómo no tokì** 'the time when [I] was a child'; **byoóki no tokì**; **gakúsee no tokì**; **samûi toki**; **isóḡasìi toki**, etc. More will be said about **tokî** in later lessons.

Tokî also occurs in reduplicated (= doubled) form: /**tokî** + **tokî**/ = **tokídokì** 'sometimes.'

Tuuziru, an affective vowel verbal, has a wide range of meanings that share in the notion of passing through—either in the sense of a railroad that runs from one point to another, or a telephone call that goes through, or a person who is understood by—gets through to—his/her audience. Note /**X de tuuziru**/ = 'get through by means of X.'

No in **îma no wa** is a contraction of /connective **no** + nominal **no**/, the latter a replacement for **deñwa**.

Rusubañ as an independent word usually refers to the person in charge of an apartment, home, or any kind of building during the absence of the regular occupants. Performing the duties of a **rusubañ** is conveyed by the phrase **rusubañ (o) suru**.

4. In CC4, an office employee (N) is speaking with a supervisor (J) about a telephone that is out of order. (N) uses careful-style with distal predicates in sentence-final position and before **kara**. (J), in contrast, uses casual-style, with direct-style predicates exclusively.

(N)a. **Kosyoo-suru** 'break down' is an affective verbal. Note: **kosyóo-sitè (i)ru** 'it has broken down'; 'it is broken down.' In this pattern, it is similar in meaning to **kosyóo dà**. The extended predicate here connects the broken-down condition of the telephone with the fact that no calls will go through on the instrument in question.

(J)a. **Nâ(a)**, a sentence-particle, is closely related to **nê(e)**. However, it is (1) used more commonly, though not exclusively, in blunt-style; and (2) it is particularly common in deliberative utterances addressed to oneself. The extended predicate links (J's) having important business with his consternation.

(N)b. The **no** of **tonári nò** is a contraction of /connective **no** + nominal **no**/, the latter a replacement for **deñwa**.

5. In CC5, the participants of a telephone call are having trouble hearing each other because of a bad connection. The speech-style on both sides is careful, although Tâkano-sañ (J) says little more than **môsimosi**. Distal-style is used exclusively except for the request form **kudásài**, which, although not distal-style, is polite.

(J)a. Note that (J) identifies herself when answering the telephone. This is a very common—although not universal—practice.

(N)a. As usual, the extended predicate serves to connect and explain: 'it's that it's hard to hear that explains my talking loudly, repeating, etc.'

The accented alternate of **toói** is **toóì** (i.e., **toóì desu**, **toóì no**, etc.). Note also: **tooku** 'the far away' (a nominal).

Kikoeru is a double-**ḡa**, affective verbal. Both the person who can hear and what is audible are followed by **ḡa** (or **wa**).

N(b). **Ôoki na** occurs as an alternate of **oókìi** *only as the modifier of a following nominal*. It consists of a **na**-nominal derived from the adjectival followed by **na**. This kind of alternation occurs in the case of only a few adjectivals. Examples: /**tîisa na** + nominal/ and /**okâsi na** + nominal/. Be careful to note (1) the loss of adjectival final **-i** in the derivative form that takes **na**; and (2) the difference in accent of the two forms.

Structural Patterns

*1. /INTERROGATIVE + **mo**/: **dâre mo***

The pattern /interrogative + **mo**/ regularly implies the inclusion of everything (or, in some cases, a large quantity) in the question-word category. Thus:

îtu 'when?'	**îtu mo** 'all the whens' = 'always'
dôo 'how?'	**dôo mo** 'all or many of the hows' = 'in every way,' 'in many ways'; (in some contexts:) 'somehow or other'
dôtira 'which of two?'	**dôtira mo** 'both'

For a number of these combinations, there is a requirement for a negative predicate, in which case everything in the relevant category is excluded:

dâre 'who?'	/**dâre mo** + negative/ 'nobody'
nâni 'what?'	/**nâni mo** + negative/ 'nothing'

Some /interrogative + **mo**/ combinations may occur with both affirmative and negative predicates:

Dôtira mo îi desu.	'Both are good.'
Dôtira mo yôku nâi desu.	'Neither one is good.'

An /interrogative number + **mo**/ regularly indicates a significantly large number—but not every one in existence. Thus:

nâñ-niñ mo 'any number of people' (i.e., a great many people)
nâñ-do mo 'over and over again,' 'any number of times'
îku-tu mo 'any (large) number of objects'

These number combinations also occur with both affirmative and negative predicates:

Nâñ-ḡeñ mo arimasu. 'There are any number of buildings.'

Nâñ-ḡeñ mo nâi desu. 'There aren't a large (significant) number of buildings.'

As usual, phrase-particles **ḡa** and **o** are dropped before **mo**, but other phrase-particles required by the context do occur preceding **mo**.² Compare:

Dâre ḡa simasu ka⤴ 'Who will do it?'
Daré mo simaseñ. 'No one will do it.'

Nâni o kaímàsita ka⤴ 'What did you buy?'
Naní mo kaimaseñ desita. 'I didn't buy anything.'

Dôko e ikímàsita ka⤴ 'Where did you go?'
Dokó e mo ikimaseñ desita. 'I didn't go anywhere.'

Dâre to hanásimàsita ka⤴ 'With whom did you speak?'
Daré to mo hanasimaseñ desita. 'I didn't speak with anyone.'

Dôko ni arimasu ka⤴ 'Where is it?'
Dokó ni mo arimaseñ. 'It isn't anywhere.'

Note that /interrogative + **mo**/ often occurs with an unaccented alternate.

The following chart indicates the occurrence and meaning of commonly used /interrogative + **mo**/ combinations:

Interrogative	*+ mo*	*+ Negative*	*+ Affirmative*
dâre 'who?'	**dâre mo**	'nobody,' 'not anybody'	
nâni 'what?'	**nâni mo**	'nothing,' 'not anything'	
dôko 'what place?'	**dôko mo**	'no place,' 'not any place'	'everywhere'
îtu 'when?'	**îtu mo**		'always'
dôtira 'which (of two)?'	**dôtira mo**	'neither one,' 'not either one'	'both'
dôre 'which (of three or more)?'	**dôre mo**	'not one (of three or more)'	'every one (of three or more)'
îkura 'how much?'	**îkura mo**	'no large amount'	'ever so much'
îku-tu 'how many?'	**îku-tu mo**	'no large number'	'a large number, ever so many'
dôno X 'which X?'	**dôno X mo**	'no X'	'every X'
dôñna X 'what kind of X?'	**dôñna X mo**	'no kind of X'	'every kind of X'
nâñ-boñ 'how many long cylindrical units?'	**nâñ-boñ mo**	'no large number of long cylindrical units'	'a large number of long cylindrical units'

2. Since phrase-particles **wa** and **mo** are in direct contrast, they of course never occur in the same phrase.

2. /kâ mo sirenai/

/Predicate X + **kâ mo sirenai**/ = 'X may be true'; 'maybe X.' The predicate in this pattern is either imperfective or perfective, and is regularly direct-style. However, **da**—that very unstable form—disappears here, too. The accent of inflected words before **ka** is the same as before **kara, no,** etc. Following an unaccented word or phrase, **ka** is accented. Thus:

yamérù	+	**ka mo sirenai**	'[someone] may quit'
yamétà	+	**ka mo sirenai**	'[someone] may have quit'
takâi	+	**ka mo sirenai**	'[it] may be expensive'
tâkâkatta	+	**ka mo sirenai**	'[it] may have been expensive'
tâkâku nâi	+	**ka mo sirenai**	'[it] may not be expensive'
byooki	+	**kâ mo sirenai**	'[someone] may be sick'
byoóki dàtta	+	**ka mo sirenai**	'[someone] may have been sick'
tomodati kara	+	**kâ mo sirenai**	'[it] may be from a friend'
tomódati dà kara	+	**ka mo sirenai**	'[it] may be because s/he's a friend'

Sirenai is a negative adjectival; it may also occur in its distal-style equivalents: **sirénài desu** or **sirémaseñ**. Literally, the entire pattern means something like 'it can't even be known [for sure] whether ——.' It implies more doubt than /predicate + **daròo** or **desyòo**/ or /predicate + **to** + **omôu**/. Thus:

Muzúkasìi desyoo. 'It's probably difficult.' *Cf. more doubtful*

Muzúkasìi ka mo siremaseñ. 'It may be difficult.'

Yaméru to omoimàsu. 'I think he'll quit.' *Cf. more doubtful*

Yamérù ka mo siremaseñ. 'He may quit.'

3. GERUND OF THE ADJECTIVAL

We have already learned that verbals have forms we call 'gerunds,' which end in **-te** (or **-de**), and that nominal predicates have corresponding forms consisting of /nominal (particle) + **de**/. Given the structure of Japanese, with its three predicate types, all of which tend to behave in parallel fashion, one would suspect that there is a corresponding form to be called the gerund of the adjectival. That suspicion is entirely correct. The gerund of adjectivals is made by adding **-te** to the **-ku** form. It is always accented: if the **-ku** form is accented, the derived gerund is accented on the same mora. If the **-ku** form is unaccented, the derived gerund is regularly accented on the mora immediately preceding the **-kute** ending. Examples:

Adjectival	Gerund
takâi	tâkâkute
oisii	oísìkute
samûi	sâmûkute
aôi	âôkute
îi/yôi	yôkute

Remember that **-tai** ('want to') forms and **-nai** (negative) forms are also adjectivals. Thus:

ikitai	**ikítàkute**	**tabétài**	**tabétàkute**
ikanai	**ikánàkute**	**tabênai**	**tabênakute**

The meaning of this form is predictably similar to the meaning of all gerunds: 'X being the case,' 'X being actualized,' 'X is/was true, and ——.' The patterns in which the adjectival occurs are parallel to other gerund patterns.³ (In particular, reread 7B-SP5 and 8A-SP5). Examples:

    Uti wa, êki kara toôkute, hûbeñ desu. 'My home is far from the station and inconvenient'; 'My home is inconvenient, being far from the station.'

    Anó zìsyo, atáràsìkute takâi desu. 'That dictionary is new and expensive.' (*lit.* 'being new, it's expensive')

    Kyôo wa, aítàkàkute îi desu nêe. 'Isn't it nice and warm today!' (*lit.* 'being warm, it's nice')

    Wakárànakute komárimàsu yo. 'I'm upset at not understanding.'

Note the difference in linkage that relates to particles:

    Anó gakusee ḡa dekìnakute / komárimàsita. 'I became upset at that student's inability.' (*lit.* 'That student being incapable, I became upset.')

    Ano gakusee wa / dekînakute komárimàsita. 'That student became upset at his/her inability.' (*lit.* 'That student, being incapable, became upset.')

The importance of knowing the word-class to which a Japanese word belongs becomes apparent once more, as we examine the equivalents of three English sentences which contain no word-class differences:

    (a) 'I was amazed at the numbers' being different.'
    (b) 'I was amazed at the numbers' being red.'
    (c) 'I was amazed at the numbers' being strange.'

In the Japanese equivalents, the *structural* pattern of all three is the same, but (a) contains a verbal gerund, (b) an adjectival gerund, and (c) a /nominal + **dà**/ gerund as nonfinal predicate.

    (a) **Suuzi ḡa tiḡatte, biḱkùri-simasita.**

    (b) **Suúzi ḡa akàkute, biḱkùri-simasita.**

    (c) **Suúzi ḡa hèñ de, biḱkùri-simasita.**

4. COMPOUNDS

The Japanese language has many verbals, adjectivals, and nominals which we will designate as COMPOUNDS. A compound consists of one or more nonfinal members + a final member combining to form a single word:

Nonfinal members		*Final member*
(V) verbal stem *or*		(V) verbal *or*
(A) adjectival root	+	(A) adjectival *or*
(**-i** form minus **-i**) *or*		
(N) nominal		(N) nominal

Any combination is possible. The compound belongs to the word-class of its final member. Examples:

---

3. Note, once again, that this is not the same as saying that the adjectival gerund necessarily occurs in *every* pattern in which *any* gerund is found. For example, the adjectival gerund does not occur in /+ **kudasài**/ request patterns.

(V) + (V) = Verbal Stem + Verbal:
  kakêru 'suspend'; 'telephone' + **naôsu** 'repair' > **kakenaosu** 'suspend over again';
    'telephone over again'
  kâku 'write' + **naôsu** 'repair' > **kakinaosu** 'write over again'; 'rewrite'
(V) + (A) = Verbal Stem + Adjectival:
  kikoeru 'can hear' + **-nikùi** 'is marked by difficulty' > **kikóenikùi** 'is hard to hear'
  kâku 'write' + **-yasùi** 'is marked by ease' > **kakíyasùi** 'is easy to write (*or* write with
    or write on)'
(V) + (N) = Verbal Stem + Nominal:
  dêru 'go out' + **kuti** 'mouth'; 'orifice' > **dêḡuti** 'exit'
  môosu 'say' + **wâke** 'reason' > **moosiwake** 'excuse'
(N) + (V) = Nominal + Verbal:
  beñkyoo 'study' (the noun) + **suru** 'do' > **beñkyoo-suru** 'study' (the verb)
  soodañ 'consultation' + **suru** 'do' > **soodañ-suru** 'consult'
(N) + (N) = Nominal + Nominal:
  Tookyoo 'Tokyo' + **êki** 'station' > **Toókyòo-eki** 'Tokyo Station'
  hai 'ash' + **irô** 'color' > **haiiro** 'gray'
  deñwa 'telephone' + **bañ́ḡòo** 'number' > **deñwabàñḡoo** 'telephone number'
  miḡi 'right' + **tonari** 'next door'; 'adjoining' > **miḡídònari** 'next door to the right'

Additional examples will be introduced in later lessons.

Note the following points:

  a. In some instances, some or all parts of a compound also occur as independent words, but in other cases they occur only as parts of a compound word.

  b. A compound has a meaning of its own which must be distinguished from that of the related phrase formed according to a particular structural pattern. Compare:

  Tookyoo + **êki** > compound **Toókyòo-eki** 'Tokyo Station' (a particular station in
    Tokyo), but phrase **Toókyoo no èki** 'station(s) in Tokyo'
  kâku + **naôsu** > compound **kakinaosu** 'write over again' but phrase **kâite naôsu**
    'write and (then) fix'

The creation of phrases is comparatively free; but compounds either do or do not exist in the language of the native speaker and therefore cannot be freely created by foreigners, except in the case of families of compounds like those ending in **-nikùi** and **-yasùi**, which are *comparatively* predictable.

  c. If the non-initial member of the compound begins with **k, s, t,** or **h,** that sound *may* undergo change: **k** > **ḡ**; **s** > **z**; **t** > **d**;[4] and **h** > **b** (or **p**). This accounts for the changes observed in **dêḡuti** and **miḡídònari**, as well as those that occur in many numeral and number compounds (cf. *h*yakû and sâñ-*b*yaku; *s*êñ and sañ́-*z*èñ; nî-*k*eñ and sañ-*ḡ*eñ).

  d. The accent of a compound is not always predictable simply on the basis of the accent pattern of the component parts.

---

4. Before **i, u,** and **y, t** > **z.**

Drills

A 1. **Kâre, mâtte (i)ru ñ desu ka⌒**
'(Is it that) he's waiting?'

Îya, tyôtto mâe made wa mâtte (i)ta ñ desu kedo . .
'No, (it's that) until a little while ago he was waiting, but . . .' (not now).

2. **Kâre, utí karitè (i)ru ñ desu ka⌒**
'(Is it that) he's renting a house?'

Îya, tyôtto mâe made wa karítè (i)ta ñ desu kedo . .
'No, (it's that) until a little while ago he was renting, but . . .' (not now).

3. syotyóo to hanàsite; 4. kono ryokañ ni tomatte; 5. señsèe to soodañ-site; 6. zimûsyo kasite; 7. gaikokuḡo osiete; 8. tyuuḡokugo beñkyoo-site

B 1. **Suḡîura-sañ, îma syuttyoo dèsu ka⌒**
'Is Mr/s. Sugiura away on business?'

Êe. Syuttyoo-tyuu dèsu.
'Yes, s/he's on (lit. in the middle of) a business trip.'

2. **Suḡîura-sañ, îma kâiḡi desu ka⌒**
'Is Mr/s. Sugiura in conference?'

Êe. Kaíḡi-tyuu dèsu.
'Yes, s/he's in (the middle of) a conference.'

3. deñwa; 4. siḡoto; 5. yasúmì; 6. rûsu; 7. zyûḡyoo; 8. beñkyoo

C 1. **Dâre ḡa dêta ñ desu ka⌒**
'Who is it that answered (the phone)?'

Daré mo dènakatta ñ desu yo⌒
'(The fact is) nobody answered.'

2. **Dôko e ikû ñ desu ka⌒**
'Where is it you're going?'

Dokó e mo ikanài ñ desu yo⌒
'(The fact is) I'm not going anywhere.'

3. dâre to soodañ-sita; 4. dôre o obôete (i)ru; 5. nâni ḡa âru; 6. dôtira ḡa kûru; 7. dâre to âtta; 8. dôko ni âru; 9. dâre o yoñda; 10. dâre ni reñraku-sita; 11. dâre kara karita; 12. nâni o nôñda; 13. dôno kyoositu o tukau; 14. dôñna gakusee ḡa dekîru

D 1. **Dôtira ḡa sirôi desu ka⌒**
'Which one is white?'

Dôtira mo sirôi desu kedo . .
'Both are white, but . . .' (is that all right?)

2. **Îtu koó simàsu ka⌒**
'When do you do it like this?'

Îtu mo koó simàsu kedo . .
'I always do it like this, but . . .' (is that all right?)

3. dôre ḡa muzúkasìi desu; 4. dôno kuruma ḡa takâi desu; 5. dôno hurosiki ḡa kîree desu; 6. dôno huutoo o kirâsite (i)masu; 7. dôno gakusee to aímàsita

E 1. **Gaíkokuḡo mo takusañ beñkyoo-simàsita ka⌒**
'Did you study many foreign languages, too?'

Îya, sońna ni ìku-tu mo beńkyoo-simasèñ desita yo⌒
'No, I didn't study that many' (lit. a large number to that extent).

2. **Gakúsee-sañ mo takusañ miemàsita ka⌒**
'Did many of your students show up, too?'

Îya, sońna ni nàñ-niñ mo miémasèñ desita yo⌒
'No, not that many showed up.'

3. **atárasìi kuruma/mimâsita**; 4. **kissateñ/arímàsu**; 5. **biñseñ/irímàsu**; 6. **hanâ/kaímàsita**; 7. **kyoókàsyo/tukáimàsu**

• Repeat this drill, giving affirmative responses with /number + **mo** + affirmative predicate/.

F 1. **Heñ desu nêe.**
 'Isn't it strange!'

    Sôo desu nêe. Watasi mo dôo mo heñ da to omoimasu nêe.
    'Isn't it! I think it's somehow or other strange, too.'

2. **Okásìi desu nêe.**
 'Isn't it strange!'

    Sôo desu nêe. Watasi mo dôo mo okásìi to omoimasu nêe.
    'Isn't it! I think it's somehow or other strange, too.'

3. **sitûree desu**; 4. **komárimàsu**; 5. **iyâ desu**; 6. **muzúkasìi desu**; 7. **hûbeñ desu**; 8. **tumáràanai desu**

G 1. **Kânozyo, eeḡo obôete (i)masu neʔ**
 'She remembers English—right?'

    Âa, obôete (i)ru ka mo siremaseñ nêe.
    'Oh, she may remember—that's right!'

2. **Kânozyo, byoóki dèsu neʔ**
 'She's sick—right?'

    Âa, byoóki kà mo siremaseñ nêe.
    'Oh, she may be sick—that's right!'

3. **nihoñḡo ni yowâi desu**; 4. **moñbùsyoo yamémàsita**; 5. **rikóñ-site (i)màsu**; 6. **Nihôñ ḡa nâḡakatta desu**; 7. **syotyoo to reñraku-simàsita**; 8. **nikkèeziñ desu**; 9. **Sañhurañsìsuko desita**; 10. **nihóñḡo ḡa tuuzimàsu**

H 1. **Anó kàiḡi, myôoniti desyoo?**
 'That conference is tomorrow, isn't it?'

    Sâa. Myôoniti zya nâi ka mo siremaseñ yo↗
    'Hm. It may not be tomorrow, you know.'

2. **Morimoto-sañ, eeḡo ni tuyôi desyoo?**
 'Mr/s. Morimoto is good (*lit.* strong) in English, isn't s/he?'

    Sâa. Tûyôku nâi ka mo siremaseñ yo↗
    'Hm. S/he may not be good, you know.'

3. **Suḡîura-sañ/osókù made iru**; 4. **Yamanaka-sañ/syotyóo to àtta**; 5. **sono huta-ri/iśsyo (dà)**;[5] 6. **asoko/îma samûi**; 7. **are/zisíñ dàtta**; 8. **anó zimùsyo/kinoo isóḡasìkatta**

I 1. **Mîtiko-sañ wa, eeḡo zéñbu wasúretà desyoo?**
 'Michiko has forgotten all her English, don't you think?'

    Mîtiko-sañ desu ka↗ Sôo ka mo siremaseñ nêe.
    'Michiko? That may be.'

2. **Syotyoo wa, îma sêki hazúsite (i)rassyàru desyoo?**

    Syotyóo dèsu ka↗ Sôo ka mo siremaseñ nêe.

5. In the pattern being drilled, **dà** is dropped. As usual, this is signaled by parentheses.

'The institute head is away from his desk (*lit.* seat) now, don't you think?'	'The institute head? That may be.'

3. **omâwarisañ/sore wa 'zeñzeñ siranai**; 4. **gaiziñ/amari 'meesi tukawanai**; 5. **îma no Wasiñtoñ/atˊtakài**; 6. **asoko no deñwa/kosyóo (dà)**[5]

J	1. **Matá kimasyoò ka.**	Êe, ohíma na tokì ni kitê kudasai.
	'Shall I come here again?'	'Yes, please come when you have (free) time.'
	2. **Deńwa kakemasyòo ka.**	Êe, ohíma na tokì ni kâkete kudasai.
	'Shall I telephone?'	'Yes, please call when you have (free) time.'

3. **konó kèeki kirímasyòo**; 4. **tîzu kakímasyòo**; 5. **anó kyookàsyo katˊte kimasyòo**; 6. **anó tèepu karímasyòo**; 7. **syotyóo ni kikimasyòo**

K	1. **Yôku mîruku nomímàsu ka**↗	Kodómo no tokì ni wa yôku nôñda kedo, îma wa 'amari nomímasèñ nêe.
	'Do you drink milk often?'	'When I was a child I drank [it] a lot, but now I don't drink it very much.'
	2. **Yôku têñisu simâsu ka**↗	Kodómo no tokì ni wa yôku sitâ kedo, îma wa 'amari simásèñ nêe.
	'Do you play tennis often?'	'When I was a child I played a lot, but now I don't play very much.'

3. **aísukurìimu tabémàsu**; 4. **koñna zassi mimâsu**; 5. **durañsugˊo tukáimàsu**

L	1. **Tuúzimasèñ desita yo**↗	Tuúzinàkatta ñ desu ka. Komâtta nâa.
	'I didn't get through.'	'(You mean) you didn't get through? Oh, dear!'[6]
	2. **Sore wa kosyóo dèsu yo**↗	Kosyóo nà ñ desu ka. Komâtta nâa.
	'That's broken.'	'(You mean) it's broken? Oh, dear!'[6]

3. **deńwabàñgˊoo wa sirímasèñ**; 4. **wâiñ wa koré dakè desu**; 5. **kamî wa kirâsite (i)masu**; 6. **asítà kara syutˊtyoo dèsu**; 7. **asoko wa mazûi desu**

M	1. **Toôì desu nêe.**	Êe, toôkute komárimàsu nêe.
	'Isn't it far!'	'Yes, I'm bothered by how far it is.' (*lit.* 'Being far, it's bothersome, isn't it!')
	2. **Eego ni yowâi desu nêe.**	Êe, yôwâkute, komárimàsu nêe.
	'Isn't s/he weak in English!'	'Yes, I'm bothered by how weak s/he is.' (*lit.* 'Being weak, it's bothersome, isn't it!')

3. **mâiniti atûi**; 4. **zimûsyo gˊa isógˊasìi**; 5. **zeñzeñ wakárànai**; 6. **koko wa mazûi**; 7. **kono sigˊoto tumárànai**; 8. **konó zìsyo hurûi**

N	1. **Kosyóo-sitè (i)ru ñ desu ka**↗	Êe, kosyóo-sitè (i)te ne!
	'(Is it that) it's broken down?'	'Yes, being broken down—you know (what that means)!'

---

6. Please substitute your own favorite expletive!

2. **Tuúzinàkatta ñ desu ka**⤴ Êe, tuúzinàkute ne!
'(Is it that) you didn't get through?' 'That's right, not getting through—you know (what that means)!'

3. **atûi**; 4. **taíheñ dàtta**; 5. **isóḡasìi**; 6. **hûbeñ na**; 7. **yukî datta**; 8. **biḱkùri-sita**

O 1. **Hetâ?** Ñ. Hetâ de komâru (no)⁷ yo.
'Is s/he poor at it?' 'Yeah. S/he's poor at it, and it causes me problems.'

2. **Okásìi?** Ñ. Okâsìkute komâru (no)⁷ yo.
'Is it funny (i.e., strange)?' 'Yeah. It's strange, and it causes me problems.'

3. **kikoenai**; 4. **hûbeñ (da)**; 5. **samûi**; 6. **tooi**; 7. **tiḡáttè (i)ru**; 8. **muzukasii**; 9. **nâḡaku kakâru**

P 1. **Kore, simâsu ka**⤴ Iya, tyôtto sinîkùi kara . .
'Are you going to do this one?' 'No, it's a bit hard to do, so . . .' (I'm not going to do it).

2. **Koko kara kakémàsita⁸ ka**⤴ Iya, tyôtto kakénìkùkatta kara . .
'Did you call from here?' 'No, it was a bit hard to call, so . . .' (I didn't).

3. **kore, obóemàsita**; 4. **sore, iímàsu**; 5. **konó taipuràitaa, tukáimàsu**; 6. **końna pèñ de kakímàsu**

Q 1. **Dôre o tukáù ñ desu ka**⤴ Sôo desu nêe. Koré ḡa tukaiyasùi kara, koré o tukaimasyòo.
'Which one is it you're going to use?' 'Let's see. *This one* is easy to use, so I guess I'll use *this one*.'

2. **Dôno peñ de kâku ñ desu ka**⤴ Sôo desu nêe. Koré ḡa kakiyasùi kara, koré de kakimasyòo.
'Which pen is it you're going to write with?' 'Let's see. *This one* is easy to write with, so I guess I'll write with *this one*.'

3. **dôre o obóeru**; 4. **nâni o suru**; 5. **nâñ de tukûru**; 6. **nâñ de tabêru**; 7. **dôtira kara dêru**

R 1. **Moó iti-do iimasyòo ka**⤴ Êe. Ôoki na kôe de iťte kudasài.
'Shall I say it again?' 'Yes. Please say it in a loud voice.'

2. **Nihóñḡo de hanasimasyòo ka**⤴ Êe. Ôoki na kôe de hanâsite kudasai.
'Shall I speak in Japanese?' 'Yes. Please speak in a loud voice.'

3. **ano gakusee yobímasyòo**; 4. **ano gaiziñ ni kikímasyòo**

S 1. **Kakímàsita ka**⤴ Êe, kakímàsita kedo, moó iti-do kakinaositài ñ desu.
'Did you write [it]?'

7. The addition of **no** converts blunt-style to a gentle-style extended predicate.
8. Remember that **kakêru** refers to telephoning only when **deñwa (o)** is, if not stated, at least understood through the context.

2. **Kakémàsita**[8] **ka**⤴
'Did you hang (or apply) [it] (or telephone)?

'Yes, I wrote [it], but I'd like to write it over again.'
Êe, kakémàsita kedo, moó iti-do kakenaositài ñ desu.
'Yes, I hung (or applied) [it] (or telephoned), but I'd like to hang (or apply) [it] (or telephone) over again.'

3. **yomímàsita**; 4. **tukúrimàsita**; 5. **simâsita**

Application Exercises

A1. Leave the following messages on Ms. Morimoto's **rusúbañ-dèñwa**:
   a. Ask for a call this evening after 7:00. Leave your telephone number.
   b. You have something to attend to and can't meet the day after tomorrow. (Apologize!)
   c. You'll come (*lit.* 'go') to her office tomorrow morning at about 10:30.
   d. You'll be waiting for her at the American Embassy entrance tomorrow from 2:30 on.

2. Express the following puzzling situations in Japanese, and suggest possible explanations, using /——**ka mo siremaseñ**/:
   a. Mr. Hashimoto didn't attend class today.
   b. Mr. Kubota wasn't in the office yesterday.
   c. You telephoned Ms. Carter's office any number of times this morning but nobody answered.
   d. It was a 9:30 appointment but Ms. Morimoto didn't appear.
   e. That visitor's name is Tanaka, but he doesn't understand Japanese at all.
   f. You thought there was a meeting today, but nobody has come.
   g. You thought you couldn't make a U-turn on this street, but that taxi just did.
   h. You thought the office manager was probably coming early today. You're wondering what happened.
   i. You thought Mr. Yamamoto would probably drink a lot, but he didn't drink anything.

B. Core Conversations: Substitution

The Core Conversations of this lesson section include a number of examples of ritual speech in addition to exchanges which permit variation and substitution. One type of variation results from changing the rank of the participants, with corresponding alteration of language style.

As you practice, be sure that your facial expressions are appropriate—in Japanese terms—to what you are saying. Use the video as a model.

SECTION B

Core Conversations

1(J)a. **Môsimosi.**

(N)a. **Môsimosi. Syatyóo-sañ irassyaimàsu ka**⤴

b. **Moósiwake gozaimaseǹ g̃a, tadâima gaísyutu-tyuu de gozaimàsu g̃a, hîsyo to kawárimàsu no de, syôosyoo omáti-kudasài.**
2(J)a. **Môsimosi. Yamámori-keñkyùuzyo de gozaimasu.**
　　b. **Tadâima syuttyoo-tyuu de gozaimàsu g̃a ..**
　　c. **Hâa.**
　　d. **Hâi.**
　　e. **Sayóo de gozaimàsu ka. Gurêe wa 'raisyuu no kayôobi ni wa modôtt(e) orimasu kara ..**
　　f. **Suíyòobi no sań-zi-g̃òro de gozaimasu neˎ Kêkkoo de gozaimasu.**
　　g. **Sitûree-itasimasita. Goméñ-kudasài.**

　　b. **Osôre-irimasu.**
(N)a. **A. Môsimosi. Gurêe-sañ irássyaimàsu ka⤴**
　　b. **Âa, sôo desu ka. Kotira wa Końtinentaru-g̃iñkoo no Kâataa de gozaimasu g̃a ..**
　　c. **Zitû wa, tikâi uti ni Gurêe-sañ ni omé ni kakaritài to omóimàsite ..**
　　d. **Gotúg̃oo o ukag̃aitàkatta ñ desu g̃a ..**
　　e. **Soré dè wa |desu nêe.| Raisyuu no suíyòobi no sań-zi-g̃òro wa ikâg̃a desyoo.**
　　f. **Dê wa, sań-zi-g̃òro ni kotíra kara ukag̃aimàsu no de, yorósiku oneg̃ai-itasimàsu. Goméñ-kudasài.**

ENGLISH EQUIVALENTS

1(J)a. Hello.
　　b. I'm sorry, but s/he's out just now; but I'll put the secretary on (instead of me), so just a moment.
2(J)a. Hello. Yamamori Research Institute.
　　b. S/he's away on business just now, but ... (can I help you?)
　　c. Yes.

(N)a. Hello. Is the president in?
　　b. Thank you.
(N)a. Oh, hello. Is Mr/s. Gray in?
　　b. Oh. This is [John] Carter from the Continental Bank ...
　　c. The reason I called is that (I've been thinking) I'd like to see Mr/s. Gray in the near future, and ...

d. Yes.

e. Oh. [Mr/s.] Gray will be back by next Tuesday (at least) so . . . (you can see him/her after that).

f. That's (about) three o'clock Wednesday—right? That will be fine.

g. Goodbye.

d. I wanted to inquire about when it would be convenient for him/her but . . . (would you know?)

e. In that case . . . how would about three o'clock next Wednesday be?

f. Then I'll come over (from here) at about three, so (I request your consideration). Goodbye.

BREAKDOWNS
(AND SUPPLEMENTARY VOCABULARY)

1. **syatyoo** — company president (the president of a **kaisya**)
  +**butyoo** — division manager (the manager of a **bû**)
  +**katyoo** — section manager (the manager of a **kâ**)
  +**iñtyoo** — hospital director (the director of a **byooiñ**)
  +**gakutyoo** — academic president (the president of a **daiḡaku**)
  +**kyoozyu** — professor
  +**kyôosi** — instructor
  +**tâisi** — ambassador
  +**ryôozi** — consul
  gaísyutu-tyuu dà — be out
  hîsyo/hisyô — secretary
  kawaru /-u; kawatta/ — undergo change; change places
  kawárimàsu no de (SP1) — being the case that [I]'ll change, [I]'ll change so . . .

2. **Yamâmori** — (family name)
  +**Yamâḡuti** — (family name)
  keñkyuuzyò — research institute
  Yamámori-keñkyùuzyo — the Yamamori Research Institute
  hâa — /polite affirmation/
  zitû — truth, reality
  tikâi /-katta/ — is near
  uti — interval
  tikâi uti ni (SP2) — in the near future
  omé ni kakàru ↓ **/-u; kakâtta/** — meet, see (a person) /humble-polite/

(go)tuğoo	convenience
sayoo	/formal equivalent of **sôo**/
modôru /-u; modôtta/	return, go/come back; back up
soré dè wa	that being the case
|desu nê(e)| (SP3)	/filler/
kêkkoo /na/	fine, great
ukaḡau ↓ /-u; ukaḡatta/	visit; inquire /humble-polite/
ukáḡaimàsu ↓ no de	being the case that I'll visit (or inquire), I'll visit (or inquire) so . . .

MISCELLANEOUS NOTES

The two Core Conversations of this lesson section are careful-style, polite telephone conversations between a foreign caller (N) and office personnel (J). Both conversations include many examples of ritual language.

1(J)a. In this conversation, the person answering the telephone does not identify him/herself in any way. This is always a possible option.

(N)a. The compounds in **-tyoo** all refer to the head of a particular type of organization or organizational unit. Compare **syotyoo**, the manager of an office or institute.

Kyôosi is the most generalized term for an instructor or pedagogue, on any level of instruction, but it is never used as a term of address. This word has none of the honorific implications of **seńsèe** and therefore can be used in reference to oneself. **Kyoozyu**, which refers to a professor at the college/university level, is not used in referring to oneself.

(J)b. This utterance is extremely polite and formal, with a preponderance of distal-style predicates.

Tadâima occurs here as a more formal equivalent of **îma**.

Gaisyutu also occurs in the compound **gaisyutu-suru** 'go out'; **gaísyutu-sitè (i)ru** 'be out.'
Kawari 'change,' introduced in 11B, is a nominal derivative of the verbal **kawaru** 'undergo change,' 'become changed,' '(ex)change';[9] **kawáttè (i)ru** '[it] has changed,' 'it is different.' The **-tè (i)ru** combination used in reference to people describes those who are different, strange, unusual. Note: **X ni kawaru** 'change into X'; **X to kawaru** '(ex)change with X.' The latter combination is frequently used when a telephone call is turned over to another speaker. Note also: **deńwa (o) kawaru** 'make a replacement on the telephone.'

2. CC2 is an example of the special speech style described in 10A-SP5, in which long sentences are broken down into shorter spans, with the listener confirming his continuing attention and interest at each break. This style is extremely common on the telephone. Note the amount of repetition of the appointment time; and note also that the time is repeatedly mentioned in terms of **-ḡòro**, even though it is a business appointment.

(J)a. The compound **keńkyuuzyò** includes **keńkyuu** 'research.' Note also **kenkyuu-suru** 'do research'; **keńkyùusitu** 'laboratory.' The **-zyo** portion occurred previously in its basic form **syo** in the compound **zimûsyo** (cf. 13A-SP4).

(N)b. Note again the polite designation of self as **kotira**, basically a locational word.

(J)c. **Hâa** is a polite, rather stiff, and often humble equivalent of **hâi**.

---

9. The Japanese writing system distinguishes between two separate **kawaru** verbals—'change' versus 'exchange (with),' the former being affective and the latter operational.

(N)c. **Zitû** is a nominal: **zitû o iu** 'speak the truth'; **zitu no namae** 'real name'; **zitû ni yôku ′siḡoto (o)suru** 'really work hard.' Perhaps its most common usage is in the combination **zitû wa**, signaling the start of a particularly meaningful part of a conversation. On the telephone, the caller uses it to divide the initial ritual exchange of identification, greetings, and pleasantries, from an explanation for the true reason for the call.

Tikâi is the opposite of **tooi**. The combination /nominal X + **ni** + **tikâi**/ 'near X,' 'close to X' may be used in a concrete, spatial sense (**Toókyoo ni tikài**),[10] or in a temporal sense (**kû-zi ni tikâi**), or in a general sense of close resemblance (**nihóñḡo ni tikài**). Like **osoi** and **tooi**, **tikâi** has a nominal derivative in the **-ku** form: **tikâku** 'vicinity.'

Omé ni kakàru ↓, like **oai-suru** ↓, is a humble-polite equivalent of **âu**, 'have contact with a person' (particularly the person addressed), but is more formal and elegant than the **oai-suru** form. Literally it expresses 'suspension within the sight of another.' In the introduction ritual, the combination **hazímète ome ni kakarimasu** may occur as a more formal replacement for **hazímemàsite**. **Matá ome ni kakarimasyòo** occurs in formal, polite leave-taking, expressing a suggestion for further meetings.

(J)d. Here (J) uses **hâi** after a previous **hâa** of acknowledgment, both examples of **aizuti** (cf. 10A-SP5). It is not unusual to lower the politeness level, within a limited range, as a unit of conversation progresses. But it would be most unusual to jump from **hâa** to **ñ**!

(N)d. **Tuḡoo**, polite **gotuḡoo**, refers to personal convenience. Note: **tuḡóo ḡa ìi** 'is convenient (for someone)'; **tuḡóo ḡa warùi** 'is inconvenient (for someone).' These combinations should not be confused with **bêñri** and **hûbeñ**, which refer to inherent convenience and inconvenience, as in the case of the location of something. **Gotuḡoo wa?** is a commonly occurring question that seeks to determine what is convenient for the person addressed.

(J)e. Note the use of **Gurêe** without a polite title by someone who is undoubtedly a subordinate of Gray's. Why? Because this is a member of Gray's in-group talking to an out-group member. For the same reason, **orímàsu** ↓ is used.

Compare: **kayôobi ni modôru** 's/he'll return on Tuesday' and **kayôobi ni wa modôtte (i)ru** 'on Tuesday (at least) s/he'll [already] be back.' **Modôru** is an operational verbal; it refers to the return to a former position, covering everything from backing up a car to going back to Lesson 1. It is totally lacking in the connotations of **kâeru**, which implies a return to *one's own* home, country, office, etc.

Soré dè wa is the full, uncontracted phrase upon which the abbreviated sentence initial **zyâ(a)** (or uncontracted **dê wa** [cf. (N)f following]) 'well then' is based.

Dè here is the gerund of the copula; the pattern represented by this phrase will be analyzed in a later lesson.

(J)f. **Kêkkoo** overlaps with **îi** and **yorósìi** in some of its uses, but also reflects a number of differences. In those situations in which all three expressions can occur, **kêkkoo** is definitely the most formal and elegant. Note: (1) **kêkkoo** is a **na**-nominal, whereas **îi** and **yorósìi** are adjectivals (example: **kêkkoo na yasúmì** 'a fine vacation'); (2) **kêkkoo** does not occur in negative statements or affirmative questions; (3) like **îi** and **yorósìi**, **kêkkoo** may occur as a polite refusal, i.e., 'I'm fine as I am without accepting what you offered.'

(N)f. **Ukaḡau** occurred in 6A in the polite, ritual introduction to a request for information: **Tyôtto ukáḡaimàsu ḡa..** 'I'm just going to inquire.' In (N)d of CC2 it occurs again with the 'inquire' meaning. A second, very different meaning of this verbal is 'visit,' 'call on' (cf. [N]g of CC2). Like **neḡau**, this verbal is itself humble-polite, but occurs in the

---

10. In this usage, /**X kara tikâi**/ occurs as a less common alternate.

derivative /o-stem + -suru/ humble-polite pattern as well: **oukaḡai-suru.** This is a still more polite alternate. Once again the ritual **yorósiku oneḡai-itasimàsu** occurs as a request for future consideration, favorable treatment, and smooth interaction. Note that at this point in a comparable English conversation, we would probably say 'Thank you'—for the appointment already made.

(J)g. **Sitûree-itasimasita**, with absolutely no close English equivalent in this context, covers anything that could possibly have been considered **sitûree** in the preceding conversation—perhaps even the fact that Gray wasn't in.

Structural Patterns

1. **no de**

In 8A-SP3, we discussed the occurrence of nonfinal gerunds in examples in which their connection with the following predicate was causal. Examples:

   Byooki de kimáseñ desita. 'I didn't come, because I was sick.' (*lit.* 'Being sick, I didn't come.')

   Zîko ḡa âtte, okúrete kimàsita. 'There was an accident, and [so] I was late.'

In this construction, whether or not a causal relationship exists really depends upon the individual example. The construction itself signals only actualization of the gerund portion, followed by another predicate. Thus, **Durañsu e itte, huráñsuḡo o beñkyoo-simàsita.** 'I went to France and studied French' (*lit.* 'having gone to France, I studied French') describes the *circumstances* under which I studied French but not the *cause*.

However, when the gerund in this kind of construction is the gerund of an extended predicate (cf. 9B-SP3), the relationship is regularly causal. In this pattern, too, **no** may be contracted to **ñ**, the more usual alternate in other contexts. Examples:

   Wakàrànai no de, moó iti-do itte kudasài. 'I don't understand so (*lit.* the case being that I don't understand), please say it again.'

   Asíta ikù no de, kyôo wa 'ikanai. 'Given that I'm going tomorrow, I'm not going today.'

   Tumárànai no de, yamémàsita. 'Because (i.e., being that) it's boring, I quit.'

   Kikóenàkatta no de, mâe no hôo e itta ñ desu. '(It's that) I went to the front, inasmuch as I couldn't hear.'

   Syatyoo ḡa osêki o hazúsite (i)rassyàru no de, reñraku-dekimaseñ. 'Given that the president is away from his desk (*lit.* seat), I can't get in touch with him.'

We sometimes encounter 'node' written as a single word and treated as if it were a particle like **kara**, but this is misleading: (1) it misses the identification of **no de** with the extended predicate pattern, which helps in its interpretation; and (2) it ignores the important fact that **dà** before **no de** occurs as **nà**, a form which occurs *only before nominals*. Thus:

   Byoóki dà > (extended predicate alternate) **byoóki *nà* ñ da; byoóki *nà* no** (or **ñ**)

   de, dekînai 'because of being sick, I can't do it' (compare: **byoóki *dà* kara, dekînai**)

While **no de** and **kara** are structurally very different, they are similar in meaning. In /**X kara, Y**/, we are stating that *from* the occurrence of X comes Y; in /**X no de, Y**/, we acknowledge the existence of X as a given, and that being the case, Y occurs. Obviously, these meanings are close, but the use of **kara** often implies slightly more interest in what precedes, while the use of **no de** emphasizes what follows.

The nominal **no** of **no de** may be preceded by distal-style as well as direct-style predicates. Thus:

    kawárù no de *or* **kawárimàsu no de**
    omósiròi no de *or* **omósiròi desu no de**
    iyâ na no de *or* **iyâ desu no de**

2. **tikâi uti**

Previously we encountered the nominal **uti** as an equivalent for 'house' or 'home' (particularly one's own), and in the phrase **uti no** as the modifier for items connected with one's own in-group: **utí no syùziñ, uti no ko, uti no gakkoo, uti no kaisya,** etc.

Actually, in reference to in-group/out-group in Japanese society, it is **uti** which is the regular designation for the in-group.

Among the extended meanings of **uti** is 'interval' in the sense of 'an interval inside which,' i.e., 'an interval before something contrastive becomes involved.' When **uti** indicates the time *when* something occurs, it is followed by the particle **ni**. Examples:

    tikâi uti ni   'in an interval close at hand,' 'before long'
    wakâi uti ni   'while one is young,' 'before one gets old'
    âsa no uti ni   'during the morning,' 'before the morning is over'
    mik-ka no uti ni   'inside three days,' 'before three days are over'

Other kinds of examples will be introduced in later lessons.

3. |**desu nê(e)**|

It is of the utmost importance always to keep in mind the tremendous differences between the two active language skills, writing and speaking. When we write—even though we may have a particular audience in mind—we are detached from that audience at the time of production, and we have the opportunity to make changes and corrections before we declare a manuscript finished. However, except when we are talking to ourselves or reading a prepared speech, speaking is interactive at the time of production. This means that we have the advantage of being able to notice how our listeners are reacting, affording us the luxury of being able to adjust our timing and to amplify and correct and amend what has just been said, as appropriate. But this also means that we are thinking and plotting our linguistic strategies as we talk, with the result that what we say is often significantly less well organized than what we write.

We have already discussed a number of hesitation words and their functions. Another very common 'filler' in this category is |**desu nê(e)**|,[11] which is inserted at the end of a structural phrase and thereby ends a minor sentence. The following sentence connects structurally with what precedes as if it were part of the same sentence minus |**desu nê(e)**|.

When |**desu nê(e)**| is used as a filler, it does *not* itself link up with the items around it to form regular structural patterns. To show this difference, bars | | will be used to set it apart.

This use of |**desu nê(e)**| reflects interaction between speaker and listener, at the same

---

11. **Nê(e)** occurs in its usual variants—**ne! ne?** and **nêe.**

time providing the speaker with an instant to organize, and the listener an instant to process, what is being said. Examples:

> **Hutú-ka no uti nì wa |desu nêe.| Daré mo dekìnai to omoimasu.** 'Within two days—you know—I don't think anyone can do it.'
>
> **Kotíra è wa modóranai no de |desu ne!| Awânai to omoimasu.** 'Inasmuch as I'm not coming back here—you know—I don't think I'll see [them].'
>
> **Zitû wa |desu neˊ| Tuúzinàkatta ñ desu yo⤸** 'Actually—you know?—I didn't get through.'

Drills

A 1. **Anó katà wa, kono kaisya desyoo?**
'S/he is [connected with] this company, isn't s/he?'

Êe, kono kaisya no syatyóo dèsu.
'Yes, s/he's the president of this company.'

2. **Anó katà wa, konó kà desyoo?**
'S/he is [connected with] this section, isn't s/he?'

Êe, konó kà no katyóo dèsu.
'Yes, s/he's the manager of this section.'

3. **zimûsyo**; 4. **byooiñ**; 5. **daiḡaku**; 6. **bû**

B 1. **Butyoo wa, îma deñwa-site (i)màsu ka⤸**
'Is the division manager telephoning now?'

Butyóo dèsu ka⤸ Êe, deñwa-tyuu dèsu.
'The division manager? Yes, s/he's in the middle of a phone call.'

2. **Syatyoo wa, îma syuttyoo-site (i)màsu ka⤸**

'Is the company president away on business now?'

Syatyóo dèsu ka⤸ Êe, syuttyoo-tyuu dèsu.
'The company president? Yes, s/he's in the middle of a business trip.'

3. **Mîyazi-kyoozyu/zyûḡyoo site (i)masu; yasúmì desu**; 6. **iñtyoo/kâiḡi desu**; 7. **arúbàito no gakusee/siḡóto site (i)màsu**; 4. **hîsyo/gaísyutu-site (i)màsu**; 5. **katyoo/** 8. **Yamâmori-sañ/hanâsite (i)masu**

C 1. **Kosyóo-sinài desyoo?**
'It doesn't break down, does it?'

Iêie, kosyóo-surù no de, komâtte (i)masu.
'Wrong! Given that it does break down, it's upsetting.'

2. **Syatyóo zya nài desyoo?**
'That's not the company president, is it?'

Iêie, syatyóo nà no de, komâtte (i)masu.
'Wrong! Given that it is the company president, it's upsetting.'

3. **toóku nài**; 4. **taísetu zya nài**; 5. **kikoeta**; 6. **tuuzita**; 7. **okâsìku nâkatta**; 8. **hazîmete datta**; 9. **wakâi**; 10. **dekîru**; 11. **bêñri (da)**; 12. **kikóeyàsùkatta**

D 1. **Kakínikùi desyoo?**
'It's difficult to write with, isn't it?'

Êe. Kakínikùi no de, tukáwanaku narimàsita yo.

'Yes. Given that it is difficult to write with, I don't use it now' (*lit.* I've become non-using).

2. **Kosyóo-sità desyoo?**
'It broke down, didn't it?'

Êe. Kosyóo-sità no de, tukáwanaku narimàsita yo.
'Yes. Given that it did break down, I don't use it now.'

3. **rakû zya nâi**; 4. **hêñ (da)**; 5. **okâsìku natta**; 6. **okúrete kùru**; 7. **tukáinikùi**; 8. **hûrûku natta**

E 1. **Syatyóo-sañ irássyaimàsu ka⤴**
'Is the company president in?'

Syatyóo dèsu ka⤴ Syatyoo no hîsyo to kawárimàsu no de, syôosyoo omáti-kudasài.
'The company president? I'll put the president's secretary on (instead of me), so just a moment, please.'

2. **Tâisi irássyaimàsu ka⤴**
'Is the ambassador in?'

Tâisi desu ka⤴ Tâisi no hîsyo to kawárimàsu no de, syôosyoo omáti-kudasài.
'The ambassador? I'll put the ambassador's secretary on (instead of me), so just a moment, please.'

3. **iñtyoo-señsee**; 4. **gakutyoo**; 5. **ryôozi**; 6. **syotyoo-sañ**

F 1. **Butyoo no otaku ni ukáĝaù ñ desu ka⤴**
'(Is it that) you're going to visit the division manager's home?'

Tikâi uti ni ukáĝaitài ñ desu ĝa..
'I'd like to visit soon, but...' (I don't know if I can).

2. **Ano kyoozyu to âu ñ desu ka⤴**
'(Is it that) you're going to meet with that professor?'

Tikâi uti ni aítài ñ desu ĝa..
'I'd like to meet [with him/her] soon, but...' (I don't know if I can).

3. **katyoo to 'soodañ-suru**; 4. **gakkoo dêru**; 5. **kono siĝoto 'yameru**; 6. **Mîyazi-iñtyoo ni 'reñraku-suru**

G 1. **Yoóròppa e ikímàsita ka⤴**
'Did you go to Europe?'

Iie, itte (i)maseñ. Yasûi uti ni ikítài ñ desu kedo..
'No, I haven't been [there]. I'd like to go while it's reasonable, but...' (I don't know if I can).

2. **Supeiñĝo beñkyoo-simàsita ka⤴**
'Did you study Spanish?'

Iie, beñkyoo-site (i)maseñ. Yasûi uti ni beñkyoo-sitài ñ desu kedo..
'No, I haven't studied [it]. I'd like to study [it] while it's reasonable, but...' (I don't know if I can).

3. **Nihôñ e kaérimàsita**; 4. **Hokkàidoo mimâsita**; 5. **deñwa kakémàsita**

H 1. **Ití-nitì de dekímàsu ka**▱
'Can you do it in (*lit.* being) one day?'

Sâa. Ití-nitì no uti ni dekîru desyoo ka nêe.
'Hm. I wonder if I can do it within one day.'

2. **Ití-zìkañ de dekímàsu ka**▱
'Can you do it in one hour?'

Sâa. Ití-zìkañ no uti ni dekîru desyoo ka nêe.
'Hm. I wonder if I can do it within one hour.'

3. **itî-neñ**; 4. **iś-syùukañ**; 5. **ik-kàḡetu**

I 1. **Go-kâḡetu no uti ni dekîru desyoo ka.**
'Would you be able to do that within five months?'

Zitû wa |desu ne!| Yoń-kàḡetu de dekîru ñ desu yo.
'Actually—you know—(the fact is) I can do it in four months.'

2. **Mui-ka no uti ni dekîru desyoo ka.**
'Would you be able to do that within six days?'

Zitû wa |desu ne!| Itú-ka de dekîru ñ desu yo.
'Actually—you know—(the fact is) I can do it in five days.'

3. **go-zîkañ**; 4. **nî-neñ**; 5. **kyuú-syùukañ**

J 1. **Myôoniti no uti ni kâeru desyoo?**
'We'll return (within) tomorrow, won't we?'

Ie, ainiku myoóḡòniti made damê na ñ desu yo.
'No, unfortunately, it's impossible until the day after tomorrow.'

2. **Kińyòobi no uti ni 'kore o naôsu desyoo?**
'We'll fix this (within) Friday, won't we?'

Ie, ainiku doyôobi made damê na ñ desu yo.
'No, unfortunately, it's impossible until Saturday.'

3. **siǵatù/kotira e modôru**; 4. **raisyuu/dekîru**; 5. **râiḡetu/kakénaòsu**

K 1. **Minâsañ kikóemàsita ne**▱
'You (all) could hear—right?'

|Anoo| Watasi wa |desu nêe.| Zeńzeñ kikoenàkatta ñ desu yo.
'Uh, the fact is—you know—I (at least) couldn't hear at all.'

2. **Minâsañ soódañ-simàsita ne**▱
'You (all) talked it over—right?'

|Anoo| Watasi wa |desu nêe.| Zeńzeñ soódañ-sinàkatta ñ desu yo.
'Uh, the fact is—you know—I (at least) didn't consult at all.'

3. **kikímàsita**; 4. **imâsita**; 5. **mimâsita**; 6. **dekímàsita**

L 1. **Kore wa, tukáiyasùi desyoo?**
'This is easy to use, isn't it?'

|Anoo| Zitû wa nêe. |Anoo| Tukáiyàsùku nâi ñ desu kedo . .

2. **Soñna siḡoto wa, omósiròi desyoo?**
'That kind of work is interesting, isn't it?'

|Anoo| Zitû wa nêe. |Anoo| Omósìròku nâi ñ desu kedo . .
'Uh—actually, you know—uh—the fact is that it's not easy to use, but . . .' (it's thought to be easy).

|Anoo| Zitû wa nêe. |Anoo| Omósìròku nâi ñ desu kedo . .
'Uh—actually, you know—uh—the fact is that it's not interesting, but . . .' (it's thought to be interesting).

3. kânozyo/Tanaka-sañ no ôkusañ (da); 4. kâre/zyoózù (da); 5. hîsyo/byoóki (dà); 6. ano kaisya/isóḡasìi; 7. asíta no kàiḡi/taísetu (dà); 8. seńsèe/irássyàru

M 1. **Gakutyoo wa, asita 'kotira e irássyaimasèñ yo**
'The university president isn't coming here tomorrow!'

Sôo desu ka. Soré dè wa |desu nêe.| Watási mo kimasèñ kara . .
'Oh? In that case—you know—I'm not coming either, so . . .' (let's plan accordingly).

2. **Tanaka-kyoozyu wa, kôñbañ no zyûḡyoo ni odé ni narimasèñ yo**
'Professor Tanaka is not attending tonight's class.'

Sôo desu ka. Soré dè wa |desu nêe.| Watási mo demasèñ kara . .
'Oh? In that case—you know—I'm not attending either, so . . .' (let's plan accordingly).

3. ryôozi/kokó è wa omódori ni narimasèñ; 4. katyoo/kâre to soódañ-nasaimasèñ; 5. tâisi/Nâḡoya ni otómari ni narimasèñ; 6. katyoo/hîsyo no kaérì o omáti ni narimasèñ

N 1. **Anó katà no 'gotuḡoo wa?**
'How about what is convenient for him/her?'

A. Gotuḡoo wa ukáḡawanàkatta ñ desu. Moósiwake arimasèñ.
'Oh. (The fact is) I didn't inquire about what would be convenient. I'm sorry.'

2. **Anó katà no osîḡoto wa?**
'How about his/her work?'

A. Osîḡoto wa ukáḡawanàkatta ñ desu. Moósiwake arimasèñ.
'Oh. (The fact is) I didn't inquire about his/her work. I'm sorry.'

3. onamae; 4. deńwabàñḡoo

O 1. **Suíyòobi de gozaimasu neʔ Kêkkoo de gozaimasu.**
'That's Wednesday—right? That will be fine.'

Dê wa, suíyòobi ni ukáḡaimàsu no de, yorósiku oneḡai-itasimàsu.
'Then I'll come on Wednesday (so I request your consideration).'

2. **Gôzeñ ku-zí-hàñ de gozaimasu neʔ Kêkkoo de gozaimasu.**

Dê wa, gôzeñ ku-zí-hàñ ni ukáḡaimàsu no de, yorósiku oneḡai-itasimàsu.

'That's 9:30 A.M.—right? That will be fine.'   'Then I'll come at 9:30 A.M. (so I request your consideration).'

3. **gôḡo sitî-zi**; 4. **si-ḡatu 'mui-ka**; 5. **raisyuu no mokúyòobi**

P 1. **Asíta no kàiḡi wa, zyûu-zi kara desu kedo, gotuḡoo wa?**   **Asita no zyûu-zi kara desu ka⤴ Kêkkoo desu. Asita no zyûu-zi ni ukaḡaimasu.**

'Tomorrow's conference is from 10:00 on; is that convenient for you?' (*lit.* how about your convenience?)   'From 10:00 on tomorrow? That's fine. I'll come at 10:00 tomorrow.'

2. **Asíta no zèmi wa, yôru desu kedo, gotuḡoo wa?**   **Asita no yôru desu ka⤴ Kêkkoo desu. Asita no yôru ukaḡaimasu.**

'The seminar tomorrow is in the evening; is that convenient for you?' (*lit.* how about your convenience?)   'Tomorrow evening? That's fine. I'll come tomorrow evening.'

3. **raísyuu no zyùḡyoo/kińyòo**; 4. **râiḡetu no siḡoto/mui-ka kara**; 5. **myôoniti no soodań/nî-zi kara**

Application Exercises

A. Practice making telephone calls, covering the following types of situations. Remember to include |**desu nê(e)**|, as appropriate. Your task is not to *translate* these outlines, but rather to convey the message in *appropriate Japanese,* using the ritual language you have learned. Use real telephones in order to become accustomed to the increased distortion of telephone conversations as well as the difficulty of speaking with someone you cannot see. (Remember that there is no necessity to limit your Japanese-language telephone calls to class hours!)

    1. Mr. Nakamura, from Oriental Trade, calls Ms. Carter at the Continental Bank. He makes arrangements to see her tomorrow at about 2:30.
    2. Mrs. Carter calls her husband at the Continental Bank, but he is out. She leaves a message with his secretary that she will meet him at the Okura Hotel at 6:30 this evening. (Remember your in-groups and out-groups!)
    3. Ms. Miyazi, from Tokyo University, calls Mr. Gray at the American Embassy, but he is out. She is connected with his secretary. When she explains that she would like to see him soon, she learns that he is on a business trip but will be back next Monday. An appointment is arranged for next Tuesday at 10:30.
    4. Takashi Ito calls the home of his close friend, Bill Carter, but Carter is at school. He will return home at about 6:30 this evening, so Ito will call again a little after 7:00.
    Remember to use ritual expressions, as appropriate, and hesitation noises and fillers. (Be sure to avoid English 'uh'!)

B. Core Conversations: Substitution
    Return to the Core Conversations and practice them with appropriate vocabulary substitutions. Make sure that at least some of your practice uses actual telephones.

SECTION C

Eavesdropping

(Once again, the following questions are to be answered on the basis of the accompanying tape. A = the first speaker and B = the second speaker in each conversation.)

1a. Whose home is B calling?
 b. What is the problem?
2a. Who called Mr/s. Morimoto?
 b. What was the problem?
3a. What is A's problem?
 b. What does A learn from B?
 c. What does B offer to do?
 d. What is A's reaction?
4a. Whose home is being discussed?
 b. What is one of its advantages?
 c. How is the neighborhood described?
5a. Who is the child over there?
 b. What possible identification is offered for the person next to the child?
 c. Why is B not certain?
6a. What is being discussed?
 b. What are its advantages?
 c. Where is it sold, in general?
 d. Where is it possibly also sold, in particular?
7a. What is A's problem?
 b. What does B suggest?
 c. What is the outcome?
8. What is A checking on? Why?
9a. Who has just returned?
 b. What occurred during that person's absence? Give details.
10a. Who is currently using the adjoining room?
 b. What organization is Matsuda associated with?
 c. What is Matsuda doing here?
11a. What organization did B call?
 b. With whom did B speak? For how long?
12a. Who is B?
 b. What is B turning down?
 c. How does B account for this refusal?
13a. What does A admire?
 b. Who previously used it?
 c. How old is it?
14a. Who answers the phone?
 b. Who does B think has answered?
 c. Why did B make an error in identifying the speaker?
 d. With whom does B want to speak?
 e. Where is that person?
15a. What is A's problem?
 b. What does A learn from B?
 c. Why is A particularly concerned?
16a. What is A's concern?
 b. Who is B?

c. Why is B not attending?
   d. Who may possibly attend? Why?
17a. Who is the second person to answer the phone?
   b. Who is making the call?
   c. What is the caller's position? In what organization?
   d. Why is the caller making this call?
18a. Where is Gray?
   b. Why does A apologize?
   c. Who is A? From what organization?
   d. When will Gray be back?
   e. What is A going to do?
19a. What evidence does A cite that indicates how busy Dr. Ito is?
   b. Who saw Dr. Ito? When?
   c. What news of Dr. Ito is provided by that person?
   d. What is the current effect of this on Dr. Ito?
20a. Who is B?
   b. What close friend of B's is mentioned?
   c. How did they become friends?
   d. What current association do they have?
   e. What is B going to do for A?
21a. Who is being called by B?
   b. With what organization is that person connected?
   c. Where is that person now?
   d. What does B intend to do?
22a. Who is making the call? From what organization?
   b. Why is the call being made?
   c. What is A's first reaction?
   d. What is A's later suggestion?
23a. What is A trying to find out?
   b. What solution does B suggest?
   c. What is the problem with that solution?
   d. What is B's next solution?
24a. What is under discussion?
   b. What is A's comment about it?
   c. How does B praise it?
   d. What does A request of B?
   e. When will B comply?

Utilization

(As usual, provide a stimulus and/or a response for each item, developing natural conversational sequences. Be sure to include appropriate fillers and hesitation noises.)
   1. Telephone the Takano household and ask if Takashi is in.
   2. You are talking on the telephone, struggling with a bad connection. Ask the person you're speaking with to talk a little louder.
   3. Tell a colleague that you telephoned Oriental Trade, but no one answered. Comment on how strange it is.
   4. You answered the telephone, but it's a wrong number. What would you say?
   5. You have just reached a wrong number. What would you say?
   6. Tell a colleague that you bought any number of dictionaries, but they're all no good.

7. You've just finished a telephone call. Tell your colleague that it was a bad connection, and you couldn't hear.

8. Tell a colleague that you called the U.S. last night, but you didn't get through.

9. Leave these messages for Dr. Miyaji on the telephone answering machine (be sure to identify yourself):
    (a) You're not coming to class tomorrow because you're sick.
    (b) You'd like Dr. Miyaji to call when he's free.
    (c) You'll call again tomorrow morning.

10. Express your consternation over the fact that:
    (a) the telephone is out of order.
    (b) you don't understand the teacher's Japanese.
    (c) nobody answers (the telephone).
    (d) Dr. Morimoto's telephone is always busy.

11. You've been asked to cut a pie. Ask what you should cut it with.

12. Your call from Europe is a bad connection. Ask the caller to place the call over again.

13. Tell a friend that you went to Professor Takano's seminar yesterday, but he talked in a low voice, so you couldn't hear at all.

14. Tell a colleague that a friend of yours is on a business trip, so you are house-sitting.

15. A friend hasn't appeared for class. Suggest that she may be sick.

16. A colleague is waiting for some overdue reports from Nishida. Suggest that maybe they were difficult and he couldn't do them.

17. Comment on how easy this pen is to write with.

18. You're listening to a television news commentator. Comment on what a strange voice [he has].

19. Tell a colleague that you have some important business to attend to and are going home a bit early today.

20. Tell a friend that you went to Europe once fifteen years ago, and you'd like to go back while you're [still] young.

21. A call has come in for the president of the company. Explain that since he's out of the office now, you'll put his secretary on the line. Tell the caller to wait a moment.

22. Find out when the section chief will return here.

23. Telephone the office of Division Manager Yamamori (in another company). Explain that you'd like to see him soon, and find out when it will be convenient.

24. Explain to a colleague that Dr. Morimoto was a professor at the German Language Research Institute, but has become a college president.

25. You're talking on the telephone to the head of the Toranomon Hospital. Tell him that you'll visit him at 10:00 tomorrow morning, so you'd like 'his favorable consideration.'

26. In a telephone conversation with your language instructor, move from the ritual beginnings to the real reason for your call: you'll be on a business trip from Monday to Thursday of next week, so you won't be attending class until Friday. Apologize!

27. You have just learned something new from the company president. React (i.e., 'Oh, really?') in your most polite language.

28. Someone has suggested a time for a meeting. Tell her that will be fine.

29. You've just learned that the instructor you wanted to see won't be back until tomorrow. Tell the secretary that in that case, you'll come again the day after tomorrow.

30. A friend is wondering why he never sees you. Explain that you are studying Japanese all day long.

Check-up

1. What is the underlying meaning of /interrogative + **mo**/? Describe the occurrence of such patterns with affirmative and negative predicates. (A-SP1)

2. How does the meaning of /interrogative number + **mo**/ differ from that of most other interrogatives occurring in this pattern? (A-SP1)

3. What forms of the predicate precede **ka mo sirenai**? What happens to predicates ending in **da**? (A-SP2)

4. How does the addition of **ka mo sirenai** to a predicate change its meaning? (A-SP2)

5. How is the gerund of the adjectival formed? Give an example of its use. (A-SP3)

6. What is the difference in meaning between:

   Kâre ğa wakáránakute komâtte imasu. *and*

   Kâre wa wakáránakute komâtte imasu. (A-SP3)

7. Contrast the Japanese equivalents of:
   (a) 'a bank and a post office'
   (b) 'is new and (is) expensive'
   (c) 'is pretty and (is) expensive'
   (d) 'turn the corner and stop' (A-SP3)

8. What is a compound? What types are there? To what word-class does a compound belong? Give three examples. (A-SP4)

9. What is the meaning of /predicate + **no de**/? How do we analyze **no de**? What forms of the predicate precede **no de**? (B-SP1)

10. What evidence is there that the **no** of **no de** is a nominal? (B-SP1)

11. Describe the use of **uti** as a time expression. Give two examples. (B-SP2)

12. What is a commonly occurring distal-style 'filler' in the spoken language? (B-SP3)

Lesson 14

SECTION A

Core Conversations

1(J)a. **Môo, ohîru tabémàsita?**
  b. **Mâda. Onáka suità desyoo.**
  c. **Môo, ití-zi-hàñ desu yo⤴ Rañti-sàabisu wa, nî-zi made desyoo.**

  (N)a. **Iya, mâda tâbete (i)nâi ñ desu.**
  b. **Êe. Îma nâñ-zi desu ka⤴**
  c. **Âa, sôo desu ne! Zyâa, tyôtto it́te kimàsu.**

2(J)a. **Môo gotyúumoñ-nasaimàsita ka⤴**
  b. **Kotira to kotira de gozaimàsu.**
  c. **Hâi. Pâñ ni nasáimàsu ka⤴**

  (N)a. **Ie, mâda desu. Kyôo no 'teesyoku wa?**
  b. **Zyâa, eé-kòosu ni simasu.**
  c. **Ie, râisu oneḡai-simasu.**

3(J)a. **Onómìmono wa?**
  b. **Atûi no desu ka⤴—tumétài no desu ka⤴**
  c. **Koótya de gozaimàsu ne⤴**

  (N)a. **Mîruku.**
  b. **Tumétài no. ... A, tyôtto .. Yappàri koótya ni site kudasài.**
  c. **Sôo. Dôo mo sumímaseñ.**

English Equivalents

1(J)a. Did you eat lunch yet?
  b. Not yet. You must be hungry!
  c. It's 1:30 already. Isn't the special lunch served [only] until 2:00?

  (N)a. No, (the fact is) I haven't eaten yet.
  b. Yes. What time is it (now)?
  c. Oh, that's right. Well then, I'll go and grab a bite (lit. I'll go for a bit and come).

2(J)a. Did you order yet?
  b. [Pointing to menu] They're here and here.

  (N)a. No, not yet. How about today's specials?
  b. Well, I'll have (lit. make [it] into) the 'A' lunch.

c. Certainly. Will you have (*lit.* make [it] into) bread?

3(J)a. How about [something to] drink?
b. Is that hot (stuff), or cold (stuff)?

c. That's tea, then—right?

c. No, I'd like rice.

(N)a. [I'll have] milk.
b. Cold (stuff). . . . Oh, just a minute. Please make [that] (into) tea, after all.
c. Yes. Thanks very much.

BREAKDOWNS
(AND SUPPLEMENTARY VOCABULARY)

1. **môo** /+ affirmative predicate/ (SP1) — already, yet
   ohîru — noon; noon meal
   +**hirúgòhañ** — lunch
   +**aságòhañ** — breakfast
   +**bañgòhañ** — dinner
   tabémàsita? (SP2) — did you eat?
   mâda /+ negative predicate/ (SP1) — not yet
   onaka — stomach
   suku /-u; suita/ — become empty
   onaka (ğa) suku — become hungry
   +**nôdo** — throat
   +**kawâku** /-u; kawâita/ — become dry
   +**nôdo (ğa) kawâku** — become thirsty
   rañti-sàabisu — special lunch
   +**syokudoo** — dining room, restaurant

2. **tyuumoñ-suru/gotyúumoñ-nasàru** ↑ — place an order
   +**tanômu** /-u; tanôñda/ — request, ask for
   mâda da — not yet (*lit.* it is yet [to happen])
   teesyoku *or*
   kôosu — a meal of several courses involving a fixed menu

   eé-kòosu — the 'A-meal' (so labeled on the menu)
   eé-kòosu ni suru (SP3) — make [it] (into) the 'A-meal'; decide on the 'A-meal'

   pâñ — bread
   râisu — cooked rice (usually served on a plate)

3. **nomîmono/onómìmono** — beverage, a drink
   +**tabémòno** — food
   tumetai /-katta/ — is cold

Supplementary Food and Drink Vocabulary (SP4)

(o)sakana	fish
susî/(o)sûsi	cold, vinegared rice served with raw fish, seaweed, egg, and so forth
sasímì/osasimi	raw fish served with horseradish and soy sauce
teñpura	batter-fried fish and vegetables
sukiyaki	a stew of vegetables and meat or chicken cooked in a broth
(o)sôba	buckwheat noodles
beñtòo/obeñtoo	box lunch
sâñdo *or* sañdoìtti	sandwich
gôhañ	cooked rice (usually served in a bowl)
komê/okome	uncooked rice
bâtaa	butter
siô/osîo	salt
kosyôo	pepper
(o)syooyu	soy sauce
tamâḡo	egg
(o)mizu	cold water
yû/oyu	hot water
koori	ice

Miscellaneous Notes

1. In CC1, two business colleagues discuss lunch—in particular, the fact that (N) hasn't eaten yet. Both speakers use careful-style, with distal-style predicates occurring in the major sentences which are used throughout the conversation, with the single exception of the echo use of **mâda**.

(J)a. **Ohîru** is a time word that refers to the noon hour; **hiru**, without the **o**-prefix, may also refer to daytime in general. In daily conversation, **ohîru** is a commonly occurring word for 'lunch,' a more informal equivalent of **hirúgòhañ**. With the usual difference of focus and emphasis, (N)a might also occur with phrase-particle **o** or **wa** following **ohîru**.

(J)b. **Suku** is an affective, double-**ḡa** verbal describing a change of state: 'become empty' or 'become vacant.' It can apply to everything from stomachs to streetcars. Note: **suítè (i)ru** 'it is empty'; **suítè (i)ta** 'it was empty'; **suita** 'it emptied out'; **sukánàkatta** 'it didn't empty out,' etc. Note also: **Tomodati ḡa onáka ḡa suítè (i)ru kara** 'because my friend is hungry.' In (J)b, phrase-particle **ḡa** might also occur following **onaka.**
Kawâku and **nôdo (ḡa) kawâku** pattern in exactly parallel fashion. **Kawâku** can also be used in reference to laundry, hair, dishes, etc. becoming dry.

(J)c. **Sâabisu**, a borrowing from English 'service,' covers both regular services performed as well as special services and gifts for which customers do not pay, i.e., treats that are 'on the house.' **Rañti-sàabisu** usually refers to a special lunch menu offered at a reduced price.

Syokudoo is a dining room in a public building or a private home. It may also refer to a small, inexpensive restaurant.

2. CC2 and 3 take place in a restaurant: (J), a waiter, uses polite careful-style, with distal-style predicates and a heavy preponderance of major sentences; (N), the customer, uses plain careful-style for the most part, but includes a number of fragments which further point up the difference between the speech style of the two participants.

(J)a. **Tyuumoñ**, a nominal, is a general term for an order—for food or merchandise of any kind. This word forms a **-suru** compound which is an operational verbal; it occurs in the pattern **X (o) tyuumoñ-suru** 'order X.' **Gotyúumoñ-nasàru**, a polite ↑ equivalent, refers to someone else's ordering.
Tanômu 'ask for' is a general verbal of requesting, without the humble-polite connotations of **neḡâu**. With **tanômu**, the item requested is followed by (**o**), and the person to whom the request is directed is followed by **ni**.

☠ WARNING: Do not confuse

Tomódati ni kikimàsita. 'I asked a friend' (e.g., to answer a question). *and*

Tomódati ni tanomimàsita. 'I asked a friend' (to do or provide something).

Tyuumoñ-suru, which covers requesting only in the specific sense of 'place an order,' is of more restricted use than **tanômu**.

(J)c. Japanese-style meals regularly include rice, but Western-style meals often offer a choice of rice or bread. Note that the identical kind of rice may be named differently depending on the meal with which it is served. This points up the tremendous importance Japanese place on fixed role and appropriateness. In general, unexpected and individualistic multipurpose usage is not high on the Japanese list of virtues, although there has been some change in this area in recent years. But rice cookers are not used to bake pound cakes, teacups are not used to serve punch, and **obi** (kimono sashes) are not used as dining-room table runners.

Râisu o is, of course, also possible here, although less likely to occur, since **râisu** is the regular contrast with **pañ**: there is not an emphasis on selection.

3. (J)a. **Nomîmono** and **tabémòno** are examples of compound nominals of the /verbal + nominal/ class. Note that in such cases, the nonfinal verbal is regularly in its stem form (**-màsu** form minus **-màsu**). **Monô** as an independent nominal means 'thing'; more will be said about it in a later lesson. Note also: **wasuremono** 'a thing left behind'; **kaimono** 'shopping.'

(J)a. **Tumetai** contrasts with **samûi** in the items to which it may refer. **Tumetai** is the more general term, which can be applied to anything cold to the touch. **Samûi** is reserved for coldness of the atmosphere. A day or a winter or a room or a house may be described as **samûi**; but cold coffee or soup or hands or bath water can only be **tumetai**. Compare also: **tumetai hito** 'a cold(-hearted) person'; **samûi hito** 'a person who feels cold.'

Japanese drink hot milk as well as cold. In this alternate question, **no** is the nominal, replacing the more specific **mîruku**. Note how different the meaning would be if **no** were omitted: in reference to some specific milk, one might ask, **Atûi desu ka⤴—tumétài desu ka⤴** 'Is it hot, or cold?' But in this context the waiter is asking, 'Is it hot (milk), or cold (milk)—i.e., that you want?' hence the requirement for either **mîruku** or its replacement (**no**).

(N)c. With **sumímaseñ**, (N) both thanks the waiter and apologizes for changing the order.

Supplementary Vocabulary

The **beńtòo** is an important item in any discussion of Japanese food. It ranges from the box lunch packed at home for children to take to school or on an outing and the one many office workers carry in their briefcases to the lunches sold in theaters and in trains and on station platforms. It can also be a very elaborate, catered 'box lunch' served at special parties and receptions. It is often cold, Japanese-style food including cold rice, but the possible variety of foods included is tremendous.

Sâńdo is a shortening of the borrowing **sańdoìtti**, particularly common in compounds: **hamú-sàńdo**, **tuná-sàńdo**, etc. It frequently turns up in Japanese-style English contexts as 'sand.' (Cookies and biscuits designated as 'Sand Variety' are NOT gritty!)

Gôhań is sometimes used as a general term for food or a meal, as in the combination **Gôhań ḡa dekímàsita** (*lit.* 'Food has been completed,' i.e., 'Dinner is ready').

Komê '*uncooked* rice,' is bought in a rice shop (**komêya**) or a **sûupaa** or a **depâato**. It is grown but never eaten (except in discussing the eating habits of an entire society): compare **komê o tukûru** 'grow rice (to be cooked),' but **gôhań o tukûru** 'make rice (for eating).'

A **tamâḡo**, when joined by **hâmu** ('ham') or **bêekoń** ('bacon'), usually becomes an **êggu**!

Structural Patterns

*1. /***môo** + *AFFIRMATIVE PREDICATE/*; */***mâda** + *NEGATIVE PREDICATE/*

In Lesson 5A-SP5, we encountered **moo** occurring in combination with—and in the same accent phrase as—an immediately following quantity expression, indicating an additional amount. Examples:

    moó sukòsi 'a little more'

    moó ni-kàḡetu 'two more months'

    moo hyaku-eń '¥100 more'

    moó hitò-ri 'one more person'

Note that **takúsàń** does not occur in this pattern.

We now add **môo**, which links up with a predicate and implies a change of state occurring 'already' or 'yet.'[1] In this section, we will examine only its occurrences with affirmative predicates. Examples:

    Môo ohîru (o) tabémàsu ka↗ 'Are you going to eat lunch already (*or* yet)?'

    Âkatyań wa, môo gôhań (o) tabémàsu ka↗ 'Does the baby eat rice already (*or* yet)?'

    Môo ohîru (o) tâbete (i)masu ka↗ 'Are you eating lunch already (*or* yet)?' *or* 'Have you eaten lunch already (*or* yet)?'

    Môo gaḱkoo e itte (i)màsu ka↗ 'Are you going to (i.e., attending) school already (*or* yet)?'

    Môo ohîru (o) tabémàsita ka↗ 'Did you eat lunch already (*or* yet)?'

    Môo ohîru (o) tâbete (i)masita ka↗ 'Were you eating lunch already (*or* yet)?' *or* 'Had you eaten lunch already (*or* yet)?'—i.e., as of a particular point in time in the past.

    Môo îi desu ka↗ 'Is it all right (ready, enough, etc.) yet?'

    Môo damê desita ka↗ 'Was it broken (no good, out of order, etc.) already?'

---

1. Native speakers of English vary in their use of 'yet'. As an equivalent of **môo**, it occurs only in the 'yet' = 'already' sense, *not* as 'yet' = 'still.'

As the above examples demonstrate, /**môo** + predicate/ sequences may refer to single instances or repeated occurrences, depending on the form of the predicate and the context. Note the contrast in pronunciation and meaning between /**moo** + quantity/ and /**môo** + predicate/:

    Moó sañ-niñ kitè (i)masu. 'Three more people have come.' *but*
    Môo sañ-niñ kitè (i)masu. 'Three people have come already.'
    Moó sukòsi tukáimàsita. 'I used a little more.' *but*
    Môo sukôsi tukáimàsita. 'I used a little already.'

In direct negative replies to **môo** questions, we find **mâda**, which regularly implies continuation, referring to an activity or state that goes on 'still' (or 'yet'). With a negative predicate, the continuation of non-occurrence means that something is 'not happening yet.' In other words, if Mr. Ito continues to 'not-eat,' he 'hasn't eaten yet' or 'isn't going to eat yet.'

When describing present non-activity that is continuing, the /**mâda** + **-te (i)nai**/ pattern is usual, particularly in reference to an individual's volitional activity. Thus:

    Môo Sapporo e ikimàsita ka⤴ 'Did you go to Sapporo already (*or* yet)?'
    Iie, mâda itte (i)masèñ. 'No, I haven't gone yet.'
    Hîsyo, môo kimâsita ka⤴ 'Did the secretary come already (*or* yet)?'
    Ie, mâda kité (i)masèñ. 'No, she hasn't come yet.'

With this last sentence, compare:

    Siñbuñ, môo kimâsita ka⤴ 'Did the paper come yet?'
    Mâda kimásèñ. 'It hasn't come yet' (*lit.* continues to not-come).

Here the arrival of the newspaper is looked on as a happening outside the control of the conversation participants, and the expression of its non-arrival shows less direct connection with the speaker.

Also possible are exchanges of the following types:

    Môo kaérimàsu ka⤴ 'Are you going home already (*or* yet)?'
    Ie, mâda kaérimasèñ. 'No, I'm not going home yet.'
    Katyoo wa, môo kâette (i)masu ka⤴ 'Has the *kacho* come back already (*or* yet)?'
    Ie, mâda kâette (i)másèñ. 'No, he hasn't come back yet.'
    Môo konó siḡoto o site (i)màsu ka⤴ 'Are you doing this work already (*or* yet)?'
    Ie, mâda sité (i)masèñ. 'No, I'm not doing it yet.' *or* 'No, I haven't done it yet.'
    Môo beñkyoo-site (i)màsita ka⤴ 'Were you studying already (*or* yet)?' *or* 'Had you studied already (*or* yet)?' (as of a particular point in the past)
    Ie, mâda beñkyoo-site (i)masèñ desita. 'No, I wasn't studying yet.' *or* 'I hadn't studied yet.' (as of a particular point in the past)

Môo/mâda pairs also occur with adjectival and nominal predicates:

    Asoko wa, môo samûi desu ka⤴ 'Is it cold there already (*or* yet)?'
    Iie, mâda sâmuku nâi desu. 'No, it isn't cold yet.'
    Môo hâtati desu ka⤴ 'Is s/he twenty already (*or* yet)?'
    Iya, mâda hâtati zya nâi desu. 'No, s/he isn't twenty yet.'

Mâda da, although an affirmative in form, always implies a continuation of non-occurrence: 'it's still—as it was,' 'it is yet—to happen,' 'it hasn't happened yet.'
    Yomímàsita ka⤴   'Did you read it?'
    Mâda desu.   'Not yet.'

2. MORE ON QUESTIONS WITHOUT **ka**: **Tabémàsita?**

Thus far we have encountered five question types:
    (a) Distal-style questions ending in **ka** or **ne**:
        Wakárimàsu ka⤴   'Do you understand?'
        Wakárimàsu ne⤴   'You understand—right?'
    (b) Information questions without a question-particle, ending in period intonation:
        Sore, nâñ desyoo.   'What would that be?'
    (c) Direct-style, perfective or imperfective, yes-no questions without a question-particle, ending in question intonation:
        Dekîru?   'Can you do it?'
    (d) Questions consisting of fragments without a question-particle, ending in question intonation:
        Kore wa?   'How about this one?'
    (e) Yes-no questions ending in **desyòo** (or **daròo**) with question intonation:
        Takâi desyoo?   'It's expensive, don't you think?'

We now extend the final type to include perfective and imperfective forms. In such questions, a final **su** syllable always has full voicing. This pattern is slightly more gentle than the corresponding pattern with **ka**, but otherwise is similar in meaning. Examples:

Dekímàsu?	'Is it possible?'
Môo tabémàsita?	'Have you eaten [it] yet?'
Irássyaimasèñ?	'Won't you go/come/stay?'
Kimásèñ desita?	'Didn't you come?'
Tumétài desu?[2]	'Is it cold?'
Hêñ zya arímasèñ?	'Isn't it strange?'

3. /NOMINAL + **ni** + **suru**/

The verbals **nâru** and **suru** complement each other in their meanings: **nâru** refers to a 'coming into being,' 'a becoming,' whereas **suru** denotes a 'bringing into being,' 'a causing to be.'

We have already encountered the patterns /nominal X + **ni** + **nâru**/ and /adjectival X in the **-ku** form + **nâru**/, in which X denotes the goal. Examples:
    kîree ni naru   'become beautiful'
    katyóo ni nàru   'become a *kacho*'
    âtûku naru   'become hot'
    wakárànaku naru   'become non-understanding,' i.e., 'reach a point of not-understanding'

---

2. This pattern is more gentle and is used more commonly by women.

yamétaku nàru 'become wanting-to-quit,' i.e., 'get to want to quit'

tukáitaku nàku naru 'become not-wanting-to-use,' i.e., 'get to not-want to use'

Suru (and polite equivalents **nasâru** ↑ and **itasu** ↓) also occur in parallel goal patterns, although not in all the same types of variants.³

/Nominal X + **ni** + **suru**/ = 'make [it] to be X,' 'make [it] into X,' 'decide on X'; /adjectival X in the **-ku** form + **suru**/ = 'make [it] to be X.' Examples:

Teńpura ni simàsita.	'I decided on tempura.'
Huráńsuḡo ni itasimasyòo.	'Let's make it French.'
Nâñ ni nasaimasu ka⤴	'What will it be?' (i.e., 'What will you make [your order] to be?')
Konó bìiru o tumétaku site kudasài.	'Please chill this beer.'

With time expressions that take phrase-particle **ni** of 'time when,' there is an overlap of two patterns. While **kyôo simasita** can mean only 'I did it today' and **kyôo ni simasita** only 'I decided on today,' when we examine examples like **kû-zi ni simasita**, we find that the meaning may be either 'I did [it] at 9:00' or 'I decided on 9:00,' depending on the context. When both patterns occur in the same utterance, the order is fixed: the 'time when' pattern always precedes the goal pattern. Example:

Sâñgatu ni kû-ḡatu ni simasita.   'In March I decided on September' (i.e., as the time for a particular event).

Since **nâru** regularly occurs with an expressed goal, **sâñ-zi ni narimasita** can only mean 'it has come to be 3:00.' However, when 'time when' and goal are both expressed, the same ordering rule applies for **nâru** as for **suru**: 'time when' before goal. Example:

Nâñ-neñ ni Syoówa ni narimàsita ka⤴   'In what year did it become Showa?'

4. FOOD AND DRINK

The food and drink terms that might be introduced here are limitless. We have selected a sampling of commonly used terms, and additional items will be added from time to time. In this domain, you will probably be increasing your vocabulary forever—or at least as long as you involve eating in your Japanese-language study. Note that all food and drink names are, of course, nominals, and that non-Japanese foods usually have names that are borrowed from the place of origin. Currently the language is filled with items borrowed from English—from **Makúdonàrudo** to **Misútaa-dòonatu** and **Keńtakkii-huraido-tìkiñ** among the chain stores; from **oréñzi-zyùusu** to **omûretu** and **tôosuto** and **bêeguru** for Western breakfast; from **tyokórèeto** to **nyuú-iñḡurañdo-meepuru-nàttu** and **pisútatio-h(u)àzzi** in the ice cream store.⁴

The Japanese on the whole tend to be seriously interested in food. They spend time in its preparation, emphasizing not only how it tastes but also how it looks. By Western standards, portions tend to be small, with the exception of bowlfuls of rice. However, rice consumption is markedly decreasing in Japan, while the consumption of milk and dairy products is increasing.

---

3. **Suru** does not occur following negatives or **-tai** forms.
4. Were you able to understand these transfers from English? Key: 'MacDonald('s)'; 'Mister Donut(s)'; 'Kentucky Fried Chicken'; 'orange juice'; 'omelet'; 'toast'; 'bagel'; 'chocolate'; 'New England maple nut(s)'; 'pistachio fudge.'

Food is a favorite topic of small talk when guests are invited for a meal. The more formal and elaborate the function, the more emphasis is placed on serving unusual dishes, and such food can become the subject of extended discussion. **Kore wa nâñ desyoo**, the English equivalent of which could well sound rude at a Western gathering, is a complimentary indication in Japan that the host/ess has provided a truly special and unusual treat for a guest.

Drills

A 1. **Môo daízyòobu desu ka⤴**   **Êe, okaḡesama de**[5] **daízyòobu desu.**
'Is it all right yet?'   'Yes, thank you (for asking). It's all right.'

2. **Môo wakárimàsita ka⤴**   **Êe, okaḡesama de wakárimàsita.**
'Has it become clear yet?'   'Yes, thank you (for asking). It has become clear.'

3. **dekímàsita**; 4. **daíḡaku dèsu**; 5. **aímàsita**; 6. **tuúzimàsita**

B 1. **Sonó kyookàsyo ni modôru?**   **Môo modôtta yo⤴** *or*
'Are you going back to that textbook?'   **Môo modôtta wa yo⤴** /F/
'I already did (go back).'

2. **Kono teḡami 'kakinaosu?**   **Môo 'kakinaosita yo⤴** *or*
'Are you going to rewrite this letter?'   **Môo kakínaosità wa yo.** /F/
'I already did (rewrite).'

3. **waapuro naôsu**; 4. **iñtyoo to 'reñraku-suru**; 5. **katyoo ni âu**; 6. **omâwari-sañ ni 'kiku**; 7. **kono siñbuñ yômu**; 8. **konó kyookàsyo ni kawaru**

C 1. **Môo itî-zi desu yo⤴**   **Hoñtoo? Zyuúnì-zi da to omôtta kara..**
'It's 1:00 already.'   'Really? I thought it was 12:00, so...' (I was in no hurry).

2. **Môo mokúyòo desu yo⤴**   **Hoñtoo? Suíyòo da to omôtta kara..**
'It's Thursday already.'   'Really? I thought it was Wednesday, so...' (I was in no hurry).

3. **kokono-ka**; 4. **gô-zi**; 5. **suíyòobi**; 6. **nano-ka**

D 1. **Zyûu-zi ni ukáḡaimasyòo ka.**   **Môo zyuú-zi-suḡì zya nâi desu ka⤴**
'Shall we pay a visit at 10:00?'   'Isn't it already after 10:00?'

2. **Nî-zi kara soódañ-simasyòo ka.**   **Môo ni-zí-suḡì zya nâi desu ka⤴**
'Shall we talk it over, starting at 2:00?'   'Isn't it after 2:00 already?'

3. **sâñ-zi ni 'butyoo to oái-simasyòo**; 4. **yô-zi kara hanásimasyòo**; 5. **gô-zi ni yamémasyòo**

E 1. **Môo kaísya ni modòru ñ desu ka⤴**   **Êe. Tyôtto hayâi kedo, îma modóritài to omoimasu.**
'Are you going back to the company already?'   'Yes. It's a bit early, but (I think) I'd like to go back now.'

---

5. **Okaḡesama de** 'thanks to you,' 'thanks for your interest' always implies a favorable situation.

2. **Môo syotyóo to reñraku-surù ñ desu ka**⤴
'Are you going to get in touch with the institute director already?'

Êe. Tyôtto hayâi kedo, îma reńraku-sitài to omoimasu.
'Yes. It's a bit early, but (I think) I'd like to make contact now.'

3. **atárasìi kyoókàsyo ′tyuumoñ-suru**; 4. **katyóo to àu**; 5. **amérikàziñ no kyôosi to kawaru**; 6. **kuukoo ni iku**

F 1. **Moó sukòsi tyuúmoñ-simaseñ ka**⤴
'Won't you order a little more?'

Môo takúsañ tyuumoñ-simàsita kara..
'I've already ordered a lot, so . . .' (no, thank you).

2. **Moó sukòsi kikímaseñ ka**⤴
'Won't you listen a little more?'

Môo takúsañ kikimàsita kara..
'I've already listened a lot, so . . .' (no, thank you).

3. **tukáimaseñ**; 4. **yomímaseñ**; 5. **mimáseñ**; 6. **kaímaseñ**

G 1. **Môo ohîru o tabémàsita ka**⤴
'Have you eaten lunch yet?'

Ie, mâda tâbete (i)nâi ñ desu.
'No, I haven't eaten yet.'

2. **Môo ′gakutyoo no ′gotuḡoo o kikímàsita ka**⤴
'Have you asked yet what is convenient for the university president?'

Ie, mâda kiíte (i)nài ñ desu.
'No, I haven't asked yet.'

3. **kono zassi o yomímàsita**; 4. **hisyô to soódañ-simàsita**; 5. **tokee o naósimàsita**; 6. **arúbàito no gakusee o yobímàsita**

H 1. **Môo onáka sukimàsita ka**⤴
'Are you (*lit.* have you become) hungry yet?'

Ie, mâda sukímaseñ nêe.
'No, I'm not (getting hungry yet).'

2. **Môo nôdo kawákimàsita ka**⤴
'Are you (*lit.* have you become) thirsty yet?'

Ie, mâda kawákimaseñ nêe.
'No, I'm not (getting thirsty yet).'

3. **sono suuzi wakárimàsita**; 4. **kyôo no siñbuñ kimâsita**; 5. **kû-zi no sińkàñseñ demâsita**; 6. **butyóo ni narimàsita**

I 1. **Môo ′kodomo imâsu ka**⤴
'Do you have children yet?'

Ie, mâda imáseñ.
'No. I don't have any yet.'

2. **Môo końpyùutaa tukáimàsu ka**⤴
'Do you use the computer yet?'

Ie, mâda tukáimaseñ.
'No, I don't use it yet.'

3. **supeiñḡo wakárimàsu**; 4. **keńkyuuzyò arímàsu**; 5. **tyuuḡokugo no siñbuñ yomímàsu**; 6. **końna zìsyo irímàsu**

J 1. **Môo eéḡo no siñbuñ yòñde (i)masu ka**⤴
'Is s/he reading English newspapers already?'

Iya, mâda yôñde (i)máseñ kedo..
'No, s/he's not (reading [them] yet), but . . .' (perhaps at a later date).

2. **Môo daíĝaku ni itte (i)màsu ka↗** Iya, mâda itte (i)masèñ kedo..
   'Is s/he attending university already?' 'No, s/he's not (attending yet), but...'
   (perhaps at a later date).
3. **kekkoñ-site (i)màsu;** 4. **arúbàito sité (i)màsu;** 5. **keñkyuuzyò de osíete (i)màsu;**
6. **sore kawâite (i)masu**

K 1. **Sonó wàiñ, môo tumétaku** Ie, mâda tumétaku nài desu yo↗
   narimàsita ka↗ 'No, it's not (cold yet).'
   'Is that wine cold yet?' (*lit.* Has that
   wine become cold yet?)
 2. **Yamâmori-sañ, môo katyóo ni** Ie, mâda katyóo zya nài desu yo↗
   narimàsita ka↗ 'No, s/he isn't (a *kacho* yet).'
   'Is Mr/s. Yamamori a *kacho* yet?' (*lit.*
   Has Mr/s. Yamamori become a *kacho*
   yet?)
 3. **Tanaka-kyoozyu/ohima ni;** 4. **Hokkàidoo/sâmûku;** 5. **kotosi no siĝoto/isóĝasìku;**
 6. **musukosañ/daiĝaku ni**

L 1. **Kânozyo, môo modórimàsita ka↗** Mâda desu. Asíta modòru to omoimasu.
   'Has she returned yet?' 'Not yet. I think she'll return tomorrow.'
 2. **Ano ryokañ, môo sukímàsita ka↗** Mâda desu. Asíta sukù to omoimasu.
   'Has that inn emptied out yet?' 'Not yet. I think it will empty out
   tomorrow.'
 3. **kâre/ziteñsya karímàsita;** 4. **atárasìi gaíziñ no señsèe/miémàsita;** 5. **eeĝo no atár-**
   asìi kyoókàsyo/tyuúmoñ-simàsita

M 1. **Mâda moñbùsyoo ni itte (i)nâi ñ** Iya, môo ikímàsita yo↗
   desu ka↗ 'No, I *have* gone.'
   '(Is it that) you haven't gone to the
   Education Ministry yet?'[6]
 2. **Mâda señsèe no zêmi ni dête (i)nâi** Iya, môo demâsita yo↗
   ñ desu ka↗ 'No, I *have* attended already.'
   '(Is it that) you haven't attended the
   professor's seminar yet?'
 3. **kâre no onîisañ ni âtte;** 4. **kânozyo to hanâsite;** 5. **Kyôoto no otéra to zìñzya mîte**

N 1. **Mâda oókuràsyoo ni ikánài ñ desu** Iya, môo ikímàsu yo↗
   ka↗ 'No, I *do* go (already).'
   '(Is it that) you don't go to the
   Finance Ministry yet?'

---

6. Depending on context, this Japanese utterance might also mean 'You aren't going (i.e., on a regular basis) to the Education Ministry yet?' The negative response would then be **Iya, môo itte (i)màsu yo↗** 'No, I *am* going on a regular basis already.'

2. **Mâda 'osake ḡa âtûku nâi ñ desu ka⤴**   **Iya, môo atûi desu yo⤵**
'(Do you mean) the saké isn't hot yet?'   'No, it *is* hot (already).'

3. **Mîyazi-sañ no ozyôosañ wa gakkoo zya nài**; 4. **gaímùsyoo no katâ to soódañ-sinài**; 5. **asoko wa sâmûku nâi**

O 1. **Mâda gakútyoo no deñwabàñḡoo wakáràñai ñ desu ka⤴**   **Iya, môo wakárimàsita yo⤵**
'(Is it that) you don't yet know the college president's telephone number?'   'No! I *do* know it already.' (*lit.* It has already become clear.)

2. **Mâda bañḡòhañ dekînai ñ desu ka⤴**   **Iya, môo dekímàsita yo⤵**
'(Is it that) dinner isn't ready yet?'   'No. It *is* ready already.' (*lit.* It has already become finished.)

3. **onáka sukimasèñ**; 4. **nôdo kawákimasèñ**; 5. **sono atárasìi kyoókàsyo dênai**

P 1. **Kore kara, keñkyuuzyò ni modórimàsu yo⤵**   **Hoñtoo? Modórimàsu?**
'I'm going back to the research institute now.'   'Really? You're going back?'

2. **Anó gakkoo no zyùḡyoo, omósìròku arímasèñ yo⤵**   **Hoñtoo? Omósìròku arímasèñ?**
'The classes at that school aren't interesting.'   'Really? They're not interesting?'

3. **kêsa, koñpyùutaa kosyóo-simàsita**; 4. **asita, rusubañ dekímasèñ**; 5. **sono yoozi, amari taísetu zya arimasèñ**; 6. **konó wàiñ, tumétaku arimasèñ**

Q 1. **Osûsi o tabémàsu ka⤴—osásimi o tabemàsu ka⤴**   **Osûsi o oneḡai-simasu. A, tyôtto. Yappàri osásimi ni site kudasài.**
'Are you going to eat sushi, or sashimi?'   'I'd like sushi. Oh, wait a minute. Make it sashimi, after all.'

2. **Osáke o nomimàsu ka⤴—bîiru o nomímàsu ka⤴**   **Osáke o oneḡai-simàsu. A, tyôtto. Yappàri bîiru ni sité kudasài.**
'Are you going to drink saké, or beer?'   'I'd like saké. Oh, wait a minute. Make it beer, after all.'

3. **siô/tukáimàsu/syooyu**; 4. **siñbuñ/mimâsu/zassi**; 5. **hurosiki/kaímàsu/syoppiñḡu-bàggu**

• Repeat this drill, replacing **oneḡai-simàsu** with **tanómimàsu** in the responses.

R 1. **Pâi o tyuúmoñ-simasyòo ka—pûriñ o tyuúmoñ-simasyòo ka.**   **Kokó nò wa dôtira mo oísìi desu ḡa, pûriñ ni simásyòo ka.**
'Shall we order pie, or pudding?'   'Both of those things here are good, but shall we decide on pudding?'

2. **Sukíyaki o tyuumoñ-simasyòo ka— teñpura o tyuumoñ-simasyòo ka.**
'Shall we order sukiyaki, or tempura?'

Kokó nò wa dôtira mo oísìi desu ḡa, teńpura ni simasyòo ka.
'Both of those things here are good, but shall we decide on tempura?'

3. **obeñtoo/sâñdo**; 4. **wâiñ/osake**; 5. **osôba/osûsi**; 6. **kêeki/aísukurìimu**

- Repeat this drill, replacing **ni simásyòo** with **(o) tanómimasyòo** in the responses.

S 1. **Îtu kâre to kawárimàsu ka**⤴
'When will you change with him?'

Asíta kawaritàkatta ñ desu kedo; tyôtto hayâi to omôtte, asâtte ni simasita.
'I wanted to change tomorrow, but I thought it was a bit early and made it the day after tomorrow.'

2. **Îtu keńkyuuzyò ni modórimàsu ka**⤴
'When will you go back to the research institute?'

Asíta modoritàkatta ñ desu kedo; tyôtto hayâi to omôtte, asâtte ni simasita.
'I wanted to go back tomorrow, but I thought it was a bit early and made it the day after tomorrow.'

3. **Oríeñtaru-bòoeki ni reńraku-simàsu**; 4. **tomodati o syoókai-simàsu**; 5. **kânozyo to hanásimàsu**; 6. **ano gaiziñ ni aímàsu**

T 1. **Îtu ḡa îi desu ka**⤴
'When will be good?'

Sôo desu nêe. Îtu ni simásyòo ka.
'Hm. When shall we make it?'

2. **Kyôo ḡa îi desu ka**⤴
'Will *today* be good?'

Sôo desu nêe. Kyôo ni simásyòo ka.
'Hm. Shall we make it today?'

3. **asítà**; 4. **raineñ**; 5. **myôoniti**; 6. **saraisyuu**; 7. **nâñ-ḡatu**; 8. **asíta no àsa**

U 1. **Tyôtto osôi desu nêe.**
'It's a bit late, isn't it!'

Zyâa, moó sukòsi hâyàku simásyòo ka⤴
'Then shall I make it a little earlier?'

2. **Tyôtto muzúkasìi desu nêe.**
'It's a bit difficult, isn't it!'

Zyâa, moó sukòsi yasásiku simasyòo ka⤴
'Then shall I make it a little easier?'

3. **yomínikùi**; 4. **oókìi**; 5. **naḡâi**

- Repeat this drill, making the responses more polite by replacing **simásyòo** with **itásimasyòo**.

V 1. **A, usíro no hòo ni narimasita nêe.**
'Oh, it's come to be toward the back, hasn't it!'

Sôo desu nêe. Dâre ḡa usíro no hòo ni sita ñ desyoo nêe.
'It has, hasn't it! Who do you suppose caused it to be toward the back?'

2. **A, tukáinìkùku narimasita nêe.**
'Oh, it's become hard to use, hasn't it!'

Sôo desu nêe. Dâre ḡa tukáinìkùku sita ñ desyoo nêe.
'It has, hasn't it! Who do you suppose made it hard to use?'

3. **tosyôsitu ni**; 4. **okâsîku**; 5. **hêñ ni**; 6. **mizîkàku**

Application Exercises

A1. Practice restaurant role-playing. Order specific dishes and set menus; ask if the restaurant has particular items; order drinks—specifying whether hot or cold, when appropriate; make a change in your order; ask for pepper, soy sauce, more butter, etc.

2. Take turns asking and answering questions about whether group members have yet been to specific places, eaten specific Japanese dishes, studied specific languages, met specific people, etc. Practice both /**môo** + affirmative predicate/ and /**mâda** + negative predicate/ questions.

B. Core Conversations: Substitution

Practice the Core Conversations, retaining the original sentence patterns but substituting other food and drink items. Use appropriate props and point when the dialogue requires it. Inject a degree of liveliness and enthusiasm that fits the subject matter, at the same time maintaining Japanese intonation patterns.

SECTION B

Core Conversations

1(J)a. **Moó ìp-pai, dôozo.**
  b. **Tabako wa?**
  c. **Yamétà ñ desu ka⌒**
  d. **Zyâa, môo zeñzeñ suwanài ñ desu ka⌒**

(N)a. **Zyâa, hañbuñ dake.**
  b. **Ie, kêkkoo desu.**
  c. **Êe. Keñkoo ni yòku nâi to omôtte . .**
  d. **Ie, mâda ití-nitì ni ni-hóñ-g̀ùrai wa suímàsu kedo nêe.**

2(J)a. **Sûmisu-kuñ, guái wa dòo? Môo îi no?**
  b. **Sôo. Mâda sukôsi kaóiro g̀a warùi nêe.**
  c. **A, sorya ikenai nêe.**

(N)a. **Arîg̀atoo gozaimasu. Mâda kusúri o nòñde (i)ru ñ desu.**
  b. **Êe. Naní mo tabetàku nâi no de, gêñki g̀a dênai ñ desu.**

3(N)a. **Matûzusi no deñwabàñg̀oo sitte (i)ru? Demáe tyuumoñ-sitài ñ da kedo . .**
  b. **A, dôo mo. . . . Môsimosi. Yoñ-tyoomè no Itóo-apàato no Burâuñ desu kedo, demáe oneg̀ai-dekimàsu ka⌒ . . . Zyôo o**

(J)a. **Tyôtto, sirábèru kara, mâtte. . . . Hâi, kore.**

ni-níñmae onegai-simàsu. . . .
Hâi. Go-ĝoositu desu. Onégai-
simàsu. . . . A, môsimosi.
Burâuñ desu ĝa, âto donó-ĝurai
de dekimàsu ka⌇ . . . Ie, mâda
kônai ñ desu. . . . Hâi, yorosiku.

English Equivalents

1(J)a. Have another glass(ful).
    b. How about a cigarette?
    c. Do you mean you quit?

    d. Then does that mean that you don't smoke at all any more?

(N)a. Well, just a half.
    b. No, that's all right.
    c. Yes. [I've been] thinking that it's not good for my health.

    d. No, I do still smoke about two cigarettes a day, but . . . (not as many as I used to smoke)—you know!

2(J)a. How are you, Smith? Are you all right yet?

    b. Oh. Your color is still a little bad, isn't it!

    c. Oh, that's too bad!

(N)a. Thanks [for asking]. I'm still taking medicine.

    b. Yes. Since I don't want to eat anything, I don't have any energy.

3(N)a. Do you know the telephone number for Matsuzushi? (It's that) I want to order home delivery but . . . (I don't know the number).

    b. Oh, thanks. . . . [On the telephone] Hello. This is [Sue] Brown at the Ito Apartments in 4-chome; can I order home delivery? . . . I'd like two orders of deluxe. . . . Yes. It's [apartment] #5. . . . (Please fill the order.) [After a considerable delay, on the telephone a second time] Oh, hello. This is [Sue] Brown; how much longer until it's ready? . . . No, it's still not here. . . . Yes, would you take care of it?

(J)a. I'll check, so wait a minute. . . . Here, this is it.

BREAKDOWNS
(AND SUPPLEMENTARY VOCABULARY)

1. îp-pai (see below) — one glassful; one cupful
   hānbuñ — half portion; half part
   tabako — cigarette
   keñkoo /na/ — health; healthy
   keńkoo ni ìi (SP1) — is good for one's health
   suu /-u; sutta/ — smoke
   môo /+ negative predicate/ (SP2) — no more
   mâda /+ affirmative predicate/ (SP2) — still
2. guai — condition
   kusuri — medicine
   kusúri (o) nòmu — take medicine (by mouth)
   kaoiro — (facial) color
   gêñki /na/ — pep, vim, high spirits; peppy, vigorous
   gêñki (g̃a) dêru — perk up, become energetic
   sorya — /contraction of sore wa/
   ikenai — it won't do; it's too bad
3. Matûzusi — (name of a sushi shop)
   susîya — sushi shop
   +teñpuraya — tempura shop
   +sobâya — noodle shop
   +rêsutorañ — restaurant (Western-style)
   +komêya — rice store
   +sakaya — liquor store
   +tabakoya — cigarette shop
   +kusuriya — drugstore
   demae — home delivery of prepared food
   sirábèru /-ru; sirâbeta/ — look into, investigate, check
   mâtte. (SP3) — wait!
   yoń-tyoomè (see below) — 4-chome
   apâato — apartment; apartment house
   Itóo-apàato — the Ito apartments
   zyôo — deluxe
   +tokuzyoo — super-deluxe
   +nami — regular
   ni-niñmae (see below) — two portions, two orders
   go-g̃ôositu (see below) — room #5

-hai: *Classifier for counting glassfuls and cupfuls*

îp-pai	rôp-pai		
nî-hai	nanâ-hai/sitî-hai		
sâñ-bai	hâp-pai/hatî-hai		
yôñ-hai	kyûu-hai		
go-hai	zîp-pai/zyûp-pai		

nâñ-bai 'how many glassfuls?'

-tyoome: *Classifier for naming chome*

ití-tyoomè	rokú-tyoomè
ni-tyóomè	naná-tyoomè
sañ-tyoomè	hat́-tyoomè
yoń-tyoomè	
go-tyoome	

nań-tyoomè 'what chome?'

-niñmae: *Classifier for counting portions*

iti-niñmae	roku-niñmae
ni-niñmae	nana-niñmae/siti-niñmae
sañ-niñmae	hati-niñmae
yo-niñmae	ku-niñmae/kyuu-niñmae
go-niñmae	zyuu-niñmae

nañ-niñmae 'how many portions?'

-g̃oositu: *Classifier for naming room numbers*

ití-g̃òositu	rokú-g̃oositu
ni-g̃oositu	naná-g̃òositu/sití-g̃òositu
sañ-g̃oositu	hatí-g̃òositu
yoń-g̃oositu	kyuú-g̃òositu
go-g̃oositu	zyuú-g̃òositu

nań-g̃òositu 'what room number?'

MISCELLANEOUS NOTES

1. CC1 is a conversation between two office colleagues who are out drinking together after work, a very common practice in Japan. While the distal-style final predicates indicate careful-style, the tone is relaxed, moving toward the casual: more than half of the utterances are fragments.

(J)a. **Moo** here is linked with a following number: 'one glassful more.'

(N)a. **Hañbuñ dake** may be intended to be interpreted literally or it may be a polite, restrained way of accepting more. Usually more than half a glass will be poured in response, unless there is an objection.

According to the rules of Japanese etiquette, one should not pour his/her own drinks, particularly the early rounds: the solidarity of a group that is eating and drinking together is established and maintained by reciprocal pouring.

(J)b. Japan has been comparatively slow to respond to the warnings against smoking. While there are some beginning signs, few areas are set aside for nonsmokers.

(N)c. Note: **keńkoo dà** '[s/he] is healthy; **keńkoo na àkatyañ** 'a healthy baby.'

(J)d. **Suu** is a **w**-root verbal, hence the negative **suwanai**. It is operational: **tabáko o suttè (i)ru** '[s/he] is smoking (a cigarette).' **Nômu** also occurs with **tabako**, meaning 'smoke.'

(N)d. **Mâa** again indicates reservation.

Note the use of **wa** following an extent pattern: 'about two at least I do smoke but . . .' (not the quantities I used to smoke).

2. CC2 is a conversation between a Japanese professor (J) and his foreign student (N) who has been ill. Note the contrast in styles: the professor uses casual-style with direct-style predicates, while the student uses careful-style with distal-style predicates.

(J)a. **Guai** may refer to the condition of a person or of a thing, particularly a machine. Note: **guái g̃a ìi, guái g̃a warùi, guái g̃a hèñ da.**
Môo ìi no?: here, the professor is asking whether the student's condition is 'already good,' having been bad, i.e., has he recovered yet.

(N)a. The verbal **nômu** is used with both liquid and solid medicines taken by mouth.

(J)b. **Kaoiro** is a nominal compound of the /nominal + nominal/ type: **kao** 'face' + **irô** 'color.' When one is pale and sickly, the color word to be used is **aôi**.

(N)b. **Gênki**: Commonly occurring combinations are: **gênki ḡa îi** 'is in good spirits'; **gênki ḡa nâi** 'is without pep,' 'is depressed'; **gênki ni naru** 'become peppy,' 'recover'; **gênki da** 'is healthy,' 'is vigorous'; **gênki na hito** 'a healthy, energetic person'; **gênki ḡa dêru** 'become energetic,' 'be vigorous.' Note also: **Ogênki desu ka**↙ 'Are you well?' /polite/.

(J)c. **Ikenai** is a negative derived from the vowel verbal **ikeru**, which in turn is derived from **iku**. Ikenai—distal-style **ikémasèǹ**—implies that something cannot proceed effectively, cannot 'make it': it may express sympathy, as in this CC, while at the same time implying that 'this won't do!' It may also be used as a warning: 'that won't do,' 'you mustn't do that.'

3. CC3 occurs in the apartment of Sue Brown (N) and her Japanese roommate (J). They are obviously close friends and accordingly use casual-style with direct-style predicates. However, when Sue Brown calls the local sushi shop on the telephone, she switches to careful-style with distal-style predicates.

(N)a. **Matûzusi**, the name of a sushi shop, is a compound consisting of /**matu** 'pine' + **sûsi**/ with the initial **s** of **sûsi** changed to **z**. The supplementary vocabulary includes a number of shop names that consist of /product + **-ya**/, the same pattern previously encountered in **hôñya, hanâya,** and **buñbooḡuya**. These compounds may refer to dealers as well as shops. Note that **sake** as the nonfinal member of a compound becomes **saka**; this type of /e > a/ alternation is a recurring pattern.

Demae refers to a convenient delivery system by which one can order prepared dishes—sushi, tempura, noodles, etc.—from local shops by telephone.

(J)a. **Sirábèru** is an operational vowel verbal: **X (o) sirábèru** 'consult X' or 'check into X' (examples: **nôoto (o) sirábèru** 'consult a notebook,' **deńwabàńḡoo (o) sirábèru** 'look up a phone number'); **Y de sirábèru** 'check by means of Y' (example: **zîsyo de sirábèru** 'check [something] with the dictionary').

(N)b. **Âto donó-ḡurai de dekimàsu ka**: This question asks 'Being (i.e., after the passage of) about how much remaining time will it be completed?' Compare this question with the more direct, confrontational complaint that would be typical in many other cultures: 'I've been waiting for almost an hour. Are you going to bring that sushi soon?'—or perhaps something stronger.

Classifiers:

-Hai, the classifier for counting glassfuls and cupfuls, follows the regular pattern of classifiers beginning with **-h**: with **itî, rokû, hatî,** and **zyûu**, both numerals and classifier undergo change, and with **sañ** and **nañ-**, the **h** of the classifier becomes **b**. Note that to count cups and glasses, as opposed to the contents of these containers, we would use **hitô-tu, hutá-tù,** etc.

-Niñmae is the classifier used in counting individual orders or portions. This classifier occurs in one form only: the irregularities of **hitô-ri** and **hutá-rìi** do not carry over.

-Tyoome occurs in one form only, but the numerals **itî** and **hatî** undergo change when compounded with it. Higher numbers are not listed, since they occur very rarely. The chome refers to a comparatively small geographic division within successively larger divisions of a city. The fact that Sue Brown identifies her location with only **yoń-tyoomè no Itóo-apàato** indicates that she is talking with a shopkeeper in the immediate area. Otherwise she would be required to specify *which* **yoń-tyoomè**, i.e., the **yoń-tyoomè** in which area.

-Ḡoositu compounds name individual room numbers or the numbers of suites of rooms or apartments. For those with three or more digits, alternate forms occur. Compare '#1204': **Sêñ nihyaku yoñ-ḡòositu** or **ití·nìi·marú·yoñ-ḡòositu**.

Structural Patterns

1. keńkoo ni ìi

The particle **ni**, with its basic meaning of location, and derivative meanings of goal, time when, and manner, has occurred in many combinations. Examples:

    Kokó ni arimàsu.   'It is here (in this place).'
    Kokó ni kimàsita.   'I came here (to this place).'
    Tomódati ni narimàsita.   'S/he became a friend.'
    Pâñ ni simâsita.   'I decided on bread.'
    Ni-ḡátù ni kimâsita.   'I came in February.'
    Kîree ni kakímàsita.   'S/he wrote beautifully.'

We now encounter a further extension of the locational/goal meaning of **ni**, in examples in which a condition applies in reference to a particular item, either animate or inanimate. Thus, if we wish to describe something that is good specifically in reference to health (it may be bad in the area of enjoyment!), we convey this as: **keńkoo ni ìi** 'it is good in reference to health'—i.e., 'for one's health.' Additional examples:

    kodomo ni muzukasii   'is difficult for children'
    tosíyòri ni hûbeñ da   'is inconvenient for old people'
    gaiziñ ni oisii   'is delicious to foreigners'
    âkatyañ ni abunai   'is dangerous for babies'

Affective predicates in the double-**ḡa** category may also occur with this referential **ni** following the major affect. Thus

    Tomodati ḡa eéḡo ḡa wakàru kara..   'Since my friend can understand English...'
    or
    Tomodati ni eéḡo ḡa wakàru kara..   *lit.* 'Since English is comprehensible to my friend...;' *and*
    Kodomo ḡa koré ḡa dekìru kedo..   'Children can do this, but...' *or*
    Kodomo ni koré ḡa dekìru kedo..   *lit.* 'This is possible for children, but...'

2. /mâda + AFFIRMATIVE PREDICATE/; /môo + NEGATIVE PREDICATE/

In Section A of this lesson, **môo** implying the 'already' occurrence of a state or activity with an affirmative predicate, and **mâda** implying continuation with a negative predicate, were introduced:

    Môo tabémàsita.   'I already ate [it].'
    Mâda tâbete (i)másèñ.   'I haven't eaten [it] yet' (*lit.* 'I am still not eating [it]').

Keeping these basic meanings in mind, we now examine **mâda** and **môo** with affirmative and negative predicates, respectively.

    Mâda with an affirmative predicate again implies continuation, in this case continuation of an existing state or occurring activity. Examples:

Mâda sonó zèmi ni demâsu.   'I'll still attend that seminar.'
Mâda konó siḡoto (o) site (i)màsu.   'I'm still doing this work.'
Sono ryokañ wa mâda suíte (i)màsu.   'That inn is still empty.'
Kyôneñ wa, mâda yôku aímàsita.   'Last year I still saw him/her often.'
Sonó tokì ni wa, mâda mâiniti kokó e kitè (i)masita.   'At that time I was still coming here every day.'
Asoko wa mâda samûi to omoimasu.   'I think it's still cold there.'
Sono deñwa wa mâda damê desyoo?   'That telephone is still out of order, isn't it?'

As the above examples demonstrate, continuation indicated by **mâda** may refer to a single occurrence of a condition or activity (**mâda atûi** 'it's still hot'; **mâda yôñde (i)ru** 'I'm still reading [it]') or to multiple occurrences (**mâda mâiniti âtûku naru** 'it still gets hot every day'; **mâda mâiniti konó siñbuñ o yòñde (i)ru** 'I'm still reading this newspaper every day').

Môo linked to a negative predicate implies that a negative condition has already been achieved, i.e., that the affirmative condition no longer applies. In other words, **môo dekînai**, lit. 'it is already impossible' means 'it no longer *is* possible.' Again, the reference may be to a single instance or repeated occurrences. Examples:

Môo wakárimasèñ.   'I don't understand any more.' (*lit.* 'Already I am non-understanding.')
Môo sonó zèmi ni demásèñ.   'I don't/won't attend that seminar any more.'
Môo 'hurañsuḡo wa beñkyoo-sit(e) orimasèñ.   'I'm not studying French any more.'
Sono ryokañ wa, môo suíte (i)nài desyoo?   'That inn is no longer empty, is it?'
Kâre wa, môo 'zeñzeñ sonó gakkoo è wa itté (i)nài to omoimasu.   'I believe that he isn't going to that school at all any more.'
Môo tâkâku nâi desyoo.   'It's probably not expensive any more.'
Môo kodómo zya nài yo↗   'I'm not a child any more!'
Sonó tokì made ni wa, môo tabáko o sutte (i)masèñ desita.   'By that time, I wasn't smoking any more.'

3. SENTENCE-FINAL GERUND IN INFORMAL REQUESTS

In sentence-final position and with period intonation, an affirmative verbal gerund may occur as an informal request. This usage is typical of casual-style. Examples:

Tyôtto mâtte.   'Wait a minute.'
Eñpitu kasite.   'Lend me a pen.'
Yamete.   'Quit [that].'

When sentence-particle **yo** or **ne** follows the gerund, the resulting sequence is more typical of gentle-style. Examples:

Sirâbete ne↗   'Check on it, would you?'
Deñwa kîtte yo.   'Hang up!'

These request sentences, unlike those ending in /gerund + **kudasài**/, are not classified among those ending with a regular sentence-final form.

Drills

A 1. **Îi desu ka** ⌒
    'Is it all right?'

    Watási nì wa îi kedo ..
    'It's all right for me, at least, but . . .' (I'm not commenting on anyone else).

  2. **Wakárimàsu ka** ⌒
    'Is it clear?'

    Watási nì wa wakâru kedo ..
    'It's clear to me, at least, but . . .' (I'm not commenting on anyone else).

  3. **dekímàsu**; 4. **oísìi desu**; 5. **daízyòobu desu**; 6. **hayâi desu**; 7. **hûbeñ desu**; 8. **tabénikùi desu**; 9. **muzúkasìi desu**

B 1. **Osake nomânai?**
    'Won't you have some saké?'

    Osake wa yamétà ñ da—keñkoo ni yòku nâi to omôtte.
    'Saké I've given up—believing that it's bad for me (*lit.* health).'

  2. **Tabako 'suwanai?**
    'Won't you have a cigarette?'

    Tabako wa yamétà ñ da—keñkoo ni yòku nâi to omôtte.
    'Cigarettes I've given up—believing that they're bad for me.'

  3. **satôo 'iranai**; 4. **syooyu 'tukawanai**; 5. **bîiru nomânai**; 6. **siô 'tukawanai**

• Repeat this drill, replacing the blunt **yamétà ñ da** with the gentle **yamétà no**, in the responses.

C 1. **Eégo, mâda beñkyoo-sitè (i)ru?**
    'Are you still studying English?'

    Iya, môo beñkyoo-site (i)nài.
    'No, I'm not studying any more.'

  2. **Eégàkañ, mâda suítè (i)ru?**
    'Is the movie theater still empty?'

    Iya, môo suíte (i)nài.
    'No, it's not empty any more.'

  3. **koñpyùutaa/kosyóo-sitè (i)ru**; 4. **eégo/osíetè (i)ru**; 5. **hurañsugo/obôete (i)ru**; 6. **tâkusii/mâtte (i)ru**; 7. **sonó hòñ/yôñde (i)ru**

D 1. **Kâre mâda iru?**
    'Is he still here?'

    Môo inái to omòu kedo ..
    'I believe he's no longer here, but . . .' (I'm not certain).

  2. **Kânozyo mâda dêru?**
    'Will she still attend?'

    Môo dênai to omôu kedo ..
    'I believe she will no longer attend, but . . .' (I'm not certain).

  3. **gôhañ/âru**; 4. **syatyoo/irássyàru**; 5. **kono siḡoto/dekîru**; 6. **kânozyo/kûru**

E 1. **Wâiñ wa, mâda tumétài desu ka** ⌒
    'Is the wine still cold?'

    Iya, môo tumétaku nài desu yo ⌒
    'No, it's not cold any more.'

  2. **Sonó pàñ wa, mâda atáràsìkatta desu ka** ⌒
    'Was that bread still fresh?'

    Iya, môo atárasìku nâkatta desu yo ⌒
    'No, it wasn't fresh any more.'

  3. **sono siḡoto/isóḡasìi desu**; 4. **onîisañ/osîḡoto desu**; 5. **kâre no ôkusañ/wakâi desu**; 6. **kânozyo/kâiḡi desu**; 7. **Sapporo/áttàkàkatta desu**; 8. **guai/wârûkatta desu**; 9. **kaoiro/hêñ desita**; 10. **ozîisañ/oḡeñki desu**

F 1. **Mâda kânozyo to aímàsu ka**↗
'Do you still meet with her?'

Ie, ikénai to omòtte, îma wa âtte (i)másèñ.
'No, I thought I shouldn't, and (so) I'm not seeing her now.' (*lit.* 'Thinking that it doesn't do.')

2. **Mâda osyóoyu tukaimàsu ka**↗
'Do you still use soy sauce?'

Ie, ikénai to omòtte, îma wa tukátte (i)masèñ.
'No, I thought I shouldn't, and (so) I'm not using it now.'

3. **sonó zèmi ni demâsu**; 4. **tabako suímàsu**; 5. **koóhìi nomímàsu**; 6. **kêeki tabémàsu**

G 1. **Kâre wa, môo 'kono kusuri nôñde (i)másèñ ne**↗
'He isn't taking this medicine any more—right?'

Ie, mâda nôñde (i)ru to omóimàsu kedo ..
'No, I think he's still taking it, but . . .' (I may be wrong).

2. **Kânozyo wa, môo 'tabako suítte (i)masèñ ne**↗
'She isn't smoking any more—right?'

Ie, mâda suítè (i)ru to omóimàsu kedo ..
'No, I think she's still smoking, but . . .' (I may be wrong).

3. **sonô hito/kono ryokañ ni tomátte (i)masèñ**; 4. **sonô ko/eégo obôete (i)másèñ**; 5. **sonó hìsyo/konó koñpyùutaa tukátte (i)masèñ**; 6. **sono gakusee/konó kyookàsyo yôñde (i)másèñ**

H 1. **Môo zeñzeñ tabako suwanài ñ desu ka**↗
'(Is it that) you don't smoke at all any more?'

Mâa, mâda sukôsi wa suû kedo nêe.
'Well, I do still smoke a little (at least) but . . .' (not as much as I used to).

2. **Môo zeñzeñ bìiru nomânai ñ desu ka**↗
'(Is it that) you don't drink beer at all any more?'

Mâa, mâda sukôsi wa nômu kedo nêe.
'Well, I do still drink a little (at least) but . . .' (not as much as I used to).

3. **eégo hanasànai**; 4. **pâñ tabênai**; 5. **osìo tukawanai**; 6. **himá nài**

I 1. **Mâtu?**
'Are you going to wait?'

Ññ↗ Anâta ga mâtte.⁷
'Uh-uh. *You* wait.'

2. **Yobu?**
'Are you going to call him/her?'

Ññ↗ Anâta ga yoñde.
'Uh-uh. *You* call.'

3. **kau**; 4. **mîru**; 5. **misêru**; 6. **dêru**; 7. **kûru**; 8. **iku**; 9. **sirábèru**

J 1. **Zyôo ni-níñmae dèsu ka**↗
'Is that two orders of deluxe?'

Ie, sáñ-niñmae oneḡai-simàsu.
'No, we'd like three orders.'

2. **Wâiñ îp-pai desu ka**↗
'Is that one glass of wine?'

Ie, nî-hai oneḡai-simasu.
'No, we'd like two glasses.'

3. **bîiru nî-hoñ**; 4. **nami 'iti-niñmae**; 5. **tokuzyoo 'sañ-niñmae**; 6. **kootya nî-hai**

7. These replies are extremely direct and abrupt.

K 1. **Otaku wa, sań-tyoomè desita neʃ** Iêie, ni-tyóomè desu yo⤴
'Your home was in 3-chome—right?' 'No, no. It's in 2-chome.'

2. **Hîsyo wa, nií·màru·ni-ĝôositu desita neʃ** Iêie, nií·màru·ití-ĝòositu desu yo⤴
'The secretary was in Room #202—right?' 'No, no. S/he's in Room #201.'

3. **Matûzusi/ni-tyóomè**; 4. **syokudoo/ití·màru·go-ĝôositu**; 5. **ano oísii sobàya/go-tyóomè**; 6. **iñtyoo/sáñbyaku zyuúroku-ĝòositu**

L 1. **Komê o kaʹte kimàsu.** **Dôno komêya ni ikû ñ desu ka**⤴
'I'm going to buy some rice (and come [back]).' 'Which rice store is it you're going to?'

2. **Kusúri o katte kimàsu.** **Dôno kusuriya ni ikû ñ desu ka**⤴
'I'm going to buy some medicine (and come [back]).' 'Which drugstore is it you're going to?'

3. **osake**; 4. **tabako**; 5. **hôñ**; 6. **hanâ**

M 1. **Sono tyuumoñ, âto ni-kâĝetu de dekîru desyoo ka.** **Ik-kàĝetu dakê de dekîru to omóimàsu yo**⤴
'Do you suppose you'll be able to take care of that order in two more months?' 'I think I can do it in just one month.'

2. **Sore, âto sań-zìkañ de kawâku desyoo ka.** **Ni-zîkañ dakê de kawâku to omóimàsu yo**⤴
'Do you suppose that will dry in three more hours?' 'I think it will dry in just two hours.'

3. **ano ryokañ/mik-ka/suku**; 4. **si-ĝátù kara no kyôosi/ni-syûukañ/wakâru**; 5. **sonó hòñ/go-kâĝetu/dêru**; 6. **kyôo no siñbuñ/ni-zîkañ/kûru**

Application Exercises

A1. Practice placing telephone orders for **demae**. Include your name and location; specifics of the order; a check on how long it will take. Don't neglect to incorporate the ritual language appropriate to the situation.

2. Take turns asking and answering questions about whether or not group members are continuing specific activities—still studying certain languages, still attending certain seminars, still coming to school at a specified time, still eating lunch at a specified place, still listening to Japanese tapes every evening, etc. Also check on the continuation of certain conditions: whether specified objects are still expensive, whether certain individuals are still busy, whether specified places are still cold (hot), etc. Practice both /**mâda** + affirmative predicate/ and /**môo** + negative predicate/ questions.

B. Core Conversations: Substitution

Practice the Core Conversations with substitutions. For example, in CC1, alter the situation (1) to one in which (N) is a smoker who has given up drinking; (2) to one in which (N) has given up both smoking and drinking; and (3) to one in which (N) has always been a nonsmoker/nondrinker. Convert CC2 to a situation in which (N) has recovered. For CC3, make the usual substitutions in terms of the specifics of the order, while retaining the original sentence patterns.

SECTION C

Eavesdropping

(Answer the following questions on the basis of the accompanying tape. A = the first speaker and B = the second speaker in each conversation. For the conversation with three speakers, C = the third speaker.)
- 1a. What time is it?
- b. What is A's problem?
- 2a. What is being discussed?
- b. What information about it does A provide?
- c. Why doesn't B know more about it?
- 3a. Who is A?
- b. What similar situation are A and B in?
- c. What does B suggest?
- d. What is A's reaction?
- 4a. Where does this conversation take place?
- b. Who is A?
- c. What do B and C ask for?
- 5a. How is the weather?
- b. What condition do A and B share?
- c. What solution does B offer?
- d. Why does this solution happen to be available?
- 6a. What is under discussion?
- b. What does B first suggest?
- c. Why does B offer an alternate suggestion?
- 7a. What are A and B discussing?
- b. What does B decide on?
- c. What does B decide against? Why?
- 8a. What two items does A offer?
- b. Which does B refuse? Why?
- 9a. What does A check on first?
- b. What does A then suggest?
- c. What is B's reaction?
- d. What is A's second suggestion?
- e. What is B's reaction?
- 10a. Name the person A is looking for.
- b. Where is that person?
- c. What is A's reaction upon learning this?
- d. What is the explanation? Give details.
- 11a. What is B's original order?
- b. What change is made?
- 12a. Who is B?

b. What is A urging?
c. What is B's response to the urging?
d. How is this contrary to what A knows?
e. What is the explanation?
f. Why does B apologize?
13a. How does B feel about eating right now? Why?
b. What does A notice about B?
c. What reassurance does B offer? Give details.
d. What is A's reaction?
14a. What does B usually eat for lunch?
b. What about today?
c. What does A suggest?
d. What is B's response?
15a. What does A ask for?
b. What else does B suggest?
c. What is A's response?
16a. What is under discussion?
b. What kind of place is it? Where is it?
c. When did A go there?
d. What did A order there?
e. What was A's reaction?
17a. Who is telephoning? From where?
b. What is being ordered?
c. How long will it take?
d. What time is it now?
18a. What time is it?
b. Who is B?
c. Why is A concerned about B?
d. What is B's explanation?
e. What is A's warning to B?
f. What is B going to do now?
19a. What is A trying to find out?
b. Why does B apologize?
c. What solution does B suggest?
d. Why is it of no help?
20a. What is B asked to do?
b. What does B want to do instead?
c. What was A's mistaken impression?
d. What does A then invite B to do?
21a. What does A offer B?
b. What is B's response and what is the explanation?
c. What is A's follow-up suggestion?
d. How does B respond to this, and with what explanation?
e. What is B's final request?

Utilization

(Be sure to provide a stimulus and/or response for each of the utterances that corresponds to the description below.)

1. Ask a colleague if she has had lunch yet.

2. Explain to a classmate that since you haven't had lunch yet, you're going to the dining room for a bit (and will be back).
3. Check on how late the special lunch is served here.
4. Call the waiter and tell him you haven't ordered yet.
5. Ask the waiter what today's specials are.
6. Order coffee and then change your order to cold milk.
7. You've taken your professor to lunch. Find out what he would like to order; what he would like to drink; whether he would like rice or bread; whether he would like a little more coffee.
8. Tell your colleague you are hungry. Suggest going to a noodle shop and having some noodles.
9. Tell your classmate you're thirsty. Explain that you're going to a **kissàteǹ** in the basement and invite her to go, too.
10. Suggest that you go to the restaurant in the basement now because it has probably emptied out already.
11. You are in the company dining room. Tell a colleague that you haven't ordered yet. Ask him what he thinks is good today.
12. Ask the waiter for: a little more rice; salt and pepper; soy sauce; more butter; ice; water; hot water; another cup of tea.
13. Tell a colleague that you want to have (*lit.* eat) some sashimi (sukiyaki, tempura, sushi) today. Ask him what place would be good.
14. You are shopping in a supermarket. Ask where the rice (eggs, butter, fish, pudding, ice cream, bread) is.
15. Warn a friend that the **sôba** in the new **sôba** shop in the basement isn't very good.
16. Offer a friend another glass of beer.
17. You've been offered another cup of coffee. Ask for just half.
18. Call the local sushi shop and order two portions of regular and one portion each of deluxe and super-deluxe to be delivered. Give your name and address (#405, Yamamoto Apartments, 3-chome).
19. You and a colleague are deciding on a day to meet. Suggest that you make it Wednesday.
20. Check with a colleague on whether Professor Nakamura from Tokyo University is still teaching Japanese in America.
21. Tell a friend that you've been taking this medicine since last month, but you just don't have any energy.
22. Tell a colleague that you want to buy some medicine (saké, rice, cigarettes). Ask if there is a drugstore (saké shop, rice shop, cigarette store) near the station.
23. You have just learned that a friend has been ill. Tell him that his color is still bad. Ask him if he's all right.
24. Tell a colleague that since there's something wrong with this computer (*lit.* the condition of this computer is bad), you're not using it any more.
25. You've been offered a cigarette. Explain that you don't smoke any more.
26. A close friend has asked you for someone's telephone number. Tell him to wait a minute, because you're still checking.
27. You are discussing the positions of mutual friends with a business colleague. Explain that Morimoto is still a **katyoo**, but Sugiura has already become a **butyoo**.
28. You're discussing supplies with your assistant. Tell him to order more large envelopes—since you've already run out.
29. Tell a friend you've given up smoking because it isn't good for one's health.
30. Your friend needs a dictionary. Tell him to ask the secretary.

Check-up

1. What is the basic meaning of /**môo** + predicate/? How does **môo ikímàsita** relate to **môo ikímaseǹ**? (A-SP1), (B-SP2)

2. What is the difference between /**moo** + quantity expression/ and /**môo** + predicate/? (A-SP1)

3. What is the basic meaning of /**mâda** + predicate/? How does **mâda beńkyoo-site (i)màsu** relate to **mâda beńkyoo-site (i)masèñ**? (A-SP1), (B-SP2)

4. Give the direct negative answers to the following:

   Môo simâsu ka⤴

   Môo simâsita ka⤴

   Môo sité (i)màsu ka⤴

   Môo sité (i)màsita ka⤴

   Mâda simâsu ka⤴

   Mâda sité (i)màsu ka⤴

   Mâda sité (i)màsita ka⤴   (A-SP1), (B-SP2)

5. Explain the difference between:

   Môo simâsita ka⤴

      Mâda sité (i)masèñ. *and*

   Môo kawákimàsita ka⤴

      Mâda kawákimasèñ.   (A-SP1)

6. In what two ways can **wakárimàsu** be converted into a question still in distal-style, the equivalent of 'do you understand?' How do the two patterns differ? (A-SP2)

7. Distinguish between the members of the following pairs:

   (a) **Soré (o) simàsita.**

      Soré ni simàsita.

   (b) **Âsa simasita.**

      Âsa ni simasita.

   (c) **Âsa ni narimasita.**

      Âsa ni simasita.

   (d) **Yô-zi ni narimasita.**

      Yô-zi ni simasita.

   (e) **Sasímì ni simasita.**

      Âtûku simasita.   (A-SP3)

8. What is the difference in meaning between:

   Sonó hìsyo ḡa îi desu. *and*

   Sonó hìsyo ni îi desu.   (B-SP1)

9. What alternate pattern of similar meaning is available for double-**ḡa**, affective predicates (i.e., /X ḡa + Y ḡa + predicate/)? Give an example. (B-SP1)

10. Give a more informal, casual-style equivalent of **kitê kudasai**. What sentence-particles may occur with this pattern? With what effect? (B-SP3)

Lesson 15

SECTION A

Core Conversations

1(J)a. **Ohâsi to h(u)ôoku to, dôtira g̃a îi desu ka↗**

(N)a. **Ohâsi o oneg̃ai-simasu.**

b. **Ohâsi wa, daízyòobu desu ka↗**

b. **Êe, motîroñ. Wasyoku wa, ohâsi no hôo g̃a tabéyasùi to omóimàsu yo↗**

c. **Naruhodo nêe. . . .** [To the waiter] **Sumímasèñ. Ohâsi oneg̃ai-simaasu.**

2(J′)a. **Nâñ-mee-sama desu ka↗**

(J″)a. **Hutá-rì desu.**

(J′)b. **Nî-mee-sama desu neʕ Dôozo.**

(N)a. **Seḱkaku koko màde kitâ ñ da kara, kono heñ no oísii monò g̃a tabétài desu nêe.**

(J″)b. **Kono heñ wa osákana g̃a oisìi desu yo↗—ûmi no sôba da kara.**

b. **Zyâa, sakána ni simasyòo. . . . Âa, oísìkatta. Tyôtto tabésug̃imàsita nêe.**

c. **Hoñtoo ni. Watasi mo, onáka g̃a ippai dèsu.**

c. **Oísìi kara, omíyage nì mo, tyôtto kat́te kaerimasyòo ka.**

d. **Soo simasyoo?**

3(N)a. **Tekísasu-òiru no Bêerii-sañ desu g̃a nêe.**

(J)a. **Êe.**

b. **Dôko e otúre-simasyòo ka.**

b. **Teñhana wa?**

c. **Teñ́pura dèsu ka↗**

c. **Gaíkoku no katà da kara, osûsi ya osásimi yòri îi to omôu ñ desu kedo . .**

d. **Dê mo, Teñhana wa sâabisu ḡa 'sore hodo yôku nâi desyoo.**

e. **Âa, sôo sôo. Sonó hòo ḡa îi desu neʃ Zyâa, soó simasyòo.**

d. **Sôo desu nêe. Zyâa, Uméteñ wa dòo desyoo.**

ENGLISH EQUIVALENTS

1(J)a. Which do you prefer—chopsticks, or a fork?
  b. Can you manage chopsticks?

(N)a. I'd like chopsticks.
  b. Yes, of course. For Japanese-style food I think that chopsticks are easier (for eating).

  c. Of course! . . . Excuse me! Could we have chopsticks?

2(J')a. How many (people) [in your party]?

 (J')b. That's two (people)—right? [This way,] please.
 (N)a. Since (it's the case that) we've taken the trouble to come all the way here, we'll want to eat something good from this area, won't we.

(J")a. Two (people).

  b. Well then, let's decide on fish. . . . Oh, that tasted good. I'm afraid I overate a bit . . .

(J")b. This area has delicious fish—since it's near the ocean.

  c. Since it's [so] good, shall we also take some home as a gift (*lit.* shall we return home having bought a little to be a souvenir, too)?

  c. [It] really [was delicious]. I'm full, too.

3(N)a. About Mr/s. Bailey, from Texas Oil . . .
  b. Where should we take him/her?
  c. You're suggesting tempura?

  d. Shall we do that?

(J)a. Yes . . .
  b. How about Tenhana?
  c. S/he's a person from abroad so I do think it's better than things like sushi and sashimi, but . . . (what do you think?)

  d. But [if it's] Tenhana, the service probably wouldn't be that good.

  d. That's right, isn't it. Well then, how about Umeten?

  e. Oh, right! *That* would be better, wouldn't it! Then let's make it that (*lit.* let's do it like that).

Breakdowns
(and Supplementary Vocabulary)

1. (o)hâsi — chopsticks
   h(u)ôoku — fork
   +nâihu — knife
   +supûuñ — spoon
   A to B to, dôtira ḡa îi (SP1) — which is better—A or B?
   motîroñ — of course, certainly
   wasyoku or
   +nihoñsyoku — Japanese-style food
   +yoosyoku — Western-style food
   wasyoku wa (o)hâsi ḡa tabéyasùi (SP2) — chopsticks are easy for eating Japanese-style food
   (o)hâsi no hôo (SP1) — the alternative of chopsticks
   (o)hâsi no hôo ḡa tabéyasùi — chopsticks are easier to eat with
   +kańzyòo/okańzyoo — the check

2. nâñ-mee(sama) (see below) — how many people?
   sek̀kakù — with special trouble or effort
   monô — thing (tangible)
   +nikû/onîku — meat
   +tori — chicken
   +yasai/oyâsai — vegetable
   +kudâmono — fruit
   +okâsi — cake; candy; sweets
   ûmi — ocean, sea
   +yamâ — mountain
   tabésuḡìru /-ru; tabésùḡita/ (SP3) — overeat
   ippai — full
   (o)miyaḡe — souvenir
   (o)miyaḡe ni kau (SP4) — buy as a souvenir

3. Tekísasu-òiru — Texas Oil
   Bêerii — Bailey
   tureru /-ru; tureta/ or
   oture-suru ↓ — take along (of people)
   +môtu /-u; motta/ — take hold (or possession) of
   +motte (i)ku — take (of things)
   Teñhana — (name of tempura restaurant)
   gaikoku — foreign country
   +(o)kuni — a country; one's native land or area
   osûsi ya 'osasimi (SP5) — things like sushi and sashimi

osásimi yòri (SP1)	more than sashimi, compared to sashimi
sâabisu	service
sore hodo (SP1)	to that extent
sore hodo yôku nâi	isn't that good
Umeteñ	(name of tempura restaurant)
sonó hòo ḡa îi	that alternative is better (*lit.* good)

-mee(sama): *Classifier for counting people*

itî-mee(sama)	rokû-mee(sama)
nî-mee(sama)	nanâ-mee(sama)/sitî-mee(sama)
sâñ-mee(sama)	hatî-mee(sama)
yôñ-mee(sama)	kyûu-mee(sama)
gô-mee(sama)	zyûu-mee(sama)
nâñ-mee(sama)	'how many people?'

MISCELLANEOUS NOTES

1. CC1 takes place in a restaurant where two colleagues have gone for Japanese food. Their speech style is careful, with distal-style predicates in major sentences, which make up the majority of utterances.

(J)a. J's inquiry as to whether or not the foreigner (N) can handle chopsticks has been a commonly occurring question in situations of this kind, regardless of how long the foreigner has been in Asia, particularly if the Japanese has not had extensive contact with foreigners.

(N)b. **Tabéyasùi** can be used both in reference to food and to eating implements—'is easy to eat (with)' (cf. 13A-SP4). Here, both references occur within the same utterance.

2. CC2 also takes place in a restaurant. This time, a Japanese and a foreigner have traveled some distance to an area known for its good fish. Again the speech style is basically careful. Most utterances are major sentences with distal-style predicates, but note also the direct-style final predicate **oísìkatta** (N)b, the fragment **Hoñtoo ni** (J″)c, and the inverted sentence (J″)b, features of casual-style.

The classifier **-mee**, used by (J′), a waiter, to count people, is a more formal equivalent of **-ri/-niñ**. Both may occur with the polite suffix **-sama**. The waiter's language is polite.

(N)a. **Sekkakù**, a nominal, implies special effort: it occurs commonly within sequences ending in **kara** or **no de** expressing cause ('since a special effort was made'). Note also: **Sekkakù desu ḡa** (*or* **kedo**), 'it's especially [kind of you] but,' the polite refusal of an offer; and /**sekkaku no** + nominal X/ 'an X involving special effort.'

Note how the /extended predicate + **kara**/ combines two notions: (1) the presence of (N) and (J″) in the restaurant means that they have come all this way; (2) from that fact comes the suggestion as to what they should eat.

For an explanation of the particle **ḡa** in **monô ḡa tabétài**, see 7B-SP4.

(J″)b, (N)b: Note the alternation between the use of **sakana** and **osakana**. While women use the polite forms more commonly, there is no strict gender-related rule.

(J″)c. **Ippai**, despite its ending, is a nominal: **iṕpai dà; iṕpai zya nài; iṕpai ni nàtta**.

(N)c. The Japanese are inveterate purchasers and donors of **(o)miyaḡe**, with stations, airports, and resort towns filled with **miyaḡeya** (souvenir shops). It is generally expected that travelers returning from a trip will bring **(o)miyaḡe**, particularly for their office staff, their family, and their friends.

3. In CC3, two business colleagues, using careful-style with distal-style predicates, are discussing where best to entertain a foreign client who will be visiting them. (J)'s suggestion of tempura rather than sushi or sashimi reflects the traditional Japanese assumption that foreigners dislike raw fish. This has less validity these days, although it continues to be true of some newcomers to Japan and Japanese food.

(N)a. Note how the upcoming topic of conversation is introduced: **X dèsu ḡa** (or **kedo**) . .

(N)b. **Tureru** refers to accompaniment by living beings. It frequently occurs in its gerund form in combination with the appropriate verbal of motion: **turete (i)ku** 'take to a place'; **turéte kùru** 'bring here'; **turéte kàeru** 'take/bring home.' Compare parallel combinations with **môtte**, from **môtu**, an operational verbal (**motte (i)ku, motte kùru,** and **motte kàeru**) when *things* are taken, brought, and taken/brought home. **Otúre-simasyòo** is a humble form, showing respect to Bailey. **Teñhana** is a blend of **teñpura** + **hanâ**; and **Umeteñ**, of **ume** 'plum' + **teñpura**.

Structural Patterns

1. COMPARISON OF TWO ITEMS: yòri AND hodo

/X **to** Y **to, dôtira (no hôo)**——/ = 'of X and Y, which (alternate) is [more]——?' X and Y are nominals, which may be modified. **Dôtira** is followed by /particle (usually **ḡa** or **o**) + predicate/. In this pattern, **dôtira** 'which of two?' alternates with **dôtira no hôo** 'the which-of-two alternative?' Examples:

Kore to sore to, dôtira (no hôo) ḡa kîree desu ka 'Which (alternative) is prettier—this one or that one?'

Atûi no to tumétài no to, dôtira (no hôo) ḡa oísìi desyoo ka. 'Which (alternative) would be tastier—the hot one or the cold one?'

Koñpyùutaa to taípurâitaa to, dôtira (no hôo) o yôku tukáimàsu ka 'Which (alternative) do you use more often—a computer or a typewriter?'

This use of particle **to** after both items that are being compared stresses that *only* these items are under consideration.

Note that, unlike the English equivalents, which contain a comparative degree (i.e., 'prett*ier,*' 'tast*ier,*' and '*more* often'), this Japanese pattern involves no change in, or qualification of, the predicate. The use of **dôtira (no hôo)** singles out which *one member* of the pair is to be described by the predicate. In the direct responses to the above questions, **hôo** 'alternative' may or may not be included:

Koré ḡa kìree desu. '*This one* is pretty.' or

Konó hòo ḡa kîree desu. '*This one* is petti[er].' (*lit.* This alternative is pretty.)

Atûi no ḡa oísìi desyoo? '*The hot one* would be tasty, wouldn't it?' or

Atûi no no hôo ḡa oísìi desyoo? '*The hot (one) alternative* would be tasti[er], wouldn't it?'

Koñpyùutaa o yôku tukaimasu. 'I often use *a computer.*' or

Koñpyùutaa no hôo o yôku tukaimasu. 'I use *the computer (alternative)* [more] often.'

However, if there is emphasis on the fact that, while one member of the compared pair is characterized by the predicate to a greater degree, the other member nonetheless also shares the feature, **môtto** 'more' may occur, linked with the predicate. Thus:

> **Kinôo mo âtûkatta kedo, kyôo wa môtto atûi desu nêe.** 'Yesterday was hot, too, but today is [still] hotter (*lit.* more hot), isn't it!'

When the *less* qualifying item of a comparison is expressed, it is followed by **yòri** (**yori** after an accented word): /**X yòri**/ = 'more than X,' 'compared to X.'

Study the following examples, noting the particles:

> **Soré yòri koré** (or **konó hòo**) **ḡa kìree desu.** '*This* is prettier than that.' (*lit.* 'More than that, *this* [or *this alternative*] is pretty.')
>
> **Tumétài no yori, atûi no (no hôo) ḡa oísìi desyoo?** '*The hot one* would be tastier than the cold one, wouldn't it?' (*lit.* 'More than the cold one, *the hot one* [or *alternative*] would be tasty, wouldn't it?')
>
> **Taipúràitaa yori, koñpyùutaa (no hôo) o yôku tukaimasu.** 'I use *the computer* more than the typewriter.' (*lit.* 'More than the typewriter, I use [*the alternative of*] the computer.')

In the above examples, the phrase ending with **yòri** may occur after the **ḡa** or **o** phrase without any difference in meaning other than a slight change in emphasis.

/**X wa Y yòri——**/ also occurs, when X is already under discussion or is being compared, and the focus is on what follows. Thus: **Kore wa, soré yòri kîree desu.** 'This one *is prettier than that one.*' Also possible are particles **wa** and **mo** following **yòri**. Thus: **Koré yòri wa, omósiròi desyoo kedo..** 'Compared to this (at least), it's probably interesting, but...' (it's not unqualifiedly interesting); **Kore wa, anó koñpyùutaa yori mo tukáinikùi desu yo**✓ 'This one is more difficult to use than *that* computer, *too.*'

If 'X is bigger than Y,' it follows that 'Y is not as big as X.' In such negative comparisons, Y is described as not having a quality 'as much as X,' 'to the extent of X,' expressed in Japanese as **X hodo**. Examples:

> **Bîiru wa, wâiñ hodo oísiku nài desyoo?** 'Beer isn't as good as wine, don't you agree?'
>
> **Señsèe no eeḡo wa, ano gakúsee nò hodo zyoózù zya nâi desu nêe.** 'The teacher's English isn't as good as that student's, is it!'
>
> **Kono siḡoto wa, are hodo zikáñ ḡa kakaranai to omoimasu.** 'I believe this work won't take as much time as that.'
>
> **Sore hodo omósìròku nâi desu yo**✓ 'It's not that interesting.' [This Japanese, like the English equivalent, implies 'not very interesting'.]

2. MORE ON AFFECTIVE PREDICATES

In 5A-SP1, we introduced the notion of affective predicates—those that are viewed as occurring outside the boundaries of human determination or volition. Included within the group were those predicates that may occur with two phrases ending in phrase-particle **ḡa**—the so-called double-**ḡa** predicates.

In patterns of this kind, the secondary affect is a feature of, or an area within, or a limitation of, the primary affect. That is to say, /**A ḡa + B ḡa** + predicate **C**/ may be regarded as 'C applies to A in the area of B.' Thus,

Katyoo ḡa eéḡo ḡa dekimàsu yo. 'The section manager knows English,' i.e., 'The section manager is English-capable.'

With the usual shift in focus, either affect—or both—may, of course, be followed by **wa** instead of **ḡa**.

In Lesson 5, the emphasis was on affective *verbals* as examples of affective predicates. But adjectival and /nominal + **dà**/ predicates are typically affective (non-operational), and many belong to the double-**ḡa** category. Consider these examples from the CC:

Wasyoku wa, ohâsi no hôo ḡa tabéyasùi. 'Japanese food is easier to eat with chopsticks.' (*lit.* 'Japanese food is chopsticks-alternative-easy-to-eat.')

Teñhana wa, sàabisu ḡa yôku nâi. 'Tenhana doesn't have good service.' (*lit.* 'Tenhana is service-not-good.')

In both these examples, the context requires that the primary affect be followed by **wa**. However, with the appropriate change of focus, double-**ḡa** sequences would result. For example:

Teñhana ḡa sàabisu ḡa îi kara, sokó e ikimasyòo ka. 'Since Tenhana has good service, shall we go there?'

Seńsèe ḡa huráñsuḡo ḡa ozyoozu dà kara, huráñsuḡo de hanàsite kudasai. 'Since the professor is good in French (*lit.* 'is French-skillful'), please speak in French.'

Otóotò ḡa guái ḡa warùi kara, kusúri o katte kimàsu. 'Since my brother doesn't feel well (*lit.* 'is condition-bad'), I'm going to go and buy some medicine.'

Further examples of affective patterns will be introduced in subsequent lessons.

3. COMPOUNDS IN -suḡìru

The verbal **suḡîru** occurs independently with the meaning 'go past,' 'pass by.' (Examples: **sań-neñ sùḡita** '3 years passed by'; **Toókyòo-eki (o) sùḡita** '[I] went past Tokyo Station.') It is the stem of this verbal that occurs in time expressions like **kû-zi go-hûñ-suḡi** '5 minutes past 9 o'clock.'

Suḡîru also enters into compounds with preceding verbal stems, adjectival roots, and **na**-nominals, with the meaning 'go to excess,' 'be too much.' Examples:

tabésuḡìru	'overeat'
tukáisuḡìru	'overuse'
sisúḡìru	'overdo'
takásuḡìru	'be too expensive'
oókisuḡìru	'be too big'
muzúkasisuḡìru	'be too difficult'
geńkisuḡìrù	'be too lively'

Note that **-ki-** and **-si-** within combinations like **oókisuḡìru** and **muzúkasisuḡìru** are devoiced (whispered) syllables, in contrast with their pronunciation in **oókìi** and **muzúkasìi**. (For an explanation, see Section I of the Introduction to Part 1.)

4. /(o)miyaḡe ni kau/

The phrase-particle **ni** has occurred in a number of goal and purpose constructions: **Kyôoto ni iku** 'go to Kyoto'; **byoóki ni nàru** 'become (get to be) ill'; **eé-kòosu ni suru** 'decide on (make [the order] to be) the A lunch'; **siḡóto ni kùru** 'come for work'.

As a further extension of this usage, we find examples in which /**X ni**/ indicates the capacity or role to be filled by a particular item. Thus,

Kono biñseñ o miyáḡe ni kaimàsita. 'I bought this stationery as (i.e., to be) a souvenir.'

Koko o kyoósitu ni tukatte (i)màsu. 'We're using this place as a classroom.'

Demae o bañḡòhañ ni tyuúmoñ-simàsita. 'I ordered *demae* as my dinner.'

5. PHRASE-PARTICLE **ya**

/Nominal A + **ya** + nominal B/ = 'A and B and others of a similar kind,' 'A and B and so on,' 'A and B among others,' 'items like A and B.' Compare:

otôosañ to okâasañ 'your father and mother' *and*

otôosañ ya okâasañ 'your father and mother and others in your family'

otya to koóhìi 'tea and coffee' *and*

otya ya koóhìi 'tea and coffee and other such drinks'

There may be more than two nominals in the series:

hôñ ya ′zassi ya ′siñbuñ 'books and magazines and newspapers and the like.'

A preceding modifier usually qualifies the entire following group:

hurûi hôñ ya zîsyo 'old books and dictionaries and the like.'

A series joined by **ya** occurs in the same kinds of patterns as a nominal alone.

Butyoo ya katyóo dèsu. 'They are division managers and section managers and the like.'

Koñpyùutaa ya taípuràitaa ḡa arimasu. 'There are computers and typewriters and such things.'

Drills

A 1. **Eé-kòosu to bií-kòosu to, dôtira no hôo ḡa oísìi desyoo ka⤴**   **Bií-kòosu no hôo ḡa oísìi to omôu ñ desu kedo ..**
'Which would be tastier—the 'A' lunch or the 'B' lunch?'   'I do think the 'B' lunch is tastier, but . . .' (I'm not sure).

2. **Kono kusuri to ′ano kusuri to, dôtira no hôo ḡa tuyôi desyoo ka⤴**   **Anó kusuri no hôo ḡa tuyôi to omôu ñ desu kedo ..**
'Which would be stronger—this medicine or that medicine?'   'I do think that medicine is stronger, but . . .' (I'm not sure).

3. **zyôo/tokuzyoo/îi**; 4. **katyoo/butyoo/yôku wakâru**; 5. **tosyôkañ/keńkyuuzyò/tikâi**; 6. **ni-tyóomè/yoń-tyoomè/bêñri (da)**; 7. **rokú-ḡòositu/go-ḡôositu/oókìi**

B 1. **Koko no sukiyaki wa, teńpura yòri oísìi desu ka⤴**   **Iêie, teńpura hodo oisiku nài desu yo.**
'Is the sukiyaki here tastier than the tempura?'   'No, it's not as good as the tempura.'

2. **H(u)ôoku wa, ohâsi yori tukáiyasùi desu ka⤴**   **Iêie, ohâsi hodo tukáiyàsùku nâi desu yo.**

'Is a fork easier to use than chopsticks?'
'No, it's not as easy to use as chopsticks.'

3. **asoko no yoosyoku/wasyoku/takâi desu**; 4. **sakana/tori/îi desu**; 5. **tikatetu/bâsu/bêñri desu**; 6. **durañsugo/doitugo/muzúkasìi desu**

C 1. **Koko wa, Sapporo hodo sâmûku nâi desu neʔ**
'This place isn't as cold as Sapporo—right?'
Iêie, Sápporo yòri zutto samùi desu yo⤴
'No, it's much colder than Sapporo.'

2. **Gakutyoo wa, Morímoto-señsèe hodo huráñsugo ga ozyoozu zya nài desu neʔ**
'The university president isn't as good in French as Dr. Morimoto—right?'
Iêie, Morímoto-señsèe yori zutto ozyoozu dèsu yo⤴
'No, s/he is much more skilled than Dr. Morimoto.'

3. **it-tyoome no susìya/anó sobàya/demáe ga hàyàku nâi**; 4. **gaíkoku no monò/Nihóñ no monò/yâsùku nâi**; 5. **Yoóròppa/Âzia/ikíyàsùku nâi**; 6. **kotósi no yasumì/kyôneñ no/nâgâku nâi**; 7. **asâtte no kâigi/otótòi no/taísetu zya nài**

D 1. **Otyá yòri, koóhìi no hôo ga takâi desu ka⤴**
'Is *coffee* more expensive than tea?'
Êe, mâa, otyá yòri wa takâi ka mo sirénài kedo . .
'Yes—well—it may be more expensive than tea (at least), but . . .' (it's not *that* expensive).

2. **Supéiñgo yòri, itáriago no hòo ga ozyóozu dèsu ka⤴**
'Is s/he better at *Italian* than Spanish?'
Êe, mâa, supéiñgo yòri wa ozyóozu kà mo sirénài kedo . .
'Yes—well—s/he may be better at it than Spanish (at least), but . . .' (s/he's not *that* good).

3. **sasímì/sôba/tabéyasùi**; 4. **Toodai/Wâseda/tikâi**; 5. **konó heñ no hòteru/kono ryokañ/rakû**; 6. **myôobañ/kôñbañ/tugôo ga ìi**; 7. **gaímùsyoo/oókuràsyoo/yôku wakarimasu**

E 1. **Butyoo mo 'katyoo mo, eégo ga ozyoozu dèsu ka⤴**
'Are both the division manager and the section manager good in English?'
Dôtira mo hetâ zya nâi kedo, katyóo no hòo ga tyôtto ozyóozu dà to omoimasu.
'Neither is bad at it, but the section manager is a bit better, I think.'

2. **Wâseda mo 'Keeoo mo, muzúkasìi desu ka⤴**
'Are both Waseda and Keio difficult?'
Dôtira mo yasásiku nâi kedo, Keéoo no hòo ga tyôtto muzúkasìi to omoimasu.
'Neither one is easy, but Keio is a bit more difficult, I think.'

3. **konó susìya/tonari no teñpuraya/oísìi desu**; 4. **atárasìi kusuri/hurûi no/yowâi desu**; 5. **kono zassi/ano siñbuñ/yomínikùi desu**; 6. **kono waapuro/ano waapuro/bêñri desu**

F 1. **Sûsi mo îi kedo, sasímì wa dôo desyoo.**
'Sushi will be good, too, but how about sashimi?'

A, sôo sôo. Osásimi no hòo ḡa îi desu ne!
'Oh, right! Sashimi will be better, won't it!'

2. **Yamâmori-señsee mo yôku gozôñzi da kedo, iñtyoo wa dôo desyoo.**
'Dr. Yamamori knows [that] well, too, but how about the head of the hospital?'

A, sôo sôo. Îñtyoo no hôo ḡa yôku gozôñzi desu ne!
'Oh, right! The head of the hospital knows [that] better, doesn't s/he!'

3. **Tanaka-sañ no onêesañ/kîree da/imootosañ**; 4. **osake/keñkoo ni yòku nâi/tabako**; 5. **teesyoku/oisii/sâñdo**

G 1. **Anó sakana dèsu kedo, syoóyu o tukaimasyòo ka.**
'About that fish—shall I use soy sauce?'

Êe. Ano sakana wa, osyóoyu no hòo ḡa îi to omoimasu.
'Yes. For that fish, soy sauce is better, I think.'

2. **Muzúkasii deñwa dèsu kedo, Itóo-sañ to kawarimasyòo ka.**
'About difficult telephone calls—shall I put Mr/s. Ito on instead?'

Êe. Muzukasii deñwa wa, Itóo-sañ no hôo ḡa îi to omoimasu.
'Yes. For difficult telephone calls, Mr/s. Ito is better, I think.'

3. **yuútàañ/go-tyóomè made matímasyòo**; 4. **kono kusuri/hañbuñ dake nomimasyòo**

H 1. **Kono heñ wa, sakána wa oisiku nài desyoo?**
'This area isn't good for fish, is it?'

Êe. Nâni ḡa oísìi desyoo nêe—kono heñ wa.
'That's right. What *would* be good—[in] this area?'

2. **Rañti-sàabisu wa, asóko wa yàsùku nâi desyoo?**
'The special lunch isn't cheap [at] that place, is it?'

Êe. Dôko ḡa yasûi desyoo nêe—rañti-sàabisu wa.
'That's right. What place *would* be cheap—[for] lunch service?'

3. **zassi/asóko nò/omósìroku nâi**; 4. **ano gakusee/eḡo/zyoózù zya nâi**; 5. **asoko/ kooeñ/kîree zya nâi**; 6. **koñsyuu/kiñyòobi/yôku nâi**

I 1. **Anó sobàya ḡa sôba ḡa oísìi kara, asóko e ikimàsita.**
'That soba shop has delicious soba, so I went there.'

Zyâa, yáppàri anó sobàya ni sitâ ñ desu ka⤴
'Then you mean you did decide on that soba shop after all?'

2. **Umêteñ ḡa teesyoku ḡa yasùi kara, asóko de tabemàsita.**
'Umeten has inexpensive special meals, so I ate there.'

Zyâa, yáppàri Uméteñ ni sitâ ñ desu ka⤴
'Then you mean you did decide on Umeten after all?'

3. **anó misè/sâabisu/îi/asóko ni oture-simàsita**; 4. **anó sùupaa/okome/yasûi/asóko de kaimàsita**

J 1. **Asoko no kodomo wa, gênki desu nêe.**
'Aren't the children at that place lively!'

Êe. Tyôtto geńkisuǵìru ń zya nâi desu ka⌐
'Yes. Isn't it the case that they're a bit too lively?'

2. **Kôñya no 'yakusoku wa, hayâi desu nêe.**
'Isn't tonight's appointment early!'

Êe. Tyôtto hayásuǵìru ń zya nâi desu ka⌐
'Yes. Isn't it the case that it's a bit too early?'

3. **anô ko/tamâǵɔ o takúsañ tabemàsu**; 4. **konó sèki/toòi desu**; 5. **Matûzusi no 'demae/takâi desu**; 6. **butyoo/osake o takúsañ nomimàsu**

K 1. **Îi omíyaǵe ni nàru desyoo ne!—konó kèeki.**
'It will probably make (*lit.* become) a good souvenir—this cake.'

Sôo desu ne! Zyâa, omiyaǵe ni 'mit-tu-hodo katte kaerimàsu yo.
'That's right. Well, I'll buy about three as souvenirs (and go home).'

2. **Îi omíyaǵe ni nàru desyoo ne!—konó hòñ.**
'It will probably make a good souvenir—this book.'

Sôo desu ne! Zyâa, omiyaǵe ni 'sañ-satu-hodo katte kaerimàsu yo.
'That's right. Well, I'll buy about three as souvenirs (and go home).'

3. **kabañ**; 4. **nâihu**; 5. **tîzu**

L 1. **Kyoositu wa?**
'What about a classroom?'

A. Râiǵetu made wa, kokó o kyoositu ni tukattè (i)ru ń desu kedo . .
'Oh, through next month (at least), I'm using this place as a classroom, but . . .' (after that I don't know).

2. **Zimûsyo wa?**
'What about an office?'

A. Râiǵetu made wa, kokó o zimùsyo ni tukáttè (i)ru ń desu kedo . .
'Oh, through next month (at least), I'm using this place as an office, but . . .' (after that I don't know).

3. **kaíǵìsitu**; 4. **uketuke**;[1] 5. **keńkyuuzyò**

M 1. **Zassi ya siñbuñ mo, yôku oyómi ni narimàsu ka⌐**
'Do you often read magazines and newspapers and the like, too?'

Zitû wa |desu nêe.| Zassi ya siñbuñ wa, hotôñdo yomânai ń desu yo.
'Actually—you know—I hardly read things like magazines and newspapers at all.'

2. **Ôono-kyoozyu ya Mîyazi-sañ to mo, yôku oái ni narimàsu ka⌐**
'Do you often meet with people like

Zitû wa |desu nêe.| Ôono-kyoozyu ya Mîyazi-sañ to wa, hotôñdo awânai ń desu yo.

---

1. **Uketuke** may refer to the reception desk as well as the receptionist.

Professor Ono and Mr/s. Miyaji, too?' 'Actually—you know—I hardly meet with people like Professor Ono and Mr/s. Miyaji at all.'

3. doítùziñ ya huráñsùziñ to/ohánasi ni narimàsu; 4. taípuràitaa ya końpyùutaa/otúkai ni narimàsu; 5. Kâñkoku ya Tyûuḡoku ni/irássyaimàsu

N 1. **Koóhìi nomímaseñ ka⸍**
'Won't you have some coffee?'

Seḱkakù desu ḡa, koóhìi wa nomânai ñ desu.
'It's kind of you to offer, but I don't drink coffee.'

2. **Tabako suímaseñ ka⸍**
'Won't you have a cigarette?'

Seḱkakù desu ḡa, tabako wa suwánài ñ desu.
'It's kind of you to offer, but I don't smoke.'

3. osyooyu tukáimaseñ; 4. aságòhañ tabémasèñ; 5. tênisu simáseñ

O 1. **Osákana o tabemaseñ ka⸍**
'Won't you have some fish?'

Êe. Seḱkaku koko màde kitâ ñ da kara, tabétài desu nêe.
'Yes. Since I came all the way here, I'd like to eat some.'

2. **Omíyaḡe o katte kaerimaseñ ka⸍**
'Won't you buy some souvenirs before you go home (*lit.* go home having bought)?'

Êe. Seḱkaku koko màde kitâ ñ da kara, katte kaeritài desu nêe.
'Yes. Since I came all the way here, I'd like to buy some before I go home (*lit.* go home having bought).'

3. bañgòhañ o tâbete ikímaseñ; 4. seńsèe no otaku ni ukáḡaimasèñ; 5. syotyoo to soódañ-simaseñ; 6. Matuda-kyoozyu to reńraku-simaseñ

P 1. **Teńhana e oture-simasyòo ka.**
'Shall we take [them] to Tenhana?'

A, îi âidea desu nêe. Teńhana e turete ikimasyòo.
'Oh, that's a good idea! Let's take [them] to Tenhana.'

2. **Roḱ-kai no kissateñ e oture-simasyòo ka.**
'Shall we take [them] to the coffee shop on the sixth floor?'

A, îi âidea desu nêe. Roḱ-kai no kissateñ e turete ikimasyòo.
'Oh, that's a good idea! Let's take [them] to the coffee shop on the sixth floor.'

3. **Sińzyuku no hòteru**; 4. **Gińza no depàato**; 5. **otera ya zíñzya**

Application Exercises

A1. Using pairs of objects or pictures of objects—books, magazines, dictionaries, pens, as well as foods and drinks for which the Japanese terms have been introduced—practice

asking and answering questions as to relative price, size, newness, interest, tastiness, etc., as appropriate. Concentrate on /**X to Y to, dôtira**——/, and **yòri** and **hodo** patterns.
  2. Continue practicing comparisons involving pairs, this time in reference to familiar things in the real world (for example, the closeness of two places, the difficulty of two languages, the price of two kinds of cars, etc.)
  3. Practice making restaurant small-talk:
     (a) Discuss the use of chopsticks: for example, ease or difficulty of usage, for what foods they are appropriate, etc.
     (b) Discuss the eating preferences of Japanese and foreigners.
     (c) Discuss possible things you might take home as **omiyaḡe**.
     (d) Comment on how delicious the food was (mentioning that you overate) and how good the service was.

B. Core Conversations: Substitution
  Practice the CC, making changes in the vocabulary, but not the overall dialogue structure. Include in your substitutions the supplementary vocabulary listed in the Breakdowns.

SECTION B

Core Conversations

1(N)a. **Naní mo gozaimaseñ ḡa, dôozo.**
   b. **Mâa, îp-pai dôozo.**
   c. **Môtto mesíaḡarimaseñ ka⤴**

(J)a. **A, osôre-irimasu.**
   b. **Itádakimàsu. . . .**
   c. **Arîḡatoo gozaimasu. Dê mo, Kâataa-sañ hodo tûyôku nâi kara . .**[2]

2(N)a. **Wasyoku to 'yoosyoku to tyuúka-ryòori no uti de, dôre ḡa itíbañ osuki dèsu ka⤴**

   b. **Tyûuka wa?**

(J)a. **Bôku wa, yáppàri, wasyóku dèsu nêe. Yoosyoku wa, dôo mo damê na ñ desu yo.**
   b. **Mâa, kirái zya nài kedo, wasyóku hodo tabetài to wa omówànai desu nêe.**

3(J)a. **Kyôo no seťto-mènyuu wa, kotíra ni nàtt(e) orimasu.**

   b. **Dôre mo daítai onazi dèsu ḡa, itíbañ hayài no wa, eé-sètto de gozaimasu ne!**
   c. **Ie, hoká nò wa, tyôtto zikáñ ḡa kakarimàsu no de . .**

(N)a. **Konó mit-tù no uti de, dôre ḡa 'itibañ hâyâku dekimasu ka⤴**

   b. **Soré yòri hayâi no, arímàsu?**
   c. **Zyâa, eé-sètto tanomimasu. Narubeku hâyâku sité kudasài.**

2. The video has a less common alternate pattern: **Arîḡatoo gozaimasu ḡa, Kâataa-sañ . .**

70 • Lesson 15

ENGLISH EQUIVALENTS

1(N)a. There's nothing [worth mentioning], but please have some.
   b. Do have a glass(ful).
   c. Won't you have some more?

(J)a. Oh, thank you.
   b. I'll have some, thank you. . . .
   c. Thank you but since I'm not as good a drinker as you, Mr/s. Carter . . . (I'm going to stop).

2(N)a. Which do you like best—Japanese-style food, Western-style food, or Chinese cooking?

   b. What about Chinese?

(J)a. Me, I [like] Japanese-style food (after all). (It's that) Western-style food really doesn't agree with me.
   b. Well, I don't dislike it, but I don't (believe I) like to eat it as much as Japanese-style food.

3(J)a. [Pointing to one section of the menu] Today's specials are here.

   b. They're all about the same, but the fastest is the 'A' special.

   c. No, the other things take a little time, so . . . ('A' is the fastest).

(N)a. Of these three, which can you do the fastest?

   b. Is there something that is faster than that?

   c. Then I'll order the 'A' special. Please make it as fast as possible.

BREAKDOWNS
(AND SUPPLEMENTARY VOCABULARY)

1. **mesiaḡaru ↑ /-u; mesiaḡatte/** (SP1)   eat; drink; smoke /honorific-polite/
2. **ryôori**   cooking
   tyuúka-ryòori   Chinese cooking
   +**nâka**   inside, within
   sôto   outside
   A to B to C no uti de or
   A to B to C no nâka de (SP2)   being among A and B and C
   sukî/osuki /na/   pleasing; like
   itibañ   most, to the greatest degree
   itíbañ sukì da (SP2)   is most pleasing; like best
   kirai /na/   displeasing; dislike
3. **seťto-mènyuu**   set menu (the special fixed meals on a menu)

   kotíra ni nàtt(e) orimasu + (SP3)   [it] has come to be here
   konó mit-tù no uti de or

konó mit-tù no nâka de	being among these three things
itíbañ hayài	is fastest
itíbañ hàyàku dekîru	can be done fastest
daitai	for the most part
itíbañ hayài no	the one that is fastest
eé-sètto	the 'A' meal, the 'A' special
soré yòri hayâi no	one that is faster than that
hoka	other, another, other than
zikáñ ğa kakàru	take time
narubeku (SP4)	as much as possible
narubeku hâyâku	as fast as possible
+yawárakài /-katta/	is soft; is tender
+katai /-katta/	is hard; is stiff; is tough
+amai /-katta/	is sweet; is bland
+suṕpài	is sour, is acid
+karâi /-katta/	is spicy; is salty
+usui /-katta/	is thin (of liquids); is weak (of coffee, tea, etc.); is pale (of colors)
+kôi /-katta/	is thick (of liquids); is strong (of coffee, tea, etc.); is dark (of colors)

Supplementary Vocabulary: Tableware

(o)sara	plate
koóhiikàppu ~ kâppu	coffee cup
koppu	glass
tyawañ/otyâwañ	bowl (for rice)
(o)wañ	bowl (for soup)
yunómì	teacup (Japanese-style)

MISCELLANEOUS NOTES

1. CC1 is the kind of dialogue that typically occurs whenever a guest is offered food or drink by a host. It includes many ritualistic utterances. On the accompanying video, Mr. Suzuki, (J), is the guest of his business colleague, Mr. Carter, (N). The style is essentially careful and polite, with most predicates in distal-style. While these two individuals do not ordinarily use polite-style when they converse with each other at work, the formality of the host-guest relationship has resulted in a style shift.

(N)a. This is a ritualistic utterance, regularly used by a host as refreshments are about to be eaten or drunk. The literal meaning 'there is nothing' has no validity: the implication is that there is nothing worth mentioning or worthy of the occasion.

(N)b. **Mâa**, previously introduced as a word indicating agreement with some reservation or reluctance (cf. CC2[J]b, following), occurs here to indicate persuasion.

J(c). **Tuyôi** 'is strong' is used here in reference to Mr. Carter's capacity for drinking alcoholic beverages. Comments of this kind are extremely common among the Japanese and are a favorite topic of small talk.

A direct-style predicate occurs here within a minor sentence ending in **kara**. This is less significant in identifying overall style than its occurrence as a final predicate in a major sentence would be.

2. CC2 is a conversation about food preferences between two acquaintances who maintain some distance in conversing. The style is careful, with distal-style final predicates. On the accompanying video, Ms. Miller is asking her business colleague, Mr. Yamada, about his likes and dislikes, as they enjoy a meal together sitting at a counter at a Japanese restaurant.

(N)a. **Ryôori**: Note also **ryôori-suru** 'prepare food' and **ryoórìya** 'restaurant (Japanese-style).' **Sukî da** and **kirái dà** are affective, double-ḡa predicates. Both the person who likes (or dislikes) and the thing (or person) who is liked (or disliked) are followed by **ḡa** (or **wa**, with a shift of focus). The patterning is the same as that which occurs with **wakâru, dekîru**, etc. (cf. 5A-SP1 and 15A-SP2).

(J)b. Note the contrast implied in the use of **wa**: while Yamada does not *dislike* Chinese cooking, he won't go so far as to say that he likes to eat it as much as he likes Japanese food (*lit.* 'that I want to eat it as much as Japanese food [at least] I don't believe').

3. CC3 is a restaurant conversation between a waiter (J) and a customer (N) who is in a hurry. The style is careful, with both participants using distal-style predicates; but only the waiter uses polite-style.

(J)a, b, and (N)c. **Setto-mènyuu**, like **kôosu**, is a borrowing, similar in meaning to **teesyoku**. **Eé-sètto** and **bií-sètto**, referring to particular fixed meals, parallel the forms **eé-kòosu** and **bií-kòosu**.

(J)c. Note that **kakâru** is an affective, double-ḡa verbal. Here, because of the focus, **hoká nò** is followed by **wa**: 'the other ones (in contrast) are "time-takers."' The very careful, polite speech of the waiter includes a distal-style verbal preceding **no de**.

Structural Patterns

1. VERBALS OF EATING AND DRINKING

The verbals **tabêru** 'eat' and **nômu** 'drink' have both special polite equivalents as well as predictable derived forms.
Study the following chart:

Plain	Polite	
	Humble-Polite ↓	Honorific-Polite ↑
tabêru	itadaku	mesiaḡaru *or* otábe ni nàru
nômu	itadaku	mesiaḡaru *or* onómi ni nàru

The special polite equivalents **itadaku** and **mesiaḡaru** are additional examples of polite expressions which are less specific than their plain equivalents. Only in plain-style is it always necessary to distinguish verbally between eating and drinking.

The derived polite expressions **otábe ni nàru** and **onómi ni nàru**, while definitely honorific-polite, are more specific and less elegant than **mesiaḡaru**. However, in reference to medicine and cigarettes, **onómi ni nàru** is the more common honorific-polite equivalent of **nômu**.

2. *COMPARING THREE OR MORE ITEMS:* **uti ~ nâka; itibañ**

In Section A, we learned how to compare two items. We will now examine the patterns that are used when three or more items are involved. The comparison of two items regularly involves the use of **dôtira** 'which of two items?' and/or **hôo** 'alternative.' In comparing three or more items, the required word is **itibañ** 'most,' 'to the greatest degree'; question words (other than **dôtira**) are used as appropriate in the given context. Compare:

    Dôtira (no hôo) ḡa oísìi desu ka 'Which is tastier?'

    Wasyóku no hòo ḡa oísìi desu. '*Japanese food* is more delicious.' *and*

    Dôre ḡa itíbañ oisìi desu ka 'Which is tastiest?'

    Wasyóku ḡa itibañ oisìi desu. '*Japanese food* is most delicious.'

When the two items involved in a comparison question are named, they occur in the pattern:

    /**A to B to, dôtira——**/

When three or more items are compared, a parallel pattern that includes /**A to B to C to**/ may occur, but much more frequent is the pattern /**A to B to C (no uti) de, dôre** (or **dâre, dôko, îtu,** etc.) + particle + **itibañ——**/, in which **de** is the gerund of **dà**, and **uti** refers to a particular set or in-group: *lit.* 'being (the set made up of) A + B + C.' In this pattern, the inclusion of **uti** is optional.

Nâka, a place nominal that refers to the 'inside' of tangible objects, also occurs as an alternate of **uti** in this construction, particularly when there is no overt indication of the makeup of the set under consideration.

It is of course possible to group the items compared, rather than name them individually. Thus:

    Konó osùsi (no uti ~ nâka) de, dôre ḡa itíbañ oisìi desyoo ka. 'Of this sushi, which would be the tastiest?'

    Kono sâñ-satu no zîsyo de, koré ḡa itibañ wakariyasùi to omoimasu. 'Of these three dictionaries, *this one* is the easiest to understand, I believe.'

Additional examples:

    Syatyoo to 'butyoo to 'katyoo no uti de, dâre ḡa 'itibañ eéḡo ḡa ozyoozu dèsu ka 'Of the company president, the division manager, and the section manager, who is best in English?'

    Hôñ to 'zassi to 'siñbuñ de, dôre o itíbañ yòku yomímàsu ka 'Which do you read most often—books, magazines, or newspapers?'

    Teńpura mo yòku tabêru ñ desu kedo, itíbañ sukì na no wa sasímì desu. 'I do eat tempura often, too, but what I like best is sashimi.'

    Tâkusii wa, bâsu yori hayâi kedo, itíbañ hayài no wa, deńsya zya nài desu ka 'A cab will be faster than the bus, but won't the fastest one be the train?'

3. VERBAL GERUND + ôru

In 7A-SP5, the verbal **ôru** was introduced as the humble-polite ↓ equivalent of **iru** 'be (animate).' Thus, as the polite equivalent of the exchange:

Asítà made imâsu ka 'Will you be here until tomorrow?'
Êe, imâsu. 'Yes, I will (be here).'

we learned:

Asítà made irássyaimàsu ka
Hâa, orímàsu.

Consider also:

Kono deñwa, tukátte (i)rassyaimàsu ka 'Are you using this telephone?'
Hâa, tukátt(e) orimàsu. 'Yes, I am (using).'

The verbal **ôru** also occurs following verbal gerunds, in patterns in which the referent is an inanimate. In such cases, **ôru** moves from the humble-polite category /↓/ to the neutral-polite /+/, which shows deference only to the person addressed. (Cf. **gozáimàsu**, which is also /+/.) Examples:

Koko wa, kyoósitu ni nàtt(e) orimasu. 'This place has been made into (*lit.* become) a classroom.'
Atárasìi kyoókàsyo ḡa dêt(e) orimasu yo 'A new textbook has come out.'
Kotira ni 'kuruma ḡa takúsañ tomatt(e) orimàsu nêe. 'Aren't there a lot of cars parked here!'

Note the contrast in the patterns of contraction: **-te iru > -te ru; -te irassyàru > -te rassyàru;** but **-te òru > -t òru.**

4. narubeku

Narubeku 'to the greatest extent possible' links up with predicates to indicate maximum degree. Examples:

Narubeku hâyaku kitê kudasai. 'Please come as early as you can.' (*lit.* 'Please come early to the greatest extent possible.')
Narubeku kîree ni kâite kudásaimasèñ ka 'Would you write as beautifully as possible?'
Narubeku yasásiku iimàsita kedo, daré mo wakarànakatta ñ desu. 'I said it as simply as possible, but nobody understood.'

Drills

A 1. **Gôhañ môtto mesíaḡarimasèñ ka** | **Arîgatoo gozaimasu. Zyâa, moó sukòsi itadakimasu. Oísii gòhañ desu nêe.**
'Won't you have some more rice?' | 'Thank you. Well, I'll have a little more. Isn't it delicious rice!'

2. **Osake môtto mesíaḡarimasèñ ka** | **Arîgatoo gozaimasu. Zyâa, moó sukòsi itadakimasu. Oísii osake dèsu nêe.**
'Won't you have some more saké?' |

	'Thank you. Well, I'll have a little more. Isn't it delicious saké!'

3. **kudâmono**; 4. **osûsi**; 5. **onîku**; 6. **okâsi**; 7. **pûriñ**

B 1. **Yuube, oísii sakana o tabemàsita yo.** **Dôtira de mesíaḡarimàsita ka⤴**
'I ate some delicious fish last night.' 'Where did you eat it?'

2. **Yuube, omósiròi hito ni aímàsita yo.** **Dôtira de oái ni narimàsita ka⤴**
'I met someone interesting last night.' 'Where did you meet him/her?'

3. **demáe o tyuumoñ-simàsita**; 4. **omíyaḡe o kaimàsita**; 5. **oísii wàiñ o nomímàsita**; 6. **anó deñwabàñḡoo o sirábemàsita**

C 1. **Osuki na sakana wa, dôre desyoo.** **Sakána dèsu ka⤴ Zitû wa, sakana wa, amari sukî zya nâi ñ desu.**
'Which would be the fish you like?' 'Fish? Actually, the fact is I don't like fish very much.'

2. **Osúki na okàsi wa, dôre desyoo.** **Okâsi desu ka⤴ Zitû wa, okâsi wa, amari sukî zya nâi ñ desu.**
'Which would be the sweets you like?' 'Sweets? Actually, the fact is I don't like sweets very much.'

3. **kudâmono**; 4. **teesyoku**; 5. **oyâsai**; 6. **tyuúka-ryòori**

D 1. **Sakana to nikû to 'tori no uti de, dôre ḡa itíbañ osuki dèsu ka⤴** **Yappàri, torí dèsu nêe—watasi wa.**
'Which do you like best—fish, meat, or chicken?' 'It's chicken, after all—for me.'

2. **Supûuñ to h(u)ôoku to ohâsi no uti de, dôre o itíbañ yòku tukáimàsu ka⤴** **Yappàri, ohâsi desu nêe—watasi wa.**
'Which do you use most often— spoons, forks, or chopsticks?' 'It's chopsticks, after all—for me.'

3. **eeḡo/surañsuḡo/doituḡo/dôre ḡa/zyoózù desu**; 4. **kôñya/asítà/asâtte/îtu ḡa/ohíma dèsu**; 5. **katyoo/butyoo/syatyoo/dâre ḡa/hanásiyasùi**; 6. **Ḡiñza/Toranomoñ/Mêziro/dôko ḡa/bêñri desu**

E 1. **Gaikokuḡo no uti de, dôre ḡa itíbañ muzukasìi to omóimàsu ka⤴** **Sâa, dôre mo miñna muzukasìi ñ zya nâi desu ka⤴**
'Among foreign languages, which do you think is most difficult?' 'Hmm. Isn't it the case that they're all— every one of them—difficult?'

2. **Gaikoku no uti de, dôko ḡa itíbañ omosiròi to omóimàsu ka⤴** **Sâa, dôko mo miñna omosiròi ñ zya nâi desu ka⤴**
'Among foreign countries, what place do you think is most interesting?' 'Hmm. Isn't it the case that they're all— every one of them—interesting?'

3. **ryôori/dôko no/oisii**; 4. **kono daiḡaku/dôko/rakû da**; 5. **kono teḡami/dôre/ wakárinikùi**; 6. **konó mit-tù/dôre/komâru**

F 1. **Kore, oísìi desyoo?**
'This is delicious, don't you think?'

Êe. Konó nàka de, itíbañ oisìi to omoimasu.
'Yes. Among these, it is the most delicious, I believe.'

2. **Kâre, yôku dekîru desyoo?**
'He is very capable, don't you agree?'

Êe. Konó nàka de, itíbañ yòku dekîru to omoimasu.
'Yes. Among these, he is the most capable, I believe.'

3. **kânozyo/kîree (da)**; 4. **Toodai/tikâi**; 5. **kore/miyásùi**; 6. **anô hito/keńkoo (dà)**; 7. **koko/sâabisu ḡa îi**; 8. **ano gakusee/komâru**

G 1. **Soré yòri hayâi bâsu wa, nâi no?**
'You mean there isn't a faster bus than that one?'

Ń. Soré ḡa itibañ hayài.
'Yeah. *That one* is the fastest.'

2. **Kâre yori zyoózù na hito wa, inâi no?**
'You mean there isn't anyone better at it than he is?'

Ń. Kâre ḡa itíbañ zyoozù da.[3]
'Yeah. *He's* the best.'

3. **soko/bêñri na tokóro**; 4. **kore/omósiròi zassi**; 5. **soko/tikâi êki**; 6. **Osamu-sañ/ himá na hitò**

H 1. **Koóhìi to 'kootya to 'otya no uti de, dôre ḡa itíbañ osuki dèsu ka**
'Which do you like best—coffee, black tea, or Japanese tea?'

Yappàri koóhìi desyoo nêe. Kootya ya otya mo, mâa, sukî da kedo, koóhìi hodo zya nâi desu ne!
'Coffee, I guess. I do rather like black tea and Japanese tea and such, too, but not as much as coffee.'

2. **Tikatetu to bâsu to tâkusii no uti de, dôre ḡa itíbañ hayâi desu ka**
'Which is fastest—the subway, the bus, or a cab?'

Yappàri tikátetu desyòo nêe. Bâsu ya tâkusii mo, mâa, hayâi kedo, tikátetu hodo zya nài desu ne!
'The subway, I guess. The bus and taxis and such are rather fast, too, but not as [fast] as the subway.'

3. **iñtyoo to 'Hayasi-sañ to kâre/dâre/gaikoku e yôku ikímàsu**; 4. **gês·sûi to kîñ·dôo to kâa·môku/îtu/isóḡasìi desu**; 5. **tosyôkañ to keńkyuuzyò to 'koko/dôko/beńkyoo- siyasùi desu**

---

3. Responses ending in **dà** are blunt-style. The gentle-style equivalent, which drops **dà**, is the more common alternate for women.

I 1. **Asoko wa, rêsutorañ desu ka⤴**   **Êe. Kyôneñ kara rêsutorañ ni nâtt(e) orimasu.**
'Is that place a restaurant?'   'Yes. It has been (*lit.* become) a restaurant since last year.'

2. **Kono heñ wa, koóeñ dèsu ka⤴**   **Êe. Kyôneñ kara koóeñ ni nàtt(e) orimasu.**
'Is this area a park?'   'Yes. It's been a park since last year.'

3. **kêeki to koóhìi/sêtto**; 4. **oyasumi/hutu-ka**; 5. **zêmi/maisyuu**; 6. **rañti-sàabisu/ni-zí-hàñ made**; 7. **kaisya/tonári no bìru**

J 1. **Âtuku simasyoo ka.**   **Êe, narúbeku àtuku site kudasai.**
'Shall I heat it (*lit.* make [it] hot)?'   'Yes, please make it as hot as possible.'

2. **Gôḡo ni simásyòo ka.**   **Êe, narúbeku gòḡo ni site kudasai.**
'Shall I make it the afternoon?'   'Yes, please make it the afternoon to the extent possible.'

3. **usuku**; 4. **amaku**; 5. **ippai ni**; 6. **ôoki na osara ni**; 7. **yasasiku**; 8. **nâḡaku**; 9. **tumetaku**

K 1. **Kore wa, tyòtto amâi desu nêe.**   **Moó tyòtto kâraku simásyoò ka⤴**
'This is a bit bland, isn't it!'   'Shall I make it a little spicier?'

2. **Kore wa, tyòtto wakárinikùi desu nêe.**   **Moó tyòtto wakáriyàsùku simásyòo ka⤴**
'This is a bit hard to understand, isn't it!'   'Shall I make it a little easier to understand?'

3. **yowâi**; 4. **tumetai**; 5. **muzukasii**; 6. **hayâi**; 7. **usui**

L 1. **Konó zikañ de ìi desu ka⤴**   **Tyôtto . . Hoká no zikañ ni simaseñ ka⤴**
'Will this time (i.e., being this time) be all right?'   'I'm afraid it's a bit of a problem. Won't you make it a different time?'

2. **Konó misè de îi desu ka⤴**   **Tyôtto . . Hoká no misè ni simáseñ ka⤴**
'Will this shop be all right?'   'I'm afraid it's a bit of a problem. Won't you make it a different shop?'

3. **hanâ**; 4. **omiyaḡe**; 5. **susîya**; 6. **kaisya**; 7. **kyoositu**; 8. **teesyoku**

M 1. **Hoká no zassi mo kaù ñ desu ka⤴**   **Ie, konó zassi dakè desu kedo, koré o moo is-satù kaítài ñ desu.**
'(Is it that) you're going to buy other magazines, too?'   'No, just this magazine, but I'd like to buy one more of these.'

2. **Hoká no osara mo kaù ñ desu ka⤴**   **Ie, konó osara dakè desu kedo, koré o moo itì-mai kaítài ñ desu.**
'(Is it that) you're going to buy other plates, too?'   'No, just these plates, but I'd like to buy one more of these.'

3. **hanâ**; 4. **wâiñ**; 5. **peñ**; 6. **huutoo**

N 1. **Zassi no hoka ni, nâni o katta ñ desu ka**⤴   **Zaśsi dakè desu. Hoká nì wa naní mo kaimasèñ desita.**
'What is it you bought besides magazines?'   '(It's) just magazines. I didn't buy anything else.'

2. **Itóo-señsèe no hoka ni, dâre ni âtta ñ desu ka**⤴   **Itóo-señsèe dakê desu. Hoká nì wa daré ni mo aimasèñ desita.**
'Who is it you saw other than Dr. Ito?'   '(It's) just Dr. Ito. I didn't see anyone else.'

3. **Yoòròppa/dôko e itta**; 4. **koñpyùutaa/nâni o tyuumoñ-sita**; 5. **akâi no/nâni o tanôñda**; 6. **gakusee/dâre o syookai-sita**; 7. **obasañ/dâre no sewâ ni nâtta**; 8. **butyoo/dônata ḡa irâsita**

O 1. **Osakana mo onîku mo 'osuki desyoo?**   **Sôo desu nêe. Osakana wa ne! Kirái zya nài kedo, nikû hodo tabétài to wa omóimasèñ ne!**
'You like both fish and meat, don't you?'   'Hmm. About fish, you know? I don't dislike it, but I don't believe I like to eat it as much as meat.'

2. **Bîiru mo wâiñ mo 'osuki desyoo?**   **Sôo desu nêe. Bîiru wa ne! Kirái zya nài kedo, wâiñ hodo nomítài to wa omóimasèñ ne!**
'You like both beer and wine, don't you?'   'Hmm. About beer, you know? I don't dislike it, but I don't believe I like to drink it as much as wine.'

3. **sukiyaki/teñpura**; 4. **Huráñsu-ryòori/tyuúka-ryòori**; 5. **pâñ/gôhañ**; 6. **koóhìi/kootya**; 7. **karâi monô/amái monò**; 8. **gaíkoku no bìiru/Nihóñ no bìiru**

Application Exercises

A1. Using the outlines provided in A1 and 2 of the Application Exercises of Section A of this lesson, expand the practice by comparing sets of three or more items. Cover not only the question of what is *most* endowed with a particular quality, but include also internal comparison within a set: 'A is more —— than B, but not as much as C'; 'A is more —— than B, but C is the most ——.'

2. Practice making restaurant small talk:
   (a) Play the role of a host, encouraging your guests to eat and drink more.
   (b) Play the role of a guest, being polite about not eating or drinking too much, offering compliments about the food and drink, etc.
   (c) Discuss your favorite foods and drinks.
   (d) Discuss the eating and drinking habits of Japanese and Americans—what kinds of things they eat for each meal, what time they eat, where they eat, etc. (Restrict yourself to familiar vocabulary: your aim should be to internalize what has already been introduced to the point where you can use it fluently.)

3. At a restaurant:

(a) Ask the waiter to bring the A meal as quickly as possible.
(b) Ask the waiter if he can make the coffee a little weaker.
(c) Check on which meat is most tender—that of the A, the B, or the C meal.
(d) Check on which of three items on the menu is the spiciest.
(e) Check on which of two menu items is blander.
(f) Ask for the check—as quickly as possible.

B. Core Conversations: Substitution

Practice the Core Conversations with appropriate substitutions. Put extra effort into your intonation and gestures, making certain that your own delivery is appropriate to the subject matter. Note the facial expressions of the CC participants in the accompanying video, and use these as models.

SECTION C

Eavesdropping

(Answer the following questions on the basis of the accompanying tape. For each conversation, A = the first speaker and B = the second speaker.)

1a. Which speaker is the guest?
 b. What is the guest urged to do?
2a. What does A offer B?
 b. Why does B refuse?
 c. What is A's concern?
 d. What is B's response?
3a. In what connection does B mention **Kyuusyuu**?
 b. How does the climate there compare with here?
 c. How does this match with A's assumption?
4a. Where does this conversation probably take place?
 b. What is A apparently looking at?
 c. What is A inquiring about?
 d. How does the item on the right compare with the one(s) on this side?
 e. What is A's decision?
5a. What is A trying to decide?
 b. What does B suggest? Why?
 c. What is A's decision?
6a. Where does this conversation probably take place?
 b. What does A request?
 c. Who is B?
 d. What amount of money does B mention, and what does it represent?
 e. Why does B apologize?
7a. Who is A looking for?
 b. Where is that person?
 c. What does B offer to do?
 d. Comment on the relationship between A and B as indicated by the politeness level used.
8a. What is A perplexed about?
 b. What does A learn from B?
 c. Why is A unacquainted with the item under discussion?
 d. What does B invite A to do?

e. Why does A refuse?
9a. What does this shop sell?
 b. How does this shop compare with the shop over there? Give two points of comparison.
10a. What choice is B offered?
 b. What possible reason for the choice does A check on?
 c. What is the actual reason for the choice?
11a. Where does this conversation take place?
 b. How many people are in B's group?
 c. Who is A?
 d. Why does A apologize?
12a. Where did A go yesterday?
 b. What was A's reaction? Give details.
 c. What does B wonder?
13a. What are A and B eating?
 b. How is it?
 c. What explanation does B offer?
 d. What is A's reaction?
14a. What does B accept from A?
 b. How is it?
 c. What is B's reaction?
15a. What have A and B been doing?
 b. What is A's assessment of the situation?
 c. What does B want to do?
 d. What excuse does A offer for not agreeing?
 e. How does B react?
16a. Where does this conversation take place?
 b. What is A looking at?
 c. Why is this week a good time for such activity?
 d. What request made by A cannot be satisfied?
 e. What was A's mistaken assumption?
17a. What invitation does A extend to B?
 b. What comparison does A volunteer?
 c. What possible objection does B offer?
 d. What are A's two responses to this objection?
18a. What is B asked to compare?
 b. What is B's response?
 c. What is B's preference?
 d. What does B eat for lunch?
 e. What concern does A mention?
 f. Why is it not really a concern?
 g. How does B feel about living abroad?
19a. Where does this conversation occur?
 b. What is being discussed?
 c. How do the items differ?
 d. Which does B choose? What about A?
 e. What else is being ordered?
20a. Identify A and B and the location of the conversation.
 b. What is A looking at?
 c. In what connection are plates mentioned?
 d. Where do the items being dicussed come from?
 e. Which kind does A like best?

f. What is the only advantage of the green ones?
g. What is A's final decision?

Utilization

(As usual, provide a stimulus and/or a response for each item, developing natural conversational sequences.)

1. Ask a colleague which he likes better, Western-style food or Chinese cooking.
2. Ask a colleague which is oldest, Tokyo University, Keio, or Waseda.
3. Ask a friend which is more difficult to read, French or German.
4. Tell a colleague that you like tempura more than sukyaki, but your favorite is sashimi.
5. Tell a friend you think that for Western-style food, a knife and fork are easier to eat with, but for Japanese-style food, chopsticks are easier.
6. Tell a friend that there isn't any food you like more than ice cream.
7. Ask a friend if she thinks Russian is more difficult than German.
8. Tell a colleague that you think the sushi at this sushi restaurant is better than that at Matsuzushi, but not as good as at the new sushi restaurant in the basement.
9. Ask the clerk at the bookstore if they have any English–Japanese dictionaries newer than this one.
10. Tell a friend that the pie here is good, too, but you think the cake is *more* delicious.
11. Tell your colleague that since you have made the special effort of studying Japanese, you want to speak Japanese as much as possible.
12. Tell your colleague that since you have made the special effort of coming to Japan, you want to eat as much Japanese food as possible.
13. Find out if: this area / Matsuzushi / Umeten / Japan / this restaurant } has good { fish. / service. / tempura. / coffee. / meat.
14. You've been asked by a fellow train passenger if Toranomon is the next stop. Tell her that you've already passed it.
15. Tell a colleague that you wanted to buy a large Japanese–English dictionary, but they're too expensive, so you decided on a small one.
16. Tell a friend that you overate last night, and today you don't feel very well.
17. Tell a friend that you're going to Ginza department stores tomorrow and will buy things like bowls and plates as souvenirs.
18. As a host, apologize for the meal you are offering; urge the guests to eat/drink more; suggest another cup of coffee.
19. Ask the waiter which of these three fixed dinners takes the least time (i.e., can be made fastest).
20. Tell a friend that this dictionary is easy to use, but you think the others are rather difficult (to use).
21. Ask a friend who has just come to Japan what kinds of places he wants to see, besides the temples and shrines in Kyoto.
22. Ask the person you're talking with on the phone to talk as loud as possible, because you can't hear very well.
23. You are about to receive directions on how to get to a particular destination. Request politely that they be given (*lit.* said) as simply as possible, since you don't understand Japanese very well.
24. Tell a visitor (politely) that this (place) has been a **kissaten** since last year.
25. Tell your lunch partner that you don't dislike spicy things, but you prefer bland things.

26. Warn your friend that this

coffee		cold.
meat		tough.
tea	is	weak.
saké		strong.
sushi		awful tasting.

27. Remark on how pretty these plates (cups, glasses, rice bowls) are.
28. Ask the waiter for the check.
29. A visitor is coming to town. Ask a colleague where you should take him.
30. Ask the secretary to take this letter to the reception desk.

Check-up

1. Describe the function of the pattern /**A to B to, dôtira (no hôo)**———/. (A-SP1)
2. When A is more endowed with a particular quality than B, what particle follows B? (A-SP1)
3. When A is not as endowed with a particular quality as B, what extent word follows B? (A-SP1)
4. Predicates like **tabéyasùi, sukî da,** and **kakâru** are described as double-**ḡa**, affective predicates. Explain. (A-SP2)
5. What is the meaning of compounds ending in **-suḡìru**? Describe the types of elements with which **-suḡìru** forms compounds. (A-SP3)
6. In the combinations **omiyaḡe ni kau, seǹsèe ni nâru,** and **sasímì ni suru,** in what way is the relationship between the nominal and the verbal similar? (A-SP4)
7. Contrast the meaning of **yasai to kudâmono** and **yasai ya kudâmono.** (A-SP5)
8. What is the humble-polite ↓ equivalent of **tabêru**? Of **nômu**? (B-SP1)
9. Give two honorific-polite ↑ equivalents of **tabêru**; of **nômu**. How do they differ? (B-SP1)
10. What word is indispensable in the comparison of three or more items? In such comparisons, which question word(s) may occur? (B-SP2)
11. When comparing three items, A, B, and C, what patterns are used to designate the items? (B-SP2)
12. Compare the use of **orímàsu** in the sequences (1) **kotíra ni orimàsu**; (2) **keḱkoǹ-sit(e) orimàsu**; (3) **tokêe ḡa okuret(e) orimàsu**. (B-SP3)
13. What is the meaning of **narubeku**? How is it used? Give two examples. (B-SP4)

Lesson 16

SECTION A

Core Conversations

1(J)a. **Tyôtto sâmûku nâi desu ka**⸺ **koko.**

(N)a. **Sôo desu ka⸺ Mâdo wa zêñbu simâtte (i)masu kedo neʕ . . . A, anó dòa ga aíte (i)rù ñ da. Simémasyòo ka.**

 b. **Kamáimasèñ ka.**

 b. **Êe, betu ni. Sâkki Tanáka-sañ ga aketà ñ da kedo, Tanaka-sañ môo inâi kara . .**

2(N)a. **Kagî kakémasyòo ka.**

(J)a. **Iya, îi desu yo⸺ Sonó dòa wa kagî kakárànai ñ desu.**

 b. **Daízyòobu desu ka**⸺

 b. **Mâa, daízi na monò wa naní mo hàitte (i)nâi kara . .**

 c. **Konó kàmera wa?**

 c. **A, sôo sôo. Sore wa torâñku ni irét(e) okimasyòo.**

 d. **Îma irímasèñ neʕ**

 d. **Êe. Kokó dè wa ʼsyasiñ torânai kara . .**

3(N)a. **Kêe-tyañ. Têrebi tukêt(e) oite— nyûusu mitâi kara.**

(J)a. **Têrebi? Tûite (i)ru ñ zya nai? Watasi, kesíte (i)nài wa yo**⸺

 b. **Sôo? Naní mo kikoenài kara, kesíte àru to omôtta.**

 b. **Tyôtto mâtte. . . . A, kiétè (i)ta. Tukêt(e) oku wa neʕ**

 c. **Arîgatoo.**

4(N) **Butyoo. Amérika-giñkoo no Howâito-sañ ga ʼkore o oíte (i)rassyaimàsita ga . .**

(J) **Âa, sore neʕ Hôñdana ni simâtt(e) òite.**

84 • Lesson 16

English Equivalents

1(J)a. Isn't it a little cold—here?

   b. You don't mind?

2(N)a. Shall I lock [this]?

   b. Is it safe?

   c. What about this camera?

   d. You don't need it now—right?

3(N)a. Kei! Turn the television on now—because I want to watch the news.

   b. Oh? I can't hear anything, so I thought that it was turned off.

   c. Thanks.

4(N) Division Chief! Mr/s. White, from the Bank of America, left this, but . . . (what should I do with it?)

(N)a. Oh? The windows (at least) are all closed, but (maybe something else is open) . . . Oh, (it's that) that door is open. Shall I close it?

   b. Not particularly. (It's that) Mr/s. Tanaka opened it a little while ago, but s/he's not here anymore so . . . (we can close it).

(J)a. No, that's all right. (It's that) that door doesn't lock.

   b. Well, nothing valuable is inside, so . . . (there's no need to worry).

   c. Oh, that's right. That—let's put in the trunk for the time being.

   d. That's right. I won't be taking pictures here (at least), so . . . (I don't need it).

(J)a. The television? Isn't it (the case that it's) on? I haven't turned it off.

   b. Wait a minute. . . . Oh, it was off. I'll turn it on now—O.K.?

(J) Oh, that. Put it on the bookshelf for the time being.

Breakdowns
(and Supplementary Vocabulary)

1. **mâdo**   window
   simâru /-u; simâtta/ (SP1)   become closed
   dôa *or*
  +**to**   door
  +**amîdo**   screen door
  +**amâdo**   storm door
  +**husuma**   sliding door (opaque)
  +**syoozi**   sliding door (translucent)
   aku /-u; aita/   become open
   simêru /-ru; sîmeta/   close [something]
   sâkki   a while ago
   akeru /-ru; aketa/   open [something]

2. kaḡî | key
kaḡî (o) kakêru /-ru; kâketa/ | lock [something]
kaḡî (ḡa) kakâru /-u; kakâtta/ | become locked
daízì /na/ | valuable, important
hâiru /-u; hâitta/ | go in, enter
kâmera | camera
torâñku | trunk
ireru /-ru; ireta/ | put into, insert
oku /-u; oita/ | put, place
iret(e) oku (SP3) | put in for future use, put in and leave [it]
syasiñ | photograph
tôru /-u; tôtta/ | take up, take away
syasíñ o tòru | take a picture

3. Kêe | Kei (girl's nickname)
têrebi | television
+râzio | radio
+dêñki | electricity; electric lights
tukêru /-ru; tukêta/ | attach [something]; turn on
tukêt(e) oku | turn on for future use, turn on and leave [it]

nyûusu | news
tûku /-u; tûita/ | become attached; become turned on
kesu /-u; kesita/ | turn off; extinguish, erase
kesíte àru (SP2) | has been turned off
kieru /-ru; kieta/ | go out; become turned off; become extinguished

4. Amérika-gìñkoo | Bank of America
Howâito | White (name)
oite (i)ku | leave behind (*lit.* go having put down)
+tana | shelf
hôñdana | bookshelf
simau /-u; simatta/ | put away, store
simatt(e) oku | put away for future use, put away and leave [it]

MISCELLANEOUS NOTES

1. CC1 is an essentially careful-style conversation, with a number of casual-style features. Along with a preponderance of distal-style predicates are occurrences of direct-style predicates, fragments, and an inverted sentence. On the accompanying video, Deborah Miller and her colleague, Mr. Yamada, cope with a draft in the office.

(N)a. **Mâdo wa** implies that as (N) thinks about the various items that might be involved, the windows, at least, are closed. However, the blame is then put on the **dôa**: 'it's *the door* that is open.' This latter utterance, a major sentence with a direct-style final predicate, is uttered in this context by (N) with exclamatory force; she is talking more casually for the moment as she makes the significant discovery. Note the repetition of Tanaka's name.
Amîdo is a compound of /**amî** 'net' + **to** 'door'/ with voicing of the initial consonant of the second member. **Amâdo** is a compound of /**âme** 'rain' + **to**/, which includes in addition an /e > a/ final vowel change of the first member of the compound. **Amâdo** are solid panels, traditionally of wood but recently often of aluminum, which slide out on a track from a container attached to the outside wall of a Japanese-style house.

2. CC2 is a basically careful-style conversation: the final predicates of major sentences are distal-style, but those of minor sentences are direct-style. There are also examples of fragments. On the video, Smith and Suzuki discuss the need to lock Mr. Suzuki's car.

(N)a, (J)a. The operational verbal **kakêru** 'hang [something],' 'suspend [something],' when used in combination with **kaḡî** 'key,' refers to the act of locking. Note: **X no kaḡî (o) kakêru** 'lock X.' **Kakâru** 'become suspended,' however, is a double -**ḡa,** affective verbal: **konó dòa ḡa kaḡî ḡa kakáránai kara** 'since *this door* doesn't lock.' The opposite of **kaḡî (o) kakêru** is **kaḡî (o) ʹakeru** (or ʹ**hazusu**) 'unlock.'

(J)b. **Daízi** is a **na**-nominal: **daízi na X** 'an important or valuable X,' 'X that is precious (to someone).' Note also **X o daízi ni suru** 'treat X as important.' The fragment **Odaizi ni** is a common ritual expression ('take care of yourself') used as a farewell in addressing someone about to be involved in some kind of risk.

(J)d. **Tôru** is an operational verbal that refers basically to taking up, picking up, taking hold of, or taking away. It occurs with many more specialized meanings, depending on its context. Note, for example, **Kâsa (o) tôtte kite kudasai.** 'Please go and get (come having picked up) my umbrella'; **Satôo (o) tôtte kudasai.** 'Please pass me the sugar'; **Huráñsugo (o) tòtte (i)masu.** 'I'm taking French'; **Kono syasiñ (o) torímasyòo.** 'Let's take out (i.e., remove) this picture'; **Syasíñ (o) torimasyòo.** 'Let's take some pictures' (*or* 'Let's remove the photographs'). The Japanese are the world's greatest camera enthusiasts, particularly fond of taking group pictures that commemorate social gatherings, meetings, excursions, etc.

3. CC3 is a casual-style conversation, with all predicates in the direct-style. Its minor sentences include informal requests in the gerund form. (J) is clearly female, as indicated by the utterances that end in /predicate + **wa yo**/ and /predicate + **wa ne**/. On the accompanying video, actually both participants are female: Sue Brown and her roommate, Kei, are discussing their television set.

(N)a. **Kêe** is a shortening of a given name (probably **Kêeko** 'Keiko'), used as a nickname by a close friend.

(J)b. **Kiétè (i)ta** 'it was off,' i.e., at the time when the speaker thought it was on.

4. CC4 is an exchange between a division chief (J) and his subordinate (N) regarding something a visitor left behind. On the accompanying video, Mr. Carter (N) speaks with the division chief, his superior, using distal-style, and refers to the visitor with polite-style (↑). The division chief's reply is an informal request ending with a gerund.

(J)a. **Simau** is a **w**-consonant, operational verbal: **X o Y ni simau** 'put X away into/onto Y.' Note that the direct-style perfective forms and gerunds of **simau** and **simâru** 'become closed' are identical except for accent: **simatta/simatte** from **simau**, but **simâtta/simâtte** from **simâru**.

Structural Patterns

1. VERBAL PAIRS: TRANSITIVE / INTRANSITIVE

Japanese includes a number of verbal pairs with similar roots, all of which reflect a similar meaning relationship: in each case, one partner of the pair implies an activity that operates on—and changes the state of—a person or thing *different from* the operator performing the activity; the other partner describes an activity that involves the operator only. We will call the first type 'transitive,' and the second 'intransitive.'[1] Compare

Tometa. 'I stopped [something].' I performed the act of stopping, as a result of which *something else* stopped, a transitive verbal, with

Tomatta. 'I stopped, i.e., brought myself to a halt, stopped over.' I performed the act of stopping, which affected only me—I stopped myself, an intransitive verbal.

The transitive partner of such pairs is always an operational verbal which may occur with an operand followed by particle **o**. The intransitive partner may or may not be operational, and its occurrences with /nominal + **o**/ phrases are limited to certain verbals only and certain relationships only (cf. **kono miti o iku** 'go along this street'). Consider now these verbal pairs, introduced in this lesson:

Transitive	*Intransitive*
simêru 'close [it]'	**simâru** '[it] closes'
Dôa (o) simémàsita.	**Dôa (ḡa) simárimàsita.**
'I closed the door.'	'The door closed.'
akeru 'open [it]'	**aku** '[it] opens'
Mâdo (o) akémàsita.	**Mâdo (ḡa) akímàsita.**
'I opened the window.'	'The window opened.'
kaḡî (o) kakêru 'lock [it]'	**kaḡî (ḡa) kakâru** '[it] locks'
Kurúma no kaḡî o kakémàsita.	**Kurúma no kaḡî (ḡa) kakárimàsita.**
'I locked the car.'	'The car locked.'
ireru 'put [it] in'	**hâiru**[2] '[it] enters'
Kodómo (o) iremàsita.	**Kodómo (ḡa) hairimàsita.**
'I put the child in.'	'A child came/went in.'
tukêru 'attach [it]'	**tûku** '[it] attaches'
Têrebi (o) tukémàsita.	**Têrebi (ḡa) tukímàsita.**
'I turned on the television.'	'The television went on.'
kesu 'extinguish [it]'	**kieru** '[it] goes out/off'
Râzio (o) kesímàsita.	**Râzio (ḡa) kiémàsita.**
'I turned off the radio.'	'The radio went off.'

If the operand of the transitive verbal is not expressed, it must be known from the context.

1. These terms are also applied to verbals which do not occur as partners in such pairs.
2. There is an alternate intransitive verbal **iru** (the stem of which occurs in the compound **iriḡuti** 'entrance') which matches the transitive partner according to a regular pattern. Its occurrences are limited.

Otherwise, the statement **Kesímàsita.** will invariably lead to the response, **Nâni o?** Compare: **Kiémàsita. . . . Nâni ḡa?**

An intransitive-partner /gerund + **(i)ru**/ regularly refers to a continuing state that *results from* the occurrence of the activity:

    simâtte (i)masu 'it's closed'

    tûite (i)masu 'it's attached, turned on'

    hâitte (i)masu '[person or thing] is in'

Note that **(i)ru** (or a polite equivalent) occurs whether the referent is animate or inanimate; the reference is to a previous animated activity.

Compare now the intransitive verbal occurring alone, with the corresponding /gerund + **(i)ru**/ pattern:

    Anó màdo akímàsu ka 'Does that window open?'

    Anó màdo aíte (i)màsu ka 'Is that window open?'

    Zîsyo mo haírimàsu ka 'Will the dictionaries go in, too?'

    Zîsyo mo hâitte (i)masu ka 'Are the dictionaries in, too?'

The transitive partners occur in the /gerund + **(i)ru**/ pattern much more commonly in the negative:

    Anó torañku wa mâda akéte (i)masèñ. 'I haven't opened that trunk yet.'

    Mîruku wa iréte (i)masèñ. 'I haven't put in any milk.'

Insofar as they occur in the affirmative, they usually refer to repeated occurrences:

    Ik̀-kai no màdo o zêñbu akéte (i)màsu. 'S/he is opening all the windows on the first floor.'

    Têepu o takúsañ irete (i)màsu. 'S/he is putting in lots of tapes.'

A single occurrence is usually viewed in Japanese as about to occur (imperfective) or accomplished (perfective). Thus, while 'he's opening the door,' referring to an entire activity or process, is common in English, the Japanese usually view the same single occurrence as not yet begun or finished. Only when a single opening involves a long-drawn-out process (as in the case of opening a well-wrapped package, for example) would **akete (i)ru** be used.[3]

2. /TRANSITIVE VERBAL GERUND + **âru**/

We are already familiar with the pattern /verbal gerund + **(i)ru**/, indicating a continuing activity or a continuing state resulting from a previous activity (example: **tâbete (i)ru** '[I] am eating' or '[I] have eaten (and continue to be affected by the previous activity' (cf. 9B-SP3).

The gerund of a transitive verbal may also be immediately followed by **âru**, as an indication of a non-animate state that results from the occurrence of the action of the verbal:

    akéte àru '[it] has been opened'

    sîmete âru '[it] has been closed'

    tukête âru '[it] has been attached'

    tâbete âru '[it] has been eaten'

3. A very specialized use of this pattern covers situations in which a person continues to be affected by a previous action involving something closely connected with him/herself. For example, speaking of my hands: **Pokêtto ni iréte (i)màsu.** 'I have them in my pockets.'

tukûtte âru   '[it] has been made'

In other words, the transitive activity occurred (the gerund), and the resulting state continues (**âru**). When **âru** occurs in the perfective, the reference is to a previous, already completed state (**âtta**) resulting from a still earlier activity (the gerund):

sîmete âtta   '[it] had been closed,' '[it] was closed (at some point in the past)'

In neutral-polite equivalents, forms of **âru** are replaced by corresponding forms of **gozáimàsu**.

In most occurrences, the /nominal + **o**/ linked to the /-**te (i)ru**/ pattern becomes /nominal + **g̃a**/ in construction with the corresponding /-**te âru**/:

kono sig̃oto (o) site (i)ru   '[I]'m doing this work'

konó sig̃oto (g̃a) site àru   'this work has been done'

But also possible is:

konó sig̃oto (o) site àru   'the present situation (**âru**) results from the previous doing of this work (**sig̃oto [o] site**)'

Note that while both

(1) **mâdo (g̃a) aite (i)ru**   'a window is open' *and*

(2) **mâdo (g̃a) akéte àru**   'a window has been opened'

refer to a window now open, (1) describes a window now in a state of having become open, while (2) implies that the present state results from someone's having opened the window.

The sequence **tâbete nâi kara** may be the negative of **tâbete âru kara** 'because it hasn't been eaten,' or of **tâbete (i)ru kara** with the **i** deleted: 'because I haven't eaten [it].' Only context distinguishes the two.

3. /OPERATIONAL VERBAL GERUND + **oku**/

The basic meaning of the verbal **oku** is 'put,' 'place.' It is a transitive, operational verbal:

Asoko ni konó hòñ (o) oíte kudasài.   'Put these books over there.'

Sore wa dâre g̃a kokó ni oità ñ desu ka   'Who (is it who) put that here?'

In combination with an immediately preceding transitive verbal gerund, **oku** indicates that the action of the verbal gerund is performed in advance, for future use or benefit. In such combinations, the final **e** of the gerund is often dropped, and the form of **oku** has nonfocused accent (i.e., it is either unaccented, or has accent on a lower pitch level than a preceding accent, or enters into the same accent phrase as the preceding gerund). But following an unaccented gerund, the gerund **oite** acquires a first-mora accent. Thus:

kaít(e) okimàsita   'bought in advance' (distal-style)

tukûtt(e) okimasyoo   'let's make [it] for future use' (distal-style)

aket(e) oku   'open in advance of actual need,' 'open and leave open until needed,' (direct-style)

oít(e) òite kudasai   'put [it here] for the time being'

This /gerund + **oku**/ pattern requires that there be no intervening interruption. Compare:

Atárasìi kyoókàsyo kaíte okimàsita.   'I bought the new textbook in advance.'

Atárasìi kyoókàsyo (o) katte, asóko ni okimàsita.   'I bought the new textbook and put it over there.'

Drills

A 1. **Dôa, aíte (i)màsu ka**⤴   Iie. Akémasyòo ka⤴
   'Is the door open?'   'No. Shall I open it?'
 2. **Mâdo, simâtte (i)masu ka**⤴   Iie. Simémasyòo ka⤴
   'Is the window closed?'   'No. Shall I close it?'
 3. kaĝî/kakâtte; 4. osatoo/hâitte; 5. têrebi/tûite

B 1. **Dôa o akémasyòo ka.**   Môo aíte (i)rù ñ zya nâi desu ka.
   'Shall I open the door?'   'Isn't it (the case that it's) open already?'
 2. **Siô o irémasyòo ka.**   Môo hâitte (i)ru ñ zya nâi desu ka.
   'Shall I put in some salt?'   'Isn't it (the case that it's) in already?'
 3. têrebi/kesímasyòo; 4. kaĝî/kakémasyòo; 5. kyoositu/simémasyòo

C 1. **Mâdo, môo akémàsita ka**⤴   Mâda akéte (i)maseñ kedo ..
   'Did you open the windows already?' 'I haven't opened them yet, but ... (shall I do it?)
 2. **Osara, môo simáimàsita ka**⤴   Mâda simátte (i)maseñ kedo ..
   'Did you put the dishes away already?' 'I haven't put them away yet, but ... (shall I do it?)
 3. dêñki/kesímàsita; 4. amâdo/simémàsita; 5. kaĝî/kakémàsita

D 1. **Konó heñ no depàato, môo aíte (i)màsu ka**⤴   Mâda aíte (i)maseñ yo⤴
   'Are the department stores around here open yet?' 'They're not open yet.'
 2. **Ni-kái no dèñki, môo tûite (i)masu ka**⤴   Mâda tûite (i)máseñ yo⤴
   'Are the lights on the second floor turned on yet?' 'They're not on yet.'
 3. toráñku no kaĝî/kakâtte; 4. atárasìi kyoókàsyo/dête; 5. Morímoto-sañ no ozyòosañ/kekkoñ-site; 6. kuruma/modôtte; 7. syasiñ/dêkite

E 1. **Tyôtto, toráñku akéte kudasài.**   Sumímaseñ kedo, akánai ñ desu.
   'Would you just open the trunk.'   'I'm sorry, but (the fact is) it won't open.'
 2. **Tyôtto, kaĝí kàkete kudasai.**   Sumímaseñ kedo, kakáranai ñ desu.
   'Would you just lock [it].'   'I'm sorry, but (the fact is) it won't lock.'
 3. mizu 'tomete; 4. râzio tukête; 5. syoozi sîmete; 6. dêñki 'kesite; 7. kâmera 'irete

F 1. **Sonó dòa akánai ñ desu ka**⤴   Iya, akímàsu yo⤴ Îma wa aíte (i)nài kedo ..
   '(Is it that) that door doesn't open?' 'No. It opens. It isn't open now, but ...' (it does open).
 2. **Koñpyùutaa ni haíranai ñ desu ka**⤴ Iya, haírimàsu yo⤴ Îma wa hâitte (i)nâi kedo ..
   '(Is it that) it won't go into the

computer?' 'No, it will go in. It's not in now, but . . .' (it will go in).

3. torâñku simárànai; 4. kokó no kaǧì kakárànai; 5. anó bìru no dêñki 'kienai; 6. konó tèepu 'tomaranai; 7. hurûi hoo no têrebi tukânai

G 1. Îma torâñku akémasyòo ka. Âa, akét(e) òite neˤ
'Shall I open the trunk now?' 'Oh, open it (for future purposes), would you?'

2. Îma râzio kesímasyòo ka. Âa, kesít(e) òite neˤ
'Shall I turn off the radio now?' 'Oh, turn it off (for the time being), would you?'

3. zassi simáimasyòo; 4. demae tanómimasyòo; 5. mâdo simémasyòo; 6. têrebi tukémasyòo

H 1. Osyooyu, môo irétà ñ desu ka↗ Hâi, irét(e) okimàsita kedo, îi desu ka↗
'(Is it the case that) you put some soy sauce in already?' 'Yes, I put some in (in advance). Is that all right?'

2. Kuruma, môo tométà ñ desu ka↗ Hâi, tomét(e) okimàsita kedo, îi desu ka↗
'(Is it the case that) you parked your car already?' 'Yes, I parked it (in advance). Is that all right?'

3. nâihu ya h(u)ôoku/simatta; 4. demae/tanônda; 5. hîsyo/syookai-sita; 6. dêñki/kesita; 7. osûsi/tukûtta; 8. tîzu/mîseta

I 1. Konó taipuràitaa, îma sûǧu otúkai ni nàru ñ desu ka. Ièie. Asítà made tukáwanài kara, simátt(e) okimasyòo.
'(Is it that) you're going to use this typewriter very soon now?' 'No, no, I'm not going to use it until tomorrow, so let's put it away for now.'

2. Konó kèeki, îma sûǧu mesíaǧarù ñ desu ka. Ièie. Asítà made tabênai kara, simátt(e) okimasyòo.
'(Is it that) you're going to eat this cake very soon now?' 'No, no. I'm not going to eat it until tomorrow, so let's put it away for now.'

3. konó hòñ/oyómi ni nàru; 4. konó tèepu/okíki ni nàru; 5. kono teǧami/omíse ni nàru; 6. konó suutukèesu/oáke ni nàru; 7. kono osake/mesiaǧaru

J 1. Dôa ǧa aíte (i)rù ñ desu nêe. A, sôo desu nêe. Akéte àru kedo, dâre ǧa akétà ñ desyoo nêe.
'The *door* is open, isn't it!' 'Oh, you're right! It's been opened, but I wonder who it is who opened it!'

2. Kyoósitu no kaǧì ǧa kakâtte (i)ru ñ desu nêe. A, sôo desu nêe. Kâkete âru kedo, dâre ǧa kâketa ñ desyoo nêe.
'The *classroom* is locked, isn't it!' 'Oh, you're right! It's been locked, but I wonder who it is who locked it!'

3. **koṅpyùutaa/tûite**; 4. **toraṅku/simâtte**; 5. **têrebi/kiete**; 6. **kuruma/tomatte**; 7. **satôo/hâitte**

K 1. **Dôa, akéte arimàsu ka⤴**
'Has the door been opened?'

Ie, mâda akéte nài desu nêe. Akémasyòo ka.
'No, it hasn't been opened yet, has it. Shall I open it?'

2. **Obeñtoo, tanôñde arímàsu ka⤴**
'Have the box lunches been ordered yet?'

Ie, mâda tanôñde nâi desu nêe. Tanómimasyòo ka.
'No, they haven't been ordered yet, have they. Shall I order them?'

3. **owañ/simatte**; 4. **râzio/tukête**; 5. **Teñhana/deñwa-site**; 6. **mizu/irete**; 7. **kaḡî/hazu-site**

L 1. **Kono waapuro, kesíte ìi?**
'Is it all right to turn off this word processor?'

Êe. Sâkki katyóo ḡa tukèta ñ da kedo, môo inâi kara . .
'Yes. (It's that) the section chief turned it on a while ago, but s/he's not here any more so . . .' (it's all right).

2. **Konó màdo, akéte ìi?**
'Is it all right to open this window?'

Êe. Sâkki katyóo ḡa sìmeta ñ da kedo, môo inâi kara . .
'Yes. (It's that) the section chief closed it a while ago, but s/he's not here any more so . . .' (it's all right).

3. **koṅpyùutaa/tukête**; 4. **dôa/sîmete**

M 1. **Teḡami wa, Kodáma-sañ ḡa oite ikimàsita ḡa; môo mimâsita ka⤴**
'The letter—Mr/s. Kodama put down before leaving (*lit*. put down and went), (but) did you see it (yet)?'

Kodama-sañ ḡa? Iie. Dôko ni oítà ñ desyoo.
'Mr/s. Kodama [did]? No. Where do you suppose it is s/he put it?'

2. **Huutoo wa, Itóo-sañ ḡa simatte ikimàsita ḡa; môo mimâsita ka⤴**
'The envelope—Mr/s. Ito put away before leaving (*lit*. put away and went), (but) did you see it (yet)?'

Itoo-sañ-ḡa? Iie. Dôko ni simáttà ñ desyoo.
'Mr/s. Ito [did]? No. Where do you suppose it is s/he put it away?'

3. **kuruma/Tanaka-sañ/tomete**; 4. **okâsi/hîsyo/irete**; 5. **demae/arúbàito no gakusee/tanôñde**; 6. **obeñtoo/ukétuke no hitò/tyuumoñ-site**

Application Exercises

A1. Take turns asking members of the group to open, close, lock, and unlock windows and doors, and turn lights on and off. Ask and answer questions relating to changing conditions, using information questions (who, what, and which) as well as yes-or-no questions. Be sure to distinguish between questions as to whether doors, windows, etc. *do* open or *are* open (or have been opened).

2. Using assorted pens, pencils, magazines, books, dictionaries, etc., and containers of various sizes, practice verbals **ireru, hâiru,** and **simau**: check on whether specific items will go into designated containers, what is already in, what has been put in, who put designated items where, and so forth. Utilize all the newly introduced patterns, and use this opportunity to review numbers. Example:

(a) **Eñpitu (o) yôñ-hoñ-hodo konó syoppiñġubàggu ni iréte kudasài.**

'Please put (about) four pencils into this shopping bag.'

(b) **Îma wa, koko ni 'eñpitu (ġa) yôñ-hoñ iréte arimàsu** (*or* **hâitte [i]masu**) **kedo; dâre ġa irétà ñ desu ka**⤴

'Four pencils have now been put in here (*or* are in here); who (is it) who put them in?'

3. Suggest some appropriate activity to be performed in advance, on the basis of a specific condition or need that has been described by another member of the group. Examples:

(a) **Tuġî no zyûġyoo, ni-zí-hàñ made desu nêe.**

'The next class ends at 2:30, doesn't it.'

Sôo desu nêe. Zyâa, obéñtoo o tàbete okímasyòo ka.

'That's right. Then shall we eat our lunch now?'

(b) **Sâñ-zi ni dêru to omóimàsu kedo..**

'I think I'll leave at 3:00, but...' (is that all right?)

Zyâa, îma suútukèesu o kurúma no toràñku ni irét(e) okimasyòo.

'Then why don't I put the suitcase into the trunk of the car now.'

B. Core Conversations: Substitution

Practice the Core Conversations with appropriate variations. Include changes in the participants that require stylistic adjustments, but always keep the conversation topic in mind in order to avoid creating unlikely situations.

Given your expanding repertoire of structural patterns and vocabulary, more and more substitutions are possible, but do not change the basic structure of the conversation. In particular, be sure to retain examples of new structural patterns.

SECTION B

Core Conversations

1(J)a. **Koñsyuu no doyòobi, ohíma dèsu ka**⤴

(N)a. **Hâi. Betu ni naní mo arimasèñ kedo..**

b. **Uti e syokúzi ni irassyaimaseñ ka**↗ **Amerika kara tomódati ḡa kùru ñ desu.**

c. **Sôo sôo. Burâuñ-sañ wa mâe ni mo 'iti-do irássyaimàsita ne!**

d. **Zyâa, Eéhukù-tyoo no êki ni tûite kara, odêñwa kudasai. Êki made omúkae ni ikimàsu kara..**

e. **Rokú-zi-ḡòro, ikâḡa desu ka**↗
f. **Hâi.**

g. **Soó site kudasài.**

h. **Kotíra kòso.**

2(J)a. **Burâuñ-sañ. Mâda kaérànai no?**

b. **Ñ. Îya, tyôtto 'kaze hiityatte ne! Isyá no tokorò ni yóttè kara kâeru ñ da kedo..**

c. **Dôo mo. Zya, osaki ni.**

b. **Sôo desu ka. Arîḡatoo gozaimasu. Yorókòñde ukáḡaimàsu. Otaku wa Eéhukù-tyoo desita ne**↗

c. **Êe. Dê mo, moósiwake nài ñ desu ḡa, mití o tyòtto wasúrete simattà no de..**

d. **Sumímasèñ. Nâñ-zi ni ukáḡaimasyòo ka.**

e. **Rokû-zi desu ne**↗

f. **Zyâa, sonó kòro êki kara odêñwa-simasu.**

g. **Wakárimàsita. Zyâa, tanósìmi ni sité orimàsu.**

h. **Arîḡatoo gozaimasu.**

(N)a. **Ñ, kore zêñbu yáttyattè kara.. Môo kâeru no?**

b. **Kaze? Odaizi ni.**

c. **Sayonara.**

ENGLISH EQUIVALENTS

1(J)a. Are you free this Saturday?

b. Won't you come to my home for dinner (*lit.* dining)? (It's that) a friend is coming from the States.

c. That's right. You came once before (too), didn't you, Mr/s. Brown.

d. In that case, after you arrive at the Eifuku-cho station, give me a call. (Because) I'll go to the station to meet you.

(N)a. Yes, I have nothing special, but... (why do you ask?)

b. Oh? Thank you. I'll be happy to come. Your home was in Eifuku-cho—right?

c. Yes. But—I'm very sorry but—I've completely forgotten how to get there, so ... (I need directions).

d. Thank you. What time shall I come?

e. How about around six o'clock?
f. Yes.

g. Please do.

h. *My* pleasure.

2(J)a. You're not going home yet, Sue?

b. Yeah. No, I ended up catching a bit of a cold, you know, and after I stop in at the doctor's I'll be going home, but . . . (I'm not going home immediately).
c. Thanks. Well then, (excuse me for leaving) ahead of you.

e. That's six—right?
f. Then I'll call from the station about then.
g. Fine. Well, I'm looking forward to it.
h. Thank you.

(N)a. Right. After I've finished doing all this . . . (I'll go home). You're going home already?

b. A cold? Take care.

c. Goodbye.

BREAKDOWNS
(AND SUPPLEMENTARY VOCABULARY)

1. **syokuzi** しょくじ — dining; meal
   yorókòbu /-u; yorókòñda/ よろこぶ — take pleasure in
   yorókòñde ukaḡau よろこんで うかがう — visit with pleasure
   Eéhukù-tyoo えいふくちょう — (section of Tokyo)
   wasurete simau (SP1) わすれてしまう — forget completely; end up forgetting
   tûku /-u; tûita/ つく — arrive
   tûite kara (SP2) ついてから — after having arrived
   mukaeru /-ru; mukaeta/ むかえる — meet; greet; welcome
   (o)mukae おむかえ — a meeting; a greeting; a welcoming
   (o)mukae ni iku (SP3) おむかえに行く — go to meet
   + **okuru /-u; okutta/** おくる — send; send off, see off
   sonó kòro そのころ — about that time
   tanósìmi ni suru たのしみにする — consider to be a pleasure

2. **yaru /-u; yatta/** やる — do
   yatte simau *or* やってしまう
   yattyau (SP1) やっちゃう — do completely; end up doing
   yattyattè kara やっちゃってから — after having finished doing
   kaze かぜ — a cold
   hiku /-u; hiita/ ひく — pull
   hiite simau *or* ひいてしまう
   hiityau ひいちゃう — pull completely; end up pulling
   kaze o hiku かぜをひく — catch cold
   (o)isya(-sañ) いしゃ — medical doctor
   isyá no tokorò いしゃのところ — the doctor's (place)

yoru /-u; yotta/ よる	stop in
yotté kara よってから	after having stopped in
odaizi ni おだいじに	[treat yourself] carefully

Professions

keñtikuka	architect
giñkòoiñ	banker
dâiku(-sañ)	carpenter
kaí syàiñ	company employee, company staff member
syâiñ	company employee (lower ranking)
koñsàrutañto	consultant
hâisya(-sañ)	dentist
gaíkòokañ	diplomat
uñtèñsyu(-sañ)	driver, chauffeur
gîsi	engineer
nôoka	farmer
boóekìsyoo	foreign trader, importer-exporter
ziyûuḡyoo	freelance worker
koómùiñ	government employee
roódòosya	laborer
siñbuñkìsya	journalist
beñgòsi(-sañ)	lawyer
señkyòosi	missionary
kañḡòhu(-sañ)	nurse
mêisya(-sañ)	eye doctor
seezika	politician
saráriimañ	salaried employee
teñiñ	sales clerk

MISCELLANEOUS NOTES

1. CC1 is a polite invitation to dinner. (J), after determining that his invitation is accepted, makes arrangements for (N) to reach his home: he will meet her at the station and escort her to the house. The style is careful, with most final predicates in distal-style. It is a rather polite conversation, which includes honorific-polite and humble-polite forms associated with the ritual of invitation (**irássyàru, ukaḡau,** etc.), but otherwise uses plain predicates.

(J)b. Note the negative—here an honorific-polite—used as an invitation. **Syokuzi** occurs frequently in the compound verbal **syokuzi-suru** 'dine,' 'have a meal.'

Compare: **Amerika kara tomódati ḡa kùru.** 'A friend is coming from America.' *and*
Amérika karà no tomódati ḡa kùru. 'A friend from America is coming.'

(N)b. **Yorókòbu,** as an independent verbal, occurs most commonly in reference to persons other than the speaker. However, when **yorókòñde** occurs as a gerund of manner accompanying another predicate (stated or implied), the person saying it is frequently the referent: **yorókòǹde suru** 'I'll be happy to do it,' **yorókòǹde iku** 'I'll be happy to go,' **Yorókòǹde.** 'Gladly.' (in response to requests and invitations), etc.

Note the perfective of recall: '[As I think about it, I recall that] your home was in Eifuku-cho, wasn't it?'

(J)d. Note: /place **ni** *or* (less commonly) **e** + **tûku**/ 'arrive at a place.'

(N)g. **Tanósìmi ni sité orimàsu,** a polite, ritualistic expression, implies that (N) is considering the upcoming dinner to be a pleasure: *lit.* 'I am making [it] into a pleasure.' Particle **ni** establishes **tanósìmi** as a goal. Compare: **miyaǵe ni kau** 'buy as (= to be) a souvenir.'

2. CC2 is a conversation between two graduate students who converse with each other in casual-style. Final predicates are direct-style, and there are several minor sentences, including ritual fragments. Note the extended predicates, linking the language with observation of the actual scene. For example: [Does your continuation of work indicate that] you're not going home yet?

(N)a. **Yaru** 'do' is a slightly more informal, casual equivalent of **suru** in its occurrences with that meaning. However, **yaru** does NOT replace **-suru** in /nominal + **-suru**/ compounds (**beñkyoo-suru, kekkoñ-suru,** etc.). Note **yarínaòsu** 'redo.'

(J)b. After saying yes (**ñ**), Kato qualifies his agreement with **îya**, indicating that he is now offering a negative note: he *will* return home, but only after he has seen the doctor. Note the break-up of what would be a single, long, complex utterance into two parts, with the first ending in **ne!**

Isyá no tokorò: compare English 'the doctor's.'

Note /place **ni** *or* **e** + **yoru**/ 'stop in at a place.' With verbals of motion, Japanese tend to move to places (including 'the place where someone or something is' [**isyá no tokorò, dôa no tokórò**]) rather than to people, but **isya ni yoru** is also possible in addition to the commonly occurring **isyá no tokorò ni yoru**.

Odaizi ni: See the Miscellaneous Notes in Section A of this lesson. This is a commonly used ritual expression.

Professions

The use of **suru** with terms for professions (cf. drills M and N, following) indicates the practicing of the profession.

Many of these terms are compounds, containing words that also occur independently. Some you will have recognized immediately.

The addition of **-sañ** indicates, as usual, politeness and deference. Note that it occurs with only some of the professional designations. Note also:

keñtiku	architecture
hâ	tooth
gaikoo	diplomacy
uñteñ-suru	drive a vehicle
ziyûu /na/	free, unrestricted
roodoo-suru	labor
kâñgo-suru	nurse, care for
mê	eye
seezi	politics

Structural Patterns

1. /VERBAL GERUND + simau/

In 16A-SP3, we learned the combination /verbal gerund + **oku**/, indicating the performance of an activity in advance, for future reference or benefit. We also learned a new verbal, **simau** 'put away,' 'store.'

We now find that **simau** may occur in combination with an immediately preceding operational verbal—transitive or intransitive—indicating finality: depending on context, the combination has one of three shades of meaning: (1) 'end up doing—often contrary to one's original plan'; or (2) 'finish doing,' 'do completely'; or (3) 'do without any follow-up activity or contact.' Thus:

(1) **Betu ni ikítaku nàkatta kedo, ítte simaimàsita.** 'I didn't especially want to go, but in the end I went.'

(2) **Kyôneñ señsèe no otaku e ití-do ikimàsita kedo; môo mití o wasurete simaimàsita.** 'I went to the teacher's home once last year, but I've already completely forgotten the way.'

(3) **Nakamura-kuñ kara naní mo kiite (i)nài? ... Ñ. Kâre wa neꜜ Kyôneñ Yoóròppa e 'ittyatte ..** 'You haven't heard anything from Nakamura?' ... 'That's right. He went off to Europe last year and ...' (no word since).

In the last example above, /**-te** + **simau**/ is contracted into /**-tyau**/, a common occurrence in the spoken language. The combination is then inflected as if it were a single verbal ending in **-tyau**. Thus:

    wasurete simau > wasuretyau

    komâtte simau > komâttyau

    tâbete simau > tâbetyau

When the gerund ends in **-de**, the combination with **simau** is contracted to **-zyau**:

    nôñde simau > nôñzyau

    yôñde simau > yôñzyau

Note that **oku** and **simau** have the specialized connotations described in this lesson only when they occur immediately following a verbal gerund, and have nonfocus accent—either no accent, or accent on a pitch-level significantly lower than that of the preceding gerund, or in the same accent phrase as the preceding gerund. Compare these examples:

simatte simau/simattyau	'finish putting away'
oit(e) oku	'place [here] for future use'
simatt(e) oku	'put away for future use'
oite simau/oityau	'finish putting [here]'
oite, (sore kara,) simau	'place [here] and (then) put away'
katte, (sore kara,) koko ni oku	'buy and (then) put here'

2. /VERBAL GERUND + kara/

The phrase-particle **kara** has occurred both following nominals and following predicates with the same underlying meaning: **X kara** 'from X,' 'stemming from X,' 'proceeding from

X.' Thus: **soko kara** 'from there'; **sore kara** 'from that point,' 'after that'; **sonó tokì kara** 'from that time'; **sonô hito kara** 'from that person.' Predicates before **kara** have occurred only in the perfective, imperfective, or tentative form (distal or direct) indicating origin in a causal sense:

   byoóki dà kara   'because [I] am sick,' i.e., 'stemming from being sick'
   wakárimasèñ desita kara   'because [I] didn't understand'
   kâraku nâi desyoo kara   'because it probably isn't spicy'

We now add a new combination, the gerund of a verbal **X** + **kara**, indicating origin in a temporal sense: 'after X has been realized,' 'after having X-ed,' 'after X-ing.' An unaccented gerund assumes a final-mora accent before **kara**. Thus:

   tûite kara   'after having arrived' (i.e., 'proceeding from having arrived, next——')
   yotteˋ kara   'after having stopped in'
   yattyatteˋ kara   'after having finished doing'

Examples:
   Mâdo (o) sîmete kara, koko wa attàkàku narimasita.
   'After [I] closed the window(s) (proceeding from the closing of the window[s]), this place warmed up.'
   Kore (o) zêñbu yôñzyatte kara, señsèe to soódān-simasyòo.
   'After (proceeding from) reading all of this, let's have a discussion with the teacher.'

Compare now these three types of utterances:
   (1) **Byoóki ni nàtte, sigoto (o) yamémàsita.**   'Having become ill, I quit work.' (I became ill and quit work.)
   (2) **Byoóki ni nàtte kara, sigoto (o) yamémàsita.**   'After I became ill, I quit work.'
   (3) **Byoóki ni nàtta kara, sigoto (o) yamémàsita.**   'Because I became ill, I quit work.'

In (1), we are told of work stoppage simply in terms of a particular condition's having been realized. In (2), a temporal connection between the two occurrences is emphasized: after I became ill, I quit. In (3), the /——/ **kara** sequence provides the reason for quitting. Note that the only difference between (2) and (3) is a single vowel sound, **nàtte** versus **nàtta**, reminding us again of the importance of accurate pronunciation. Also possible is **Byoóki ni nàtte, sore kara, sigoto (o) yamémàsita.** 'I became ill, and after that, I quit work,' which combines the meanings of (1) and (2).

3. EXPRESSING PURPOSE

The particle associated with goal or purpose is **ni**, the most basic particle of location—original, continuing, or final. Compare now

   (a) **Kyoositu ni itta.** 'I went to the classroom.' *and*
   (b) **Beñkyoo ni itta.** 'I went for study.'

In (a), **kyoositu** describes the location ultimately arrived at as a result of the action of going. In (b), **beñkyoo** describes the purpose of the action of going, with the person involved ultimately 'in study,' describing location in a figurative sense.

Nominals referring to activity—**soodañ, beñkyoo, kekkoñ, rikoñ, kaimono**, etc.—frequently occur followed by particle **ni** and linked to a verbal of motion (particularly **iku, kûru,** or **kâeru**), as expressions of purpose. Examples:

Asoko e soódañ ni ikimasyòo. 'Let's go to that place for consultation.'

Asita kaímono ni ikimaseñ ka⤴ 'Wouldn't you [like to] go (for) shopping tomorrow?'

The form of the verbal most closely associated with the nominal class is the stem. In fact, if a nominal is derived from a verbal, it is identical with the stem, except for a possible shift in accent. And as an honorific-polite equivalent of verbals, we learned a pattern that includes a polite nominal derivative of the verbal, i.e., /o + stem/:

kau > okái ni nàru ↑ ;

kâku > okáki ni nàru ↑ ; etc.

In this pattern /o + stem/ is identified as a polite nominal rather than a 'polite stem' because the prefix **o-** never attaches to verbal forms; it is a nominal and adjectival prefix. Accordingly, we describe **omukae ni iku** as a /nominal + **ni** + **iku**/ pattern, 'go for a welcoming' (**mukaeru**→stem **mukae**→nominal **mukae**→polite nominal **omukae**).

However, the stem of the verbal may also occur /+ **ni** + motion verbal/, expressing purpose but at the same time retaining its original verbal properties. This means that other nominal phrases may hook up with this stem—something that is normally impossible for a nominal in a /nominal + **ni** + motion verbal/ pattern. Examples:

kyoókàsyo o ˈkai ni iku 'go to buy a textbook'

tomódati ni ài ni kûru 'come to see a friend'

têrebi o mî ni kâeru 'return home to watch television'

Compare now:

beñkyoo ni kùru 'come for study' *but*

nihóñgo o beñkyoo-si ni kùru 'come to study Japanese'

Please note that a very limited number of polite /o- + stem/ nominals retain a verbal-like operational function, with operands politely referring to humans. In this category are **omukae** and **ookuri** (**señsèe o omúkae ni mairimàsita** 'I went to meet the teacher').

Other purpose constructions that are used in combination with verbals other than **iku**, **kûru**, etc., will be introduced in later lessons.

Drills

A 1. **Kore simâsita?**
'Did you do this?'

Êe, yappàri sité simaimàsita. Kore dakê wa sitáku nàkatta ñ desu kedo ne!
'Yes, I ended up doing it, after all. (The fact is) it was just this I didn't want to do, but—you know!'

2. **Hayasi-sañ ni tanómimàsita?**
'Did you ask Mr/s. Hayashi?'

Êe, yappàri tanôñde simaimasita. Hayasi-sañ ni dakê wa tanómitàku nâkatta ñ desu kedo ne!
'Yes, I ended up asking him/her, after all. (The fact is) it was just Mr/s. Hayashi I didn't want to ask, but—you know!'

3. kazé hikimàsita; 4. oyu tukáimàsita; 5. amái monò o tabésuğimàsita; 6. Yamamoto-sañ ni aímàsita

B 1. Îtu surû ñ desu ka⤴   Môo sité simaimàsita yo⤴
'When is it you're going to do it?'   'I already finished doing it.'

2. Îtu tôru ñ desu ka⤴   Môo tôtte simáimàsita yo⤴
'When is it you're going to remove it?'   'I already finished removing it.'

3. tyuumoñ-suru; 4. kîru; 5. kariru; 6. soodañ-suru; 7. naôsu

C 1. Kâre, Amérika e ittà ñ desu ka⤴   Êe, kyôneñ itte simatte ..
'(Is it the case that) he went to the States?'   'Yes. He went off last year, and ...' (nothing further to report).

2. Kâre, kekkon-sità ñ desu ka⤴   Êe, kyôneñ kekkoñ-site simatte ..
'(Is it the case that) he got married?'   'Yes. He got married last year and ...' (nothing further to report).

3. kuní e kàetta; 4. kaisya o yameta; 5. daíğaku ni hàitta; 6. Kyûusyuu ni modôtta

D 1. Kazé hiità no?[4]   Ñ. Kinôo kara 'kaze hiityatte ne!
'You caught cold?'   Komâtte (i)ru ñ da.
    'Yeah. I came down with a cold (from) yesterday—and, you know, it's a terrible nuisance.'

2. Deñwa ğa tuúzinaku nàtta no?   Ñ. Kinôo kara tuúzinaku nàttyatte ne!
'You can't get through on the phone?'   Komâtte (i)ru ñ da.
(lit. Has the phone become nonconnecting?)   'Yeah. It went down (from) yesterday—and, you know, it's a terrible nuisance.'

3. waapuro ğa kosyoo-sita; 4. meési o kiràsita; 5. hîsyo ğa yameta

E 1. Mâda 'sono siğoto sinâi no?[4]   A, môo 'sityatta yo—zuttó màe ni.
'You're not going to do that work yet?'   'Oh, I already finished doing it—a long while ago.'

2. Mâda 'siñbuñ ya zassi simáwanài no?   A, môo 'simattyatta yo—zuttó màe ni.
'You're not going to put the newspapers and magazines away yet?'   'Oh, I already finished putting them away—a long while ago.'

3. mâdo akenai; 4. demae tyuumoñ-sinai; 5. syasiñ torânai; 6. ohîru tabênai

F 1. Môo 'reñraku wa sité arimàsu ne⤴   Reñraku? Ñ, sityátte àru kedo ..
'Contact has been made already—right?'   'Contact? Yeah, it's been made (and finished), but ...' (is there a problem?)

2. Môo dôa wa akéte arimàsu ne⤴   Dôa? Ñ, akétyatte àru kedo ..
'The doors have been opened already—right?'   'The doors? Yeah, they've been opened up, but ...' (is there a problem?)

3. kağî/kâkete; 4. demae/tanôñde; 5. siğoto/yatte; 6. tosyôsitu/akete; 7. têrebi/kesite

4. The stimuli of this drill are gentle, and the responses blunt.

G 1. **Ôono-sañ, sêki hazúsite (i)màsu?**
'Is Mr/s. Ono away from his/her desk (*lit.* seat)?'
Êe, hazúsityatte (i)màsu nêe.
'Yes, s/he has slipped away somewhere, hasn't s/he!'

2. **Kuruma no kaḡi kâkete arimasu?**
'Has the car been locked?'
Êe, kâketyatte arimasu nêe.
'Yes, it has been locked up, hasn't it!'

3. **mâdo simâtte (i)masu**; 4. **zêñbu simátte arimàsu**; 5. **koṅpyùutaa kesíte arimàsu**; 6. **miñna kitê (i)masu**; 7. **kazé hiite (i)màsu**

H 1. **Osîgoto?**
'Are you going to work?' (*lit.* 'Work?')
Hâi, siḡóto ni mairimàsita.
'Yes, I came for work.'

2. **Omukae?**
'Are you meeting someone?' (*lit.* A welcoming?)
Hâi, mukáe ni mairimàsita.
'Yes, I came to meet [someone].'

3. **gosoodàñ**; 4. **zyûḡyoo**; 5. **goreñraku**; 6. **arúbàito**; 7. **kâiḡi**; 8. **zêmi**

I 1. **Saki ni syokúzi-simasyòo.**
'Let's eat first' (i.e., in advance of something else).
Syokúzi-sitè kara, dôo simasu?
'After eating, what will you do?'

2. **Saki ni syatyóo ni ome ni kakarimasyòo.**
'Let's meet the company president first.'
Syatyóo ni ome ni kakàtte kara, dôo simasu?
'After meeting the president, what will you do?'

3. **kono siḡoto yattyaimasyòo**; 4. **hôñ o zêñbu simáimasyòo**; 5. **mêisya ni yorímasyòo**; 6. **tikatetu no zikañ o sirábemasyòo**; 7. **koṅpyùutaa ni irémasyòo**; 8. **atárasìi waa-puro o mimásyòo**

J 1. **Mata koko e irássyàru desyoo?**
'You're coming back here, aren't you?'
Êe, dê mo, iti-do uti ni deṅwa-sitè kara kimâsu kara . .
'Yes, but I'm coming after I call home (once), so . . .' (not right away).

2. **Keṅkyuuzyo ni oyóri ni nàru desyoo?**
'You're stopping in at the institute, aren't you?'
Êe, dê mo, iti-do uti ni deṅwa-sitè kara yorímàsu kara . .
'Yes, but I'm stopping in after I call home (once), so . . .' (not right away).

3. **kissateñ ni irassyàru**; 4. **Yamâḡuti-sañ ni oái ni nàru**; 5. **ohîru o 'mesiaḡaru**; 6. **tâkusii o oyóbi ni nàru**; 7. **râzio okíki ni nàru**

K 1. **Katyóo ni soodañ-simàsu ka⌐**
'Are you going to discuss [things] with the section chief?'
Êe. Soódañ-sitè kara, kaérimàsu.
'Yes. After discussing, I'm going home.'

2. **Sonó kàmera naósimàsu ka⌐**
'Are you going to fix that camera?'
Êe. Naôsite kara, kaérimàsu.
'Yes. After fixing it, I'm going home.'

3. **sono siḡoto yarímàsu**; 4. **meesi tyuúmoñ-simàsu**; 5. **tosyôkañ ni yorímàsu**

L 1. **Maḡatte, tukíatari màde ikû ñ desu neʕ**
'(It's that) I turn and go to the end of the street—right?'

Iêie. Tukíatari màde ittê kara maḡátte kudasài.
'No, no. Please turn after you go to the end of the street.'

2. **Modôtte, deńwa o kakèru ñ desu neʕ**
'(It's that) I go back and telephone—right?'

Iêie, deńwa o kàkete kara modôtte kudasai.
'No, no. Please go back after you telephone.'

3. **tâbete/kusúri o nòmu**; 4. **kâite/seńsèe ni 'soodañ-suru**; 5. **têrebi tukête/dôa o simêru**; 6. **kaisya ni turete itte/tanômu**

M 1. **Uńtèñsyu-sañ desita neʕ**
'You were a driver—right?' (recalling)

Êe, kokó e kitè kara uńtèñsyu o site (i)masu.
'Yes, I've been a driver since coming here.'

2. **Oísya-sañ dèsita neʕ**
'You were a doctor—right?'

Êe, kokó e kitè kara isyá o site (i)màsu.
'Yes, I've been a doctor since coming here.'

3. **ziyûuḡyoo**; 4. **mêisya-sañ**; 5. **nôoka**; 6. **kyôosi**; 7. **sińbuñkìsya**; 8. **końsàrutañto**; 9. **boóekìsyoo**; 10. **beńgòsi-sañ**; 11. **hâisya-sañ**

N 1. **Nakámura-sañ no onìisañ, îtu koómùiñ ni nâtta ñ desu ka**
'When is it Mr/s. Nakamura's (older) brother became a government employee?'

Go-néñ-hodo màe kara koómùiñ no siḡoto o sité (i)rù ñ da to omóimàsu kedo . .
'He's been doing government work since about five years ago, I believe, but . . .' (I'm not sure).

2. **Nakámura-sañ no onìisañ, îtu gaíkòokañ ni nâtta ñ desu ka**
'When is it Mr/s. Nakamura's (older) brother became a diplomat?'

Go-néñ-hodo màe kara gaíkòokañ no siḡoto o sité (i)rù ñ da to omóimàsu kedo . .
'He's been doing diplomatic work since about five years ago, I believe, but . . .' (I'm not sure).

3. **dâiku**; 4. **seezika**; 5. **gîsi**; 6. **keńtikuka**; 7. **syâiñ**[5]; 8. **seńkyòosi**; 9. **gińkòoiñ**; 10. **sarárìimañ**

Application Exercises

A1. Practice extending and accepting/refusing invitations. Discuss the date, time, location, and how to get there (with the host[ess] offering to draw a map or to meet the guest at the station). Use all the appropriate ritual expressions that have been introduced.

---

5. As opposed to **arúbàito**, for example.

After completing the invitation and acceptance, ask and answer questions on the content of the invitation: who is going, where, when, and how.

2. Make up a schedule for Mr/s. Nakamura's whole day, covering activities you are able to express in Japanese. Ask and answer questions relating to what s/he does after doing specific activities on the schedule.

3. Describe five situations in which you ended up doing something contrary to your original wishes.

B. Core Conversations: Substitution

Practice the CCs with appropriate variations, being careful to retain the ritual expressions without change.

SECTION C

Eavesdropping

(Answer the following questions on the basis of the accompanying tape. For each conversation, A = the first speaker and B, the second.)
1a. What is A going to do?
  b. What does A check on first?
  c. What does A learn?
2a. How is the weather?
  b. What does A suggest doing?
  c. What is B apparently concerned about?
  d. What reassurance does A offer?
3a. What is A concerned about?
  b. What response of B's is further cause for concern?
  c. What reassurance does B offer?
4a. What is the setting?
  b. What does B suggest?
  c. Why does A refuse?
5a. What has happened to the door?
  b. What did B forget?
  c. Why does B ask A to wait?
6a. What is A leaving with B?
  b. What does A urge B to do?
  c. Where will A put the object in question?
7a. What is A inquiring about? Why?
  b. What does B inquire about?
  c. What is A's plan?
8a. Where does this conversation probably take place?
  b. Who is B?
  c. What does A suggest?
  d. What does B request? Why?
9a. What is A wondering about?
  b. What explanation does B offer? Give details.
10a. What comment does A make about B?
  b. What is B's explanation?
  c. Who is B?

d. What offer does A make?
   e. What is B's response? Why?
11a. What is A about to do?
   b. What is B's reaction? Why?
   c. What does B inquire about?
   d. What is their present condition?
12a. What is A inquiring about?
   b. Where does B think A will find the information?
   c. What is the problem?
   d. What does A request?
   e. What does B request? Why?
   f. Compare the styles used by A and B.
13a. What is A looking for?
   b. Where does B assume those things are? Why?
   c. Why is A having difficulty in locating them?
   d. What happens at the end of the conversation?
14a. Who has not arrived?
   b. What possible explanation does B offer?
   c. What does A offer to do?[6]
   d. What is B's reaction to the offer?
15a. What does A suggest doing?
   b. What is B's reaction?
   c. What does B ask about?
   d. Where is it?
   e. What causes the interruption in the conversation?
   f. What location does B suggest for the proposed activity?
16a. What is located in this building?
   b. How does B account for this?
   c. Why have A and B come to this building?
   d. Who is Morimoto and who is Hayashi?
   e. What does 403 refer to?
17a. Where did B arrive yesterday?
   b. Where else has B been?
   c. Which of these places did A already know about?
   d. How does B account for having been in so many places?
18a. Where does this conversation take place?
   b. Who is B?
   c. Where is A going?
   d. What does A want to know?
   e. What information does B provide?
   f. What is A's reaction?
19a. What kind of work is Ono doing? Since when?
   b. What kind of work did A think that Ono did?
   c. What kind of work did Ono do previously? For how long? Starting when?
20a. What does A suggest? Give details.
   b. What is B's reaction?
   c. What does A discover?
   d. What evidence proves A is correct?

6. **Sokó màde** frequently occurs as a vague indication of destination, 'for a distance.'

        e. What explanation does B offer?
        f. What alternate solution does A offer?
 21a. Who is expected? At what time?
        b. What is A's mistaken assumption?
        c. What correction does B provide?
        d. Why is B not concerned?
 22a. What linguistic clues indicate that B is Watanabe?
        b. How long has B been back from France?
        c. Whose French was better than B's?
        d. Why does B want to study French?
        e. Why isn't B studying French?
 23a. Who is B?
        b. What kind of invitation is A extending to B? Give details: what, where, what day, what time.
        c. Who else has been invited?
        d. How does B respond to the invitation?

Utilization

(Follow the usual procedures, developing each item into a conversation which includes at least a stimulus and/or response.)

1. Ask a friend to: (a) open the window; (b) shut the door; (c) turn on the light; (d) turn off all the lights and lock the door.
2. Address the requests of the preceding to a colleague, politely.
3. You have just arrived at the office. Comment that the windows are all open and express wonder as to who opened them.
4. Check on whether the windows in this classroom open.
5. Inform the secretary that the lights next door have gone out.
6. Tell a colleague that you'd like to: (a) open this window, but it won't open; (b) lock this trunk, but it won't lock; (c) turn on this light, but it won't go on; (d) turn off this light, but it won't go off; (e) close this door, but it won't close.
7. A friend is helping you unpack some books. Tell him to put them here for now (i.e., to be used later).
8. Tell a friend that you didn't want to read the letter from Ms. Nakamura, but you ended up reading it.
9. A friend has asked what time the conference begins. Exclaim that you have completely forgotten.
10. You have just realized that you have two 9:00 appointments tomorrow. Exclaim over your predicament (using a form of **simau**).
11. A colleague has inquired about a friend of yours whom he knows slightly. Explain that she went off to England, and no one has heard anything.
12. A colleague is looking for the secretary. Explain that she was talking with a visitor at the reception desk a little while ago, but she's not there anymore, so . . . [I don't really know where she is].
13. Comment on how hot it's become. Ask if it's all right to open the window.
14. Find out what is in: (a) that trunk; (b) this suitcase; (c) that large, red shopping bag.
15. You've been asked if you need your camera. Explain that since you are not going to take any pictures here . . . [I don't need it].
16. Ask a friend to turn on the radio (now, in advance), because you want to listen to the 6:00 news.
17. You've been asked by your roommate to turn off the television. Ask if it isn't off. Explain that you haven't turned it on.

18. You've just noted that the student worker left his camera. Ask a colleague where you should put it for the time being.
19. Invite a colleague to dinner next Saturday.
20. Accept the preceding invitation with pleasure and find out what time you should come.
21. Telephone your school and explain that you won't be attending class today because you've caught a cold and will be going to the doctor's.
22. Ask a friend what she is going to do after she finishes listening to those tapes.
23. Tell a colleague that you went to the third floor to see Ms. Yamaguchi, but she wasn't in.
24. You are describing your plans for the remainder of the day to your classmate. Explain that after you stop in at the library you're going (a) to the bookstore to buy a new Japanese–English dictionary; (b) to the airport to meet (see off) your professor.
25. A colleague is going to Kyoto on company business. Ask him to give you a call after he arrives at his hotel.
26. A slight acquaintance has come to your town on a visit. Explain to a friend that you really didn't want to go to meet her, but you ended up going after all.
27. You have been invited to attend kabuki with an acquaintance. Tell her you are looking forward to it.
28. A friend has caught cold. Express concern.
29. Ask a friend when Ms. Hashimoto became: (a) a lawyer; (b) a doctor; (c) a consultant; (d) a nurse; (e) a journalist; (f) a professor.
30. Confirm your recollection that Ms. Watanabe's (older) brother is: (a) a banker; (b) an engineer; (c) a diplomat; (d) an architect; (e) an importer-exporter; (f) a politician; (g) a government employee.

Check-up

1. What do we mean by transitive/intransitive verbal pairs? Give three examples. (A-SP1)
2. What is the difference in meaning between **aku** and **aite (i)ru**? Between **tûku** and **tûite (i)ru**? (A-SP1)
3. What is the difference in meaning between **akenai** and **akete (i)nai**? (A-SP1)
4. Insofar as a /transitive-partner gerund + (i)ru/ occurs in the affirmative, to what kinds of action does it usually refer? (A-SP1)
5. What is the difference in meaning between **tâbete (i)ru** and **tâbete âru**? What kind of verbals may occur in their gerund form in construction with **âru**? (A-SP2)
6. /Nominal **X** + **ḡa**/ before **tâbete (i)ru** refers to the person who is eating (or has eaten). How does /Nominal **X** + **ḡa**/ before **tâbete âru** differ? What particle sometimes occurs instead of **ḡa** and with what slight difference in meaning? (A-SP2)
7. What is the basic meaning of **oku**? Of **simau**? What do these verbals mean in combination with an immediately preceding verbal gerund? (A-SP3), (B-SP1)
8. What contraction may occur in the combination /gerund + **oku**/? /Gerund + **simau**/? (A-SP3), (B-SP1)
9. What is the underlying meaning of the particle **kara**? Compare its use following an imperfective or perfective or tentative predicate with its use following a gerund. (B-SP2)
10. How do the following sentences compare?
    (a) **Byoóki ni nàtte, tabáko (o) yamemàsita.**
    (b) **Byoóki ni nàtte kara, tabáko (o) yamemàsita.**
    (c) **Byoóki ni nàtta kara, tabáko (o) yamemàsita.** (B-SP2)
11. What particle is associated with expressions of purpose? How is the difference between 'I went for consultation' and 'I went to consult with the section chief' represented in Japanese? (B-SP3)

Lesson 17

SECTION A

Core Conversations

1(J)a. **Atárasìi têrebi kaímàsita nêe.**

  b. **Hee⁀ Zyâa, hurûi no wa sutétyattà ñ desu ka⁀**

  c. **Âa, sôo na ñ desu ka.**

2(J)a. **Konó hòñ omósiròi?**

  b. **Îi?**

  c. **Zyâa, kariru ne⁀ Sâñkyuu.**

3(N)a. **Ni-kai ḡa suḱkàri kîree ni katázùita nêe.**

  b. **Hitô-ri de yatta no?**

  c. **Sôo. Zyâa, tyañto 'oree o aḡeta?**

4(N)a. **Dôo sita no?**

  b. **A, akáku nàtte (i)ru nêe.**

(N)a. **Têrebi? Iya, sore wa Yamâḡuti-sañ ḡa kudásàtta ñ desu.**

  b. **Iêie, are wa tomódati ni aḡemàsita.**

(N)a. **Ñ. Yômu? Kasíte aḡerù wa yo⁀**

  b. **Ñ. Môo yôñzyatta kara . .**

(J)a. **Hurûi monô o zêñbu sutéte simattà kara . .**

  b. **Tońde mo nài. Kîñzyo no 'gakusee-sañ ḡa tetúdàtte kurétà ñ desu yo.**

  c. **Êe. Oree mo aḡete, daíḡaku màde 'kuruma de okútte aḡetà wa⁀**

(J)a. **Gomî ḡa hâitte, mê ḡa itâi ñ da.**

  b. **Tyôtto mîte kureru?**

ENGLISH EQUIVALENTS

1(J)a. You bought a new television, didn't you!

  b. Wow! Then (is it that) you threw away the old one?

  c. Oh, is that it.

2(J)a. Is this book interesting?

(N)a. A television? No, (it's that) Mr/s. Yamaguchi gave me that one.

  b. No, no. That one I gave to a friend.

(N)a. Yeah. Will you read it? I'll lend it to you.

b. Is that O.K.?

   c. Then I'll borrow it—O.K.? Thanks.
3(N)a. Upstairs has been put in perfect order, hasn't it!

   b. Did you do it alone?

   c. Oh. Then did you pay him/her properly?

4(N)a. What's the matter?

   b. Oh, it's turned red, hasn't it!

   b. Yeah. I finished reading it already, so . . . (I can lend it to you).

(J)a. [That's] because I finished throwing away all the old things.

   b. Heavens, no! A student from the neighborhood gave me some help.

   c. Yes. I both paid him/her and got him/her to the university by car.
(J)a. My eye has something in it. (*lit.* Dust having entered [it], my eye hurts.)

   b. Would you take a look at it for me?

BREAKDOWNS
(AND SUPPLEMENTARY VOCABULARY)

1. **suteru /-ru; suteta/**	throw away
ağeru /-ru; ağeta/ *or*	
+**sasiağeru /-ru; sasiağeta/** ↓ (SP1) *or*	
+**yaru /-ru; yatta/** (SP1)	give (to you/him/her/them)
2. **kasite ağeru** (SP2)	lend (to you/him/her/them)
sâñkyuu	thank you
3. **suḱkàri**	completely, utterly
katázùku /-u; katázùita/	become tidy, be put in order
+**katázukèru /-ru; katázùketa/**	make tidy, put in order
+**soozi-suru**	clean
+**naôsu /-u; naôsita/**	fix, repair; correct
kîree ni katázùku	be put in order neatly
hitô-ri de yaru	do alone (*lit.* do, being one person)
+**(go)zibuñ de yaru**	do by oneself
kîñzyo	neighborhood
tetúdàu /-u; tetúdàtta/	help, lend a hand
kureru /-ru; kureta/ (SP1)	give (to me/us/you)
tetúdàtte kureru (SP2)	give help (to me/us/you)
tyañto	properly; exactly; neatly
(o)ree	reward; thanks, expression of appreciation
daíğaku màde 'kuruma de okuru	send *or* take to the university by car
okutte ağeru	send/send off (for you/him/her/them)
4. **gomî**	trash; dust

mê		eye	
itâi /-katta/		is painful; hurts	
mîte kureru? (SP3)		will you look at (for me/us)? will he/she/they look at (for me/us/you)?	

Parts of the body

2.	**atámà**	head	11.	**munê**	chest
3.	**siñzoo**	heart	12.	**senaka**	back
4.	**i**	stomach	13.	**kosi**	lower back
5.	**hana**	nose	14.	**udê**	arm
6.	**kuti**	mouth	15.	**tê**	hand
7.	**hâ**	tooth	16.	**asî**	leg, foot
8.	**mimî**	ear	17.	**yubî**	finger
9.	**kubi**	neck	18.	**karada**	body
10.	**kâta**	shoulder			

MISCELLANEOUS NOTES

1. In CC1, Sue Brown (N) and her office coworker (J) are discussing her new television. The style used by the two women is careful, with distal-style predicates occurring in major sentences. Note the use of extended predicates in an explanatory statement ([N]a) and two explanatory questions ([J]b, c). Note also the contrastive use of particle **wa—sore wa, hurûi no wa,** and **are wa.**

2. In CC2, Sue Brown (N) and her fellow graduate student, Kato (J), discuss a book of hers that he is interested in reading. The style is extremely casual, with very short sentences. All predicates are direct-style. Sue Brown's use of sentence-final **wa yo** is feminine.

(J)c. The English borrowing **sañkyuu** occurs quite commonly, particularly in the 'in' speech of young people. Here because Kato is speaking with a foreigner, he would be especially apt to use it.

3. CC3 is a conversation between Mr. Carter (N) and his Japanese wife (J) regarding the straightening up of the second floor of their home, completed today by Mrs. Carter with the help of a student. Mr. Carter uses casual-style, with direct-style predicates. His use of sentence-final **yatta no?** is gentle-style, commonly, though not exclusively, used by men when addressing women and children informally. Mrs. Carter's style is also casual, with direct-style predicates, though she does include one distal-style extended predicate ([J]b). Her use of sentence-final **wa** is feminine.

(N)a. The intransitive **katázùku** and its transitive partner, **katázukèru**, refer not only to putting places in order, but also to straightening out or settling tasks and problems—even the marrying off of a daughter!

(N)b. **Hitô-ri de yaru** 'do alone (*lit.* being one person).' Compare **hutá-rì de iku, sañ-niñ de suru,** etc. **Zibuñ** (polite **gozibuñ**) refers to one's own self. Whereas **hitô-ri de yaru** emphasizes the fact that only *one* person was involved, **zibuñ de yaru** indicates accomplishment through one's own ability, power, or strength, without assistance. Note also: **zibuñ no kuruma** 'one's own car,' **zibúñ no koñpyùutaa** 'one's own computer,' etc.

(J)b. The addition of **-san** to **gakusee** adds both politeness and a more personalized touch.

Tetúdàu occurs commonly in its humble-polite derivative in offers of help: **Otêtudai-(ita)simasyoo ka; Otêtudai-(ita)simasu.** Note that particle **o** may follow the person or the task that is helped.

(O)ree covers not only thanks or gratitude that is expressed verbally, but also an expression of appreciation that takes the form of money or a gift. The basic meaning of **(o)ree** relates to etiquette and decorum. To describe someone as **ree o siranai** is to describe a person who is rude, ill-bred, ill-mannered—a boor. Compare also **situree** 'lacking **ree**.' Note also **(o)ree o iu** 'express thanks'; **(o)ree o suru** 'reward,' 'make recompense'; **(o)miyaḡe no oree ni** 'in return for a souvenir [received].' Often what is simply regarded as doing a favor that calls for no reward in the West is considered by the Japanese to be an obligation which should be repaid. This should not be confused with Western patterns of tipping.

Okuru covers not only the sending of articles through the mail, but also sending people on their way, seeing them off—the opposite of **mukaeru**—or accompanying them to a destination. Thus, **gakusee o 'kuruma de okuru** 'send a student by car' or 'take a student by car'; **tomodati o utí màde arûite okuru** 'walk a friend home.'

4. Kato (J) has something lodged in his eye and is asking his friend Smith (N) for help. The style is casual, with direct-style predicates.

(N)a. Compare: **nâni o suru?** 'what will (*or* do) you do?' **dôo suru?** 'how will (*or* do) you proceed *or* handle the situation?' **nâni o sita?** 'what did you do?' **dôo sita** 'what happened?' (i.e., 'how did you act that this kind of situation resulted?').

(J)a. **Itâi** is a double-ḡa affective adjectival: **Tomodati ḡa atámà ḡa itâi kara . .** 'Since my friend has a headache . . .' (i.e., 'my friend is head-painful'). Compare: **Ano kodomo wa mê ḡa oókìi nêe.** 'What big eyes that child has!' From the Japanese point of view, one does not 'have' headaches, large eyes, a bad heart, and so forth; rather, these are matters of description—the head is painful, the eyes are big, and the heart is bad. These descriptions are related to individuals through the usual particles—**ḡa** or **wa** or **mo**. Note that the hypothetical pattern *****tomódati no atamà ḡa itâi** sounds a bit as though the severed head of your friend is causing pain to someone!

Itâi! is the Japanese equivalent of 'Ouch!' Also, **Dôko ḡa itâi?** is equivalent to 'Where does it hurt?' (*lit.* 'What place is painful?')

(N)b. Remember that **nâtte (i)ru** refers to a present state resulting from a previous activity: 'it has become.'

Structural Patterns

1. VERBALS OF GIVING

The importance of in-group/out-group distinctions, as well as vertical (hierarchical) distinctions in Japanese, means that the concept of giving is very complex. In English, no matter who the giver or who the recipient, the verb 'give' is used; in Japanese, on the other hand, a teacher's giving something to a student, for example, is distinguished from what occurs when a student gives something to a teacher.

We are concerned with five different verbals of giving. First we divide them on the basis of whether the giving proceeds away from the speaker (for example, the speaker gives to the addressee) or toward the speaker (for example, the addressee gives to the speaker).

Next one must consider the relative ranks of the conversation's participants, the formality of the topic/situation, etc.—all the features that play a role in the determination of Japanese speech styles.

When in-group[1] gives to out-group, the speaker chooses one of three possible verbals: **yaru, ageru,** or **sasiageru.** These verbals cover any situation involving giving in which either the speaker is the giver or the giver has a closer connection with the speaker than the recipient.

Now, how do these verbals differ? **Yaru** (distinct from **yaru** 'do') covers giving to inanimates (water to plants, for example), animals, and, in the language of some people, to subordinates, younger relatives, and close friends. This verbal is gradually becoming less frequently used.

Ageru, which formerly implied giving to a superior, has now become more neutral in its implication: for some speakers, it is used in reference to all recipients, animate and inanimate, except those to whom one is being overtly polite and deferential; for those who continue to use **yaru,** it covers all other situations, except those involving polite deference to a superior.

Sasiageru is the verbal that covers those situations of giving in which the giver politely defers to the recipient as superior.

We now turn to giving by the out-group to the in-group, covering situations involving giving in which either the speaker is the recipient or the recipient has a closer connection with the speaker than the giver. Two verbals cover this kind of situation, one already familiar, **kudásàru,** and the other, a verbal newly introduced in this lesson, **kureru. Kudásàru** is a polite verbal, elevating the position of the giver, whereas **kureru** places the giver at the same level as the speaker or at a lower level.

The interrelationship of all these verbals can be diagrammed thus:

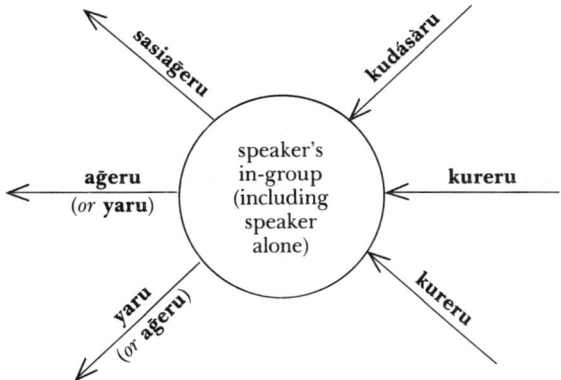

Note the following:

All the giving verbals are operational, and occur in the pattern /Y **ni** X **o** + verbal of giving/ = 'give X to Y,' provided recipient and thing given are expressed. The use of **ni**

---

1. Remember that we view the speaker alone as a 'minimal in-group.'

following the recipient is another example of the use of this particle to indicate goal, the ultimate location.

2. In statements, **kudásaru** and **kureru** regularly imply the speaker (and/or the speaker's in-group) as a recipient without any overt mention of such. Remember: **Kudásài** = 'Please give it *to me*'; 'to me' is implied by the verbal; in contexts where the in-group is larger than one person, 'to us' may be implied.

3. If 'I' give something 'to you,' the movement is necessarily away from the speaker ('me'), and only one of the left-hand verbals in the diagram above is possible. But if 'he' gives something 'to you,' any one of the giving verbals is possible: the choice depends first on whether 'I' consider myself in 'your' in-group or in 'his' in-group at the moment, and second on the degree of politeness.

4. Often the verbal used in direct address may differ from the verbal used in reporting the same event. Thus I may ask a store clerk for a shopping bag, saying **kudásaimaseñ ka,** but later describe the occurrence to others as **kurémàsita**. The nature of the event, the formality of the situation, the personality of the speaker, even nonparticipants who are present—all influence the choice of the verbal. Examples:

    Konó tèepu (wa) tomódati ḡa kuremàsita. 'This tape a friend gave me.'

    Dâre ḡa sonó zassi (o) kuretà ñ desu ka⤻ 'Who [out there] (is it who) gave you [who are closer to me] that magazine?'

    Obâasama ḡa kudásàtta no? '(Is it that) Grandmother gave you [that]?' (mother to her own child)

    Mizú (o) yarimasyòo ka⤻ 'Shall I give [the plant, the dog, the cat] some water?'

    Mizú/omízu o aḡemasyòo ka⤻ 'Shall I give you some water?'

    Omízu o sasiaḡemasyòo↓ ka⤻ 'Shall I give you some water?'

In the last two examples, there is a difference in the level of politeness accorded the addressee. A professor or doctor or honored guest, for example, would appropriately be addressed with the alternate which includes **sasiaḡeru**.

2. /GERUND + VERBAL OF GIVING/

We have long been familiar with the request patterns /gerund + **kudásài**/ and /gerund + **kudásaimaseñ ka⤻**/, which request the 'giving' of the actualized action represented by the verbal. We now extend those patterns to include not only all forms of **kudásàru**, but also all forms of the other four verbals of giving.

In general terms, /verbal gerund X + verbal of giving/ = 'performance of X for the benefit of someone.' The performer of the activity, if expressed, is followed by **ḡa** (or **wa**) and the benefactor (the person 'to whom' the action is given) by particle **ni**. The choice of verbal of giving follows the guidelines in SP1, above. Examples:

    Tomodati ḡa syasíñ o tòtte kuremasita. 'A friend took a picture for me.'

    Kaḡî o kâkete aḡemasyoo ka⤻ 'Shall I lock the door for you?'

    Señsèe ḡa 'kono 'muzukasii nihoñḡo o oyómi ni nàtte↑ kudasaimasita↑. 'The teacher read this difficult Japanese for me.'

    Dâre ḡa sonó tokee o katte kuremàsita ka⤻ 'Who [out there] bought that watch for you [who are closer to me]?'

Señsèe. Deñwabàñḡoo o sirâbete sasiaḡemasyoo ↓ ka⤴ 'Doctor, shall I look up the telephone number for you?'

Kêe-tyañ ni têrebi o tukêt(e) oite aḡemasita. 'I turned on the television (for future viewing) for Kei.'

The verbal of giving may, of course, occur in a negative derivative form:

Kâre ni mití o kikimàsita kedo, itte kuremasèñ desita. 'I asked him the way, but he didn't tell me.'

or, in the cases of **yaru, aḡeru,** and **sasiaḡeru,** it can appear in a **-tai** derivative form:

Kêe-tyañ ni kêeki o tukûtte aḡétàkatta kedo, zikâñ ḡa nàkute .. 'I wanted to make a cake for Kei, but not having time ...'

The accentuation of this pattern is parallel to that of /gerund + **oku**/ and /gerund + **simau**/.

The frequency of the pattern using a verbal of giving cannot be overestimated. Probably the greatest difficulty it poses for the foreign student is simply to remember to use it. It often occurs in Japanese when the English equivalent contains nothing parallel—a further reminder that Japanese is not a translation of English! Consider these examples:

English: [I explained something to a friend, but] *he didn't understand.*

Japanese: **Wakâtte kurémasèñ desita.**

English: [I took a friend to a Japanese movie as a special treat, and] *she really enjoyed it.*

Japanese: **Yorókòñde kuremasita.**

In both cases, Japanese overtly indicates the relationship of the speaker to the action as that of benefactor, and assigns directionality to the activity.

3. ADDITIONAL REQUEST PATTERNS

We can now expand our request patterns by replacing **kudásaimasèñ ka⤴** with **kurémasèñ ka⤴**, thus forming a less deferentially polite pattern.

Mâtte kuremaseñ ka⤴ 'Would (*lit.* won't) you wait for me?'

Kasíte kuremaseñ ka⤴ 'Would (*lit.* won't) you lend [it] to me?'

Kâre ni aḡéte kuremaseñ ka⤴ 'Would (*lit.* won't) you give [it] to him for me?'

All **-maseñ ka⤴** request forms can be changed to direct-style, in which case **ka** may be replaced by question intonation:

Mâtte kurenai?

Kasíte kudasarànai?

The latter example, while retaining its politeness, is now more familiar and informal. This type of utterance occurs more commonly in the speech of women.

Also possible are blunt direct-style requests ending in **kurenai ka**, which are more typical of male speech.

The negative of these request forms implies politeness through indirectness. (Compare English '*Won't* you have some cake?') But in CC4(J)b, Kato asks Smith to check his eye, saying **Tyôtto mîte kureru?** This is a more direct (therefore less polite and more familiar) request form appropriate to the conversation of these two male graduate students who have established a friendly relationship.

At this stage, using how many different request patterns are you able to ask someone to wait? Can you come up with at least ten? (Don't forget **omáti ni nàru** alternates!)

Drills

A 1. **Yamamoto-sañ ni râzio o aḡétai to omòtte iru ñ desu ḡa ..**
'I've been thinking I'd like to give Mr/s. Yamamoto a radio, but ...' (what do you think?)

Râzio o? Âa, îi desu nêe. Yorókobimàsu yo.
'A radio? Oh, that's great! S/he'll be pleased.'

2. **Osamu-kuñ ni eéḡo no hòñ o aḡétai to omòtte (i)ru ñ desu ḡa ..**
'I've been thinking I'd like to give Osamu an English book, but ...' (what do you think?)

Eéḡo no hòñ o? Âa, îi desu nêe. Yorókobimàsu yo.
'An English book? Oh, that's great! He'll be pleased.'

3. **Mîtiko-sañ/hañdobàggu**; 4. **Suḡîura-sañ/kâmera**; 5. **Nakáda-sañ no òkusañ/kîree na biñseñ**; 6. **Huráñsùziñ no tomodati/tokee**

B 1. **Kono syasiñ, irímàsu ka.**
'Do you need this photograph?'

Sono syasiñ? A, irímaseñ. Sasíaḡemàsu yo.
'That photograph? Oh, I don't need it. I'll give it to you.'

2. **Kono huutoo, irímàsu ka.**
'Do you need this envelope?'

Sono huutoo? A, irímaseñ. Sasíaḡemàsu yo.
'That envelope?' Oh, I don't need it. I'll give it to you.'

3. **syoṕpiñḡubàggu**; 4. **tîzu**; 5. **kabañ**; 6. **hurosiki**; 7. **têepu**

C 1. **Ano syasiñ, Yukio-tyañ no?**
'Is that photograph Yukio's?'

Ñ. Yukío ni yattà no.
'Yeah. I gave it to Yukio.'

2. **Anó tèrebi, imootosañ no?**
'Is that television your (younger) sister's?'

Ñ, imóotò ni yaťtà no.
'Yeah. I gave it to my (younger) sister.'

3. **osara/Kêe-tyañ**; 4. **omiyaḡe/otootosañ**; 5. **kâsa/Kimura-kuñ**; 6. **pâñ/anô ko**

• Repeat this drill, replacing gentle **no** with blunt **ñ da** in the responses.

D 1. **Kâre ḡa zéñbu kâita ñ desu ka.**
'(Is it that) *he* wrote it all?'

Iêie. Hotôñdo zéñbu watási ḡa kàite aḡétà ñ desu yo.
'No, no. (It's that) almost all of it *I* wrote for him.'

2. **Kâre ḡa zéñbu yattà ñ desu ka.**
'(Is it that) *he* did it all?'

Iêie. Hotôñdo zéñbu watási ḡa yatte aḡetà ñ desu yo.

3. **tukûtta**; 4. **katázùketa**; 5. **yônda**; 6. **simatta**; 7. **sirâbeta**

E 1. **Hurûi zassi môo sutétyattà ñ desu ka.**
'(Is it that) you threw away the old magazines already?'

'No, no. (It's that) almost all of it *I* did for him.'

Hurûi zassi? Âa, are wa ne! Tomódati ni aḡemàsita.
'The old magazines? Oh, those, you know, I gave to a friend.'

2. **Nyuúyòoku no tîzu môo sutétyattà ñ desu ka.**
'(Is it that) you threw away the map of New York already?'

Nyuúyòoku no tîzu? Âa, are wa ne! Tomódati ni aḡemàsita.
'The map of New York? Oh, that, you know, I gave to a friend.'

3. **gaikokuḡo no siñbuñ**; 4. **ano gurêe no syoṕpiñḡubàggu**; 5. **Amérika karà no syasiñ**

F 1. **Toodai no Yamáda-señsèe ḡa okáki ni nàtta ñ desu ne?**
'(It's that) Prof. Yamada from Tokyo University wrote it—right?'

Zitû wa ne! Utí no hìsyo ḡa kâite sasíaḡetà ñ desu yo
'Actually, you know, (the fact is) our secretary wrote it for him/her.'

2. **Toodai no Yamáda-señsèe ḡa onáosi ni nàtta ñ desu ne?**
'(It's that) Prof. Yamada from Tokyo University corrected it—right?'

Zitû wa ne! Utí no hìsyo ḡa naôsite sasíaḡetà ñ desu yo
'Actually, you know, (the fact is) our secretary corrected it for him/her.'

3. **otúkuri ni nàtta**; 4. **osírabe ni nàtta**; 5. **ośsyàtta**; 6. **omíse ni nàtta**

G 1. **Yukio-tyañ wa îi ko desu nêe. Zêñbu hitô-ri de yaítta ñ desyoo?**
'Isn't Yukio a good child! (It's that) he did all that alone, didn't he?'

Tońde mo nài. Zêñbu watási ḡa yattà ñ desu yo
'Heavens, no! (The fact is) *I* did it all.'

2. **Yukio-tyañ wa îi ko desu nêe. Zêñbu hitô-ri de katázùketa ñ desyoo?**
'Isn't Yukio a good child! (It's that) he straightened everything up alone, didn't he?'

Tońde mo nài. Zêñbu watási ḡa katazùketa ñ desu yo
'Heavens, no! (The fact is) *I* straightened it all up.'

3. **aketa**; 4. **sita**; 5. **kiita**

H 1. **Kîree na owáñ dèsu nêe.**
'What beautiful bowls!'

Kîree desyoo? Sono owañ ne! Tomódati ḡa kuretà ñ desu yo
'Aren't they beautiful? Those bowls, you know, a friend gave me.'

2. **Ôoki na kêeki desu nêe.**
'What a big cake!'

Oókìi desyoo? Sonó kèeki ne! Tomódati ḡa kuretà ñ desu yo
'Isn't it big? That cake, you know, a friend gave me.'

3. **karâi osûsi**; 4. **oisii otya**; 5. **okâsi na tokee**; 6. **tîisa na kâmera**
• Repeat this drill, substituting **señsèe** for **tomodati** and **kudásàtta** for **kureta** in the responses.

I 1. **Tâkano-sañ g̃a tukûtta ñ desu ka⤴—sono tana.**
'Was it [you], Mr/s. Takano, who made it—that shelf?'

Iya, tomódati g̃a tukùtte kurétà ñ desu yo⤴
'No, (it's that) a friend made it for me.'

2. **Tâkano-sañ g̃a katta ñ desu ka⤴—sonó ràzio.**
'Was it [you], Mr/s. Takano, who bought it—that radio?'

Iya, tomódati g̃a katte kuretà ñ desu yo⤴
'No, (it's that) a friend bought it for me.'

3. **tanôñda/isya**; 4. **suteta/gomî**; 5. **tetúdàtta/sig̃oto**; 6. **akétè kita/mâdo**

J 1. **Yaru?**
'Are you going to do it?'

Iya, môo Hayási-sañ g̃a tyañto yatte kuretà kara, watási wa ìi desyoo?
'No, Mr/s. Hayashi already did it for me just as it should be done, so I'm okay [without doing anything]—right?'

2. **Kau?**
'Are you going to buy it?'

Iya, môo Hayási-sañ g̃a tyañto katte kuretà kara, watási wa ìi desyoo?
'No, Mr/s. Hayashi already bought it for me just as it should be done, so I'm okay [without doing anything]—right?'

3. **okuru**; 4. **sasiag̃eru**; 5. **simêru**; 6. **turete (i)ku**; 7. **yoru**

K 1. **Hitô-ri de ittà ñ desu ka⤴**
'(Is it that) you went alone?'

Iya, imóotò mo issyo ni itte kuremàsita kara ..
'No, my (younger) sister went along, too, (for me), so ...' (I didn't go alone).

2. **Hitô-ri de soózi-sità ñ desu ka⤴**
'(Is it that) you did the cleaning alone?'

Iya, imóotò mo issyo ni soozi-site kuremàsita kara ..
'No, my (younger) sister cleaned, too, together [with me] (for me), so ...' (I didn't do it alone).

3. **tâbeta**; 4. **kâetta**; 5. **sirâbeta**; 6. **àtta**; 7. **modôtta**

L 1. **Dâre g̃a issyo ni itte kuretà ñ desu ka⤴**
'Who went with you (for you)?'

Iya, hitô-ri de ittà ñ desu yo.
'No no, I went alone.'

2. **Dâre g̃a issyo ni soozi-site kuretà ñ desu ka⤴**
'Who did the cleaning with you (for you)?'

Iya, hitô-ri de soózi-sità ñ desu yo.
'No no, I did the cleaning alone.'

3. **tâbete**; 4. **kâette**; 5. **sirâbete**; 6. **âtte**; 7. **modôtte**

M 1. **Tyôtto 'kore mîte kurenai?**
'Would you just look at this for me?'

    Tyôtto mâtte⁄ Îma sûĝu mîte aĝeru kara . .
'Just a minute. I'll look at it for you right away now so . . .' (wait!)

2. **Tyôtto 'sore mîsete kurenai?**
'Would you just show me that?'

    Tyôtto mâtte⁄ Îma sûĝu mîsete aĝeru kara . .
'Just a minute. I'll show it to you right away now so . . .' (wait!)

3. **deńwatyoo sirâbete**; 4. **konó meesi yòńde**; 5. **êki made 'okutte**; 6. **tetúdàtte**

N 1. **Dâre ĝa it́te kurerù no?**[2]
'Who will go (for you)?'

    Ôono-sań ĝa it́te kurerù ń zya nai?
'Isn't it (the case) that Mr/s. Ono will (go for me)?'

2. **Dâre ĝa kat́te kurerù no?**
'Who will buy it (for you)?'

    Ôono-sań ĝa kat́te kurerù ń zya nai?
'Isn't it (the case) that Mr/s. Ono will (buy for me)?'

3. **tukûtte**; 4. **tanôńde**; 5. **osiete**

O 1. **Mîte aĝemasyoo ka⁄**
'Shall I look at [this] for you?'

    A, zya, warûi kedo, tyôtto mîte kudasaimasu?
'Oh, well, I really shouldn't bother you, but will you (look at it for me)?'

2. **Sutéte aĝemasyòo ka⁄**
'Shall I throw [this] away for you?'

    A, zya, warûi kedo, tyôtto sutéte kudasaimàsu?
'Oh, well, I really shouldn't bother you, but will you (throw it away for me)?'

3. **irete**; 4. **simatte**; 5. **tanôńde**; 6. **turete itte**; 7. **yotte**; 8. **kawatte**

P 1. **Mimi, dôo sita no? Itâi no?**[2]
'What happened to your ear? Does it hurt?'

    Mimi? A, îe. Betu ni îtâku nâi ń desu ĝa, tyôtto . .
'My ear? Oh, no, it doesn't especially hurt, but [there's something] a bit [wrong].'

2. **Senaka, dôo sita no? Itâi no?**
'What happened to your back? Does it hurt?'

    Senaka? A, îe. Betu ni îtâku nâi ń desu ĝa, tyôtto . .
'My back? Oh, no, it doesn't especially hurt, but [there's something] a bit [wrong].'

3. **asî**; 4. **yubî**; 5. **udê**; 6. **kubi**; 7. **tê**; 8. **nôdo**; 9. **atámà**; 10. **kâta**; 11. **hana**

Q 1. **Anô hito, mê ĝa wârûkute nêe.**
'S/he has bad eyes and (you know

    Âa, mê ĝa warûi ń desu ka. Sirímaseń desita.

---

2. The stimulus questions are gentle-style.

what that means).'

'Oh, (you mean) his/her eyes are bad? I didn't know.'

2. **Anô hito, siñzoo ga wàrùkute nêe.**
'S/he has a bad heart and (you know what that means).'

Âa, siñzoo ga warùi ñ desu ka. Sirímaseñ desita.
'Oh, (you mean) his/her heart is bad? I didn't know.'

3. **kosi**; 4. **i**; 5. **asî**; 6. **hâ**; 7. **mimî**

Application Exercises

A1. Take a few minutes to put your immediate surroundings into some disarray: rearrange the furniture inappropriately, place various objects in places where they don't belong, leave trash in unexpected places, etc. Then restore the area to its normal condition, using the new patterns of 17A. In one type of practice (1), instruct various members of the class to perform specific tasks, and then report to the group on who did what for you. For additional practice (2), ask and answer questions about events as an onlooker. Examples:

(1) **A-sañ. Sono hurûi siñbuñ (o) zêñbu sutéte simatte kudasài. ... A-sañ (ga) ′sono hurûi siñbuñ (o) zêñbu sutéte simatte kuremàsita.** 'Mr/s. A. Please throw away all the old papers.' ... 'Mr/s. A threw away all the old papers for me.'

(2) **Dâre ga ′sono hurûi siñbuñ (o) zêñbu sutéta simattà ñ desu ka** 'Who threw away all those old papers?'
Dâre ga sutéte simatte kuretà ñ desu ka 'Who threw [them] away for you?'
Dâre ga ′B-sañ ni sutéte simatte agetà ñ desu ka 'Who threw [them] away for Mr/s. B?'
Dâre ni sutéte simatte agetà ñ desu ka 'Who did you throw [them] for?'
A-sañ wa dâre ni sutéte simatte agetà ñ desu ka 'Who did Mr/s. A throw [them] away for?'

Examples of tasks:

hôñ o hôñdana ni ′simau	siñbuñ ya zassi o katázukèru
gomî o ′suteru	sonó kamì o konó nàka ni ′ireru
kore o mâdo no mâe ni ′oku	mâdo o simêru
kore o ′tonari ni ′motte iku	dêñki o tukêru

2. Practice all the patterns of the preceding exercises in reference to more general situations. Add requests for one person to perform activities in behalf of another. Example:

A-sañ. B-sañ ni kyôo no siñbuñ o katte agete kudasaimaseñ ka 'Mr/s. A. Would you (for my benefit) buy today's paper for Mr/s. B?'

In accordance with how different roles are assigned to different students, vary the verbals of giving (**kureru/kudásàru; yaru/ageru/sasiageru**) and the patterns of request (**site kurenai (ka)?/kurémaseñ ka/kudásaranai?/kudásaimaseñ ka**) appropriately. However, be sure that the requests you are making are in keeping with the assumed roles. (The use of the most polite, deferential patterns will still not justify asking the company president to throw out the rubbish!) Examples of tasks:

otáku màde no tîzu o kâku	zîsyo o 'kariru
konó teḡami o yòmu	demae o 'tyuumoñ-suru
atárasìi koñpyùutaa o mîru	miti o 'kiku
têrebi o tukêru	Itóo-sañ no deñwabàñḡoo o sirábèru
syasíñ o tòru	sûsi o tukûru
wâiñ o 'kau	

3. Practice presenting problems for which another member of the group can offer a solution. Examples:

Hurûi desu nêe—kore wa. 'Isn't this old—this one!'

Atárasìi no o katte aḡemasyòo ka⁄ 'Shall I buy a new one for you?'

4. In response to questions as to what happened (**Dôo sita ñ desu ka⁄**) practice 'body-aches.' Insofar as possible, tie in explanations for the problem. Examples:

Kaze o hiite, atámà ḡa itâi ñ desu. 'I caught a cold and have a headache.'

Tumétai mìruku o nôñde, hâ ḡa itâku nâtta ñ desu. 'I drank some cold milk, and my teeth hurt.'

B. Core Conversations: Substitution

Practice the Core Conversations, altering the language style according to changes introduced in the participants and their relationships. Include questioning relating to the contents.

SECTION B

Core Conversations

1(N)a. **Konó keesàñki naôsite moráitai ñ desu kedo..**

(J) **Sâa. Naórimàsu ka nêe. Koré to onazi tàipu ḡa îma hizyóo ni oyasuku nàtt(e) orimasu yo⁄ Atárasìi no o okái ni narimasèñ ka⁄**

b. **Zyâa, soó simasyòo.**

2(N)a. **Kono teeburu wa dôko desu ka⁄**

(J)a. **Ué e mottè (i)tte kudasai. Tatámi no heyà desu.**

b. **Kore mo?**

b. **Iya, soré wa màda kiméte (i)nài kara, tyôtto mâtte. Îma zyamá ni nàru kara, sôto ni oít(e) okimasyòo.**

c. **Kotti no komákài monô wa dôo simasyoo ka.**

3(N)a. **Hôñ mo zêñbu katázukimàsita yo⌒**

   b. **Ie, betu ni. Tyôtto kâta ğa korímàsita kedo..**

   c. **Âa, îi desu nêe.**

   d. **Ie.... Niwa no ohana ni mizú yatte okimasyòo ka.**

   c. **A. Daídokoro-dòoğu desu neʃ Zêñbu 'daidokoro e moítè (i)tte moraimasyoo. Âto de 'todana ya hikidasi ni simáimàsu kara..**

(J)a. **Gokûroosama. Tukâreta desyoo.**

   b. **Otyá ni simasèñ ka⌒ Îma oísii otya o iremàsu kara..**

   c. **Kyôo wa Burâuñ-sañ ni tetúdàtte itádaità no de, hoñtoo ni tasukarimàsita wa⌒**

   d. **A, soré wa ìi desu yo.**

ENGLISH EQUIVALENTS

1(N)a. I'd like to have this calculator repaired, but ... (can you do it?)

   b. Then why don't I do that.

2(N)a. Where [does] this table [go]?

   b. This, too?

   c. What shall I do with the little things that are over here?

3(N)a. The books have all been put in order, too.

(J) Hm. I wonder if it can be repaired. [Ones of] the same type as this one have become extremely cheap, you know. Wouldn't you [like to] buy a new one?

(J)a. Take that upstairs. It [goes to] the tatami room.

   b. No, that one I haven't decided yet, so wait [on that one]. It will get in the way now, so let's put it outside for the time being.

   c. Oh, you mean the kitchen utensils. Why don't I have you take them all to the kitchen. Later I'll put them (away) in the cupboards and the drawers so ... (they should be in the kitchen).

(J)a. Thanks for your trouble. You're probably tired.

b. No, not especially. My shoulders have become a bit stiff, but . . . (I'm not tired).

c. Oh, that will be nice!

d. Oh, no! . . . Shall I take care of watering the flowers in the garden?

b. Won't you have some tea? I'm going to make some (tea) now that will be tasty so . . . (please have some).

c. Today it's because I've had you help me, Sue, that I've survived (*lit.* I have really been rescued).

d. Oh, that's all right.

BREAKDOWNS
(AND SUPPLEMENTARY VOCABULARY)

1. **keésàñki** — calculator
   morau /-u; moratta/ (SP1) — receive, accept, get
   naôsite morau (SP2) — have [something] fixed
   naôru /-u; naôtta/ — become repaired; recover
   tâipu — type, style, variety; typing
   koré to onazi tàipu — a type the same as this
   hizyoo ni — extremely
   oyasui [+] — is cheap /polite/
   oyásuku nàtt(e) oru [+] (SP3) — it has become cheap /polite/
2. **teeburu** — table
   +**tukue** — desk
   +**isu** — chair
   +**tañsu** — chest
   +**bêtto/bêddo** — bed
   +**sutañdo** — lamp
   +**osiire** — closet
   +**kâgu** — furniture
   uê/ue — top; up; over
   +**sita** — bottom; down; below, under
   +**yoko** — side
   tatami — (Japanese-style floor mat, roughly 3′ × 6′)
   heyâ — room
   tatámi no heyà — room with mats
   kimeru /-ru; kimeta/ (SP4) — decide [something]
   +**kimaru /-u; kimatta/** — become decided
   (o)zyama — nuisance, bother; interruption
   (o)zyamá ni nàru — become a nuisance

+dâsu /-u; dâsita/		put out, take out
komákài /-katta/		occurs in small units; is small, is detailed
daidokoro		kitchen
+huroba		bathroom
+geñkañ		entry hall
+rooka		corridor
+imâ		(Western-style) living room
+tyanoma		(Japanese-style) living room, sitting room
+syosai		study
+siñsitu		bedroom
doógù		tools, implements
daídokoro-dòogu		kitchen utensils
mot́tè (i)tte morau		have [something] taken
+arau /-u; aratta/		wash
+huku /-u; huita/		wipe
todana		cupboard
hikidasi		drawer
3. Gokûroosama.		it's been trouble for you; thanks for your trouble
tukárèru /-ru; tukâreta/		become tired
kôru /-u; kôtta/		become stiff
otya o ireru		make tea
itadaku ↓		receive, get (*also:* eat, drink) /polite/
tetúdàtte itadaku ↓ (SP2)		receive helping, be helped /polite/
tasúkàru /-u; tasúkàtta/		become rescued, saved
+tasúkèru /-ru; tasúkèta/		rescue, save
niwa		garden
hanâ/ohana		flower
+kî		tree; wood
+ueki/ûeki		plant
+inu		dog
+nêko		cat

Miscellaneous Notes

1. Mr. Carter (N) has stopped in at a stationery store to inquire about having a calculator repaired, but he is talked into buying a new one by the clerk (J). Both speakers use careful-style with distal-style predicates. Mr. Carter's speech is plain, but the clerk's is polite (**oyasuku** ↑, **orímàsu** ↓, **okái ni narimasèñ** ↑).
   (N)a. **Keésàñki**: note also **keesañ-suru** 'calculate.'
   (N)a, (J). **Naôru** 'become repaired, fixed, corrected, cured' is the intransitive partner

of **naôsu** 'repair, fix, correct, cure.' (Cf. **deñwa o kakenaosu** 'place a call again [to correct problems].')

(J). **Onazi** has already been pointed out as a special nominal because of its occurrence immediately before other nominals without a connective. Note now that, like **issyo**, it may be preceded by a /nominal + **to**/ phrase with a parallel meaning: **tomodati to issyo** 'together with a friend'; **tomodati to onazi** 'same as a friend.'

Hizyoo has as its most basic meaning 'emergency' (cf. **hizyôoḡuti** 'emergency exit'; **hizyóoburèeki** 'emergency brake'). As a **na**-nominal it is equivalent to 'extraordinary,' 'extreme.' In (J), it occurs with particle **ni** as an expression of manner: 'extremely.'

Note the use of **nâtt(e) orimasu** in reference to an inanimate. With a **-te (i)ru** pattern, even an inanimate referent is viewed as being connected with an animate type of activity or the state resulting from such an activity. The polite equivalent of **iru** in such occurrences is **ôru**, identified as a neutral-honorific⁺ rather than humble-polite ↓ (its value when linked with animate referents).

The clerk's honorific ↑ negative is a polite invitation to the customer to buy a new calculator.

2. Sue Brown (N) is helping Mrs. Carter (J) get settled in the Carters' new home. The speech style is careful with plain, distal-style final predicates. Mrs. Carter's use of several direct-style nonfinal predicates and of an informal request form in (J)b (**mâtte.**) indicates a degree of informality.

(N)a. **Bêddo** is a new-style borrowing which contains a double (long) **d**, a sound not found in traditional Japanese. The older form of this word is **bêtto**, which represents more traditional pronunciation.

Kâgu: note also **kaḡûya** 'furniture store or dealer.'

(J)a. Remember the contrast between **turete (i)ku** 'take [a person]' and **motte (i)ku** 'take [a thing].' **Môtu** as an independent verbal is equivalent to 'take hold of'; **môtte (i)ru** = 'be holding'; 'have'; 'own.'

Note: **yoko ni oku** 'place on its side' or 'place at the side (of something).'

Tatámi no heyà: Many homes in Japan are a Japanese version of Western style, with only one tatami room that has mats instead of a wooden floor.

(J)b. **(O)zyama** occurs in several polite ritual expressions: initially, **Ozyáma desyòo ḡa..** 'Excuse me for interrupting you...'; at departure, **Ozyáma-(ita)simàsita.** 'Excuse me for having interrupted you.'

Dâsu 'put out' is the transitive partner of **dêru** 'go out,' 'come out,' 'leave.' Both are operational. A /nominal + **o**/ phrase precedes **dêru** only when the nominal is a place nominal describing the area through which the motion occurs: **Toókyoo o dèru** 'leave Tokyo.' Compare: **kono miti o iku** 'go along this street' and **kâdo o maḡaru** 'turn the corner,' which also are /place nominal + **o** + intransitive verbal/ examples. **Dâsu** is the opposite of **ireru**, just as **dêru** contrasts with **hâiru**. Note also: **hôñ o dâsu** 'publish a book'; **teḡámi o dàsu** 'mail a letter'; **sôto ni** (*or* **e**) **dâsu** 'put outside.'

(N)c. **Komákài**: Note also **komâkàku suru** 'break into small pieces or units' (including making change); **komâkàku kîru** 'cut up fine,' 'chop fine'; **komákài âme** 'drizzle.'

Arau and **huku** are both operational consonant verbals: **X o arau** 'wash X'; **X o huku** 'wipe X.'

Todana is a compound of **to** 'door' and **tana** 'shelf,' with voicing of the initial consonant of the second item.

3. CC3 is a continuation of CC2, with the same participants and essentially the same speech style.

(N)a. Sue Brown's use of the intransitive **katázukimàsita** politely avoids assigning credit to herself for having done the work.

(J)a. **Gokûroosama (desita)** is a ritual expression based on the nominal **kûroo** 'toil,' 'hardship,' 'care.' It is used, as in this CC, to thank a subordinate for effort expended in behalf of the speaker, or to comment politely to equals or superiors on their toils, performed for themselves or for others. Mrs. Carter, as the wife of a professional banker, outranks Sue Brown, the student; accordingly, this is an appropriate setting for the use of **gokûroosama** by Mrs. Carter to express thanks for the help she has received.

Tukárèru is an affective verbal that occurs commonly in its **-te (i)ru** form ('be tired') and in combination with **simau** (**tukâretyatta** 'I've become exhausted'). The ritual expression **Otúkaresama (dèsita)** is based on the nominal derived from the stem of this verbal. In a society of hard work, once described as 'a nation of workaholics,' being tired is often regarded as one proof of serious endeavor.

Kâta ḡa kôru: The parallel to Westerners' tension and exhaustion headaches are the stiff shoulders of the Japanese, suggesting that even some of our ailments may be culture specific. As we export some of our many headache remedies and the accompanying ads and commercials to Japan, we may spread the related malady as well, but traditionally the shoulders have been the area of weariness and tension for the Japanese. They even manufacture armchairs with built in 'shoulder-pounders' to aid in relaxation.

(J)b. **Otyá ni simasèñ ka⤳** *Lit.* 'Won't you make it to be tea?' 'Won't you decide on tea?' **Otya o ireru**: The Japanese 'put *in* the tea'; English speakers 'put the tea *on*.'

(J)c. **Tasúkàru** 'become rescued' is the intransitive partner of **tasúkèru** 'rescue.' Besides its literal use, **Tasúkarimàsita** occurs in many situations similar to those in which we use 'You saved my life' in a figurative sense in English. Note also: **Tasuketeeee!** 'Heeeelp!' (Politeness can be abandoned in such situations.)

(N)d. **Ueki** is a compound of **uê**, the stem of **ueru** 'plant,' and **kî** 'tree.' Note also **uekiya** 'gardener.'

Household pets—dogs and cats—are becoming more popular in Japan, particularly in the large cities, where pet supply stores can now be found. Traditionally dogs were watchdogs, regularly kept out-of-doors.

Structural Patterns

1. VERBALS OF RECEIVING

Any act of giving must also involve an act of receiving. If I give a book to a friend, that friend receives the book from me; the event can be described from either point of view. It is not surprising that the patterns of giving described in Section A of this lesson have parallel patterns of receiving.

There are two basic verbals of receiving: **morau**, a **w**-consonant verbal, and **itadaku**, its humble-polite equivalent (which is already familiar in reference to eating and drinking). These verbals regularly refer to receiving by the in-group.

The particle **ḡa** follows the *recipient* (if expressed), particle **o** follows the *thing* received, and **ni** or **kara** follows the *person from whom* the thing is received. Of course, shifts in focus lead to the usual particle variations. Examples:

  Kono teḡami, imóotò ḡa kêsa moráttà ñ desu. 'This letter my sister received this morning.'
  Kêsa Dôitu no tomodati ni (~ kara) deñwa o moraimàsita yo. 'This morning I received a call from a friend in Germany.'
  Konó kyookàsyo, señsèe kara (~ ni) itádakimàsita. 'I received this textbook from the teacher.'
  Hisyô kara (~ ni) huútoo o moratte kudasài. 'Please get (*lit.* receive) some envelopes from the secretary.'
  Kore 'itadaite yorósìi desu ka. 'May I have (*lit.* receive) this?'
  Kono biñseñ, arúbàito ḡa hisyô kara (~ ni) morátte kuremàsita. 'This stationery the part-timer got (received) for me from the secretary.'
  Asítà made ni 'ano teḡami moráitài ñ desu kedo . . 'I'd like to receive that letter by tomorrow, but . . .'

Note that this use of **ni** is an example of its use in indicating *original* location: the thing received was located with the source first, and *then* it was received into a new location. This is similar to its use with **kariru: X ni** (or **kara**) **kariru** 'borrow from X.'
  The honorific-polite **omórai ni nàru** ↑ is polite to the recipient.

2. /GERUND + VERBAL OF RECEIVING/

Parallel to /gerund + verbal of giving/, indicating performing an activity for someone, /gerund + verbal of receiving/ represents receiving the benefit of an activity performed in one's behalf. Compare:
  Sore o yôñde aḡemasita. 'I read that for someone.' *and*
  Sore o yôñde moraimasita. 'I had that read by someone.'

Literally, **yôñde aḡeru** refers to 'giving reading (to the out-group),' and **yôñde morau** to 'receiving reading (by the in-group).' Again, the person from whom the performance of the activity is received is followed by **ni** or ~~**kara**,~~ with a definite preference for **ni**. Examples:
  Gakusee ni syosái o katazùkete moraimasita. 'I had a student straighten up the study.'
  Señsèe ni 'kono 'muzukasii nihoñḡo o yôñde (or **oyómi ni nàtte** ↑) **itadakimasita** ↓ . 'I had the teacher read this difficult Japanese for me.'

Note that the 'had' of these English glosses is used with an implication of benefit. It does NOT mean 'had done' in the sense of causation.
  Compare now:
  Naôsite kudasai. 'Please fix it.' *and*
  Naôsite moratte kudasai. 'Please have it fixed.'

A /gerund + **moraitai** (*or* **itadakitai**)/ pattern is frequently used in indirect—and therefore polite—requests. Instead of directly asking someone to do something, it is common to remark that you'd 'like to have it done.' Often the addressee is obviously the person who is expected to perform the action, but avoiding a direct request is more polite. Thus,
  Kono isu o tonári no heyà ni móttè (i)tte moráitài ñ desu kedo . . 'I'd like to have these chairs taken to the next room, but . . .' (will someone/you do it?)

While in the real world for every giving there is a receiving, not every activity can be described from both points of view. Compare

    Seńsèe ḡa otóotò ni konó syasiñ o kudasaimàsita. 'The teacher gave my brother this photograph.' *and*

    Otóotò ḡa seńsèe ni konó syasiñ o itadakimàsita. 'My brother received this photograph from the teacher.'

Also,

    Arúbàito ḡa atárasìi zîsyo o simátte kuremàsita. 'The part-timer put the new dictionaries away for me.' *and*

    Arúbàito ni atárasìi zîsyo o simátte moraimàsita. 'I had the part-timer put the new dictionaries away for me.' *but*

    Daidokoro o soózi-site moraitài ñ desu kedo . . 'I'd like to have the kitchen cleaned, but . . .'

    Kore, kurúma no toràñku ni iréte moratte kudasài. 'Please have these things put in the trunk of the car.'

The situations described by the last two examples cannot be expressed in terms of a verbal of giving. In those cases which can be expressed in terms of both giving and receiving, the particles are absolutely crucial. An initial /**X ni**/, if hooked up to a verbal of giving occurring later in the sentence, expresses the recipient or benefactor of the action; but linked to a verbal of receiving, it expresses the agent—the person by whom the action is performed.

3. oyasui

The prefix **o-** (or **go-**) associated with neutral politeness to the person addressed (example: **osakana**) or honorific-type politeness to the referent of the word (example: **oḡêñki**),³ is most commonly a nominal prefix. The nominal class includes derivatives of verbals based on the verbal stem, a group which occurs with the **o-** prefix in a number of fixed patterns: /+ **ni nâru**/, /+ **-suru**/.

This prefix may also occur with some adjectivals. Again, depending on the adjectival, the politeness may be directed toward the referent of the adjectival or to the addressee. Thus, if I comment on an expensive item as **otakai**, I am being polite to the person I am addressing, but **oísoḡasìi** implies politeness to the person who is busy—who may be the person addressed or a third person, but never myself (the speaker).

Note that some adjectivals lose their accent when the polite prefix is added.

☠ WARNING: Prefix **o-** does not occur with verbal forms.

4. kimeru/kimaru

Kimeru 'decide' is the operational transitive partner of affective, intransitive **kimaru** 'be(come) decided.' Note the combinations in which they occur:

/**X o kimeru**/ 'decide X, settle X'

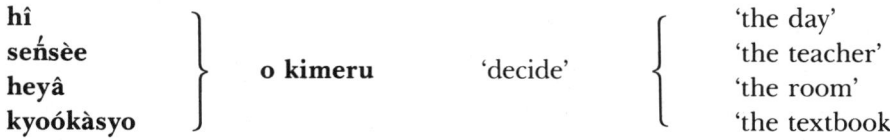

    3. Of course, the referent may *be* the addressee.

/Y ni kimeru/ 'decide on Y, settle on Y'

getúyòobi			'Monday'
Nakámura-señsèe	ni kimeru	'decide on'	'Dr. Nakamura'
konó heyà			'this room'
anó kyookàsyo			'that textbook'

In both sets of examples, **kimeru** can be replaced by **kimaru**, but /X o kimeru/ becomes /X ga kimaru/ 'X gets decided.'

By combining members of the two sets, we form examples like:

Kâiḡi no hî o kayôobi ni kimémàsita. 'We set Tuesday as the day for the conference.'

In other words, in /X o kimeru/ and /X ḡa kimaru/, X is the *category* of the decision (time, place, kind of person or thing), but in /Y ni kimeru or kimaru/, Y is the *particular* item decided on.

We have already encountered sequences of /time nominal + ni/ indicating the time *when* an action or state occurred. In some contexts, **Kayôobi ni kimémàsita.** means that 'I decided [something] on Tuesday.' With time words which occur *without* particle **ni** in 'time when' patterns, there is a contrast.

Îtu kimémàsita ka⤴ 'When did you decide?'

Kyôo kimémàsita. 'I decided today.'

Îtu ni kimémàsita ka⤴ 'When did you decide on?' (as the time for something)

Kyôo ni kimémàsita. 'I decided on today.' (as the time for something)

If a 'time when' pattern occurs in the same sentence as /nominal + **ni** [= goal]/, the 'time when' pattern must precede.[4] Thus:

Tuḡî no kâiḡi wa, getúyòobi ni raísyuu no doyòobi ni kimémàsita. 'For the next conference, on Monday we decided on next Saturday.'

The pattern /X ni suru/ 'make it X,' introduced previously, is similar in meaning to /X ni kimeru/ 'decide on X.' In both cases, /X ni/ is, of course, a goal pattern.

Note also:

kimatte (i)ru 'a decision has been made'

kiméte àru 'it has been decided'[5]

mâda 'kimete (i)nai '[I] haven't yet decided'

Drills

A 1. **Omíyaḡe o moraimàsita.**   **Omiyaḡe o? Dâre ni?**
    'I received a souvenir.'   'A souvenir? From whom?'

---

4. It is also possible to replace the **ni** of goal/manner with another particle of similar (though stiffer, more bookish) meaning: **to**.

5. Emphasizes a state resulting from operational deciding, i.e., 'someone decided it, and the result is now in existence.'

2. **Keésàñki o moráimàsita.**
   'I received a calculator.'

   Keésàñki o? Dâre ni?
   'A calculator? From whom?'

3. **oree**; 4. **kâmera**; 5. **okâsi**

• Repeat this drill, replacing **dâre ni** with **dâre kara** in the responses.

B 1. **Kimí ḡa tukùtta no?—dâiku-sañ ni tanôñda no?**[6]
   'Did *you* make it, or did you ask the carpenter?'

   Zitû wa, dâiku-sañ ni tanôñde, tukûtte morátta ñ desu.
   'Actually, (the fact is) I asked the carpenter and had him make it.'

2. **Kimí ḡa deñwa ni dèta no?—hîsyo ni tanôñda no?**
   'Did *you* answer the phone, or did you ask the secretary?'

   Zitû wa, hîsyo ni tanôñde, dête morátta ñ desu.
   'Actually, (the fact is) I asked the secretary and had her answer the phone.'

3. **yatta/beñgòsi**; 4. **okutta/teñiñ**; 5. **kâita/końsàrutañto**; 6. **reñraku-sita/syâiñ**

C 1. **Kore, ané ḡa tukùtta ñ zya nâi desyoo ka.**
   'Isn't it the case that my (older) sister made this?'

   Êe. Onêesañ ni tukûtte itadakimasita.
   'Yes. Your (older) sister made it for me.'
   (*lit.* I received the making by your sister.)

2. **Kore, hâha ḡa naôsita ñ zya nâi desyoo ka.**
   'Isn't it the case that my mother fixed this?'

   Êe. Okâasañ ni naôsite itadakimasita.
   'Yes. Your mother fixed it for me.'

3. **âni/syookai-sita**; 4. **otóotò/tetúdàtta**; 5. **tîti/sirâbeta**; 6. **sôbo/moʹtte kita**

D 1. **Anó hàisya ni mîte moraù ñ desu ka╱**
   '(Is it that) you're going to have that dentist see you?'

   Ie, hoká no hàisya ni mîte moraitai to omôtte . .
   'No, [I've been] thinking I'd like to have another dentist see me . . .'

2. **Anó kyòosi ni osíete moraù ñ desu ka╱**
   '(Is it that) you're going to have that instructor teach you?'

   Ie, hoká no kyòosi ni osíete moraitài to omôtte . .
   'No, [I've been] thinking I'd like to have another instructor teach me . . .'

3. **uńtèñsyu/turete (i)tte**; 4. **seezika/hanâsite**; 5. **boóekìsyoo/âtte**; 6. **teñiñ/mîsete**

E 1. **Deńwabàñḡoo o morátte kudasài.**
   'Please get the phone number.'

   Deńwabàñḡoo desu ka╱ |Anoo| Dâre ni moráimasyòo ka.
   'The telephone number? Uh . . . Who should I get it from?'

2. **Kusúri o moratte kudasài.**
   'Please get the medicine.'

   Kusúri dèsu ka╱ |Anoo| Dâre ni moráimasyòo ka.

---

6. The stimulus questions are gentle-style.

3. oturi; 4. gôhañ; 5. ohâsi

F 1. **Hîsyo ḡa irû kara, kore kâite moratte kudasai.**
'The secretary is here, so please have him/her write this.'

Hîsyo ni kâite moráù ñ desu neʔ Wakárimàsita.
'(That's) have the secretary write it—right? I understand.'

2. **Doítùziñ ḡa irû kara, kono 'doituḡo no teḡami yôñde moratte kudasai.**
'There's a German here, so please have him/her read this German letter.'

'The medicine? Uh . . . Who should I get it from?'

Doítùziñ ni yôñde moráù ñ desu neʔ Wakárimàsita.
'(That's) have the German read it—right? I understand.'

3. arúbàito no gakusee/koko katázùkete; 4. uñtèñsyu/kono huutoo moʼtè (i)tte;
5. dâiku-sañ/kono tukue naôsite

G 1. **Tukue wa, dôo simâsu ka⤴**
'What are you going to do with the desk?'

Tukúe dèsu ka⤴ Koʼti no heyà e moʼtè kite moraimasyoo.
'The desk? Why don't I have it brought into the room over here.'

2. **Ueki wa, dôo simasu ka⤴**
'What are you going to do with the plant?'

Uéki dèsu ka⤴ Koʼti no heyà e moʼtè kite moraimasyoo.
'The plant? Why don't I have it brought into the room over here.'

3. todana; 4. isu; 5. hôñdana; 6. kono dooḡu

H 1. **Aʼtì o soózi-site moraitài ñ desu ḡa, dâre ni tanómimasyòo ka nêe.**
'I want to have that place over there cleaned up. I wonder who I should ask.'

Aʼtì desu ka⤴ Âa, watási ḡa soozi-site aḡemàsu yo.
'Over there? Oh, *I*'ll clean it up for you.'

2. **Konó ràzio o naôsite moráitài ñ desu ḡa, dâre ni tanómimasyòo ka nêe.**
'I want to have this radio repaired. I wonder who I should ask.'

Konó ràzio desu ka⤴ Âa, watási ḡa naòsite aḡemasu yo.
'This radio? Oh, *I*'ll repair it for you.'

3. niwa/kîree ni site; 4. waapuro/moʼtè kite; 5. arúbàito no gakusee/okutte;
6. syatyoo/mukae ni itte

I 1. **Yasûi desu ka⤴**
'Is it cheap?'

Êe, oyásùi desu yo⤴
'Yes, it's cheap.' /polite/

2. **Takâi desu ka⤴**
'Is it expensive?'

Êe, otákài desu yo⤴
'Yes, it's expensive.' /polite/

3. tuyôi; 4. hayâi; 5. isóḡasìi; 6. atûi

- Repeat this drill, using the polite forms in the questions as well.

J 1. **Anó màdo, akéte itadakitài ñ desu ḡa . .**
'I'd like to have [you] open those windows but . . .' (is it possible?)

  Sâa. Akímàsu ka nêe.
  'Hm. I wonder if they open.'

2. **Konó keesàñki, naôsite itádakitài ñ desu ḡa . .**
'I'd like to have [you] repair this calculator but . . .' (is it possible?)

  Sâa. Naórimàsu ka nêe.
  'Hm. I wonder if it can be repaired.'

3. ué no hikidasi no kaḡì/kâkete; 4. anó ràzio/tukête; 5. ano husuma/sîmete; 6. anó tàkusii/tomete; 7. anó tèrebi/ôókìku site; 8. zikañ/kimete

K 1. **Kore to onazi isu arímàsu ka**↗
'Do you have any chairs the same as this one?'

  Tyoódo onazi isu dè wa gozaímasèñ ḡa, ikâḡa desyoo ka.
  'They're not exactly the same chair, but how about these?'

2. **Kore to onazi osara arímàsu ka**↗
'Do you have any plates the same as this one?'

  Tyoódo onazi osara dè wa gozáimasèñ ḡa, ikâḡa desyoo ka.
  'They're not exactly the same plate, but how about these?'

3. kusuri; 4. hanâ; 5. huutoo

L 1. **Îma simásyòo ka**↗
'Shall I do it now?'

  Êe. Sumímasèñ ḡa, îma sit(e) ôite kudasaimaseñ ka↗
  'Yes. I'm sorry [to bother you], but would you do it now (for future reference)?'

2. **Îma kimémasyòo ka**↗
'Shall I decide it now?'

  Êe. Sumímasèñ ḡa, îma kimét(e) òite kudasaimaseñ ka↗
  'Yes. I'm sorry [to bother you], but would you decide it now (for future reference)?'

3. yomímasyòo; 4. okúrimasyòo; 5. naósimasyòo; 6. motte kimasyòo; 7. katázuke-masyòo; 8. yarímasyòo

- Repeat this drill, substituting **kurémasèñ ka** for **kudásaimasèñ ka** in the responses.

M 1. **Beñḡòsi o kimémàsita yo**↗
'I decided the lawyer.'

  Hee↗ **Dâre ni kimétà ñ desu ka**↗
  'Oh! Who (i.e., which lawyer) is it you decided on?'

2. **Sêki o kimémàsita yo**↗
'I decided the seats.'

  Hee↗ **Dôko ni kimétà ñ desu ka**↗
  'Oh! Where (i.e., the seats located where) is it you decided on?'

3. keñtikuka; 4. kyoositu; 5. tyuumoñ; 6. kâiḡi no hî

N 1. **Beñḡòsi ḡa kimárimàsita yo**↗

  A. **Dâre ni kimáttà ñ desu ka**↗

'The lawyer has been decided.'   'Oh. Who is it that's been decided on?'

2. **Irô g̃a kimárimàsita yo**⁄
'The color has been decided.'
A. **Dôre ni kimáttà ñ desu ka**⁄
'Oh. Which one is it that's been decided on?'

3. **ryokañ**; 4. **arúbàito no hito**; 5. **isya**; 6. **heyâ**

O 1. **Kyôo wa wasyóku ni kimemàsita.**
'For today, I decided on Japanese food.'
Âa, yáppàri wasyóku g̃a ìi desu ka nêe.
'Oh, I suppose Japanese food will be good, after all!'

2. **Asítà wa aítì ni kimémàsita.**
'For tomorrow, I decided on that place.'
Âa, yáppàri aítì g̃a îi desu ka nêe.
'Oh, I suppose that place will be good, after all!'

3. **oree/asítà**; 4. **kuruma/guríìñ no**; 5. **heyâ/tonari**; 6. **tyuumoñ/tokuzyoo**; 7. **Siñzyuku màde/tikatetu**

P 1. **Zyûg̃oo wa, g̃es·sûi·kîñ ni kimárimàsita kara . .**
'For class, it's been decided on Mon-Wed-Fri, so . . .' (plan accordingly)
Âa, yáppàri g̃es·sûi·kîñ ni narímàsita ka.
'Oh, is it (*lit.* did it become) Mon-Wed-Fri after all.'

2. **Oyasumi wa, asâtte ni kimárimàsita kara . .**
'For a day off, it's been decided on the day after tomorrow, so . . .' (plan accordingly).
Âa, yáppàri asâtte ni narímàsita ka.
'Oh, is it (*lit.* did it become) the day after tomorrow after all.'

3. **nomîmono/wâiñ**; 4. **kono isu/ué no heyà**; 5. **kâig̃i/âsa kara**

Q 1. **Mâdo wa, zêñbu sîmete arímàsu kara . .**
'The windows have all been shut, so . . .' (you don't have to worry about them).
A, dôo mo. Sîmete itadaite, tasúkarimàsita.
'Oh, thanks. It's really been a help, having had you shut them.'

2. **Kag̃i wa, zêñbu kâkete arímàsu kara . .**
'The locks have all been locked, so . . .' (you don't have to worry about them).
A, dôo mo. Kâkete itadaite, tasúkarimàsita.
'Oh, thanks. It's really been a help, having had you lock them.'

3. **sig̃oto/tanôñde**; 4. **reñraku/site**; 5. **gomî/sutete**; 6. **daidokoro/katázùkete**

R 1. **Mâdo wa, zêñbu sîmete arímàsu yo**⁄
'The windows have all been shut.'
A, sîmet(e) oite kudásàtta ñ desu ka. Tasúkarimàsita.
'Oh, did you shut them (in advance) for me? What a help!'

2. **Otyâwañ wa, zêñbu simátte arimàsu yo**✓   **A, simátt(e) òite kudásàtta ñ desu ka. Tasukarimàsita.**
'The bowls have all been put away.'   'Oh, did you put them away (in advance) for me? What a help!'

3. **amâdo/akete**; 4. **hikídasi no nàka/katázùkete**; 5. **kyôo no siḡoto/site**

Application Exercises

A1. Extend the Application Exercises in Section A to include requests to have tasks performed by designated individuals and follow-up descriptions of what happened. Example:

X-sañ. Y-sañ ni 'ano teeburu o kotíra ni mottè kite moratte kudasai. 'Mr/s. X. Have Mr/s. Y bring that table over here.'

After the direct request is carried out,

Y-sañ ni 'kono teeburu o 'asoko kara kotíra ni mottè kite moraimasita. 'I had Mr/s. Y bring this table here from over there.' *or*

Y-sañ wa 'X-sañ ni . . . móttè kite aḡemasita. 'Mr/s. Y brought . . . for Mr/s. X.'

2. Describe activities you would like to have performed and inquire about possibilities for carrying them out. Have other class members respond appropriately. Examples:

Kono tokee o naôsite moraitai kedo, dôko ḡa îi desyoo ka nêe. 'I'd like to have this watch repaired. I wonder what place would be good.'

Señsèe ni 'uti e irássyàtte itádakitài ñ desu kedo, îtu ḡa yorósìi desyoo ka✓ 'I'd like to have you come to my home, Teacher. When would be good?'

3. Engage in short conversations regarding decisions. Have student A inquire about the area of the decision, and B announce the actual decision. Examples:

Môo raíneñ no señsèe o kimémàsita ka✓ 'Did you decide next year's teacher yet?'
  Êe. Yamáda-señsèe ni kimémàsita. 'Yes. We decided on Dr. Yamada.'

Môo kâiḡi no hî wa kimárimàsita ka✓ 'Was the day for the conference decided?'
  Êe. Mokúyòobi ni kimárimàsita. 'Yes. It was decided that Thursday [would be the day].'

4. While one student describes his/her living quarters (real or imaginary) in detail, have other students draw an overall plan that fits the description. Include not only identification of rooms but also the placement of the doors, windows, and furniture, practicing the new words that have been introduced in this lesson.

B. Core Conversations: Substitution

Return now to the Core Conversations and practice them with appropriate substitutions. Include subsequent questioning regarding what happened in each conversation.

SECTION C

Eavesdropping

Answer the following on the basis of the accompanying tape. A = the first speaker and B, the second speaker, in each conversation.

1a. What is the topic of discussion?
  b. How did B acquire it?
  c. What is A's reaction?
2a. What is the topic of discussion?
  b. What happened to it?
  c. Why is B not inconvenienced?
3a. What is the topic of discussion?
  b. Who received them from whom?
  c. What comment does B make about items in this category? With what explanation?
4a. What is A looking for?
  b. Why can't A find it?
  c. Why is A upset?
  d. What explanation does B offer?
5a. How is the temperature outside and inside? Give details.
  b. What physical response to cold is mentioned?
6a. What request does A make of B?
  b. What is B's two-part response?
7a. What does A offer to do?
  b. How does B react to the offer?
  c. What is B's reaction to what then occurs?
8a. What is A's mistaken suggestion about the item under discussion?
  b. What is it actually? Acquired how?
  c. What does B request?
9a. Why does B ask A to wait?
  b. What alternative does A propose?
10a. Where are the tatami rooms?
  b. Who is occupying them now?
  c. What personal preference does B mention?
11a. What is the probable setting of this conversation?
  b. Why does A apologize?
  c. What is B's reaction?
  d. What does B offer to do?
12a. Why was A able to return home early? Give details.
  b. What does B check on?
  c. Who are A and B? Offer a probable identification of their relationship.
13a. What is A going to do for B?
  b. What does B select?
  c. What is the problem?
  d. How is the problem resolved?
14a. Why does A request help?
  b. Why does B ask A to wait?
  c. What does A ask B to do?
  d. What items does B ask about?
  e. What is B told to do with those items?
  f. What is A's probable relationship to B?
15a. How is B's baby's current health?
  b. Describe the baby's general physical condition.
16a. What is the problem with this plant?
  b. What does B offer to do?
  c. How does A tell B to handle the task?
  d. What is to be done with that small plant?

17a. What kind of work has B decided on?
  b. What family connection is there?
  c. What different expectation did A have regarding B's future employment? Why?
  d. What influenced B's decision?
18a. What does B want to do? By when?
  b. What difficulty is B encountering?
  c. What would A like to do?
  d. What is A going to do?
19a. Why is B still in the office?
  b. Why is A concerned about B?
  c. What does A offer to do?
  d. What task does B specify?
20a. What happened to B's finger? When? How? Give details.
  b. What does A assume about the present situation?
  c. What is the actual situation?
21a. What is B's immediate problem?
  b. What does A offer?
  c. What other problems does B sometimes have?
  d. What help does B regularly seek?
  e. What possible solution does A offer?
  f. How does B react to the suggestion?

Utilization

(For each item, to the extent possible, develop a short conversation that includes at least a stimulus and/or a response.)

  1. Tell your colleague that you received a letter from a German friend in German, but you didn't understand it, so you had a student read it for you.
  2. A friend is admiring the tape recorder you are using. Explain that it's not yours. Prof. Hayashi kindly lent it to you.
  3. You want to send a message to a Japanese business associate in Japanese. Ask a Japanese friend if he'll write it for you.
  4. Ask your helper if she finished watering the flowers and plants yet.
  5. Tell your helper that you're going to use the room next door for a conference from 11:00 on, so [he should] open the windows now.
  6. A friend has suggested closing the windows. Explain that it gets hot starting at noon every day, so ask her to leave them open.
  7. There's something wrong with your computer. Ask a close friend if he'll look at it for you.
  8. Your Japanese instructor has asked to borrow an English-language magazine. Tell her that you will give it to her, inasmuch as you have finished reading it.
  9. A friend is looking for yesterday's newspaper. Tell her that unfortunately you threw all the old papers away this morning, but yesterday's paper may still be in the library.
  10. Exclaim to a friend that this place has been put in perfect order, and express wonder as to who did it.
  11. A friend has just described some difficult work he is about to begin. Ask who will give him help.
  12. A colleague is concerned about getting a visitor to the train station at a time when he has an appointment. Offer to see her off for him.
  13. Tell a colleague that you want to send these plates to England. Check on whether the post office in this neighborhood will do (*lit.* 'Will it be all right if it's the post office in this neighborhood?').
  14. Tell a colleague that your calculator has broken. Inquire as to who might fix it for you.

15. Tell a friend that you need a map to the Toranomon Hospital. Ask if she will draw one for you.

16. A stranger, who appears to be a typewriter repairman, has just entered the office. Ask if he is going to look at the typewriters for you.

17. Find out who gave your friend his map to Mr. Ito's house.

18. There are some brochures on top of the receptionist's desk. Ask politely if it is all right to take (*lit.* receive) one.

19. Ask the secretary to have the division manager read this letter.

20. Ask your colleague to have Nakamura (the **arúbàito no gakusee**) (a) leave the computer on; (b) wash the coffeecups; (c) wipe the top of this table; (d) mail this letter.

21. Confirm your assumption that your colleague is tired, and suggest that you make tea.

22. Find out where in Tokyo (it is that) one buys (a) inexpensive chests; (b) comfortable chairs; (c) tables and desks and such; (d) furniture of this type [showing picture].

23. In explaining the present location of particular items, tell a friend that you had Takashi: (a) take the new desk to the second floor; (b) put the kitchen utensils into that bottom drawer; (c) put the suitcase in the entry hall; (d) put the rice bowls away in the kitchen cupboard; (e) bring the small plant from outside, and put it on top of the table in the study; (f) put all the small things on top of the table in the bedroom into the drawer of the chest in that room.

24. Your friend looks upset. Ask her what happened.

25. Explain to a colleague (a) that you've caught cold and have a headache; (b) that you've been using the computer since this morning and your shoulders have stiffened up.

26. In reply to the doctor's question as to what (*lit.* what place) hurts, explain (a) that you have an earache; a stomachache; a backache; (b) that you cut your finger; (c) that your right eye has become red and is very painful.

27. A colleague has inquired about a mutual acquaintance's health. Explain that he has a bad heart (i.e., his heart is bad), and he has been in the hospital since last week.

28. Exclaim on how big (in body) a colleague's young son is.

29. You've been having some problems with your back. Tell the doctor that until yesterday it wasn't too bad, but now it's become very painful.

30. Complain that you caught cold last week, and it just doesn't get better.

31. Exclaim politely on how hot it is.

32. Tell a colleague that the day of the next conference has been decided, but you wonder who made the decision.

33. You are describing last evening's dinner at a restaurant. Explain that they had both meat and fish, but you decided on fish.

34. Complain that you really would like to get a decision on next week's classroom, but no one will decide!

35. Exclaim on your exhaustion.

36. Offer to help your professor.

37. Express thanks to a colleague for his help, indicating how much it has meant to you.

38. Apologize for interrupting (a) as you begin a conversation; (b) as you end.

39. Thank your helper for her trouble.

40. Express thanks to your professor for coming all the way to your home.

41. A friend is wearing a pretty sweater. Ask her if she made it herself.

42. You've just discovered that all the dishes have been put in the cupboards. Ask Kei if she did it alone.

43. You've heard that a friend drove to Osaka last week. Ask if he went in his own car.

44. A part-time helper did some special work at your office. Ask your colleague if he has already given the helper payment (i.e., a token of thanks).

45. You are about to go down for the third time. Yell for help!!!

Check-up

1. What are the five verbals of giving discussed in this lesson? Describe how they differ in meaning. (A-SP1)
2. What is the difference in meaning between /**tomodati ḡa** + verbal of giving/ and /**tomodati ni** + verbal of giving/? (A-SP1)
3. Under what circumstances does **kureru** occur as the equivalent of 'give to you'? (A-SP1)
4. Compare

    Hôñ o kurémàsita. *and*

    Hôñ o yôñde kuremasita.

and then discuss the use of /gerund + verbal of giving/ in general. (A-SP2)

5. Describe the use of the verbal *kureru* in request patterns. How do they differ from patterns that include forms of the verbal **kudásàru**? (A-SP3)
6. What two verbals of receiving are discussed in this lesson? How do they differ in meaning? (B-SP1)
7. In /**X ḡa morau**/, /**X kara morau**/, and /**X ni morau**/, in which X is a person, what is the relationship between X and **morau**? (B-SP1)
8. Compare

    Hôñ o moráimàsita. *and*

    Hôñ o yôñde moraimasita.

    Also,

    Hôñ o yôñde kudasai. *and*

    Hôñ o yôñde moratte kudasai. *and*

    Hôñ o yôñde agete kudasâi.

    And finally,

    Hôñ o kaítài ñ desu kedo.. *and*

    Hôñ o kátte moraitài ñ desu kedo.. (B-SP2)

9. What is the relationship between **kimaru** and **kimeru**? Which of these verbals may be linked to a /nominal + **ḡa**/ phrase? A /nominal + **o**/ phrase? A /nominal + **ni**/ phrase? Define each possible combination and give examples. (B-SP3)

Lesson 18

SECTION A

Core Conversations

1(J)a. Haâi.
  b. Mâa, Burâuñ-sañ. Yôku irássyaimàsita.
  c. Kotíra kòso. Sâa, dôozo oágari-kudasài.

2(N)a. Kore, tumáràhai monô desu ğa..
  b. Ie, hoñ no kimóti dakè desu kara..
  c. Iie.

3(N)a. Ûmi mo yamâ mo mîete, totémo kìree na tokórò desu nêe.
  b. Hâi. Zyâa, sitûree-simasu.

4(J)a. Okúti ni àu ka dôo ka wakárimasèñ kedo, dôozo.
  b. Dôozo. Samémàsu kara, goéñryo nàku.

5(N)a. Môo koñna zikañ dèsu ka. Sôrosoro sitûree-simasu. Osókù made 'ozyama-site..
  b. Arîgatoo gozaimasu. Goméñ-kudasài.

(N)a. Burâuñ desu ğa..
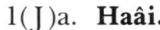
  b. Señzitu wa dôo mo sitûree-simasita.
  c. Sitûree-simasu.

(J)a. Sore wa wâzawaza dôo mo. Okízùkai itadaite, moósiwake arimasèñ.
  b. Zyâa, sek̀kakù desu kara, aríğàtàku tyoódai-itasimàsu. Arîgatoo gozaimasu.

(J) Osôre-irimasu. Dôozo oráku ni nasàtte kudasai.

(N)a. Arîgatoo gozaimasu. Dôozo okámai nàku....
  b. Hâi. Itádakimàsu.

(J) Tońde mo arimasèñ. Matá iràsite kudasai.

English Equivalents

1(J)a. Ye-es!
  b. Oh, [Sue] Brown! I'm so glad you've come.
  c. (No, excuse *me*.) Please come in (*lit.* come up).
2(N)a. This is [just] a trifle but . . . (please accept it).
  b. No, it's nothing (*lit.* just my feeling only), so . . .
  c. Don't mention it.
3(N)a. With both the ocean and mountains in view, this is a very beautiful place, isn't it.
  b. Thank you. I will.
4(J)a. I don't know whether this will suit your taste or not, but please [have some].
  b. Please have some. It will get cold, so don't hold back.
5(N)a. Is it this (kind of) time already? I'll be going now. [Forgive me,] bothering you until late.
  b. Thank you. Goodbye.

(N)a. It's [Sue] Brown . . .
  b. (Excuse my rudeness the other day.)
  c. Thank you.

(J)a. Thank you [for bringing] that specially [for me]. I'm sorry to have you take this trouble for me.
  b. Well, you've gone to all this trouble, so I'm going to accept it with gratitude. Thank you.

(J) Thank you. Please make yourself comfortable.

(N)a. Thank you. Please don't go to any trouble.
  b. All right. I'll have some.

(J) Heavens, no! Please come again.

Breakdowns
(and Supplementary Vocabulary)

1. **haâi** — ye-es!
   mâa — oh, my! /exclamation of surprise; F/
   yôku irássyaimàsita — welcome!
   señzitu *or*
   +**konaida** — the other day
   +**sibâraku** — a while (of indeterminate length)
   +**Sibâraku desu.** — It's been a while (since our last meeting)!
   sâa — here, now! come, now! /exclamation of urging/
   ağaru /-u; ağatta/ — go/come up; rise
   oáğari-kudasài (SP1) — please come up

2. **wâzawaza** — purposely, specially
   kizûkai/okízùkai — concern; solicitude
   kimoti — feeling, mood
   hoñ no kimoti — mere feeling, just feeling
   arígatài /-katta/ (SP2) — is grateful; is obliged
   tyoodai-suru ↓ — accept
   arígàtàku tyoodai-suru ↓ — accept gratefully
3. **mièru /-ru; mîeta/** — be visible
   +**kêsiki** — scenery
   rakû ni suru/oraku ni nasâru ↑ — make comfortable
4. **âu /-u; âtta/** — match up with
   (o)kúti ni àu — suit one's taste
   âu ka dôo ka wakárànai (SP3) — can't tell whether it matches or not
   okámai nàku (SP4) — don't bother; don't go to any trouble
   samêru /-ru; sâmeta/ — get cold
   eñryo/goeñryo — reserve, holding back
   goéñryo nàku — don't hold back
5. **sôrosoro** — slowly; gradually

Terms describing terrain

simâ	island	**mizúùmi**	lake
minato	harbor	**ikê**	pond
oka	hill	**sakura**	cherry
tanî	valley	**mâtu**	pine
kawâ	river	**take**	bamboo

Miscellaneous Notes

The CC of this lesson section present a typical informal visit to a private home. As might be expected, this kind of situation involves a great deal of ritual language, which should be memorized verbatim. It should be internalized to the point where it will pour forth effortlessly when needed. The style throughout is careful, with distal-style predicates. Politeness is particularly evident in the language of the hostess.

1. CC1 covers the arrival: Sue Brown, a graduate student, has come to the Carter home for a visit with Mrs. Carter, the Japanese wife of Mr. Carter of the Continental Bank.

(J)a and (N)a. Mrs. Carter responds to the bell, and Sue Brown calls out identifying herself.

(N)b. This ritual expression covers virtually any kind of recent direct contact (*not* rudeness). A literal translation of it makes no more sense in English than would the use of **Dôo simasu ka** in Japanese as an equivalent of English 'How do you do,' for example.

If Sue Brown and Mrs. Carter had not been in contact recently, we would expect **Hisásiburi dèsu.** or **Sibâraku desu.**

(J)c. **Kotíra kòso**, transferring applicability to oneself—i.e., **kotira** 'this side'—is the ritual reply.

Sâa, in this context an expression of urging, must be distinguished from **sâa** 'hmm.'

The use of verbal **aḡaru** 'go/come up,' 'rise' reflects the stepping up into the hallway from the lower level of the entry of a Japanese-style home. It covers not only the going/coming up of people, but also the rise of prices, salaries, rents, etc.

Aḡaru is the intransitive partner of transitive **aḡeru** 'raise' (**te o aḡeru** 'raise one's hand'; **atámà o aḡeru** 'lift up one's head'), whose derived meaning is 'give,' originally viewed as a polite giving upward to an out-group. Both **aḡaru** and **aḡeru** are operational.

(N)c. The ritual use of **sitûree-simasu** in this situation covers the "rudeness" of entering someone else's home.

2. CC2 covers the presentation of a gift, a regular procedure in paying a visit. Traditionally the gift is not opened in the presence of the giver, although this is not always true today, particularly when the giver is a foreigner. In this kind of situation, the giver regularly belittles the value of the gift, while the recipient, before accepting it, apologizes for the fact that the giver took so much trouble on his/her behalf.

(J)b. **Tyoodai-suru**, like **itadaku**, is a humble-polite(↓) equivalent of **tabêru, nômu**, and **morau**. Unlike **itadaku**, which is native Japanese in origin, it is based on Chinese roots. The two words occur in similar contexts, except that only **itadaku** can follow gerunds in the **(site) itadaku** 'have [something] done' pattern.

3. CC3 covers small talk preceding the serving of refreshments.

(N)a. **Miêru** occurred previously as an equivalent of 'appear,' 'put in an appearance.' Here it occurs as a double-**ḡa** affective verbal referring to visibility, balancing **kikoeru**, which refers to audibility. Thus: **Dôre ḡa miênai ñ desu ka**✓ 'Which one can't you see?' **Dâre ḡa miênai ñ desu ka**✓ 'Who can't see?' or 'Whom can't you see?'

(N)b. Here the ubiquitous **sitûree-simasu** occurs as an apology for relaxing and making oneself comfortable in someone else's home.

4. CC4 covers the offering of refreshments, an expected procedure during a visit to someone's home. Even a visitor to a Japanese business office is frequently served tea or coffee. The host(ess) regularly indicates some reservation about what s/he is serving and urges the guest not to hold back. The guest, in reply, requests that the host(ess) not go to any trouble (obviously at a point beyond which any such adjustment can be made).

(N)a. **Okamai** is a polite nominal based on the stem of the verbal **kamau** 'mind,' 'care,' 'trouble [oneself] about.' See SP4, following, for a discussion of the pattern.

(J)b. Note that things which become cold (**samêru**) are then **tumetai**, not **samûi**. In other words, **samêru** means **tumétaku nàru**, not **sâmûku naru**. **Eñryo** 'holding back,' 'reserve,' 'standing on ceremony' is highly regarded in Japanese society. Note also: **eñryo-suru** 'hold back,' 'stand on ceremony'; **eñryo-site oku** 'hold back for the time being,' 'take a rain check.'

5. CC5 covers the departure, which includes an apology by the visitor for intruding upon the hostess and staying so long, countered by the latter's denial and invitation to the visitor to come again.

(N)a. Now **sitûree-simasu** becomes an apology for leaving. Given the many different situations covered by this expression, the appropriateness of **señzitu wa sitûree-simasita** upon meeting up with someone again after recent contact is hardly surprising.

(N)b. Note the use of **goméñ-kudasài** as a farewell, which is similar to its use on the telephone.

Structural Patterns

1. POLITE REQUESTS: oágari-kudasài

In a society as hierarchically structured as the Japanese, it is not surprising that there are many different request patterns, differing only in their level of politeness and formality. Thus far, we have encountered the following types:

Yôñde.
Yôñde kurenai?
Yôñde kurenai ka.
Yôñde kuremaseñ ka⤴
Yôñde kudasai.
Yôñde kudásarànai?
Yôñde kudásaimasèñ ka⤴
Oyómi ni nàtte.
Oyómi ni nàtte kudasai.
Oyómi ni nàtte kudásarànai?
Oyómi ni nàtte kudásaimasèñ ka⤴

All these combinations are requests that someone read. Of the above patterns, the first is the most casual and informal; those that include forms of **kureru** are less polite than those including corresponding forms of **kudásaru**↑; distal-style forms in **-maseñ** are more formal and careful than the corresponding direct-style forms in **-(a)nai**; the imperative **kudásài** is more direct and confrontational than negative question forms of the same verbal; **oyómi ni nàtte**↓ is more polite than **yôñde**.

We now add a new request pattern: a nominal consisting of /**o-** + verbal stem/ compounded with **-kudasài**. One example of this pattern occurred earlier in the combination **Syôosyoo omáti-kudasài**. 'Please wait a moment.' With its **-kudasài** ending, this combination is direct and imperative; but the polite /**o-** + verbal stem/ makes the combination more polite than /gerund + **kudásài**/.

Also possible in this pattern are polite nominals referring to actions, which compound with **-suru** to form verbals. Examples: **gosyóokai-kudasài** 'please introduce'; **gosóodañ-kudasài** 'please consult'; **goréñraku-kudasài** 'please get in touch.'

As an extension of this pattern, it is also possible to replace **-kudasài** with the less confrontational negative question forms:

Oágari-kudasarànai?
Oágari-kudasaimasèñ ka⤴

And all occurrences of direct imperative **kudásài** can be made into the slightly more deferential distal imperatives by the addition of **-màse** (cf. **irássyài** and **irássyaimàse**). Examples:

Oágari-kudasaimàse.
Oyómi ni nàtte kudasaimase.

2. SPECIAL POLITE ADJECTIVAL FORMS: arígatài > arîgatoo

Thus far, we have discussed /plain versus polite/ and /direct versus distal/ in relation to verbal and /nominal + **da**/ predicates. For adjectivals, only the distinction between direct and distal (**takâi** and **takâi desu**) and the occurrence of the polite prefix **o-** before regular adjectival forms (**otakai**) have been introduced. Actually, there is another polite adjectival pattern involving special forms, which we have been using in two of our most common ritual expressions: **ohayoo** and **arîḡatoo**. Study the following:

	Plain	Polite
Direct	hayâi arîḡatài	ohayoo arîḡatoo
Distal	hayâi desu arîḡatài desu	oháyoo gozaimàsu arîḡatoo gozaimasu

A similar chart can be made for adjectivals in general, subject to the following restrictions:

1. In forming the special polite forms, **-ai** and **-oi** adjectival endings become **-oo, -ui** becomes **-uu**, and **-ii** becomes **-yuu**.[1] Usually, the new form is unaccented.
2. Whether or not **o-** is also prefixed to the adjectival must be learned for each adjectival.
3. Except for those forms which occur in ritualized contexts, special polite adjectivals occur only in distal-style, followed by a form of **gozáimàsu**.
4. These special polite forms are more polite than /**o-** + regular forms/.
5. Except for those used ritually, which occur very commonly, these special forms are extremely polite and are becoming comparatively rare. Insofar as they do occur, they are used most commonly in formal speeches and in very polite conversation, especially among women. For those learning Japanese as a foreign language, they are important primarily for passive recognition rather than active use.

Examples:

takóo gozaimàsu	< takâi
tukáitoo gozaimàsu	< tukaitai
(o)tuyóo gozaimàsu	< tuyôi
toóo gozaimàsu	< tooi
osámuu gozaimàsu	< samûi
oátuu gozaimàsu	< atûi
oókyuu gozaimàsu	< oókìi
(o)yorósyuu gozaimàsu	< yorosii

3. EMBEDDED ALTERNATE QUESTIONS

In cases where the answer to a yes-no question is unknown, forgotten, not remembered, and so forth, the question, in direct style, can be embedded within a longer sentence, followed immediately by a second direct-style question to form an alternate question pattern. The second question may occur in one of three forms:

1. **dôo ka** (direct-style equivalent of **dôo desu ka**) 'how is it?' Examples:

   Oísìi ka dôo ka, wakárimasèn̄. 'I can't tell whether it will taste good or not (*lit.* does it taste good, how is it?).'

   Daízyòobu ka dôo ka, sirímasèn̄. 'I don't know whether it's all right or not.'

---

1. Note that a simple rule of this kind is impossible if one uses Hepburn romanization, in which **ookyuu** > **okyu**, but **yorosyuu** > **yoroshu**.

Môo 'huutoo o tanôñda ka dôo ka, obôete imáseñ. 'I don't remember whether I ordered envelopes (already) or not.'

2. An opposite or negative of the first question. Examples:
   Takâi ka yasûi ka, gozôñzi desu ka⌐ 'Do you know whether it's expensive or cheap?'
   Asita kûru ka kônai ka, zoñzímaseñ. 'I don't know whether s/he is coming tomorrow or not (coming).'
3. A second, free alternative. Examples:
   Eéḡo de hanàsita ka, nihóñḡo de hanàsita ka, sirímaseñ. 'I don't know whether they talked in English or (talked in) Japanese.'
   Kânozyo, kinoo utí ni ità ka, rûsu datta ka, sitte (i)màsu ka⌐ 'Do you know whether she was at home or out (of the house) yesterday?'

Note that in this pattern, once again, **dà** (but not **dàtta**) is dropped before **ka**.

☠ WARNING: This pattern is appropriate only for embedding yes-no questions. For embedded information questions (comparable to English 'I forgot who is coming') see 18B-SP2, following.

4. **Okámai nàku.**

An adjectival in its **-i** form in sentence-final position ends a major sentence and makes a statement in the direct-style:
   Omósiròi. 'It's interesting.'
   Yorósìi.[2] 'It's fine.'
   Hayâi. 'It's fast.' *or* 'It's early.'

A few adjectivals in their **-ku** form may end minor sentences as wishes or indirect expressions of request: 'Let it be ———.' Examples:
   Yorosiku. 'May things go well [between us].' *or* 'Treat me favorably.'
   Okámai nàku. 'Don't go to any trouble.' (*lit.* 'Let there be no special concern on your part.')
   Goéñryo nàku. 'Don't stand on ceremony.' (*lit.* 'Let there be no holding back on your part.')

These kinds of **-ku** adjectival forms of course occur within sentences as manner expressions:
   Eñryo nàku itádakimàsu. 'I'll accept [some] without holding back.'

Drills

A 1. **Otooto, yobímasyòo ka.**   **Hâi. Zya, tyôtto oyóbi-kudasài.**
   'Shall I call my (younger) brother?'   'Yes, (then) would you (just) call him?'
   2. **Deñwa, kakémasyòo ka.**   **Hâi. Zya, tyôtto okáke-kudasài.**
   'Shall I telephone?'   'Yes, (then) would you (just) call?'
   3. **kore/irémasyòo**; 4. **husuma/simémasyòo**; 5. **deñwa/kawárimasyóo**

---

2. Unaccented adjectivals regularly acquire an accent in sentence-final position.

B 1. **Reńraku-simasyòo ka.**   Hâi. Dê wa, âto de goréńraku-kudasài.
   'Shall I get in touch?'   'Yes, well then, would you get in touch later?'

2. **Tyuúmoń-simasyòo ka.**   Hâi. Dê wa, âto de gotyúumoń-kudasài.
   'Shall I order?'   'Yes, well then, would you order later?'

3. **soodań**; 4. **syookai**

C 1. **Osámuu gozaimàsu nêe.**   Hońtoo ni samùi desu nêe.
   'Isn't it cold!' /polite/   'It really is cold, isn't it!'

2. **Owákoo gozaimàsu nêe.**   Hońtoo ni wakài desu nêe.
   'Isn't s/he young!' /polite/   'S/he really is young, isn't s/he!'

3. **otuyoo**; 4. **oatuu**; 5. **oyorosyuu**; 6. **onağoo**

D 1. **Dâre ğa miênai ń desu ka↗**   Yamâğuti-sań desu. Yamâğuti-sań ğa miênai ń desu.
   'Who (is it who) can't see?'³   'It's Mr/s. Yamaguchi. (It's the case that) Mr/s. Yamaguchi can't see.'

2. **Dâre ğa wakáránai ń desu ka↗**   Yamâğuti-sań desu. Yamâğuti-sań ğa wakáránai ń desu.
   'Who (is it who) doesn't understand?'   'It's Mr/s. Yamaguchi. (It's the case that) Mr/s. Yamaguchi doesn't understand.'

3. **iranai**; 4. **dekîru**; 5. **atámà ğa itâi**; 6. **sakána ğa kirai nà**; 7. **mimî ğa tooi**; 8. **kikoenai**

E 1. **Dôre ğa miênai ń desu ka↗**   Aré dèsu. Aré ğa miênai ń desu.
   'Which one can't you see?'   'It's that one. (It's that) I can't see that one.'

2. **Dôre ğa wakáránai ń desu ka↗**   Aré dèsu. Aré ğa wakaránai ń desu.
   'Which one don't you understand?'   'It's that one. (It's that) I don't understand that one.'

3. **iru**; 4. **dekînai**; 5. **kirái nà**; 6. **sukî zya nâi**; 7. **kikoeru**

F 1. **Kokó karà wa, ûmi mo yamâ mo miêru desyoo?**   Êe. Ûmi mo yamâ mo mîete, kêkkoo na kêsiki desu nêe.
   'From here you can see both the ocean and the mountains, can't you?'   'Yes. With both the ocean and the mountains in view, it's wonderful scenery, isn't it!'

2. **Kokó karà wa, minato mo simâ mo miêru desyoo?**   Êe. Minato mo simâ mo mîete, kêkkoo na kêsiki desu nêe.
   'From here you can see both the harbor and the island, can't you?'   'Yes. With both the harbor and the island in view, it's wonderful scenery, isn't it!'

3. **yamâ/tanî**; 4. **ikê/oka**; 5. **kî/hanâ**; 6. **ûmi/sakura**; 7. **kawâ/mizúùmi**; 8. **mâtu/ûmi**

3. Or 'Who is it you can't see?'

G 1. **Samûi desyoo?—asoko.**
'It's cold, isn't it?—that place.'

Sâa. Samûi ka dôo ka, wakárimaseñ nêe.
'Hm. It's not clear whether it's cold or not (*lit.* how it is).'

2. **Koómùiñ desyoo?—kâre.**
'He's a government employee, isn't he?—him.'

Sâa. Koómùiñ ka dôo ka, wakárimaseñ nêe.
'Hm. It's not clear whether he's a government employee or not (*lit.* how it is).'

3. **daízì/kore**; 4. **tukârete (i)ru/ano kodomo**; 5. **yawárakài/sonó nikù**; 6. **tukáinikùi/koñna nàihu**; 7. **sâmeta/ano osake**; 8. **muzúkasìkatta/señsèe no eeḡo**

H 1. **Aťtakài desyoo?—si-ḡátu-ḡòro.**
'It's warm, isn't it?—around April.'

Iya, aťtakài ka aťtàkàku nâi ka, tyôtto wakárimaseñ nêe.
'No, it's a bit unclear whether it's warm or not.'

2. **Tanî desyoo?—ano heñ.**
'It's a valley, isn't it?—that area.'

Iya, tanî ka tanî zya nâi ka, tyôtto wakárimaseñ nêe.
'No, it's a bit unclear whether it's a valley or not.'

3. **naôru/Morimoto-sañ no byooki**; 4. **sûḡu/kâiḡi no zikañ**; 5. **komâtta/miñna**; 6. **kosyóo dàtta/ano waapuro**; 7. **tâkàkatta/sonó kudàmono**

I 1. **Omósiròi desyoo?—konó hòñ.**
'It's interesting, isn't it?—this book.'

Sâa. Omósiròi ka tumàrànai ka, obôete (i)máseñ nêe.
'Hm. I don't remember whether it's interesting or dull.'

2. **Miḡí dàtta desyoo?—anó susìya.**
'It was on the right, wasn't it?—that sushi shop.'

Sâa. Miḡí dàtta ka hidári dàtta ka, obôete (i)máseñ nêe.
'Hm. I don't remember whether it was on the right or the left.'

3. **karâi/are**; 4. **aite (i)ru/geñkañ no to**; 5. **uê/kyoositu**; 6. **tukêta/koñpyùutaa**

J 1. **Ikê desu ka⤴—mizúùmi desu ka⤴**
'Is it [what we're discussing] a pond, or is it a lake?'

Sâa. Ikê ka mizúùmi ka, zitû wa watási mo yòku siránài ñ desu.
'Hm. (The fact is) actually *I* don't know whether it's a pond or a lake, either.'

2. **Sutémàsita ka⤴—tôtt(e) okimasita ka⤴**
'Did s/he throw it away, or keep it (for future reference)?'

Sâa. Sutétà ka tôtt(e) oita ka, zitû wa watási mo yòku siránài ñ desu.
'Hm. (The fact is) actually *I* don't know whether s/he threw it away or kept it, either.'

3. **yawárakài desu/katâi desu**; 4. **komárimàsu/kamáimaseñ**; 5. **onêesañ desu/imóotosañ dèsu**; 6. **îma sûḡu desu/moó sukòsi âto desu**

K 1. **Ikánài ñ desu neŝ**
'(It's that) you're not going to go—right?'

Iya, ikánài ka dôo ka, wakárimaseñ.
'No, it isn't clear whether I won't go, or what [I'll do].'

2. **Moráwanài ñ desu neŝ**
'(It's that) you're not going to accept [it]—right?'

Iya, moráwanài ka dôo ka, wakárimaseñ.
'No, it isn't clear whether I won't accept [it], or what [I'll do].'

3. **naósànai**; 4. **okuranai**; 5. **yoranai**; 6. **sasiağenai**; 7. **tanómànai**

L 1. **Okúti ni àu ka dôo ka wakárimaseñ ğa; konó kèeki, dôozo goéñryo nàku.**
'I don't know whether this will suit your taste or not, but please [have some of] this cake (without holding back).'

Osôre-irimasu. Eńryo nàku itádakimàsu. . . . Âa, oisii—konó kèeki.
'Thank you. I'll have some (without holding back). . . . Oh, it's delicious—this cake.'

2. **Okúti ni àu ka dôo ka wakárimaseñ ğa; konó onìku, dôozo goéñryo nàku.**
'I don't know whether this will suit your taste or not, but please [have some of] this meat (without holding back).'

Osôre-irimasu. Eńryo nàku itádakimàsu. . . . Âa, oisii—konó onìku.
'Thank you. I'll have some (without holding back). . . . Oh, it's delicious—this meat.'

3. **osakana**; 4. **osasimi**; 5. **tori**; 6. **pâi**

M 1. **Tyuúka-ryòori, osuki desyoo? Kôñbañ dôo desu ka⤴**
'You like Chinese cooking, don't you? How about this evening?'

Âa, sekkakù desu ğa, kôñbañ wa eńryo-sit(e) okimàsu.
'Oh, it's very kind of you, but this evening, I'll take a rain check (*lit.* I'll hold back for now).'

2. **Gôruhu, osuki desyoo? Asâtte dôo desu ka⤴**
'You like golf, don't you? How about the day after tomorrow?'

Aa, sekkakù desu ğa, asâtte wa eńryo-site okimàsu.
'Oh, it's very kind of you, but the day after tomorrow, I'll take a rain check (*lit.* I'll hold back for now).'

3. **Kyôoto/râiğetu**; 4. **teñpura/raisyuu**; 5. **tênisu/asû**

Application Exercises

A1. Act out home visits, taking turns playing the role of guest and of host(ess). Do not be overimaginative! Most important is mastering the ritualistic utterances that are appropriate: they must be delivered smoothly, fluently, and convincingly. Study the accompanying video for visual guidance on details of delivery. Repeated practice is essential.

2. Practice replying to yes-no questions with responses that use the alternate question pattern. Include **X ka dôo ka**; **X ka** /opposite/ **ka**; **X ka** /negative X/ **ka**; and /**X ka Y ka**/ within answers incorporating **wakáràṇai, siranai, obôete (i)nai**, and **wasureta** (or their distal and/or polite equivalents). Examples:

(1) **Konó zìsyo, takâi desu ka** 'Is this dictionary expensive?' ... **Sâa. Takâi ka dôo ka obôete (i)nâi kedo; totémo ìi zîsyo desu yo** 'Hmm. I don't remember whether it's expensive or not, but it's a very good dictionary.'

(2) **Sonó zèmi wa, maísyuu no mokuyòobi desu ka** 'Is that seminar every Thursday?' ... **Sôo desu nêe. Mokúyòobi ka kiɴ́yòobi ka wasúremàsita kedo; Y-sañ ḡa yôku dêru kara, Y-sañ ni kiíte kudasài.** 'Let's see. I forgot whether it's Thursday or Friday, but Mr/s. Y attends often, so ask him/her.'

3. In response to various **-masyòo ka** offers, respond using the newly introduced /**o** + verbal stem + **-kudasai**/ request pattern. Insofar as possible, perform the requested activity and then describe what was done for whom. Example:

A: **Mâdo o akémasyòo ka.** 'Shall I open the window?'
B: **Êe. Oáke-kudasài.** 'Yes. Please open it.' ...
B: **A-sañ ni mâdo o akéte moraimàsita.** 'I had Mr/s. A open the window for me.' or
 A-sañ ḡa mâdo o akéte kuremàsita. '*Mr/s.* A opened the window for me.'
A: **B-sañ ni mâdo o akéte aḡemàsita.** 'I opened the window for Mr/s. B.'

Of course, the choice of the verbal of giving or receiving will depend on the individuals involved and the relationships among them.

B. Core Conversations: Substitution

Practice the Core Conversations, making substitutions that do not violate the constraints of ritual language. These will, for the most part, be limited to changes in politeness levels (example: **X desu > X de gozaimasu**), in time words (example: **señzitu > yuúbè**), and in expressions for which a synonym has already been introduced (examples: **tyoódai-itasi-màsu > itádakimàsu; samémàsu > tumétaku narimàsu**). For the CC of this lesson, internalization to the point that you will never forget them is crucial. They must still be on the tip of your tongue even in a socially pressured situation which has simultaneous graceful shoe removal and retrieval as an added hazard!

SECTION B

Core Conversations

1(N)a. A. **Sâkki deɴ́wa ḡa arimàsita yo** (J')a. **Hñ? Dâre kara?**
 b. **Sûmi-sañ te oṡsyaimàsita kedo ..** b. **Sûmi?**
 c. **Hâi. Dônata ka gozôñzi zya nâi desu ka**
   c. **Ñ. Nâñ te itte (i)ta?**
 d. **Áto de matá deñwa irerù tte oṡsyàtte (i)masita.**
   d. **Hâi. Dôo mo. ... Môsimosi.**

(J″) Môsimosi. A, Sûmi to moósimàsu g̃a . .

2(N)a. Seńsèe. Têrebi ni odé ni nàru ñ desu tte?

b. Nâñ te iu bañgumi dèsu ka↗

c. Hoka ni dôo iu katâ g̃a odé ni nàru ñ desu ka↗

d. Sôo desu ka. Dê mo, tanósìmi desu nêe.

3(J)a. Asítà wa, syoóg̃o-sug̃ì ni irâsite kudasai.

b. Tyoódo ohìru no zyuúnì-zi tte iu îmi desu.

e. A, sakihodo wa sitûree-itasimasita.

(J)a. Êe. Tyôtto iñtabyuu-bàñg̃umi de ne!

b. Zitû wa ne! Nâñ te iítà ka yôku obôete (i)nâi ñ da yo. Keézai-kàñkee da kedo . .

c. Iya, mâda dâre g̃a dêru ka kiíte (i)nài ñ da.

d. Iya, omósiròi ka dôo ka, wakâñnai yo↗

(N) Syôog̃o? Syôog̃o tte iû no wa, dôo iu îmi desu ka↗

English Equivalents

1(N)a. Oh, there was a phone call a little while ago.
b. His name was Sumi, but . . . (that's all I know).
c. Yes. You don't know who he is?
d. He was saying that he'd put in a call again later.

(J″) Hello. Oh, my name is Sumi . . .

2(N)a. Professor, did I hear (*lit.* do they say) that (it's that) you're going to appear on television?

b. What is the name of the program? (*lit.* It is a program called what?)

(J′)a. Huh? Who from?
b. Sumi?
c. No. What was he saying?
d. O.K. Thanks. . . . [Answering the phone] Hello.
e. Oh, I'm sorry [I was out] a little while ago.

(J)a. Yes. Just on some talk show—you know.

b. Actually, you know, the fact is I don't remember for sure what it was called. It's connected with economics, but . . . (I don't remember anything more).

c. Who else will be on? (*lit.* In addition, what kind of person will appear?)
  d. Oh. But it's something to look forward to, isn't it!

3(J)a. Tomorrow please come after 'shogo.'
  b. It means exactly twelve o'clock noon.

  c. I haven't heard yet who will be on.
  d. Oh, I can't tell whether it will be interesting or not.

(N) Shogo? What does 'shogo' mean?

BREAKDOWNS
(AND SUPPLEMENTARY VOCABULARY)

1. **Hñ?** (= puff of breath + **ñ**)   Huh?
   Sûmi   (family name)
   to *or*
   (t)te (SP1)   /quotative particle/
   X to/tte iu *or*
   X to/tte ośsyàru ↑ *or*
   X to moosu ↓   be named X *or* say "X"
   dônata ka gozôñzi da ↑ (SP2)   know who it is /polite/
   nâñ te iu (SP1)   say what? *or* is named or called what?
   deñwa (o) ireru   put in a call
   deñwa (o) irerù tte ośsyàru ↑   say that s/he'll put in a call /polite/
   sakihodo   a while ago
2. **têrebi ni dêru**   appear on television
   dêru tte (SP1)   they say [someone] will appear
   bañgumi/báñgùmì   program
   iñtabyuu-bàñgumi   interview program, talk show
   +**supóotu-bàñgumi**   sports program
   +**teńki-yòhoo**   weather forecast
   +**zadâñkai**   round-table discussion; symposium
   +**kôogi**   lecture
   +**kooeñ**   speech; lecture
   +**hoómudòrama**   soap opera
   +**êega/eega**   movie
   +**sibai/osîbai**   show
   nâñ te iu bañgumi (SP1)   a program called what?
   nâñ te itta ka obôete (i)nai (SP2)   doesn't remember what it was called *or* what [someone] said

   kêezai   economics

kañkee	connection
keézai-kàñkee	a connection with economics
+seezi	politics
+gêñgo	language
+bûñḡaku	literature
+syakâiḡaku	sociology
dôo iu katâ (SP1)	a person described how? what kind of person? /polite/
dâre ḡa dêru ka 'kiku (SP2)	ask *or* hear who will appear
wakâññai	/casual-style equivalent of **wakáràṅai**/
3. syôoḡo	noon
syoóḡo-suḡì	after noon
syôoḡo tte iu no *or*	
syôoḡo tte	the thing called "shogo"
îmi	meaning
dôo iu îmi	a meaning described how? what kind of meaning?
+setumee-suru	explain
ohîru	noon; daytime
zyuúnì-zi tte iu îmi	the meaning "twelve o'clock noon"

MISCELLANEOUS NOTES

1. In CC1, the office supervisor receives word of a telephone call that came in while she was away from her desk. Immediately after this, the caller telephones again. The supervisor uses casual-style with plain, direct-style predicates in speaking to Deborah Miller, her employee, but polite careful-style, with a distal-style predicate, to the stranger on the telephone. The employee uses polite careful-style with distal-style predicates in speaking with her supervisor.

(N)a. Remember the contrast between **saki** 'ahead' in reference to space and **sâkki** 'ahead of this,' 'a while ago' in reference to time. But in the more formal compound with **hodo** (cf. [J']e), the alternate with short *k*, **sakihodo**, also refers to time.

2. In CC2, Sue Brown discusses with Professor Ono his upcoming appearance in a television interview. Such appearances by academics are extremely common in Japan. Sue Brown exhibits serious interest in the program and suggests that she will enjoy it, whereas he plays down its importance by stating that he has forgotten the name of the program, hasn't heard who else will participate, and doesn't really know whether it will be interesting or not. The professor uses blunt casual-style with direct-style predicates in talking to Sue; her speech is polite and careful, with distal-style predicates.

(N)a. The use of the extended predicate suggests that Sue Brown is confirming that what was reported to her is fact.

(J)b. The perfective **itta** is perfective of recall. That Professor Ono doesn't remember explains why he can't answer Sue Brown's question.

(N)c. Again an extended predicate: here Sue Brown ties in the notion of the interview format with the participation of someone besides the professor.

(J)c. Professor Ono turns aside Sue Brown's question with an **iya**, explaining this in terms of his not having heard the relevant information.

3. In receiving directions from her full-time coworker, the part-time worker Sue Brown hears a word she does not understand and asks for its meaning. Both speakers use generally careful-style with distal-style predicates. The direct **kudásài** request form is softened by the polite gerund (**irâsite**) that precedes it.

Setumee-suru is an operational verbal: **X ni Y o setumee-suru** 'explain Y to X'; **setumee** 'explanation.'

Structural Patterns

1. /X to ~ (t)te iu/

The quotative particle **to** was first introduced together with the verbal **omôu**, following the sequence expressing the thought:

Wakâtta to omóimàsu.   'I think I understood.'

Hêñ da to omówànai?   'Don't you think it's strange?'

We next encountered **to** in the combinations

$$\text{X to} \begin{Bmatrix} \text{iu} \\ \text{ośsyàru} \uparrow \\ \text{moosu} \downarrow \end{Bmatrix} \quad \text{'be named or called X'}$$

The quotative particle **to** has a slightly more casual equivalent **tte** (**te** following **ñ**) which occurs very commonly in the spoken language when linked with the verbal **iu**. Thus:

Anô ko wa Tâkasi tte (*or* **to**) **iimasu.**   'That child is named Takashi.'

The combination **X (t)te** (*or* **to**) **iu** (or a more polite equivalent) may occur immediately before a nominal Y,[4] meaning 'a Y named X or called X.' Examples:

Tâkasi to iu kodomo   'a child named Takashi'

Oókura to iu hòteru   'the hotel Okura'

Tanáka Yukio to ośsyàru seńsèe   'a professor named Yukio Tanaka'

nâñ te iu daiḡaku   'a university named what?'

To/(t)te also occurs in quotations immediately following the item that is quoted. Although direct quotation of the exact language that was originally used may occur, usually the quoting is indirect, with the predicate of the quotation in the direct-style. The choice between the perfective and imperfective within the quotation is determined on the basis of which was originally used. Examples:

Kâre wa, asíta kùru tte itta.   'He said he'd come tomorrow.'

Kôñbañ 'mata tetúdàtte aḡeru tte iímàsita kara . .   'I said I'd help [him/her] again this evening, so . . .' (I'll be busy).

---

4. The implications of this combination are far-reaching. Once again we must think of the three predicate types. Just as a direct-style adjectival may precede a nominal (**takâi zîsyo**), so may a direct-style verbal occur in the same kind of pattern. We must wonder about the nominal predicate. This will be discussed in detail in the next lesson.

Arúbàito wa, ano sigoto o môo yaĺte simattà tte iímàsita kedo .. 'The part-timer said s/he had already finished doing that work, but . . .' (I'm not sure).

Note the following points:

1. The verbal **iu** may of course be replaced by the honorific-polite **ośsyàru** ↑ or the humble-polite **moosu** ↓ wherever appropriate.

2. The quotative particle must immediately follow the quotation, but the verbal of speaking has no requirement involving order. Thus,

Kânozyo wa, môo wakâtta tte, sûgu seńsèe ni iímàsita. She immediately said to the teacher that she had already understood.'

3. **(T)te** and **to** are interchangeable when linked with **iu** and **ośsyàru** ↑, except that **to** is slightly more formal and less common in conversation. However, only **to** regularly occurs with **moosu** ↓. A normally unaccented sequence may acquire an accent preceding the quotative.

4. In the combinations **X (t)te itta** and **X (t)te itte**, **i-** is often contracted: **X (t)te (i)tta** and **X (t)te (i)tte.**

5. **(T)te** in sentence-final position indicates that what precedes is being reported as something that has been said. Who said it may or may not be identified, but it can never be the person reporting it. The quotation may be direct- or distal-style. This pattern is more casual than one that includes a verbal of speaking. Examples:

Are takâi tte. 'They say that's expensive.'

Yukî da tte? 'Did you say it's snow[ing]?'

Nakámura-sañ no àkatyañ, sûgôku kawáìi ñ desu tte. 'They say Mr/s. Nakamura's baby is terribly cute.'

Suzuki-sañ wa, raisyuu geńgo-kàñkee no terébi-bàñgumi ni demâsu tte. 'Mr/s. Suzuki says s/he's appearing on a television program with a language connection next week.'

6. When the reporting of a quotation is removed in time or specificity from its original occurrence, **X to ~ (t)te (i)tte (i)ta** replaces **X to ~ (t)te (i)tta.** Thus,

Râigetu 'kono sigoto yamérù daroo tte (i)ttè (i)ta. 'S/he was saying (a while back) that s/he would probably give up this work next month.'

7. Verbals other than **iu** and its polite equivalents may follow a /quotation + **to ~ (t)te**/ (e.g., **kâku** 'write,' **osieru** 'inform,' **kiku** 'hear,' 'ask,' **ukagau** 'inquire'). With the exception of **kiku**, the **to** alternate of the quotative occurs more commonly with such verbals than with **iu**. With verbals of asking, the quotation ends with question-particle **ka**⌒, preceding which **da**, as usual, is dropped.

Getúyòo ni ikánài to kâita. 'I wrote that I'm not going on Monday.'

Kâre wa, atárasìi kyoókàsyo ga dête (i)ru to 'osiete kureta. 'He informed me that a new textbook has come out.'

Môo seńsèe o kimétà to kiítà kedo, hońtoo dèsu ka⌒ 'I heard they've already decided the teacher, but is it true?'

Dônata ni kimétà ka tte kiítà kedo, daré mo osiete kuremasèñ desita. 'I asked who they decided on, but no one gave me the information.'

Kooeñ wa nâñ-zi kara ka to, seńsèe ni ukáğaimàsita. 'I inquired of the teacher what time the lecture will begin (*lit*. the lecture is from what time?.)'

8. /**X + (t)te**/ may occur as a more casual equivalent of /**X + to ~ (t)te iû no wa**/. Examples:
    Teesyoku tte, nâñ desu ka⤴ 'What is a "teishoku"?'
    Huróṣiki o katte kimàsita yo⤵ . . . Hurosiki tte? 'I went and bought a furoshiki . . .'
    '[What do you mean by] a "furoshiki"?'

The quotation may be a request form:
    Seńsèe wa, kôñbañ deńwa o irete kudasài to ośsyaimàsita yo⤵ 'The teacher said you should telephone (*lit*. said, 'Telephone . . .') tonight.'

When the quoted request is casual, ending in a gerund, it is only the final vowel of the quotation that distinguishes it from an utterance of a very different meaning. Compare:
    Kâre, deńwa o iretè tte (i)tta yo⤵ 'He said [you should] telephone.'
    Kâre, deńwa o iretà tte (i)tta yo⤵ 'He said he telephoned.'

The quotation is replaced by **nâñ** in a corresponding question: **Nâñ te iímàsita ka⤵** 'What did [s/he] say?' With this, compare: **Dôo iímàsita ka** 'How did [s/he] say or express it?' which was introduced previously. Parallel to the pattern **nâñ to** (*or* **te**) **iu X** 'an X named or called what?' is the combination **dôo iu X** 'an X described how?' 'what sort of X?' Compare also **koo iu X** 'this sort of X' and **soo iu X, aa iu X** 'that sort of X.' **Kôo, sôo, âa, dôo** are examples of another **ko-so-a-do** series.

2. EMBEDDED INFORMATION QUESTIONS

In 18A-SP3, we learned how to embed yes-no questions:

yes-no question + { **dôo ka** *or* / opposite + **ka** *or* / negative + **ka** *or* / other alternative + **ka** } + { **siranai** / **wakárànai** / **sitte (i)ru?** / **obôete (i)nai,** / **wasureta,** etc. }

The pattern always ends up involving alternate questions—the original question plus a balancing question of the kinds described above.

In contrast, the embedding of information questions involves at most only changing any distal-style predicates to direct-style. Again, **da** is regularly dropped before **ka**, and with the loss of **da**, a preceding **ñ** becomes **no**. Examples:
    Dâre ğa 'kono tokêe o naôsite kureru ka wakárimaseñ. 'It isn't clear who will fix this watch for us.'
    Nâñ-zi ni dêru ka mâda kiméte (i)nài. 'I haven't decided yet what time I'm leaving.'
    Dôre ğa itíbañ ìi ka osíete kudasài. 'Tell me which one is best.'
    Sore wa nâni ka gozôñzi desu ka⤵ 'Do you know what that is?'
    Anó kàiği wa nâñ-niti datta ka wasúremàsita. 'I forgot what date that conference was.'

Kooeñ wa nâñ-zi kara ka itte kuremaseñ desita. 'He didn't tell me what time the lecture starts.'

Îtu kimérù no ka sirímaseñ. 'I don't know when it is they'll decide.'

Particularly common are embedded questions followed by verbals of asking. Examples:

Îma nâñ-zi ka kikímasyòo. 'Let's ask what time it is now.'

Atárasìi seńsèe wa nâñ te ossyàru ka kikímàsita ka⌒ 'Did you ask what the name of the new teacher is?'

Dôno zîsyo ḡa itíbañ ìi ka kiíte kuremaseñ ka⌒ 'Would you ask (for me) which dictionary is best?'

When the embedded question occurs with a verbal of asking (particularly in the perfective), the embedded question may be immediately followed by the quotative particle, in which case the structure becomes one of quotation, as described in SP1, above. Example:

Îtu kara nihóñḡo o beñkyoo-site (i)rù ka to, ano gakusee ni kikímàsita. 'I asked that student how long (*lit.* since when) s/he has been studying Japanese.'

The quotative particle here is optional, and more commonly omitted.

Drills

A 1. **Kâre, asita kûru?**
'Is he coming tomorrow?'

    Kûru tte (i)tte (i)tà kedo..
'He was saying he'd come, but...' (I can't be sure).

  2. **Kâre, tosyôsitu ni yoru?**
'Is he stopping in at the library?'

    Yorû tte (i)tte (i)tà kedo..
'He was saying he'd stop in, but...' (I can't be sure).

  3. **kodómo turete kùru**; 4. **mata tetúdàtte kureru**; 5. **êki made okuru**; 6. **demae tanômu**

B 1. **Seńsèe, hitô-ri de irássyàru?**
'Is the doctor going (*or* coming) alone?'

    Hitô-ri de irássyàru tte (i)tte (i)rassyàtta kedo..
'S/he was saying s/he'd go (*or* come) alone, but...' (I can't be sure).

  2. **Seńsèe hitô-ri de mesiaḡaru?**
'Is the doctor going to eat alone?'

    Hitô-ri de mesíaḡarù tte (i)tte (i)rassyàtta kedo..
'S/he was saying s/he'd eat alone, but...' (I can't be sure).

  3. **nasâru**; 4. **omíe ni nàru**; 5. **okíme ni nàru**; 6. **otúki ni nàru**

C 1. **Kânozyo ni-kái ni kùru?**
'Is she coming to the second floor?'

    Iya, kônai tte.
'No, she says she isn't coming.'

  2. **Kânozyo deńwa ni dèru?**
'Is she going to answer the phone?'

    Iya, dênai tte.
'No, she says she isn't going to answer.'

  3. **tukue 'tukau**; 4. **ohâsi ḡa iru**; 5. **miti obôete (i)ru**

D 1. **Kânozyo ni-kái ni kimàsu?**

    Ie, kimáseñ te.

'Is she coming to the second floor?'   'No, she says she isn't coming.'

2. **Kânozyo deńwa ni demàsu?**   **Ie, demáseñ te.**
'Is she going to answer the phone?'   'No, she says she isn't going to answer.'

3. **keésàñki kaímàsu**; 4. **ni-kai katázukemàsu**; 5. **kôñbañ tomárimàsu**

E 1. **Dôno hôteru desu ka⬈ Oókura dèsu ka⬈**   **Êe, Oókura tte iu hòteru desu.**
'Which hotel is it? Is it the Okura?'   'Yes, it's the hotel called the Okura.'

2. **Dôno otóko no hitò desu ka⬈ Morímoto-sañ dèsu ka⬈**   **Êe, Morímoto-sañ te iu otoko no hitò desu.**
'Which man is it? Is it Mr. Morimoto?'   'Yes, it's the man named (Mr.) Morimoto.'

3. **teñpuraya/Teñhana**; 4. **bañgumi/seézi-zadañkai**; 5. **kaisya/Toókyoo-bòoeki**; 6. **daigaku/Keeoo**

F 1. **Tanaka tte iu hito, inâi desyoo ka.**   **Sâa. Tanáka tte iu hitò wa, kokó nì wa inái to omoimàsu kedo nêe.**
'Would(n't) there be a person named Tanaka [here]?'   'Hm. I believe there isn't a person named Tanaka here, but . . .' (I may be wrong).

2. **Mezíro-birù tte iu bîru, nâi desyoo ka.**   **Sâa. Mezíro-birù tte iu bîru wa, kokó nì wa nâi to omóimàsu kedo nêe.**
'Would(n't) there be a building named the Mejiro Building [here]?'   'Hm. I believe there isn't a building named the Mejiro Building here, but . . .' (I may be wrong).

3. **Yamâguti/gakusee**; 4. **Matûzusi/susîya**; 5. **Nihoñ no mizúùmi/hôñ**; 6. **Sâtoo/arúbàito no hito**

G 1. **Oókura tte iu hòteru, gozôñzi desu ne⬈**   **Oókura dèsu ka⬈ Êe, motîroñ zôñzite orimasu kedo ..**
'You know the hotel called Okura—right?'   'The Okura? Yes, of course I know it, but . . .' (why do you ask?)

2. **Kyôo no nyûusu tte iu bañgumi gozôñzi desu ne⬈**   **Kyôo no nyûusu desu ka⬈ Êe, motîroñ zôñzite orimasu kedo ..**
'You know the program called "Today's News"—right?'   '"Today's News?" Yes, of course I know it, but . . .' (why do you ask?)

3. **Kimura/kóñpyùutaa no kyôosi**; 4. **Pâruko/depâato**; 5. **Toránomoñ-byòoiñ/byooiñ**

H 1. **Ano kata, dônata?**   **A, dônata ka gozôñzi zya nâi ñ desu ka⬈**
'Who is that?'   'Oh, (you mean) you don't know who it is?'

2. **Anó osìbai, dôko?**   **A, dôko ka gozôñzi zya nâi ñ desu ka⬈**
'Where is that play?'   'Oh, (you mean) you don't know where it is?'

3. **ano bañgumi/nâñ-zi kara**; 4. **ano ueki/nâni**; 5. **anó misè/dôtti no hoo**; 6. **asóko no syàiñ/nâñ-niñ**; 7. **anó kàmera/îkura**

I 1. **Anó kaisya ni hàiru ñ desu ka⤴**
'(Is it that) you're going to join that company?'

Iya, mâda dôo iu kaisya ka yôku wakáràuai kara ..
'No, it's not yet clear what kind of company it will be, so . . .' (I can't tell you whether I'll join).

2. **Anó sibai o mìru ñ desu ka⤴**
'(Is it that) you're going to see that show?'

Iya, mâda dôo iu sibai ka yôku wakáràuai kara ..
'No, it's not yet clear what kind of show it will be, so . . .' (I can't tell you whether I'll see it).

3. **kôogi ni dêru**; 4. **kooeñ o kiku**; 5. **zadáñkai ni dêru**; 6. **señsèe ni soodañ-suru**

J 1. **Koo iu ueki wa, Toókyoo ni àru desyoo?**
'There are plants like this in Tokyo, aren't there?'

Sâa. Soó iù no wa, Tookyoo no dokó ni mo nài to omóimàsu yo⤴
'Hm. There aren't ones like that anywhere in Tokyo, I believe.'

2. **Koó iu keesàñki wa, konó misè ni âru desyoo?**
'There are calculators like this in this store, aren't there?'

Sâa. Soó iù no wa, kono mise no dokó ni mo nài to omóimàsu yo⤴
'Hm. Ones like that don't exist anywhere in this store, I believe.'

3. **kî/Hôñsyuu**; 4. **minato/Hokkàidoo**; 5. **misê/Amerika**

K 1. **Kâre, nâñ te (i)tta?**
'What did he say?'

Nâñ te (i)tta ka, obôete (i)nâi ñ desu.
'I don't remember what he said.'

2. **Kâre, îtu tte (i)tta?**
'When did he say [something would occur]?'

Îtu tte (i)tta ka, obôete (i)nâi ñ desu.
'I don't remember when he said [something would occur].'

3. **dôko**; 4. **dâre**; 5. **îtu made**; 6. **nâñ-zi**; 7. **nâñ-zìkañ**

L 1. **Anâta no kâmera, dôko ni okímàsita?**
'Where did you put your camera?'

Sumímasèñ. Dôko ni oítà ka wasúrete simaimàsita.
'I'm sorry. I completely forgot where I put it.'

2. **Anâta no kâmera, motte kimàsita?**
'Did you bring your camera?'

Sumímasèñ. Mottè kita ka dôo ka, wasúrete simaimàsita.
'I'm sorry. I completely forgot whether I brought it or not.'

3. **dôko de kaímàsita**; 4. **îtu moráimàsita**; 5. **tomódati ni karimàsita**; 6. **îtu hazîmete tukáimàsita**; 7. **Nakamura-sañ ni misémàsita**

M 1. **Sûmi-sañ wa kyôo tukû ñ desu ka⤴**
'Is it today that Mr/s. Sumi is going to arrive?'

Iya, îtu tukû no ka, kiíte (i)masèñ yo.
'No, I haven't heard when it is s/he's arriving.'

2. **Ni-kai wa Hayási-sañ ḡa katazùkete kurérù ñ desu ka↗**
   'Is it Mr/s. Hayashi who is going to straighten up the second floor for us?'

   Iya, dâre ḡa katázùkete kurérù no ka, kiíte (i)masèñ yo.
   'No, I haven't heard who it is who will straighten it up for us.'

3. **ohîru/osûsi o tanôñda**; 4. **teñpura/Teñhana ḡa itibañ oisìi**; 5. **ano syasiñ/Oota-sañ ni moratta**

N 1. **Kânozyo, îtu kûru?**
   'When is she coming?'

   Sâa nêe. Îtu kûru ka, mâda kiíte (i)nài ñ desu kedo . .
   'Hm. I haven't yet heard when she's coming, but . . .' (would you like me to check?)

2. **Kânozyo, dôñna supôotu ḡa sukî?**
   'What kind of sports does she like?'

   Sâa nêe. Dôñna supôotu ḡa sukî ka, mâda kiíte (i)nài ñ desu kedo . .
   'Hm. I haven't yet heard what kind of sports she likes, but . . .' (would you like me to check?)

3. **dôko ni yotte kàeru**; 4. **dâre o turéte kùru**; 5. **dâre to kekkoñ-suru**

O. Identify questioner and respondent on the basis of the stylistic differences.

1. **Îtu kûru ka 'kiita?**
   'Did you ask when s/he was coming?'

   Hâi, ukáḡaimàsita kedo, kônai to ośsyaimàsita.
   'Yes, I inquired, but s/he said s/he wasn't coming.'

2. **Donó-ḡurai sore obòete (i)ru ka 'kiita?**
   'Did you ask to what extent s/he remembered that?'

   Hâi, ukáḡaimàsita kedo, obôete (i)nâi to ośsyaimàsita.
   'Yes, I inquired, but s/he said s/he didn't remember.'

3. **îtu kâmera naôsite moratta**; 4. **îtu sokó e modòru**; 5. **dôko de bûñgaku beñkyoo-suru**; 6. **dâre ni siḡóto o tetudàtte moratta**

P 1. **Îtu kitâ ka 'kiita?**
   'Did you ask when s/he came?'

   Ñ. Kiítà kedo, kîte (i)nâi tte.
   'Yeah. I asked, but they said s/he hasn't come.'

2. **Nâñ-zi ni tûita ka 'kiita?**
   'Did you ask when s/he arrived?'

   Ñ. Kiítà kedo, tûite (i)nại tte.
   'Yeah. I asked, but they said s/he hasn't arrived.'

3. **dôko ni simatta** 4. **dôo site sutetyatta**; 5. **dâre ni tanôñda**; 6. **îtu isyá ni mìte moratta**; 7. **dôo site eñryo-sita**

Q 1. **Aśita no zadàñkai ni nâñ-niñ kûru ka gozôñzi desu ka↗**

   Zadâñkai desu ka↗ Yo-níñ-ḡùrai kûru tte kiíte (i)màsu kedo . .

'Do you know how many people are coming to tomorrow's round-table discussion?'

'The discussion? I've heard that about four are coming, but . . .' (I'm not sure).

2. **Tikâ ni 'kissateñ ga nâñ-geñ âru ka gozôñzi desu ka⤴**
'Do you know how many **kissateñ** there are in the basement?'

Kissateñ dèsu ka⤴ Yoń-keñ-g̀ùrai âru tte kiíte (i)màsu kedo . .
'Kissateñ? I've heard there are about four, but . . .' (I'm not sure).

3. **tukue ga îku-tu iru**; 4. **niwa no ueki o nâñ-boñ tyuumoñ-sita**; 5. **kuruma ga nâñ-dai tomatte (i)ru**; 6. **koñna osara o nâñ-mai tukau**

Application Exercises

A1. Practice relaying information, incorporating the newly introduced patterns of quotation. Use the following format:

A asks a question.
B replies.
C reports what A asked and what B replied.

Include practice on various politeness levels and speech styles appropriate to assigned roles.

2. Practice relaying requests, using /-te (kudasai)/ within quotations. Example:

A to B: **C-sañ ni myôoniti 'kotira ni deńwa o irete moratte kudasài.** 'Please have Mr/s. C call here tomorrow.'

B to C: **A-sañ wa, myôoniti 'kotira ni deńwa o iretè (kudasài) tte (iímàsita).** 'Mr/s. A said to call here tomorrow.'

3. Practice requesting—and providing—simple definitions for Japanese words such as the following: **samêru, naôru, myoóg̀òniti, ane, otóotò, oba, sôhu**. Example:

Naôsu to iu no wa, dôo iu îmi desu ka⤴ 'What does "naosu" mean?'
Yôku surû to iu îmi desu. 'It means "make good."'

4. Practice eliciting and providing information that incorporates the identification of items by name, using the /**X to iu Y**/ pattern. Examples:

a. **JSL to iu kyoókàsyo de nihóñg̀o o beñkyoo-site (i)màsu.** 'I'm studying Japanese with the textbook *JSL*.'

b. **X to iu daig̀aku de nihóñg̀o o beñkyoo-site (i)màsu.** 'I'm studying Japanese at X University.'

c. **Yuube nâñ to iu êeg̀a o mîta ñ desu ka⤴** 'What movie (*lit.* a movie named what) is it you saw last night?'

5. Practice replying to information questions (as opposed to yes-no questions) with responses that indicate an inability to answer directly, using the newly acquired embedded question pattern. Examples:

Tâkano-señsee no 'kooeñ wa, îtu desu ka⤴ 'When is Professor Takano's lecture?'

Îtu ka obôete (i)nâi kedo, koñsyuu zya nài to omoimasu. '(The fact is) I don't remember when it is, but I don't think it's this week.'

Tuĝî no yasúmi ni dôko e ikû ñ desu ka⌐ 'Where is it you're going on your next vacation?'

Dôko e ikû ka mâda wakáràñai ñ desu kedo, râiĝetu made ni wa kimárù to omoimasu. '(The fact is) it's not yet clear where I'll go, but I think it will be decided by next month.'

B. Core Conversations: Substitution

Practice the Core Conversations with appropriate substitutions, and then follow each new version with questioning relating to the new contents.

SECTION C

Eavesdropping

(Answer the following on the basis of the accompanying tape. A = the first speaker, and B = the second speaker, in each conversation.)

1a. Where does this conversation probably take place?
 b. Identify A and B.
2a. Identify A and B.
 b. For whom does A apologize?
 c. What is B about to do?
3. What was A's error?
4a. What message does B receive from A? Give details.
 b. What do the speech levels used by A and B suggest about their relative positions?
5a. What is A inquiring about?
 b. How may A learn the answer?
6. Describe the situation. What interaction occurs between A and B?
7a. What invitation does A extend? Give details.
 b. Why does B refuse?
8a. What is A inquiring about?
 b. What is B's assumption in that connection?
 c. What is B's opinion of the possible interest level?
9. Describe the situation. Describe A and B in terms of their roles and interaction.
10a. What is A presenting to B?
 b. What message does A pass on to B?
 c. What ritual apology does B offer?
11a. What has A heard about the place under discussion?
 b. What question does A still have regarding the place?
 c. What information is B able to provide in direct response?
 d. What further information does B provide?
 e. What course of action is A considering?
12a. What is A's problem?
 b. What possible solution does B offer?
 c. How does A react to the suggestion?
 d. What other course of action did A take?

e. What is B's discouraging assessment of the situation?
13. Describe the situation. Describe A and B in terms of their roles and interaction.
14a. Who are A and B?
   b. What is B offering A?
   c. How does A react to the offer?
   d. How does B react to A's comments regarding personal habits?
   e. What does B invite A to do?
15a. What is the topic of discussion? Give details.
   b. Why did A see it?
   c. Why is B surprised?
   d. What was A's reaction to the item under discussion?
16a. What is A about to do? Why?
   b. What is B particularly interested in? Why?
   c. What information is A able to provide?
   d. What comment does A make that relates to B's plans?
17a. What is it that B thinks must be beautiful?
   b. What invitation does A extend? To whom?
   c. How does B respond? Give details.
18a. What has captured A's interest? Give details as to topic, medium, day, and time.
   b. What is B's reaction?
   c. What specific information does B request?
   d. How does A respond?
19a. What is A offering B?
   b. List the ingredients in precise detail.
   c. After receiving this information, what is B interested in learning?
   d. How does A explain the reply?
20a. Describe the probable setting of this conversation.
   b. What does A single out for special praise?
   c. How does B explain this?
   d. What would A like to do?
   e. What is A's concern?
   f. What reassurance does B offer?
21a. What does A ask B to do? Why?
   b. What does B learn?
   c. What information does A provide? Give details.
   d. What information is A unable to provide?
22a. Who is the topic of discussion and what are that person's profession and specialization?
   b. What is A's opinion of that person? On what basis?
   c. What has B heard? From whom?
   d. What explanation does B offer?
23a. Where does this conversation take place?
   b. What does B not understand?
   c. What explanation does A offer?
   d. What change does B make in the course of the conversation?
   e. What is A's final request?
24a. What sports does B participate in? Give details.
   b. What is A's involvement in sports?
   c. What is A's concern in regard to golf?
   d. What is B's reaction?

Utilization

(For each item, to the extent possible, develop a short conversation that includes at least a stimulus and/or a response.)

1. Welcome a guest to your home and invite him in.
2. Present a gift to your hostess.
3. You've met your hostess of a few days ago. What would you say?
4. You've just received a gift from your guest. What would you say?
5. Invite a guest to make herself comfortable.
6. Your hostess is making preparations to serve tea. Tell her not to go to any trouble.
7. Offer a guest refreshments, expressing concern over whether or not he'll like what you are serving.
8. You are serving coffee. Urge a guest not to hold back, since it will get cold.
9. Express to your host at how late it is, and make preparations to leave.
10. Apologize to your host for staying so late.
11. Invite a guest to come again.
12. Comment on how pleasant tatami rooms are.
13. Comment on what a beautiful place this is, since you're able to see both the mountains and the harbor.
14. Tell a friend you've been thinking you'd like to go to Japan to see the cherry blossoms. Ask what month is best.
15. Comment on what a beautiful garden this is, with both a pond and pine trees.
16. You've just come across an unfamiliar place name. Explain that you can't tell whether it's the name of a lake or of a river.
17. You are looking at a Japanese map. Find out the name of (a) this island; (b) this valley; (c) this river; (d) this lake. (Use the **X to iu Y** pattern.)
18. Tell a colleague that there are many pines and bamboo trees in your garden, but no cherry trees at all.
19. You've been asked about today's visitor. Say that you don't remember whether he can speak English or not.
20. Tell a friend that you have forgotten whether Yukiko is Haruko's older or younger sister.
21. Tell a colleague that you don't know whether the **arúbàito** student threw away last week's papers or kept them.
22. You've been invited to a dinner and movie on Saturday. Refuse politely, implying that a future date might be possible.
23. Introduce yourself politely.
24. A friend has just enrolled in a seminar. Ask her who else (i.e., what kind of people) will attend.
25. You've been asked about this French dish. Explain that you don't remember what it's called.
26. Tell a friend that Mr. Suzuki said she should telephone him tonight.
27. Ask a colleague if he knows who this is (showing a picture).
28. Ask a colleague the meaning of **syôogo; zadânkai; sameru; kôogi; seńkyòosi.**
29. You are unable to attend a particular meeting. Ask a colleague what the company president said.
30. Tell a friend that you attended Professor Ono's lecture last week, but the fact is you didn't understand what he said. Ask your friend for an explanation.
31. Tell a fellow student that in the U.S. you never watch television soap operas, but in Japan you watch them often because of the connection with language.
32. Tell a fellow student that you heard that your professor is going to appear on a talk show on television, but unfortunately you don't know the name of the program.

33. You are discussing television with a friend. Tell her that you like sports programs more than soap operas but not as much as round-table discussions.

34. Ask a friend which he prefers—movies or plays.

35. Tell a colleague that you asked the secretary what time Mr. Nakamura was coming today, but she said that it wasn't clear. You're wondering who does know.

◦ 36. Ask a colleague if she knows (a) a book named *Rivers of Japan*; (b) a magazine named *Mrs.* (*Misesu*); (c) an inn called the Yamamoto-ya; (d) the Okura Hotel; (e) a car called Golf; (f) a professor called Ono Takashi.

Check-up

1. Using the verbal **mâtu,** give examples of at least ten request patterns, all of which ask someone to wait. (A-SP1)

2. How do we describe (i.e., what are the component parts of) the request pattern exemplified by **oáḡari-kudasài**? What other category of word may compound with **kudásài** to form a parallel request pattern? (A-SP1)

3. Describe the special polite adjectival forms, including examples of adjectivals ending in **-ai, -oi, -ui,** and **-ii**. To what extent do these polite forms occur in direct-style? How do they differ from forms like **otakai, oyasui,** etc?

4. Compare the Japanese equivalents for 'I don't know whether the students are coming (or not)' and 'I don't know when the students are coming.' How do we differentiate the two types of embedded questions? (A-SP3), (B-SP2)

5. Describe three types of questions that may occur as the second member of embedded alternate questions. What happens to **dà** in embedded questions? To **dàtta**? (A-SP3)

6. In the embedding of an information question before the verbal **kiku,** what particle may occur following the question? (B-SP2)

7. Compare the occurrence of **yorosii** with that of **yorosiku** in sentence-final position. How do combinations ending in **nâku** (**okámai nàku, goéñryo nàku**) in sentence-final position parallel the occurrence of **yorosiku**? (A-SP4)

8. What are the polite equivalents of the verbal **iu**? How do they differ? What is the more casual equivalent of the quotative particle **to**? (B-SP1)

9. Describe the pattern **X to iu Y**, in which X and Y are both nominals. What does **X to iu** as a complete utterance mean? (B-SP1)

10. What is the difference in meaning between **Nâñ te iu gakúsee dèsu ka** and **Dôo iu gakúsee dèsu ka**✓? What nominals fill out the series that includes **dôo** and **sôo**? (B-SP1)

11. How is quotation expressed in Japanese? What must immediately follow any quotation? On what basis is the choice between perfective and imperfective within the quotation made? Which is more common, direct or indirect quotation? Name three verbals other than **iu** that occur with quotations. (B-SP1)

12. When the reporting of a quotation is separated from the actual occurrence in time, what form of the verbal of saying is regularly used? (B-SP1)

13. Describe the occurrence of quotative **(t)te** in sentence-final position. (B-SP1)

14. What is the difference in meaning between **yôñde tte (i)tta.** and **yôñda tte (i)tta.**? (B-SP1)

15. Give an abbreviated, more casual equivalent of **X tte iû no wa.** (B-SP1)

Lesson 19

SECTION A

Core Conversations

1(N)a. Irú monò arimasu ka╱
   b. Hâi. Dôozo.
2(N) Îtu mo tukáù no wa tikátetu dèsu ka╱

3(J) Tanáka-sañ no mottè kita nîmotu wa, koré dakè desu ka╱
4(N)a. Kokútetu no kippu o utte (i)rù no wa, kokó dèsu ka╱

   b. Señeñsatu ryoóḡae-suru kikài mo arímàsu neˀ
5(N)a. Katyóo ḡa tùku no wa, îtu desu ka╱
   b. Hakkìri-sita zikañ wa, wakâtte (i)masu?

   c. Zyâa, issyo ni mukáe ni ikimasyòo.

(J)a. A. Zikókuhyoo arimàsu ka.
   b. Dôo mo.

(J) Ie. Tokídokì wa tikátetu mo tukaimàsu kedo, hutuu wa kokútetu dèsu.

(N) Iie. Azûkete âru no ḡa moó hitò-tu arimasu.

(J)a. Iya. Mukoo ni 'hito ḡa oózee narañde (i)ru tokorò ḡa âru desyoo? Asúko dèsu.
   b. Ryoóḡaeki desu ka╱ Êe, asoko ni.

(J)a. Asâtte desu ḡa ..

   b. Êe. Sîatoru kara kûru Noósuuèsuto de ne! Zyuúrokù-zi gozyûp-puñ-tyaku desu.
   c. Kokó o dèru mâe ni, moo ik-kai deñwa-site, okúrete (i)nài ka dôo ka kiíte mimasyòo.

English Equivalents

1(N)a. Is there [any]thing you need?   (J)a. Oh, do you have a timetable?

b.	Yes. Here you are.
2(N)	Do you always use the subway? (*lit.* Is the one you always use the subway?)
3(J)	Is the luggage that Mr/s. Tanaka brought just this?
4(N)a.	Is here (the one) where they sell national railway tickets?
b.	There's also a machine that changes ¥1000 bills—right?
5(N)a.	When is the section chief arriving? (*lit.* When is [the time] when the section chief will arrive?)
b.	Are you clear as to the exact time?
c.	Then let's go to meet him/her together.

b.	Thanks.
(J)	No. I do use the subway, too—sometimes, at least—but ordinarily it's the national railway [that I use].
(N)	No. There is one more thing that's been checked.
(J)a.	No. There's a place over there where lots of people are lined up—see it? That's the place.
b.	A money-changer? Yes, over there.
(J)a.	It's the day after tomorrow, but . . . (why do you ask?)
b.	Yes. It's a 16:50 arrival on Northwest coming from Seattle.
c.	Before leaving here, let's telephone again (*lit.* one more time) and find out if it's on time (*lit.* ask and see whether it's not late, or how it is).

BREAKDOWNS
(AND SUPPLEMENTARY VOCABULARY)

1. **irú monò** (SP1) — a thing [someone] needs or wants
   zikokuhyoo — timetable
   +**deñwatyoo** — telephone book
2. **itu mo tukáù no** (SP2) — one [someone] always uses
   tokídoki — sometimes
   hutuu — ordinary, regular, usual
   kokutetu — national railway
   +**z(i)ee·aaru(-señ)** — Japan Railway (Line) (JR)
3. **nîmotu** — luggage; things to be carried
   Tanáka-sañ ḡa mottè kita nîmotu *or*
   Tanáka-sañ no mottè kita nîmotu (SP1) — luggage that Mr/s. Tanaka brought
   azúkèru /-ru; azúketa/ — hand over for temporary keeping; check
   +**azúkàru /-u; azúkàtta/** — accept for temporary keeping

	azûkete âru no	one that has been checked
4.	kippu きっぷ	ticket
	uru /-u; utta/ うる	sell
	kíppu o utte (i)rù no きっぷ を うって	one where [someone] is selling tickets
+	kíppu-ùriba きっぷ うりば	ticket counter
+	zyoósyàkeñ じょうしゃけん	passenger ticket
+	kyuúkòokeñ きゅうこうけん	express ticket
+	tokkyùukeñ とっきゅうけん	special express ticket
+	sitêeseki していせき	reserved seat
+	ziyûuseki じゆうせき	free (unreserved) seat
+	guriîñsya グリーン車	"green car"
+	hutúu(rèssya)/hutûusya ふつう車	regular train (i.e., a local)
	oózèe おおぜい	large numbers of people; a crowd
	narabu /-u; narañda/ ならぶ	form a line, get in line
+	naraberu /-ru; narabeta/ ならべる	place in line
	oózee narañde (i)ru tokorò	place where many people are lined up
	señèñsatu 千円札 千円札	¥1000 bill
+	okane お金	money
+	(o)satu お札 おさつ	a bill
	ryoogae-suru りょうがえする	make change; exchange (money)
	kikâi きかい	machine
	ryoógae-suru kikài りょうがえするきかい	machine that makes change
	ryoógàeki りょうがえき	money-changing machine
5.	katyóo ḡa tukù no かちょうがつくの	(the one) when the section chief will arrive
+	hâru はる	spring
+	natû なつ	summer
+	âki あき	fall, autumn
+	huyû ふゆ	winter
	hakkìri はっきり	clear(ly), precise(ly), exact(ly)
	hakkìri-suru はっきりする	become exact
	hakkìri-sita zikañ はっきりしたじかん	exact time
	Sîatoru シアトル	Seattle
	Noósuuèsuto	Northwest (the airline)
	Sîatoru kara kûru Noósuuèsuto	Northwest that comes from Seattle
	X-tyàku	arrival at X (X = time and/or place)
+	demukaeru /-ru; demukaeta/ (also demúkàeru) でむかえる	meet, greet
+	miokuru /-u: miokutta/ (also miókùru) みおくる	see off
	dêru mâe (SP3) 出る 前	before going out
	ik-kài 一かい	one time (see below)
	kiíte mìru (SP4) きってみる	try asking, ask and see

Japanese money

itieńdama	¥1 coin	gohyákueǹsatu	¥500 bill
goeńdama	¥5 coin	seńeǹsatu	¥1,000 bill
zyuueńdama	¥10 coin	goséǹeǹsatu	¥5,000 bill
gozyuueńdama	¥50 coin	itímaǹeǹsatu	¥10,000 bill
hyakueńdama	¥100 coin		
gohyakueńdama	¥500 coin		

Classifier for counting number of times

iḱ-kài	roḱ-kài
ni-kâi	nanâ-kai/sitî-kai
sań-kài	haḱ-kài/hatí-kài
yôń-kai	kyûu-kai
go-kâi	zyuḱ-kài/ziḱ-kài
nâń-kai	'how many times?'

MISCELLANEOUS NOTES

All the CC of this lesson section are conversations between business colleagues or casual acquaintances who speak to each other in careful-style, major sentences with few fragments. Final predicates are distal-style.

1. In CC1, Mr. Carter is able to provide his colleague, Mr. Suzuki, with a timetable, which he needs. In Japan, a **zikokuhyoo** which covers the schedules for the entire nationwide rail system is available for purchase. Telephone books are used much less generally than in the West. The **meesi** of acquaintances provide most telephone numbers that anyone needs. To check on other numbers, it is usually easier—particularly for foreigners—to call directory assistance than to try to cope with the complications of listings that use Chinese characters.

2. In CC2, the participants, Sue Brown and her coworker, discuss the latter's use of public transportation.

The Japan National Railway went private in April 1987, and was renamed the Japan Railway, **JR-seń** 'JR Line.' The use of initial letters of the English name of organizations is becoming increasingly popular in Japan. Note that the **z(i)e** syllable of **z(i)ee** is innovative, not found in native Japanese words.

(J) **Tokídokì** is a compound of /**tokî** + **tokî**/, with voicing of initial **t-** to **d-** within the compound.

Hutuu: note **hutuu no X** 'average X,' 'ordinary X'; **hutuu ni suru** 'do in an ordinary way'; **hutuu wa suru** 'ordinarily do [it].' **Hutuu** is also used in reference to non-express trains, for which the more elaborate form is **hutúureǹssya**. In (J), **hutuu wa** is in contrast with **tokídokì wa**.

3. In CC3, Mr. Yamada and his colleague, Deborah Miller, discuss Mr/s. Tanaka's luggage. **Azúkèru** and **azúkàru**, related verbals that look like a typical transitive/intransitive pair, are actually both transitive operational verbals occurring with operands followed by particle **o**. The basic meaning of these verbals relates to temporary assumption of responsibility: with **azúkèru**, responsibility is handed over to another; with **azúkàru**, one accepts such responsibility oneself. These verbals cover everything from the checking of objects to the depositing of money in a bank and the leaving of children with a friend. Examples:

giñkoo ni okáne o azukèru 'deposit money in a bank'; Señ-eñ oazukari-simàsu. 'I accept ¥1000 (for now).' (clerk accepting overpayment); nîmotu ḡa azûkete âru 'the luggage has been checked.'

4. In CC4, which takes place at a station, Smith is making inquiries of his acquaintance Mr. Suzuki about where to buy particular kinds of tickets and how to make change.

Japan's transportation system is a model of speed, efficiency, and dependability. With the exception of long-distance tickets, ticket purchasing is totally mechanized in the large cities. Machines dispense tickets and change with remarkable speed. For long-distance travel, multiple tickets are required: the **zyoósyàkeñ** is required of all passengers; if one is traveling not by **hutúu(rèssya)** (**ressya** 'train') but by some kind of express (**kyuukoo**), an appropriate ticket is also required: a **kyuúkòokeñ** for a regular express and a **tokkyùukeñ** for a special express (**tokubetu** 'special' + **kyuukoo** 'express' > **tokúbetu-kyùukoo**, usually abbreviated to **tokkyuu**). A reserved seat (**sitêeseki**) requires yet another ticket, not required of passengers sitting in unreserved seats (**ziyûuseki** [**ziyûu** /na/ 'free,' 'unrestricted'[1]]). The more deluxe cars on a long-distance train are referred to as **guríiñsya**; they are not green, but they do have a green stripe.

(N)a. **Uru** 'sell,' an operational consonant-verbal, is the opposite of **kau**. In situations that refer to the actual offering of things for sale by a vendor, the **-te (i)ru** pattern is used: **Anó hòñya de ʼAmerika no zassi o utte (i)ru**. 'They sell American magazines at that bookstore.'

(J)a. Unlike **takúsàñ**, which can refer to large numbers of animates or inanimates, **oózèe** refers only to crowds of people.

Narabu 'get in line' is the intransitive partner of transitive **naraberu** 'put in line.' Both animates and inanimates can line up or be lined up: both verbals are operational, but only **naraberu** links up with /nominal + o/ phrases.

5. In CC5, Mr. Suzuki and his colleague Mr. Carter make plans for meeting their section chief, who is returning from the U.S. This is an expected courtesy shown a superior in Japan.

(N)b. Note **wakâtte (i)masu**, referring to Suzuki's present condition: 'are you now in a state resulting from its having become clear?'

(J)b. Note the use of the 24-hour clock, common in discussing transportation schedules. The clock begins with **rêe-zi** 'zero o'clock.' The nominal suffix **-tyàku** attaches to place or time nominals, or a combination of both, referring to arrival: **Toókyoo-tyàku** 'arrival in Tokyo'; **itî-zi-tyaku** 'arrival at one o'clock'; **Tookyoo itî-zi-tyaku** 'arrival in Tokyo at one o'clock.' When a **-tyàku** compound describes a following nominal, it is followed by **no**: **itî-zi-tyaku no bâsu** 'a bus arriving at one o'clock.' Combinations with **-tyàku** occur typically in contexts of travel.

(N)c. **Mukaeru** 'meet,' 'greet' was previously introduced with **okuru** as its opposite. Alternating with **mukaeru** is the compound **demukaeru**. **Okuru** occurs both with the general meaning 'send' and the more specialized 'send off,' 'see off,' but the compound **miokuru** occurs with the latter meaning only.

(J)c. **Ik-kài** is similar in meaning to **iti-do**, but is slightly more casual.

Note the negative question as the first member of the embedded alternate question: Mr. Suzuki and Mr. Carter will be telephoning to make sure the plane is *not* late before they leave to meet their section chief.

1. **Ziyûu** does NOT mean 'free' = 'not requiring payment.'

Structural Patterns

1. SENTENCE MODIFIERS WITH VERBAL AND ADJECTIVAL FINAL PREDICATES

Since the earliest lessons, we have been using the pattern /adjectival + nominal/, as in **takâi zîsyo, oókìi hôñ**, etc. If we examine this pattern, we find that it consists of a direct-style, imperfective adjectival followed directly by a nominal. Thus, **takâi** 'it is expensive' (NOT SIMPLY 'expensive') + **zîsyo** 'dictionary' = 'a dictionary which is expensive,' 'an is-expensive dictionary.'

We have already learned that in general, in whatever kind of context an adjectival occurs, the corresponding form of a verbal can also occur. This pattern is no exception. Thus we find direct-style imperfective verbals immediately preceding nominals as descriptions of the nominals: **irú monò** 'things [I] need'; **dekîru siḡoto** 'work [I] can do'; **tabêru sakana** 'fish [I] eat (*or* am going to eat).'

The order of the items is crucial: the above are either parts of longer sentences, or, as entire utterances, only fragments. Thus:

    atárasìi koñpyùutaa   'new computers' *but*
    Koñpyùutaa atárasìi.   'The computers are new.'
    tukáu koñpyùutaa   'computers [I] use' *but*
    Koñpyùutaa 'tukau.   '[I] use computers.'

The underlying meaning of /verbal *or* adjectival + nominal/ is that the nominal is described *in some relationship* by the verbal or adjectival. Note the various kinds of relationships that are possible:

    kaú hòñ   'the book [I]'m going to buy'
    kaú hitò   'the person who is going to buy [it]'
    kaú misè   'the shop where [I] will buy [it]' *or* 'the shop [I]'m going to buy'
    kaú tokì   'times when [I] buy'
    ikítai tokorò   'a place where [I] want to go'
    wakárànai tomodati   'a friend who doesn't understand'
    wakárànai nihoñḡo   'Japanese [I] don't understand'
    siránai nihoñzìñ   'a Japanese [I] don't know' *or* 'a Japanese who doesn't know'

In cases with more than one possible interpretation, context makes clear which one applies.

Most patterns that permit occurrences of an imperfective also permit a perfective, as long as the perfective makes sense in the context. This applies in this pattern:

    nôñda koóhìi   'the coffee [I] drank'
    nôñda hito   'the person who drank [it]'
    nôñda kissateñ   'the coffee shop where [I] drank [it]'
    nôñda toki   'the time when [I] drank [it]'
    muzúkasìkatta nihoñḡo   'Japanese which used to be difficult'
    beñkyoo-sitàkatta gakusee   'the student who wanted to study'
    ikítàkatta tokoro   'the place where [I] wanted to go'

We know that a Japanese verbal or adjectival in the perfective or imperfective can constitute a major sentence by itself:

Wakâtta. '[I] understood.'
Abúnài. 'It's dangerous.'
Dekînai. '[I] can't do [it].'

Accordingly, we call the occurrences of these forms as modifiers of following nominals SENTENCE MODIFIERS. They are sentences which modify—describe—the following nominal.

Like independent sentences, sentence modifiers are by no means limited to one word. They can be very long indeed, and may even contain nominals which are themselves modified by sentence modifiers which contain nominals which are modified by sentence modifiers.... This is "house-that-Jack-built patterning" in reverse order! It is the order that creates initial difficulty for the English speaker: we must be reprogrammed to reverse our thought processes. Study these examples:

Suzuki Tâkasi to iu gakusee 'a student named Takashi Suzuki'
eéḡo no hòn o ú**tte (i)ru hòn̄ya** 'a bookstore that sells English-language books'
nihon̄go o ben̄kyoo-site (i)ru tomodati 'a friend who is studying Japanese'
sên̄ḡetu Nihôn̄ ni tûita toki 'the time when [I] arrived in Japan last month'
sen̄sèe ḡa kyôn̄en̄ Yoóròppa de okái ni nàtta zîsyo 'the dictionary the teacher bought in Europe last year'
êki no tonári ni àru hôn̄ya de ká**tta kyookàsyo** 'the textbook [I] bought at the bookstore that's next to the station'
watákusi mo kyòn̄en̄ made itte (i)ta gakkoo ni îma í**tte (i)ru tomodati kara karita keesàn̄ki** 'the calculator I borrowed from the friend who's attending the school I too was attending until last year'

The above sequences, of course, may occur within a sentence, occupying any position that a nominal alone may occupy. It is also possible for one nominal to have several independent modifiers:

kono 'kinoo katta atárasìi tukue 'this new desk [I] bought yesterday'
Oósaka kara dèru Sîatoru ni iku gakusee 'the students who are going to Seattle, who are leaving from Osaka'

With this last example, compare:

Oósaka kara dète Sîatoru ni iku gakusee 'the students who are leaving from Osaka and going to Seattle'

in which **gakusee** is described by one complex modifier. In the previous example, we distinguished more than one group of students going to Seattle on the basis of whether or not they will leave from Osaka. In the second example, we are distinguishing those students who are leaving from Osaka *and* going to Seattle from all others.

A verbal or adjectival sentence occurring as a sentence modifier is distinguished from an independent sentence in only two respects: (1) the predicate of a sentence modifier can never be followed by a sentence-particle; and (2) the operator of an operational predicate and the affect(s) of an affective predicate, if expressed, are followed by **ḡa** or **no**, but not **wa**. This is a new kind of **no**. Compare:

Tomodati ḡa azuketa. '*A friend* deposited [it]' *but*
tomódati ḡa (*or* **no**) **azùketa okane** 'money my friend deposited'

Gakusee wa wakâru. 'The student (for one) understands.' *but*
gakúsee g̃a (*or* **no**) **wakàru nihoñg̃o** 'the Japanese the student understands'
Nihóñg̃o g̃a wakâru. '[I] understand *Japanese*.' *but*
nihóñg̃o g̃a (*or* **no**) **wakàru gakusee** 'the student who understands Japanese'

In general, **g̃a** and **no** are interchangeable in such examples, except that there is a preference for **g̃a** when it is far removed from its predicate or when the **no** alternate would be followed by another nominal, particularly a number or quantity word. Thus:

arúbàito g̃a końpyùutaa o tukátta heyà 'the room where the part-timer used the computer'

kodomo g̃a oózee narañde (i)ru tokorò 'the place where a crowd of children is lined up'

Note that Japanese does not usually distinguish between restrictive and nonrestrictive descriptions: **Nâg̃oya ni irú àni** can mean 'my older brother, (who is) in Nagoya' (I have only one older brother), *or* 'my older brother (who is) in Nagoya' (as opposed to my other older brother[s]).

2. ANTICIPATORY **no**

We have already encountered the nominal **no** 'one,' 'some' used as a replacement for an already familiar, more specific nominal. Examples:

Kore wa muzúkasii nihoñg̃o dèsu kedo, sore wa yasásìi no desu. 'This is difficult Japanese, but that is (some that is) easy.'

Tîzu wa, oókìi no mo tiísài no mo arimasu. 'Maps—we have big ones and small ones.'

Nominal **no** may also occur in anticipation of the more specific nominal, until the occurrence of which its particular reference is indeterminate. Thus, a sequence like **tukáù no** 'the item "use"' may refer to such varied notions as the user, the thing used, the location of the use, and the time of use. Compare the following examples:

Tukáù no wa, dâre desu ka⤴ 'Who is the one who uses (or will use) [it]?'

Compare **Dâre g̃a tukáù ñ desu ka⤴**

Tukáù no wa dôre desu ka⤴ 'Which is the one you use (or are going to use)?'

Compare **Dôre o tukáù ñ desu ka⤴**

Tukáù no wa, dôko desu ka⤴ 'Where is the place where you use (or are going to use) [it]?'

Compare **Dôko de tukáù ñ desu ka⤴**

Tukáù no wa, îtu desu ka⤴ 'When is the time when you use (or are going to use) [it]?'

Compare **Îtu tukáù ñ desu ka⤴**

In each case, the alternate with **tukáù no wa** puts special focus on what follows, specifically in relation to the **wa**-phrase: 'in reference to "use" (at least)—*who, which thing, where, when* is it?' In contrast, the alternate with the extended predicate, stressing shared information, relates the specific question of who, which one, where, or when to something already known by speaker and addressee: both recognize that something will be used, but question who or which one or where or when is it that it will be used. In other words, these two patterns are similar but not identical in meaning.

3. déru mâe

The nominal **mâe**, referring both to previous time and front location, has appeared in a number of patterns:

    Mâe wa sôo datta kedo . . 'It was like that before (at least), but . . .'
    Tyôtto mâe ni tukáimàsita. 'I used it a little while ago.'
    Kâre wa zíp-puñ mâe made imâsita yo↗ 'He was here until ten minutes ago.'
    Yô-zi sáñ-pùñ-mae desu. 'It's three minutes to four.'
    Anó hòteru no mâe desu. 'It's in front of (*or* the front of) that hotel.'

We now introduce **mâe** preceded by a sentence modifier ending with, or consisting of, a verbal. The modifier describes an occurrence that *follows* the occurrence of another event covered by the context. Keeping in mind that the choice between imperfective and perfective is regularly a matter of incomplete/complete *as of a point in time set by the context,* the verbal before **mâe** must ALWAYS be imperfective, since it is always incomplete as of the established context. Thus:

    Nihôñ e ikú màe ni, nihóñḡo o beñkyoo-simàsita. 'I studied Japanese before I went to Japan (i.e., in the time preceding a later going to Japan).'
    Nihóñḡo o beñkyoo-sità no wa, Nihôñ e ikú màe desita. 'The time I studied Japanese was before I went (i.e., previous to going) to Japan.'
    Sore wa narábu màe desita. 'That was before we lined up (i.e., the time before we would line up).'
    Kéḱkoñ-suru màe wa, Amérika dèsita kedo; keḱkoñ-sitè kara wa, Toókyoo dèsu. 'Before getting married I was in the U.S., but since getting married it's been Tokyo.'
    Tomódati ḡa kùru mâe ni, utí o katazukemàsita. 'Before my friend came, I straightened up the house.'
    Tomodati wa, kûru mâe ni utí o katazukemàsita. 'My friend straightened up the house before coming.'

4. /VERBAL GERUND + mîru/

We have been introduced to a number of special combinations of /verbal gerund X + verbal Y/ in which the combination occurs as a unit without intervening pause or break, and verbal Y has either no accent or reduced accent, or enters into a single accent phrase with X. Examples are **tâbete (i)ru, tâbete âru, tâbete simau** (∼ **tâbetyau**), and **tâbet(e) oku.** We now introduce /verbal gerund X + **mîru**/ 'do X and see how it turns out,' 'try X-ing.' Thus: **tâbete mîru** 'try eating,' **tukátte mìru** 'try using,' **kiíte mìru** 'ask and see (what we find out),' **naôsite mîru** 'fix it and see (if it works).' Compare:

    Pâi o tukûtte mîte moratta. 'I had [someone] try making a pie.' *and*
    Pâi o tukûtte, mîte moratta. 'I made a pie and had [someone] look at it.' (*lit.* 'having made a pie, I received looking at it.')

Drills

A 1. **Kore, sutémàsu ka⤴**
'Are you going to throw these away?'

  Êe, sore wa zêñbu sutéru monò desu.
  'Yes, those are all things I'm going to throw away.'

2. **Kore, okúrimàsu ka⤴**
'Are you going to send these?'

  Êe, sore wa zêñbu okúru monò desu.
  'Yes, those are all things I'm going to send.'

3. naórimàsu; 4. moíte ikimàsu; 5. irímàsu; 6. tukáimàsu; 7. katázukemàsu

B 1. **Yosída-sañ ḡa kimàsu neʔ**
'Mr/s. Yoshida is coming—right?'

  Hâi, kûru no wa Yosída-sañ dèsu kedo . .
  'Yes, the one who is coming is Mr/s. Yoshida, but . . .' (is there a problem?)

2. **Yamánaka señsèe ḡa kudásaimàsu neʔ**
'Dr. Yamanaka is giving it to us—right?'

  Hâi, kudásàru no wa Yamánaka-señsèe desu kedo . .
  'Yes, the one who is giving it to us is Dr. Yamanaka, but . . .' (is there a problem?)

3. Tanáka-kyòozyu/oyómi ni narimàsu; 4. butyoo/yamémàsu; 5. hîsyo/tetúdàtte kuremasu; 6. gakusee/okúremàsu; 7. arúbàito no hitô/sirábemàsu; 8. ryôozi/syoókai-simàsu

C 1. **Zêñbu obôete (i)ru?**
'Do you remember the whole thing?'

  Ñ̄ñ⤴ Obôete (i)ru no wa 'hañbuñ dake.
  'Uh-uh. What I remember is just half.'

2. **Zêñbu naôtte (i)ru?**
'Are all of them repaired?'

  Ñ̄ñ⤴ Naôtte (i)ru no wa 'hañbuñ dake.
  'Uh-uh. What is repaired is just half.'

3. tûite; 4. katázùite; 5. káḡi ḡa kakâtte; 6. utte; 7. narañde

D 1. **Kyôo señsèe ni tanómimàsu neʔ**
'You're going to ask the teacher today—right?'

  Iya, tanômu no wa asítà desu yo⤴
  'No, the time (lit. one) when I'll ask is tomorrow.'

2. **Kyôo misê ḡa akímàsu neʔ**
'The shop is going to open today—right?'

  Iya, akû no wa asítà desu yo⤴
  'No, the time when it will open is tomorrow.'

3. kaísya ni yorimàsu; 4. deñwa o iremàsu; 5. êeḡa o mimàsu; 6. isyá ni mìte moraimasu; 7. syatyóo ni ome ni kakarimàsu; 8. mâdo o naósimàsu

E 1. **Sonó ràzio, naôsita ñ desu ka⤴**
'(Is it that) you fixed that radio?'

  Êe, naôsita râzio desu yo⤴
  'Yes, that's the radio I fixed.'

2. **Sonó amìdo, tukûtte moráttà ñ desu ka⤴**
'(Is it that) you had those screens made?'

  Ee, tukûtte moratta amîdo desu yo⤴
  'Yes, they're the screens I had made.'

3. husuma/simâtte (i)ta; 4. tana/katta; 5. tyuúka-ryòori/osiete moratta; 6. gîsi/tanôñda; 7. teñiñ/yameta; 8. têrebi/yattyatta

F 1. **Konó tìzu, dâre ḡa kâita ka gozôñzi desu ka⤴**

  Sâa, dâre no kâita tîzu desyoo nêe.
  'Hm. I wonder who did draw it . . .' (lit.

'This map—do you know who drew it?'
    'It would be a map that who drew...')

2. **Kono teeburu, dâre ḡa moíte kita ka gozôñzi desu ka**
'This table—do you know who brought it?'
    Sâa, dâre no moíte kita teéburu desyòo nêe.
    'Hm. I wonder who did bring it...' (*lit.* 'It would be a table that who brought...')

3. asoko no ueki/okutte kureta; 4. anó èeḡa/tukûtta; 5. kyôo no otya/ireta; 6. **kono siñbuñ/suteta**; 7. konó tokkyùukeñ/wasureta; 8. ano sibai/kâita

• Repeat this drill, replacing particle **no** with particle **ḡa** in the responses.

G 1. **Señèñsatu de goséñ-eñ kudasài.**
'Please give me ¥5,000 in ¥1,000 bills.'
    Goséñ-eñ dèsu ka⌐ Zyâa, señèñsatu go-mái dèsu neʃ
    '¥5,000? Then that will be five ¥1,000 bills—right?'

2. **Hyakueñdama de sañbyakù-eñ kudasài.**
'Please give me ¥300 in ¥100 coins.'
    Sañbyakù-eñ desu ka⌐ Zyâa, hyaku-eñdama sâñ-mai desu neʃ
    '¥300? Then that will be three ¥100 coins—right?'

3. zyuueñdama/yoñzùu-eñ; 4. itímañèñsatu/hatimañ-eñ; 5. goséñèñsatu/itimañ-eñ; 6. gozyuueñdama/nihyákù-eñ; 7. gohyakueñdama/sêñ gohyákù-eñ

H 1. **Kânozyo, môo nîmotu azúkemàsita ka**
'Did she check her luggage yet?'
    A. Îma azúke ni ittà ñ desu kedo..
    'Oh, she [just] now went to check it, but...' (is that all right?)

2. **Kânozyo, môo 'kippu kaímàsita ka**
'Did she buy her tickets yet?'
    A. Îma kaí ni ittà ñ desu kedo..
    'Oh, she [just] now went to buy them, but...' (is that all right?)

3. zikokuhyoo sirábemàsita; 4. daidokoro katázukemàsita; 5. otya irémàsita; 6. amâdo simémàsita; 7. tomodati miókurimàsita

I 1. **Utí o dète kara reñraku-simasyòo ka.**
'Shall I get in touch after leaving the house?'
    Ie, dêru mâe ni sité kudasaimasèñ ka⌐
    'No, would you do it before you leave?'

2. **Kodómo o azùkete kara reñraku-simasyòo ka.**
'Shall I get in touch after leaving off the children?'
    Ie, azúkèru mâe ni sité kudasaimasèñ ka⌐
    'No, would you do it before you leave them off?'

3. siḡóto o katazùkete; 4. kaisya ni 'deñwa o irete; 5. tosyôkañ o sirábète; 6. nîmotu o azûkete; 7. zikañ o kimete

J 1. **Ano ike, konó heñ ni arimàsita ka**
'Was that pond around here?'
    Sâa, âtta ka dôo ka, tyôtto yôku obôete (i)nâi kedo; sirâbete mimasyoo ka.

2. **Ano byooiñ, nitíyòo mo aíte (i)màsu ka**⤵
'Is that hospital open on Sunday, too?'

'Hm. I just don't remember very well whether it was or not; shall I check and see?'

Sâa, aíte (i)rù ka dôo ka, tyôtto yôku obôete (i)nâi kedo; sirâbete mimasyoo ka.

'Hm. I just don't remember very well whether it's open or not; shall I check and see?'

3. ano gakusee/tetúdàtte kuremasu; 4. anó iḡirisùziñ/nihóñḡo tuuzimàsu; 5. kono osake/tuyôi desu; 6. sonó ràzio/kosyóo dèsu; 7. anó misè/keésàñki uʹtte (i)màsu

K 1. **Hasímoto-sañ ni tanomimasyòo ka**⤵
'Shall I ask Mr/s. Hashimoto?'

Âa, konaida môo tanôñde mimâsita kedo, yaṕpàri damê desita.

'Oh, I already tried asking him/her the other day, but it didn't work out after all.'

2. **Konó keesàñki naósimasyòo ka**⤵
'Shall I fix this calculator?'

Âa, konaida môo naôsite mimâsita kedo, yaṕpàri damê desita.

'Oh, I already tried fixing it the other day, but it didn't work out after all.'

3. zéñbu narábemasyòo; 4. atárasìi isu okímasyòo; 5. zikókuhyoo sirabemasyòo; 6. señsèe ni ukáḡaimasyòo; 7. asóko no ryooḡàeki tukáimasyòo

L 1. **Koré o naòsite kudasai. Naôru desyoo?**
'Would you fix this? It can be fixed, can't it?'

Koré ò desu ka. Naôsite mimàsu kedo; naôru ka dôo ka, wakárimas̱èñ yo⤵

'This? I'll try fixing it, but I can't tell whether it can be fixed or not.'

2. **Kânozyo ni aḡéte kudasài. Yorókòbu desyoo?**
'Would you give her [this]? She'll be pleased, won't she?'

Kânozyo ni desu ka. Aḡéte mimàsu kedo; yorókòbu ka dôo ka, wakárimasèñ yo⤵

'(To) her? I'll give it to her and see, but I can't tell whether she'll be pleased or not.'

3. teńiñ ni mìsete/naôsite kureru; 4. señsèe o yoñde/miêru; 5. anó booekìsyoo ni iñtabyuu-site/omósiròi

M 1. **Anó mizuùmi e môo ikímàsita neʔ**
'You already went to that lake—right?'

Ie, zitû wa mâda na ñ de, iḱ-kai itte mitài to omôtte (i)ru ñ desu yo⤵

'No, actually (being the case that it's) not yet; I've been thinking I'd like to try going some time (*lit.* one time).'

2. **Ano bañḡumi môo mimâsita neʔ**
'You already saw that program—right?'

Ie, zitû wa mâda na ñ de, iḱ-kai mìte mitâi to omôtte (i)ru ñ desu yo⤵

'No, actually (being the case that it's) not

yet; I've been thinking I'd like to try seeing it sometime (*lit.* one time).'

3. **ano keézai-kàṅkee no hôñ/yomímàsita**; 4. **anó hàisya ni/mîte moraimasita**; 5. **Ôono-señsee no kooeñ/kikímàsita**; 6. **asoko no teñiñ ni/kikímàsita**

N 1. **Kono nihoñḡo naôsu?**
'Are you going to correct this Japanese?'

|Anoo| **Suḡîura-kuñ ni naôsite mîte moráitài to omôtte . .**
'[I've been] thinking I'd like to have Sugiura try fixing it up . . .'

2. **Asâtte no zadâñkai ni dêru?**
'Are you going to take part in the round-table discussion the day after tomorrow?'

|Anoo| **Suḡîura-kuñ ni dête mîte moráitài to omôtte . .**
'[I've been] thinking I'd like to have Sugiura try participating . . .'

3. **todána no nàka sirábèru**; 4. **zikókuhyoo mìru**; 5. **konó kikài tukau**; 6. **okane komâkàku suru**

O 1. **Sono deñsya, gôḡo sitî-zi ni tukímàsu?**
'Does that train arrive at 7 P.M.?'

Êe, **zyuúkù-zi-tyaku desu ne!**
'Yes, it's a 19:00 arrival.'

2. **Sono deñsya, gôzeñ sitî-zi ni tukímàsu?**
'Does that train arrive at 7 A.M.?'

Êe, **sitî-zi-tyaku desu ne!**
'Yes, it's a 7:00 arrival.'

3. **gôḡo itî-zi**; 4. **gôzeñ nî-zi sâñzyuu gô-huñ**; 5. **gôḡo yô-zi zîp-puñ**

Application Exercises

A1. Set up the kind of model town used in earlier lessons and practice asking and answering questions that include sentence modifiers ending in verbals or adjectivals. For example:

A to B no aída ni àru no wa, nâñ to iu misê desu ka

A ni itíbañ tikài hôteru wa, nâñ to iu hôteru desu ka

A-sañ ḡa (*or* **no**) **îma hâitte (i)ru misê wa, dôñna no desu ka**

2. Using a local timetable or a specially designed one, practice asking and answering questions that include sentence modifiers. For example:

/Time/ **ni** /place A/ **o dêru bâsu wa, nâñ-zi ni** /place B/ **ni tukímàsu ka**

/Time/ **ni** /place B/ **ni tûku bâsu wa, nâñ-zi ni** /place A/ **o demâsu ka**

3. Practice responding to information questions (who, when, where, etc.) with replies that incorporate anticipatory **no**, the nominal which can refer to persons, things, places, and times. For example:

Kyôo nâñ-zi-ḡòro otáku ni kaerimàsu ka

Kâeru no wa, rokú-zi-ḡòro desyoo nêe.

Îma tukátte (i)rù kyoókàsyo wa, dôko de kaímàsita ka

Kattá no wa, A to iu misê desu kedo . .

4. Ask members of the class to perform two activities in sequence (examples: open the window, and then shut the door; read this, and then throw it away; order home-delivered food, and then read the paper.) After performing the activities requested, describe what was done, using **mâe**. (For example, 'Before opening the window, I shut the door.')

5. Practice requesting an amount of money, designating how it is to be made up. For example, ask for $50 in tens, ¥20,000 in ¥5000 bills, etc. In reply, state how many of the specified denomination are involved. Use real or facsimile money. (See Drill G, above.)

B. Core Conversations: Substitution

The Core Conversations of this section present innumerable possibilities for substitution. As you practice new versions of the conversations, be sure to retain the original framework, including basic sentence structure and sentence-particles.

SECTION B

Core Conversations

1(N)a. **Kêsa tâkusii ni nóttà ñ desu ğa neʃ Uńtèñsyu ğa zyosée no tàkusii na ñ desu yo.**

(J) **Heeˌ Mezúrasìi nêe.**

b. **Desyoo? Watasi mo biḱkùri-simasita.**

2(J)a. **Kińyòobi kara no tûaa ni ikú hito no nàka de, mâda kiṕpu o mòtte (i)nái hitò wa, inâi desyoo ne!**

(N)a. **Señsyuu oyásumi dàtta hito wa, mâda morátte (i)maseñ yoˌ**

b. **Sôo desu ka. Zyâa, toózitu no àsa atúmàtta tokî ni watásimasyòo.**

b. **Atúmàru no wa, Sińzyukù-eki Hiğásìğuti no kaísatùğuti no tokórò desu neʃ**

c. **Sôo. Zyûuzi-hatu no toḱkyuu ni norù ñ da kara neʃ Ku-zí-hàñ made ni atúmàtte (i)tâi desu ne!**

3(N)a. **Utí ğa tikài hito wa, îi desu nêe.**

(J)a. **Mâa, tuúkiñ-zìkañ ğa mizíkài kara..**

b. **Zitû wa, kinoo kâeru no ğa kânari osôkatta ñ desu kedo neʃ**

b. **Ñ.**

c. **Tukârete, deńsya no nàka de gûuguu netyáttà ñ desu yo.**

c. **Sôo desu ka.**

d. **Sore de neʔ**
  e. **Hâtto ki ḡá tùita tokî wa, môo orîru êki o dête simátta àto de . .**
  f. **Awátete tàtta kedo, dôa wa môo simâttyatte (i)ru desyoo? Hazúkàsìkatta desu nêe.**

  d. **Êe.**
  e. **Taiheñ da.**

  f. **Sôo desyoo nêe.**

ENGLISH EQUIVALENTS

1(N)a. I rode in a taxi this morning, but do you know what? I'm talking about a taxi with a woman driver.
  b. Isn't it? I was amazed, too.
2(J)a. Among the people going on the tour starting on Friday, there probably aren't any people who don't have their tickets yet, are there?

(J) Wow! That's amazing, isn't it!

(N)a. The people who were on vacation last week haven't received them yet.

  b. Oh. In that case, let's hand them over [to them] when we assemble on the morning of the actual day.

  b. The gathering [place] will be (the place) where they take tickets at the East Entrance of Shinjuku Station—right?

  c. Yes. We're taking the special express that leaves at 10:00, so we want to be gathered by 9:30, don't we.
3(N)a. People with homes that are close by are fortunate, aren't they!

(J)a. Well, commuting time is short, so . . .

  b. As a matter of fact, my return home yesterday was quite late . . .
  c. Exhausted, I fell sound asleep on the train.
  d. That being the case . . .
  e. When I came to, with a start, it was (*lit.* being) after we'd already left the station where I get off . . .
  f. I stood up in confusion, but the door was (*lit.* is) already shut tight—you know? I was so embarrassed.

  b. (Yeah.)

  c. You did?
  d. Yes.

  e. How awful!

  f. You must have been!

Breakdowns
(and Supplementary Vocabulary)

1. **noru /-u; notta/** — get on; board a vehicle; ride
   +**noseru /-ru; noseta/** — place on [something]; take on board; give a ride

   tâkusii ni noru — take a taxi
   zyosee — woman, female
   +**dañsee** — man, male
   uńtèñsyu ḡa zyosée no tàkusii (SP1, SP2) — a taxi whose driver is a woman
   mezúrasìi /-katta/ — is amazing, surprising, unexpected
   Desyoo? — Don't you agree? I thought you'd say that!

2. **tûaa** — tour
   kińyòobi kara no tûaa — a tour which is from Friday (begins Friday)
   ikú hito no nàka de — (being) among the people who are going
   señsyuu oyásumi dàtta hito (SP1) — people who were on vacation last week
   toozitu — the very day, the day in question
   atúmàru /-u; atúmàtta/ — come together
   +**atúmèru /-ru; atûmeta/** — bring together
   atúmàtta toki — (the time) when [we've] assembled
   watasu /-u; watasita/ — hand over
   +**wataru /-u; watatta/** — go over, go across
   atúmàru no — the gathering together
   hiḡasi — east
   +**nisi** — west
   +**kita/kitâ** — north
   +**minami** — south
   Hiḡásìḡuti — the East Entrance
   kaísatùḡuti — ticket-checking gate, wicket
   kaísatùḡuti no tokoro — the place where the wicket is
   X-hàtu — departure at X time or from X place
   zyûu-zi-hatu no tokkyuu — special express leaving at 10:00
   +**tâtu /-u; tâtta/** — depart
   ku-zí-hàñ made ni atúmàru — gather by 9:30
   ku-zí-hàñ made ni atúmàtte (i)ru — be gathered by 9:30

3. **utí ḡa tikài hito** — people with homes that are close by
   tuukiñ — commuting
   tuúkiñ-zìkañ — commuting time
   kâeru no — the returning (home)
   kâeru no ḡa osôi — going home is late

kânari	fairly, rather, quite
neru /-ru; neta/	go to sleep; go to bed
+nekasu /-u; nekasita/	put to sleep; lay [something] on its side
+nemûi /-katta/	is sleepy
gûuguu netyau (SP3)	fall sound asleep
ki ḡá tùku	notice; become aware
+ki ó tukèru	pay attention; be careful
hâtto/hatto	with a start, in surprise
hâtto ki ḡá tùku	become aware with a start
ki ḡá tùita toki	(time) when [I] became aware
orîru /-ru; ôrita/	descend; get off (a vehicle)
+orôsu /-u; orôsita/	lower; unload; let off (a vehicle)
orîru êki	station where [I] get off
dête simátta àto de (SP4)	(being) after having left
awateru /-ru; awateta/	become confused, disconcerted, disorganized
tâtu /-u; tâtta/	stand up; become built
+tatêru /-ru; tâteta/	stand [something] up, erect [something]
+suwaru /-u; suwatta/ *or*	
+(kosí)kakèru /-ru; (kosí)kàketa/	sit down
hazúkasìi /-katta/	is shy, embarrassed

Miscellaneous Notes

1. In CC1, Sue Brown tells her professor, Dr. Ono, about an unusual experience on the way to the university. The topic and setting are informal—reflected in Sue Brown's use of **yo** and **Desyoo?**—but she, of course, uses distal-style. Professor Ono's single utterance is direct-style.

(N)a. **Noru**, an operational, intransitive consonant-verbal, has as its transitive partner the operational vowel-verbal **noseru**. Although these verbals usually refer to getting on or riding on vehicles, they can also refer to general location on top of something. Note these combinations: **hikôoki ni noru** 'board a plane'; **anó kàdo de noru** 'get on at that corner'; **Ano tana ni nâni ḡa notte (i)ru?** 'What is on that shelf?' **bâsu ni ′kodomo o noseru** 'put the children on the bus'; **Noíte kudasài.** 'Please get on.' **Noséte kudasài.** 'Please let me on.' **tomodati ni ′kodomo o bâsu ni ′nosete morau** 'have a friend put the children on the bus'; **koko ni bâsu ni noíte kùru** 'come here (riding) on a bus.'

Zyosee and **dañsee** are impersonal equivalents for 'woman' and 'man' which avoid the politeness choices posed by **katâ/hitô**, and **kâre/kânozyo**. Note **zyoseeḡo** 'women's language' and **danseeḡo** 'men's language.'

(J). **Mezúrasìi**: compare /**mezúrasìi** + nominal/ and /**mezúràsìku** + predicate/, as in **Mezúrasìi hôn o kâita.** '[He] wrote an amazing book.' **Mezúràsìku hôn o kâita.** 'Believe it or not, he wrote a book.' **Mezúrasìi nihóñḡo dèsu.** 'It's unusual Japanese.' **Mezúràsìku nihóñḡo dèsu.** 'Unexpectedly, it's Japanese.' In these examples, **mezúrasìi** hooks up with the immediately following nominal only, but **mezúràsìku** describes a predicate—the verbal, **kâita**, and the /nominal + **da**/ predicate, **nihóñḡo dèsu**.

(N)b. **Desyoo?** occurs as an informal sentence indicating agreement which is totally according to expectation with a judgment or comment just mentioned by one's partner in a conversation. Sue Brown is in complete agreement with Professor Ono's reactions to her experience, which she expected.

2. In CC2, Mr. Yamada and Deborah Miller are discussing final arrangements for the tour group they are organizing. As always, their language is careful, with distal-style, but not polite-style, predicates.

(J)a. **Môtu**, an operational consonant-verbal, has been frequently encountered in the combinations **motte iku** and **moíte kùru** (but note the accent change). By itself, it refers to taking hold of: **môtte kudasai** 'please take hold [of this],' 'please hold [it].' **Môtte (i)ru** refers to holding, having, or possessing. Unlike **âru**, a double-**ḡa** affective verbal that can also refer to having, **môtu** occurs with particle **o** following an operand: **okáne ḡa àru**, but **okáne o mòtte (i)ru**. Only the latter can also mean 'I'm holding money.'

(J)b. Note the grammatical contrast between 'when' clauses in English, and the Japanese use of the nominal **tokî** 'time,' 'occasion' preceded by a sentence modifier. Although (J)b refers to the future, the handing over of tickets will occur at a time when the group *will have already assembled*; accordingly, the perfective occurs before **tokî**.

Watasu 'give over' is the transitive partner of intransitive **wataru** 'go over,' 'go across.' Both are operational consonant-verbals. Compare **teḡami o watasu** 'hand over a letter' and **kawâ o wataru** 'cross over the river.' Intransitive **wataru** links up with a /nominal + **o**/ phrase, provided the nominal is a place word that describes the area through or over which the crossing occurs. Compare **miti o iku, kâdo o maḡaru, mití o arùku**.

(N)b. Note the identification of a place in terms of /name of larger unit (**Siñzyukù-eki**) + name of smaller unit (**Hiḡásiḡuti**)/ without a connecting particle **no**. The -**ḡuti** of **Hiḡásiḡuti** and **kaísatùḡuti** is derived from **kuti** 'mouth,' 'orifice'; compare also **dêḡuti** 'exit' and **iriḡuti** 'entrance.' Note **kaisatu** 'ticket-checking.'

(J)c. The suffix -**hàtu** is attached to nominal expressions indicating the place and/or time of departure: **Toókyoo-hàtu** 'leaving from Tokyo'; **sitî-zi-hatu** 'leaving at 7:00'; **Tookyoo sitî-zi-hatu** 'leaving Tokyo at 7:00.' A /-**hàtu** + -**tyàku**/ sequence, without connecting particle, indicates both departure and arrival; but the sequence requires **no** to hook up with a following nominal: **Nâḡoya kû-zi-hatu 'Tookyoo zyuúitì-zi-tyaku no kyuukoo** 'the express leaving Nagoya at 9:00 arriving in Tokyo at 11:00.' Like -**tyàku**, -**hàtu** is used most commonly in relation to transportation. **Tâtu**, an operational verbal, occurs in contexts having to do with travel. **Dêru**, a verbal of much broader and more general usage, includes the domain of **tâtu**. Note **Toókyoo ni** (*or* **e**) **tâtu** 'leave for Tokyo.'

Compare **ku-zí-hàñ made ni atúmàru** 'gather by 9:30' and **ku-zí-hàñ made ni atúmàtte (i)ru** 'be (already) gathered by 9:30.' **Atúmèru** 'bring together' is the transitive partner of **atúmàru** 'come together.' Both are operational verbals, with **atúmèru** a vowel verbal and **atúmàru** a consonant verbal; but only **atúmèru** occurs with /nominal + **o**/ phrases.

3. In CC3, Deborah Miller describes for Mr. Yamada an embarrassing experience she had in the train. Ms. Miller is the principal speaker, using careful-style with distal-style predicates. She involves her listener by breaking up long sentences into segments that call for appropriate input. Mr. Yamada's remarks are all supportive comments.

(J)a. Note **tuukiñ-suru** 'commute to an office.'

(N)b. The **no** of **kâeru no** refers here to the time of going home, made clear by **osôkatta**.

Kânari: Note **kânari no okane** 'a fair amount of money'; **kânari no hito** 'quite a few people.'

(N)c. **Neru** 'go to bed,' an operational vowel verbal, is the intransitive partner of transitive **nekasu**, an operational consonant verbal which occurs with /nominal + o/ phrases and covers not only putting people to bed but also laying objects on their side.

(N)e. **Ki ḡá tùku** 'notice' (*lit.* 'attention becomes attached') is an affective expression which contrasts with operational **ki ó tukèru** 'pay attention' (*lit.* 'attach attention'). These phrases have just about achieved single-word status, as evidenced by the polite-honorific **okíotuke ni nàru** ↑, rather than *__ki o otúke ni nàru__ ↑, the expected form for a /nominal + particle + verbal/ phrase.

Orîru 'get off,' 'get down' is the intransitive partner of transitive **orôsu** 'let off,' 'lower.' These verbals refer to downward movement in general, as well as to disembarking from vehicles, and both are operational. **Orîru** is a vowel-verbal and **orôsu** a consonant-verbal. Note the following combinations: **Ôrite kudasai.** 'Please get off (*or* down).' **Orôsite kudasai.** 'Please let me off (*or* down).' **nîmotu o orôsu** 'unload luggage'; **kodómo o orosu** 'let the children off (*or* down)'; **Orímàsu.** 'Getting off!' **yamâ o orîru** 'go down a mountain'; **kurúma kara orìru** 'get out of a car.'

Note **X tokî wa Y âto de** 'the time X being after Y.' Here —— **tokî wa** hooks up with a /nominal + **dà**/ predicate. This contrasts with —— **tokî ni,** which indicates the time at which something *happens*.

Compare **simâttyatta** 'it shut tight' and **simâttyatte (i)ru** 'it is shut tight.'

(N)f. **Tâtu** 'stand up,' 'become built' is the intransitive partner of transitive **tatêru** 'stand [something] up,' 'build' (cf. **tatêmono**), **tâtu** belonging to the consonant class and **tatêru** to the vowel class. Only **tatêru** may occur with a /nominal + o/ phrase. Note that **tâtu** 'stand up' is operational, but **tâtu** 'become built,' affective.

Suwaru is the general verbal for sitting, used most commonly in reference to Japanese-style sitting on the floor. For sitting on chairs (or benches, beds, tables, etc.), **kakêru** (or the longer form **kosíkakèru**) is usually used. **Kakêru** and **kosíkakèru**, which refer to hanging or suspending, are never used in reference to sitting on the floor.

Structural Patterns

1. SENTENCE MODIFIERS WITH /NOMINAL + COPULA/ FINAL PREDICATES

In Section A-SP1, we were introduced to sentence modifiers whose final predicates were verbals or adjectivals. There remains the third predicate type, /nominal + copula/.

We learned in Section A that the final predicate of a verbal or an adjectival sentence modifier is perfective or imperfective and direct-style. If the /nominal + copula/ sentence modifier followed the same pattern, it would consist of:

/nominal + **dà**/ + nominal *or*

/nominal + **dàtta**/ + nominal,

with the possibility, of course, of longer sentence modifiers ending in this way. Returning to Lesson 5B-SP1, in which we talked about nominal connectors to be analyzed later, we learned sequences like:

niséñ-eñ no hòñ 'a ¥2000 book'

guriîñ no hôñ 'a green book'

kîree na hoñ 'a beautiful book'

We are now prepared to analyze those phrases. When a sentence consisting of or ending with /nominal + **dà**/ occurs as a modifier of a following nominal, **dà** acquires the special form **no**, unless the preceding nominal is a **na**-nominal, in which case it becomes **na**. Thus:

/**byoóki dà** + **gakusee**/ > **byooki no gakusee** 'a student who is sick,' 'a sick student'

/**gêñki da** + **kodomo**/ > **gêñki na kodomo** 'a child who is healthy,' 'a healthy child'

Byooki is not a **na**-nominal, but **gêñki** is. However, we learned, in connection with the extended predicate, that every /nominal (particle) + **dà**/ before the extended predicate ending becomes /nominal (particle) + **na**/. Thus, **na** does follow nominals that do not belong to the **na**-class, in an extended predicate construction, and it is accented after unaccented sequences.

Byoóki nà ñ desu. '(It's that) [s/he]'s sick.'

Nihóñziñ na no? '(Is it that) [s/he]'s Japanese?'

Kyôo kara na ñ desyoo? '(It's that) it's starting today—right?'

In other contexts involving /nominal (particle) + **dà** + nominal **no**/, the resulting sequence depends on whether or not the nominal of the sentence modifier is a **na**-nominal. Compare:

/**gurîiñ da** + **no** 'one'/ > *gurîiñ no + no > gurîiñ no

Gurîiñ no wa, hurûi desu. 'The one that is green is old.' (The contraction is similar to that of particle **no** + nominal **no**).²

/**kîree da** + **no** 'one'/ > **kîree na no**

Môtto kîree na no wa, arímasèñ ka 'Isn't there one that is prettier?'

In the perfective equivalent of the sentence modifier with a nominal predicate, **dàtta** retains its normal form:

byoóki dàtta gakusee 'a student who was sick'

gêñki datta kodomo 'a child who was healthy'

The negative of a nominal predicate, as usual, becomes an adjectival predicate:

nihóñziñ zya nâi señsèe 'the teacher who isn't Japanese'

Extending sentence modifiers with a nominal final predicate to include **ḡa**- affects, we find parallelism with the sentence modifiers introduced earlier, including preference for **-ḡa** over **no** in cases of ambiguity:

/**tomódati ḡa sukì da** + **monô**/ > **tomódati ḡa** (*or* **no**) **sukì na mono** 'things my friend likes'

/**otóotò ḡa gakúsee dàtta** + **tokî**/ > **otóotò ḡa gakúsee dàtta toki** 'the time when my younger brother was a student'

But not every **no** that connects nominals in an **X no Y** pattern is the special form of the copula. We must also recognize a particle which specifies that Y is a part of, a possession of, or a derivative of X. Consider the phrase **nihóñziñ no señsèe**. This has two distinct meanings, depending on whether /**no** = **dà**/ ('the teacher who is Japanese') or /**no** = partitive particle/ (then 'the teacher of the Japanese people'). Note some additional differences between the two:

---

2. For some nominals, an alternate consisting of /**dà** > **na** + **no**/ is also possible. Example: **byooki no** *or* **byoóki nà no** 'the one who is sick.'

If /**no** = **dà**/,[3] there is a predictable negative equivalent, **nihóñzìñ zya nâi señsèe,** which can only mean 'the teacher who isn't Japanese.'

Only if /**no** = **dà**/ can the sequence be changed to the perfective: **nihóñzìñ datta señsèe** 'a teacher who was Japanese.'

Consider, now, the various different **no** that we have encountered:

(1) nominal **no** as a replacement or anticipatory nominal, or the **ñ/no** nominal of the extended predicate.
   Oókìi no o kudasai.   'Give me a big one.'
   Kaû no wa dôko?   'Where do you buy it?'
   Wakâru ñ desu.   'It's that I understand.'

(2) **no** as a special pre-nominal form of **dà**.
   byooki no gakusee   'a student who is sick'

(3) **no** as a particle connecting nominals, where the following nominal is a derivative or part of the preceding.
   watási no hòñ   'my book'
   kawa no mizu   'water in the river'
   Toókyoo no tàkusii   'Tokyo taxi'

(4) **no** as a particle that alternates with **ḡa**, following the operator or affect of the predicate of a sentence modifier.
   âni no (*or* **ḡa**) **tukátta kikài**   'the machine my older brother used'
   ane no kirai na sakana   'fish my older sister dislikes'

(5) **nò** as the contraction of /particle (3) **no** + nominal **no** (1)/ or as the contraction of /**no** (2) = **dà** + nominal **no** (1)/.
   watási nò desu   'it's mine (i.e., my one)'
   gurêe no desu   'it's the one that's gray'

2. SENTENCE MODIFIERS AS PARTITIVE DESCRIPTORS

In situations in which a larger unit is described in terms of one of its parts, Japanese uses sentence modifiers whose predicate is the description and the specific part its affect. In other words, 'a child with big eyes' becomes an 'eyes-are-big child'; 'a river with clean water' becomes a 'water-is-clean river'; 'a taxi with a woman driver' becomes a 'driver-is-a-woman taxi.' Note the following examples:

   mê no oókìi kodomo   'a child with big eyes'
   utí ḡa tikài zimûsyo   'an office with one's home close by'
   mizú no kìree na kawâ   'a river with clean water'
   uñteñsyu ḡa zyosée no tàkusii   'a taxi with a woman driver'
   atáma no itài Tanaka-sañ   'Mr/s. Tanaka who has a headache'
   mimí no tooi tosiyòri   'an old person who's hard of hearing'
   eéḡo ḡa zyoozù na gakusee   'a student with good English'

---

3. In the unlikely event that the modifier of **nihóñzìñ no señsèe** = 'the teacher of the Japanese people' were negated, it would turn out to be **nihóñzìñ no zya nâi señsèe,** which many native speakers reject as extremely unusual.

gaíkokuḡo ḡa dekìru kyôosi 'an instructor proficient in foreign languages'
hisyô ḡa dáñsee no zimùsyo 'an office with a male secretary'

In all the above examples, particle **ḡa** can be replaced by particle **no** and vice versa, except that **ḡa** is preferred between nominals where **no** might be ambiguous.

Note that the sequence **X no Y Z**, in which X and Z are nominals and Y a predicate, may represent two different patterns. In the sequence /**X no** + **Y Z**/, **no** is the connective particle between nominals, but in /**X no Y** + **Z**/, **no** is the particle that alternates with **ḡa**, connecting a nominal to the predicate of a sentence modifier. Compare:

Tookyoo no takâi kissateñ = **Tookyoo no** + **takâi kissateñ** 'expensive coffee shops in Tokyo' *and*

koóhìi no (*or* **ḡa**) **takâi kissateñ** = **koóhìi no** (*or* **ḡa**) **takâi** + **kissateñ** 'coffee shops where the coffee is expensive'

The accent phrasing of the two patterns is distinct: following the particle **no** which connects nominals, an accented word has high pitch, and an unaccented word starts a new accent phrase. Thus, in the sequence **hôñ no omósiròi tokoro**, with high pitch on **omósiròi** (at least as high as the high pitch of **hôñ**), the sequence is equivalent to 'interesting places in the book,' but with the high pitch of **omósiròi** lower than that of **hôñ,** it means 'a place where the books are interesting.'

3. ONOMATOPOEIA

Onomatopoeia refers to words in a language which are supposed to suggest their meaning by their sound. When in English we use terms like bowwow, meow, and cock-a-doodle-doo, we are using onomatopoeia. The fact that these terms are far from universal indicates how culture specific onomatopoeia is. Japanese dogs say **wâñwañ** and their cats **niâo.** Which sounds have pleasant connotations or "sound beautiful" are totally different, depending on the culture.

Japanese has a particularly large inventory of onomatopoeic vocabulary. There are entire dictionaries devoted exclusively to the category, which in Japanese distinguishes between words which are connotative of sound (**giseeḡo**) and those that are meant to suggest their meaning (unrelated to sound) through their general makeup (**gitaiḡo**). For example, **gâtagata**, denoting a rattling sound, is an example of **giseeḡo**, whereas **girigiri**, describing an activity that is barely achieved, reached by the skin of one's teeth, is an example of **gitaiḡo**. For native speakers, who have grown up with countless examples, the associations which particular combinations of sounds are meant to evoke are similar, with the result that they have predictable reactions even to items they have never heard before. But for the foreigner, Japanese **giseeḡo** and **gitaiḡo** can actually be more difficult to master than other new vocabulary.

In this lesson, we are introduced to two new onomatopoeic words: **gûuguu** and **hâtto**. They represent two common shapes for this kind of vocabulary. Like **gûuguu** and the two onomatopoeic examples cited above, many onomatopoeic words are reduplicated—i.e., they consist of a sequence repeated twice. Note that in examples of this category that begin with **g**, the repeated **g** in the middle of the word is never **ḡ**.

The final **-to** of **hâtto** is also typical of many onomatopoeic words. Those in this category are usually nominals that occur principally in combination with a predicate as manner constructions. Some form compounds with **suru**.

/Gûuguu + neru/ refers to very sound sleep. (Could **gûuguu** be suggesting the snoring sound associated with deep sleep?) **Hâtto** describes occurrences accompanied by surprise. Note also: **hâtto-suru** 'become startled.'

Undoubtedly **biḱkùri** also belongs to the onomatopoeia category. Its **-ri** ending, like the **-to** of **hâtto**, is typical. Like **hâtto**, **biḱkùri** also forms a compound with **suru**: **biḱkùri-suru** 'become amazed.' However, **biḱkùri** does not occur as a manner expression modifying a following predicate.

4. **dête simátta àto de**

We have previously encountered **âto** in the combination **âto de** 'being a later time' and /**âto** + a time expression of extent/ indicating time remaining until a designated time.

Âto is a nominal, and it is often preceded by a sentence modifier. You will remember that a sentence modifier preceding **mâe** 'before' is always imperfective, since it describes an activity that has not occurred by the time that the related occurrence takes place. **Âto** 'after' is the exact opposite: since the action of its modifier has always already happened by the time the related predicate occurs, its verbal modifier is ALWAYS perfective. Thus:

> **Katyóo ḡa tùita no wa, môo demáe o tyuumoñ-sita àto desita.** 'When the section chief arrived, it was already after I had ordered the food to be delivered.'
>
> **Demáe o tyuumoñ-sita àto de, katyóo ḡa tukimàsita.** 'After I ordered the food to be delivered, the section chief arrived.'
>
> **Moó sukòsi sirâbeta âto de, atárasìi kyoókàsyo o tyuúmoñ-simasyòo.** 'After we check a little more, let's order new textbooks.'

The **de** following **âto** in the preceding examples is the gerund of **dèsu**, indicating that only at the point when the later time (**âto**) is actually realized—i.e., arrived at—does the related activity occur.

We already know another Japanese pattern for sequential occurrences:

> **Utí e kàette kara, demáe o tyuumoñ-simàsita.** 'After returning home, I ordered food to be delivered.'

Compare now:

> **Utí e kàetta âto de, demáe o tyuumoñ-simàsita.**

In both cases, returning home preceded the ordering of food. But in the example with **kara**, the second activity stems from the first: proceeding from the return, the ordering occurred soon after. With **âto de**, the emphasis is on the fact that the ordering took place after—not before—the return home.

☠ WARNING: Remember that **âto** is a nominal but **kara** a particle: **sitá àto** but **sitê kara** 'after having done.'

5. SPOKEN NARRATIVE STYLE

Until this lesson, our conversing in Japanese has been limited to exchanges between two individuals, with each person contributing more or less equally to the conversation. In CC3 of this lesson section, we encounter our first example of "storytelling," as Deborah Miller describes a personal experience. Mr. Yamada is her audience.

It is important to note that the relating of a narrative is not a matter of simply lining up countless ——**te**, ——**te**, ——**te**, sequences, with an occasional **sore kara** and **-màsita**. Note the style that Miller uses:

(1) She signals the start of her story with **zitû wa** to separate it from the general comments that have preceded.
(2) Her first statement, ending in **n desu kedo**, provides useful information for future comprehension. It was the lateness of her return that explains why she was so tired.
(3) The first event (falling asleep) is presented as a complete independent unit, ending in **yo**.
(4) The transition to what follows is handled by **sore de** 'being that condition just described.'
(5) The remainder of the story is handled in one long, complex sentence that includes —— **tokî wa**, —— **âto de**, —— **kedo**, —— **desyoo?** This is broken up into two parts to engage the listener better. Note that the four parts—going past the station, noticing, standing up, and having the doors shut—are interrelated in a complex pattern which creates interest. They are not simply related in terms of sequential ordering, 'A, then B, then C, then D.' Vividness and immediacy are further heightened by the use of the imperfective for the final predicate: **simâttyatte (i)ru desyoo?**
(6) The story ends with a description of the storyteller's reaction.
(7) Of crucial importance is the involvement of the listener. In Japanese spoken narrative the speaker and the listener must be in perfect sync, with the speaker providing clear signals at regular intervals for the listener to demonstrate his interest and continuing attention. A **kedo neˀ** or a pause at the end of a grammatical phrase from Miller are signals for at least a grunt from Yamada—although a **taihen da** shows greater concern. The direct-style of this comment emphasizes Yamada's close involvement. A sentence-final **yo** from Miller provides a major break, eliciting a **Sôo desu ka** from Yamada that is like a conversational paragraph marker. And Miller's **nêe**, terminating the story, calls for an appropriate **nêe** comment from Yamada.

Drills

A 1. **Kokó no tàkusii, unten ga zyoozù desu nêe.**
'The taxis here are well driven, aren't they!'

Hontoo ni unten ga zyoozù na tâkusii desu nêe.
'They really are well-driven taxis, aren't they!'

2. **Konó zyùgyoo, sensèe ga amérikàzin desu nêe.**
'These classes have American teachers, don't they!'

Hontoo ni sensèe ga amérikàzin no zyûgyoo desu nêe.
'They really are classes with American teachers, aren't they!'

3. **kono kaisya/syain ga hima**; 4. **konó depàato/tenin ga damè**; 5. **kono gakkoo/kodómo ga gènki**; 6. **kono sigoto/àsa ga taihen**; 7. **konó zimùsyo/tuúkin ga rakù**; 8. **kono ryokan/okyáku ga oozêe**

B 1. **Anó untènsyu, unten ga zyoózù desita nêe.**

Âa, ano unten ga zyoozù datta untensyu desu ka. Îma dôo site (i)ru desyoo nêe.

'That driver was really skilled in driving, wasn't he!' | 'Oh, that driver who was skilled in driving? I wonder how he's doing now.'

2. **Ano daiĝaku, gaiziñ no gakusee ĝa oózèe desita nêe.**
   'That college had many foreign students, didn't it!' | **Âa, ano gaíziñ no gakusee ĝa oozèe datta daíĝaku dèsu ka. Îma dôo nâtte (i)ru desyoo nêe.**
   'Oh, that college that had many foreign students? I wonder what has become of it now.'

3. kaisya/siĝoto ĝa taiheñ; 4. hisyô/tâipu ĝa zyoózù; 5. gaíkòokañ/Yamada-sañ ĝa kirai

C 1. **Ano kodomo, mê ĝa oókìi desu nêe.**
   'Doesn't that child have big eyes!' | **Hoñtoo ni mè no oókìi kodómo dèsu nêe.**
   'S/he really is a child with big eyes, isn't s/he!'

2. **Ano hanasi, îmi ĝa nâi desu nêe.**
   'That story doesn't have any meaning, does it!' | **Hoñtoo ni ìmi no nâi hanásì desu nêe.**
   'It really is a story with no meaning, isn't it!'

3. âkatyañ/kaóiro ĝa warùi; 4. señsèe/kôoĝi ĝa omósiròi

D 1. **Tokidoki koítì ni kimâsu kara . .**
   'I sometimes come here, so . . .' | **Zyâa, kitâ tokî ni wa, reñraku-site kudasài.**
   'Well then, when you come (*lit.* have come), please get in touch.'

2. **Tokidoki kíppu moraimàsu kara . .**
   'I sometimes receive tickets, so . . .' | **Zyâa, morátta tokì ni wa, reñraku-site kudasài.**
   'Well then, when you receive (*lit.* have received) [some], please get in touch.'

3. kurúma karimàsu; 4. konó èki de orímàsu; 5. kokó ni yorimàsu

E In the following drill, note the difference in status between the questioner and referent, and the respondent, indicated by the politeness levels.

1. **Kokó ni tùita toki ni âtta ñ desu ka**⌐
   '(Is it the case that) you saw him/her when you arrived?' | **Ie, tûita tokî ni wa mâda irássyarànakatta kara, âto de omé ni kakarimàsita.**
   'No, when I arrived s/he wasn't in yet, so I saw him/her later.'

2. **Dêkita toki ni âtta ñ desu ka**⌐
   '(Is it the case that) you saw him/her at the time it was completed?' | **Ie, dêkita tokî ni wa mâda irássyarànakatta kara, âto de omé ni kakarimàsita.**
   'No, at the time it was completed s/he wasn't in yet, so I saw him/her later.'

3. **otya ireta**; 4. **kimatta**; 5. **kodomo o miokutta**; 6. **okáne o azukàtta**

F 1. **Îtu watásimasyòo ka.** | **Miñna atúmàtta toki ni watásimasyòo yo.**
'When shall we hand it over?' | 'Let's hand it over when all [of the group] have assembled.'

2. **Îtu azúkemasyòo ka.** | **Minna atúmàtta toki ni azúkemasyòo yo.**
'When shall we check [the luggage, for example]?' | 'Let's check it when all [of the group] have assembled.'

3. **yaɩ́te mimasyòo**; 4. **deńwa iremasyòo**; 5. **kimémasyòo**; 6. **sasíaḡemasyòo**

G 1. **Sono toki, mâda 'gakusee desyoo?** | **Êe, mâda gakúsee no tokì datta kara . .**
'At that time you were (*lit.* are) still a student—right?' | 'Yes, that was still the student period, so . . .' (you can draw appropriate conclusions).

2. **Sono toki, môo 'hima desyoo?** | **Êe, môo himá na tokì datta kara . .**
'At that time you were (*lit.* are) already free—right?' | 'Yes, that was already free time, so . . .' (you can draw appropriate conclusions).

3. **môo seńkyòosi**; 4. **mâda gêñki**; 5. **mâda 'kodomo**; 6. **mâda hitô-ri**; 7. **mâda hûbeñ**; 8. **môo 'syatyoo**; 9. **mâda 'Amerika**

H 1. **Sore wa, Yamámoto-kuñ ni àu mâe desita neʕ** | **Iêie, âtta âto desu yo.**
'That was before you met (Mr.) Yamamoto—right?' | 'No, no, (it's) after I met him.'

2. **Sore wa, nîmotu o azúkàru mâe desita neʕ** | **Iêie, azúkàtta âto desu yo.**
'That was before you took charge of the luggage—right?' | 'No, no, (it's) after I took charge of it.'

3. **kippu o morau**; 4. **guríìñsya no kippu o tanômu**; 5. **isu o naraberu**; 6. **zikáñ ḡa hakkìri-suru**

I 1. **Sakí ni hairimàsu yo** | **Dôozo. Kodáma-sañ ḡa hàitta âto de haírimàsu kara . .**
'I'll go in ahead.' | 'Please do. I'll go in after Mr/s. Kodama has gone in, so . . .' (you go ahead).

2. **Sakí ni orimàsu yo** | **Dôozo. Kodáma-sañ ḡa òrita âto de orímàsu kara . .**
'I'll get off ahead.' | 'Please do. I'll get off after Mr/s. Kodama has gotten off, so . . .' (you go ahead).

3. **demâsu**; 4. **nemâsu**; 5. **aḡárimàsu**; 6. **torímàsu**; 7. **yarímàsu**

J 1. **Miñna biḱkùri-simasita yo** | **Desyoo? Biḱkùri-suru daroo to omôtte (i)masita.**
'Everyone was surprised.'

2. **Zêñbu obôete (i)masita yo↗**
   'They remembered it all.'

   Desyoo? Obôete (i)ru daroo to omôtte (i)masita.
   'Weren't they? I thought they would probably be surprised.'
   'Didn't they? I thought they would probably remember.'

3. **hotôñdo zêñbu wasúremàsita**; 4. **kânari tukáremàsita**

K 1. **Atúmàru no wa, kaísatùg̃uti no tokórò desita ne↗**
   'The place where we will get together was [to be] the place where they check tickets—right?'

   Êe, kaísatùg̃uti no tokórò ni atúmàtte ne!
   'Yes, gather at the place where they check tickets.'

2. **Atúmàru no wa, gôg̃o kû-zi desita ne↗**
   'The time when we will get together was [to be] 9:00 P.M.—right?'

   Êe, gôg̃o kû-zi ni atúmàtte ne!
   'Yes, gather at 9:00 P.M.'

3. **nisí-dèg̃uti**; 4. **toozitu**; 5. **syôog̃o**; 6. **katyoo no otaku**; 7. **êki no mâe no 'kissateñ**

L 1. **Ano tokkyuu wa, zyûu-zi-hatu desu ne↗**
   'That special express leaves at 10:00—right?'

   Êe, zyûu-zi ni dêru tokkyuu dèsu.
   'Yes, it's the special express that leaves at 10:00.'

2. **Ano kyuukoo wa, zyûuku-zi-tyaku desu ne↗**
   'That express arrives at 19:00—right?'

   Êe, zyûuku-zi ni tûku kyuúkoo dèsu.
   'Yes, it's the express that arrives at 19:00.'

3. **tokkyuu/zyuúyò-zi gozyûp-puñ-tyaku**; 4. **kyuukoo/rêe-zi nî-huñ-hatu**; 5. **bâsu/gôg̃o gô-zi-hatu**

M 1. **Ano sig̃oto zêñbu sitâ ñ desu ka↗ Tukâreta desyoo?**
   '(Is it the case that) you did all of that work? You got tired, didn't you?'

   Êe, sitá àto de tukârete simatte, imá màde gûuguu neté (i)màsita.
   'Yes, after having done it I became exhausted, and I was sleeping soundly until now.'

2. **Kodomo o miñna nekasità ñ desu ka↗ Tukâreta desyoo?**
   '(Is it the case that) you put all the children to bed? You got tired, didn't you?'

   Êe, nekásita àto de tukârete simatte, imá màde gûuguu neté (i)màsita.
   'Yes, after having put them to bed I became exhausted, and I was sleeping soundly until now.'

3. **zêñbu yôñda**; 4. **zêñbu katázùketa**; 5. **miñna miokutta**; 6. **asóko màde 'mukae ni itta**

N 1. **Nîmotu, azúkàtte (i)masu neˢ** **Êe, tomódati g̃a azùkete kurétà kara . .**
'The luggage is checked—right?' 'Yes, a friend checked it for me, so . . .' (it is checked).

2. **Atárasìi isu, naránde (i)màsu neˢ** **Êe, tomódati g̃a narabete kuretà kara . .**
'The new chairs are lined up—right?' 'Yes, a friend lined them up for me, so . . .' (they are lined up).

3. kodomo/bâsu ni noʹtte (i)màsu; 4. âkatyañ/neté (i)màsu; 5. amâdo/simâtte (i)masu; 6. torâñku no kag̃î/kakâtte (i)masu; 7. têrebi/kiéte (i)màsu; 8. sôto no dêñki/tûite (i)masu

Application Exercises

A1. Using a timetable—real or specially prepared—practice asking and answering questions about departures and arrivals using /place and/or time + **-hàtu/**, /place and/or time + **-tyàku/**, and sentence modifiers ending in **dêru** (or **tâtu**) and **tûku**.

2. Practice asking and answering questions that relate to what is done at specified times. For example:

Mití g̃a wakarànai tokî ni wa, dôo suru ñ desu ka 'What is it you do at times when you don't know the road?'

Omâwari-señ ni mití o kikù ñ desu nêe. 'You ask a policeman (the road).'

Tabesug̃ite, guái g̃a wàrùku natta tokî ni wa, dôo suru ñ desu ka 'When you've overeaten and don't feel well, what is it you do?'

Taitee kusúri o nòñde, yasûmu ñ desu nêe. 'You usually take medicine and rest.'

3. Following the procedures of Application Exercise A4 of Section A of this lesson, describe each second activity as having occurred *after* the first, using an **âto de** pattern.

4. Using magazines or specially drawn pictures, describe items within them in terms of particular features they exhibit. For example:

mâdo no nâi heya 'a room with no windows'

pâi g̃a sukî na hito 'a person who likes pie'

isya g̃a ʹzyosee no byooiñ 'a hospital where the doctors are women'

hisyô g̃a dañsee no zimùsyo 'an office where the secretaries are men'

mâdo no tiísài heya 'a room with small windows.'

B. Core Conversations: Substitution

After practicing the Core Conversations with minor replacements—individual vocabulary items (time and place words and personal names) in CC1 and 2—develop a related narrative, following closely the format developed in CC3.

SECTION C

Eavesdropping

(Answer the following on the basis of the accompanying tape. A = the first speaker; B = the second speaker.)

1a. What is A inquiring about?
  b. What does B have in this category?
 2a. What is A looking for? Why?
  b. What information does B provide?
  c. Why does A ask B to wait?
 3. What kind of activity is going to take place? Involving what two categories of items?
 4a. What does A offer to do?
  b. Why does B turn down the offer?
 5a. What is A perplexed about?
  b. What information does B provide?
  c. What prediction does B make? Why?
 6a. Where will the tour group gather? On what day?
  b. Why does B believe this place will be easy to find?
  c. What is the departure time? On what kind of train?
 7a. What is B's usual time for leaving the office?
  b. What is A's reaction?
  c. What departure from the regular pattern does B mention?
 8a. What does A think about the subway here?
  b. What explanation does B offer?
  c. How old is the subway?
  d. How did A commute before?
  e. What has been the effect on A of switching to the subway?
 9a. When does B usually work? For how long?
  b. What comment does this elicit from A? With what supporting evidence?
  c. What differing opinion does B mention?
10a. Where does A suggest that the luggage be put? Why?
  b. How does B proceed?
  c. How does A handle the luggage?
11a. How much money is there?
  b. Describe how it is constituted.
  c. What does A ask B to do with the money?
  d. What is B's concern?
  e. What is A's response?
12a. What is A trying to find out?
  b. Why is B unable to answer immediately?
  c. Why does B ask A to wait? Give details.
13a. Why does A apologize?
  b. What is B's reaction?
  c. What is A's explanation?
  d. How did A react to the situation?
14a. Which tickets has B already purchased, and which tickets have not yet been bought?
  b. How is B traveling (what kind of train, car, seat, etc.)?
  c. Why did B decide on this?
  d. Why does B thank A?
15a. Where does this conversation probably take place?
  b. What is A trying to find out?
  c. What is the problem that A did not anticipate?
  d. Where is A at the present time?
  e. Where must A go now?
  f. Who is B?

16a. Who is standing over there?
   b. What does B offer to do?
   c. How does the person being discussed react?
   d. What suggestion is made as to why that person has come here? What led to that conclusion?
17a. Identify A and B.
   b. What seems to be the general problem?
   c. Where did B put the books?
   d. What instructions does B receive from A?
18a. Identify A and B.
   b. In what connection is a schedule mentioned?
   c. What three amounts (in yen) are mentioned? Identify each.
19a. What is the topic of conversation?
   b. Where did it come from, and how did B acquire it?
   c. What does B collect? Since when?
   d. What does B offer to do?
   e. What is A's response?
20a. Give details regarding the company president's arrival.
   b. Who is going to meet the president?
   c. What time will they leave?
   d. What does A tell B to do? Why?
   e. Comment on the relative ranks of A and B.
21a. What does A ask B to do?
   b. When will B do this?
22a. How is A feeling? Why?
   b. In what connection is 'two o'clock' mentioned?
   c. At what time did A leave home?
   d. What happened at 8:30?
23a. Where does A want to go? Which entrance is mentioned first?
   b. What is located at that entrance?
   c. What error does B uncover?
   d. What is located at the south entrance?
   e. What request does A make of B?
24a. What is the topic of discussion? When did it occur?
   b. Why did B think it would be interesting?
   c. Why is B embarrassed?
25a. Who is B?
   b. What is A inquiring about?
   c. What two categories of people does B mention, and how does B distinguish them in connection with A's inquiry?
   d. What is the reason for A's inquiry? Give details.
   e. What is B's reaction?
   f. What does B agree to do?
26a. Who is B?
   b. What happened the day before yesterday?
   c. What was the result?
   d. What does A request of B initially?
   e. How are the people under discussion described?
   f. Why does A ask B to wait?
27a. What did A hear this morning?
   b. What is interesting about this?

c. What additional categories of people does B mention?
d. What is B's overall reaction?

Utilization

(Use each of the following as the basis for a short conversation that includes at least a stimulus and/or response. If conversation participants are not identified, use plain distal-style.)

  1. Inquire about the identity of the place where they sell (a) green car tickets; (b) special express tickets; (c) reserved seat tickets; (d) bus tickets. (Use anticipatory **no**.)
  2. Inquire as to the time when (a) the special express from Kyoto will arrive; (b) the next bus for Nagoya will leave; (c) the part-timer will come to pick up the section chief's luggage; (d) the people going on the tour will gather. (Use anticipatory **no**.)
  3. Inquire about the identity of the person who (a) (just) now left the office; (b) is going to the airport to see the division chief off; (c) arrived late this morning because of the earthquake; (d) needs a timetable. (Use anticipatory **no**.)
  4. Inquire about the identity of the things that (a) the secretary handed over to the head of the institute; (b) the part-timer bought at the stationery store; (c) Takashi checked at the airport. (Use anticipatory **no**.)
  5. Tell a colleague that you don't know whether or not the train that Mr. Suzuki is taking is a special express.
  6. Confirm that the ticket counter where they sell reserved seat tickets is near the north entrance of the station.
  7. Ask a colleague which is furthest south—Kyoto, Osaka, or Kobe.
  8. Tell a friend that you are keeping (taking charge of temporarily) the luggage that Mr. Suzuki brought from home.
  9. Check on what it is the people who are lined up over there are waiting for.
  10. Ask what a machine that makes change is called in Japanese.
  11. Explain that you want to change a thousand-yen bill. Ask if you can do it with this machine.
  12. Tell a friend that you know what day the new Japanese teacher is coming, but you have forgotten the exact time.
  13. Find out from a colleague if his study of English occurred (*lit.* was) before going to England or after.
  14. Explain that the train that leaves Kyoto at 9:30 and arrives in Tokyo at 1:00 does not stop in Nagoya.
  15. Point out that there is a crowd of people lined up in front of the hotel. Suggest that you try asking why it is they are there.
  16. Find out if you buy your ticket (a) before boarding the bus; (b) after you board the bus.
  17. Explain that you want to use a public phone. Ask a friend if he has a ten-yen coin.
  18. Inform a colleague that you (a) rode a bus with a woman driver; (b) attend a school where all the teachers are women; (c) want to rent a home with short commuting time; (d) want to buy a car with comfortable seats.
  19. Inform a colleague that yesterday (in contrast with other days) you (a) came (riding) here in a cab; (b) walked home; (c) took the Japan Railway in Tokyo Station.
  20. Tell a colleague that you fell sound asleep in the train this morning, and when you came to, it was already after you'd left the station where you get off.
  21. A group is going to see a movie together. Explain that since the movie starts at 6:30, you want to be assembled in front of the theater by 6:00.
  22. Exclaim about (a) a child with big eyes; (b) a student proficient in English; (c) a person who likes sake; (d) a place close to the ocean *and* the mountains; (e) an office with easy (relaxed) commuting; (f) a place where the winters are cold (summers are hot); (g) a spring (fall) with no free time.

23. Using a very polite request form, ask a group you are connected with to (a) stand up; (b) sit down (on chairs); (c) sit down here (on tatami); (d) assemble over here; (e) line up at the place where they check tickets; (f) board the bus; (g) get off at the next station; (h) hand over their tickets; (i) unload their luggage; (j) cross over to the other side of the street.

24. Complain to a friend that this morning you wanted to get on (off) the bus at the West Entrance of the station, but they wouldn't let you get on (off) there.

25. Comment that your return home last night was (a) amazingly early; (b) quite early; (c) awfully late; (d) later than usual.

26. Check on the identity of the part-time students who were on vacation last week.

27. Comment that you have become (a) sleepy; (b) exhausted; (c) embarrassed.

28. Ask your associate to (a) line up the people who want to take taxis; (b) keep these textbooks until tomorrow; (c) assemble the people who want to hear Professor Kato's lecture, at 2:30 on the day in question, in front of this building.

29. Find out the hour at which the average Japanese mother puts a child of about five to bed.

30. Tell a colleague that you did this work (a) carefully; (b) in confusion.

31. Exclaim that spring (fall, summer, winter) has come. (*lit.* It has become ——.)

Check-up

1. What do we mean by a sentence modifier? What form do sentence modifiers take? In what ways do they differ from independent sentences? (A-SP1), (B-SP1)

2. What is the basic pattern of a sequence that provides a description A of a part or feature B of a larger unit C? (B-SP2)

3. What is meant by anticipatory **no**? Give examples. (A-SP2)

4. What form of the sentence modifier precedes **mâe**? **âto**? How does **sitá àto de** differ from **sitê kara**? (A-SP3), (B-SP4)

5. Describe the use of /verbal gerund + **mîru**/. (A-SP4)

6. Identify the **no** in each of the following sequences:
    (a) **Tomódati no kyookàsyo desu.**
    (b) **Tomódati no karita kyookàsyo desu.**
    (c) **Tomódati nò desu.**
    (d) **Hazúkasìi no wa, watási dèsu.**
    (e) **Hutúu no susì desu ka**↗
    (f) **Hutúu nò desu ka**↗
    (g) **Hutùu nà no?**   (B-SP2)

7. What is meant by onomatopoeia? Name two types recognized in Japanese. How do they differ? Give examples of each type. (B-SP3)

8. Describe the involvement of the listener in a Japanese storytelling situation. (B-SP5)

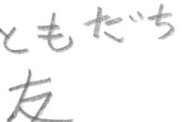

Lesson 20

SECTION A

Core Conversations

1(N)a. Tônai kara Nârita e ikû no ni wa, rimúziñ-bàsu o tukáù no ḡa itíbañ bèñri desyoo ne!

b. Dê mo, Uéno màde nîmotu moťte (i)kù no ḡa 'taiheñ desyoo?

2(J)a. Nîmotu oôi ñ desu ka⌐

b. Soñna ni?

c. Zyâa ne! Zibúñ de motte ikû yori, taḱkyuubiñ o tanòñda hoo ḡa rakû desu yo⌐

d. Sirímasèñ desita? Deñwa ìp-poñ de utí màde nîmotu tôri ni kite neˤ Kuúkoo màde hakóñde kurerù ñ desu yo.

3(J)a. Goórudeñ-uìiku wa, dôo suru tumóri dèsu ka⌐

b. Hee⌐ Dôko mo kômu daroo kedo, mâa, yaṕpàri îi desu nêe— ryokoo wa.

(J)a. Anó bàsu wa bêñri da kedo nêe. Uéno e dète, deńsya de itta hòo ḡa tâsika desu yo⌐ Go-zí-ḡòro tte iù no wa, raśsyuàwaa desu kara ne!

b. Mâa, soré wa sòo desu nêe.

(N)a. Êe. Oókìi suútukèesu ḡa nî-ko to |desu ne!| Hako ḡa îk-ko desu.

b. Êe. Sore ni, suútukèesu no hitô-tu ḡa, monósùḡòku omôi ñ desu yo⌐

c. Takkyuubiñ te?

d. Soré wa ìi desu ne! Zitû wa dôo siyoo ka to omôtte (i)ta ñ desu yo⌐ Tasúkàrimasita.

(N) |Anoo| Si-gô-niti ryokóo ni deyòo to omôtte (i)ru ñ desu.

English Equivalents

1(N)a. For going from metropolitan Tokyo to Narita, I suppose using the limo-bus is most convenient, isn't it.

(J)a. That bus is convenient, but—going out to Ueno and going by train is more reliable. Because the time around 5:00 is rush hour, you know.

b. But taking luggage as far as Ueno is difficult—isn't it?

b. Well, that is true, isn't it.

2(J)a. (Is it that) you have lots of luggage?

(N)a. Yes. It's two big suitcases and—uh—one box.

b. That much?

b. Yes. What's more, (it's that) one of the suitcases is terribly heavy.

c. Well, then, you know, rather than taking it by yourself, it will be easier to arrange for "takkyubin."

c. "Takkyubin"?

d. Didn't you know? (It's that) with one phone call they come all the way to the house to pick up the luggage, you know, and transport it as far as the airport for you.

d. That's great! Actually I was wondering what I should do. You saved my life.

3(J)a. What do you plan to do for Golden Week?

(N) Uh—I've been thinking I'd go off on a trip for about four to five days.

b. Really! It will probably get crowded everywhere, but—well—it is (indeed) wonderful, isn't it—travel.

Breakdowns
(and Supplementary Vocabulary)

1. **tônai** — within the city of Tokyo
   + **sînai** — within a city (which is a **si**)
   + **matî** — town, small city
   + **murâ** — village
   Nârita — (name of airport and city)
   + **Haneda** — (name of airport)
   ikû no ni wa (SP1) — for going
   + **kayou /-u; kayotta/** — commute
   rimúziñ-bàsu — limousine bus

+monórèeru	monorail
+hâiyaa	limousine available for hire
tukáù no ḡa bêñri da	using [it] is convenient
itta hòo	the alternative of having gone
tâsika /na/	certain, positive, reliable
deńsya de itta hòo ḡa tâsika da (SP2)	it's more reliable to go (*lit.* have gone) by train
go-zí-ḡòro tte iû no	what is designated 'about 5 o'clock'
motte (i)kù no ḡa ′taiheñ da	taking [it] is difficult
2. oôi/ôoi /-katta/	are many; are frequent
+sukúnài /-katta/	are few, are rare; are infrequent
nî-ko	two pieces
hako	box
îk-ko	one piece
suútukèesu no hitô-tu	one of the suitcases
omoi /-katta/	is heavy
+karui /-katta/	is light (of weight)
monósuḡòi /-katta/	is dreadful, awful
monósùḡòku omoi	is awfully heavy
zibúñ de motte (i)kù yori	more than taking by oneself
takkyuubiñ	/special delivery service/
tanôñda hoo	the alternative of having requested
tanôñda hôo ḡa rakû da	it's easier to request (*lit.* have requested)
deńwa ìp-poñ de (SP3)	by means of one phone call
hakobu /-u; hakoñda/	transport, carry
+todôku /-u; todôita/	be delivered, reach, extend
+todókèru /ru; todôketa/	deliver
3. goórudeñ-uìiku	Golden Week (April 29–May 5)
surú tumori dà (SP4)	[I] plan to do
si-gô-niti (SP5)	4–5 days
ryokoo	trip; travel
ryokóo ni dèru	leave on a trip
deyôo (SP6)	/direct-style equivalent of **demásyòo**/
deyôo to omôu	I think I'll leave
kômu /-u; kôñda/	become crowded, congested, filled up

-ko: *Classifier for counting pieces*

îk-ko	rôk-ko
nî-ko	nanâ-ko/sitî-ko
sâñ-ko	hâk-ko
yôñ-ko	kyûu-ko
gô-ko	zîk-ko/zyûk-ko

nâñ-ko 'how many pieces?'

MISCELLANEOUS NOTES

1. In CC1, Sue Brown, a part-time worker, discusses transportation to the airport with her supervisory coworker. The style is careful, with distal-style final predicates.

(N)a. Note the contrast between **tônai** and **sînai**: Tokyo is the only city designated as a **tô** (this has no connection with the **too** of **Tookyoo**!). Other major cities are **sî**.
Kayou, an operational **w**-consonant verbal, refers to regularly repeated travel between two points. **Tuukiñ-suru** refers to traveling specifically to work. While these meanings overlap, they are not identical.

(J)a. **Tâsika**, a **na**-nominal, occurs both before forms of **dà** and in two manner patterns that have significantly different meanings: /**tâsika ni** + predicate/ = 'certainly,' 'positively,' 'surely'; /**tâsika** + predicate/ = 'if I'm correct,' 'if I remember correctly,' 'most likely.'

The use of **tte iù no** following **go-zí-g̃òro** places special focus on the item preceding the quotative.

2. CC2 is a continuation of CC1, with the same participants using the same style. Here Sue Brown's coworker has a concrete suggestion for how Sue can solve her baggage problem.

(J)a. **Oôi** and **sukúnài** are adjectivals that occur as predicates *following* the item to which they specifically refer: **suútukèesu g̃a oôi** 'there are lots of suitcases' (*lit.* 'suitcases are many'); **kâzi g̃a sukúnài** 'there are few fires' (*lit.* 'fires are few'). These are double-**g̃a**, affective predicates: **Nihôñ g̃a zisíñ g̃a oòi kara** 'since Japan has many earthquakes'; **konó matì g̃a tâkusii g̃a sukúnài kara** 'since this town has few taxis.' A particularly common pattern is **X no** (*or* **g̃a**) **oôi/sukúnài Y** 'a Y with many/few X's': **zîko no oôi koósàteñ** 'a crossing with many accidents'; **eég̃o no hòñ g̃a sukúnài tosyôkañ** 'a library with few English-language books'; **inû g̃a ôoku nâi tokoro** 'a place without many dogs'; **kâig̃i g̃a sukûnàku nâtta kaisya** 'a company where conferences have become infrequent.' Note that **oôi** is similar in meaning to **takúsañ àru**, although structurally it is very different.

(N)a. The classifier **-ko** is used to count units of inanimate objects of various shapes—boxes, suitcases, eggs, bars of soap. These are objects which can also be counted with the **hitô-tu**, **hutá-tù** series.

Note the distal-style filler |**desu ne!**|, which functions like **ne** alone in dividing a sentence into shorter units, but is stylistically different.

(N)b. Compare: **hitô-tu no suútukèesu** 'one suitcase' and **suútukèesu no hitô-tu** 'one of the suitcases.'

(J)c. **Zibuñ**: Note again **zibúñ no monò** 'one's own things'; **zibuñ de suru** 'do by oneself' (i.e., by one's own efforts), compared with **hitô-ri de suru** 'do alone.'

(J)d. **Tôri ni kûru** 'come to take (i.e., pick up).'
Hakobu is an operational consonant verbal which occurs with /operand + **o**/: **omói torañku o 'kuruma de hakobu** 'transport a heavy trunk by car.' **Hakoñde kureru**: 'the out-group transports for the in-group'; here 'they transport for you.'

3. In CC3, Smith, a graduate student, tells his acquaintance Mr. Suzuki, the banker, his plans for Golden Week. The week is so named because it includes three national holidays—April 29, the Emperor's Birthday, May 3, Constitution Day, and May 5, Children's Day. Understandably this is a popular week for traveling, with trains, planes, and inns and hotels filled to capacity.

The conversation is careful-style, with distal-style final predicates. Note that Mr. Suzuki uses an inverted sentence, and direct-style **daròo** before **kedo**. Smith begins his reply to Mr. Suzuki's question politely with the filler |**anoo**|.

(N) **Ryokoo**: note also **ryokoo-suru** and **ryokoo o suru** 'take a trip'; **Amerika o ryokoo-suru** 'travel through America.'

(J)b. **Kômu** is an affective, double-g̃a consonant verbal: **ano heñ g̃a utí g̃a kòñde (i)ru** 'that area is crowded with houses' ('house-congested'). Its opposite is **suku** 'become empty' (introduced in **onáka g̃a sukimàsita**).

Structural Patterns

1. **ikû no ni wa**

We previously encountered the nominal **no** used in reference to an already familiar item (**kôi koóhìi mo usûi no mo** 'both strong coffee and some that's weak') and the anticipatory nominal **no** whose specific relationship with a sentence modifier is identified later in the sentence (**Tâtu no wa îtu?** 'When is the time [*lit.* one] when you are going to leave?') In this lesson, we are introduced to a number of contexts in which the nominal **no** is preceded by a sentence modifier—usually one ending with a verbal—and refers to general occurrence: **tukáù no** 'the act of using,' 'using,' 'to use'; **Nârita e kurúma ni notte (i)kù no** '(the act of) going to Narita (riding) in a car.' Such sequences, which are structurally /modifier + nominal/, occur in contexts in which nominals in general regularly occur. Compare:

    Otyá g̃a sukì desu yo✓ 'I like tea.' *and*

    Otyá o nòmu no g̃a sukî desu yo✓ 'I like to drink tea.'

Also:

    Soñna sig̃oto g̃a taiheñ dèsu nêe. 'Work like that is terrible, isn't it!' *and*

    Soñna sig̃oto o surù no g̃a taíheñ dèsu nêe. 'Doing work like that is terrible, isn't it!'

Note the contrast in structural meaning between this pattern and the /gerund + predicate/ pattern:

    Koré o tukaù no wa omósiròi desyoo? 'Using this one is fun, isn't it?' (general statement)

    Kore o tukatte îi desyoo? 'It's all right to use this one, isn't it?' (*lit.* 'having used this one will be all right'; usually refers to one occasion or one purpose)

In the combination /verbal sentence modifier + **no ni (wa)** + predicate X/, sentence modifier + **no** is viewed as an activity, and the entire sequence states that X is involved or required for the purpose of performing the sentence modifier. Example:

    Kuúkoo e ikù no ni wa, konó miti o ikù to omóimàsu kedo.. 'For (the purpose of) going to the airport, I think you go along this road, but... (I'm not sure).'

Notice that **ni** is once again the particle of goal or purpose, indicating ultimate location, but in a figurative sense. **Wa** has its usual meaning, indicating that what follows is to be applied at least to what precedes; it is regularly included when the pattern refers to a general condition posed as a topic for explanatory comment.

2. COMPARISON OF ACTIVITIES

In Lesson 15, we learned patterns for the comparison of two items and of three or more items:

(1) **X to Y to, dôtira no hoo ḡa îi desu ka⤴**
(2) **(Y yòri) X no hôo ḡa îi desu.**
(3) **X to Y to Z (no uti) de, dôre ḡa itíbañ ìi desu ka⤴**
(4) **X ḡa itíbañ ìi desu.**

In these patterns, X, Y, and Z were nominals. To compare activities, we can follow the procedure described in SP1 above: we can replace unit nominals with the nominal **no** preceded by a sentence modifier ending with a verbal predicate—in all but one of the sentences above. In the pattern (2) above, when one activity is described as more —— than another, the sentence modifier precedes the nominal **hôo** 'alternative' directly. Particularly when the sequence takes the form of advice applicable to a specific situation, an affirmative predicate is regularly in the perfective, implying that 'the alternative of *having done*' is the one that will conform to the predicate, i.e., it won't conform until it has been done. Thus:

Yasai o môtto tâbeta hoo ḡa îi desu yo⤴ 'You'd better eat more vegetables.' (*lit.* 'The alternative of having eaten more vegetables will be good.')

Tikátetu de itta hòo ḡa bênri desyoo? 'Wouldn't it be more convenient to go by subway?'

Hâiyaa ni nótta hòo ḡa tâsika desu yo⤴ 'It will be more reliable to take a limousine.'

However, in the case of negative sentence modifiers, the imperfective is used, pointing up the fact that non-occurrence is a continuing state, represented in Japanese by adjectivals. Examples:

Anó isu ni kosikakènai hoo ḡa îi desu yo⤴ 'You'd better not sit on that chair.'

Satôo o irénai hòo ḡa oísìi desyoo? 'It's tastier not putting sugar in, isn't it?'

Zyûḡyoo no tokî wa, eeḡo o tukáwanai hòo ḡa omósiròi to omóimàsu yo⤴ 'I think it's more interesting not to use English in class.'

The affirmative imperfective may also occur when an affirmative alternative refers to general, repeated activity:

Hikôoki de ikú hòo ḡa hayâi desu yo⤴ 'It's faster to go by plane.'

Returning to example (2) above, **yòri** is regularly preceded by an imperfective verbal (or derivative negative adjectival) in the comparison of activities (or non-occurrence of them). Following an accented verbal or adjectival, **yòri** loses its accent; following an unaccented verbal or adjectival, there are alternate patterns, illustrated by:

iku + **yòri** > ikû yori *or* ikú yòri

ikanai + **yòri** > ikánài yori *or* ikánai yòri

Thus,

Hâiyaa ni nótte kùru yori, rimúziñ-bàsu de kitá hòo ḡa zútto yasùi desu yo⤴ 'It will be much cheaper to come (*lit.* have come) by limo-bus than to come in a limousine.'

Hôteru de atúmàru yori, êki de atúmàtta hoo ḡa bêñri zya nâi desyoo ka. 'Wouldn't it be more convenient to assemble (*lit.* have assembled) at the station than to assemble at the hotel?'

Returning now to examples (1) through (4) above, we are able to expand all the patterns to cover activities:

(1) **Têrebi o mîru no to, râzio o kikû no to, dôtira ḡa omósiròi to omóimàsu ka⤴** 'Which do you think will be more interesting—watching television or listening to the radio?'

(2) **Râzio o kikû yori, têrebi o mîta hoo ḡa omósiròi desyoo?**[1] 'It will be more interesting to watch television than to listen to the radio—right?'

(3) **Nihoṅḡo o hanâsu no to, yômu no to, kâku no (no uti) de, dôre ḡa itíbaṅ sukì desu ka⤴** 'Which do you like best—speaking Japanese, reading [it], or writing [it]?'

(4) **Yáppàri hanâsu no ḡa itíbaṅ sukì desu nêe—watasi.** 'I do like speaking best, I [do], after all is said and done.'

Note that if (2) is changed to a **hodo** pattern, we find:

Râzio o kikû no wa, têrebi o mîru hodo omósìròku nâi desyoo? 'Listening to the radio is not as interesting as watching television—right?'

Like **yòri**, **hodo** is directly preceded by an imperfective sentence modifier. With the loss of **hôo**, the /sentence modifier + **no**/ pattern occurs once more as the topic of discussion.

3. deṅwa ìp-poṅ de

A quantity expression without a following phrase-particle expresses the extent to which a following predicate applies:

Mík-ka tomarimàsita. 'I stopped for three days' (Compare: **Mík-ka ni tomarimàsita.** 'I stopped on the third').

Zassi o sâṅ-satu karímàsita. 'I borrowed three books' (*lit.* 'I borrowed books to the extent of three volumes').

Ĝîsi ḡa hutá-ri miemàsita. 'Two engineers appeared.'

Isya mo hitô-ri kimâsita. 'One doctor came, too.'

Sore wa takúsaṅ gozaimàsu. 'We have lots of those.'

Sukôsi kudásài. 'Give me a little.'

Donó-ḡurai irimàsu ka⤴ 'About how much do you need?'

When a quantity expression describes a nominal that is linked to a predicate by a particle other than **ḡa**, **o**, **wa**, or **mo**, the quantity expression follows the nominal directly:

Tomódati huta-rì to, ûmi e ítte kimàsita. 'I went (and came [back]) to the ocean with two friends.'

Tâkusii nî-dai de, kuúkoo e ikimàsita. 'We went to the airport in two taxis.'

Sore wa, môo tomódati huta-rì ni íttà ñ desu. '(It's that) I already told that to two friends.'

Note the difference in meaning that results from a change in order:

deṅwa ìp-poṅ de tanômu 'order with one phone call'
deṅwa de îp-poṅ tanômu 'order one (long, cylindrical object) by phone'

---

1. In contexts in which this sentence refers to a general condition, **mîru** is also possible.

4. **tumori**

Tumori is a nominal which is always preceded by a modifier—a sentence modifier or a prenominal—and followed by some form of the copula **dà**. It indicates intentions or personal expectations:

Kotosi no natu ryokóo-suru tumori dèsu. 'I expect to travel this summer.'

Âsa hâyâku anó gakusee o atumèru tumóri dàtta ñ desu kedo, yappàri damê desita. 'I did plan to assemble those students early in the morning, but after all, it fizzled.'

Môo yaítyatta tumori dà kedo . . 'I assume I already did it all, but . . .' (am I wrong?)

Kâre wa, dôo iu tumori de soó ittà ñ desyoo nêe. 'What do you suppose he had in mind when he said that?' (*lit.* 'being what kind of intention . . .')

Asítà made ni kokó o tàtu? . . . Sonó tumori dà kedo . . 'Are you going to leave by tomorrow?' . . . 'That's my intention, but . . .'

Most **tumóri dà** statements refer to the speaker, and questions to the addressee. When used of a third person, there is usually an added qualification—'I believe,' 'someone said,' 'isn't it the case?' etc.

For a negative equivalent, either the predicate of the sentence modifier or the **tumóri dà** sequence may be negated. Negating the sentence modifier is more common.

Anó nìmotu, orósànai tumori desu. 'I intend not to unload that luggage.'

Anó nìmotu, orôsu tumori zya nâi desu. 'I don't intend to unload that luggage.'

There is, of course, a slight difference in meaning between these two alternates: in the first example, there is a definite plan—namely not to unload that luggage. In the second, less common alternate, the speaker contradicts the notion of a plan to unload.

In this lesson section, the only /sentence modifier + **tumóri dà**/ sequences introduced are those in which the sentence modifier does not have its own expressed operator (different from the referent of **tumóri dà**). Additional patterns will be introduced in Section B.

5. APPROXIMATE NUMBERS

The pattern /two consecutive numerals + classifier/ indicates an approximate number somewhere within the boundaries of the two numerals. Examples:

ni-sañ-puñ '2 to 3 minutes'
sañ-yoñ-dai '3 or 4 vehicles'
go-rók-kàḡetu '5 to 6 months'
sití-happyakù-eñ '¥700–¥800'
ni-sáñ-zyùu-niñ '20 to 30 people'

Note the following constraints:

1. Approximate numbers count; they do not name. In other words, they are all quantity expressions.

2. Except for a few instances of **yo** 'four,' the Japanese series of numerals (**hito-**, **huta-**, **mi-**) does not occur in this pattern.

3. The combinations for approximate numbers of days are irregular, and only a few combinations occur with any frequency:

hutu-ka + mik-ka > nî-sañ-niti/ni-sâñ-niti

mik-ka + yok-ka > sâñ-yok-ka
yok-ka + itu-ka > sî-go-niti/si-go-niti/si-gô-niti
itu-ka + mui-ka > gô-roku-niti/go-roku-niti

6. THE DIRECT-STYLE CONSULTATIVE

The **-masyòo** form of verbals, meaning 'let's ——' or 'I guess I'll ——,' 'why don't I ——,' is a distal-style form, as indicated by the **-mas-**. In this lesson, its direct-style equivalents are introduced.

Once again, we must distinguish between vowel-verbals and consonant verbals in order to describe a Japanese pattern. To form the consultative, we add **-yòo** to the root of vowel verbals and **-òo** to the root of consonant verbals. The root, you will remember, is a vowel verbal minus the **-ru**, and a consonant verbal minus the **-u**, of the imperfective ending. Thus:

	Imperfective	Root	Direct-style consultative
Vowel verbals	tabêru	tabe	tabéyòo
	akeru	ake	akéyòo
	simêru	sime	siméyòo
	iru 'be'	i	iyôo
	orîru	ori	oríyòo
	mîru	mi	miyôo
Consonant verbals	iku	ik	ikôo
	hanâsu	hanas	hanásòo
	mâtu	mat	matôo
	yobu	yob	yobôo
	nômu	nom	nomôo
	nâru	nar	narôo
	kau (< *kawu)	kaw	kaôo (< *kawôo)
	kayou (< *kayowu)	kayow	kayóòo (< *kayówòo)
Irregular verbals	kûru	ku/ki/ko	koyôo
	suru	su/si/se	siyôo

Note the following:

1. Since the consultative implies volitional decision making, only operational verbals regularly occur in this form.

2. The special polite verbals in **-aru** do not have a consultative form: honorific-polite ↑ verbals never refer to the speaker (always a referent of consultative forms) and **gozâru** + is affective, not operational.

3. The consultative of the verbal **-màsu**, which identifies distal-style, has an irregular consultative ending: in spite of the fact that it is a consonant verbal, it takes the **-yoo** ending ordinarily found only in vowel verbals: /**-mas** + **-yoo** > **-masyòo**/.

The direct-style consultative may occur as the final predicate of a major sentence. In such occurrences, it is typical of casual-style, particularly blunt speech used by men. Examples:

Zyâa, ikôo. 'Well then, let's go.'
Kaéròo ka. 'Sh'we go home?'

Yaméyòo ka naa. 'I wonder if I should quit.'

One of the most frequent uses of this form is in the pattern /direct-style consultative X + **to omôu** = '[I] think that [I]'ll X.' In such cases, identification with blunt-style is lost. Examples:

Raíneñ no àki Yoóròppa e ikôo to omoimasu. 'I think I'll go to Europe next fall.'

Îma môtte (i)ru zîsyo yori oókìi no o kaôo to omôtte (i)ru ñ desu kedo.. 'I've been thinking of buying a larger dictionary than the one I have now, but...' (I'm not certain).

Thinking a question constitutes wondering:

Îma yátte (i)ru arubàito o yaméyòo ka to omôtte (i)ru ñ desu kedo.. 'I've been wondering if I should quit the part-time work I'm doing now, but...' (I'm undecided).

In this pattern, the person who is thinking is also the person to whom the consultative form refers. With other forms preceding **to omôu**, there is no such requirement:

Dekímàsu ka⤴ ... Dekîru to omoimasu. 'Can you do it?' ... 'I think I can.'

Onîisañ dekîru desyoo ka.... Dekîru to omoimasu. 'Can your brother do it?' ... 'I think he can.'

Kôñbañ nań-zi-ḡòro kâeru ñ desu ka⤴ ... Hatî-zi made ni wa kâette (i)ru daroo to omóimàsu kedo.. 'About what time will you return home tonight?' ... 'By 8:00 I think I'll probably be back, but...' (I'm not sure).

Okâasañ wa? ... Itá daròo to omoimasu. 'How about your mother?' ... 'I think she was probably here.'

The sequences that include the consultative report thinking about a *suggested* behavior—consideration of a plan—whereas those with the imperfective (with or without a following **daroo**) simply report beliefs that certain activities or conditions (probably) will (or do or did) occur. Underlying this distinction are the basic distinctions of these forms:

Iku. 'Going will or does occur.'

Ikú daròo. 'Going probably will or does occur.'

Ikôo. 'Let's go' *or* 'Why don't I go.'

Drills

A 1. **Îńtyoo ni reńraku-sitài ñ desu kedo..**
'I'd like to get in touch with the hospital director...'

Îńtyoo ni? Âa, îńtyoo ni reńraku-surù no ni wa ne! Hîsyo no Yamâḡuti-sañ ni tanômu ñ desu yo⤴
'With the hospital director? Oh, for getting in touch with the hospital director, you ask Mr/s. Yamaguchi, the secretary.'

2. **Syotyóo ni watasitài ñ desu kedo..**
'I'd like to hand this over to the institute director...'

Syotyoo ni? Âa, syotyóo ni watasù no ni wa ne! Hîsyo no Yamâḡuti-sañ ni tanômu ñ desu yo⤴

'To the institute director? Oh, for handing it over to the institute director, you ask Mr/s. Yamaguchi, the secretary.'

3. **sińkàñseñ no kippu o kaitai**; 4. **dôru o ryooḡae-sitai**; 5. **nîmotu o azúketài**; 6. **arúbàito no hito o atúmetài**; 7. **mêsseezi o tutaetai**; 8. **okyakusañ o okutte moraitai**

B 1. **Anó deñsya ni norù no ni wa, mukóo no hòo ni itá hòo ḡa îi desyoo nêe.**
'For getting on that train, it would probably be better to be on the other side, wouldn't it.'

Êe, mukóo no hòo ni irû no ḡa ịtíbañ ìi to omóimàsu yo
'Yes, being on the other side is best, I think.'

2. **Mití no mukòo ni watarù no ni wa, kâdo made modôtta hoo ḡa îi desyoo nêe.**
'For crossing the street, it would probably be better to go back to the corner, wouldn't it.'

Êe, kâdo made modôru no ḡa itíbañ ìi to omóimàsu yo
'Yes, going back to the corner is best, I think.'

3. **Yoòròppa ni iku/tûaa ni hâitta**; 4. **kuukoo e iku/rimúziñ-bàsu ni notta**; 5. **konó nìmotu o hakobu/dañsee ni tanòñda**; 6. **anó señsèe ni âu/îma deńwa o iret(e) òita**; 7. **koré tabèru/nâihu to h(u)òoku o tukatta**

C 1. **Anô hito, tabako suu?**
'Does s/he smoke?'

Ñ, konaida sut́te (i)rù no mîta (wa)² yo
'Yeah, I saw him/her smoking the other day.'

2. **Kânozyo, zitêñsya ni noru?**
'Does she ride a bicycle?'

Ñ, konaida not́te (i)rù no mîta (wa) yo
'Yeah, I saw her riding the other day.'

3. **anô ko/rosíaḡo yòmu**; 4. **kokó no misè/bâsu no kippu uru**

D 1. **Bâsu de kayóù no to, tikátetu de kayoù no to, dôtti ḡa hayâi?**
'Which is faster, to commute by bus or to commute by subway?'

Tikátetu de kayotta hòo ḡa hayâi desyoo?
'It would be faster to commute by subway, wouldn't it?'

2. **Kyôo todókèru no to, asíta todokèru no to, dôtti ḡa îi?**
'Which is better, to deliver [it] today or to deliver [it] tomorrow?'

Asíta todòketa hoo ḡa îi desyoo?
'It would be better to deliver [it] tomorrow, wouldn't it?'

3. **Nârita kara tâtu/Oosaka kara/yasûi**; 4. **kaísatùḡuti de atúmàru/dêḡuti de/wakári-yasùi**; 5. **deñwa de kiku/âtte/yôku wakâru**; 6. **hi-tôri de katázukèru/oózèe de/hayâi**; 7. **kot́tì ni narabu/tonari ni/zyamá ni narànai**

2. The inclusion of **wa** before **yọ** marks the utterance as feminine.

E 1. **Konó hutuu ni norimasyòo ka—moó tyòtto matímasyòo ka.**
'Shall we take this local, or shall we wait a little longer?'

Konó hutuu ni norù yori, moó tyòtto mâtta hoo ḡa yôku arímasèñ ka⁄
'Isn't it better to wait a little longer than to take this local?'

2. **Moíte kaerimasyòo ka—todôkete moraimasyoo ka.**
'Shall we carry [it] home, or shall we have [it] delivered?'

Moíte kàeru yori, todôkete morátta hòo ḡa yôku arímasèñ ka⁄
'Isn't it better to have [it] delivered than to carry [it] home?'

3. tuḡî no êki made ikímasyòo/kokó de orimasyòo; 4. turéte ikimasyòo/azúkemasyòo; 5. îma kiméte simaimasyòo/móo iti-do soodañ-simasyòo; 6. zibúñ de hakobimasyòo/taḱkyuubiñ o tanomimasyòo

F 1. **Asóko ni oite ìi?**
'Is it all right to put [it] over there?'

A, asóko nì wa okánai hòo ḡa îi desu yo⁄
'Oh, you'd better not put [it] over there!'

2. **Kodómo ni watasite ìi?**
'It is all right to hand [it] over to children?'

A, kodómo nì wa watásanai hòo ḡa îi desu yo⁄
'Oh, you'd better not hand [it] over to children!'

3. asoko o watatte; 4. asoko ni nekasite; 5. asóko ni tàtete; 6. asóko ni oròsite

G 1. **Kyôo reñraku-sinàkute îi?**
'Is it all right not to get in touch today?'

Îya, yáppàri kyôo reñraku-sita hòo ḡa îi desu yo⁄
'No, as I think about it, you'd better get in touch today.'

2. **Îma tôri ni ikánakute îi?**
'Is it all right not to go to get [it] now?'

Îya, yáppàri îma tôri ni iíta hòo ḡa îi desu yo⁄
'No, as I think about it, you'd better go to get [it] now.'

3. kyôo naósànakute; 4. îma deñwa irenàkute; 5. asâtte azúkarànakute; 6. zêñbu narábet(e) okanàkute; 7. mińna atumarànakute; 8. zêñbu nâkute

H 1. **Deñwa de sûḡu wakâtta desyoo?**
'It became clear right away by phone, right?'

Hâi, deñwa ìp-poñ de wakárimàsita.
'Yes, it became clear with one phone call.'

2. **Tâkusii de zêñbu todôita desyoo?**
'Everything was delivered by taxi, right?'

Hâi, tâkusii itî-dai de todókimàsita.
'Yes, it was delivered with one taxi.'

3. hako ni zêñbu hâitta; 4. bâsu ni 'miñna notta; 5. suútukèesu de 'sore 'motte (i)tta

I 1. **Sono sûḡôku omói suutukèesu mo 'hako mo zêñbu seńsèe no desyoo?**
'Those extremely heavy suitcases *and* boxes are all the professor's—right?'

Iya, hakó no ìk-ko wa seńsèe no zya nâi to omóimàsu kedo..
'No, I think one of the boxes is not the professor's, but...' (I'm not sure).

2. **Kokó ni oite àru hôñ mo 'zassi mo zêñbu hurûi desyoo?**
'The books *and* the magazines that have been put here are all old—right?'

Iya, zaśsi no is-satù wa hûrûku nâi to omóimàsu kedo . .
'No, I think one of the magazines is not old, but . . .' (I'm not sure).

3. **asóko ni tàtte (i)ru dañsee/zyosee/miñna arubàito (da)**; 4. **îma katta teeburu/isu/dôre mo todókèru**; 5. **konó heñ no hòteru/ryokañ/zêñbu takâi**

J 1. **Îtu watasu?**
'When will you hand it over?'

Îma watásòo.
'Why don't I hand it over now?'

2. **Îtu iku?**
'When will you go?'

Îma ikôo.
'Why don't I go now?'

3. **tanômu**; 4. **kau**; 5. **noru**; 6. **orôsu**; 7. **atúmèru**; 8. **orîru**; 9. **suru**; 10. **yobu**; 11. **tâtu**; 12. **âu**.

K 1. **Tuĝî no êki de orímàsu?**
'Are you going to get off at the next station?'

Êe, oríyòo to omôtte (i)masu.
'Yes, I'm thinking of getting off [there].'

2. **Nâĝoya made kayóimàsu?**
'Are you going to commute all the way to Nagoya?'

Êe, kayóòo to omôtte (i)masu.
'Yes, I'm thinking of commuting [there].'

3. **râiĝetu ryokóo-simàsu**; 4. **sûĝu tatímàsu**; 5. **môo nemàsu**; 6. **otyá o iremàsu**; 7. **asítà mo kimàsu**; 8. **mukóo e hakobimàsu**; 9. **hikídasi ni iret(e) okimàsu**

L 1. **Îtu simâsu ka**↗
'When are you going to do [it]?'

Sôo desu nêe. Îtu siyôo ka to omôtte (i)ru ñ desu ĝa nêe.
'Well, I've been wondering when I should do [it], but . . .' (I haven't decided).

2. **Îtu kaérimàsu ka**↗
'When are you going to go back?'

Sôo desu nêe. Îtu kaéròo ka to omôtte (i)ru ñ desu ĝa nêe.
'Well, I've been wondering when I should go back, but . . .' (I haven't decided).

3. **urímàsu**; 4. **sasíaĝemàsu**; 5. **mótte ikimàsu**; 6. **kimémàsu**; 7. **tabémàsu**; 8. **yorímàsu**

M 1. **Komímàsu ka nêe—kono zikañ.**
'I wonder if it gets crowded—at this hour.'

Êe, kômu daroo to omóimàsu yo↗
'Yes, I think it probably does get crowded.'

2. **Haírimàsu ka nêe—zêñbu.**
'I wonder if it will go in—all of it.'

Êe, hâiru daroo to omóimàsu yo↗
'Yes, I think it probably will go in.'

3. **todókimàsu/zêñbu**; 4. **awátemàsu/miñna**; 5. **komárimàsu/oózèe**

N 1. **Hokkàidoo made ikû desyoo?**
'You are going as far as Hokkaido, aren't you?'

Êe, mâa, ikú tumori dèsu kedo . .
'Yes, well, I plan to go [that far], but . . .' (what do you think?)

2. **Kyôoto de orîru desyoo?** **Êe, mâa, orîru tumóri dèsu kedo..**
'You are going to get off in Kyoto, aren't you?' 'Yes, well, I plan to get off [there], but...' (what do you think?)

3. **ryoogae-suru**; 4. **kuúkoo màde 'miokuru**; 5. **kono omói hako mo oròsu**; 6. **taḱkyuubiñ o tanòmu**; 7. **sînai made 'kayou**

O 1. **Hokkàidoo made ikû no?** **Iya, ikánai tumori dà kedo..**
'(Is it that) you are going as far as Hokkaido?' 'No, I plan not to go [that far], but...' (is there a problem?)

2. **Kyôoto de orîru no?** **Iya, orînai tumóri dà kedo..**
'(Is it that) you are going to get off in Kyoto?' 'No, I plan not to get off [there], but...' (is there a problem?)

3. **ryoogae-suru**; 4. **kuúkoo màde 'miokuru**; 5. **kono omói hako mo oròsu**; 6. **taḱkyuubiñ o tanòmu**; 7. **sînai made 'kayou**

P 1. **Zyûgyoo ni dêta?** **Ñ. Denâi tumóri dàtta kedo, yappàri nêe.**
'Did you attend the class?' 'Yeah. I planned not to attend, but after all, you know.'

2. **Sitêeseki no kippu 'katta?** **Ñ. Kawánai tumori dàtta kedo, yappàri nêe.**
'Did you buy reserved-seat tickets?' 'Yeah. I planned not to buy [them], but after all, you know.'

3. **hurûi mono 'utta**; 4. **gakkoo màde hôñ o tôri ni itta**; 5. **kabañ azúkàtta**; 6. **tônai e kitâ**

Q 1. **Señsèe ni omé ni kakàru no wa, nî-zi desu ka↗—sâñ-zi desu ka↗** **Nî-zi no tumóri dàtta ñ desu ga, yappàri sâñ-zi no hôo ga îi ka mo siremaseñ ne!**
'Is the time you're going to see the teacher two o'clock, or three o'clock?' 'I planned for two o'clock, but when I think about it, three o'clock may be better.'

2. **Señsèe ga onóri ni nàru no wa, hutûusya desu ka↗—guríñsya desu ka↗** **Hutûusya no tumóri dàtta ñ desu ga, yappàri guríñsya no hôo ga îi ka mo siremaseñ ne!**
'Is the [train] you, professor, are going to take the regular coach, or the green car?' 'I planned for the regular coach, but when I think about it, the green may be better.'

3. **señsèe o 'omati-suru/nisiǵuti/higasiǵuti**; 4. **señsèe o 'oture-suru/koñsyuu/goóru-deñ-uìiku**; 5. **señsèe ni 'omise-suru/seézi no zyùgyoo/kêezai no zyûgyoo**

R 1. **Kono tukue, Sugìura-sañ ga okái ni narimàsita.** **Sôo desita ka. Dôo iu tumori de kattà ñ desyoo nêe.**
'This desk Mr/s. Sugiura bought.' 'S/he did? I wonder what his/her intention was to have bought it?'

2. **Anó hòñ, butyóo ga osute ni narimàsita.** **Sôo desita ka. Dôo iu tumori de sutétà ñ desyoo nêe.**

'That book the division chief threw away.'	'S/he did? I wonder what his/her intention was to have thrown it away?'

3. konó nìmotu/onîisañ/moʹtte (i)rassyaimàsita; 4. konó osòba/Watanabe-sañ/tyuúmoñ-nasaimàsita; 5. ano kippu/Ôono-sañ/oúri ni narimàsita; 6. anó zadàñkai/Sâtoo-sañ/odé ni narimàsita; 7. ano osatu/katyoo/owátasi ni narimàsita

S 1. **Kyôoto e ikû no ni wa, ni-zíkañ-g̃ùrai kakâru desyoo?**
'It will probably take about two hours to go to Kyoto—right?'
 Êe, ni-sáñ-zìkañ kakâru desyoo ne!
'Yes, it will probably take two to three hours.'

2. **Kore zéñbu surû no ni wa, sañ-kag̃etu-g̃ùrai kakâru desyoo?**
'It will probably take about three months to do all of this—right?'
 Êe, sañ-yoñ-kàg̃etu kakâru desyoo ne!
'Yes, it will probably take three to four months.'

3. ni-kai o suḱkàri katázukèru/yok-ka; 4. kore o iu/gô-huñ; 5. konó kikài o naôsu/mik-ka; 6. kore zéñbu sirábèru/zyuúgo-zìkañ; 7. konó hanasì o setumee-suru/itízìkañ

T 1. **Kono gakkoo, señsèe g̃a sukúnài desu nêe.**
'This school has few teachers, doesn't it!'
 Sôo desu nêe. Hoñtoo ni señsèe no sukúnài gakkoo dèsu nêe.
'Isn't that true! It really is a school with few teachers, isn't it!'

2. **Kono kyoositu, mâdo g̃a oôi desu nêe.**
'This classroom has lots of windows, doesn't it!'
 Sôo desu nêe. Hoñtoo ni màdo no oôi kyoósitu dèsu nêe.
'Isn't that true! It really is a classroom with lots of windows, isn't it!'

3. kaisya/waápuro g̃a oôi; 4. daíg̃aku/zyosée g̃a oôi; 5. hito/nîmotu g̃a sukúnài

U 1. **Kono heñ wa, kurúma g̃a oòi desu nêe.**
'There are lots of cars around here, aren't there!'
 Sôo desu nêe. Kurúma g̃a òokute komárimàsu nêe.
'That's true. It's a bother that there are [so] many cars, isn't it!'

2. **Kono heñ wa, tâkusii g̃a sukúnài desu nêe.**
'Taxis are scarce around here, aren't they!'
 Sôo desu nêe. Tâkusii g̃a sukûnàkute komárimàsu nêe.
'That's true. It's a bother that taxis are [so] scarce, isn't it!'

3. zîko/oôi; 4. koósyuu-dèñwa/sukúnài; 5. kâzi/oôi; 6. zisiñ/oôi

V 1. **Hakóñde morattà no?**
'You had [someone] carry it?'
 Iya, zibúñ de hakoñdà ñ da yo.[3]
'No, I carried it myself.'

2. **Watásite morattà no?**
'You had [someone] hand it over?'
 Iya, zibúñ de watasità ñ da yo.[3]
'No, I handed it over myself.'

---

3. Blunt-style. The gentle-style equivalent has **no yo** in place of **ñ da yo**.

3. **atûmete**; 4. **narabete**; 5. **azûkete**; 6. **irete**

W1. **Sore, gozíbuñ no kàmera?**   **Konó kàmera? Ñ, zibúñ nò da kedo . .**
'Is that your own camera?'   'This camera? Yeah, it's my own, but . . .'
                                                       (why do you ask?)

2. **Sore, gozíbuñ no kyookàsyo?**   **Konó kyookàsyo? Ñ, zibúñ nò da kedo . .**
'Is that your own textbook?'   'This textbook? Yeah, it's my own, but . . .'
                                                       (why do you ask?)

3. **têrebi**; 4. **waapuro**; 5. **heyâ**

Application Exercises

Have each class member plan an imaginary trip, including duration, dates of departure and return, means of transportation, destination, etc. Take turns discussing and asking and answering questions pertaining to these travels, using the new patterns of this lesson section. For example:

1a. Plans: **tumori**
    'Where do you intend to go?'
    'When do you intend to leave/return?'
    'How long do you expect to stay in /place/?'

1b. Plans: **-(y)òo to omôu**
    'I'm thinking of going to /place/.'
    'I think I'll go by train and return by plane.'
    'I think I'll take a special express' (*or* green car, reserved seat, bullet train, express, regular train).
    'I think I'll buy my tickets in advance.'

2. Process: **x no ni wa**
    'It takes /approximate duration of time/ to go from A to B.'
    'For taking the train leaving at 9:00, I'll need a passenger ticket *and* an express ticket.'
    'For going to the airport, the train is more reliable than the limo-bus.'

3. Alternatives: **hôo, itibañ**
    'It's faster to go to the airport by train than to take a cab.'
    'It's easier to hire **takkyuubiñ** than to carry heavy luggage by yourself.'
    'Which is cheaper—to fly to Hawaii or to go by ship?'
    'Since it's Golden Week travel, you'd better buy your tickets early.'
    'Taking a reserved seat on a green car is most expensive.'
    'Traveling with friends is most fun.'

    The possibilities are limitless: at this stage in your study of Japanese, you have reached the point where you can say a great deal. The main problem in participating in this kind of conversation will be your delivery. You must avoid the temptation to plan what you want to say in English and then translate that directly into Japanese with an overlay of English intonation that reflects the original. Instead, work on incorporating the structural patterns for conversation that you have learned, by internalizing the CC and Drills.

B. Core Conversations: Substitution

After practicing the Core Conversations, making the usual appropriate vocabulary substitutions, go over them again, altering the relationship between the participants: close friends (blunt/gentle, blunt/blunt, gentle/gentle); supervisor/employee; slight acquaintances.

SECTION B

Core Conversations

1(J)a. **Osôi nêe—Suzuki-kuñ. Koko ni kû-zí-hàñ tte (i)tte àru ñ daroo?**

(N)a. **Êe. Soré wa tyañto sitte (i)ru hazu nà ñ desu kedo nêe.**

b. **Suzúki-kuñ no tokorò kara wa, norîkae ḡa oòi ñ daroo ka.**

b. **Sâa nêe.**

2(J)a. **Tyôtto 'zikañ ḡa siñpai nêe.**

(N)a. **Tâkusii de itta hòo ḡa îi desyoo ka.**

b. **Iya, îma no zikañ wa, mûsiro tikátetu no hòo ḡa hayâi wa. Kâiḡi wa tâsika zyûu-zi kara desyoo?**

c. **Mâda daízyòobu na hazú dà kedo, isôide ikímasyòo.**

b. **Hâi. Ma ní àu desyoo ka.**

3(N)a. **Tâsika konó èki ni mîdori no madôḡuti ḡa âtta hazú nà ñ da kedo..**

(J) **Hañtai no hòo zya nai?**

b. **A, sôo ka. Kottì ḡa minámiḡuti no tumori dàtta kedo, matíḡàete (i)ta ñ da.**

4(N)a. **Dôo desita—gakkai wa.**

(J)a. **Dôo mo nêe. Mâa, iroiro beñkyoo-suru tumori de ittà ñ da kedo nêe.**

b. **Puróḡùramu ni wa zûibuñ rippa na namae ḡa dète (i)masita kedo nêe.**

b. **Soré wa sòo na ñ da kedo nêe. Yakû ni tatânai hanásì no oôi puróḡùramu de nêe. Gakkàri-sityatta.**

c. **Sôo desu ka.**

English Equivalents

1(J)a. He's late, isn't he—Suzuki. (It's the case that) he has been told (*lit.* it's been said) [to be] here at 9:30—right?

(N)a. Yes. (It's the case that) he is expected to know that (at least) exactly, but . . . (I wonder what happened).

b. From Suzuki's place would it be the case that there are lots of transfers?

b. I wonder.

2(J)a. Time is a bit of a worry, isn't it.

(N)a. Would it be better to go by cab?

b. No, at this hour, rather the subway is faster. If I remember correctly, the conference starts at 10:00—right?

b. Yes. Do you suppose we'll be on time?

c. We should still be all right, but let's hurry.

3(N)a. (It's that) there should be (*lit.* have been) a green [-car] ticket window in this station if I remember correctly, but . . . (I don't see it).

(J) Isn't it in the opposite direction?

b. Oh. I was under the impression that *this way* was the south entrance, but (it's that) I was mistaken.

4(N)a. How was it—the academic conference?

(J)a. Somehow—you know . . . (It's that) I went with the expectation of learning all kinds of things, but . . . (it didn't turn out that way).

b. On the program, very eminent names appeared, but . . . (was there a problem?)

b. (It's the case that) that is so, but it was a program with lots of useless talks, and—you know! It was a letdown.

c. Really!

Breakdowns
(and Supplementary Vocabulary)

1. **itte àru**　　　　　　　　　　　it has been said
   koko ni kû-zi tte itte àru　　'here at 9:30' has been said

hazu (SP1)	general expectation
sítte (i)ru hazu dà	it is expected that [s/he] knows; [s/he] should know
+kaeru /-ru; kaeta/	change [something]
+noríkàèru /-ru; noríkàeta/	transfer to another vehicle
norikae	a transfer
2. siñpai	worry, concern
mûsiro	rather, more than that
mûsiro X no hôo ḡa hayâi	rather X is faster
ma ní àu	be on time
daízyòobu na hazu da	it is expected to be all right; it should be all right
isôḡu /-u; isôida/	be in a hurry, make haste
isôide 'iku	go hurriedly
3. madôḡuti	ticket window
mîdori no madôḡuti	ticket window for green-car tickets
âtta hazu da	it is expected that there was; there should have been
hañtai	opposite
minámiḡuti no tumori dàtta (SP2)	I expected it to be the south entrance
matíḡàèru /-ru; matíḡàeta/	make a mistake
+matíḡàu /u; matiḡatta/	be(come) wrong, in error
4. gakkai	learned society
iroiro /no ~ na/	various
puróḡùramu	program
rippa /na/	splendid, magnificent, great, eminent
+yuumee /na/	famous; notorious
namáe ḡa dèru	names appear
namáe ḡa dète (i)ru	names are carried, published, printed, etc.
yakû ni tâtu	be of use
+yakû ni tatêru	put to use
yakú ni tatànai hanásì	a useless talk
hanásì ḡa (or no) oôi puróḡùramu	a program with many talks
gaḱkàri-suru	become discouraged; be disappointed

MISCELLANEOUS NOTES

1. In CC1, Mr. Carter and his division chief are waiting at a coffee shop for Mr. Suzuki, whose failure to appear on time can't be explained. The division chief uses blunt, casual-style, with direct-style final predicates. Mr. Carter's speech, in contrast, is careful, with a

distal-style predicate. The **nee** that ends his two utterances shows empathy and lack of confrontation.

(J)a. **Ítte àru** conveys the notion that something (in this context, **koko ni kû-zi**) has been said without any indication of who said it. **Daroo?** and **daroo ka** (in [J]b) in sentence-final position are typical of blunt-style, particularly men's speech.

(N)a. Mr. Carter is clearly more ambivalent in his reply, using both **hazu** (see SP1, following) and **kedo**, with an empathetic **nêe** added for good measure. He wants to keep his boss happy without damaging his colleague, Mr. Suzuki.

(J)b. **Norikae** is a nominal derivative (stem form) of the compound verbal **noríkaèru** < /stem of **noru** + **kaeru** 'change [something]'/. **Kaeru**, an operational vowel verbal (compare **kâeru** 'return,' a consonant verbal) is the transitive partner of **kawaru** '[something] changes.' (Given these two related verbals, we can assume that **kaeru** comes from an earlier *__kaweru__, with the **w** lost, as it usually is, everywhere except before **a**.) Compare also **iíkaèru** 'rephrase,' 'say again in a different way'; **kakikaeru** 'rewrite'; **torikaeru** 'exchange.'

(N)b. Mr. Carter continues to wonder "cooperatively" with his boss, at the same time providing no concrete information or comment on Mr. Suzuki.

2. In CC2, Deborah Miller and her supervisor, Ms. Sakamoto, are hurrying to a conference. There is some question as to whether they will arrive on time. Ms. Sakamoto uses gentle casual-style, with a feminine sentence-final **wa**↗. Her final predicates **hayâi** and **siñpai** (the latter with deleted **dà**) are direct-style, but **desyòo** and **ikímasyòo** reflect the avoidance of corresponding direct-style forms in women's gentle-style speech. Both of Ms. Miller's utterances end in distal-style **desyòo ka.**, not significant in identifying a woman's speech-style, but careful-style is assumed in this situation.

(J)a. **Siñpai** covers a range that includes uneasiness and concern as well as real worry. The related verbal is **siñpai-suru**. A Japanese is apologetic about causing others to worry about his/her own personal problems or concerns; hence the ritual expression **Siñpai o kàkete, sumímasèñ**. 'I'm sorry to have made you worry (*lit*. having hung worries on you).'

(J)b. **Mûsiro** emphasizes the validity of the alternate that follows, in contrast with what was previously mentioned.

Remember the distinction between /**tâsika** + predicate/ and /**tâsika ni** + predicate/. The former implies some lack of certainty, in contrast with the latter, which stresses the predicate 'positively.'

(N)b. **Ma** refers to an interval of time or space—in some contexts, appropriate timing and spacing, an important component of a well-adjusted life for the Japanese. **Ma ní àu** implies meeting up with the fixed timing, i.e., being on time. Note: **X ni ma ní àu** 'be on time for X.'

(J)c. **Isôḡu** is our first example of a consonant verbal whose root ends in **-ḡ**. The perfective and the gerund of such verbals end in **-ida/-ide**, with the **-ḡ-** lost. Compare verbals with roots ending in **k: aruku/aruita**.

3. In CC3, Smith and Kato, male graduate students, are in a station, looking for the ticket window where green-car tickets are sold. Both use casual-style, with direct-style predicates. Smith's **sôo ka** and sentence-final **dà** are blunt-style.

(N)a. **Madôḡuti**: compare **dêḡuti**, **minamiḡuti**, etc. The use of **átta** before **hazu** is the perfective of recall.

(J) **Hañtai**: Compare **hañtai-suru** 'oppose'; **X ni hañtai-suru** 'oppose X'; **tûyôku hañtai-suru** 'oppose strongly'; **hañtai ni** 'conversely.'

(N)b. **Matíḡàu** is an intransitive, affective verbal whose partner is **matíḡaèru**, a transitive, operational verbal. Note: **matíĝàtte (i)ru** 'it's wrong'; **matíĝàtta X** 'wrong X,' 'mistaken X'; **X o matíĝaèru** 'mistake X' (as in **mití o matíĝaèru** 'take the wrong road'); **X o 'Y ni/to matíĝaèru** 'mistake X for Y.'

4. In CC4, Sue Brown discusses with Professor Ono a recent conference he attended. It proved to be a disappointment. Brown uses basically careful-style, with distal-style predicates. However, her inverted sentence and question without **ka** ([N]a) are casual features that move her language slightly toward the casual on the casual-careful continuum. Professor Ono's language is clearly casual-style, with direct-style predicates, a preponderance of fragments and minor sentences, and the contracted form **sityatta**.

(J)a. **Dôo mo** is regularly an intensifier; when it occurs alone as a fragment, it intensifies whatever notion is established by the context and/or intonation and gestures. Here, Professor Ono is emphasizing his ambivalent feelings about the conference.

Iroiro is a nominal which is followed by either the **no** or the **na** alternate of **dà** at the end of a sentence modifier: **iróiro no hitò** or **iróiro na hitò** 'people (who are) of various kinds.' /**Iroiro na** + nominal/ has a contracted equivalent /**iroñ na** + nominal/. **Iroiro** also occurs without a following particle as a manner pattern, hooking up with a predicate: **iróiro hanàsu** 'talk about all kinds of things'; **iróiro àru** 'there exist various kinds.'

Beñkyoo-suru covers not only studying over a period of time but also acquisition of knowledge on one occasion. Consider **Beñkyoo ni narimàsita**, the polite ritual remark to make after hearing a lecture by one's professor or a guest. Compliments like 'That was a good lecture,' or 'Your ideas are very stimulating' are not the kind of remarks one makes to a superior in Japan!

(J)b. **Yakû ni tâtu**: **Yakû** is a nominal which refers to 'duty,' 'office,' 'role'; the combination **yakû ni tâtu** covers being useful, serving a purpose. The transitive partner of this intransitive combination is **yakû ni tatêru**: /X o yakû ni tatêru/ 'put X to use.'

Note that **puróguràmu** is preceded by a sentence modifier (**hanásì no** [or **ĝa**] **oôi**), the nominal of which (**hanásì**) is also preceded by a sentence modifier (**yakû ni tatânai**).

Structural Patterns

1. **hazu**

In Section A-SP1 we introduced **tumori**, referring to a personal intention or expectation. We now introduce a nominal which directly contrasts with this: **hazu**.

Hazu indicates general expectation not personally motivated; it may refer to an impersonal condition or to something associated with a person other than the speaker:

Suzuki-sañ, kyôo kimâsu ka⌐ . . . **Kûru hazú dèsu kedo . .** 'Is Mr/s. Suzuki coming today?' . . . 'S/he's expected to come, but . . .' (I'm not sure).

Anó dàiku-sañ, kore dekímàsu ka⌐ . . . **Dekîru hazú dèsu yo**⌐ 'Can that carpenter do this?' . . . 'S/he should be able to.'

Koré ĝa wakàru hazu no gakusee wa, inâi desyoo? 'There aren't any students who are expected to understand this—right?'

Soó iu dooĝù wa bêñri na hazú dèsu kedo, dôo desyoo ka nêe. 'Tools like that are supposed to be convenient, but I wonder.'

Môo huyû ni nâtte (i)ru kara, Sapporo wa îma samûi hazú dèsu nêe. 'It's already (become) winter, so Sapporo should be cold now, shouldn't it!'

Note that **hazu** can be preceded by both operational and affective predicates. Instead of a direct negative of **hazu desu** following a regular /nominal + da/ negation pattern (*__hazu zya nâi__), we find —— **hazu ḡa/wa nâi** 'there is no expectation.' The sentence modifier preceding **hazu** may also be negative. Compare the following answers to the question: **Koóhìi wa?**

    Âru hazú dèsu yo⤴ 'There should be some.'

    Âru hazu wa nâi desu yo⤴ 'There's no reason to expect there is any.'

    Nâi hazú dèsu yo⤴ 'The expectation is that there isn't any.'

    Nâi hazu wa nâi desu yo⤴ 'There's no reason to expect there isn't any.'

There is also the question of perfective/imperfective both before and after **hazu**. Compare the following:

    Kâre wa daíḡaku ni hàiru hazú dà kedo; hâiru ka dôo ka wakárimasèn̄ nêe. 'It is expected that he'll enter college, but it's not clear whether he'll enter or not.'

    Kâre wa daíḡaku ni hàitta hazú dà kedo; tâsika ni hâitta desyoo ka nêe. 'He is supposed to have entered college, but I wonder if he definitely did enter.'

    Kâre wa daíḡaku ni hàiru hazú dàtta kedo; gakkoo o yamete, dâiku ni naťtyaimàsita. 'It was expected he would enter college, but he quit school and ended up becoming a carpenter.'

    Kâre wa kyônen̄ made ni daíḡaku ni hàitta hazú dàtta kedo; hon̄too wa, haíràna-katta n̄ desu nee. 'It was expected that he had entered college by last year but actually he didn't enter.'

Several different Japanese patterns have now been glossed with English that includes 'should.' The distinctions must be kept in mind. Compare these examples:

    'You should take this medicine.' (advice) = **Kono kusuri o nôn̄da hoo ḡa îi desu yo⤴**

    'S/he should have arrived in Osaka by now.' (expectation that s/he arrived) = **Môo Oósaka ni tùita hazu desu.**

    'S/he should have arrived here by now.' (expectation that proved wrong) = **Môo kokó ni tùite (i)ru hazú dèsita kedo ..**

    'What time should we leave?' (suggestion) = **Nân̄-zi ni tatímasyòo ka.**

2. MORE ON **tumori**

In Section A-SP4, we were introduced to examples of **tumori** preceded by sentence modifiers consisting of, or ending with, operational verbals whose operators were the same as the person with the intention (usually the speaker, or, in questions, the addressee).

    Bâsu ni noríkaèru tumori desu. 'I intend to transfer to the bus.' (*My* intention is that *I* will transfer.)

    Soodan̄-suru tumori de ukáḡaimàsita. 'I visited with the intention of talking things over.' (*My* intention was that *I* would consult.)

Tumori also occurs in reference to beliefs or assumptions or personal expectations in which the sentence modifier may be operational or affective, and the operator or affect, expressed or understood from context, different from the 'intender.'

Sore wa gaíziñ ni wakariyasùi nihoñḡo no tumori? 'Do you expect that to be Japanese that's easy for foreigners to understand?'

Arúbàito ḡa tetúdàtte kuréru tumori dàtta kedo.. 'I intended for the part-timer to give me help, but...' (it didn't work out).

Kyôo ḡa doyôobi no tumóri dèsita kara.. 'Since I assumed that *today* is Saturday...' (I acted accordingly).

As an alternate for this /**tumori + dà**/ pattern, we find /**tumori de + iru**/, which substitutes a /**tumori de** + predicate/ pattern for the more usual /nominal + **dà**/. Example:

Kâre ḡa tukúe o todòkete kuréru tumori de imàsita ḡa.. 'I intended (existed with the intention) for him to deliver a desk for me, but...' (I wonder what happened).

Drills

A 1. **Omôi desu ka↗—anó nìmotu.**
'Is it heavy—that luggage over there?'

   Omói hazu dèsu kedo, dôo desyoo ka nêe.
   'It's supposed to be heavy, but I wonder.'

2. **Kyuúkoo dèsu ka↗—ano ressya.**
'Is it an express—that train over there?'

   Kyuúkoo no hazu dèsu kedo, dôo desyoo ka nêe.
   'It's supposed to be an express, but I wonder.'

3. **sakúra dèsu/anó kì**; 4. **kîree desu/ano otera**; 5. **arímàsu/sono syasiñ**; 6. **tuyôi desu/kono osake**; 7. **zyoózù desu/ano gakusee**

B 1. **Îtu kara narábu to omòu?**
'When do you think they will start to line up?'

   Môo naráñde (i)ru hazu dà kedo..
   'They should be lined up already, but...' (I'm not sure).

2. **Îtu tôri ni kûru to omôu?**
'When do you think they will come to pick [it] up?'

   Môo tôri ni kitê (i)ru hazú dà kedo..
   'They should have come to pick [it] up already, but...' (I'm not sure).

3. **îtu kara tetúdàu**; 4. **îtu todóku**; 5. **îtu kara uru**; 6. **îtu kara yaru**; 7. **îtu tûku**; 8. **îtu ki ḡá tùku**

C 1. **Syatyóo ḡa hañtai-simasèñ ka↗**
'Won't the company president oppose?'

   Iya, hañtai-sinai tte (i)ttè (i)ta kara, hañtai-suru hazu wa arimasèñ yo.
   'No, s/he was saying s/he wouldn't oppose, so there's no reason to expect that s/he will (oppose).'

2. **Beñḡòsi ḡa yamémasèñ ka↗**
'Won't the lawyer quit?'

   Iya, yaménai tte (i)ttè (i)ta kara, yaméru hazu wa arimasèñ yo.
   'No, s/he was saying s/he wouldn't quit, so there's no reason to expect that s/he will (quit).'

3. **uñtèñsyu/komárimasèñ**; 4. **dâiku/okúremasèñ**; 5. **Tanaka-sañ/yarímasèñ**

D 1. **Koṅsyuu atumarimàsu ka⤴—minâsañ.**
'Are they getting together this week—all of them?'

Ie, koṅsyuu wa màda atúmarànai hazú dèsu yo⤴
'No, the expectation is that they won't get together yet this week (at least).'

2. **Gozeṅ-tyuu komímàsu ka⤴—ano miti.**
'Does it get crowded during the morning—that street?'

Ie, gozéṅ-tyuu wa màda komânai hazú dèsu yo⤴
'No, the expectation is that it doesn't get crowded yet during the morning (at least).'

3. îma útte (i)màsu/tokkyùukeñ; 4. îma sûḡu yakû ni tatímàsu/konó dooḡù; 5. kotósi demàsu/ano atárasìi kyoókàsyo; 6. asíta akimàsu/anó misè

E 1. **Kêe-tyañ zêmi ni denâi no ka nâa.**
'I wonder if (that means) Kei isn't going to attend the seminar.'

Iyaa, dênai hazu wa nâi to omôu kedo nêe.
'No, I believe it's not likely that she won't attend, but . . .' (I'm not sure).

2. **Rokû-zi no tokkyuu ni ma ní awànai no ka nâa.**
'I wonder if (that means) they won't be on time for the six o'clock special express.'

Iyaa, ma ní awànai hazu wa nâi to omôu kedo nêe.
'No, I believe it's not likely that they won't be on time, but . . .' (I'm not sure).

3. miñna ki ḡá tukànai; 4. kaḡî kakárànai; 5. oyâ wa ′siñpai-sinai; 6. zeñzeñ awatenai; 7. kokó karà wa yamâ wa miênai; 8. anó èki wa mîdori no madôḡuti ḡa nâi

F 1. **Miñna gô-zi ni tukímàsu ne⤴**
'Everybody's going to arrive at five—right?'

Êe, |anoo| gô-zi ni tûku hazú dèsu kedo nêe. Hoṅtoo ni tyañto tùku ka dôo ka hakkìri sinâi ñ desu.
'Yes, uh, they are supposed to arrive at five. But whether or not they will actually arrive as planned isn't clear.'

2. **Kokó ni atumarimàsu ne⤴**
'They're going to gather here—right?'

Êe, |anoo| kokó ni atumàru hazú dèsu kedo nêe. Hoṅtoo ni tyañto atumàru ka dôo ka hakkìri sinâi ñ desu.
'Yes, uh, they are supposed to gather here. But whether or not they will actually gather as planned isn't clear.'

3. Oósaka de norimàsu; 4. hatí-zìkañ neté (i)màsu; 5. giṅkoo ni azukemàsu; 6. tokkyuu ni ma ni aimàsu

G 1. **Miñna rokû-zi ni tûita ñ desyoo?**
'(It's that) everybody arrived at six—right?'

Zitû wa nêe. Rokû-zi ni tûku hazú dàtta ñ desu kedo nêe. Tukânakatta ñ desu yo.
'Actually, (it's that) they were supposed to arrive at six, you know, but (the fact is) they didn't (arrive).'

2. **Uénò-eki de ôrita ñ desyoo?**
'(It's that) they got off at Ueno Station—right?'

Zitû wa nêe. Uénò-eki de orîru hazú dàtta ñ desu kedo nêe. Orînakatta ñ desu yo.
'Actually, (it's that) they were supposed to get off at Ueno Station, you know, but (the fact is) they didn't (get off).'

3. hiǧásiǧuti ni atumàtta; 4. Hanéda màde kitê kureta; 5. zibúñ de mottè kita; 6. hitôri de katázùketa; 7. tomódati o turetè kita

H 1. **Butyoo wa, mukóo màde irássyaimàsu ne⤴**
'The division chief will go over there, won't s/he?'

Hâi, irássyàru hazu desu. Watási wa sitùree-suru tumóri dèsu ǧa . .
'Yes, s/he is expected to go. I intend to excuse myself, though . . .'

2. **Señsèe wa, zadâñkai ni odé ni narimàsu ne⤴**
'The professor will take part in the round-table discussion, won't s/he?'

Hâi, odé ni nàru hazu desu. Watási wa sitùree-suru tumóri dèsu ǧa . .
'Yes, s/he is expected to participate. I intend to excuse myself, though . . .'

3. syatyoo/okyákusàma ni oái ni narimàsu; 4. okyákusàma/kokó de omati ni narimàsu; 5. iñtyoo/omíokuri ni narimàsu; 6. anó katà/kokó ni oyori ni narimàsu

I 1. **Tumárànai hanàsì desu nêe. Koñna hanasì wa ôôkatta ñ desu ka⤴—sono gakkai wa.**
'It's a boring talk, isn't it! Were there many talks like this—at that conference?'

Êe, tumárànai hanásì no oôi gakkai de nêe.
'Yes, it was a conference with many uninteresting talks, and . . .' (you know what that means).

2. **Omósiròi hitô desu nêe. Koñna hitô wa sukûnàkatta ñ desu ka⤴—sonó zadâñkai wa.**
'S/he's an interesting person, isn't s/he! Were there few people like this—at that round-table discussion?'

Êe, omósiròi hitô no sukúnài zadâñkai de nêe.
'Yes, it was a round-table discussion with few interesting people, and . . .' (you know what that means).

3. yaríyasùi siǧoto/mezúràsìkatta/kaisya; 4. beñri na êki/tîkâkatta/uti; 5. kîree na kêsiki/ôôkatta/tûaa

J 1. **Añmari yakù ni tatânai hôñ desu nêe. Koñna hòñ o yômu ñ desu ka⤴—konó zèmi wa.**
'This is a book which is not very useful! (Does it mean) they read books like this—in this seminar?'

Êe, añmari yakù ni tatânai hôñ o yômu zêmi de nêe.
'Yes, it is a seminar in which they read books that are not very useful, and . . .' (you know what that means).

2. **Mezúrasìi yasái dèsu nêe. Koñna yasai ǧa takusañ hàitte (i)ru ñ desu**

Êe, mezúrasìi yasai ǧa takúsañ hàitte (i)ru ryôori de nêe.

ka↗—**kokó no ryòori wa.**
'These are unusual vegetables! Are there a lot of vegetables like this—in the cooking here?'

'Yes, it's cooking that has a lot of unusual vegetables in it, and . . .' (you know what that means).

3. **yuúmee na beñḡòsi/ḡa 'oozee iru/kokó no zimùsyo**; 4. **tîisa na simâ/ḡa yôku miêru/ano oka**; 5. **zûibuñ kôñde (i)ru miti/o iku/rimúziñ-bàsu**; 6. **kânari toói tokorò/kara kayotte (i)ru/ano gakusee**

K 1. **Hañtai-sita hòo ḡa îi ñ zya arímasèñ ka**↗

'Wouldn't it be better to oppose?'

Iya, mûsiro hañtai-sinai hòo ḡa îi desyoo.

'No, rather it would probably be better not to oppose.'

2. **Kusúri o nòñda hoo ḡa îi ñ zya arímasèñ ka**↗

'Wouldn't it be better to take some medicine?'

Iya, mûsiro nomânai hoo ḡa îi desyoo.

'No, rather it would probably be better not to take any medicine.'

3. **Yamâḡuti-sañ ni tanôñda**; 4. **sitêeseki o kaít(e) òita**; 5. **monóreèru ni notta**; 6. **toozitu deñwa ireta**; 7. **sînai made todôketa**

L 1. **Kippu-ùriba wa, tâsika minámiḡuti no hòo desita ne**↗

'The ticket counter, if I'm not mistaken, was on the south gate side, wasn't it?'

Kippu-ùriba? Iya, kitáḡuti no hòo zya nâi?

'The ticket counter? No, isn't it the north gate side?'

2. **Mîdori no madôḡuti wa, tâsika nisíḡuti no hòo desita ne**↗

'The green [-car] ticket counter, if I'm not mistaken, was on the west gate side, wasn't it?'

Mîdori no madôḡuti? Iya, hiḡásiḡuti no hòo zya nâi?

'The green [-car] ticket window? No, isn't it the east gate side?'

3. **arúbàito no gakusee/zyosee**; 4. **anó tùaa/kitá no hòo**; 5. **suútukèesu/sôto**; 6. **ziyûuseki/mâe**; 7. **minato/hidari**

M 1. **Mîdori no madôḡuti wa, nisíḡuti zya nài?**

'Isn't the green [-car] ticket window at the west gate?'

Âa, sôo da. Kokó ḡa nisiḡuti no tumori dàtta kedo, matíḡàete (i)ta ñ da.

'Oh, that's right. I assumed *this* was the west gate, but (it's that) I was mistaken.'

2. **Zadâñkai wa, suíyòobi zya nâi?**

'Isn't the round-table discussion on Wednesday?'

Âa, sôo da. Kyôo ḡa suíyòobi no tumóri dàtta kedo, matíḡàete (i)ta ñ da.

'Oh, that's right. I assumed *today* was Wednesday, but (it's that) I was mistaken.'

3. **goórudeñ-uìiku/gô-ḡatu**; 4. **Kodáma-sañ no zyùḡyoo/getúyòobi**; 5. **kyoositu/rokkai**

N 1. Zûibuñ takâi ñ zya nai?—kono tukue.
'Isn't it (the case that it's) awfully expensive—this desk?'

Ñ, tâkâkute gak̄kàri-sityatta.
'Yeah, I was disappointed that it was [so] expensive.'

2. Añmari yakù ni tatânai ñ zya nai?—konó zìsyo.
'Isn't it (the case that it's) not very useful—this dictionary?'

Ñ, yakû ni tatânakute gak̄kàri-sityatta.
'Yeah, I was disappointed that it was not useful.'

3. zûibuñ karui/kono hako; 4. añmari yòku nâi/kono kuruma; 5. zûibuñ sukúnài/oree; 6. zûibuñ tooi/kaisya; 7. añmari atatàkàku nâi/ryôori; 8. añmari wàkàku nâi/asóko no syàiñ

Application Exercises

A1. Make up two detailed weekly schedules, one for your division head and the other for your helper (an **arúbàito no gakusee**). Practice answering questions (from in-group and from out-group members) as to what these people are expected to be doing at specific times, using **hazu**, based on the schedules. Examples:

Îma wa suíyòobi no âsa ku-zí-hàñ desu. Arúbàito wa nâni o sité (i)rù desyoo ka. 'It's now 9:30 Wednesday morning. What is the part-timer doing?'

Arúbàito desu ka⌒ Bûñḡaku no zêmi ni dête (i)ru hazú dèsu kedo.. 'The part-timer? The expectation is that he's attending a literature seminar, but...' (I'm not sure).

2. Using each of the following as a mistaken assumption, describe something you did which was inappropriate. Example:

Yuúmee na señsèe ḡa odé ni nàru. 'Famous professors will participate.'

Yuúmee na señsèe ḡa odé ni nàru tumóri dàtta kara, anó zèmi ni it́tà ñ da kedo, matíḡàete (i)ta ñ desu. 'I expected famous professors to participate so I went to that seminar, but I was wrong.'

a. **Ití-zi-hàñ no kaisoku-deñsya ḡa ni-zí-màe ni tûku.**
b. **Kyôo ḡa doyôobi da.**
c. **Aré ḡa kono tuḡì ni tukáu kyookàsyo da.**
d. **Kânozyo ḡa tetúdàtte kureru.**
e. **Konó èki no kaísatùḡuti no tokórò ḡa atúmàru tokórò da.**
f. **Kâre ḡa ué no tokorò ni not́te (i)ru nìmotu o orôsite kureru.**
g. **Koko ḡa nihoñḡo no kyoositu da.**
h. **Anó kippu-ùriba ḡa mîdori no madôḡuti da.**
i. **Kono ressya ḡa kaisoku da.**
j. **Konó wàiñ no hôo ḡa amâi.**
k. **Konó hòñ no hôo ḡa nihóñḡō ḡa yomiyasùi.**

B. Core Conversations: Substitution

Practice the Core Conversations, making substitutions that do not alter the basic framework of the conversations. Again, introduce variation in the relationships of the participants. Practice asking and answering questions on content.

SECTION C

Eavesdropping

(Answer the following on the basis of the accompanying tape. A = first speaker; B = second speaker.)
1a. What task are A and B apparently involved in?
 b. According to A, what is needed?
 c. What does B offer to do?
 d. What concern does A raise?
 e. What is B's expectation?
2a. What are A and B concerned about?
 b. What was the situation earlier today?
 c. What is A's advice?
3a. Of the two alternatives A is considering, which may be the better one? What are the two alternatives?
 b. What does B offer to do? Why?
 c. How does B politely turn aside A's thanks?
4a. What is A about to do?
 b. What alternative does B suggest? Why?
 c. What specific question is B unable to answer?
5a. What time is it?
 b. What suggestion does A make?
 c. What is B's objection?
 d. What alternate suggestion does A make? Why?
6a. From whom does A request help?
 b. What request does A make?
 c. What difficulty does B encounter? The solution?
7a. What two types of people are compared?
 b. For B, which category may have the more difficult life?
 c. What supporting evidence does A offer?
8a. What is happening tomorrow? Where?
 b. What does A offer to do?
 c. Why is the offer turned down?
9a. What problem has B encountered?
 b. Why does A find the situation unusual?
 c. What explanation does A suggest?
 d. What is B's reaction?
10a. Who is B?
 b. What is A's mistaken assumption?
 c. What change of plans occurred? Why?
11a. What is A inquiring about?
 b. What is B's opinion on the subject?
 c. Why does B come to that conclusion?

d. What is B's comment on taxicabs?
12a. How is B's luggage being sent?
   b. What does B request from A?
   c. How does A respond to the request?
13a. What is A inquiring about?
   b. Why is A surprised?
   c. How does B counteract A's reaction about the difficulty of the situation?
14a. Where is the other green-car ticket window located?
   b. What advantage does it offer at the moment?
   c. What is the explanation for the situation described as **suḡôi**?
15a. Who is being discussed?
   b. What is happening to that person today?
   c. Where is that person well known? Where not?
   d. What information supplied by B elicits surprise from A?
   e. How does B feel about the work of the person under discussion?
16a. Where is Dr. Morimoto?
   b. What explanation does B offer?
   c. What is the explanation for A's surprise?
   d. Compare the language styles of A and B.
17a. What does A suggest?
   b. What problem does B raise?
   c. What is the explanation for the problem?
   d. What was the situation in the past?
   e. What are A and B going to do?
18a. What request does A make of B? With what change?
   b. Comment on the contents and weight of the objects under discussion.
19a. Where is A apparently going? By what means of transportation?
   b. What alternate means does B suggest? Leaving from where?
   c. How long does this take?
   d. Why is this means of transportation described as easier for A?
20a. Describe B's transportation plan.
   b. What is A's alternate plan?
   c. Describe A's objection to B's original plan. Give details.
21a. What is A looking for?
   b. Where is that object supposed to be? Put there by whom?
   c. Where is it found?
   d. Why is A surprised?
22a. What reaction does A expect to 'this idea'?
   b. What is the actual situation?
   c. Who is Yamada?
   d. What is Yamada's recommendation, as reported by B?
   e. What is A's reaction?
   f. Where does B stand on the subject?
23a. What is the general topic of discussion?
   b. How is it described in general terms?
   c. What problem did B encounter?
   d. What had B hoped to do?
   e. Why was B surprised to have encountered this problem?

Utilization

(For each item, provide at least a stimulus or a response. Whenever possible, develop a short conversation.)

1. Find out where one goes to buy tickets for the bullet train; change dollars into yen; check luggage; call a cab; mail a letter.
2. You are planning a trip. Find out which is cheaper—to fly from Haneda or to go by bullet train from Tokyo Station.
3. You and a colleague are on your way to a meeting. Explain that it will be faster to get off here and take a cab than to go to the next station and walk.
4. Warn a friend against crossing the street here; drinking the water here; eating at that sushi shop.
5. Tell a colleague that all the furniture you bought yesterday was delivered to your home in one car.
6. Warn a friend that she'd better go to the corner where the traffic light is to cross a street like this.
7. Explain to the porter that all the suitcases over there are yours, but one of the boxes isn't.
8. Tell a colleague that you have been thinking about buying a new car. Ask for advice on what kind would be good.
9. Tell a friend that you are going to Professor Nakamura's home for dinner. You are wondering what you should give him.
10. Tell a colleague that you plan to study Japanese in Kyoto next year, but you are wondering what school to attend.
11. Tell a colleague that you planned not to sell your car until next year, but you ended up selling it to a friend last week.
12. Express wonder as to what the section chief's intention was in gathering all the **arúbàito** students together.
13. Exclaim on how few foreigners this school has; how many word processors this office has.
14. Comment on the fact that accidents have become rare around here.
15. Exclaim on the frequency of earthquakes in Japan.
16. Someone is looking for Ms. Nakamura. Explain that since it is after 9:00, she should be in the classroom already.
17. Professor Ito is going to address a group of foreign students and would like to speak in Japanese. Assure him that since they have been studying for three years now (already), they should understand.
18. Tell a colleague that the teacher for next year was supposed to be decided by now, but the decision may not be made until next year.
19. A friend is inquiring about Ms. Yamada. Explain that since she left Tokyo on the 4:30 special express, she should have arrived in Nagoya by now.
20. There is concern over Mr. Hayashi's possible opposition to the purchase of a new computer. Assure the group that since it is a useful computer, there is no reason to expect that he will oppose.
21. A friend has asked about crowding on the subway on Sunday. Explain that since it gets crowded every day, there's no reason to expect that it won't get crowded on Sunday, too.
22. You have boarded the wrong car on the train. Explain to the conductor that you assumed *this* was the green car, but you were mistaken.
23. You've been standing in the wrong line. Explain that you assumed that *this* was the ticket window for the bullet train.
24. Tell a colleague that you plan to drive to Osaka and stay for 3–4 days.
25. Commenting on a new dictionary you have recently bought, express discouragement at how useless; difficult to understand; difficult to read it is.

26. Exclaim on a magnificent home; heavy luggage; an interesting trip; a boring town; amazingly proficient English.
27. You've been asked about the availability of tickets for a lecture. Explain to your colleague that, as far as you can remember, they will also be selling tickets on the actual day.
28. Warn your colleague against carrying a box that is that heavy by himself.
29. Your colleague has suggested taking a cab in the interest of speed. Point out that (rather) the subway will be faster.
30. Suggest to a close friend that you go home early; transfer to the JR; take a limited-express; get off at the next station; hurry to that meeting.

Check-up

1. In sequences like **sûsi ḡa sukî da, sonó zassi ḡa omosiròi, tabako o yameta**, how can the nominals be replaced by a sequence denoting an activity, such as **êeḡa o mîru**? (A-SP1)
2. In describing an occurrence that takes place 'in the process of, or in direct connection with, the performance of a particular activity,' what pattern is used? (A-SP1)
3. Compare the Japanese equivalents of: 'Planes are faster than cars' and 'Taking a plane would be faster than going by car.' How do you account for the form of the verbal that occurs before **hôo**? What happens when the form is negative? What form of a verbal regularly occurs before **yôri**? (A-SP2)
4. Under what circumstances is there a requirement that quantity expressions, including numbers, directly follow the nominal they qualify? Give two examples. (A-SP3)
5. Under what circumstances does a number consist of /two consecutive numerals + classifier/? The numerals of which numeral series occur in such patterns? Which classifiers—naming, or counting—occur? Which numeral sequence does not occur? (A-SP5)
6. How is the direct-style consultative of verbals formed? What is the distal-style equivalent? How is the distal form analyzed? In what way is it irregular? Which of the verbal subclasses—consonant, vowel, special polite, and irregular—does not occur in the consultative? Why is this predictable? (A-SP6)
7. What is the difference in meaning between **ikôo** and **ikú daròo**? Compare the occurrence of operational and affective verbals in these two patterns (A-SP5).
8. Compare the difference in meaning of the following:

   (a) **Surú to omoimàsu.**
   (b) **Surú daròo to omoimasu.**
   (c) **Siyôo to omoimasu.**
   (d) **Siyôo to omôtte (i)masu.**   (A-SP5)

9. What is the basic meaning of **tumori**? To what word-class does it belong? Describe what may precede it and what may follow it. Who is the usual referent of **tumori** in statements? In questions? In what negative patterns does it occur? (A-SP4)
10. Compare the use of **tumori** in:

    (a) **Surú tumori dàtta kedo..**
    (b) **Kâre ḡa síte kureru tumori dàtta kedo..**
    (c) **Nihóñḡo no tumori dàtta kedo..**   (A-SP4, B-SP2)

11. When stating that something is done 'with a particular intention,' in what pattern does **tumori** occur? (A-SP4)
12. What is the basic meaning of **hazu**? How does it contrast with **tumori**? To what word-class does it belong? Describe what may precede it and what may follow it. What regularly serves as the negative of a **hazú dèsu** sequence? Who is regularly *not* the referent of a **hazu** pattern? (B-SP1)
13. Compare the following:

(a) **Hâiru hazú dèsu.**
(b) **Haírànai hazú dèsu.**
(c) **Hâiru hazu wa nâi desu.**
(d) **Haírànai hazu wa nâi desu.**
(e) **Hâiru hazú dèsita.**
(f) **Hâitta hazú dèsu.**
(g) **Hâitta hazú dèsita.**   (B-SP1)

Lesson 21

SECTION A

Core Conversations

1(N)a. **Miñsyuku dè mo syokúzi demàsu ka⌒**

　b. **Sâñ-syoku desu ka⌒**

(J)a. **Êe, mâa, bôku no keékeñ dè wa, kimátta monò sika dasânai kedo..**

　b. **Ie, taitee 'ni-syoku-tuki de, âsa sika dasânai tokórò mo âru soo desu.**

2(N) **Miñsyuku no koto, gozôñzi desu ka⌒**

(J) **Ie, bôku wa 'amari.. Dê mo, Oóta-sañ ğa tàbuñ yôku sitté (i)ru hazu dèsu yo⌒ Ryokóo-suru tokì wa, miñsyuku nì sika tomáranai sòo desu kara..**

3(J)a. **Môsimosi, Tokíwa-hòteru de gozaimasu.**

　b. **Kâkari ni mawásimàsu no de, syôosyoo omáti-kudasài.**

(J')a. **Omátase-itasimàsita. Îtu kara otómari ni narimàsu ka⌒**

(N) **A, môsimosi. Yoyáku oneğai-simàsu.**

　b. **Raisyuu no doyôobi kara nî-haku de..**

　b. **Nâñ-mee-sama de gozaimasu ka⌒**

　c. **Goíssyo de gozaimàsu ka⌒**

　c. **Nî-mee desu.**

　d. **Ie, betubetu no sîñguru o oneğai-simasu.**

　d. **Onamae wa?**

　e. **Mîraa to iimasu.**

e. **Mîraa-sama. Dê wa, zyuú-hati-niti no doyôobi kara, nî-haku to iú kotò de, siṅguru-rùumu o hutâ-heya otóri-site okimàsu kara ..**

4(J) **Íp̀-paku ìkura ka ʹkiita?**

f. **Yorósiku oneḡai-simàsu.**
(N) **A, simâtta. Nedañ no koto, wasúretè (i)ta.**

English Equivalents

1(N)a. Are meals served in minshuku, too?

(J)a. Yes, well, in my experience (at least), they serve only certain (*lit.* decided upon) things, but ... (they do serve).

b. Is that three meals?

b. No, usually it's (with) two meals, and there are also places where they serve only breakfast, I hear.

2(N) Do you know anything about minshuku?

(J) No, me, [not] very much ... But Mr/s. Ota should probably know a good deal. Because when s/he travels, s/he stays only in minshuku, I hear.

3(J)a. Hello. (It's) Tokiwa Hotel.

(N) Oh, hello. I'd like (to make) a reservation.

b. I'll transfer you to the person in charge, so just a moment.

(J′)a. I'm sorry to have kept you waiting. (From) when will you be staying [here]?

b. (Being) two nights, starting Saturday of next week.

b. How many people will it be?
c. Will this be one room (*lit.* together)?
d. Your name?

c. It will be two (people).

d. No, I'd like separate singles.
e. (My name is) Miller.

e. Mr/s. Miller. Well then, (being a matter described as) two nights, starting Saturday, the eighteenth; I'll hold two single rooms, so ...

f. Please take care of everything.

4(J) Did you ask how much it is for one night?

(N) Oh, damn! I forgot about the price.

Breakdowns
(and Supplementary Vocabulary)

1. **miñsyuku**   private homes offering bed and board to tourists

syokúzi (g̃a) dèru	meals are served
keekeñ	experience
bôku no keékeñ dè wa	in my experience (at least)
kimátta monò (SP1)	things that have been decided
dâsu	put out; take out; serve (of meals)
kimátta monò sika dasânai (SP2)	not serve except fixed things, serve nothing but fixed things
sâñ-syoku	three meals
ni-syoku-tuki	with two meals; two meals included
âsa sika dasânai	not serve except in the morning, serve only in the morning
âru soo da (SP3)	I hear that there are, it is said that there are
2. kotô (SP4)	fact; act
miñsyuku no kotò	facts concerning minshuku
Oota	(family name)
tâbuñ	probably
ryokóo-suru tokì	time(s) when one travels
miñsyuku ni tomaru	stay in a minshuku
miñsyuku nì sika 'tomaranai	not stay except in minshuku, stay only in minshuku
tomáranai sòo da	I hear that [someone] doesn't stop/stay, they say that [someone] doesn't stop/stay
3. Tokíwa-hòteru	Tokiwa Hotel
yoyaku	reservation
kâkari or	
kâkari no hito/kata	person in charge
mawasu /-u; mawasita/	send around; pass around; transfer
+mawaru /-u; mawatta/	go around; be passed around; be transferred
nî-haku[1]	two nights of a stay
+hitô-bañ[1]	one night
+syuumatu	weekend
goissyo	together /polite/
betubetu	separate
siñguru/siñguru-rùumu	single room
+dâburu/dabúru-rùumu	double room
+tuíñ/tuíñ-rùumu	room with twin beds

1. For a more complete list, see below, "classifiers."

+yooma		Western-style room
+nihoñma *or*		
+wasitu		Japanese-style room
+basu-tuki		with bath
nî-haku to iú kotò de		being a fact described as a stay of two nights
huta-heya¹		two rooms
tôtt(e) oku		put aside, set aside
4. simâtta		damn! oh, dear!²
nedañ		price
nedáñ no kotò		facts concerning the price

-haku: *Classifier for counting nights of a stay*	**-bañ:** *Classifier for counting nights*	**-heya:** *Classifier for counting rooms*
ip-paku	hitô-bañ	hitô-heya
nî-haku	huta-bañ	hutâ-heya
sâñ-paku	mî-bañ	mî-heya
yôñ-paku	yô-bañ	yô-heya
go-haku		itû-heya
nâñ-paku 'how many nights of a stay?'	îku-bañ 'how many nights?'	îku-heya 'how many rooms?'

MISCELLANEOUS NOTES

1. In CC1, Smith asks his acquaintance, Mr. Suzuki, about minshuku, Japan's equivalent of bed-and-board lodgings. Minshuku are organized into a nationwide network, making it possible to make reservations from the large cities where offices are located. Minshuku are significantly less expensive than hotels and inns. The language style, as is usual between these two individuals, is careful, with distal-style final predicates. (Remember that since **kedo** is not a sentence-particle, a predicate preceding **kedo** is not a final predicate.)

    1. (J)a. **Keekeñ**: Note also **keékeñ g̃a àru** 'have experience'; **keekeñ-suru** 'experience,' 'go through.'

    (N)b, (J)b. **Syoku** regularly occurs as a classifier only with one, two, and three, to count meals within a day. **-Tuki**, a nominal suffix derived from the stem of the verbal **tûku**, forms unaccented nominal compounds in combination with other nominals: /nominal X + **-tuki**/ 'with X attached.' Examples: **sañ-syoku-tuki** 'with three meals included'; **deńwa-tuki no kaig̃ìsitu** 'a conference room with a telephone'; **basú-tuki no heyà** 'a room with bath.'

    2. In CC2, Smith and Mr. Suzuki continue their conversation about minshuku in the same basic style. However, in direct questioning about Mr. Suzuki's knowledge, Mr. Smith, a graduate student, uses a polite/honorific ↑ form (**gozôñzi desu ka**), and Mr. Suzuki, a more senior professional, uses a fragment in direct reply.

    2. Substitute your favorite expletive!

(J) Because Mr. Suzuki's utterance begins with **ie** in response to Mr. Smith's question, we can presume that the fragment **amari . .** implies a negative.

Tâbuñ: Probability can be expressed without **tâbuñ**—i.e., with **daròo** and **desyòo**—but a sentence with **tâbuñ** must contain a further indication of lack of certainty. Frequently **tâbuñ** occurs in combination with a **daròo/desyòo** form. Here, **hazú dèsu** reinforces the uncertainty.

3. In CC3, Deborah Miller makes a hotel reservation by telephone. She uses careful-style (with distal-style final predicates), but as the customer, she feels no requirement to use polite-style. In contrast, the switchboard operator and the room clerk use polite careful-style. The fragment **Onamae wa?** is also polite, and the fragment **Mîraa-sama.** is a confirmation of the guest's name, in a very polite form.

(N) **Yoyaku**: Note also **yoyaku-suru** 'make a reservation'; /**X o yoyaku-suru**/ 'reserve X.' **Yoyaku** also covers restaurant and transportation reservations and subscriptions to newspapers and magazines.

(J)b. **Mawasu** is the transitive partner of intransitive **mawaru**. Both are operational consonant verbals. **Mawasu** covers spinning a wheel, sending around a notice, transferring a telephone call to someone else, and so forth.

Mawaru, on the other hand, describes a wheel that goes around, a tape recording that runs, a notice that circulates, and people who tour an area. For this last example, the pattern is /place nominal + **o** + **mawaru**/, with **o** following the nominal indicating the place through which the action occurs: **Yoóròppa o 'mawatte (i)ru** 's/he's going around Europe.'

(J')a. **Omátase-itasimàsita**: Remember to use this polite ritual expression when resuming a telephone conversation after a delay during which the other party has been kept waiting.

(J')b, (N)c. Note the contrast between the very polite **nâñ-mee-sama** and Ms. Miller's plain reply, **nî-mee**. The clerk repeats the very polite suffix with the guest's name: **Mîraa-sama** ([J']e).

(J')e. **Otori-site** is the humble-polite ↓ equivalent of **tôtte**. The combination **tôtte oku** implies taking up and holding temporarily for future use, hence 'put aside,' 'set aside.'

Note the lengthening and stressing of phrase-final mora, typical of a new intonation pattern becoming popular, particularly in the speech of young people. It alternates with the use of **ne!/ne?**

(N)f. **Yorósiku onegai-simàsu** is one of the most commonly used of all Japanese ritual expressions. It expresses a request for favorable, considerate treatment from the person addressed and occurs frequently at the conclusion of a conversation.

4. CC4 is a brief exchange between Deborah Miller and the office consultant, Ms. Tanaka, with whom she has become friendly. The style is casual, with direct-style final predicates.

(N) **Simâtta** is a mild expletive expressing consternation and annoyance.

Numbers: The classifiers introduced in this lesson occur commonly with low numerals; the higher the numeral, the rarer they become. In those uncommon instances when a higher number is called for, a classifier that ordinarily combines with Japanese numerals (**-bañ** 'night,' for example) may occur with the corresponding Chinese series numerals. Note

    ip-paku-suru   'stay one night'
    nî-haku-suru   'stay two nights' (etc.)

Note also **yôñ-paku**, with **h > p**, following the irregular pattern of **yôñ-puñ** 'four minutes.'

Structural Patterns

1. kimátta monò

In Japanese, significantly more frequently than in English, verbals represent the realization of a new state rather than a process: 'become tired,' 'become decided,' 'become comprehensible.' To represent the result of such 'becoming,' we find either a perfective (= 'the becoming happened') or a **-te (i)ru** pattern (= 'continue to be affected by the becoming which already happened'). Compare

'I own ——'	môtte (i)ru
'I know ——'	sitte (i)ru
'I see!'	wakâtta
'I forget!'	wasureta
'Here comes ——!'	kitâ
'There goes ——!'	itta

In each case, the Japanese alternate in **-ta** stresses the occurrence of the change of state, whereas the **-te (i)ru** alternate emphasizes the continuing result of the change.

Many of these 'becoming' verbals occur in the perfective form as the description of a following nominal. As such, they constitute a verbal sentence modifier: just as **takâi zîsyo** 'an it-is-expensive dictionary' is an example of /adjectival sentence modifier + nominal/, **kimátta monò** 'an it-became-decided thing' is a /verbal sentence modifier + nominal/. Examples:

tukâreta hito	'a tired person'
kawâita mono	'dried things'
kôñda deñsya	'a crowded train'
tiḡátta hitò	'a different person'
matíḡàtta ryokañ	'the wrong inn'
karíta kyookàsyo	'a borrowed textbook'

2. PHRASE-PARTICLE sika

/Nominal (particle) + **sika** + negative predicate/ = 'the situation is negative except for the nominal (+ particle),' 'the situation is positive only in the case of the nominal (+ particle).' Preceding **sika**, an unaccented /nominal + particle/ acquires an accent on the particle (**kokó nì sika**). As in the case of **wa** and **mo**, only phrase-particles other than **ḡa** and **o** occur before **sika**. These three particles—**wa**, **mo**, and **sika**—complement each other.

Using circles to represent sets, we can illustrate these three particles as follows:

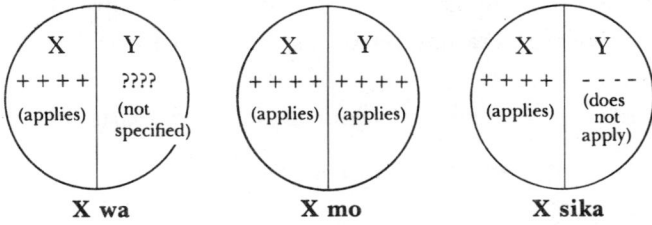

X wa: Of a given set (which is clearly defined or only implied), 'X at least' applies, in

reference to a predicate (stated or implied). The applicability of the remainder (Y) is not explicitly stated.

X mo: In addition to Y (which is clearly defined or only implied), 'X also,' 'even X' applies, forming a set made up of /X + Y/.

X sika: 'Except for X,' the remainder of the set (Y) (clearly defined or only implied) does *not* apply in reference to the predicate.

(The smallest set is a single item; the largest is everything relevant in the given context.)

Note that **wa**, **mo**, and **sika** are all in marked contrast to **ḡa** and **o**, which imply an exhaustive, closely intertwined involvement of the preceding nominal without reference to its membership in any set. Compare

(1) **Gakúsee ḡa tukaimàsita.** **Gakúsee o tukaimàsita.**
   '*Students* used [it].' '[I] used *students* [for a task].'

(2) **Gakúsee wa tukaimàsita.** **Gakúsee wa tukaimàsita.**
   'Students (at least) used [it].' 'Students (at least) [I] used.'

(3) **Gakúsee mo tukaimàsita.** **Gakúsee mo tukaimàsita.**
   '*Students* used [it], *too*.' '[I] used *students*, *too*.'

(4) **Gakúsee sika tukaimaseñ desita.** **Gakúsee sika tukaimaseñ desita.**
   'No one used [it] except students'; '[I] didn't use anyone except students';
   'Only students used [it].' '[I] used only students.'

Examples (2), (3), and (4) are ambiguous out of context. In these, **gakusee** may be the user or the used.

The question that immediately arises relates to the difference between **sika** and **dakê**. **X dakê** means that just X—no more, no less—is relevant. In contrast, **X sika** definitely implies an occurrence less than might be expected: as indicated by the negative that follows, there was no occurrence with the exception of X. Thus, in reply to **Oózee miemàsita ka‿** 'Did many people attend?' if attendance was actually fifty and considered a small number under the circumstances, the reply must be: **Iie, gozyûu-niñ sika miémaseñ desita.** Compare: **Nâñ-niñ miémàsita ka‿** 'How many attended?' **Go-zyûu-niñ dakê desu. Gozyûu-niñ dake miémàsita.** 'Just (= exactly) fifty people. Just fifty people attended.'

Additional examples of **sika**:

   Nihóñziñ sika wakáranai. 'Only Japanese understand.' (*lit.* 'Except for Japanese, understanding doesn't occur.')

   Nihóñḡo sika dekìnai. 'I can handle only Japanese.'

   Zikókuhyoo sika kawanàkatta. 'I didn't buy anything except a timetable.'

   Toókyoo è sika ikánàkatta. 'I didn't go anywhere except to Tokyo.'

   Gôhañ wa hâsi de sika tabênai. 'I eat rice only with chopsticks.'

   Kore, watasi no iś-satù sika nâi zîsyo desu. 'This is my only (*lit.* there's only one) dictionary.'

   Nihôñ ni sika nâi monô desu. 'It's something which exists only in Japan.'

☠ WARNING: **Sika** occurs only with negative predicates!

3. /PREDICATE + **sôo da**/

/Direct-style perfective or imperfective predicate X + **sôo da**/ = 'X is said to be true,' 'I hear that X is true.' The source of the information need not be made clear. **Sôo** is one of the very few nominals preceding which the **da** form of the copula (ending a sentence modifier) occurs in an unchanged form.

The **da** following **sôo** may of course occur in distal-style as well. Following an accented word or phrase, **sôo** regularly loses its accent. Examples:

Modôru			s/he'll return.'
Modôtta			s/he returned.'
Modôtte (i)ru			s/he has returned.'
Modôtte (i)ta			s/he had returned.'
Hurûi			it's old.'
Hûrûkatta	soo desu.	'They say	it was old.'
Modóràhai			s/he won't return.'
Modóràhakatta			s/he didn't return.'
Modôtte (i)nâi			s/he hasn't returned.'
Modôtte (i)nâkatta			s/he hadn't returned.'
Gêñki da			s/he's well.'
Gêñki datta			s/he was well.'

We now have three patterns for reporting information:

(1) **Âsa sika dasânai soo da.**

(2) **Âsa sika dasânai tte ′kiita.**

(3) **Âsa sika dasânai tte.**

Pattern (2) refers specifically to information that was *heard*; (3) states what someone *said*; but (1) is imprecise as to how the information was transferred, indicating only what the general report is.

The Japanese are very specific in differentiating between facts based on direct observation and knowledge and those that reflect secondhand information. Accordingly, the /predicate + **soo da**/ construction is *very* common.

4. kotô

Kotô is a nominal that refers to an intangible thing, act, fact. It is regularly preceded by a modifier—a pre-nominal, /nominal + particle **no**/, or a sentence modifier. Following an accented word or phrase, it regularly loses its accent. Examples:

konó kotò 'this fact'

kêezai no koto 'things about economics'

komâtta koto 'circumstances that have become troublesome'

zeñzeñ wakaràhai koto 'facts I don't understand at all'

In some of its occurrences **kotô** overlaps with **no**:

Sûsi o tabêru koto (*or* **no**) **ğa sukî desu.** 'I like to eat sushi' (i.e., the act of eating *or* the item described as "eat sushi").

/Sentence X + **to** *or* **(t)te iú kotò**/ = 'the fact stated as X.' In this pattern, X may be a major or a minor sentence.

Katyoo ğa Yokóhama kara kayotte (i)rù to iú kotò wa sirímaseñ desita. 'I didn't know (the fact) that the section chief is commuting from Yokohama.'

Hitô-bañ nimâñ goséñ-eñ to iu kotò de, syokúzi wa hàitte (i)nâi. 'It's (a fact stated as) ¥25,000 for one night, and meals are not included.'

Ano syokudoo, seťto-mèñyuu to iú kotò de, kimátta monò sika dasânai soo desu. '(In) that dining room it's (a matter of) a fixed menu, and they serve only certain things, I hear.'

Drills

A 1. **Oóta-sañ nì wa, reñraku-sita neʔ**
'You contacted Mr/s. Ota (at least)—right?'

Êe, zitû wa, Oóta-sañ nì sika reñraku-sinàkatta ñ desu ḡa . .
'Yes, actually I didn't contact anyone but Mr/s. Ota, but . . .' (is that all right?)

2. **Teñki-yòhoo wa, kiita neʔ**
'You listened to the weather forecast (at least)—right?'

Êe, zitû wa, teñki-yòhoo sika kikánàkatta ñ desu ḡa . .
'Yes, actually I didn't listen to anything but the weather forecast, but . . .' (is that all right?)

3. **butyoo/hañtai-sita**; 4. **arúbàito no hito/matíḡàeta**; 5. **gakkai ni/dêta**; 6. **guríìñsya no kippu/âtta**; 7. **miñsyuku/tanôñda**

B 1. **Oóta-sañ karà mo, Tanáka-sañ karà mo, deñwa àtta?**
'Were there telephone calls from both Mr/s. Ota and Mr/s. Tanaka?'

Ie, Tanáka-sañ karà sika arímaseñ desita.
'No, there was [a call] only from Mr/s. Tanaka.'

2. **Asoko no miñsyuku mo, ryokañ mo, takâi?**
'Are both the minshuku and the inns there expensive?'

Ie, ryokáñ sika tàkaku arímaseñ.
'No, only the inns are expensive.'

3. **aságòhañ/bañgòhañ/dâsita**; 4. **nisiḡuti de/hiḡasiḡuti de/siñkañseñ no kippu 'utte (i)ru**; 5. **teeburu/isu/hakoñde kureta**; 6. **kêezai no zyûḡyoo/seézi no zyûḡyoo/tôtta**; 7. **Nârita e/Haneda e/mukae ni iku**; 8. **dañsee/zyosee/arúbàito (da)**; 9. **otona/kodomo/yakû ni tâtta**

C 1. **Konó osara sika tukawanài ñ desu ka**↗
'(Is it that) you'll use only these dishes?'

Iêie, hoká no osara mo tukaimàsu yo↗
'No, no, we'll use other dishes, too.'

2. **Nyuúsu-bàñgumi sika mînai ñ desu ka**↗
'(Is it that) you watch only news programs?'

Iêie, hoká no bañgumi mo mimàsu yo↗
'No, no, I watch other programs, too.'

3. **kono miñsyuku ni/tomáranài**; 4. **yuúmee na hitò/kônai**; 5. **nî-bañ no madôḡuti de/uranai**; 6. **isôḡu tokî/iranai**; 7. **Oóta-sañ kara/karínài**

D 1. **Kimura-sañ, yamémàsita ka**↗   **Êe. Yaméta sòo desu kedo . .**
    'Did Mr/s. Kimura quit?'   'Yes. I hear s/he quit, but . . .' (I'm not sure).

2. **Watanabe-sañ, ryokóo-simàsu ka**↗   **Êe. Ryokóo-suru sòo desu kedo . .**
    'Does Mr/s. Watanabe travel?'   'Yes. I hear s/he travels, but . . .' (I'm not sure).

3. syatyoo-sañ/miémàsita; 4. miñna/gaḱkàri-site (i)masita; 5. oyaḡosañ/siṅpai-site (i)màsita; 6. anó èeḡa/omósiròi desu; 7. asoko/hûbeñ desu; 8. kono kippu/guríiñ-sya no desu; 9. zyûu-zi-hatu/toḱkyuu dèsita; 10. ano ryokañ/tâkâkatta desu

E 1. **Ryokóo no hì wa, kâre ḡa kimérù ñ desu ne**↗   **Êe, kâre ḡa kiméru sòo desu kedo, îtu kiméte kurerù ka wakárimaseñ nêe.**
    'About the date of the trip—(it's that) *he's* going to decide—right?'   'Yes, I hear that *he* will decide, but when he will (decide for us), I don't know.'

2. **Tomaru miñsyuku wa, Yamâḡuti-sañ ḡa yoyáku-surù ñ desu ne**↗   **Êe, Yamâḡuti-sañ ḡa yoyáku-suru sòo desu kedo, îtu yoyáku-site kurerù ka wakárimaseñ nêe.**
    'About the minshuku we're going to stay in, (it's that) *Mr/s. Yamaguchi* is going to make the reservation—right?'   'Yes, I hear that *Mr/s. Yamaguchi* will make the reservation, but when s/he will (make the reservation for us), I don't know.'

3. gaḱkai ni kùru hito ni/Tâkano-sañ ḡa reñraku-suru; 4. koko no ueki/otókò no ko ḡa hakobu; 5. taná no ue no nìmotu/kânozyo ḡa orósu; 6. tûaa no kippu/hisyô ḡa kátte kùru

F 1. **Ano ryokañ wa, aságòhañ mo dâsu soo desu nêe.**   **Êe, watasi mo, dâsu tte kiítà kedo, hoṅtoo desyòo ka nêe.**
    'They say that inn serves breakfast too, don't they.'   'Yes, I too heard that they serve it, but I wonder if that's true.'

2. **Konó kikài wa, yakû ni tâtu soo desu nêe.**   **Êe, watasi mo, yakû ni tâtu tte kiítà kedo, hoṅtoo desyòo ka nêe.**
    'They say this machine is useful, don't they.'   'Yes, I too heard that it is useful, but I wonder if that's true.'

3. oyâ wa, kekkoñ ni 'hañtai-site (i)ru; 4. atárasìi zimûsyo o tatêru tumori da; 5. anó señsèe no zêmi wa, monósùḡòku omósiròi; 6. hikôoki ni ma ní awànakatta

G 1. **Miñsyuku dè wa, syokúzi dasimàsu ka**↗   **Êe, taítee dasimàsu kedo ne! Dasânai miñsyuku mo âru soo desu yo**↗
    'At minshuku, do they serve meals?'   'Yes, they usually do (serve), but I hear there are also minshuku where they don't (serve).'

2. **Êki de wa, ryoóḡae-dekimàsu ka**↗   **Êe, taítee ryooḡae-dekimàsu kedo ne! Ryoóḡae-dekìnai êki mo âru soo desu yo**↗
    'At stations, can one make change?'

'Yes, one usually can (make change), but I hear there are also stations where one cannot (make change).'

3. depâato/kâĝu ut́te (i)màsu; 4. daiĝaku/gaíkokuĝo osiemàsu; 5. susîya ya sobâya/demáe todòkete kuremasu; 6. Nihoñ no kaisya/okyakusañ ni koóhìi ya otyá dasimàsu

H 1. **Rosiaĝo wa, kânari omósiròi soo desu ne!**
'They say the Russian language is quite interesting.'

A, watasi, rosíaĝo no kotò wa, zeńzeñ wakarànai ñ desu.
'Oh, (it's the case that) me, I don't know anything about Russian.'

2. **Sî-ĝatu no 'gakkai wa, oózee atumàru soo desu ne!**
'They say that a lot of people will gather for the April academic conference.'

A, watasi, sî-ĝatu no gaḱkai no kotò wa, zeńzeñ wakarànai ñ desu.
'Oh, (it's the case that) me, I don't know anything about the April academic conference.'

3. mońbùsyoo/konó àidea ni 'hañtai da; 4. miñsyuku/iróiro bèñri da; 5. toozitu/syatyóo-sañ ĝa okaeri ni nàru; 6. kono kuruma/totémo mezurasìi tâipu da; 7. Mîyazi-sañ/atíra no daiĝaku o ode ni nàtta

I 1. **Kêezai no koto, gozôñzi desu ka**
'Do you know anything about economics?'

Kêezai no koto? Watasi ni wakâru ka dôo ka sińpai dèsu kedo . .
'About economics? I'm concerned about whether or not it's clear to me, but . . .' (what can I do?)

2. **Booeki no koto, gozôñzi desu ka**
'Do you know anything about foreign trade?'

Booeki no koto? Watasi ni wakâru ka dôo ka sińpai dèsu kedo . .
'About foreign trade? I'm concerned about whether or not it's clear to me, but . . .' (what can I do?)

3. Yoóròppa; 4. sibai; 5. Iĝirisu no seezi; 6. Nihóñ no supòotu

J 1. **Arúbàito no kotô da kedo, ití-zìkañ îkura?**
'About part-time work, how much is it for one hour?'

A, simâtta. Ití-zìkañ îkura ka kikánàkatta.
'Oh, damn! I didn't ask how much it is for one hour.'

2. **Kôoĝi no kotô da kedo, iḱ-kai nàñ-puñ?**
'About lectures, how many minutes is it for one time?'

A, simâtta. Iḱ-kai nàñ-puñ ka kikánàkatta.
'Oh, damn! I didn't ask how many minutes it is for one time!'

3. oree/ití-niti ìkura; 4. miñsyuku/iṕ-paku ìkura; 5. tûaa/hitô-ri îkura; 6. heyâ/hitô-heya nâñ-niñ

K 1. **Doyôobi kara nî-haku de, sîñguru o hitô-heya onéḡai-simàsu.**
'I'd like one single room for (*lit.* being) two nights, starting Saturday.'

Dê wa, doyôobi kara nî-haku to iú kotò de, sîñguru o hitô-heya otóri-site okimàsu kara . .
'Then that's (*lit.* being a matter described as) two nights starting Saturday; we'll reserve one single room (for you), so . . .' (everything is taken care of).

2. **Doyôobi kara sâñ-paku de, sîñguru o hitô-heyà oneḡai-simàsu.**
'I'd like one single room for (*lit.* being) three nights, starting Saturday.'

Dê wa, doyôobi kara sâñ-paku to iú kotò de, sîñguru o hitô-heya otóri-site okimàsu kara . .
'Then that's (*lit.* being a matter described as) three nights starting Saturday; we'll reserve one single room (for you), so . . .' (everything is taken care of).

3. doyôobi/sâñ-paku/tuîñ; 4. kińyòobi/sâñ-paku/tuîñ; 5. kińyòobi/ip-paku/tuîñ;
6. kińyòobi/ip-paku/dâburu; 7. getúyòobi/yôñ-paku/sîñguru

L 1. **Asoko no kaisya ḡa abúnài tte iú kotò o, utí no beñḡòsi kara kiítà ñ desu ḡa . .**
'(It's that) I heard from our lawyer this thing about that company (over there) being in danger (e.g., of bankruptcy), but . . .' (did you know that?)

Hee⤴ Asóko no kaisya ḡa abunài ñ desu ka. Soñna koto, zeńzeñ sirimasèñ desita.
'Really? You mean that company (over there) is in danger? I didn't know anything about that at all.'

2. **Anó misè wa nedáñ ḡa takài tte iú kotò o, gakúsee kara kiità ñ desu ḡa . .**
'(It's that) I heard from the students this thing about prices being high at that shop, but . . .' (did you know that?)

Hee⤴ Anó misè wa nedáñ ḡa takài ñ desu ka. Soñna koto, zeńzeñ sirimasèñ desita.
'Really? You mean the prices are high at that shop? I didn't know anything about that at all.'

3. uńtèñsyu ḡa mití o matiḡàeta/hisyô; 4. kokó no kaḡì wa Nakáda-kuñ sika mòtte (i)nai/kâre no ôkusañ; 5. hotôñdo no gakusee wa zibúñ no kuruma o mòtte (i)ru/daíḡaku no señsèe; 6. oókìi nîmotu wa iê made todôkete kureru/tomodati; 7. asóko kara kaisya màde zyuúḡò-huñ sika kakáràinai/Kûbota-katyoo

Application Exercises

A1. Once again, set up the model town, and ask questions that either contain **sika** or require **sika** in the reply. Examples:

Konó matì ni hôteru mo 'ryokañ mo arímàsu ka/ 'Are there hotels *and* inns in this town?'

   Iie, hôteru sika arímaseñ nêe. 'No, there are only hotels.'

Eéḡo no hòñ ḡa kaítài kedo, konó heñ nì wa 'kono tiísài hôñya sika nâi ñ desu ka/ 'I want to buy some English books; in this area is there only this small bookstore?'

   Iie, oókìi no mo arímàsu yo/ 'No, there's a big one, too.'

Tâkusii wa êki no mâe ni sika naráñde (i)nâi ñ desu ka/ 'Are the taxis lined up only in front of the station?'

   Iie, hôteru no mâe ni mo naráñde (i)rù desyoo? 'No, they are lined up in front of the hotel, too—aren't they?'

   2. Practice relaying information. After having student A inform student B of a piece of new information:

   a. Have student B relay the information using the new **sôo desu** pattern. Example:

   A to B: **Anó buñbooḡuya de utte (i)ru koñpyùutaa, damê desu yo.** 'The computers they're selling in that stationery store are no good!'

   B to C: **Anó buñbooḡuya de utte (i)ru koñpyùutaa, damê da soo desu yo/** 'I hear the computers they're selling in that stationery store are no good.'

   b. Have student B relay the information as a fact he didn't know. Example:

   B to C: **Anó buñbooḡuya de utte (i)ru koñpyùutaa ḡa damê da tte iú kotò wa, sirímaseñ desita.** 'I didn't know (the fact) that the computers they're selling in that stationery store are no good.'

3. Practice making hotel and restaurant reservations by telephone. Distribute cards to each member of the class outlining the kind of reservation to be made, with date and number of people: for a hotel, add the kind of accommodations, length of stay, questions regarding meals and price; for restaurants, decisions regarding food and drink to be served, time, price per person. Remember to use ritual expressions!

B. Core Conversations: Substitution

Practice the Core Conversations with substitutions in details and in types of participants as appropriate. Following this practice, ask and answer questions on the content of each conversation.

SECTION B

Core Conversations

1(J)a. **Ohûro ni ohâiri ni narimàsu ka/**

(N)a. **Saki ni syokúzi ni sitè mo îi desu ka/**

b. **Hâa. Dotíra de mo kèkkoo de gozaimasu yo/ Îma sûḡu odásisitè mo yorósìi desu ka/**

b. **Êe, oneḡai-simàsu.**

2(J)a. **Ôókìkute, kîree de, kimóti no ìi ohûro datta wa nêe.**

b. **Zyâa, haíránakatta no?**

3(J)a. **Sôrosoro ohútòñ osíki-itasimasyòo ka**

b. **Asú no àsa wa, ikâḡa itásimasyòo ka.**

c. **Iya, osôkute mo, zyûu-zi ni wa odé ni nàtta hoo ḡa ..**

d. **Kasíkomarimàsita.**

e. **Hâi, syoóti-itasimàsita.**

4(N)a. **Tonari, nâni sitê ñ daroo.**

b. **Kinóo no ryokañ mo yattè (i)ta nêe.**

(N)a. **Mâa, bôku ni wa mizú iretè mo nâni sitê mo âtûkute âtûkute ..**

b. **Ñ. Totémo mùri datta.**

(N)a. **Onéḡai-simàsu.**

b. **Zyuú-zi-hàñ-hatu no siñkàñseñ na ñ da kedo .. Koko zyûu-zi zyûppuñ de, ma ní aimàsu ka**

c. **To iu kotò wa, kû-zi made ni wa syokúzi o sumàset(e) oita hoo ḡa îi desu ne!**

d. **Warûi kedo, sití-zi-hàñ ni okôsite kuremaseñ ka.**

(J)a. **Eñkai da sòo yo**

b. **Îma sîizuñ da kara, dokó e ittè mo niḡîyaka nêe.**

English Equivalents

1(J)a. Are you going to take baths?

b. Yes. Either (way) will be fine. May I serve you right away now?

2(J)a. Wasn't it a big and beautiful and pleasant bath!

b. Then does that mean you didn't get in?

3(J)a. Shall I begin to (*lit.* slowly) spread the futon?

b. How shall we handle tomorrow morning?

c. No, at the latest (*lit.* even if it's late), (you'd better) leave at 10 ...

(N)a. May we have dinner first?

b. Yes, would you please?

(N)a. Well, for me, even if I added cold water, or no matter what I did, it was HOT and ... (therefore I didn't enjoy it).

b. That's right. It was too much.

(N)a. Please.

b. It's (connected with) the bullet train leaving at 10:30 ... Will we be on time leaving (*lit.* being) here at 10:10?

c. That means we'd better finish eating by 9:00, at least, hadn't we.

     d. I understand.
     e. Yes, certainly.
4(N)a. What do you suppose they're doing next door?
   b. They were doing [the same kind of thing] at the inn (where we were) yesterday, too, weren't they!

   d. I'm sorry to bother you, but would you wake us at 7:30?

(J)a. They say it's a dinner party.

   b. It's the season now, so wherever you go, it's lively and noisy.

BREAKDOWNS
(AND SUPPLEMENTARY VOCABULARY)

1. **hurô/ohûro**   bath
   hurô/ohûro ni hâiru   take a bath
   saki ni   ahead (of time or place)
   syokuzi ni suru   make it dinner; have dinner
   sitê mo (SP1)   also (or even) having done
   sitê mo îi? (SP2)   will also (or even) having done [it] be all right? may [I] do [it]?

   hâa   /polite equivalent of **hâi**/
   dotíra dè mo (SP3)   whichever (of two) it is; wherever it is
   dotíra de mo kèkkoo da   either one is fine; anywhere is fine
   odási-sitè↓ mo   also (or even) having put [it] out /humble-polite/

   odási-sitè↓ mo yorósìi?   will also (or even) having put [it] out be all right? may I put [it] out? may I serve [it]? /humble-polite/

2. **kimóti ḡa ìi**   is pleasant
   ôókìkute, kîree de, kimóti no (or **ḡa**) **ìi ohûro**   a bath which is big and beautiful and pleasant
   +**tokonoma**   alcove
   mizú (o) iretè mo   also (or even) having put in cold water
   nâni (o) sitê mo   whatever (someone) has done
   mûri /na/   unreasonable, excessive, forced, impossible
3. **hutoñ/ohútòñ**   Japanese-style quilt for sleeping; futon
   siku /-u/; siita/   spread out
   osôkute mo   also (or even) being late; at the latest
   to iu kotò wa   the fact expressed thus (i.e., as what you just said); that is to say

   sumásèru /-ru; sumâseta/   bring to an end, finish

+sûmu /-u; sûnda/	come to an end
okôsu /-u; okôsita/	wake [someone] up
+okîru /-ru; ôkita/	wake up; get up
syooti-suru	agree to; consent to
4. sitê ñ daroo	/contraction of sité (i)rù ñ daroo/
eñkai	dinner party (Japanese-style)
+hirôoeñ	(wedding) reception (Japanese-style)
+kôñpa	(student) party (Japanese-style)
+pâat(e)ii	party
sîizuñ	the season
iťtè mo	also (or even) having gone
dokó e ittè mo	wherever [someone] has gone
niḡîyaka /na/	lively; bustling; prosperous

MISCELLANEOUS NOTES

1. CC1 is a conversation between a maid at a Japanese inn (J) and a foreign guest, Mr. Carter (N).

It is not unusual for Japanese stopping at inns to take baths before having dinner. If the inn is located in a hot spring area, the bath may be the main purpose of the stay, and a guest may take several baths in a day. In traditional Japanese inns, meals are served in the guests' rooms rather than in a communal dining room. Predictably, the maid uses polite careful-style, with distal-style predicates. Mr. Carter's speech is careful-style, with distal-style final predicates, but is plain rather than polite.[3]

(J)b, (N)b. Note that the maid asks about serving dinner with a polite permission pattern. Mr. Carter's reply is in the form of a request.

2. In CC2, Mr. Carter and his Japanese wife have just returned to their room at the inn after having been to the inn baths. Mrs. Carter has enjoyed her bath tremendously, but Mr. Carter found it so hot—a common reaction of foreigners—that he did not go into it at all.

In the traditional Japanese bathing ritual, one washes before entering the tub, using a small bucket for splashing water over the body. The tub, filled with very hot water, is for soaking and relaxing. Baths at inns range from small individual units, which may or may not adjoin an individual guest room, to large units, the size of small pools, which several guests may enter at the same time. But even the smallest bath is deep compared to American bathtubs. The speech style of both Mr. and Mrs. Carter is casual, with direct-style predicates. Mrs. Carter's language is gentle, with feminine **wa nee** ending one utterance, while Mr. Carter's **ñ** and **muri datta** are blunt.

(J)a. **Ohûro** is preceded by one complex sentence modifier: **ôókìkute** hooks up with **kîree de**, which in turn hooks up with **kimóti no** (or **ḡa**) **ìi**. Compare **oókiì, kîree na, kimóti no** (or **ḡa**) **ìi ohûro** 'a large, beautiful, pleasant bath' in which **ohûro** is modified by three independent modifiers. **Kimóti ḡa ìi** refers to good feelings. It can be used in reference to oneself ('I feel good') or, as here, in reference to one's reactions to something:

---

3. While **onéḡai-simàsu** is, in form, humble-polite, its ritual use has resulted in its no longer being marked as particularly polite. If **-itasimàsu** replaces **-simàsu**, then the form becomes a significant signal of polite speech.

since it makes me feel good, 'it is pleasant.' The opposite is **kimóti ga warùi** 'I don't feel well'; 'it is unpleasant' (because of the way it makes me feel).

The **tokonoma** is the special alcove in a Japanese-style room where an ornamental object or flower arrangement is displayed, along with a hanging scroll. The seat in front of the **tokonoma** at a Japanese-style dinner party is the place of honor.

(N)a. **Bôku ni wa** 'for me (at least)—in comparison with you.' The particle **ni** connects **bôku** with **âtûkute** 'being hot for me.' **Âtûkute** is repeated for emphasis.

(N)b. **Mûri**: note /**mûri na X**/ 'an unreasonable X'; /**mûri ni** + predicate X/ 'do X unreasonably, with unreasonable effort'; **mûri (o) suru** 'strain,' 'lean over backwards.'

3. In CC3, Mr. Carter and the maid at the inn discuss plans for the next morning. The speech style of the two participants is the same as that of CC1.

(J)a. **Sôrosoro**, referring to gradual, nonprecipitate activity, is meant to suggest its meaning by the form of the word—an example of **gitaigo**.
Siku is a transitive operational consonant-verbal: **X o siku** 'spread X.' This verbal includes spreading bedding or carpeting or newspapers on the floor, as well as such activities as laying bricks for a road. **Sikimono** refers to carpets, rugs, mats, etc. The traditional Japanese style of sleeping uses quilts (futon) laid on the tatami. Futon are brought out each night and put into a closet each morning. One sleeps on top of the **sikíbùtoñ** (< **siki** [stem of **siku**] + **hutoñ** [**h** > **b** within a compound]) and under a **kakébùtoñ** (< **kake** [stem of **kakêru** 'hang,' 'suspend,' 'apply'] + **hutoñ**).

(N)b. **Koko zyûu-zi zyûp-puñ de**: Mr. Carter is checking on whether they will be on time for their train if 10:10 is the time for leaving there (= the inn). The notion of leaving is understood from the context. This use of **de** was first introduced in the sequence **rakû de îi desu nêe** (8A-SP5).

(J)c. The maid's advice to a guest as to what he should do is softened by her trailing off without actually finishing her sentence.

(N)c. **To iu kotò wa**: The quotative **to** applies to what was just said by the maid: 'in reference to the fact expressed in terms of what you just said,' 'that is to say,' 'in other words.' The close connection with the preceding is reflected in the accentuation: **to iu koto** is pronounced on level high pitch before the drop to **wa**. Ordinarily we would expect the initial mora of the phrase (**to**) to have low pitch.
Sumáseru, an operational vowel-verbal, is the transitive partner of intransitive **sûmu**, an affective consonant-verbal; thus **X o sumáseru** 'end X,' but **X ga sûmu** 'X ends.' Note also: **sûñda koto** 'finished things.' The root **sum** relates to closure, suggesting the underlying meaning of the ritual apology and thank-you **sumímaseñ**, *lit.* 'this [regret and/or obligation] doesn't end.' The combination **sumáset(e) oku** implies finishing in advance of the scheduled departure time.

(N)d. **Okôsu**, a consonant-verbal, is the transitive partner of the intransitive vowel-verbal **okîru**. Both are operational.

(J)e. **Syooti-suru** frequently occurs in combination with verbals of giving and receiving: **syoóti-site kurenàkatta** 's/he didn't give me his/her consent.'
Syoóti-(ita)simàsita is a ritual expression occurring in many of the same situations as **Kasíkomarimàsita**.

4. In CC4, Mr. and Mrs. Carter are getting ready for bed at the inn, but a noisy party is in progress in the next room. Mr. Carter seems a bit annoyed, but Mrs. Carter is resigned. Again, the speech of both is casual-style with direct-style predicates, but Mr. Carter uses blunt-style, while his wife's language is more gentle.

(N)a. **Sitê ñ daroo** is contracted by dropping **iru** before **ñ**: **sité irù ñ daroo** > **sité rù ñ daroo** > **sitê ñ daroo**. Note also **sité àru ñ daroo** > **sité à ñ daroo**. This type of contraction is common in rapid, blunt-style speech.

(J)a, b. Mrs. Carter's dropping of **dà** in final predicates is typical of gentle-style.

(J)b. **Sîizuñ** refers to season as 'the season for something.' Note also **siizuñ-tyuu**.

Structural Patterns

1. /GERUND⁴ + mo/

Particle **mo** signals "additionalness," either neutral or out of the ordinary, thus 'also' or 'even,' depending on context. /Gerund X + **mo**/ = also (*or* even) if x has been actualized prior to the actualization of the predicate with which it hooks up. Before **mo**, an unaccented gerund acquires a final-mora accent. Examples:

tukáttè mo   'also/even having used'

yâsûkute mo   'also/even being cheap'

seńsèe de mo   'also/even being a teacher'

Thus: **Zîsyo o tukáttè mo wakáràna i.** 'Also/even if I use a dictionary, I don't/won't understand.' (The usage of the dictionary begins *before* understanding is expected to occur; thus, the literal meaning is 'having used.')

Sore wa yâsûkute mo 'kawanai. 'Also/even if that's cheap, I won't buy it.'

Seńsèe de mo dekînai. 'Also/even if it's a teacher, s/he can't/won't be able to do it.'

Compare:

sitê mo *and*

sitâ kedo

The first reflects a proposition—an occurrence or condition that is introduced *as if* realized—whereas the second describes an actual occurrence.

The pattern /gerund X + **mo** + gerund Y + **mo**/ = 'whether X or Y' (*lit.* 'also/even X, also/even Y'). Examples:

Tomódati ḡa zèmi ni dête mo yasûñde mo, watási wa demàsu. 'Whether my friend attends the seminar or takes the day off, I'm going to attend.'

Soré wa tàkàkute mo yâsûkute mo, kaú tumori dèsu. 'Whether that is expensive or cheap, I plan to buy it.'

Wasítu dè mo yoóma dè mo, kamáimasèñ. 'Whether it's a Japanese-style room or a Western-style room, it doesn't matter.'

Contrast:

Wasitu ka yooma ka wasúremàsita. 'I forgot whether it's a Japanese-style room or a Western-style room.'

Unlike the /—— **mo** —— **mo**/ pattern, the /—— **ka** —— **ka**/ pattern contains underlying alternate questions, the answers to which are under consideration.

---

4. In this lesson, only affirmative gerunds are taken up. Negative gerunds will be handled in Lesson 22, Section A.

2. PERMISSION

We have already encountered the pattern /gerund X + îi/, meaning 'it will be all right for X to have been actualized.' Examples:

    Koré o sutete ìi desu ka 'Is it all right to throw this away?'

    Kôkute îi desu yo 'It's all right for it (coffee, for example) to be strong.'

    Hâsi de îi desu ka 'Will chopsticks do?' (I.e., 'Will it be all right for it to be chopsticks, given the present situation?')

However, in circumstances in which other alternatives are clearly acceptable, the gerund is followed by **mo** 'also,' 'even.' Examples:

    Situation: I know that that sweater can be washed in cold water.

    Question: **Oyú de arattè mo îi desu ka** 'May I wash it in hot water, too?' 'Even if I wash it in hot water, will it be all right?'

    Situation: I prefer weak coffee.

    Statement: **Kôkute mo îi desu yo** 'Also/even if it's strong, it will be all right.'

    Situation: I know you would prefer a knife and fork.

    Question: **Hâsi de mo îi desu ka** 'Also/even if it's chopsticks, will it be all right?'

In many situations, even though other specific alternatives are not obvious from the context, it becomes polite to imply their existence by using the pattern that includes **mo**. In other words, the speaker indicates that in addition to other possibilities (which may be no more than the non-occurrence of the action or state mentioned), also/even this particular course of action or condition is all right. Thus:

    Hâitte mo îi desu ka 'May I come in?' (I assume not coming in is fine.)

    Muzúkasìkute mo îi desu yo 'It's all right even if it's difficult.' (I assume no one raises any objections to easiness.)

    Yoósyoku dè mo îi desu ka 'Will Western-style food be all right?' (I assume there are other types of food that will also be all right.)

The use of **mo** emphasizes the fact that the option mentioned is not the only possibility. It is therefore softer and more polite.

In place of **îi** in this pattern, it is also possible to use **yorosii** and **kamáimasèñ**. **Kêkkoo da** is another alternative for statements.

3. INTERROGATIVES WITH /GERUND + **mo**/ SEQUENCES

When an interrogative (**nâni, dâre, dôko, îtu**), with or without a following phrase-particle, hooks up with a /gerund + **mo**/ sequence, the question meaning is lost and the sequence takes on a generalized, indefinite meaning. Again, the gerund refers to an occurrence or state actualized prior to that of the predicate with which the sequence hooks up. Some combinations, particularly /—— de mo/ sequences, occur with alternate accent patterns (i.e., an accent on the interrogative or on the gerund, or no accent).

Compare the members of the following pairs:

    Dâre ḡa 'yaru? 'Who will do it?'   **dâre ḡa yaítè mo** 'whoever does it,' 'no matter who does it'

Nâni o mawasu? 'What will you send around?'	**nâni o mawásitè mo** 'whatever [you] send around,' 'no matter what [you] send around'
Dôko kara kayou? 'Where do you commute from?'	**dôko kara kayóttè mo** 'wherever [you] commute from'
Îkura haráu? 'How much will you pay?'	**îkura harâtte mo** 'however much [you] pay'
Dôo suru? 'What will you do?' 'How will you proceed?'	**doó sitè mo** 'whatever [you] do'
Dôñna ni muzúkasìi? 'To what extent is it difficult?'	**dôñna ni muzúkasìkute mo** 'however difficult it is'
Nâñ desu ka⌇ 'What is it?'	**nâñ de mo** 'whatever it is'
Îtu desu ka⌇ 'When is it?'	**îtu de mo** 'whenever it is'
Nâñ-zi kara desu ka⌇ 'What time does it start?'	**nâñ-zi kara de mo** 'whatever time it starts'

Be careful to distinguish between /interrogative + **mo**/ and /interrogative (particle) + **dè mo**/. Compare:

    Dôtira mo îi desu yo⌇ 'Both are fine.' *and*

    Dôtira de mo îi desu yo⌇ 'Whichever one (of the two) it is will be fine.' 'Either one will be fine.'

Examples:

    Kono-ḡoro, dôñna ni beñkyoo-sitè mo wakáranàkute, komâtte (i)masu. 'I'm upset because no matter how much I study these days, I don't understand.'

    Nañyoobi de mo yorosìi desu kara, dôozo irâsite kudasai. 'Any day will be fine; (so) please come [anytime].'

    Doó sitè mo ʼkono siḡoto o hâyaku sumásetài to omôtte (i)ru ñ desu. 'I've been thinking that I want to finish this work quickly, no matter what.'

    Îkura[5] **yamétàkute mo, yaménai hòo ḡa îi desyoo nêe.** 'No matter how much I want to quit, it will probably be better not to (quit), won't it.'

Drills

A 1. **Ohûro ni hâitte mo îi desu ka⌇**   **Dôozo, oháiri-kudasài.**
    'May I take (*lit.* go into) a bath?'   'Please (go in).'

2. **Kono teḡami dâsite mo îi desu ka⌇**   **Dôozo, odàsi-kudasài.**
    'May I mail this letter?'   'Please (mail).'

3. **tyôtto ôrite;** 4. **tomodati ni kasite;** 5. **mukoo e itte;** 6. **koré yòñde**

B 1. **Narubeku hâyaku syokúzi ni sitài ñ da kedo ..**   **A, îma syokúzi ni sitè mo îi desu yo⌇**
                                                     'Oh, it will be all right even if you have

---

5. Note that **îkura** 'how much?' does not necessarily refer to price in these sequences.

'We'd like to have dinner as early as possible, but . . .' (can we?)

2. **Narubeku hâyâku katázuketài ñ da kedo . .**
'We'd like to put things in order as early as possible, but . . .' (can we?)

dinner now.'

A, îma katázùkete mo îi desu yo⤴
'Oh, it will be all right even if you put things in order now.'

3. **todóketài**; 4. **watasitai**; 5. **tutaetai**; 6. **nekasitai**; 7. **mukae ni ikitai**; 8. **motte (i)tte ağetai**

C 1. **Ohútòñ sikímasyòo ka⤴—gozíbuñ de sikimàsu ka⤴**
'Shall I spread the bedding, or will you spread [it] yourself?'

2. **Teğami dasímasyòo ka⤴—gozíbuñ de dasimàsu ka⤴**
'Shall I mail the letter, or will you mail [it] yourself?'

Síite moratte mo îi kedo, zibúñ de siìte mo îi desu yo.
'I could also have you spread [it], but it will be all right if I spread [it] myself, too.'

Dâsite moráttè mo îi kedo, zibúñ de dàsite mo îi desu yo.
'I could also have you mail [it], but it will be all right if I mail [it] myself, too.'

3. **señsèe ni reñraku-simasyòo**; 4. **osatu watásimasyòo**; 5. **suútukèesu hakóbimasyòo**; 6. **obeñtoo tukúrimasyòo**; 7. **syasiñ torímasyòo**

D 1. **Sûgu nemâsu ka⤴—moó sukòsi ôkite (i)masu ka⤴**
'Are you going to go to bed right away, or are you going to stay up a little longer?'

2. **Motte ikimàsu ka⤴—azúkemàsu ka⤴**
'Are you going to take [it], or are you going to check [it]?'

Sûğu netê mo, moó sukòsi ôkite (i)te mo, îi desu yo⤴
'It's O.K. whether I go to bed right away or stay up a little longer.'

Motte ittè mo, azûkete mo, îi desu yo⤴
'It's O.K. whether I take [it] or check [it].'

3. **kyôo atúmemàsu/asítà made matímàsu**; 4. **ziyûuseki de ikímàsu/sitêeseki ni simâsu**; 5. **îma tutáemàsu/toózitu iimàsu**; 6. **zibúñ de hakobimàsu/takkyuubiñ tanomimàsu**

E 1. **Issyo dè mo kamáimasèñ ka⤴**
'Will it be all right also/even if they're together?'

2. **Ué dè mo kamáimasèñ ka⤴**
'Will it be all right also/even if it's upstairs?'

Iya, betúbetu no hòo ğa îi desu yo.
'No, [being] separate will be better.'

Iya, sitá no hòo ğa îi desu yo.
'No, downstairs will be better.'

3. **usiro**; 4. **kodomo**; 5. **omótè**

F 1. **Kôñbañ osóku nàru ka mo siremaseñ.**

Osôkute mo kamáimasèñ yo⤴
'It won't matter even if it's late.'

'I may be(come) late tonight.'
2. **Nedañ tâkâku nâru ka mo siremaseñ.**
'The price may be(come) high.'

Tâkâkute mo kamáimaseñ yo↗
'It won't matter even if it's expensive.'

3. nîmotu omóku nàru; 4. okyakusañ ôôku nâru; 5. señsèe no 'kooeñ wakárinìkùku nâru

G 1. **Dôre ni simásyòo ka.**
'Which shall we decide on?'

Doré de mo ìi to omóimàsu ğa nêe.
'I think any one of them will be fine, but . . .' (don't you agree?)

2. **Dâre ni tanómimasyòo ka.**
'Whom shall we ask?'

Daré de mo ìi to omóimàsu ğa nêe.
'I think anybody will be fine, but . . .' (don't you agree?)

3. îtu deńwa iremasyòo; 4. nâñ-niñ ni dête moraimasyoo; 5. dôno madôğuti de kikímasyòo; 6. dôñna heyâ o yoyáku-simasyòo; 7. dôko ni tomárimasyòo; 8. nâñ-niti made ni sumásemasyòo

H 1. **Nâni o tukúrimasyòo ka.**
'What shall we make?'

Nâni o tukûtte mo, îi ñ zya arímaseñ ka↗
'Isn't it the case that whatever we make will be all right?'

2. **Nâñ-paku-simasyoo ka.**
'How many nights shall we stay?'

Nâñ-paku-site mo, îi ñ zya arímaseñ ka↗
'Isn't it the case that however many nights we stay will be all right?'

3. dâre ni watásimasyòo; 4. dôko de orósimasyòo; 5. nâñ-zi ni okósimasyòo; 6. nâñ-zi ni okímasyòo; 7. nańyòobi ni yorímasyòo

I 1. **Mizú iretà no?**
'(Is it the case that) you put in cold water?'

Ñ. Dê mo, mizú iretè mo nâni sitê mo, yappàri damê de ne!
'Yeah. But whether I put in cold water or no matter what I do, it's no good, and . . . you know!'

2. **Oóta-sañ ni tanòñda no?**
'(Is it the case that) you asked Mr/s. Ota?'

Ñ. Dê mo, Oóta-sañ ni tanòñde mo nâni sitê mo, yappàri damê de ne!
'Yeah. But whether I ask Mr/s. Ota or no matter what I do, it's no good, and . . . you know!'

3. wasítu no hòo 'soozi-sita; 4. yuúmee na señsèe ni kiíte mìta; 5. kâkari no hito yoñde hanâsita; 6. kyoó-zyuu ni sumasèru tte 'itta; 7. mâdo zêñbu sîmeta; 8. kippu katt(e) òita

J 1. **Zyûu-zi zyúp-puñ ni dête, ma ní aimàsu ne?**

Iya, soré yòri ni-sáñzyùp-puñ wa hâyaku odé ni nàtta hoo ğa tâsika desu yo↗

'We'll make it in time, leaving at 10:10, won't we?'	'No, it will be safer to leave at least twenty or thirty minutes earlier than that.'
2. **Hatí-zi-hàñ ni atúmàtte, ma ní aimàsu ne⸮** 'We'll make it in time, getting together at 8:30, won't we?'	**Iya, soré yòri ni-sáñzyùp-puñ wa hâyâku oátumari ni nàtta hoo ga tâsika desu yo**↗ 'No, it will be safer to gather at least twenty or thirty minutes earlier than that.'

3. **kû-zi ni naraǹde**; 4. **syôogo ni tyuumoñ-site**; 5. **gozí-sugì ni deñwa irete**; 6. **rokû-zi ni ôkite**; 7. **sití-zi-g̀oro tâbete**

K 1. **Kippu wa, rokû-mai de itímañ niséñ-eñ dàtta to omoimasu.**
'The tickets were ¥12,000 for six, I think.'

To iu kotò wa, itî-mai niséñ-eñ dèsu ne⸮
'That means they are ¥2,000 for one—right?'

2. **Heyâ wa, dâburu de nimáñ-eñ dàtta to omoimasu.**
'The room was ¥20,000 for a double, I think.'

To iu kotò wa, hitô-ri itímañ-eñ dèsu ne⸮
'That means it's ¥10,000 for one person—right?'

3. **syokuzi/go-nìñ de ′itimañ-eñ**; 4. **isu/yoť-tù de ′yoñmañ-eñ**; 5. **wâiñ/nî-hoñ de ′rokuseñ-eñ**

L 1. **Kyôo wa, atûi (wa)**⁶ **nêe.**
'It's hot today, isn't it!'

Koko wa, îtu de mo atûi ñ zya nai?
'Isn't it the case that it's hot here no matter when it is?'

2. **Kyôo wa, rakû da (wa) nêe.**
'We have it easy today, don't we!'

Koko wa, îtu de mo rakû na ñ zya nai?
'Isn't it the case that we have it easy here no matter when it is?'

3. **oózèe da**; 4. **nig̀îyaka da**; 5. **hitó ga sukunài**; 6. **kimóti ga ìi**

M 1. **Anó señèñ-satu, dôko ni oíte à(ru) ñ daroo.**⁷
'Where do you suppose that thousand yen bill has been put?'

Dokó ni mo oite nài daroo?⁷ **Hêñ da nêe.**⁸
'It hasn't been put anywhere—has it? Isn't it strange!'

2. **Anó nìmotu, dâre ni todôite ([i]ru) ñ daroo.**
'Who do you suppose that baggage has been delivered to?'

Daré ni mo todòite nâi daroo? Hêñ da nêe.
'It hasn't been delivered to anyone—has it? Isn't it strange!'

3. **anó heyà/nâni siíte à(ru)**; 4. **ano sigoto/dâre ga yaťtè ([i]ru)**; 5. **ano okane/îkura ryóogae-site à(ru)**

N 1. **Tonari, nâni sitê ([i]ru) ñ daroo.**⁷ **Kôñpa ka nâa.**

Tonari? Ñ, kôñpa sitê ([i]ru) ñ daroo.⁷
'Next door? Yeah, they're probably

---

6. **Wa** occurs in this drill only in feminine-style.
7. A female speaker is more apt to use **desyoo**.
8. In a more gentle equivalent of this blunt-style utterance, **da** is dropped.

'What do you suppose they're doing next door? I wonder if it's a student party.'

partying.'

2. **Kâre, nâni sińpai-sitè ([i]ru) ń daroo. Pâat(e)ii no kotô ka nâa.**
'What do you suppose he's worrying about? I wonder if it's about the party.'

Kâre? Ń, pâat(e)ii no koto sińpai-sitè ([i]ru) ń daroo.
'Him? Yeah, he's probably worrying about the party.'

3. **ue/nâni yaťtè/eńkai**; 4. **Osamu-kuń/nâni mâtte/reńraku**; 5. **Yamâġuti-kuń/nâni atû-mete/hako**; 6. **îńtyoo/nâni tukûtte/atárasìi puróġùramu**

Application Exercises

A1. Make up a number of permission questions relating to an institution—school or office—with which you are connected. Examples: Is it all right to study two foreign languages at the same time? Is it all right to smoke in the classroom/office? Is it all right for people who don't own their own computers to use the school's/office's? Is it all right to take library books home? Is it all right to use the school's/office's computers and stationery to write letters to friends? Is it all right to take food and drinks into the classroom/office? Is it all right to bring box lunches to the school/office?

In replying, provide more than simple **hâi/iie** answers: where appropriate, give qualified approval, alternate suggestions, advice, or explanations. Direct negative replies, at this point, must be restricted to **damê desu**, or **ikémaseń**, or **tyôtto**.

2. Practice **-masyòo ka** questions that are (a) yes/no questions and (b) information questions containing interrogatives. In reply to the first type, give answers that offer alternatives. Example:

Tyôtto atûi desu nêe. Mâdo o akémasyòo ka.
'It's rather hot, isn't it! Shall I open the window?'
  Mâdo o akétè mo, dôa o akétè mo îi desu yo.
  'It will be fine whether you open the window or the door.'

In reply to the second type, give answers that encompass the entire category of the interrogative. Example:

Kôńbań kôńpa ġa arímàsu nêe. Nâni o mótte ikimasyòo ka.
'There's a party tonight, isn't there! What shall I take?'
  Nâni o mótte ittè mo îi desu yo.
  'Whatever you take will be fine.'

B. Core Conversations: Substitution

Practice the Core Conversations, making changes in the participants that affect the viewpoint. For example, have Mr. and Mrs. Carter discuss when they want to take baths and have dinner (CC1). Have Mrs. Carter comment on her bath, and Mr. Carter on the party next door, to the maid (CC2 and 4). Following each conversation, ask and answer questions on content.

SECTION C

Eavesdropping

(Answer the following on the basis of the accompanying tape. A = the first speaker; B = the second speaker.)
 1. Name everything that B bought.
 2a. Where does the person under discussion come from?
  b. When did that person come?
  c. How long is that person expected to stay?
 3a. Where does this conversation probably take place?
  b. Identify A and B.
  c. What is A requesting?
 4a. What has A heard about B's trip?
  b. When did B take the trip?
  c. What does B mention as having been good?
  d. What were the meal arrangements?
 5a. Who is A?
  b. Why is B calling? Give details.
  c. Why does A ask B to wait?
 6a. Where is Ota? Since when? Until when?
  b. Why is A upset?
  c. What do the speech styles used by A and B suggest about their relative positions?
 7a. Where is A going?
  b. Why is B glad?
  c. In what connection is 'sixty' mentioned?
  d. What do the speech styles used by A and B suggest about their relative positions?
 8a. What is A offering B?
  b. When is it to be used?
  c. What is B's reaction?
 9a. What is B going to do before A?
  b. Why is A waiting until later?
10a. What book is being discussed?
  b. Who has already read it?
  c. Why is B surprised?
  d. What is going to be done with the book?
  e. Who is B?
  f. What do the speech styles used by A and B suggest about their relative positions?
11. Why is A upset? Give details.
12a. What is the topic of discussion?
  b. What time does the plane leave?
  c. What does B suggest?
  d. What is A's concern?
  e. What is the final decision?
13a. Where does B stay when traveling? Why? Give B's two reasons.
  b. What does A suggest as another possible reason for the choice?
14a. When does the party begin?
  b. Why isn't B leaving for the party immediately?
  c. What is A's concern?
  d. How does B reassure A?

e. What is A going to do?
15a. Why does A ask B what happened?
  b. How does B account for what A has noted?
  c. What time did B go to bed last night and get up this morning?
  d. What is the explanation for such hours?
  e. Why is B discouraged?
16a. What is the topic of discussion?
  b. What was originally requested? The second choice?
  c. What was finally settled on?
  d. What explanation is given for the lack of choice available?
17a. What time is it now?
  b. At about what time is the visitor expected?
  c. What did A want to do before the guest's arrival?
  d. Why is A upset? Give details.
18a. Where is A?
  b. Where is A going next?
  c. At what time does A expect to be there, at the earliest?
  d. What is B's reaction?
19a. What time does B get up in the morning?
  b. Why does A want to know?
  c. In what connection are 7:00 and 8:30 mentioned?
  d. Why is A worried?
  e. What is B going to do?
20a. What request does A make?
  b. How does B react? Why?
  c. What problem does B foresee?
  d. What is A's reaction?
  e. What alternate solution does B offer? Why?
21a. What is the topic of discussion?
  b. How many people are involved?
  c. How much did it cost last year?
  d. Why will that amount probably be adequate this year, too?
22a. Identify A and B.
  b. What does A comment on?
  c. What does B invite A to do?
  d. Compare the number of Japanese-style and Western-style rooms in the house.
  e. How does this compare with the buildings of today?
  f. What comment does B make to A about the use of the room they are in?
23a. What difference between Japanese-style inns and hotels is mentioned?
  b. What are A and B looking at?
  c. What is A concerned about?
  d. What is B's advice?
  e. What difficulty does A raise?
24a. Give details pertaining to A's request for a reservation: when, how long, special arrangements, number of people.
  b. What possible problem does B raise, and how does A react?
25a. What apparently accounts for the gaiety upstairs?
  b. What, involving how many people, is mentioned in connection with downstairs?
  c. What question does B raise?
  d. Why is Ota introduced into the conversation?

e. In what connection do A and B know Ota?

Utilization

(For each item, develop a short conversation that includes at least a stimulus and/or response.)

1. Tell a colleague you've heard that in minshuku they serve nothing but fixed things, but in the large hotels they serve everything ('no matter what'). Ask if it's true.

2. Ask a colleague if she knows anything about inns in Kyoto; minshuku in Hokkaido; American economics; British politics; French literature.

3. Tell a colleague that when you travel on business, you stop nowhere except in hotels.

4. You've been asked about English-language schools in this town. Explain that you don't know very much about them, but the part-time student worker probably knows, because he is studying English now at that kind of school.

5. You are speaking to the Okura Hotel on the telephone. Explain that you want to make a reservation for three nights starting next Tuesday, for a double room for two people. Give your name. (Remember ritual statements!)

6. On the telephone, explain that you will transfer the call to the (a) secretary; (b) person in charge; (c) division chief; (d) director of the institute.

7. There's a new show at the nearby theater. Tell a friend that you've had tickets put aside for Saturday night. Invite her to go with you.

8. You are checking on prices. Find out how much it is for a limousine for a day; a single room for a night; a bicycle for an hour; a twin-bed room for a week.

9. Tell a friend that you asked the time of the train, but you forgot about the price.

10. Inform a colleague that there is a report that (a) the secretary is sick; (b) Mr. Nakamura wants to enter the Foreign Ministry; (c) the textbook we'll use next is awfully difficult; (d) Mr. Miller, the missionary, used to be an engineer; (e) Mr. Carter is married to a person of Japanese ancestry; (f) Ms. Suzuki has experience in teaching (*lit.* having taught) French; (g) the section chief is supposed to arrive the day after tomorrow.

11. At an inn: you've been asked if you want dinner now. Find out if it's all right to take a bath first.

12. Ask permission to come in; go home early; look at this textbook; borrow this dictionary; clear off the top of this desk; throw away these old newspapers; read the letter from Takashi.

13. You've been asked your preference on a particular point. Explain that it will be fine (a) whether you eat right away or take a bath first; (b) whether you sleep on quilts or in a bed; (c) whether it's a 10:00 appointment or an 11:00 one; (d) whether the coffee is weak or strong; (e) whether you stay in an inn or a minshuku; (f) whether it's a Japanese-style room or a Western-style room.

14. You have just bought several small items. Tell the clerk that it doesn't matter whether she puts them together (*lit.* makes [them] to be together) or (makes them) separate.

15. You are setting up a schedule for your helper. Tell him to come every day by nine o'clock (at least), at the latest.

16. Apologize to the maid, but tell her that even if you add cold water to the bath, it's too hot for you.

17. Tell your colleague that even if you leave right away now, you probably won't be on time for the meeting.

18. Tell an acquaintance you've heard that usually Japanese inns include two meals [in the charge], but there are also some that include one meal. Ask if this is true.

19. Your friend has been concerned about his tape recorder. Tell him the tape is now going around, so it should be all right.

20. You've just left a restaurant. Comment on what a delicious and attractive and pleasant place it was; how beautiful the flowers in the alcove were.

21. You've been busy unpacking. Tell your friend that you don't feel well (i.e., you've 'become' that way). Ask if it's all right to rest for a bit.

22. You and your friend have been visiting your professor, and it's getting late. Suggest to your friend that you begin to (i.e., slowly) take your leave.

23. Ask the maid to spread the futon; serve dinner; bring some beer; call you at 7:00 A.M. tomorrow.

24. Tell a friend that when your mother came to wake you up, you were already awake.

25. Tell a colleague that you wanted to be awakened when you were staying at a minshuku last week, but no one woke you up, and you didn't make it to the train in time.

26. Tell a friend that you wanted to travel through Europe, but your parents wouldn't give their consent.

27. Comment to a friend that wherever you go now, since it's the season [for it], they're having parties (include dinner parties, wedding receptions, and student parties).

28. You've been asked what you would like to drink. Reply that anything at all will be fine.

29. You've been asked what time will be convenient for an appointment. Reply that any day from Monday to Friday is fine, but the weekend is a bit difficult (a strain for you).

30. You are concerned that your colleague is overworking. Tell him that he should not overdo.

31. Tell a friend that you are reading your Japanese-language textbook every day, but newspapers are still too much.

32. You've just recalled something important that you forgot to do. Exclaim!

Check-up

1. What form of verbals that denote change to a new state ('become ——') frequently occurs as a modifier describing a following nominal? What type of nominal modifier does this constitute? Give examples. (A-SP1)

2. What is the meaning of phrase-particle **sika**? With what kind of predicates does it occur? In what way are particles **wa**, **mo**, and **sika** similar? In what way do they complement each other? Compare the use of **sika** and **dake**. (A-SP2)

3. What is the meaning of **sôo da** attached to a predicate? What forms does the predicate preceding **soo da** take? Which of these forms is unusual? (A-SP3)

4. Describe three patterns for indicating that a statement is being reported as secondhand information. How do they differ? (A-SP3)

5. What is the meaning of **kotô**? Compare the difference in meaning between:

   Nedáñ o sitte (i)màsu. *and*
   Nedáñ no kotò o sitte (i)màsu.

With what other nominal does **kotô** overlap in some of its uses? Give an example. (A-SP4)

6. What types of sequences precede **to/(t)te iu koto**? When does **to iu kotò wa** occur initially in a sentence, and what is unusual about its acccentuation? (A-SP4), (B-MN)

7. What form of a predicate occurs before **mo**? What is the meaning of such a sequence? Of two such sequences in combination? What is the difference between /predicate + **mo**/ and /predicate + **kedo**/ in form and meaning? (B-SP1)

8. How is permission expressed in Japanese? (B-SP2)

9. Describe the differences in the use of **asità de ii desu ka** and **asíta de mo ii desu ka**. (B-SP2)

10. When an interrogative occurs in sequences that end with /predicate + **mo**/, how is the meaning of the interrogative altered? What form of the predicate occurs before **mo**? (B-SP3)

11. Compare the meaning of members of pairs like:
    dôre mo *and* **dôre de mo**
    dôtira mo *and* **dôtira de mo**
    îtu mo *and* **îtu de mo**   (B-SP3)

Lesson 22

SECTION A

Core Conversations

1(J)a. Âme ni narânakute yôkatta desu nêe.

   b. Kâsa moƚte (i)kanàkute mo îi desyoo nêe.

(N)a. Êe. Seḱkaku no pìkunikku desu kara ne!

   b. Mâa, hitúyoo nài to omóimàsu yo⌐ Mâda kumôtte (i)ru kedo, teńki-yòhoo ni yoru to, gôḡo kara wa hârete kuru soo desu kara..

2(N)a. Hîdôku[1] hûtte kimasita nêe.

   b. Zyâa, tuyú zya nài ñ desu ne!—konó àme wa.

   c. Mâdo o sîmet(e) okánàkute mo daízyòobu desyoo ka.

(J)a. Taíhùu ḡa tikázùite kite (i)ru soo desu yo⌐

   b. Êe. Hôra, kazé mo hùite kita desyoo?

   c. Sîmet(e) oita hoo ḡa îi desu yo⌐

3(J)a. Mâiniti konó dèñsya de irássyàru ñ desu ka⌐

   b. Kû-zi made ni irássyarànakute mo îi ñ desu ka⌐—kâisya wa.

(N)a. Mâa, hi ní yotte tiḡaimàsu kedo, daitai imá-ḡoro dèsu ne!—suítè (i)te rakû desu kara.

   b. Êe. Uti wa zisá-syùkkiñ desu kara..

1. On the accompanying videotape, **hîdôku** is replaced by **zûibuñ**, with similar meaning.

4(J)a. **Yuube zisíñ g̃a àtta soo desu nêe.**

b. **Iya, zitû wa, syuttyoo de kot́tì ni inâkatta ñ de, siránàkatta ñ desu.**

(N)a. **E? Ki g̃á tukànakatta ñ desu ka⤴ Kânari ôoki na zisíñ dàtta desyoo?**

b. **Âa, naruhodo.**

ENGLISH EQUIVALENTS

1(J)a. Isn't it great that it didn't rain!

b. I probably won't have to take an umbrella, will I!

(N)a. Yes, because this is a very special picnic, isn't it!

b. Well, I don't think there's any necessity. It's still cloudy, but according to the weather forecast, from the afternoon on (at least), it will begin to clear (they say), so . . . (it won't be necessary).

2(N)a. It's begun to rain hard, hasn't it!

b. Then that means it's not [part of] the rainy season, is it—this rain.

c. Do you suppose it will be all right for me not to close the windows (in advance)?

(J)a. They say a typhoon is approaching (*lit.* has begun to get close), you know.

b. That's right. Look! The wind has started blowing, too, hasn't it?

c. You'd better close them (in advance).

3(J)a. Is it that you take (*lit.* go by) this train every day?

b. Does that mean you don't have to get (*lit.* go) there by nine—[at] your company?

(N)a. Well, it's different depending on the day, but for the most part it's about this time (*lit.* about now)—since it's comfortable, being empty.

b. That's right. Because our place uses (*lit.* is) staggered hours.

4(J)a. I hear there was an earthquake last night, wasn't there.

b. No, actually (it's that) I didn't know because I was away on business and wasn't here.

(N)a. What? You mean you didn't notice? It was a pretty big earthquake, wasn't it?

b. Oh, of course.

BREAKDOWNS
(AND SUPPLEMENTARY VOCABULARY)

1. **âme ni nâru** get to be rain; start to rain

+(o)têñki	weather; good weather
+(îi) (o)têñki ni nâru	get to be good weather
pîkunikku	picnic
sekkaku no pìkunikku	a picnic involving special effort
motte (i)kanàkute mo (SP1)	also (or even) not having taken
mótte (i)kanàkute mo îi	doesn't have to take (lit. even not having taken will be all right)
hituyoo /na/	necessary; necessity
hitúyoo (ḡa) nài	there's no necessity
kumôru (-u; kumôtta/	become cloudy
kumôtte (i)ru	be cloudy
yoru /-u; yotta/	rely, depend; lean
teńki-yòhoo ni yoru to (SP2)	according to (lit. with relying on) the weather forecast
harêru /-ru; hâreta/	become clear
hârete kuru (SP3)	come to be clear; begin to clear
2. hidôi /-katta/	is severe
hûru /-u; hûtta/	fall (of rain, snow, etc.)
hîdôku hûru	fall severely; rain (or snow) hard
hûtte kuru	begin to fall
+yamu /-u; yañda/	stop (of rain, snow, etc.)
taíhùu	typhoon
+ôomizu/oómizù	flood
tikázùku /-u; tikázùita/	approach, draw near; become acquainted
tikázùite kuru	begin to approach; come to be near
tikázùite kite (i)ru	has begun to approach
+tikázukèru /-ru; tikázùketa/	bring close; associate with
tuyu	rainy season
hôra	look! hey!
kaze	wind
hûku /-u; hûita/	blow
hûite kuru	begin to blow
+kamínarì	thunder, thunderbolt
+naru /-u; natta/	sound
+kamínarì ḡa 'naru	it thunders
sîmet(e) okánàkute mo	also (or even) not having shut (in advance)
sîmet(e) okánàkute mo daízyòobu da	doesn't have to shut (in advance) (lit. even not having shut will be all right)
3. hi/hî	day; sun
hi ni yotte (SP2)	depending on the day

hi ni yotte tiǧau	differ depending on the day
irássyaràna kute↑ mo	also (*or* even) not having gone *or* come *or* been there /honorific-polite/
irássyaràna kute↑ mo îi	doesn't have to go *or* come *or* be there /honorific-polite/
zisá-syùkkiñ	staggered work hours

MISCELLANEOUS NOTES

1. In CC1, Mrs. Carter (J) and a neighborhood acquaintance, Sue Brown (N), are discussing the weather. They are happy that it isn't raining, in view of the picnic that has been specially planned. The speech-style is careful, with distal-style final predicates, as is usual in the conversation of these two individuals. Since Mrs. Carter is the wife of a bank executive and Sue Brown is a graduate student, there is a difference of rank which precludes truly relaxed casualness.

(O)teñki without a modifier usually refers to good weather; but with modifiers it can be favorable, as in **îi teñki**, or unfavorable: **warûi teñki** 'bad weather'; **iyâ na teñki** 'unpleasant weather.' Note that in Japanese we regularly speak of 'becoming' good weather, seasons, etc., with an /**X ni nâru**/ pattern. Compare English 'spring has come.'

(N)b. Note: **hitúyoo dà** 'it's a necessity' or 'it's necessary'; **hitúyoo ǧa àru** 'there is a necessity'; **hitúyoo na monò** 'a thing which is necessary,' 'a necessity.'

Kumôru and **harêru** are intransitive, affective verbals, **kumôru** a consonant-verbal and **harêru** a vowel-verbal. Note: **kumôtta hi** 'a cloudy day'; **hâreta hi** 'a clear day.'

2. In CC2, Smith, the graduate student, discusses an approaching typhoon with his landlady. The style is careful, with distal-style final predicates.

(N)a. Compare (1) **hidôi 'tumetai kaze** 'cold wind which is severe,' 'severe, cold wind' (**hidôi + tumetai kaze**); (2) **hîdôku tumetai kaze** 'severely cold wind' (**hîdôku tumetai + kaze**); (3) **hîdôkute 'tumetai kaze** 'wind which is severe and cold,' 'severe and cold wind' (**hîdôkute 'tumetai + kaze**). In (1), **hidôi** and **tumetai** are mutually independent modifiers of **kaze**. In (2), **hîdôku** describes **tumetai** in a manner pattern. In (3), **hîdôkute** hooks up with **tumetai** in the usual /gerund X + predicate Y/ relationship: 'being severe, it's cold.' **Hûru** is an intransitive, affective consonant-verbal, as is **yamu** (the intransitive partner of **yameru**). Both are used only in reference to rain, snow, etc.

(J)a. **Tikázùku** is an intransitive consonant-verbal, a compound of **tika** (root of **tikâi**) and **tuku** (**t > z** in a compound); it has a transitive vowel-verbal partner, predictably **tikázukèru**. Both are operational verbals, but only the latter occurs with /nominal + **o**/ phrases; **X o tikázukèru** 'bring X closer,' 'associate with X.'

(N)b. **Tuyu** refers to the Japanese rainy season, which begins in mid-June and lasts for about three or four weeks.

(J)b. **Hûku** 'blow,' distinct from **huku** 'wipe' (although both are operational consonant-verbals, identical in form except for accent), refers both to the blowing of the wind (**kazé ǧa hùku**) and 'operationally' blowing on something (**koóhìi o hûku**). Note the use of **mo** in **kazé mo hùku** in this context: it refers to the blowing of the wind as additional to the falling of the rain.

Naru, an intransitive, affective consonant-verbal (distinct from **nâru** 'become'), covers many types of sound: the noise of thunder, the ringing of bells, even the growling of a stomach!

3. In CC3, Mrs. Carter talks with an acquaintance, Deborah Miller, a regular employee of the Oriental Foreign Trade, about her commuting. They both use careful-style, with distal-style final predicates. Mrs. Carter's language is polite, with honorific-polite **irássyàru**↑ used in reference to Ms. Miller. Examining Ms. Miller's utterances, we find that there is no opportunity for her to use polite-style unless she were to replace **dèsu** with **de gozaimàsu**. This would constitute an extremely subservient, unusual usage in the given context. What is significant is that she uses distal-style consistently, even before **kedo** and **kara**. Under these circumstances, this can be regarded as a match for Mrs. Carter's politeness.

(N)b. **Uti** is the in-group, which can refer to one's home, family or—as in this case—one's own workplace.

Zisá-syùkkiñ is a compound of **zîsa** 'time difference' (cf. **zyuúyo-zìkañ no zîsa** 'a fourteen-hour time difference') and **syukkiñ** 'attendance at the office.' The compound refers to a system under which individual employees elect different work hours.

4. In CC4, Mr. Suzuki and his young acquaintance, Smith, are talking about last night's earthquake. Both use careful-style, with distal-style final predicates. (Smith's use of **naruhodo** is not significant as a style marker, since it regularly occurs as a fragment.)

(J)a. Suzuki's use of **âtta soo desu** immediately signals that his knowledge of the earthquake is second-hand. This accounts for Smith's use of an extended predicate in (N)a.

(J)b. **Iya** signals general rejection by Mr. Suzuki of what Smith is thinking. Note Mr. Suzuki's use of two extended predicates: It's that he wasn't in town that explains his not noticing; and that being the case, it's a matter of not having known about it.

Structural Patterns

1. /NEGATIVE GERUND + **mo***/; NEGATIVE PERMISSION*

In Lesson 21B-SP1 and 2, we encountered the /gerund + **mo**/ pattern, including its use in permission patterns. We discussed only affirmative gerunds.

We now consider /negative gerund + **mo**/, the meaning of which is parallel to that of affirmative sequences:

mótte ikanàkute mo	'also/even not having taken [it]' (as of the time of the sequence with which this hooks up)
amáku nàkute mo	'also/even not being sweet'
tuyú zya nàkute mo	'also/even not being the rainy season'

Examples:

Isóḡanakute mo, ma ní àu to omoimasu. 'Even if we don't hurry, we'll be on time, I think.'

Tukáitaku nàkute mo, waapuro o tukátta hòo ḡa îi desu yo↙ 'Even if you don't want to use a word processor, you'd better use [one].'

Tumétaku nàkute mo, oísìi desyoo? 'Even if it's not cold, it's tasty—isn't it?'

Tuyú zya nàkute mo, kono-ḡoro wa âme ḡa oôi desu ne! 'Even if it's not the rainy season, there's lots of rain these days, isn't there!'

A /negative gerund + **mo**/ frequently occurs as the second part of a /gerund **mo** + gerund **mo**/ sequence, i.e., as the negative equivalent of the first part:

    kimétè mo, kiménàkute mo 'whether [you] decide or not'

    katázuketàkute mo, katázuketàku nâkute mo 'whether [you] want to straighten it up or not'

    at́tákàkute mo, at́tàkàku nâkute mo 'whether it's warm or not'

    yuúmee dè mo, yuúmee zya nàkute mo 'whether [s/he]'s famous or not'

Be sure to distinguish:

    Nihóñgo dè mo, nihóñgo zya nàkute mo, wakáràngai desyoo? 'Whether it's Japanese or not, [s/he] probably won't understand—right?'

    Nihóñgo ka dòo ka wakáràngai desyoo? '[S/he] probably won't understand [e.g., the answer to the question] whether it's Japanese or not—right?'

When a /negative gerund + **mo**/ is followed by **îi**, **yorosii**, **kêkkoo**, or **kamáwànai**, permission for non-occurrence is indicated:

    Mînakute mo îi desu yo⤴ '[You] don't have to look at it.'

    Omáti-sinàkute↓ **mo yorósìi desu ka**⤴ 'Is it all right for me not to wait?'

    Wâkaku nâkute mo kamáwànai. 'It doesn't matter even if [s/he]'s not young.'

    Kyôo zya nâkute mo îi desu yo⤴ 'It doesn't have to be today.'

Compare, now, sequences with and without **mo**:

    Yomânakute îi desu yo⤴

    Yomânakute mo îi desu yo⤴

The first alternative simply states that it will be all right not to read (i.e., not to have read [something] by a designated time). But in the second alternative, the **mo** indicates that 'not having read will *also/even* be all right,' implying that other satisfactory alternatives exist—particularly the corresponding affirmative. As in the case of the parallel affirmative pattern, the /negative gerund + **mo**/ sequence is required if another option is overtly supplied by the context. Where no second choice is supplied, using this pattern is softer and a bit more polite, because it implies the existence of other alternatives.

2. /**X ni yoru to**/; /**X ni yotte**/

The verbal **yoru** 'depend,' 'lean' occurs in two frequently used, special combinations:

    a. /Nominal X + **ni yoru to**/ = 'according to X.' This is our first example of the occurrence of **to**, the particle of accompaniment—'with'—following a predicate. Literally, **X ni yoru to** means 'with depending on X.' This pattern is frequently used in indicating the source of the information contained in a /predicate + **sôo da**/ pattern.

    Siñbuñ ni yoru to, kôñbañ âme ga hûru soo desu. 'According to the newspaper, it's going to rain tonight (they say).'

Note that an occurrence of /**X ni yoru to**/ is regularly paired with an occurrence of /predicate + **sôo da**/, or with a predicate that contains some other indication that the information is second-hand. (Later lessons will expand the use of **to** following imperfective predicates.)

    b. /**X** + **ni yotte**/ = 'depending on X' (*lit.* 'having depended on X'). X is a nominal or an interrogative sentence. Examples:

Hitó ni yotte tiğaimàsu. 'It differs depending on the person.'
Nâñ-zi ni tûku ka ni yotte kimémasyòo. 'Let's decide depending on what time we arrive.'

In clause- or sentence-final position, **yotte** occurs in the form appropriate to the context.

Sore wa hí ni yorimàsu. 'That depends on the day.'

Note these other commonly occurring combinations:

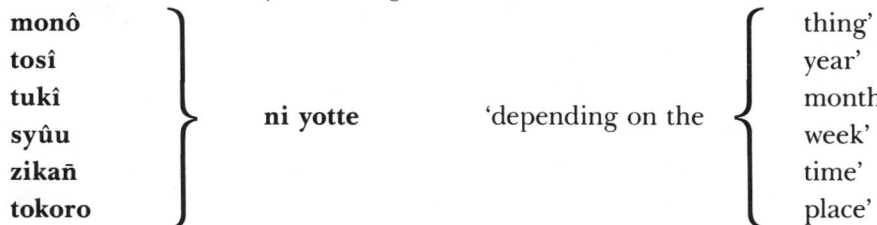

monô — thing'
tosî — year'
tukî — month'
syûu ni yotte 'depending on the week'
zikañ — time'
tokoro — place'

3. hârete kuru

Kûru may indicate not only coming to (or toward) the speaker's physical location but also arriving at the speaker's time frame. Thus, **hârete kuru** implies arriving at the present moment in terms of a change (often gradual) to becoming clear (**harêru**), i.e., 'get to be clear,' 'begin to clear.' Compare the English use of *come* in combinations like 'come to understand,' 'come to like,' 'come to hate,' 'come to appreciate.'

In this pattern, the gerund preceding **kûru** is regularly that of an intransitive verbal (and often that of an affective intransitive). The combination is pronounced as a unit: **kûru**, or any of its derivative forms, either loses its accent or, if accented, shows only a slight rise in pitch following an accented gerund. Following an unaccented gerund, /gerund + **kûru**/ is pronounced as one accent phrase, with the accent on the **kûru** verbal. Examples:

wakâtte kuru 'come to understand'
nâtte kuru 'begin to become'
kumôtte kuru 'begin to cloud up'
hârete kuru 'begin to clear'
tukârete kuru 'come to be tired'
hûtte kuru 'begin to rain *or* snow'
yańde kùru 'gradually stop raining *or* snowing'
kôñde kuru 'begin to get crowded'
suíte kùru 'begin to empty out'

Drills

A1. **Isóğimasyòo ka**◞ **Isóğànakute mo îi desyoo?**
    'Shall we hurry?' 'We don't have to hurry, do we?'

 2. **Kâre okósimasyòo ka**◞ **Okósànakute mo îi desyoo?**
    'Shall we wake him up? 'We don't have to wake him up, do we?'

 3. **inû dasímasyòo**; 4. **waápuro tukaimasyòo**; 5. **dêñki tukémasyòo**; 6. **hisyô matímasyòo**; 7. **zikókuhyoo mimasyòo**; 8. **kyuúkòokeñ kaímasyòo**

B 1. **Kodomo o okósànakute mo îi desyoo ka.**
'Do you suppose it's all right even if I don't wake up the children?'

Yappàri okôsita hoo ḡa îi desyoo.
'You'd probably better wake [them] up, after all.'

2. **Kâkari ni mawásanàkute mo îi desyoo ka.**
'Do you suppose it's all right even if I don't send [this] around (or transfer [this call]) to the person in charge?'

Yappàri mawásita hòo ḡa îi desyoo.
'You'd probably better send [it] around (or transfer [it]), after all.'

3. **kâiḡi ni ma ní awànakute**; 4. **ryoóḡae-sit(e) okanàkute**; 5. **okyakusañ o miókuranàkute**; 6. **namae o obôet(e) okánàkute**; 7. **atúmàru zikañ o kiménàkute**

C 1. **Nôḡuti-sañ wa, miênai soo desu yo⌒**
'I hear Mr/s. Noguchi isn't going to make an appearance.'

Mâa, Nôḡuti-sañ ḡa miênakute mo, watási wa kamaimaseñ kara . .
'Well, even if Mr/s. Noguchi doesn't make an appearance, I don't mind, so . . .' (please don't be concerned).

2. **Watánabe-kàtyoo wa, ma ní awànai soo desu yo⌒**
'I hear Section Chief Watanabe isn't going to make it on time.'

Mâa, Watánabe-kàtyoo ḡa ma ní awànakute mo, watási wa kamaimaseñ kara . .
'Well, even if Section Chief Watanabe doesn't make it on time, I don't mind, so . . .' (please don't be concerned).

3. **Tâkano-señsee/mesiaḡaranai**; 4. **Kûbota-sañ/wakáràtnai**; 5. **gakúsee no arubàito/inai**; 6. **Oóta-syòtyoo/obôete (i)rássyaràtnai**; 7. **Yamâḡuti-kuñ/kônai**

D 1. **Atûi hoo ḡa îi desyoo?**
'It had better be hot—right?'

Iya, âtûkute mo âtûku nâkute mo kamáwànai to omóimàsu kedo . .
'No, whether it's hot or not (hot), I don't think it matters, but . . .' (does it?)

2. **Kiíta hòo ḡa îi desyoo?**
'We'd better ask—right?'

Iya, kiítè mo kikánàkute mo kamáwànai to omóimàsu kedo . .
'No, whether [we] ask or not (ask), I don't think it matters, but . . .' (does it?)

3. **yooma no**; 4. **karui**; 5. **mîta**; 6. **kîree na**; 7. **maḡatta**

E 1. **Tâkâkute mo kamáimaseñ ka⌒**
'Does(n't) it matter even if it is expensive?'

Zitû wa, yâsûkute mo tâkâkute mo îi ñ desu yo⌒
'Actually, whether it's cheap or expensive, it will be all right.'

2. **Tiḡátte (i)tè mo kamáimaseñ ka⌒**
'Does(n't) it matter even if they are

Zitû wa, onázi dè mo tiḡátte (i)tè mo îi ñ desu yo⌒

different?' 'Actually, whether they're the same or different, it will be all right.'

3. muzúkasìkute; 4. sitá dè; 5. urâ de; 6. kôkute; 7. sôto de; 8. nâĝakute

F 1. **Âme ni nâru ka to siṅpai-sityaimàsita nêe.**
'We did worry that it might rain, didn't we!' (*lit.* 'worry "will it rain?" ')

Êe, dê mo, âme ni narânakute yôkatta.
'Yes, but it didn't rain, and that was great!'

2. **Sonó zyùĝyoo ĝa yakû ni tatânai ka to siṅpai-sityaimàsita nêe.**
'We did worry that that course might not be useful, didn't we!'

Êe, dê mo, yakû ni tâtte yôkatta.
'Yes, but it was useful, and that was great!'

3. anô hito no kao o 'wasurete (i)ru; 4. hôñdana ĝa todókànai; 5. taíhùu ĝa kûru; 6. okyakusañ ĝa gaḱkàri-suru

G 1. **Kâsa moṫte ikimaseñ ka⤴**
'Aren't you going to take an umbrella?'

Daízyòobu desyoo?—moṫte (i)kanàkute mo.
'Isn't it all right—even if I don't take [one]?'

2. **Nisîzaka-sañ okósimaseñ ka⤴**
'Aren't you going to wake up Mr/s. Nishizaka?'

Daízyòobu desyoo—okósanakute mo.
'Isn't it all right—even if I don't wake [her/him] up?'

3. giṅkoo ni yorimaseñ; 4. zikáñ o kimemaseñ; 5. tuĝóo kiite mimaseñ

H 1. **Oisyasañ ni mîte moráwanàkute mo, sûĝu yôku naru desyoo?**
'Even if I don't have a doctor look at it, it will get better soon, won't it?'

Iya, mîte morátta hòo ĝa îi desu yo—yaṕpàri.
'No, you'd better have it looked at, after all.'

2. **Isóĝanakute mo ma ní àu desyoo?**
'Even if I don't hurry, I'll make it in time, won't I?'

Iya, isôida hoo ĝa îi desu yo—yaṕpàri.
'No, you'd better hurry, after all.'

3. osíete aĝenàkute/zibúñ de ki ĝa tùku; 4. roóka ni dasànakute/zyamá ni narànai; 5. deñki o tukênakute/sono syasiñ ĝa miêru

I 1. **Anó eñkai nì wa dênakute mo îi desyoo?**
'We don't have to go to that party (at least), do we?'

Êe, betu ni, mûri site dêru hituyoo wa nâi to omóimàsu kedo nêe.
'Right. I don't think there is any necessity to go out of our way to attend, but . . .' (don't you agree.)

2. **Sitêeseki o kaṫte okanàkute mo îi desyoo?**
'We don't have to buy reserved-seat [tickets] in advance, do we?'

Êe, betu ni, mûri site 'katte oku hituyoo wa nâi to omóimàsu kedo nee.
'Right. I don't think there is any necessity to go out of our way to buy [them] in advance, but . . .' (don't you agree.)

3. nîmotu o zêñbu tê de hakóbanàkute; 4. kooeñ o yuúmee na señsèe ni onéǵai-sinàkute

J 1. Yôku señsèe to soódañ-suru sòo desu ne!
'I hear you consult with the teachers often.'

Mâa, señsèe ni yorímàsu kedo neʕ
'Well, it depends on the teacher, but—you know?'

2. Yôku miñsyuku ni tomaru sòo desu ne!
'I hear you stay at minshuku often.'

Mâa, miñsyuku ni yorimàsu kedo neʕ
'Well, it depends on the minshuku, but—you know?'

3. gaḱkai ni ode ni nàru; 4. arúbàito ni tanômu; 5. okyakusañ o 'miokuru

K 1. Watanabe-syotyoo ḡa syotyoo o yamérù ñ da tte?
'They're saying that Institute Director Watanabe is going to resign as institute director?'

Hâi. Râzio ni yoru to, yaméru sòo desu nêe.
'Yes. According to the radio, (they say) s/he is going to resign.'

2. Kôñbañ kara yukî ḡa hûru ñ da tte?
'They're saying it's going to snow (starting) tonight?'

Hâi. Râzio ni yoru to, hûru soo desu nêe.
'Yes. According to the radio, (they say) it's going to snow (*lit.* fall).'

3. atárasìi tikatetu o tukûru; 4. Kyûusyuu no hôo de oómizù ḡa dêta; 5. kotósi no taihùu wa hîdôkatta; 6. sibái o mìru hito ḡa sukûnàku nâtta; 7. îma no Kyôoto wa niḡîyaka na

• Repeat this drill, substituting **to iú kotò desu nêe** for **sôo desu nêe** in the responses.

L 1. Râzio ni yoru to, yukî ḡa hûru soo desu yo⌐
'According to the radio, it's going to snow (I hear).'

Âa, yukî ḡa hûru tte? Râzio de kiítà ñ desu ka⌐
'Oh, they say it's going to snow? You mean you heard [that] on the radio?'

2. Têrebi ni yoru to, gôḡo kara harêru soo desu yo⌐
'According to the television, starting in the afternoon it's going to clear (I hear).'

Âa, gôḡo kara harêru tte? Têrebi de mîta ñ desu ka⌐
'Oh, they say it's going to clear starting in the afternoon? You mean you saw [that] on television?'

3. siñbuñ/Tâkano-señsee wa yuúmee dà; 4. tomodati/ohûro wa keñkoo ni ìi; 5. râzio no teńki-yòhoo/hîdôku tuyôi kaze ḡa hûku; 6. ano zassi/ miñsyuku no hòo ḡa yâsùkute îi

M 1. Siñbuñ wa yòñde (i)nâi kedo, Yosida-sañ no byooiñ ḡa damê[2] ni nâtta tte kiítà ñ desu ḡa ..
Êe. Watási mo siranàkatta ñ desu ḡa; siñbuñ ni yoru to, damê ni nâtta soo desu nêe.

2. **Damê** here means 'no good' either in terms of the quality of the hospital's medical care or its financial standing.

'I haven't read the paper, but I heard that Mr/s. Yoshida's clinic has gone down the drain, but . . .' (is this true?)

'That's right. (The fact is) I didn't know either, but according to the paper, (it's reported) it has gone bad.'

2. **Nyûusu wa mîte (i)nâi kedo, yuube no zisiñ wa ôókìkatta tte kiítà ñ desu ğa ..**

'I haven't seen the news, but I heard the earthquake last night was strong (*lit.* big), but . . .' (is this true?)

Êe. Watási mo siranàkatta ñ desu ğa; nyûusu ni yoru to, ôókìkatta soo desu nêe.

'That's right. (The fact is) I didn't know either, but according to the news, (I hear) it was strong (*lit.* big).'

3. râzio wa kiíte (i)nài/hûbeñ na tokórò de mo iê o 'utte (i)ru; 4. kâkari no hitô ni wa kiíte (i)nài/amari ríppa na señsèe wa anó gakkai nì wa kônai; 5. koñsyuu no zassi wa yôñde (i)nâi/Suğîura-sañ no kaisya ğa 'abunai[3]

N 1. **Dâre de mo syoóti-site kurerù ñ desyoo ka.**

'Do you suppose (it's that) everyone (*lit.* whoever it is) will give us their consent?'

Sâa, sore wa, yappàri hitó ni yotte tiğaù desyoo.

'Well, actually that probably will depend on the person (*lit.* differs, depending on the person).'

2. **Maineñ taíhùu ğa kûru ñ desyoo ka.**

'Do you suppose (it's that) typhoons come every year?'

Sâa, sore wa, yappàri tosî ni yotte tiğaù desyoo.

'Well, actually that probably depends on the year (*lit.* differs, depending on the year).'

3. mâiniti okôsite ağeru; 4. nañyòo de mo gô-zi ni siğóto ğa sùmu; 5. dôko de mo 'siízuñ-tyuu wa kômu; 6. dâre de mo kekkoñ-suru tokì wa rippa na hiròoeñ o yaru; 7. dôno ryokâñ dè mo tomáru tokì wa yoyáku ğa hituyoo nà; 8. maísyuu Hurañsu kara deñwa ğa hàiru

O 1. **Mâiniti isóğasìi ñ desu ka⤴**

'(Is it that) you are busy every day?'

Iêie. Hi ni yotte neʃ Isóğasìi hi mo isoğàsìku nâi hi mo âtte ne!

'No, no. Depending on the day, you know, there are (*lit.* being) both busy days and days that aren't busy . . .'

2. **Dôre mo yakû ni tatû ñ desu ka⤴**

'(Is it that) all of them are useful?'

Iêie. Monô ni yotte neʃ Yakû ni tâtu monô mo yakû ni tatânai monô mo âtte ne!

'No, no. Depending on the thing, you know, there are (*lit.* being) both useful things and things that are not useful . . .'

3. **Abunai** here refers to financial standing.

3. **dôko mo kôñde (i)ru**; 4. **minâsañ ryokóo ḡa sukì na**; 5. **maitosi ryokoo-suru**; 6. **maítuki isya ni mìte morau**; 7. **dôno kuni mo komâtte (i)ru**

P 1. **Âme ḡa hûtte (i)masu yo**
'Say, it's raining.'

Sôo desu ka. Kyôo wa hurânai daroo to omôtta kedo, yaṕpàri hûtte kimâsita ka.
'It is? I thought it probably wouldn't rain today, but has it started to rain after all?'

2. **Hitó ḡa atumàtte (i)masu yo**
'Say, people are gathering.'

Sôo desu ka. Kyôo wa atúmarànai daroo to omôtta kedo, yaṕpàri atúmàtte kimâsita ka.
'They are? I thought they probably wouldn't gather today, but have they started to gather after all?'

3. **hârete**; 4. **yukî ḡa hûtte**; 5. **kazé ḡa hùite**; 6. **hi ḡá dète**; 7. **kôñde**; 8. **yamâ ḡa mîete**

Q 1. **Yuube zisíñ ḡa àtta soo desu nêe.**
'I hear there was an earthquake last night, wasn't there.'

E? Siránàkatta ñ desu ka Kânari ôoki na zisíñ dàtta desyoo?
'What? You mean you didn't know? It was a rather strong (*lit.* big) earthquake, wasn't it?'

2. **Yuube kâzi ḡa àtta soo desu nêe.**
'I hear there was a fire last night, wasn't there.'

E? Siránàkatta ñ desu ka Kânari ôoki na kâzi datta desyoo?
'What? You mean you didn't know? It was a rather big fire, wasn't it?'

3. **zîko**; 4. **kôñpa**; 5. **eñkai**; 6. **kâiḡi**; 7. **kooeñ**; 8. **pâat(e)ii**

Application Exercises

A1. Collect weather reports from local newspapers and translate their contents into Japanese. Do *not* attempt literal translations; simply describe, in terms of the Japanese patterns you have learned, the information contained in the reports.

2. Practice asking and answering questions about the weather in the hometowns of class members, including the instructor. Discuss the seasons, rain- and snowfall, wind, floods, heat and cold, etc.

3. Following the procedure outlined in Application Exercises A of Lesson 21B, ask now about the acceptability of *not* doing specified things. For example: (a) In studying foreign languages at your institution, is it all right even if you don't (1) listen to tapes? (2) buy a dictionary? (b) Do you not have to study a foreign language? (c) Is it all right even if you don't attend class every day? (e) Is it all right even if you don't come here on weekends?

B. Core Conversations: Substitution

Follow the usual procedures, making appropriate substitutions in the Core Conversations, including changing the relationships of the participants. After practicing the new versions, ask and answer questions on content.

SECTION B

Core Conversations

1(J)a. Kâataa-san. Byoóki nà ñ desyoo? Mûri sitya ikémaseñ yo.

(N)a. Êe. Dê mo, koré dakè wa, zettai ni kyôo sité simawanàkutya ikénai to omòtte..

b. Hoká no hitò zya dekînai ñ desu ka⌐

b. Kore wa, bôku de nâkutya wakáranai to omôu ñ desu yo.

2(N) Kore kiméru màe ni, Sâtoo-san ni soódan-sinàkutya ikénài desyoo ka.

(J) Mâa, naíyoo nì mo yorímàsu kedo nêe. Yappàri tyôtto kiíte mìta hoo ḡa îi desu yo.

3(N)a. Kêsa itta 'kissateñ no 'kootya, mâzûkatta to omówànai?

(J)a. Ñ. Ańna ni usùkutya, azi wa zeńzen wakaràanai yo.

b. Soré dè mo 'okane haráwànakutya ikénài ñ da kara, harâ ḡa tâtte syoó ḡa nài wa ne!

b. Mattaku ne!

4(N)a. Nihóñḡo de hanasimasyòo ka⌐

(J)a. Soó simasyòo. Sonó hòo ḡa tasúkarimàsu.

b. Mâa, watasi no nihoñḡo mo hetâ da kedo; sekkaku Nihòñ ni irû kara, narubeku tukátta hòo ḡa îi to omôtte..

b. Kotóbà wa, rensyuu-sinàkutya sûḡu wasúrete simaimàsu kara nêe. Yômu hoo mo kânari dekímàsu ka⌐

c. Iêie. Yômu no wa, zîsyo ḡa nâkutya.. To iu yòri, zîsyo ḡa âtte mo 'nakanaka muzúkasìi desu neˤ

English Equivalents

1(J)a. Mr/s. Carter. Isn't it the case that you're ill? You must not overdo!

(N)a. I know. But I feel (*lit.* thinking) that just this (at least) I absolutely must finish doing today...

b. Can't someone else do it? (*lit.* Do you mean it can't be done being another person?)

2(N)a. Before deciding this, do you suppose I have to consult with Mr/s. Sato?

    b. It's that I don't think this will be understood unless I'm the one [to do it].

(J) Well, it depends on the contents, too, but . . . After all is said and done, it would be better to ask him/her and see [what s/he thinks].

3(N)a. The (black) tea at the "kissaten" we went to this morning—don't you think it tasted awful?

    b. Even so, (it's the case that) you have to pay (money), so you can't help getting angry, can you!

(J)a. Yeah. With it *that* weak, you can't make out the flavor at all.

    b. Absolutely!

4(N)a. Shall we speak in Japanese?

(J)a. Let's do that. That will be more helpful [to me].

    b. Well, *my Japanese* is weak, too, but here I am all the way over in Japan, so thinking I'd better use it as much as possible . . . (I try to do that).

    b. Language—without practicing it, you completely forget it right away, so . . . (you must use it). Are you able to read pretty well, too?

    c. No, no! When it comes to reading, unless I have a dictionary . . . Rather, I should say, *even if* I have a dictionary, it's quite difficult, you know?

BREAKDOWNS
(AND SUPPLEMENTARY VOCABULARY)

1. **sitê wa** *or*
   sityâ(a) (SP1)   having done it
   sitê wa 'ikenai *or*
   sityâ(a) 'ikenai (SP2)   [one] must not do [it] (*lit.* having done [it], it will not do)

   zettai ni   absolutely
   sitê simawanàkute wa *or*
   site simawanàkutya(a)   not having finished doing [it]

sité simawanàkute wa (*or* -nàkutya[a]) 'ikenai (SP2)	[one] must finish doing [it] (*lit.* not having finished doing [it], it won't do)
hoká no hitò de wa *or*	
hoká no hitò zya(a)	being another person
hoká no hitò de wa dekînai *or*	
hoká no hitò zya(a) dekînai	being another person (i.e., if it's someone else), it can't be done
bôku de nâi	it's not me
bôku de nâkute wa (*or* nâkutya[a])	not being me
bôku de nâkute wa (*or* nâkutya[a]) wakáràanai	not being me (i.e., unless it's me), there's no understanding
2. soódañ-sinàkute wa (*or* -nàkutya[a])	not having consulted
soódañ-sinàkute wa (*or* -nàkutya[a]) 'ikenai	[one] must consult (*lit.* not having consulted, it won't do)
naiyoo	contents; subject matter, substance
+mokuteki	purpose
+kekka	result
3. usûkute wa *or*	
usûkutya(a)	being weak (of coffee, tea, etc.)
usûkutya wa (*or* -kutya[a]) wakáràanai	being weak, you can't tell
azi	taste
+niôi	smell
harâu /-u; harâtta/	pay
haráwànakute wa (*or* -nakutya[a])	not having paid
haráwànakute (*or* -nakutya[a]) wa 'ikenai	[one] must pay (*lit.* not having paid, it won't do)
harâ	belly, abdomen
harâ g̃a tâtu	become angry
+sikata *or*	
+siyoo *or*	
syoo (SP3)	way of doing
sikáta g̃a nài *or*	
syoó g̃a nài	nothing can be done; it can't be helped
harâ g̃a tâtte syoó g̃a nài	[one] can't help having become angry
mattaku	precisely, totally, entirely
4. kotóbà	(spoken) language, utterance; phrase, word

reñsyuu-suru	practice
reñsyuu-sinàkute wa (*or* -nàkutya[a])	not having practiced
reñsyuu-sinàkute wa (*or* -nàkutya[a]) 'wasurete simau	not having practiced, [one] completely forgets
yômu hoo	the reading alternative
yômu no	the act of reading
nâkute wa *or* nâkutya(a)	there not being; not having
to iu yòri (SP4)	more than saying what was just said; that is to say, rather

MISCELLANEOUS NOTES

1. In CC1, the secretary, Ms. Yamamoto, expresses her concern for Mr. Carter, one of her supervisors, who is continuing to work in spite of being ill. Both use careful-style, with distal-style final predicates. One of Mr. Carter's utterances ([N]a) is a minor sentence ending in a direct-style gerund; here, a distal-style gerund would be excessively polite.

(N)a. **Zettai ni** occurs with predicates—often negative—as an expression of manner: 'absolutely,' 'positively.'

2. In CC2, Deborah Miller checks with her colleague, Mr. Yamada, on the necessity for consulting with Mr/s. Sato before making a particular decision. While Mr. Yamada's reply is qualified by the use of **mâa** and **tyôtto**, and the suggestion that the contents affect the decision, the message nonetheless comes through clearly: consult! The extent to which even the most marginally involved person is consulted in connection with every decision in Japan is surprising—and often extremely frustrating—to Westerners. Some of this consultation takes place in meetings, the number and length of which far exceed any foreign parallel. This is another manifestation of the group approach: all in-group members involved in a task must be active participants. Decisions that affect groups are not usually made unilaterally by individuals.

As usual, Ms. Miller and Mr. Yamada speak to each other in careful-style, with distal-style final predicates.

3. In CC3, Sue Brown is ANGRY. She is expressing her anger in no uncertain terms to her fellow graduate student, Kato, who understands her complaint: He too was served awful-tasting tea at the kissaten for which full price was charged.

Both participants use casual-style, with direct-style predicates. Except for Sue Brown's feminine **wa ne!** (3[N]b), the language is blunt. Sue Brown's anger is reflected by the unusual speed of her speech and by a facial expression that shows her annoyance. Note that even here we have no confrontation, since she is speaking with Kato, who shares her complaint. This kind of outburst at the kissaten would be considered by many to be crass.

(J)a. **Añna ni**: Remember that when the referent is familiar to both speaker and addressee, the **-a** member of a **ko-so-a-do** series is used.

Azi: Note also **azí ḡa àru** 'there is a taste'; **azi ḡa suru** 'have a taste,' 'taste (a certain way).' **Niôi** 'smell' occurs in exactly parallel patterns.

(N)b. **Harâ** is the seat of the emotions for the Japanese. Note: **harâ ga oókìi** 'is bighearted, magnanimous'; **harâ o kimeru** 'make up one's mind'; **hitó no harà o yômu** 'read a person's mind.' (These particular expressions are more common in men's speech.) Note also **harákirì** (from **harâ o kîru**) and **haragee** (the art of reading the thoughts of others without resorting to language). When a person becomes angry the **harâ** stands on end (**harâ ga tâtu**).

(J)b. **Mattaku** is an intensifier, implying completeness and totality: **Maítaku soò desu**. 'That's exactly the way it is'; **Maítaku siranài**. 'I know nothing about it.'

4. CC4 is a brief discussion of language between Ms. Miller and Mr. Suzuki, preliminary to a substantive conversation in which Japanese will be the language used. Both use carefulstyle, with distal-style final predicates. A few minor sentences occur: (N)b and c (first sentence) and (J)b (first sentence).

When a Westerner who speaks Japanese begins a conversation with a Japanese (who can be assumed to have studied English for many years in school), there is the question of which language to use. It should be handled thoughtfully. A situation to be avoided at all costs is one in which an English speaker with minimal Japanese insists on speaking Japanese with a Japanese who is fluent in English. Of course, even this is permissible if a preliminary agreement has been made (to provide the English speaker with practice in Japanese, for example), but otherwise . . .

(J)a. **Sonó hòo** refers to the alternative of Japanese as opposed to another language.

(N)b. **Watasi no nihoñgo mo**: since Mr. Suzuki has implied that his foreign-language capability is limited, Ms. Miller also modestly downplays her Japanese ability.

(J)b. **Kotóbà** regularly refers to some unit of the spoken language, without clear differentiation: 'the word,' 'a word,' 'an utterance,' 'a phrase,' etc. The Japanese writing system is organized as a continuum with no spaces, and the Western concept of a word is missing. This explains the lack of uniformity in word division when Japanese write in romanization, a system which calls for spaces between words. In this text, "words" have been arrived at on the basis of a linguistic analysis.

Yômu hoo is the reading alternative, as opposed to **hanâsu hoo** 'the speaking alternative.'

Structural Patterns

*1. /GERUND + **wa**/*

We note again how parallel and complementary **mo** and **wa** are in their patterning, with **X mo** indicating 'X in addition' and **X wa** 'X at least,' 'X, for one.' In lessons 21B and 22A, we introduced **mo** following a gerund. Now we come to /gerund + **wa**/.

Whereas **koré o tukattè mo** 'also/even having used this' assumes other possibilities as valid, **koré o tukattè wa** implies applicability in this context only: 'at least having used this.' (As usual, the gerund implies actualization as of the following clause, not in reference to the present time.) Thus, **konó zìsyo o tukáttè wa wakáranai** states that 'assuming at least that [one] [will] have used this dictionary, then there will be no comprehension.' The /gerund + **wa**/ pattern regularly occurs only when the following clause is negative—if not in form, at least in connotation. Preceding **wa** or **mo**, a regularly unaccented gerund acquires an accent on the final mora.

In the spoken language, /e + w + a/ is frequently contracted to **ya** or **yaa**. An example already encountered: **sore wa** > **sorya(a)** (Lesson 14B). This type of contraction is particularly common in the case of /gerund + **wa**: **-te wa** > **-tya(a)** and **-nakute wa** > **-nakutya(a)**.[4] When the gerund ends in **-de**, the contraction would end in **-dya(a)**, an alternate spelling for **-zya(a)** that is used in some romanization systems.

Zya was first encountered in the negative of the nominal predicate:

zîsyo desu $\begin{cases} \text{zîsyo zya arímasèñ} \\ \text{zîsyo zya nâi desu} \end{cases}$

This **zya** is also a contraction of **dè wa**: 'as for being a dictionary (at least), there's none of it.' The pattern may be altered by omitting the **wa** (**zîsyo de arímasèñ/nâi desu**) or by replacing the **wa** with **mo** (**zîsyo de mo arímasèñ/nâi desu**). In the spoken language, the former pattern (without **wa**) frequently occurs *within* another pattern—particularly one which itself ends with **wa**—in cases where no notion of comparison or set-membership is implied (cf. CC1[N]b). In the standard language, it rarely occurs independently. In the pattern with **mo**, once again "additionalism" is involved: 'it isn't a dictionary, either.' Examples:

Kodómo dè wa (*or* **zyà[a]**), **dekînai.** 'If it's a child [who is to be involved], then it can't be done.'

Zîsyo g̃a nâkute wa (*or* **nâkutya[a]**), **wakáràneai.** 'Without a dictionary (i.e., in the event that there is no dictionary), I don't/won't understand.'

Nedañ g̃a ańna ni tàkàkute wa (*or* **tàkàkutya[a]**), **komáru desyoo?** 'Isn't it upsetting for the prices to be that high?'

Note the important difference between

Wakáràneakute wa siñpai dèsu. 'Without understanding (i.e., unless [I] have understood), it's a worry'; 'it's a worry not to understand' *and*

Wakáràneakute siñpai dèsu. 'Not having understood, it's a worry'; 'I'm worried about my not understanding.'

In the first, **wakáràneai** is proposed as a condition to consider, but in the second, **wakáràneai** is an actuality.

2. NECESSITY AND PROHIBITION

The /gerund + **wa**/ pattern occurs in expressing necessity and prohibition in combination with **ikenai** 'it can't go,' 'it won't do,' 'it's no good,' 'no, no!' **Narânai** 'it won't become [anything]' occurs as a less common alternate of **ikenai** in this pattern in the spoken language.

Thus, /affirmative gerund X + **wa** + **ikenai**/ = '[one] must not X,' 'it must not be X' (*lit.* 'it will not do to have Xed *or* to be X [at least]'), but /negative gerund X + **wa** + **ikenai**/ = '[one] must X,' 'it must be X' (*lit.* 'it will *not* do *not* to have Xed *or not* to be X [at least]'). **Ikenai** may be replaced by **narânai** 'it won't become [anything]' as a slightly less forceful equivalent. These Japanese patterns do indeed express definite necessity and prohibition. They should NOT be thought of as regular equivalents of English 'must,' which has many different shades of meaning besides necessity and prohibition. Consider 'You must be hungry,' 'that must be a church,' and 'that must not be accurate,' which have no connection with these Japanese patterns.

---

4. Note that this simple rule is invalid when one uses Hepburn romanization: **kore wa** > **korya**, but **-te wa** > **-cha** (and **-nakute wa** > **-nakucha**), and **-de wa** > **-ja**.

Note how the **-te mo** ~ **-te wa** patterns complement each other:
   Hâitte mo îi? 'May I come in?'
      Iya, hâittya(a) ikénài. 'No, you must not come in.'
   Yomânakute mo îi? 'Is it all right even if I don't read it?'
      Iya, yomânakutya(a) ikénài. 'No, you must read it.'

These patterns should be avoided in situations where the social context would make it rude to require or prohibit. Do not ignore the softer patterns you have already learned, including **tyôtto . .**

The prohibition and necessity patterns may also occur in questions, with the negative answers indicating permission to do or not do.

3. -kata ~ -yoo

Syoó ḡa nài and **sikáta ḡa nài** (and their distal and polite equivalents) express a fatalistic reaction to a given situation: 'that's it!' 'there's nothing to be done,' 'it can't be helped.'

Syoo (a contraction of **siyoo** 'way of doing') reflects a more casual style than **sikata**, which has a similar meaning.

The **-kata** suffix of **sikata** (and, less commonly, the **-yoo** suffix of **s[i]yoo**) regularly combines with verbal stems to form nominal compounds meaning 'way of ——ing,' 'manner of ——ing.' Examples:

hanásikàta		talking'
yomíkàta		reading'
iikata		saying'
kakíkàta		writing'
tanómikàta	'way of'	requesting'
tukúrikàta		making'
tukaikata		using'
arúkikàta		walking'
narabikata		lining up'
sikikata		spreading out'

Note that the compound is accented (on the **ka** of **-kata**) only if the verbal stem is derived from an accented verbal.

Following a gerund, **syoo/sikata ḡa nai** indicates the inevitability of the action or state of the gerund.

Harâ ḡa tâtte		'[I] can't help getting angry.'
Komâtte		'[I] can't help getting upset.'
Siñpai-site	**syoó/sikáta ḡa nài.**	'[I] can't help worrying.'
Âtûkute		'There's no way to avoid the heat.'
Itâkute		'There's no way to avoid the pain.'
Yamétàkute		'[I] can't help wanting to quit.'

Note also: **X suru yòri syoó/sikáta ḡa nài** 'there's nothing to be done other than doing X,' and **X sitè mo, syoó/sikáta ḡa nài** 'even if one does X, it's no use.'

4. SELF-CORRECTION

One of the important ways in which speaking and writing differ is in how we self-correct. In writing, we are able to delete or correct any mistakes we detect before releasing the manuscript, but once something has been said, the utterance itself cannot be wiped out, no matter how quickly we become aware of it. What is required is a spoken signal that indicates a retroactive deletion and provides a substitute item to counteract or improve on what was just said. Consider how we use 'I mean' in spoken English: 'On Tuesday—I mean Wednesday—I'll be back.'

One self-correction pattern in Japanese is introduced in CC4(N)c. Deborah Miller started out as if to say **zîsyo ḡa nâkutya(a) muzúkasìi desu** 'without having a dictionary... it's difficult.' But immediately upon saying this, she decided she wanted to correct to a stronger statement. Accordingly, as soon as she completed the initial, weaker comment ('without having a dictionary'), she began a new sentence with **To iu yòri** with **to** pronounced as in **To iu to** [cf. 21B-CC3]): 'more than saying what was just said,' i.e., the quotative particle **to** refers to the previous sequence. She then proceeded to furnish the upgraded version, **zîsyo ḡa âtte mo**. This correction pattern covers situations in which a speaker self-corrects a sequence judged after being uttered to be too weak.

Drills

A 1. **Kore wa, oǹnà zya, dekînai ñ desu ka**⤴
'Is it that (being) women (they) can't do this?'

Iêie, oǹnà de mo dekímàsu yo⤴
'No, no. Also/even (being) women (they) can do it.'

2. **Kore wa, kodomo zya, wakárànai ñ desu ka**⤴
'Is it that (being) children (they) don't understand this?'

Iêie, kodómo dè mo wakárimàsu yo⤴
'No, no. Also/even (being) children (they) understand it.'

3. **arúbàito/yakû ni tatânai**; 4. **asíta/ma ní awànai**; 5. **tiísài hoo no hako/haírànai**; 6. **usiro/miênai**; 7. **mukoo kara/kikoenai**

B 1. **Bâsu de ittya, ma ní awànai desyoo ka.**
'Do you suppose they won't make it in time, going by bus?'

Îe, bâsu de iťtè mo, ma ní àu hazú dèsu yo⤴
'No, also/even going by bus, they should make it in time.'

2. **Nedáñ ḡa tàkàkutya, kaťte kurenài desyoo ka.**
'Do you suppose they won't buy it for us, the price being high?'

Îe, nedáñ ḡa tàkàkute mo, kaťte kureru hazu dèsu yo⤴
'No, also/even if the price is high, they can be expected to buy it for us.'

3. **miñsyuku ni tomattya/omósìròku nâi**; 4. **kodómo ḡa tanòñzya/syooti-site kurenai**; 5. **âme ḡa hîdôkutya/supôotu wa dekînai**; 6. **kazé ḡa tûyôkutya/hûne wa dênai**; 7. **takúsañ matiḡàetya/kyoo-zyuu ni sumânai**

C 1. **Kore wa, ońnà de mo dekîru siḡóto dèsu ka**⤴
'Is this a job that also/even (being) a woman can do?'

Iya, ońnà zya, dekînai ń zya nâi desu ka⤴
'No, isn't it the case that (being) a woman can't do it?'

2. **Kore wa, arúbàito de mo wakâru kotô desu ka**⤴
'Is this a thing that also/even (being) a part-time worker can understand?'

Iya, arúbàito zya, wakárànai ń zya nâi desu ka⤴
'No, isn't it the case that (being) a part-time worker can't understand it?'

3. **soko/hoká no hitò/wakâru tokórò**; 4. **are/wakâi hito/wakâru hôń**; 5. **soko/îma sûḡu/todôkete kureru tokórò**; 6. **sore/otona/omósiròi to omôu bańgumi**

D 1. **Kore, mâzûkute mo tâbete kurérù desyoo ka.**
'Do you suppose they'll eat this (for us), even if it tastes bad?'

Ńñ⤴ **Mâzûkutya, tâbete kurenai yo.**[5]
'Uh-uh. Assuming that it tastes bad, they won't eat it.'

2. **Ano mise, kôńde (i)te mo iréte kurerù desyoo ka.**
'Do you suppose that shop will let us in, even if it's crowded?'

Ńñ⤴ **Kôńde (i)tya, 'irete kurenai yo.**
'Uh-uh. Assuming that it's crowded, they won't let us in.'

3. **ano miti, isôide mo abúnaku nài**; 4. **anô hito, yukî ḡa hûtte mo dekîru**; 5. **siḡoto ḡa sukûnàkute mo komárànai**; 6. **osóku nàtte mo ôkite mâtte (i)ru**; 7. **mâdo ḡa tîisàkute mo yôku miêru**

E 1. **Kore wa, otókò zya, zeítai ni dekìnai ń desyoo ka.**
'Do you suppose it's that this is absolutely impossible if you are (*lit.* being) a man?'

Sôo desu nêe. Yahâri ońnà de nâkutya, dekînai desyoo nêe.
'Hmm . . . It probably *is* impossible unless you are a woman.'

2. **Kore wa, otona zya, zeítai ni hairànai ń desyoo ka.**
'Do you suppose it's that you absolutely don't go into this if you are (*lit.* being) an adult?'

Sôo desu nêe. Yahâri kodómo de nàkutya, haírànai desyoo nêe.
'Hmm . . . You probably *don't* go into it unless you are a child.'

3. **zyosee/tuuzinai**; 4. **titioya/soodań-sinai**; 5. **hidári no hòo/miênai**; 6. **uê/todókànai**

F 1. **Mâdo o sîmet(e) oitya, kikóenài ń desyoo ka.**
'Do you suppose (it's that) you can't hear with the windows kept closed?'

Êe, akét(e) okanàkutya, kikóenai tte iù ń desu yo.
'That's right. (It's that) they say you can't hear unless you keep them open.'

2. **Têrebi ḡa tûite (i)tya, zyamá ni nàru ń desyoo ka.**

Êe, kiéte (i)nàkutya, zyamá ni nàru tte iù ń desu yo.

5. The responses of this drill are blunt-style.

'Do you suppose (it's that) it is (*lit.* becomes) a disturbance with the TV on?'

'That's right. (It's that) they say it becomes a nuisance unless it's turned off.'

3. **kôe ḡa tîisàkutya/wakáràna**i; 4. **tamâḡo ḡa hûrûkutya/mazûi**; 5. **isú ḡa yawaràka-kutya/karáda ni yòku nâi**; 6. **nîmotu ḡa omôkutya/hakoñde kurenai**; 7. **kodómo ḡa òkite (i)tya/komâru**

G 1. **Zisá-syùkkiñ de mo îi?**
'Will (also/even being) flex-time be all right?'

Zisá-syùkkiñ zya, ikénài desyoo.
'Flex-time probably won't do.'

2. **Tikázùite mo îi?**
'Is it all right (also/even) to get closer?'

Tikázùitya, ikénài desyoo.
'You probably must not (get closer).'

3. **komâkàkute**; 4. **hañtai-site**; 5. **daítai dè**; 6. **nemûkute**; 7. **tuíñ de**; 8. **kôkute**; 9. **kumôtte (i)te**; 10. **tukátte àtte**; 11. **hutóñ dè**; 12. **yowâkute**

H 1. **Eeḡo, matíḡaete mo îi desu ka⤴**
'Is it all right even if I make mistakes in English?'

Mâa, yappàri matíḡaènai hoo ḡa îi desu kedo nêe.
'Well, it is, after all, better not to make mistakes, but . . .' (it may be unavoidable).

2. **Siḡoto, goóruden-uìiku de mo îi desu ka⤴**
'Is it all right even if the work is in Golden Week?'

Mâa, yappàri goóruden-uìiku zya nâi hoo ḡa îi desu kedo nêe.
'Well, it is, after all, better if it's not Golden Week, but . . .' (it may be unavoidable).

3. **mâe, minîkùkute**; 4. **kodomo ni watasite**; 5. **koko ni narabete**; 6. **mâdo, kitá dè**; 7. **oyasumi, mizîkàkute**

I 1. **Yoyáku-sit(e) okanàkute mo îi?**
'Is it all right even if I don't make a reservation in advance?'

Dame, dame. Tyañto yoyáku-sit(e) okanàkutya ikénài desyoo?
'No, no! You must surely make an advance reservation—isn't that right?'

2. **Rippa na kyoozyu de nàkute mo îi?**
'Is it all right even if it's not a well-recognized professor?'

Dame, dame. Tyañto rippa na kyoozyu de nàkutya ikénài desyoo?
'No, no! It must surely be a well-recognized professor—isn't that right?'

3. **orée aḡenàkute**; 4. **reñraku-sinàkute**; 5. **onázi hì de nâkute**; 6. **sirâbete mînakute**; 7. **wakáriyàsùku nâkute**; 8. **sîroku nâkute**; 9. **tiísài koto ni ki ḡá tukànakute**

J 1. **Gôḡo made inâkute mo îi desyoo?**
'I don't have to stay until the afternoon—right?'

Iya, gôḡo made itá hòo ḡa yôku nâi desu ka⤴
'No, won't it be better to stay (*lit.* have stayed) until the afternoon?'

2. **Mâiniti ukáḡawanàkute mo îi desyoo?**

Iya, mâiniti ukáḡatta hòo ḡa yôku nâi desu ka⤴

'I don't have to pay a visit every day—right?'	'No, won't it be better to visit (*lit.* have visited) every day?'

3. kusuri nomânakute; 4. zêñbu osíete yaranàkute; 5. Nârita made miókuranàkute; 6. sûḡu katázùkete simáwanàkute; 7. sûḡu haráwànakute; 8. kekka sirábènakute; 9. mokuteki iwánàkute

K 1. Iḱ-kai no sèki zya nâkute mo îi desyoo?	Iya, iḱ-kai no sèki no hoo ḡa yôku nâi desu ka⟋
'It doesn't have to be a first-floor seat, right?'	'No, isn't a first-floor seat better?'
2. Wâkâku nâkute mo îi desyoo?	Iya, wakâi hoo ḡa yôku nâi desu ka⟋
'S/he doesn't have to be young, right?'	'No, isn't [a] young [person] better?'

3. kotóbà ḡa yasásiku nàkute; 4. azi ḡa usúku nàkute; 5. naiyoo ḡa wakáriyàsuku nâkute; 6. siḡoto ḡa sûñda âto de nâkute

L 1. Âto de harâttya, ikenai?	Iya, îi yo—âto de harâtte mo.
'I can't (*lit.* is it no good for me to) pay later?'	'No (i.e., that's not the case), it's all right—even if you pay later.'
2. Koko de réñsyuu-sityà, ikenai?	Iya, îi yo—koko de réñsyuu-sitè mo.
'I can't (*lit.* is it no good for me to) practice here?'	'No (i.e., that's not the case), it's all right—even if you practice here.'

3. hisyô ni mawasitya; 4. sôba made tikázùitya; 5. tuḡî no êki de ôritya; 6. otóotò ni tasúkète morattya; 7. zîsyo mîte kâitya

M 1. Teḡami wa, îma dâsi ni ikánàkutya ikénài no?	Iya, betu ni îma dâsi ni ikánàkute mo îi ñ desu kedo ne!
'(Is it that) I have to go and mail the letter now?'	'No, (it's that) you don't especially have to go and mail it now, but . . .' (you'd better do it soon).
2. Ryokañ wa, kyôo yoyáku-sinàkutya ikénài no?	Iya, betu ni kyôo yoyáku-sinàkute mo îi ñ desu kedo ne!
'(Is it that) I have to make reservations for the inn today?'	'No, (it's that) you don't especially have to make the reservations today, but . . .' (you'd better do it soon).

3. tonari/îma katázukènakutya; 4. sonó kamì/îma suténàkutya; 5. okane/koñsyuu harawànakutya; 6. kâsa/kyoó-zyuu ni kawanàkutya; 7. gakkai/miñna dènakutya; 8. okyakusañ no namae/zêñbu obôet(e) okánàkutya

N 1. Gaikokuḡo wa, reñsyuu-sinàkutya, damê desu ne!	Êe, reñsyuu-sinàkutya, gaikokuḡo wa sûḡu wasúretyaimàsu kara nêe.
'Foreign languages are no good unless you practice them, are they!'	'Yes, not practicing [them], you completely forget [foreign languages] right away, so . . .' (you must practice).
2. Kotóbà wa, tukáwanàkutya, damê desu ne!	Êe, tukáwanàkutya, kotóbà wa sûḡu wasúretyaimàsu kara nêe.

'Languages are no good unless you use them, are they!' | 'Yes, not using [them], you completely forget [languages] right away, so . . .' (you must use them).

3. hanásikàta/reńsyuu-sinàkutya; 4. kakíkàta/kakânakutya; 5. yarikata/mîte (i)nâkutya; 6. tukaikata/tukátte mìnakutya

O 1. **Yômu hoo mo kânari dekímàsu ka** | **Ie, yômu no wa, tyôtto dekímaseń.**
'Can you manage reading (*lit.* the reading alternative) fairly well, also?' | 'No, reading I can't quite handle.'

2. **Kâku hoo mo kânari dekímàsu ka** | **Ie, kâku no wa, tyôtto dekímaseń.**
'Can you manage writing fairly well, also?' | 'No, writing I can't quite handle.'

3. **hanâsu**; 4. **tukûru**; 5. **osieru**; 6. **hakobu**; 7. **naôsu**

P 1. **Zîsyo ḡa nâkutya, dekímaseń ka** | **Êe, zîsyo ḡa nâkutya . . To iu yòri, zîsyo ḡa âtte mo, dekímaseń nêe.**
'Can't you do it without a dictionary?' | 'Right. Unless I have a dictionary—or rather I should say, even if I have a dictionary, I can't do it.'

2. **Seńsèe ni kikánàkutya, dekímaseń ka** | **Êe, seńsèe ni kikánàkutya . . To iu yòri, seńsèe ni kiítè mo dekímaseń nêe.**
'Can't you do it without having asked the teacher?' | 'Right. Unless I've asked the teacher—or rather I should say, even if I've asked the teacher, I can't do it.'

3. hitó ni tasukète moráwanàkutya; 4. końpyùutaa o tukáwanàkutya; 5. mâiniti kayówanàkutya; 6. zeńbu yarínaosànakutya

Q 1. **Kore, tukáttè mo îi desu ka** | **Êe, tukáttè mo îi . . To iu yòri, tukátte moratta hòo ḡa îi desu nêe.**
'May I use this?' | 'Yes, you may use it—or rather I should say, it will be better to have you use it, won't it!'

2. **Kore, deńwa irétè mo îi desu ka** | **Êe, irétè mo îi . . To iu yòri, deńwa iréte moratta hòo ḡa îi desu nêe.**
'May I put in a call about this?' | 'Yes, you may call—or rather I should say, it will be better to have you call, won't it!'

3. sukôsi isôide; 4. moo iti-do reńsyuu-site; 5. hakkìri site; 6. mińnà ni mîsete

Application Exercises

A1. Formulate statements of necessity and prohibition that apply to your daily life. Examples: We can't[6] smoke in the classroom; we can't bring food into the classroom; we

---

6. Note that 'can't' in this context does not refer to ability.

must listen to tapes in studying Japanese at this school; we must study a foreign language at this school; we must speak nothing but Japanese with our Japanese (= Japanese person) teacher; we can't look at our textbooks during classtime.

2. Using examples from the preceding exercise, ask related permission questions that will elicit these statments as **iie** answers.

3. On the basis of a bus or train timetable—actual or made up—ask and answer questions—containing permission, necessity, and prohibition patterns—that relate to reaching an announced destination in time for a set appointment. Example (using as destination a 3:00 conference in Tokyo):

> **Môtto hâyâku dêru bâsu mo âru kedo; itî-zi no bâsu ni noʹtte ittè mo, ma ní aù desyoo ka.** 'There are also buses that leave earlier, but do you suppose I'll be on time even if I go on the 1 o'clock bus?'
>> **Iie, soré yòri hâyâku dêru bâsu ni noránàkutya ikémasèñ yo.** 'No, you must take a bus that leaves earlier than that.'

4. Practice answering questions, self-correcting in terms of strengthening your answers, by changing from a **-nakutya(a)** to a **-te mo** pattern. Examples:

> **Asítà no pâat(e)ii, dôo desyoo nêe.** 'How do you think the party tomorrow will be?'
> **Sôo desu nêe. Tomodati o turéte ikanàkutya . . To iu yòri, tomodati o turéte ittè mo, tumárànai daroo to omóimàsu nêe.**
> 'Hm. Unless I take a friend . . . rather I should say, even if I take a friend, I think it will probably be boring.'

B. Core Conversations: Substitution

Follow the usual procedures, making appropriate substitutions in the Core Conversations, including changing the relationships of the participants wherever possible. After practicing the new versions, ask and answer questions on content.

SECTION C

Eavesdropping

(Answer the following on the basis of the accompanying audiotape. A = the first speaker, and B = the second speaker, of each conversation.)

1. When is A supposed to do this?
2a. What is the topic of discussion?
 b. On what does it probably depend, according to B?
 c. Who is quoted?
 d. What is that person's opinion?
3a. What problem does A note?
 b. What question does B raise?
 c. What is B going to do?
4a. What is A glad about?
 b. Why was B worried?
 c. What is the weather forecast?
5a. Who is B?
 b. In general, when does B have time?

c. What qualification does B mention?
6a. What is being complained about?
 b. What was the result for B?
 c. What change occurred this week?
 d. How did it affect B?
7a. What course of action does A assume to be advisable?
 b. What is A concerned about?
 c. Why does B expect that the cost will not be very high?
 d. What other factor will affect the cost?
8a. Why does A assume B had a tough time?
 b. What did B do, and what was the result?
 c. What didn't A notice?
9a. What is imminent?
 b. When does it start in this area? With what variation?
 c. How does this compare with Tokyo?
10a. Identify A and B.
 b. What is B concerned about?
 c. What does B think might be necessary?
 d. Why does A apologize?
 e. What does B warn A against doing?
11a. What problem have A and B encountered?
 b. What is A complaining about?
12a. What is A's complaint?
 b. What reaction does B have to the matter A is complaining about?
13a. Describe the weather.
 b. Why is B surprised?
 c. Why is B upset?
14a. What is the topic of discussion?
 b. Who bought it? Where?
 c. What is the problem?
 d. What is on top of it?
 e. What one good point is mentioned about the thing being discussed?
 f. Why is A angry?
 g. According to A, what can be done about the problem?
15a. What does A ask B to do? Why?
 b. What is B's reaction to the item in question?
 c. What advice and warning does B give?
16a. Describe the weather.
 b. What season is it?
 c. How does B feel?
 d. What does A suggest? When?
 e. What is B's reaction?
 f. What kind of weather is A expecting? For how long?
 g. What is the source of A's prediction?
17a. Describe the weather.
 b. What is A trying to decide?
 c. What advice does B give? On what basis?
18a. What language does B use when speaking with Carter?
 b. Compare Carter's speaking and writing proficiency in Japanese.
 c. In what connection is a dictionary mentioned?
 d. According to B, what does Carter need to do?

19a. What does B comment on just before drinking the coffee offered by A?
  b. Why does A urge B to go ahead and drink the coffee?
  c. What possible problem does A raise in connection with the coffee?
20a. What is the topic of discussion?
  b. When did B not attend?
  c. Why does B not attend more often?
  d. What did Yamaguchi say?
  e. What is B's reaction?
21a. What time is it?
  b. Why does A think it is necessary to hurry?
  c. What information does B provide to convince A that there is no need to hurry?
22a. What is the topic of discussion?
  b. On what day and at what time did it occur?
  c. Why did neither A nor B notice it?
23a. What compliment does A pay B?
  b. What is B's reaction?
  c. Who is A?
  d. How does A explain a lack of improvement?
  e. What is B's conflicting situation?
  f. What is B's reaction to A's repeated compliments?
24a. What has A heard about B's company?
  b. Why is this a help for B?
  c. What time does B start work in the morning?
  d. What is A's reaction, and what does A think might be a problem?
  e. What actual problem does B mention?
25a. What is the topic of conversation?
  b. How is the weather in Shikoku? Give details.
  c. How does B know?
  d. What has now begun here?
  e. What does this indicate?

Utilization

(For each item, develop a short conversation that includes at least a stimulus and/or response.)

1. Request permission from your supervisor not to (a) come until 9:30 tomorrow morning; (b) telephone Mr. Nakamura until next week; (c) finish this work until Monday; (d) have this typewriter repaired until tomorrow.

2. Check with a friend on whether it's all right (also/even) if you don't (a) put ice in this drink; (b) lock the car; (c) give Mr. Sato some (monetary) expression of thanks; (d) throw away these old magazines; (e) mail this letter right away.

3. Comment on how glad you are that (a) it didn't rain; (b) it didn't get cold; (c) the sun came out; (d) it got warm; (e) it got to be nice weather; (f) there was no (it didn't become a) flood.

4. Tell a colleague that according to the weather report (a) it will begin to clear up starting this evening; (b) it will cloud up starting tomorrow morning; (c) it will become very cold tomorrow; (d) it may snow tonight; (e) a typhoon is on the way; (f) the wind will become strong, starting in the afternoon.

5. Tell a colleague that you heard there was a rather strong earthquake last evening, but you were riding in the subway and didn't notice it.

6. Tell an acquaintance that since your company is on flex-time, you don't have to be (*lit.* go) there by 9:00.

7. You've been asked about the winters in your home town. Explain that it differs depending on the year, but usually it snows a great deal.

8. Your friend has asked whether he should lock his car. Tell him it probably isn't necessary, but maybe it would be better to lock it.

9. You're talking on the telephone to an acquaintance out of town. Tell her that it's raining hard and you wonder if this isn't the rainy season already.

10. You are posing a group in preparation for taking a picture. Tell them to come a bit closer (to the camera).

11. You've been asked the age at which American children enter school. Explain that it differs depending on the child, but for the most part, they enter at age six.

12. You've been asked by an acquaintance how your Japanese studies are progressing. Explain that recently you've come to understand more than before. (Express thanks for the concern!)

13. Check with a friend on whether (a) the rain has stopped; (b) it's thundering.

14. Tell a friend that he mustn't (a) smoke in this room; (b) drink the water here; (c) overdo; (d) use this telephone; (e) wash this in hot water; (f) write in English; (g) spread the futon in this room.

15. Tell the secretary that she must (a) finish doing this work by noon; (b) practice her English more; (c) use this typewriter for writing English letters.

16. In discussing various tasks that must be done, explain to a colleague that this one (at least) anyone can probably do, but that one is impossible if it's anyone else.

17. Tell your colleague that since—no matter what—you absolutely must finish this work today, you are going to be here until late.

18. Ask a colleague if he thinks it's necessary to consult with Mr. Suzuki before changing the time of next week's conference.

19. You've been asked your opinion of a certain procedure. Reply that it depends on (a) the purpose; (b) the people who will do it; (c) the place where they will do it; (d) the results of the work they are doing now.

20. You've been asked by a close friend for your opinion of a recent lecture. Comment that the professor's manner of speaking was excellent, but the contents!

21. Comment to a friend that (a) when coffee is this weak, you can't detect any taste; (b) when you've caught a cold, you can't detect any odor; (c) when it's this hot, you get a headache; (d) when one's way of speaking is that fast, you don't understand the meaning.

22. Warn a colleague that (a) taking the 4:45 train, one probably won't be on time; (b) unless it's a young person, this kind of work won't be possible; (c) without practicing, one forgets quickly.

23. Exclaim about (a) a way of writing that is easy to read; (b) a way of speaking that is difficult to understand; (c) a way of lining up that is strange; (d) a way of doing [things] that is upsetting; (e) a way of reading that is wrong.

24. You have just been informed about a particular set of circumstances. Reply that in that case, you can't help (a) becoming angry; (b) becoming annoyed; (c) forgetting; (d) being poor [at something]; (e) wanting to quit; (f) wanting to talk it over.

25. Comment that unless you practice language—or rather, even if you practice it, becoming good at it is awfully difficult.

Check-up

1. What is the basic meaning of /negative gerund + **mo**/? Of /affirmative gerund X + **mo** + negative gerund X + **mo**/? What is the difference in meaning between /negative gerund + predicate/ and /negative gerund + **mo** + predicate/ (example: **âme ga hurânakute komâru** vs. **âme ga hurânakute mo komâru**)? (A-SP1)

2. What pattern represents negative permission, i.e., permission *not* to do something? (A-SP1)

3. Describe a pattern by which the source of secondhand information, reported in a /——**sôo**

desu/ pattern, is made explicit. What is the basic meaning of the verbal it includes? Of the particle that follows the verbal? (A-SP2)

4. What is the meaning of **X ni yotte/yoru**? Define X. Give five commonly occurring examples of this pattern. (A-SP2)

5. **Kûru** 'come' usually refers to motion to or toward the speaker's location. In what other sense is it commonly used? Describe its use following the gerund of intransitive verbals like **wakâru**, **kômu**, **harêru**. What feature of meaning do these verbals often share besides intransitivity? (A-SP3)

6. How do the particles **wa** and **mo** resemble each other? Complement each other? Apply these relationships to explaining their use following gerunds. (B-SP1)

7. What kind of predicate usually follows a /gerund + **wa**/ pattern? What contraction of the combination occurs commonly in the spoken language? What is the general rule covering this contraction? In what combination did we first encounter this? (B-SP1)

8. Describe a pattern that expresses necessity and one that expresses prohibition. How do these patterns interrelate with patterns expressing permission? (B-SP2)

9. The suffix **-kata** forms compounds with what form of the verbal? What do these compounds mean? Contrast **sikata**, **siyoo**, and **syoo**. (B-SP3)

10. Describe one Japanese pattern of self-correction. What type of correction does it cover? (B-SP4)

Lesson 23

SECTION A

Core Conversations

1(N)a. **Kâataa-sañ. Odékake dèsu ka⌇**
   b. **Îi desu nêe. Môo natû na ñ desu nêe. Yakémàsu yo⌇—kyôo wa.**
   c. **Âa, sôo na ñ desu ka.**

2(J)a. **Îma okáeri dèsu ka.**
   b. **Okáimono dèsu ka⌇**
   c. **Îi no ḡa arímàsita?**

3(J)a. **Burâuñ-sañ. Kyôo wa îtu mo to tiḡáimàsu ne!**
   b. **Pâat(e)ii de mo âru ñ desu ka⌇**
   c. **Zyâñpaa to ziípañ ni nàrete (i)ru kara, tiḡáu hitò ni miémàsita yo⌇**

(J)a. **Êe, tyôtto ûmi e.**
   b. **Iya, añmari kùròku narítàku nâi kara, koñna ôoki na boosi kabûtte (i)ru ñ desu yo⌇**

(N)a. **Êe. Tyôtto depâato ni yoťtè kita kara, osóku nàttyatte..**
   b. **Êe, raísyuu no kekkòñsiki ni kité iku tamè no hukû o mî ni iťtà ñ desu kedo..**
   c. **Mâa, nakánaka ki ni ittà no ḡa mitúkaranài si, nedâñ ḡa takài si, kyôo wa sikáta ḡa nài kara, akíràmete kâette kimasita.**

(N)a. **Sôo desu ka⌇ Âa, sûutu kité (i)rù si; kutû mo, kîree na no haíte (i)rù kara..**
   b. **Ie, tyôtto hitó ni awànakutya narânai no de..**
   c. **Sôo desu ka⌇**

English Equivalents

1(N)a. Mrs. Carter. Are you going out?

(J)a. Yes, to the beach (*lit.* ocean) for a bit.

b. That's great! (It's that) it's summer already, isn't it! You're going to get burned—today.

c. Oh, is that it.

2(J)a. Are you on your way home now?

b. (Is it) shopping?

c. Were there any nice ones?

3(J)a. Ms. Brown! Today you're different from usual (*lit.* always), aren't you.

b. (Is it that) there's a party or something?

c. I'm used to your jacket and blue jeans, so you seemed like a different person.

b. No, I don't want to get too suntanned (*lit.* black), so that explains my wearing this kind of large hat.

(N)a. Yes. I stopped in (*lit.* came having stopped in) at a department store, so I'm late (*lit.* having ended up becoming late . . .).

b. Yes, (it's that) I went to look at clothes to wear to a wedding next week, but . . . (there were problems).

c. Well, what with just not finding anything that appealed to me, and the prices being high, today it's hopeless, so I gave up and came home.

(N)a. Oh? Oh, because I'm wearing a suit, and my shoes, too—I'm wearing nice looking ones.

b. No, (being the case that) I just have to meet (or see) some people . . . (I'm dressed like this).

c. Really?

BREAKDOWNS
(AND SUPPLEMENTARY VOCABULARY)

1. **dekakeru /-ru; dekaketa/**   go out; set out
   odékake dà ↑ (SP1)   /honorific-polite equivalent of **dekakeru**/
   yakeru /-ru; yaketa/   get burned; get baked; get roasted
+ **yaku /-u; yaita/**   burn [something]; bake; roast
   boosi   hat
   kabúru /-u; kabútta/   put *or* wear on the head
2. **okáeri dà ↑**   /honorific-polite equivalent of **kaeru**/
   kekkòñsiki   wedding ceremony
   kiru /-ru; kita/   put *or* wear on the body
   kite (i)ku   wear (to a place) (*lit.* go, having put on)

kité (i)ku tamè da (SP2)	it's for the sake of wearing (to a place)
+nûĝu /-u; nûida/	take off (of clothing)
hukû	clothing
kité (i)ku tame no hukù	clothing for wearing (to a place)
+wahuku	Japanese-style clothing
+yoohuku	Western-style clothing
ki ni iru /-u; ki ni itta/	appeal
mitukaru /u; mitukatta/	be(come) found, be(come) discovered
+mitukeru /-ru; mituketa/	find, locate, turn up [something]
mitúkaranài si (SP3)	it isn't found and (what is more)
takâi si	it's expensive and (what is more)
akíramèru /-ru; akíràmeta/	give up, forego; resign oneself to
kâette kuru	come back; come home
akíràmete kâette kuru	give up and come back (lit. come back, having given up)
3. îtu mo to 'tiĝau	be different from [what is] always [normal]
sûutu	man's or woman's suit
+sebiro	man's suit
kité (i)rù si	is wearing and (what is more)
kutû	shoes
haku /-u; haita/	put or wear on the feet or legs
kutû mo, kîree na no (o) haítè (i)ru	as for shoes, too—be wearing nice looking ones
pâat(e)ii de mo (SP4)	a party or something (lit. also/even being a party)
zyâñpaa	windbreaker; jacket
ziipañ	blue jeans
narêru /-ru; nâreta/	become accustomed
ziípañ ni narèru	become accustomed to blue jeans
miêru /-ru; mîeta/	appear, seem
tiĝáu hitò ni miêru	appear as if a different person

Clothing

geta	wooden clogs (for out-of-doors)
surîppa	slippers worn in the home
zoori	sandals (for out-of-doors)
suràkkusu *or*	
pâñtu	slacks, pants
sukâato	skirt
syâtu	shirt

waisyatu	man's dress shirt
burâusu	blouse
dôresu	dress
sitaḡi	underwear
nêkutai	necktie
nêkutai (o) simêru *or* nêkutai (o) 'suru	put on (tie) a necktie

-tyaku; *Classifier for counting suits*

it́-tyakù	rokú-tyakù		
nî-tyaku	nanâ-tyaku		
sâñ-tyaku	hat́-tyakù		
yôñ-tyaku	kyûu-tyaku		
gô-tyaku	zyut́-tyakù/zit́-tyakù		
nâñ-tyaku			

-soku: *Classifier for counting pairs of footwear*

ís-sokù	rokú-sokù
nî-soku	nanâ-soku
sâñ-zoku	haś-sokù
yôñ-soku	kyûu-soku
gô-soku	zyuś-sokù/ziś-sokù
nâñ-zoku	

MISCELLANEOUS NOTES

1. In CC1, Sue Brown has run into Mrs. Carter as she (Mrs. Carter) takes off for a visit to the beach. The conversation style is basically careful, with distal-style final predicates, but notice that Mrs. Carter uses one fragment ([J]a) and a direct-style predicate before **kara**, indicating a slightly relaxed style in this setting. Sue Brown's polite conversation-opener is typical, particularly since it refers to Mrs. Carter's own actions.

(N)a. **Dekakeru**, a compound of **dê**, the stem of **dêru**, and **kakêru**, is an intransitive, operational vowel verbal. **Kakeru** as the second member of compound verbals usually indicates 'starting' or 'setting out' or 'being about to' (cf. **ikikakeru** 'be about to go').

(N)b. **Yakeru** is an affective vowel verbal, the intransitive partner of **yaku**, an operational consonant verbal. **Yaku** covers dry cooking—baking, broiling, grilling, toasting, and roasting. Note also **hi ni yakeru** 'become sunburned.'

(J)b. Note: **kurôi > kûroku naru > kûroku narítài > kûroku narítàku nâi**.

(N)b, (J)b. With exposure to the sun, one gets burned (**akáku nàru**) or tanned, brown (*lit.* black) (**kûroku naru**). Traditionally, pale skin has been considered beautiful in Japan, and many Japanese avoid direct sunning.

Kabûru is a transitive, operational consonant verbal. Note: **X o kabûru** 'put X (on the head)'; **kabûtte (i)ru** 'be wearing (on the head)'; **kabûtte iku** 'wear (on the head) to a place'; **hutóñ o kabùru** 'pull a quilt over one's head.'

2. In CC2, Sue Brown, on her way home from a shopping expedition, has run into Mrs. Carter. The conversation style is careful, with distal-style final predicates. Mrs. Carter opens the conversation with a commonly occurring polite inquiry (cf. CC1[N]a). Her use of **okaimono** ([J]b) is particularly typical of women's language, and her use of a question without final **ka** in (J)c is gentle. Sue Brown uses two minor sentences and one major sentence. Note that in this generally relaxed conversation, she uses direct-style in all nonfinal predicates except for **dèsu kedo** ([N]b) in its occurrence at the end of a minor sentence. The direct-style alternative would be **dà**, less likely to be used in this context by Sue Brown in talking to Mrs. Carter.

(N)b. The **sikî** of **keḱkòṅsiki** refers to ceremonies and rites. **Kiru** is a transitive, operational vowel verbal. Note: **X o kiru** 'put X on (the body)'; **kite (i)ru** 'be wearing (on the body); **kite iku** 'wear (on the body) to a place.' We now have a challenging group of sound-alikes! Be sure to distinguish:

   kité (i)màsu (from **kiru** 'put on')   **kiíte (i)màsu** (from **kiku** 'ask,' 'listen')
   kitê (i)masu (from **kûru** 'come')   **kîtte (i)masu** (from **kîru** 'cut')

Nûgu is an operational, transitive consonant verbal, the opposite of all the verbals of putting on: **X o nûgu** 'take off X.'

(N)c. **Ki ni iru**: **Ki** 'mind,' 'spirit,' 'feelings,' 'attention' was previously encountered in **ki ḡá tùku**, **ki ó tukèru**, and **kimoti** (< **ki** + **môti** [stem of **môtu**]). **Iru** 'enter,' which occurs in its stem form in **iriḡuti** 'entrance,' is the intransitive consonant verbal partner of transitive vowel verbal **ireru** 'put in.' Except for its occurrences in special combinations like **ki ni iru**, this verbal regularly occurs in its alternate form, **hâiru**. (Both verbals are operational.)

Mitukeru, the transitive vowel verbal partner of intransitive consonant verbal **mitukaru**, is an operational verbal with a connotation of self-will. When 'finding' lacks that implication, affective **mitukaru** occurs. Thus, finding a job, a place to live, something to wear, etc., from the Japanese point of view, is a matter of the item in question 'becoming located,' without self-determination.

Akírameru is an operational, transitive vowel verbal: **X o akírameru** 'give up *or* abandon hope of X' as in **gaíkoku de beṅkyoo-surù no o akírameru** 'give up [the idea of] studying abroad.'

Kâette kuru 'come back (home)' implies 'getting here, having come back (home).' Note also: **kâette iku** 'go back (home)'; **hâitte kuru** 'come in'; **hâitte iku** 'go in'; **dête kuru** 'come out'; **dête iku** 'go out.'

3. In CC3, Sue Brown's supervisor is surprised to see her at the office in clothing more formal than usual. (As a part-time student worker, her normal garb is blue jeans and windbreaker.) As usual, Sue Brown and her colleague use careful-style in speaking with each other, with distal-style final predicates. Sue Brown's two longest utterances are minor sentences (ending in /direct-style + **kara**/ and the gerund of the extended predicate, /direct-style + **no de**/), indicating a generally relaxed tone, which is not surprising given the topic of conversation and the only slight difference of rank between the two.

(N)a. **Haku** is a transitive, operational consonant verbal. Note: **X o haku** 'put X on (the feet or legs)' (includes shoes, socks, pants, and skirts); **haite (i)ru** 'be wearing (on the feet or legs)'; **haite iku** 'wear (on the feet or legs) to a place.'

In (N)a, **kutû** is given added focus by introducing it initially with **mo**, separated from its modifier, **kîree**. Compare this patterning with unfocused **kîree na kutû mo 'haite (i)ru**.

(J)b. **Pâat(e)ii** includes an example of innovative pronunciation representing a foreign combination, the **t** of **te** followed by the **i**-vowel, a mora not found in native Japanese words.

(J)c. **Narêru**, an intransitive, affective vowel verbal, is another example of a verbal whose basic meaning implies realization of a state: 'become accustomed'; 'get used to.' Note: **nârete (i)ru** '[I] am used to [it]'; **X ni narêru** 'become accustomed to X'; **nâreta hito** 'a person used to [something].'

Miêru was previously introduced as 'put in an appearance,' 'appear,' and as 'can see,' 'be visible.' In this lesson, it is introduced with another meaning, 'appear to be,' 'seem to be.' Note the combination **X ni miêru** 'seem to be X,' 'appear as X.' Compare this use of **ni** with that of **omiyaḡe ni kau** 'buy as a souvenir.'

Supplementary Vocabulary: **Geta**, **zoori**, and **kutû** are all for outdoor wear only. Within the home, Japanese wear only **surîppa**, similar in style to American scuffs; however, when walking on **tatami**, they remove even their **surîppa**. A separate pair of **surîppa** is kept for use in the toilet. Extra pairs of **surîppa** are kept in the **gêñkañ** for use by guests in private homes, inns, and Japanese-style restaurants.

Until very recently, **pâñtu** referred only to underpants, but now it is used along with **surâkkusu** in reference to slacks. The earlier term for the latter was **pâñtaroñ**, a borrowing from French.

Waisyatu was originally borrowed from 'white shirt,' but its use today has no special color limitation.

Sitaḡi is a compound of **sita** 'under' and **ki**, the stem of **kiru** 'put on the body,' with the commonly occurring change of **k** to **ḡ** in this position. Articles of clothing like blouses, shirts, skirts, dresses, etc. are counted with classifier **-mai**, but trousers, slacks, etc., with **-hoñ**.

Structural Patterns

1. /o- + VERBAL STEM + dà/

/**O-** + verbal stem + a form of the copula/ is an honorific-polite ↑ equivalent of the verbal. Note the following:

 1. While both patterns are honorific-polite, this new pattern is not quite as polite as /**o-** + stem + **ni** + **nâru**/.

 2. In the imperfective, this new pattern may refer to a future, a present, or a repeated activity or state. Thus: **Oyóbi dèsu ka**↗ 'Will you *or* do you call?' or 'Are you calling?' **Oyobi** is a polite nominal, and literally the question asks, 'Is it or will it be a calling by you (that is involved)?' Thus, the distinction between **yobímàsu ka** and **yońde (i)màsu ka** disappears.[1]

The use of the perfective is parallel to the imperfective: **Oyóbi dèsita ka**↗ 'Did you call?' or 'Were you calling?'

 3. The negative equivalents reflect regular nominal patterning. Since this is a polite pattern, **dè wa** occurs frequently (particularly with **gozáimasèñ**), but **zya** is also possible. Thus:

> **Odékake dè wa gozáimasèñ ka**↗
>
> **Okáeri zya nài?**
>
> **Oyóbi zya arimasèñ ka**↗

 4. Remember that the replacement form for /**o-** + **i** (**iru**) or **ki** (**kûru**) or **iki** (**iku**)/ is **oide**. Thus, **Oíde dèsu ka**↗ 'Are you staying/coming/going?' However, other verbals for which there is a special honorific-polite ↑ (**suru, iu**, etc.) do not occur in this pattern.

Note that we now have an operational nominal pattern which may occur with /operand + **o**/: **Nîmotu o oázuke dèsu ka**↗ 'Are you checking your luggage?'

2. **tamê**

Tamê 'reason,' 'sake,' 'benefit' is a nominal usually preceded by a modifier. Without a preceding modifier, it refers to benefit, as in **tamê ni nâru mono** 'a thing which is beneficial

---

 1. This is not true of the /**o-** + stem + **ni nâru**/ pattern, which distinguishes **oyóbi ni nàru** and **oyóbi ni nàtte (i)rassyaru**.

(*lit.* becomes a benefit).' When **tamê** is preceded by an imperfective verbal, it expresses reason as *purpose*; it expresses reason in the sense of *cause* when the preceding verbal is perfective. In the case of nonverbal predicates, context distinguishes between reason = purpose and reason = cause.

Tamê may be followed (1) by the copula (including the **no** [but **na** + **no/ñ**] form before another nominal) or (2) by particle **ni** of purpose/goal/manner, or (3) as a slightly stiffer alternate of (2), it may occur without a following particle, linking up with a predicate as a manner construction. For some speakers, **tamê** has an unaccented alternate before **no**. Examples:

    Kyôosi ni nâru tamê (ni), konó gakkoo ni hairimàsita. 'I entered this school for the purpose of becoming a teacher.'

    Byoóki ni nàtta tamê (ni), daigaku o yameta. 'I quit school because of having become ill.'

    Dekînai tamê (ni) 'yameta. 'I quit because of not being able to do it.'

    Hâha no tamê (ni) kattâ ñ desu. '(It's that) I bought it for my mother.'

    Byoóki no tamè (ni) kônakatta. 'I didn't come because of illness.'

    Sonó tamè desyoo? 'It's for that reason, isn't it?'

    Kaísya ni kite iku tamè no sûutu desu. 'It's a suit for wearing to the office.'

    Nâñ no tamê (ni) sitâ ñ desu ka↗ 'For what purpose is it you did [that]?'

Previously, purpose involving activity was expressed by /verbal stem + **ni**/, but that pattern occurred most commonly in combination with a following verbal expressing change of location (**iku, kûru, kâeru,** etc.): **kai ni iku** 'go to buy.' The contexts in which **tamê** occurs are much more extensive, including those in which /stem + **ni**/ may also occur.

3. PARTICLE **si**

/Predicate X (imperfective, perfective, or tentative) + **si**/ = 'X (among other things leading to a single result) and . . .'

    Consider some typical examples:

    Kawánài no? . . . Êe. Takâi si, amari kîree zya nâi si . . 'You're not going to buy it?' . . . 'That's right. It's expensive, and (what is more) it isn't very pretty, and . . .'

    Yamâ mo mièru si, ûmi mo tikâi kara, îi tokórò desu nêe. 'You can see the mountains, and (what is more) the ocean is near, so it's a wonderful place.'

Si is often simply identified as equivalent to English 'and.' There are important differences:

(1) /Predicate **X** + **si**/ always implies other related predicates which may or may not be overtly stated.

(2) The sequence **X si, Y si, Z** (in which X, Y, and Z end with, or consist of, predicates) may mean that Z is another example in the set to which X and Y belong (X, and what is more, Y, and what is more, Z), or Z may express the result of things like X and Y (X, and what is more, Y, and so Z). In the second example above, **kara** can be replaced by **si** with little actual difference in meaning. Note also that in CC2(N)c, **kyôo wa sikáta ga nài** is the result of two problems mentioned, both of them followed by **si**.

What is the difference, now, between /gerund, + predicate/ and /predicate **si**, + predicate/? Compare:

(a) **Sûutu o kite, boósi o kaburimàsita.** 'I put on a suit, and (then) I put on a hat.'
   (b) **Sûutu o kitâ si, boósi mo kabùtta (si. .)**[2] 'I put on a suit, and (what is more) I put on a hat (and) . . .' (all this led to my being quite dressed up.)

In (a), whatever activities were involved are stated, and the order of the two parts of the sentence cannot be changed without markedly changing the meaning of the sentence. In (b), the activities mentioned are not necessarily the entire inventory; all activities involved were leading to a single result; and the order of the **. . . si** sequences can be changed with no appreciable difference in meaning. In (a), a connective between the two clauses would be **sore kara**, but in (b), **sono ue** or **sore ni**.

Predicates preceding **si** may be direct- or distal-style, but if a final predicate is direct, predicates before **si** can be expected to be direct-style only. Before **si** (as before **kara, kedo, no**), an unaccented predicate acquires an accent.

Even if the activity or state described by a **si**-clause has already occurred, the imperfective may occur before **si**, since it is stressing the type of activity or state rather than focusing on the occurrence itself.

4. pâat(e)ii de mo

/Nominal X (ptc) + **dè mo**/ *lit.* 'also/even being X (ptc),' occurs in situations in which 'being X' is one possibility among several. In other words, being X, too, is valid in addition to other possibilities. If the relationship between the nominal preceding **dè** and the following predicate represents that of a particle other than **ḡa** or **o**,[3] the particle is retained before **dè mo**. Examples:

   kêeki de mo tukûru   'make a cake or something'
   hôteru ni de mo 'tomaru   'stop at a hotel or someplace'
   yamâ e de mo 'iku   'go to the mountains or somewhere'
   tomódati karà de mo 'kariru   'borrow from a friend or someone'

Drills

A 1. **Odékake dèsu ka**⌇   **Ie, kyôo wa dekákemasèñ.**
   'Are you going out?'   'No, today I'm not going out.'
  2. **Oázuke dèsu ka**⌇   **Ie, kyôo wa azúkemasèñ.**
   'Are you going to check [it]?'   'No, today I'm not going to check [it].'
  3. **odasi**; 4. **oatumari**; 5. **oyari**; 6. **oai**

B 1. **Koré kara tyòtto dekákemàsu kara . .**   **A, seńsèe mo odékake da sòo desu yo**⌇
   'After this I'm going to go out for a bit, so . . .' (I'll see you later).   'Oh, the professor is also going out, I hear.'
  2. **Koré kara tyòtto norímàsu kara . .**   **A, seńsèe mo onóri da sòo desu yo**⌇
   'After this I'm going to ride [it] for a bit, so . . .' (I'll see you later).   'Oh, the professor is also going to ride [it], I hear.'

---

2. If **si** is included, the sentence becomes a minor sentence.
3. Of course the particles **wa, mo,** and **sika** do not apply here at all.

3. **kakénaosimàsu**; 4. **isóĝimàsu**; 5. **yorímàsu**; 6. **yasúmimàsu**; 7. **tukáimàsu**; 8. **miókurimàsu**

C 1. **Seńsèe wa, gakkoo ni odékake zya arimasèñ ka⤴**
'Isn't the professor going to go out to school?' or 'Hasn't the professor gone out to school?'

Êe, odekake desyoo?
'Yes, s/he is (going out), isn't s/he?' or 'Yes, s/he has (gone out), hasn't she?'

2. **Seńsèe wa, sińkàñseñ ni onóri zya arimasèñ ka⤴**
'Isn't the professor going to ride in the bullet train?' or 'Isn't the professor (riding) on the bullet train?'

Êe, onori desyoo?
'Yes, s/he is (going to ride or is riding), isn't s/he?'

3. **Wâseda no seńsèe ni oai**; 4. **zyûu-zi ni otati**; 5. **kabañ o oazuke**; 6. **seezi o oosie**; 7. **oyorokobi**; 8. **onaka osuki**

D 1. **Sore wa, nihóñĝo o reñsyuu-suru tamè no kikâi desu neʔ**
'That's a machine for practicing Japanese, isn't it?'

Êe, sonó tamè no kikâi desu.
'Yes, it's a machine for that purpose.'

2. **Sore wa, puróĝùramu o kiméru tamè no kâiĝi desu neʔ**
'That's a meeting to decide the program, isn't it?'

Êe, sonó tamè no kâiĝi desu.
'Yes, it's a meeting for that purpose.'

3. **nyûusu o wakáriyàsùku suru tamê no hanásikàta**; 4. **hikôoki o yoyáku-suru tamè no deńwabàñĝoo**; 5. **atárasìi gakkoo o tatêru tamê no okane**; 6. **daíĝaku o dète (i)nái hito ni beńkyoo-site morau tamê no tokórò**

E 1. **Konó hukù de keḱkòñsiki ni ikú tumori dèsu.**
'I intend to go to a wedding in this outfit.'

Âa, keḱkòñsiki ni ikú tamè no hukû na ñ desu neʔ
'Oh, so that's an outfit for going to a wedding, is it?'

2. **Konó kikài de têepu o kikú tumori dèsu.**
'I intend to listen to the tapes with this machine.'

Âa, têepu o kikú tamè no kikâi na ñ desu neʔ
'Oh, so that's a machine for listening to tapes, is it?'

3. **konó hòñ de kotóbà o sirábèru**; 4. **konó pèñ de komákài tîzu o kâku**; 5. **konó osara de kèeki o yaku**; 6. **konó heyà de eñkai o suru**; 7. **kono okane de kaimono o suru**

F 1. **Kotóbà o beńkyoo-si ni kità ñ desyoo?**
'(It's that) s/he came to study the language, didn't s/he?'

Hâi. Kotóbà o beńkyoo-suru tamè ni kità soo desu.
'Yes. They say s/he came for the purpose of studying the language.'

2. **Yosída-sañ ni ome ni kakàri ni kitâ ñ desyoo?**
'(It's that) s/he came to meet Mr/s. Yoshida, didn't s/he?'[4]

Hâi. Yosída-sañ ni ome ni kakàru tamê ni kitâ soo desu.
'Yes. They say s/he came for the purpose of meeting Mr/s. Yoshida.'

3. **ryokóo no kotò o kiki**; 4. **demáe o todòke**; 5. **dôresu o kari**; 6. **isu o narabe**; 7. **okáne o harài**

G 1. **Beńkyoo-si ni iràsita ñ desu ka⟋**
'(Is it that) you went in order to study?'

Ie. Motîroñ beńkyoo mo simàsita ḡa, sonó tamè ni ittà ñ zya nâi ñ desu.
'No. Of course, I studied, too, but (the fact is) it's not the case that I went for that reason.'

2. **Sibái o mì ni iràsita ñ desu ka⟋**
'(Is it that) you went in order to see some plays?'

Ie. Motîroñ sibái mo mimàsita ḡa, sonó tamè ni ittà ñ zya nâi ñ desu.
'No. Of course, I saw some plays, too, but (the fact is) it's not the case that I went for that reason.'

3. **tyuúka-ryòori o tâbe**; 4. **syotyóo ni ài**; 5. **mêisya ni mîte morai**; 6. **nîmotu o okuri**; 7. **okáne o azùke**

H 1. **Kono kîree na boosi kattè kita ñ desu ḡa, dôo desyoo.**
'I went and bought (lit. came having bought) this pretty hat; (but) how about it?'

Hee⟋ Watási no tamè ni kattè kite kudásàtta ñ desu ka⟋
'Wow! You mean you went and bought it for me?'

2. **Kono mezúrasìi omiyaḡe moráttè kita ñ desu ḡa, dôo desyoo.**
'I went and got (lit. came having received) this unusual souvenir; (but) how about it?'

Hee⟋ Watási no tamè ni moráttè kite kudásàtta ñ desu ka⟋
'Wow! You mean you went and got it for me?'

3. **omósiròi hôñ karite**; 4. **rakû na siḡoto moratte**; 5. **kimóti no ìi syâtu motte**; 6. **tukáiyasùi zîsyo katte**

I 1. **Îi apâato wa arímàsita?**
'Was there a good apartment?'

Îe neʕ Ki ní itta apâato ḡa mitúkaranài si, nedáñ wa takài si nêe.
'No—you know? In addition to not finding an apartment I liked, the prices are high, and—you know!'

2. **Îi sûutu wa arímàsita?**
'Was there a good suit?'

Îe neʕ Ki ní itta sùutu ḡa mitúkaranài si, nedáñ wa takài si nêe.

---

4. 'S/he' is a member of our in-group; deference is being shown to 'Mr/s. Yoshida.'

                                      'No—you know? In addition to not finding a suit I liked, the prices are high, and— you know!'

3. yoohuku; 4. tokórò; 5. hôñdana; 6. tûaa

J 1. **Âme g̃a hûtte (i)ru si, kazé mo hùite (i)ru si, dekáketaku nài desu nêe.**
'It's raining, and (what's more) the wind is blowing, and—I don't want to go out.'

    Dekákenàkute mo îi ñ zya arímasèñ ka⌒ Sonó hòo g̃a îi ka mo sirémasèñ yo⌒
'Isn't it (that it's) all right even if you don't go out? It might be better that way, you know.'

2. **Nemûi si, zikáñ mo osòi si, tosyôkañ ni ikítaku nài desu nêe.**
'I'm sleepy, and (what's more) it (lit. the time) is late, and—I don't want to go to the library.'

    Ikánàkute mo îi ñ zya arímasèñ ka⌒ Sonó hòo g̃a îi ka mo sirémasèñ yo⌒
'Isn't it (that it's) all right even if you don't go? It might be better that way, you know.'

3. huyû g̃a samûi/monó no nedañ mo takài/koñna tokorò ni itáku nài; 4. deñsya g̃a kòmu/kíppu mo kainikùi/goóruden-uìiku ni ryokóo-sitaku nài; 5. irô g̃a 'ki ni iranai/tyôtto oókisug̃ìru/kitáku nài; 6. azí g̃a kosug̃ìru/sâabisu mo warûi/anó misè de tabétàku nâi; 7. kotóbà g̃a wakárànai/naíyoo mo tumarànai/anó èeg̃a mitàku nâi

K 1. **Morímoto-kuñ g̃a kàette kimâsita yo⌒**
'Morimoto came back!'

    Sôo desu ka. Dôko kara kâette kitâ ñ desu ka⌒
'Did he! Where is it that he came back from?'

2. **Yamanaka-sañ g̃a kodómo o turete kimàsita yo⌒**
'Mr/s. Yamanaka brought (lit. came bringing along) a child!'

    Sôo desu ka. Dôko kara turétè kita ñ desu ka⌒
'Did s/he! Where is it that s/he brought the child from?'

3. gaíkoku no monò g̃a hâitte; 4. oózee arùite; 5. otókò mo oñ́nà mo watatte; 6. hisyô g̃a isôide; 7. tâkusii ni notte

L 1. **Asoko wa, kîree na burâusu g̃a arímàsu nêe. Dê mo, sukâato wa dôo desu ka⌒**
'That place has pretty blouses, doesn't it! But how are their skirts?'

    A, sukâato mo, kîree na no g̃a arímàsu yo⌒
'Oh, they have pretty ones in skirts, too.'

2. **Asoko wa, kimóti no ìi wasítu g̃a arimàsu nêe. Dê mo, yóoma wa dòo desu ka⌒**
'That place has pleasant Japanese-style rooms, doesn't it! But how are their Western-style rooms?'

    A, yooma mo, kimóti no ìi no g̃a arímàsu yo⌒
'Oh, they have pleasant ones in Western-style rooms, too.'

3. oísii koohìi/kootya; 4. rippa na kyoositu/tosyôkañ; 5. bêñri na tikatetu/bâsu; 6. atárasìi yasai/nikû ya 'sakana; 7. yuúmee na susìya/teñpuraya

M 1. **Pâat(e)ii de mo âru ñ desu ka⤴**   Pâat(e)ii? Êe, tyôtto⁵ âru ñ desu.
'(Is it that) there's a party or   'A party? Yes, (it's that) there is.'
something?'

2. **Kazé dè mo hiítà ñ desu ka⤴**   Kaze? Êe, tyôtto hiítà ñ desu.
'(Is it that) you caught a cold or   'A cold? Yes, (it's that) I did (catch).'
something?'

3. kakíkàta/reñsyuu-suru; 4. kaímono nì/dekakeru; 5. gaikoku e/ìttè (i)ta; 6. keḱkòñsiki ni/dêru

N 1. **Koóhìi de mo nomímasèñ ka⤴**   Koóhìi? Îi desu nêe. Nomímasyòo.
'Won't you have some coffee or   'Coffee? That'll be great! Let's have some.'
something?'

2. **Zêmi no señsèe ni de mo aímasèñ**   Zêmi no señsèe ni? Îi desu nêe.
ka⤴   Aímasyòo.
'Wouldn't you [like to] see the   'The seminar professor? That'll be great!
seminar professor or somebody?'   Let's see him/her.'

3. huráñsu-ryòori/tâbe ni ikímasèñ; 4. tiísài miñsyuku ni/tomárimasèñ; 5. Hoḱkàidoo de/atúmarimasèñ; 6. hâru ni/ryokóo-simasèñ

O 1. **Hasímoto-sañ te iù no wa, asoko no**   Sôo, sôo. Asoko no 'ano boósi o kabùtte
boósi o kabùtte (i)ru hitô desu ka⤴   (i)ru hito neʃ Aré ḡa Hasimoto-sañ dèsu.
'Is (the one named) Mr/s. Hashimoto   'Yes. That person over there wearing a
the person over there wearing a hat?'   hat—right? *That's* Mr/s. Hashimoto.'

2. **Yamánaka Mìtiko-sañ te iû no wa,**   Sôo, sôo. Asoko no 'ano aôi dôresu o
asoko no aôi dôresu o kité (i)ru hitò   'kite (i)ru hito neʃ Aré ḡa Yamanaka
desu ka⤴   Mìtiko-sañ desu.
'Is (the one named) Michiko   'Yes. That person over there wearing a
Yamanaka the person over there   blue dress—right? *That's* Michiko
wearing a blue dress?'   Yamanaka.'

3. Yosida-sañ/ziípañ o haite (i)ru hitô; 4. Nôguti-kuñ/zyâñpaa o kité (i)ru hitò; 5. Kêe-tyañ/kawáii sukâato o 'haite (i)ru ko; 6. Ôono-sañ/sirôi waisyatu o kite, guríiñ no surâkkusu o haíte (i)ru hito

P 1. **Tanáka-sañ ḡa ataràsìku katta**   Êe, pâat(e)ii ni haíte iku tamè ni katta
sukàato desu ka⤴   sòo desu.
'Is this the skirt which Ms. Tanaka   'Yes. I hear she bought it to wear to a
bought recently (*lit.* newly bought)?'   party.'

2. **Tanáka-sañ ḡa ataràsìku katta kutù**   Êe, pâat(e)ii ni haíte iku tamè ni katta
desu ka⤴   sòo desu.

---

5. **Tyôtto** in the responses of this drill serves merely to reduce the importance of the statement.

'Are these the shoes which Mr/s. Tanaka bought recently (*lit.* newly bought)?'	'Yes. I hear s/he bought them to wear to a party.'

3. **boosi**; 4. **syâtu**; 5. **sebiro**; 6. **sûutu**; 7. **hukû**

Q 1. **Kûrôku narímàsu yo**↗ 'You're going to get tan (*lit.* become black)!'	**Sôo desyoo nêe. Añmari kùròku narítàku nâi keredo, sikáta ḡa nài desu ne**ʃ 'I suppose. I don't want to get too tan, but I can't help it, can I!'
2. **Himá ni narimàsu yo**↗ 'You're going to have nothing to do (*lit.* become free time)!'	**Sôo desyoo nêe. Añmari hima ni naritàku nâi keredo, sikáta ḡa nài desu ne**ʃ 'I suppose. I don't want to become too free, but I can't help it, can I!'

3. **isóḡasìku**; 4. **nemuku**; 5. **yuumee ni**; 6. **hetâ ni**; 7. **sukî ni**; 8. **osoku**

• Repeat this drill, replacing **sikata** with **syoo** in the responses.

R 1. **Oókìi zîsyo, kasíte aḡemasyòo ka.** 'Shall I lend you a big dictionary?'	**Iya, sekkakù desu kedo, tiísài no ni nârete (i)ru kara, tiísài no de kêkkoo desu.** 'No, thank you (i.e., despite your kindness); I'm used to a small one, so (being) the small one will do.'
2. **Yawárakài ohútòñ, siíte aḡemasyòo ka.** 'Shall I spread a soft futon?'	**Iya, sekkakù desu kedo, katâi no ni nârete (i)ru kara, katâi no de kêkkoo desu.** 'No, thank you (i.e., despite your kindness); I'm used to a firm one, so (being) the firm one will do.'

3. **kôi otya/irete**; 4. **tiísài surîppa/kasite**; 5. **maé no hòo no sêki/tôtte**; 6. **atátakài tokoro/tanôñde**; 7. **atárasìi kyoókàsyo/katte**

Application Exercises

(In all of the following exercises, remember that the purpose is to practice and utilize what you have already learned, NOT to plot out questions and answers in English and fall into the 'what's the Japanese word for ——?' trap as you translate literally into Japanese of the kind that native speakers have never dreamed of using!)

A1. Discuss clothing by asking your Japanese instructor about Japan: What do children wear to school? What do office workers/part-time student workers/students/professors wear? When do Japanese wear Japanese-style clothing? etc. Next, have your instructor ask you similar questions about your society.

2. Using appropriate pictures from magazines, practice the newly introduced clothing

vocabulary together with a review of sentence modifiers. Examples: About how old is the person wearing the white dress and black shoes? Where do you suppose the person wearing the hat and heavy coat is going? What kind of work do you think the woman does who is wearing the gray suit?

3. Discuss clothing for special purposes: Ask and answer questions involving —— **tamê no hukû.** Example: **Hirôoeñ ni ikú tamè no hukû wa, dôñna hukû desyoo ka.**

4. Using the following statements as conclusions, provide appropriate build-ups, using clauses ending in **si**:

(a) **Sûĝôku îi tokórò desu nêe.**

(b) **Dekînai gakúsee dèsu nêe.**

(c) **Taíheñ na hì desita.**

(d) **Tukâretyatta.**

(e) **Tyôtto yasûñde, otyá dè mo nomítài to omôtte . .**

(f) **Koñna siĝoto yamétaku nàttyatta.**

B. Core Conversations: Substitution

Follow the usual procedures, making appropriate substitutions in the Core Conversations, followed by questioning on the contents.

SECTION B

Core Conversations

1(J)a. **Kore kara kikâete ikímàsu no de, zikáñ ĝa kakarimàsu kara, matâzu ni 'osaki ni irâsite kudasai.**

    (N) **Iya, kamáimasèñ yo⌒ Zikañ wa zyuúbuñ arimàsu kara, oísoĝi ni naránai de kudasai.**

b. **Sumímasèñ.**

2(J)a. **Okáeri-nasài.**

    (N)a. **Tadaima. Yamaĝuti-sañ. Ôobaa kinâi de dekákerù ñ desu ka⌒**

b. **Aˊttakài sêetaa kité (i)rù si, buátui kutùsita haíte irù kara . .**

    b. **Dê mo, neń no tamè ni, uwáĝi o motte (i)tta hòo ĝa îi to omóimàsu kedo ne!**

3(J)a. **Koo iu baai wa, nâni o kité ikù ñ desyoo ka.**

    (N)a. **Mâa, gaíkoku karà no okyákusañ mo mièru si, kânari h(u)ôomaru na monò desu si . .**

b. **Zyâa, kimóno wa dòo desyoo.**

    b. **Âa, îi ka mo sirémasèñ nêe.**

4(N)a. Îtu mo kâkete (i)ru mêḡane to onázi dèsu ka⤴

b. Suzuki-sañ wa, mêḡane mo yôku niâu kedo, koñtàkuto mo bêñri da sôo desu yo⤴

(J)a. Ie, dôo mo minîkùkute syoó ḡa nài ñ de nêe. Atárasìi no ni kaétà ñ desu yo.

b. Are wa mê ni rêñzu o irérù ñ desyo(o)? Kañḡàeta dakê de, kimóti ḡa wàrùku narímàsu yo.

ENGLISH EQUIVALENTS

1(J)a. Since I'm going to change now before going on (*lit.* I'll go having changed), it will take time, so you go ahead without waiting.

b. Thanks./I'm sorry.

2(J)a. Hello. You're back!

b. I'm wearing a warm sweater, and (I'm wearing) thick socks, so . . . (there's no need for concern).

3(J)a. In cases like this, what do you suppose (it is that) you wear?

b. Then how would a kimono be?

4(N)a. Are those the same as the glasses you're always wearing?

b. In your case, Mr/s. Suzuki, eyeglasses are becoming, too, but contact [lenses] are also convenient, I hear.

(N) No, it doesn't matter. There's plenty of time, so please don't hurry.

(N)a. Hello. Mrs. Yamaguchi. Do you mean you're going out without (putting on) a coat?

b. But I think you'd better take a jacket to be on the safe side, but . . . (don't you agree!)

(N)a. Well, guests from foreign countries will also attend, and it's a rather formal thing, and . . . (so this means a certain type of clothing).

b. Oh, maybe that would be good, wouldn't it!

(J)a. No, there was (*lit.* being) nothing I could do about how hard they were to see with—you know? (It's that) I changed to new ones.

b. They involve putting lenses into your eyes—right? I feel awful just to have thought about it!

BREAKDOWNS
(AND SUPPLEMENTARY VOCABULARY)

1. **kikáèru ~ kiğáèru /-ru;**
   kikâeta ~ kiğâeta/ — change clothing (worn on the body)
   kikâete iku — go having changed; change and go (i.e., change before going)

   matâzu ni (SP1), (SP2) *or*
   matânai de (SP2) — without waiting; instead of waiting
   zyuúbùñ /na/ — enough, plenty
   isóğàzu ni *or*
   isóğànai de — without hurrying; instead of hurrying
   isóğànai de kudasai *or*
   oísoği ni naránai↑ de kudasai (SP2) — please don't hurry

2. **ôobaa** — (over)coat, topcoat
   kizu ni *or*
   kinâi de — without wearing; instead of wearing (on the body)

   sêetaa — sweater
   +**atui /-katta/** *or*
   buatui /-katta/ — is thick
   +**usui /-katta/** — is thin
   kutûsita — socks, stockings
   +**tâbi** — bifurcated socks (Japanese-style)
   nêñ — care, caution
   neń no tamè — for the sake of caution, to be on the safe side
   uwağì — jacket

3. **baai** — case, circumstance
   koo iu baai wa — case(s) like this (at least)
   h(u)ôomaru /na/ — formal
   kimono — kimono
   +**yukata** — light, cotton kimono
   +**ôbi** — Japanese sash
   +**ôbi o simêru** *or*
   +**ôbi o 'suru** — put on *or* wear an obi

4. **mêğane** — eyeglasses
   mêğane o kakêru — put on *or* wear eyeglasses
   mêğane o kâkete (i)ru — be wearing eyeglasses
   miníkùi /-katta/ — is hard to see with *or* look at
   dôo mo miníkùi — is extremely hard to see with *or* look at

minîkùkute syoó g̃a nài	there's no way of avoiding their being hard to see with or look at
syoó g̃a nài no de ʼkaeru	change [something], there being no way out
atárasìi no ni ʼkaeru	change to new ones
niâu /-u; niâtta/	suit, become [someone]
końtàkuto(-rèñzu)	contact lens(es)
rêñzu	lens(es)
+**końtàkuto(-rèñzu) o ʼsuru**	put in *or* wear contacts
kañg̃aèru /-ru; kañg̃àeta/	think over, consider, ponder
kañg̃àeta dakê de (SP3)	(being) just having thought about it
kimóti g̃a wàrùku naru	get to feel bad

MISCELLANEOUS NOTES

1. CC1 is a conversation between Mrs. Carter, the Japanese wife (J) of a banker, and a neighborhood acquaintance, Sue Brown (N), a student/part-time worker. Both use careful-style with distal predicates and examples of honorific-polite ↑ verbals in their direct **kudásài** patterns.

(J)a. **Kikáèru** is a compound of verbal stem **ki** (from **kiru**) and **kaeru** 'change.' There is an alternate form which voices the initial **k** of **kaeru** to **g̃** (**kig̃áèru**). **Kaeru** 'change (something)' is the transitive, operational partner of intransitive, affective **kawaru** '(something) changes.'[6] **Kaeru** was originally *****kaweru** (cf. **tomeru/tomaru**), but **w** has been lost in modern Japanese everywhere except before **a**. Note also **noríkaèru** 'change vehicles,' 'transfer,' and **torikaeru** 'exchange.' Do not confuse transitive vowel verbal **kae-ru** with intransitive consonant verbal **kâer-u** 'return (home).'

(J)b. Mrs. Carter is grateful for both Sue Brown's willingness to wait and her assurances that there is no hurry, but she is sorry to keep Sue waiting.

2. In CC2, Smith (N), a student, expresses concern that his landlady (J) may not be dressed warmly enough as she prepares to go out. Smith's speech style is careful, with distal-style predicates, even before **kedo**. The landlady's only utterance has nonfinal predicates, all direct-style.

(N)a. **Ôobaa**, a shortening of **oóbaakòoto**, refers to a full-length coat, worn by men or women. **Uwag̃i** is a compound of **ue** and **ki** (from **kiru**, with voicing of the initial consonant: **ki > g̃i**). **Ue** comes from an earlier *****uwe** (see the preceding note on **kaeru**) and demonstrates a common phenomenon, by which word-final **e** changes to **a** when that word becomes the initial part of a compound. Compare /**âme** + **to**/ > **amâdo** 'storm doors' and /**âme** + **kâsa**/ > **amág̃àsa** 'rain umbrella.'

Uwag̃i, which may refer to suit jackets, blazers, sports jackets, etc., contrasts with **zyâñpaa**, an informal windbreaker-type jacket.

(J)b. Note the accent contrast in **atûi** 'is hot' and **atui** 'is thick.' However, the contrast disappears before **no, desu, kara**, etc., where both are accented.

---

6. Note that **kawaru** 'exchange (with)' is operational: **hisyô to kawaru** 'exchange places with the secretary.'

Usui previously occurred in reference to weak coffee and tea, and light colors as the opposite of **kôi**.

(N)b. Note the politeness and nonconfrontation reflected in the student's advice to his landlady: 'This is what I think, but (you may have other ideas, but) you probably agree, don't you!'
Note **neñ o ireru** 'be extra careful, conscientious.'

3. In CC3, the Japanese secretary, who has received an invitation to a formal social event, is seeking advice on what to wear from Mr. Carter. As usual, their speech style is careful, with distal-style final predicates. Note also the secretary's use of indirect **desyòo** questions, and Mr. Carter's use of distal-style before **si** at the end of a minor sentence.

(J)a. **Baai** has an alternate pronunciation, **bawai**. Note: **watasi no baai wa** 'in my case'; **hituyoo na baai** 'a case of necessity'; **baai ni yotte** 'depending on circumstances'; **koó sinàkutya 'ikenai baai** 'a case of having to do it like this.' Note the use of the extended predicate in asking what it is people in general wear, in the given circumstances. Compare **Nâni o kité ikimàsu ka⤴** 'What are you going to wear?' which usually refers specifically to the person addressed.

(J)b. **Kimono**, a compound of **ki** (from **kiru**) and **mono**, refers only to particular items of Japanese clothing.
Yukata, besides being worn as summer kimono, are regularly issued in Japanese hotels and inns as sleeping garments.

4. In CC4, Mr. Suzuki and his business colleague, Mr. Carter, are discussing Mr. Suzuki's new glasses. As usual, these two individuals use careful-style, with distal-style final predicates, when talking to each other.

(J)a. **Miníkùi** covers not only difficulty in reference to glasses that are hard to see with or see through; it is also used in reference to anything or anybody that is difficult to look at—i.e., is unattractive or ugly. Note **X o kaeru** 'change X'; **Y ni kaeru** 'change into Y'; **X o 'Y ni kaeru** 'change X into Y.'

(N)b. Note how (N) tactfully introduces the subject of contact lenses without suggesting any negative criticism of Suzuki's new glasses.
Niâu is an intransitive, affective consonant verbal. Note: **X ni niâu** 'suit X,' 'be becoming to X.'

(J)b. Here again the extended predicate refers to general applicability: 'These contact lenses you are talking about involve putting lenses into one's eyes—right?' Compare **Rêñzu o irérù desyoo?** which suggests the addressee as the specific referent.
Kañgaèru is a transitive, operational vowel verbal. Whereas **omôu** refers to having thoughts, **kañgaèru** implies thinking about, pondering, considering (**X o kañgaèru** 'consider X,' 'think about X'). Note **kañgàete simau** 'think twice about a matter.'

Structural Patterns

1. ALTERNATE NEGATIVE STEM IN **-(a)zu**

We have already encountered alternate forms in Japanese which result from a different order of development. For example, starting out with the verbal **mâtu**, if we derive the distal-style equivalent and then negate it, we produce the form **matímasèñ**; but if we negate it first and *then* form the distal-style equivalent, we arrive at **matânai desu**.

Prior to this lesson, our only adjectival stem form was formed by adding **-ku** to an adjectival root. This rule covered all adjectivals, including negative adjectivals, which are derived from verbals. Thus:

Imperfective	Root	Stem
yasûi	yasu	yâsûku
ikitai	ikita	ikitaku
ikanai	ikana	ikanaku

However, there is an alternate negative stem form which is derived directly from the affirmative verbal root. In this case, the ending combines the concepts of /negation + stem/. The ending is **-zu** for vowel verbals and **-azu** for consonant verbals. Examples:

	Root	Alternate Negative Stem
Vowel Verbals		
tabêru 'eat'	tabe	tabêzu
akeru 'open'	ake	akezu
kaeru 'change'	kae	kaezu
mîru 'look at'	mi	mîzu
kiru 'put on'	ki	kizu
iru 'be located' (animate)	i	izu
Consonant Verbals		
kîru 'cut'	kir	kirâzu
kâeru 'return'	kaer	kaérazu
mâtu 'wait'	mat	matâzu
hanâsu 'talk'	hanas	hanásazu
nômu 'drink'	nom	nomâzu
ośsyàru ↑ 'say,' 'be called'	ossyar	ośsyaràzu
Irregular Verbals		
suru 'do'	su/si/se	sezu
kûru 'come'	ku/ki/ko	kôzu

The **-(a)zu**-form of an accented verbal is also accented, with the accent occurring on the next-to-last mora. Corresponding forms for **âru** and **gozâru**⁺ 'be located' (inanimate) are lacking.

2. USES OF **-(a)zu/-(a)nai de**

We have already been introduced to uses of the negative stem in **-naku** and the negative gerund in **-nakute**. Examples:

(a) **Zyûĝyoo ni dênaku narímàsita.** 'I don't go to class any more.' (*lit.* 'I became not-attending-class.')

(b) **Zyûĝyoo ni denâkute, wakâru desyoo ka.** 'Do you suppose I'll understand, not having gone to class?'

In (a), the **-ku** pattern describes the goal of **nâru**, i.e., the situation of non-occurrence (**dênai**) that came to be. In (b), the gerund, as usual, describes an activity or state that has been actualized prior to that of the predicate it modifies. In other words, the question relates to whether there will be understanding that presupposes non-attendance in class.

We now introduce two new patterns which cover a different kind of situation.

1. The new alternate negative stem followed by the particle **ni** of manner (= verbal root + **-(a)zu ni**) describes a situation in which one activity (represented by a following predicate) takes place without the occurrence of another. There is no overt indication that the activity is affected by or depends on or results from the non-occurrence of the other; the **-(a)zu ni** pattern describes the manner in which the activity occurs: 'non-doing-ly,' as it were. Examples:

> **Zyûĝyoo ni dêzu ni, uti de yasúmimàsita.** 'I took it easy at home, without (i.e., instead of) going to class.'
>
> **Tomodati o matâzu ni, kaérimasyòo.** 'Let's go home without (*or* instead of) waiting for our friends.'
>
> **Kâre wa, naní mo tabèzu ni, gakkoo ni ittyatta.** 'He went off to school without eating anything.'
>
> **Wasurezu ni, seńsèe ni deńwa site kudasài.** 'Don't forget to telephone the doctor.' (*lit.* 'Telephone without forgetting.')

2. An alternate to the **-(a)zu ni** sequence in the pattern described above is /imperfective negative adjectival + copula gerund **dè**/. The resulting meaning is similar, although the construction is very different. In this case we are introducing an actualized situation (the gerund **dè**) involving generalized non-occurrence (**-[à]nai**).

In all the examples above, **-(a)zu ni** can be replaced by the corresponding **-(à)nài de** form with little change in overall meaning. Thus:

> **Tomodati o matânai de, kaérimasyòo.** *lit.* 'Let's go home, having actualized a non-waiting for our friends.'

Here the gerund **de** suggests actualization, but of a *non-occurring* rather than *non-occurred* variety. Contrast:

> **Tomodati o matânakute, kâiĝi ni ma ní aimàsita.** 'Not having waited for my friends, I was on time for the conference.'

The **-(à)nài de** pattern differs from the **-(a)zu ni** pattern in its use in negative requests. Note the following:

> **Yaménài de kudasai.** 'Please don't quit.'
>
> **Isóĝanai de kurémaseń ka.** 'Would you not go fast?'
>
> **Daré ni mo ossyarànai de kudásaimaseń ka.** 'Would you be kind enough not to tell anyone?'

In these examples, **-(a)zu ni** cannot replace **-(à)nài de**: you are, after all, requesting an actualization. In these requests, the **-(à)nài de** sequence is followed immediately, without pause, by the expression of giving, to form a single, complex pattern. This is parallel to corresponding affirmative requests. Contrast these examples, which contain comma intonation:

> **Mînai de, kudásài.** *or*
>
> **Mîzu ni, kudásài.** 'Please give [it] to me, without looking at it.'

Negative request patterns occur as less direct, and therefore more polite, negative responses to requests for permission, as compared with prohibition patterns. Compare:

    Hâitte mo îi desu ka⤻   'May I come in?'

        Haíránai de kudasai.   'Please don't (come in).' *or*

        Hâittya ikémaseǹ.   'You mustn't (come in).'

The second reply is more direct and markedly stronger.

An affirmative gerund may occur in sentence-final position (with or without following sentence-particle[s]) as a direct-style, casual request. Negatives in **-(a)nài de** follow the same patterning:

    Haíránai de. *or*

    Haíránai de yo./ne⤴   'Don't come in!'

3. kańgàeta dakê

Dakê was previously introduced following nominals:

    Soré dakè desu.   'That's all.' (*lit.* 'It's just that.')

    Sukôsi dake onéḡai-simàsu.   'I'd like just a little.'

    Katta no wa, zîsyo dakê desu.   'What I bought was (*lit.* is) just a dictionary.'

    Kono-ḡoro, zêmi dakê ni dête (i)masu.   'I'm attending just the seminar these days.'

Dakê may also follow predicates. Consider the following examples:

    Oókìi desu nêe. . . . Oókìi dakê desu yo. Zeńzeñ yakù ni tatímaseǹ.   'Isn't it big?' . . . 'All it is is big. It's of no use.'

    Ano gakusee, kîree desu nêe. . . . Kîree na dakê desu yo. Beńkyoo-sinài si, zyû-ḡyoo ni dênai si . .   'Isn't that student pretty!' . . . 'All she is is pretty. She doesn't study, and she doesn't attend classes, and . . .'

    Dekiru dake[7] **'sore o usúku kìtte kudasai.**   'Please cut that as thin as possible (*lit.* to the extent possible).'

    Sore o mîta dakê de, kimóti ḡa heñ ni nâttyatta.   'Just having looked at that I ended up feeling strange.'

The underlying meaning of **dakê** is 'extent.' In its uses following a predicate, it is clearly a nominal, demonstrated conclusively by the occurrence of the **na** alternate of the copula immediately before it. However, its occurrence immediately following nominals suggests that structurally it is a particle. Probably the simplest way to treat this kind of situation is to recognize two **dakê**—one a nominal, preceded by sentence modifiers, and the other a particle, following nominals and /nominal + particle/ phrases. (Compare English, with its verb 'practice' and noun 'practice,' its adverb 'far' and adjective 'far,' for example.)

Drills

A 1. **Tyańto reńraku-sitè kara ittà ñ desu ka⤻**   **Ie, reńraku-sinài de ittyattà ñ desu.**   'No, (the fact is) I went off without making

---

7. **Dekiru dake** alternates with **narubeku**, of similar meaning.

  '(Is it the case that) you went after making contact properly?'

2. **Tyañto deñki kesítè kara ittà ñ desu ka⤸**
'(Is it the case that) you went after having turned off the lights as you should?'

  contact.'

  Ie, deñki kesánài de ittyattà ñ desu.
'No, (the fact is) I ended up going without turning them off.'

3. **katázùkete**; 4. **harâtte**; 5. **kutû kaete**; 6. **teñki-yòhoo kiite**; 7. **âkatyañ nekasite**; 8. **kotóbà ni nârete**

- Repeat this drill, replacing the **-(à)nài de** forms in the responses with the corresponding **-(a)zu ni** forms.

B 1. **Mâtte kara ittà no?**
'(Is it that) you went after having waited?'

  Iya, matâzu ni ittyatta.
'No, I went off without waiting.'

2. **Sirâbete kara kiítà no?**
'(Is it that) you asked after having checked?'

  Iya, sirábèzu ni kiityatta.
'No, I ended up asking without checking.'

3. **yasûñde/kitâ**; 4. **kañḡaete/kâita**; 5. **kiḡaete/sita**; 6. **kité mìte/katta**; 7. **mâdo sîmete/dekaketa**

- Repeat this drill, replacing the **-(a)zu ni** forms with the corresponding **-(à)nài de** forms.

C 1. **Asita deñwa o iremàsu kara . .**
'I'll put in a call tomorrow, so . . .' (please wait).

  Wasúrenài de iréte kudasài neʃ Mâtte (i)masu kara . .
'Please don't forget (to put in [the call])—O.K.? Because I'll be waiting.'

2. **Asita îi no o mitúkemàsu kara . .**
'I'll locate a good one tomorrow, so . . .' (please wait).

  Wasúrenài de mitúkete kudasài neʃ Mâtte (i)masu kara . .
'Please don't forget to locate [one]—O.K.? Because I'll be waiting.'

3. **surîppa o mótte kimàsu**; 4. **sêetaa o todókemàsu**; 5. **Nârita made mukáe ni ikimàsu**; 6. **zikáñ o kimemàsu**; 7. **teḡámi o dasimàsu**

- Repeat this drill, replacing the **-(à)nài de** forms in the responses with the corresponding **-(a)zu ni** forms.

D 1. **Isóḡànakute mo îi desu ka⤸**
'Is it all right even if I don't hurry?'

  To iu yòri, isóḡanai de kudasai.
'Rather than saying that, please don't hurry.'

2. **Kiḡáènakute mo îi desu ka⤸**
'Is it all right even if I don't change (clothes)?'

  To iu yòri, kiḡáenai de kudasai.
'Rather than saying that, please don't change.'

3. **matânakute**; 4. **narábenàkute**; 5. **reñsyuu-sinàkute**; 6. **okósànakute**; 7. **surîppa hakánakute**

E 1. **Kôṅpa no koto, kaṅḡaemàsita?**
'Did you think about the party?'

Êe, dê mo, tyôtto kaṅḡaeta dakê de, iyâ ni nâttyatte . .
'Yes, but I became fed up just having thought about it a little, and . . .' (I've done little more).

2. **Ôbi no nedaṅ, mimâsita?**
'Did you see the price of the obi?'

Êe, dê mo, tyôtto mîta dakê de, iyâ ni nâttyatte . .
'Yes, but I became fed up just having glanced at it, and . . .' (I didn't buy it).

3. **seṅsèe no hanásì/kikímàsita**; 4. **tabako/suímàsita**; 5. **oryôori/tabémàsita**; 6. **kêezai no hôṅ/sirábemàsita**

F 1. **Zimûsyo katázùkete, kaḡî mo kâkete kitâ ṅ desyoo?**
'(It's that) you straightened up the office and locked it, too [before you came] (lit. came having straightened up)—right?'

Iya, katázùketa dakê de, kaḡî wa kakêzu ni kîtyatta. Awátetè (i)ta kara . .
'No, I just straightened it up and I ended up coming without locking it. I was flustered, so . . .' (that explains it).

2. **Isya e itte, kusúri mo morattè kita ṅ desyoo?**
'(It's that) you went to the doctor['s] and got some medicine, too, [before you came]—right?'

Iya, ítta dakê de, kusuri wa moráwàzu ni kîtyatta. Awátetè (i)ta kara . .
'No, I just went [there] and ended up coming without getting any medicine. I was flustered, so . . .' (that explains it).

3. **heyâ yoyaku-site/nedaṅ mo kiite**; 4. **omoi mono hakoṅde moratte/oree mo aḡete**; 5. **tûaa no kotô kiite/okáne mo haràtte**

G 1. **Kono aťtakài sêetaa, kité iku tumori dà si . .**
'I intend to wear this warm sweater, and . . .' (I'll have other things to keep me warm).

Dê mo, neṅ no tamè ni, moó itì-mai moťte (i)tta hòo ḡa îi desu yo
'But you'd better take one more, just in case.'

2. **Kono oókìi kâsa, moťte iku tumori dà si . .**
'We intend to take this big umbrella, and . . .' (we'll have other things to protect us against the rain).

Dê mo, neṅ no tamè ni, moó ìp-poṅ moťte (i)tta hòo ḡa îi desu yo
'But you'd better take one more, just in case.'

3. **buátui kutùsita/haite**; 4. **atárasìi yukata/kite**; 5. **aťtakài zûboṅ/haite**; 6. **oókìi uwaḡi/kite**; 7. **huyú no sùutu/kite**

H 1. **Kimóno o kite (i)rassyaimàsu ka**
'Are you going to wear a kimono?'

Ie, koo iu baai wa, kimono wa kité (i)kanai hòo ḡa îi to omôtte . .

2. **Ziípañ o haite (i)rassyaimàsu ka↗**
 'Are you going to wear jeans?'

 Ie, koo iu baai wa, ziipañ wa haíte (i)kanai hòo ga îi to omôtte . .
 'No, [since I've been] thinking that it's better not to wear jeans in this kind of situation . . .' (I'm not wearing them).

 'No, [since I've been] thinking that it's better not to wear a kimono in this kind of situation . . .' (I'm not wearing one).

3. **kurôi hukû o kite**; 4. **geta o haite**; 5. **mêḡane o kâkete**; 6. **koñtàkuto o site**; 7. **ôobaa o môtte**

I 1. **Konaida no señsèe no kooeñ wa, yôku wakâtta kedo; kyôo wa dôo desyoo nêe.**
 'The professor's lecture the other day I understood well, but I wonder how it's going to be today.'

 Wakáràniai baai wa, dôo surû ñ desu ka↗
 'What is it you'll do in case you don't understand?'

2. **Ano sibai wa, kippu ḡa takusañ àtta kedo; koré wa dòo desyoo nêe.**
 'For that play (you know about) there were lots of tickets, but I wonder how it's going to be [for] this one.'

 Nâi baai wa, dôo surû ñ desu ka↗
 'What is it you'll do in case there aren't any?'

3. **señsyuu wa, hâreta/koñsyuu**; 4. **tiísài tokî wa, kawáìi hukû ḡa yôku niâtta/îma**; 5. **Huráñsu no kotobà ni wa, sûḡu nâreta/rosiago**; 6. **Yamâḡuti-sañ no tokóro wa, sûḡu mitukatta/Yosida-sañ no otaku**

J 1. **Nihoñḡo ḡa tuúzinai baai mo àru desyoo kedo; soñna tokì ni wa, dôo nasaimasu ka↗**
 'There probably are also circumstances when Japanese isn't comprehensible (*lit.* doesn't get through); what do you do at times like that?'

 Sôo desu nêe. Mâa, taitee no baai wa, tuúzimàsu kara nêe.
 'Hmm. Well, in most circumstances, it's comprehensible (*lit.* it gets through), so . . .' (I really can't answer).

2. **Ki ní iru monò ḡa mitúkaranai baai mo àru desyoo kedo; soñna tokì ni wa, dôo nasaimasu ka↗**
 'There probably are also circumstances when things that appeal to you can't be found; what do you do at times like that?'

 Sôo desu nêe. Mâa, taitee no baai wa, mitúkarimàsu kara nêe.
 'Hmm. Well, in most circumstances, [something] can be found, so . . .' (I really can't answer).

3. **kiǵáèru zikañ ḡa nâi**; 4. **tanôñda monô o suḡu motte kònai**; 5. **tosyôkañ ḡa 'aite (i)nai**; 6. **nâni o itte (i)rù no ka wakárànai**; 7. **teḡami ḡa todókànai**

K 1. **Konó kutùsita wa?**
'What about these socks?'

Kutûsita? Âa, sore wa daré mo hakanài kara ..
'Socks? Oh, those no one is going to wear, so . . .' (don't worry about them).

2. **Kono yukata wa?**
'What about this yukata?'

Yukata? Âa, sore wa daré mo kinài kara ..
'Yukata? Oh, that no one is going to wear, so . . .' (don't worry about it).

3. **boosi**; 4. **uwaḡi**; 5. **zoori**; 6. **mêḡane**; 7. **surâkkusu**

L 1. **Sonó mèḡane, miyásùi?**
'Are those eyeglasses easy to see with?'

Ñ̂ñ↙ Minîkùkute siyóo ḡa nài no de, hoká nò ni kaéru tumori nà ñ da.[8]
'No, they're [so] hard to see with it's impossible, so I plan to change to other ones.'

2. **Sono zoori, hakíyasùi?**
'Are those Japanese sandals easy to (put on and) wear?'

Ñ̂ñ↙ Hakínikùkute siyóo ḡa nài no de, hoká nò ni kaéru tumori nà ñ da.
'No, they're [so] hard to (put on and) wear it's impossible, so I plan to change to other ones.'

3. **rêñzu/tukáiyasùi**; 4. **ôobaa/kiyásùi**; 5. **kabañ/motíyasùi**; 6. **isu/suwáriyasùi**

M 1. **Sonó mèḡane, niâu ñ zya arímaseñ ka↙**
'It's not the case that those glasses are becoming?'

Iya, añmari niawànai si, sore ni, nedáñ mo takài desu kara; kaú no wa, tyôtto kañḡaetyaimasu[9] **nêe.**
'No, they are not very becoming, and what's more, the price is high, so I'll just think twice about buying them.'

2. **Sonó sèetaa, attakài ñ zya arimaseñ ka↙**
'It's not the case that that sweater is warm?'

Iya, añmari attàkàku nâi si, sore ni, nedáñ mo takài desu kara; kaú no wa, tyôtto kañḡaetyaimasu nêe.
'No, it's not very warm, and what's more, the price is high, so I'll just think twice about buying it.'

3. **kutûsita/buatui**; 4. **kabañ/karui**; 5. **kutû/zyoobu na**; 6. **zîsyo/miyásùi**; 7. **hutoñ/rakû na**; 8. **kikâi/bêñri na**

---

8. The **na ñ da** ending is blunt-style. For gentle-style, change to **na no**.
9. The unusual accent of this verbal (i.e., not on the **ma** of **-masu**) is explained by the fact that it is a contraction of **kañḡaete simaimasu**.

Application Exercises

A1. Using pictures of Japanese wearing Japanese-style clothing, as well as of anyone wearing Western-style clothing, follow the procedures outlined in Section A, Application Exercise A2.

2. Ask and answer questions about daily activities that might involve two activities (i.e., /gerund + predicate/ or /gerund + **kara** + predicate/) to be answered negatively with the **-(a)zu ni/-(à)nài de** pattern. Examples:

    Aságòhañ o tâbete zyûĝyoo ni dêta ñ desu ka⤳ 'Did you eat breakfast before attending class (*lit.* attend having eaten)?'

    Iie, tabênai de (*or* **tabêzu ni**) **dêta ñ desu.** 'No, I attended without eating.'

    Kyoókàsyo o yôñde kara têepu o kikû ñ desu ka⤳ 'Do you listen to tapes after reading your textbook?'

    Iie, yomâzu ni (*or* **yomânai de**) **kikû ñ desu.** 'No, I listen without reading it.'

3. Respond to complimentary statements by limiting favorable characteristics just to the one mentioned. Examples:

    Oísii pài desu nêe. 'What a delicious pie!'

    Oísii dakè de, keńkoo nì wa yôku nâi desu yo⤳ 'It just tastes good; it's not good for you.'

4. Practice responding to questions asking permission to do certain things in the classroom (examples: lock the door, open the window, close the door, write in pencil, leave early, come late tomorrow, look at your textbook, smoke in the classroom, drink coffee here) with negative request patterns.

B. Core Conversations: Substitution

Again, practice the Core Conversations with appropriate substitutions, retaining the original overall structure. Vary the participants, making appropriate changes in conversation style. Follow the practice with questions and answers on the contents.

SECTION C

Eavesdropping

(Answer the following on the basis of the accompanying audiotape. A = the first speaker, and B = the second speaker, in each conversation.)

  1a. What is A's relationship to B?
   b. Who has just come?
   c. What is A asked to do?
   d. Account for the request form used by B.
  2a. When is the party? What kind will it be?
   b. Why is A relieved?
  3a. Where was A last week?
   b. What comment does A make about such places?
   c. What happened there?

d. What is B's reaction?
4a. Who is making the call?
   b. Who is being called, and where is that person?
   c. Who answered the phone?
5a. Where is B going for Golden Week?
   b. What led B to this decision?
   c. What is A's reaction?
   d. What are B's summer plans?
6a. What is A's assumption about what B wants to do?
   b. What is the actual situation?
   c. What is B's problem?
   d. What solution does A suggest?
   e. What is B's reaction?
7a. What does A suggest initially? (Be precise.)
   b. What is B's reaction?
   c. What particular item does A then suggest?
   d. What variety does B like?
8a. How do the two objects appear to A?
   b. What is actually true?
   c. How does A explain the error?
   d. How does B tactfully respond to this explanation?
9a. What is B about to do?
   b. How is the weather?
   c. What is A's concern?
   d. How does B respond to that concern? (Give two reasons for A not to worry.)
10a. Where does this conversation probably take place?
   b. What is B about to do?
   c. What is B's problem?
11a. What did A just notice?
   b. What is the explanation?
   c. How long has the change been in effect?
   d. What does A assume must have been a problem?
   e. What was the actual situation?
12a. What did A just notice?
   b. What is the explanation?
   c. What was B's reaction to A's initial comment?
   d. In what connection is a hat mentioned?
13a. Why is B wearing glasses today?
   b. Why doesn't B like them?
   c. How are B's eyes?
   d. How does B feel about contact lenses?
   e. What polite comment does A make?
14a. Where is B employed?
   b. What three types of clothing does B wear?
   c. Which one of those types is worn under special conditions, and what are those conditions?
15a. What three reasons are mentioned by A and B for not owning a kimono?
   b. In what connection are underwear, tabi, zori, and obi mentioned?
   c. Which of these is extremely expensive?
   d. What do women wear to weddings these days?
16a. What seems strange to A about the part-time worker?

b. How does A describe the part-timer?
   c. How does B explain the situation that has confused A?
   d. Who is Morimoto?
17a. Describe the general situation, identifying the roles of A and B.
   b. What does B urge A to do?
   c. Why does A not comply?
   d. What is B's concern?
   e. What is A's polite response to that concern?
18a. What season is it?
   b. How is the weather?
   c. What has happened in Hokkaido?
   d. How does B know about this?
   e. What is B about to do?
   f. What does B plan to take, and what is the concern?
   g. What is A's advice?
19a. What, located where, is the topic of discussion?
   b. What happened to it?
   c. How did A find out?
   d. What does A mention being surprised about?
20a. What is Hashimoto's profession?
   b. Why does A feel that Hashimoto doesn't appear to represent that employment category? Give three reasons.
   c. How does B explain the situation?
21a. Where does this conversation probably take place?
   b. Identify A and B.
   c. What does A initially express a desire to do?
   d. What is the basis for the decision A is trying to make? Why?
   e. What is B's advice, in spite of what possible drawback?
   f. What does A decide?
22a. What is B about to do? For how long?
   b. What is A's assumption in regard to this?
   c. What is the actual situation? Give details.
   d. How does A account for this?
23a. What is the relationship between A and B, in all likelihood?
   b. What does A suspect, initially?
   c. What does A tell B to do?
   d. As a result, what does A learn? By what evidence?
   e. What does A assume is the explanation?
   f. What explanation does B offer?
24a. Identify A and B.
   b. Where is B now?
   c. What was B concerned about?
   d. What reassures B?
   e. What is B about to do?
   f. What does A suggest as to how B should proceed?
25a. Whose wedding is the topic of conversation?
   b. What description of the bride is offered?
   c. What is the attitude of the groom's parents?
   d. What explanation is offered?
   e. What is B's reaction?

26a. Who is the topic of conversation?
  b. Where is that person employed?
  c. How well does B know that person?
  d. How does B describe that person?
  e. Where, when, and for what purpose is that person scheduled to go?
  f. What does that person want to do before that?
  g. What is A's advice in that connection?
  h. What is B's contribution to this advice?

Utilization

(For each of the following, develop a short conversation which includes at least a stimulus and/or response.)

1. You've run into an acquaintance in the station at about 5:30. Ask if he is on his way home.
2. A neighbor is leaving her home in the morning. Inquire if she's going out.
3. Tell a classmate that you came to this university to study Japanese.
4. Tell a colleague that you heard that the daughter of Mr. Tanaka, the consultant, is studying in America in order to become a doctor.
5. Tell a friend that you bought this little box in Kyoto as a souvenir for your mother.
6. Tell your instructor that you didn't attend the seminar yesterday because of illness. (Apologize!)
7. Tell a friend that you want to buy an outfit for attending a formal wedding reception. Ask her what kind of outfit she thinks would be good.
8. Tell a colleague that you've caught a cold and you have a headache, too, so you've been thinking you'd like to go home a little early today.
9. You've just returned from an extended period abroad and are talking about the place where you were. Complain that the winters were extremely cold and the summers were terribly hot, so actually it was a rather unpleasant place.
10. Compliment your hostess on her new home, pointing out that you can see the mountains, and the ocean is close by.
11. You are out shopping with a friend and getting tired. Suggest that you have some tea or something.
12. There is going to be a student party. Offer to make a pie or something.
13. It's early April in Japan. Suggest to a colleague that your family and his go to Ueno Park or someplace to see the cherry [blossoms].
14. You're on the beach with a friend. Warn her that she's going to get burned. Tell her she'd better put on a hat.
15. Find out who that person is who is wearing (a) Japanese clothing; (b) a windbreaker and blue jeans; (c) a yellow blouse and gray skirt; (d) a black suit and blue necktie.
16. You and a colleague have been disagreeing over the identification of someone who came into the office. Admit that it is Ms. Sugiura after all. Point out that because she's wearing a hat she looks like a different person.
17. Complain to a colleague that you are still not accustomed to (the way of) using this machine.
18. You've just been shopping prior to leaving for an extended trip. Tell a friend that you bought two suits, two pairs of shoes, six pairs of socks, and two sweaters.
19. Tell a friend that you want to buy a yukata, but you haven't found one yet that appeals to you.
20. You are entering a Japanese restaurant. Ask if you should take off your shoes.
21. Tell a friend that you were thinking of buying a car, but since prices are high, you gave up (with resignation!) and bought a bicycle.
22. You've just returned to your office. Tell your colleague that you came back instead of (i.e., without) going to the conference at the Park Building.

23. Remind your part-time student worker not to forget to deliver this to Mr. Yamada at Oriental Trade before 2:00 today.
24. Explain to a friend that you thought it was warm and (so) came without wearing a coat.
25. Your friend is watching the clock anxiously, thinking he's going to be late for a deadline. Tell him he doesn't have to hurry, since there's plenty of time.
26. You're setting out on a hike in the country. Tell your friend that it will probably be cold, so to be on the safe side he'd better wear a warm sweater and heavy socks.
27. You are going to take a walk with a friend. Ask your friend if it's all right not to wear a sweater.
28. You are in the midst of discussing what to wear to a friend's wedding. Explain that in your case, you haven't yet decided what you are going to wear. Ask for suggestions.
29. You've been asked what foreigners usually wear to weddings. Explain that it depends on circumstances.
30. Ask a colleague if, in cases when you must consult with a professor whom you haven't met yet, it's all right to consult by telephone.
31. Last night you were shown some gruesome pictures by a friend. Tell your colleague that you felt awful just to have seen them.
32. An acquaintance is commenting on your large home. Respond that it's just big; it's not very convenient.
33. A friend has commented on how attractive the new sushi shop is. Tell her it's only attractive; the sushi isn't at all tasty.
34. You and a colleague are going somewhere together after work and he is concerned about not changing clothes. Tell him he doesn't have to change—or rather, it would be better not to (change).
35. Compliment a colleague on how becoming his new glasses are.
36. Compliment your friend Kei on how becoming her dress is.
37. Tell your colleague that there's nothing you can do about how difficult this computer is to use, so you want to change to a better one.

Check-up

1. Describe an honorific-polite nominal pattern derived from verbals. In what way does its range of meaning differ from that of /**o-** + verbal stem + **ni nâru**/? What is its negative equivalent? (A-SP1)
2. What is the basic meaning of **tamê**? What does it mean in occurrences without a modifier? Describe the difference in meaning among the following: **hâiru tamê; hâitta tamê; dekînai tamê; byoóki no tamè; seńsee no tamê**. What occurs following **tamê**? (A-SP2)
3. What is the meaning of particle **si**? Describe what may precede **si**. What is the difference in meaning between /gerund, + predicate/, and **si** connecting two predicates? Give two possible interpretations of /—— **si**, —— **si**, ——/. (A-SP3)
4. In the sequence **otyá dè mo nomímasyòo**, what is the meaning of **otyá dè mo**? Identify **dè**. How does this meaning correlate with other uses of **dè mo**? What particles may occur immediately following the nominal in this pattern? What particles do not occur? (A-SP4)
5. Describe the formation of the alternate negative stem. What verbals are lacking this form? (B-SP1)
6. Describe one use of the alternate negative stem. How does this pattern differ from the use of the corresponding negative gerund? What other pattern may replace this alternate negative stem pattern with similar meaning? Name one pattern in which these two patterns are *not* interchangeable. (B-SP2)
7. What is the basic meaning of **dakê**? What may immediately precede **dakê** besides nominals? Why might we speak of a particle **dakê** and a nominal **dakê**? (B-SP3)

Lesson 24

SECTION A

Core Conversations

1(J)a. **Apâato o osáǧasi da sòo desu ǧa . .**

(N)a. **Êe. Moó sibàraku Nihôñ ni nokôru kotô ni simâsite nêe. Dôko ka îi tokoro sirímasèñ ka**

b. **Zitû wa neʔ Kânai no hanásì na ñ desu ǧa ne! Utí no tonari no hitò ǧa Nyuúyòoku e ikú kotò ni narímàsite ne! Dâre ka kawári ni sùñde kureru hitô o saǧásite (i)ru sòo na ñ desu.**

c. **Êe. Moó sukòsi kuwásìi koto kiítè kara, goréñraku-simásu yo.**

b. **Hoñtoo dèsu ka.**

c. **Zêhi oneǧai-simasu.**

2(J)a. **Hoñtoo ni moosiwake nài ñ desu ǧa; rêe no mâñsyoñ, hoká no hitò ni kimáttyatta-mìtai na ñ desu yo.**

(N)a. **Sôo desu ka. Zañnèñ da kedo, sikáta ǧa arimasèñ neʔ**

b. **Mâda aíte (i)ru-mìtai datta ñ de, ohánasi-sità ñ desu ǧa; koñna kotô ni nâtte simatte, hoñtoo ni sumimasèñ.**

b. **Toñde mo arimasèñ. Dôoka, ki ní nasaranai de kudasai.**

c. **Kânai ni mo, dôk(o) ka nâi ka, ki ó tukèt(e) okú yòo ni iímàsu kara . .**

c. **Arîǧatoo gozaimasu. Yorósiku oneǧai-simàsu.**

3(J)a. **Anâta-mitai ni nihóñḡo ḡa zyoozù na hitô wa mezúrasìi desu nêe.**

b. **Kokó màde ûmâku syabêru yoo ni nâru no ni wa, hutuu donó-ḡurai kakarimàsu ka.**

(N)a. **Dôo itasimasite. Narubeku tukáu yòo ni sité (i)rù kedo, yappàri dôñdoñ 'wasurete simatte . .**

b. **Sâa. Hito ni yotte tiḡáu-mìtai desu kara nêe.**

ENGLISH EQUIVALENTS

1(J)a. I hear you're looking for an apartment, but . . . (is it true?)

b. Actually, this is something my wife reported; it's turned out that the people next door to us are going to New York, and they're looking for someone who will house-sit (*lit.* reside as a substitute) for them (I've heard).

c. Yes. After I've heard a few more details, I'll get in touch with you.

2(J)a. I'm really sorry, but about that apartment—they seem to have decided on someone else.

b. Since it seemed that it was still available, I spoke to you [about it]; I'm really sorry that it turned out this way.

c. I'll tell my wife (too) to be on the lookout for someplace (*lit.* watch [for] isn't there someplace), so . . . (she may find an apartment for you).

3(J)a. People who are competent in Japanese the way you are are unusual—wouldn't you agree!

(N)a. Yes. Having decided to remain in Japan a while longer . . . (I am looking). You wouldn't know someplace good?

b. Really?

c. Would you do that?

(N)a. Oh, that's too bad, but it can't be helped, can it.

b. No, no! Please don't be concerned.

c. Thank you. I'll count on (*lit.* politely request) your consideration.

(N)a. Oh, I'm not competent! I'm trying to use it as much as possible, but after all, I do forget it quickly, and . . . (I'm not really competent).

b. For reaching the point where you speak this well, ordinarily about how long does it take?

b. Hmm. It seems to differ according to the person, so . . . (I can't really answer).

BREAKDOWNS
(AND SUPPLEMENTARY VOCABULARY)

1. **apâato** — apartment, apartment house
   sag̃asu /-u; sag̃asita/ — look for; track down
   sibâraku — a while
   moó sibàraku — a while longer
   nokôru /-u; nokôtta/ — be(come) left behind; remain, stay on
   +**nokôsu /-u; nokôsita/** — leave behind; hold in reserve; save
   Nihôñ ni nokôru — stay on in Japan
   nokôru kotô ni suru (SP1) — decide on remaining
   dôko ka (SP2) — someplace, somewhere
   dôko ka îi tokórò — some good place
   ikú kotò ni nâru (SP1) — be(come) decided that [someone] will go
   kawari — substitute, replacement
   kawari ni — as a substitute; instead
   sûmu /-u; suñda/ — take up residence; reside
   kawári ni sùmu — reside as a substitute; house-sit
   kawári ni sùñde kureru — reside as a substitute (for the in-group)
   dâre ka — someone, somebody
   dâre ka kawári ni sùñde kureru hito — some person who will reside as a substitute (for the in-group)
   kuwásìi /-katta/ — is detailed
   kuwásìi koto — details, particulars
   zêhi — by all means
2. **rêe no X** — that very X; that X known to us both
   mâñsyoñ — apartment; apartment house
   +**dañti** — apartment complex; housing development
   X-mìtai /na/ — as if X; X-like
   +**yôo /na/** — manner, resemblance, seeming
   kimáttyatta-mìtai /na/ (SP3) — as if decided
   +**kimáttyatta yòo /na/ (SP4)** — seeming to have been decided
   aíte (i)ru-mìtai /na/ — as if open or available
   +**aíte (i)ru yòo /na/** — seeming to be open or available

końna kotò ni nâtte simau	end up becoming this kind of thing, end up like this
dôoka	/alternate of **dôozo**/
ki ni suru *or*	
ki ní nasàru ↑	mind; worry about; concern oneself about
+ki ní nàru	weigh on one's mind; become a cause for concern
ki ó tukèru	take care; pay attention; watch out
ki ó tukèt(e) oku	keep watching out (for future use)
dôko ka nâi ka, ki ó tukèt(e) oku	keep watching out [to see if] there isn't someplace
ki ó tukèt(e) okú yòo ni 'iu (SP4)	tell [someone] to keep watching out
3. anâta-mitai /na/ *or*	
+anâta no yoo /na/	like you
anâta-mitai ni zyoózù da *or*	
+anâta no yoo ni zyoózù da	is skilled as you [are]
anâta-mitai ni nihóñḡo ḡa zyoozù na hito *or*	
+anâta no yôo ni nihóñḡo ḡa zyoozù na hito	a person skilled in Japanese as you [are]
tukáu yòo ni suru (SP4)	try to use
dôñdoñ	in rapid succession
umâi /-katta/	is skilled; is delicious
syabêru /-u; syabetta/	speak, talk, chat
kokó màde ûmâku syabêru	speak well as far as this level
syabêru yoo ni nâru (SP4)	reach the point of speaking
hutuu /+ predicate/	ordinarily, regularly, usually
tiḡáu-mìtai /na/	as if being different
+tiḡáu yòo /na/	seeming to be different

Miscellaneous Notes

1. CC1 is a conversation between Mr. Suzuki (J), the banker, and Smith (N), the graduate student, about possible housing for Smith. Mr. Suzuki serves as Smith's sponsor in Japan, but otherwise has no close connections with him. The style is careful, with distal-style final predicates and several polite forms.

(J)a. **Osáḡàsi da**, in this context, is an honorific-polite ↑ equivalent of **saḡasite (i)ru**. Of the honorific-polite patterns introduced thus far, this is the least honorific and exalting.

(N)a. **Sibâraku** represents a *quantity* of time; hence **moó sibàraku** 'a period of time in addition.'

Nokôru: note **nokorimono** 'leftovers.' **Nokôru** and **nokôsu** are, of course, intransitive/transitive partners, both consonant verbals and both operational.

Sirímaseǹ: the negative here is indirect and polite, comparable to English 'you wouldn't know, would you?'

(J)b. **Kânai no hanási** 'my wife's talk,' i.e., 'something my wife said,' 'a report from my wife.' Note the extended predicates: 'what this is is something my wife said'; 'what is reported is that . . .'

Sûmu occurs in the **-te (i)ru** form, i.e., **sûnde (i)ru**, when referring to one's current residence. This verbal means 'live' only in the sense of 'reside.' Note: Place X **ni sûnde (i)ru** 'live in X.' **Sûnde kureru**: note the use of **kureru**, indicating activity being performed for the benefit of the in-group. The statement here is made from the point of view of the **tonári no hitò**.

(J)c. Note: **X ni kuwásii** 'is well versed in X,' 'having detailed knowledge of X.'

(N)c. **Zêhi** is an intensifier that occurs most commonly with request and **-tai** 'want to' patterns.

2. CC2 is a follow-up conversation to CC1, with the same participants and speech style. Mr. Suzuki is being extremely polite as he apologizes for the fact that the housing he thought might be available for Smith and actually brought to Smith's attention has already been taken. Smith attempts to relieve Mr. Suzuki's concern. The more Mr. Suzuki apologizes, the more Smith must reassure him.

(J)a. **Rêe no X** refers to an X which the speaker and addressee are both acquainted with, and which is immediately identifiable to the addressee in the given context.

Mânsyon, a borrowing from English 'mansion,' refers to an apartment or apartment house in Japan. Originally these were luxury apartments in buildings that included only a small number of units, but today the term is rapidly becoming simply an alternate for **apâato**. One thing is clear: there was never any connection with a 'mansion' beyond the earlier connotation of luxury.

Note the extended predicate: 'What happened in connection with the situation we both know about is that they apparently have decided on another person.'

(N)a. By saying **sikáta ḡa arimaseǹ**, Smith relieves Mr. Suzuki—and everyone—from responsibility.

(J)b. Note Mr. Suzuki's use of the humble-polite **ohanasi-sita** within his extended apology.

(N)b. Smith responds with an emphatic denial of Mr. Suzuki's need to apologize. Note the honorific-polite **nasáràṅai**, reflecting the politeness of Mr. Suzuki's apology in a situation that calls for formality.

(J)c. Mr. Suzuki's apology for what *did* happen is followed now by an explanation of what will be done that might take care of the problem in the future.

Kânai ni mo: We can assume that Mr. Suzuki himself will be doing everything he can to help Smith. He will tell his 'wife, too' to do so.

3. In CC3, Mr. Suzuki compliments Smith on his Japanese language proficiency, which Smith, of course, politely dismisses. The style is generally careful, with distal-style final predicates in Mr. Suzuki's utterances. Smith's utterances are minor sentences—the first a polite ritual fragment. In his final utterance ([N]b), he uses distal-style before **kara**. In the casual-careful continuum, this conversation reflects a position only slightly more careful than casual: the use of **-mìtai**, **syabêru**, and **umâi** suggests a relaxed tone that matches the topic.

(J)a. Note Mr. Suzuki's use of **anâta** in reference to Smith. Mr. Suzuki is older and a professional, whereas Smith is a graduate student. However, Mr. Suzuki does not know this foreigner well. **Anâta** reflects politeness without the deference one shows a superior.

(N)a. **Narubeku** can be replaced by **dekiru dake**.

(J)b. **Koko** in **kokó màde** within this context refers to 'this point' in the acquisition of Japanese as a foreign language.

Umâi occurs as a more blunt and casual equivalent of both **zyoózù da** and **oisii**. It is used more commonly by males.

Structural Patterns

1. /—— **kotô ni suru**/; /—— **kotô ni nâru**/

Followed by /**kotô ni suru**/, an affirmative verbal or a negative adjectival derived from a verbal indicates a volitional decision process: '[someone] decides to perform (or not perform) a particular activity.' This is simply an extension of the already familiar pattern /nominal + **ni** + **suru**/ 'decide on X,' 'make [it] to be X.' (cf. **Nâñ ni simásyòo ka.; Pâñ ni nasáimàsu ka**⌐, etc.) Note that the thing decided upon is again a nominal—namely **kotô** 'act'—and the nominal is preceded by a sentence modifier describing the particular type of act. Examples:

Môtto yasûi apâato o saḡásu kotô ni simasita. 'I decided to look for (*lit.* I made [it] to be the act of looking for) a cheaper apartment.'

Kimono o kinái kotô ni simásyòo neʔ 'Let's decide not to wear kimono—O.K.?'

Miñsyuku ni tomaru kotô ni simasyoo. 'Let's decide to stop at a minshuku.'

In reference to the last example, the question arises as to the difference in meaning between it and

Miñsyuku ni tomarimasyòo. 'Let's stop at a minshuku.'

The use of the /—— **kotô ni suru**/ pattern implies more deliberation among a number of possible choices.

The relationship between **suru** and **nâru** parallels that of the many transitive/intransitive partners that we have encountered. Compare:

akeru 'cause to be open' /**aku** 'get to be open' *and*

nokôsu 'cause to remain' /**nokôru** 'get to remain' *with*

suru 'cause to be' /**nâru** 'get to be'

If /**X kotô ni suru**/ means 'make [it] to be an X-activity,' 'decide to X,' we can suspect—accurately—that /**X kotô ni nâru**/ will refer to an activity that is decided upon, outside of the control of the individual. In other words, just as **damê ni nâru** means '[it] gets to be bad,' /**X kotô ni nâru**/ states that a particular activity (or non-activity) is the outcome, i.e., 'it is decided (by whom we are not told) that X will (or will not) occur.' Examples:

Asítà kara syuttyoo-suru kotò ni narimasita. 'It was decided that I'll go on a business trip starting tomorrow.'

Môo konó koñpyùutaa o 'tukattya ikénai kotò ni nâtte (i)masu yo⌐ 'It's been decided that we must not use this computer any more.'

The /**kotô ni suru**/ pattern alternates with /**kotô ni kimeru**/, and /**kotô ni nâru**/ with /**kotô ni kimaru**/.

2. /INTERROGATIVE + ka/

We previously learned that /interrogative + **mo**/—**îtu mo**, **dâre mo**, **nâni mo**, etc.—was a pattern indicating the all-inclusiveness of the category covered by the interrogative, and that these combinations were not interrogative.

We now take up the pattern /interrogative + **ka**/. This pattern—also not interrogative—is one of indefiniteness:

nâni ka 'something'
dâre ka 'somebody'
dôk(o) ka 'someplace'
îtu ka 'sometime'
îkura ka 'some amount'
îku-tu ka 'some number (of things)'

We have already encountered examples of this pattern in **Hoká ni nàni ka?** and **Nâni ka arímàsu ka**⸝

These combinations may occur followed by phrase-particles as required. When the relationship with the following predicate is that of **g̃a** or **o**, those two particles are usually dropped unless the statement would be ambiguous without them.

Îkura ka harâtta kedo, îkura harâtta ka wasúremàsita. 'I paid some amount, but I forgot how much I paid.'
Dâre ka kara teḡámi g̃a kimàsita yo⸝ 'Say, a letter has arrived from someone.'
Kotosi no natu, dôko ka e ikítài to omôtte (i)masu kedo . . 'I've been thinking I'd like to go somewhere this summer, but . . .' (I'm not sure I can).
Matá ìtu ka aímasyòo. 'Let's meet again sometime.'
Nâni ka tabémaseñ ka⸝ 'Won't you have something to eat?'
Dâre ka nokôru desyoo ka nêe. 'I wonder if someone will stay behind.'
Dâre ka g̃a yobímàsita kara . . 'Someone called [me], so . . .'
Dâre ka o yobímàsita kara . . 'I called [someone], so . . .'

/Interrogative + **ka**/ combinations frequently occur preceding a nominal—usually one that is modified—making the nominal indefinite. Examples:

dâre ka nihóñg̃o g̃a umài gaiziñ 'some foreigner who is good in Japanese'
nâni ka mezúrasìi mono 'some unusual thing'
dôko ka tikâi tokoro 'someplace that's close'
îtu ka ohíma na tokì 'sometime when you're free'

3. -mìtai

-Mìtai (not to be confused with the adjectival **mitâi**, from **mîru**) is a nominal enclitic (an 'add-on') which attaches to perfective and imperfective verbals and adjectivals, to nominals (or /nominal + **kara** or **made**/), and to perfective **dàtta**.

We have seen this distribution before—for example, preceding **kâ mo siremaseñ**. The presumption is that the very unstable **dà** form (the only imperfective predicate form missing) has once again been dropped. It is this distribution which prevents us from simply calling **-mìtai** an independent nominal. Before freestanding nominals, **dà** changes to **na** or **no**, but is not lost.

The /**X** + **-mìtai**/ sequence functions as a **na**-nominal, and means 'like X,' 'as if X,' 'X-like.' Often 'seem' occurs as an English equivalent: there is no one English word which corresponds exactly to the Japanese.

-Mìtai loses its accent when joined with an accented sequence; otherwise it forms a single accent phrase in combination with what precedes. Examples:

    dekîru-mitai 'as if capable'
    yaméta-mìtai 'as if having quit'
    takâi-mitai 'seeming expensive'
    oísìkatta-mitai 'as if having been delicious'
    hâru-mitai 'spring-like'
    damê datta-mitai 'as if having been no good'

Examples of combinations with nominals are particularly common. Like other **na**-nominals, **-mìtai** sequences occur before various forms of the copula, and before particle **ni** in manner/goal expressions. Examples:

    Ano gakusee wa, naní mo wakarànai-mitai desu nêe. 'That student seems not to understand anything, doesn't s/he!'
    Konó àme, tuyú-mìtai desyoo? 'This rain is like the rainy season, isn't it?'
    Nihóñzìñ-mitai ni nihóñḡo o syaberimàsu yo⤴ 'You know, s/he speaks Japanese like a Japanese.'
    Konó wàiñ wa, kusúri-mìtai na azi ḡa simásèñ ka⤴ 'Doesn't this wine have a medicine-like taste?'
    Kâre wa, sûutu o kité (i)rù kara, gakúsee-mìtai ni wa miémasèñ nêe. 'Since he is wearing a suit, he doesn't look like a student, does he!'

In the last example, **-mìtai** may be omitted with little change in meaning. Compare English alternates like 'appear to be ——,' 'seem like ——,' 'look like ——.'

4. **yôo**

Yôo is a **na**-nominal meaning 'manner,' 'resemblance,' 'like.' In some of its occurrences it alternates with **-mìtai**, but there are these differences between the two:

1. **Yôo** functions as an independent nominal. It is always preceded by a modifier which is of a type that regularly occurs before nominals—specifically a pre-nominal or a sentence (including a sentence ending in the **no** or **na** alternate of **dà**). Compare:

sonó yòo	*but*	**soré-mitai** 'like that'
nihóñzìñ no yoo	*but*	**nihóñzìñ-mitai** 'like a Japanese'
sukî na yoo	*but*	**sukî-mitai** 'as if liking'
watási nò¹ no yoo	*but*	**watási nò¹-mitai** 'like mine,' 'resembling mine'

Following an accented word or phrase, **yôo** regularly loses its accent.

2. **-Mìtai** is more typical of conversational Japanese, whereas **yôo** occurs frequently in both the spoken and the written language.

3. Only **yôo** occurs in the following very important combinations.

a. /**X yôo ni iu**/ 'tell [someone] to X' or /**X yôo ni tanômu**/ 'ask [someone] to X.' X = an imperfective affirmative verbal or a derived negative adjectival. Examples:

---

1. This **no** is the contraction of /particle **no** + nominal **no**/.

> **Kânozyo ni nokôru yoo ni iímàsita.** 'I told her to stay behind.'
>
> **Señsèe ni 'asita irâsite kudásàru yoo ni tanôñde kurémaseñ ka⌇** 'Would you ask the teacher to be kind enough to come tomorrow?'
>
> **Kêe-tyañ ni kimóno o kiru yòo ni tanómimasyòo ka.** 'Shall I ask Kei to wear a kimono?'
>
> **Eéḡo o tukawanai yòo ni itte kudasài.** 'Tell [them] not to use English.'

b. /**X yôo ni suru**/ 'act in such a way as to X,' 'act as if to X,' 'try to X,' or 'act in an X-kind of manner.' X is the same as in (a) above. Examples:

> **Nihoñḡo ḡa zyoózù ni nâru yoo ni site (i)masu.** 'I'm trying to become skilled in Japanese.'
>
> **Byoóki ni narànai yoo ni simasyoo.** 'Let's try not to get sick.'

In this pattern, **suru** may be expanded to describe what is being done to achieve X, or it may be replaced by a totally different activity. Examples:

> **Zyoózù ni nâru yoo ni, âsa kara bañ màde beñkyoo-site (i)màsu.** 'I'm studying from morning till night (in such a way as) to become skilled.'
>
> **Usíro no hitò ni mo kikóeru yoo ni, ôoki na kôe de hanásimàsita.** 'I spoke in a loud voice in such a way as to be audible to the people in back, too.'
>
> **Wasúrenai yòo ni, mâiniti reñsyuu-site kudasài.** 'Practice daily so as not to forget (*or* in a non-forgetting way).'

c. /**X yôo ni nâru**/ = 'reach the point where something is generally true or regularly occurs.' Here X is usually an affirmative imperfective verbal.

> **Mâe wa wakáràanakatta kedo, kono-ḡoro sukôsi wakâru yoo ni narimasita.** 'In the past I didn't understand, but these days, I've reached the point where I understand a little.'
>
> **Nakámura-sañ no àkatyañ wa, nañ de mo tabèru yoo ni narímàsita yo⌇** 'You know, Mr/s. Nakamura's baby has reached the point where s/he eats anything at all!'
>
> **Sono gakusee wa, moó sùḡu môtto oókìi zîsyo ḡa irú yòo ni naru to omóimàsu kedo ..** 'I think those students will reach the point very soon now where they need larger dictionaries, but . . .' (what do *you* think?)

It is this pattern that may occur with affective verbals which do not themselves occur in the **-tai** form:

> **wakâru yoo ni narítài** 'I want to understand' (*lit.* 'I want to become so as to understand')
>
> **dekîru yoo ni narítài** 'I want to be able' (*lit.* 'I want to become so as to be able')

To describe the development of a negative condition, the usual pattern is the already familiar /**-(a)naku + nâru**/:

> **Zêmi ni dênaku narimasita.** 'S/he doesn't come (*lit.* s/he became non-coming) to the seminar [any more].'

Hurañsuḡo ḡa dekînaku natta to omôu. 'I think s/he's become unable to handle French.'

Muzúkasiku nàtta kara, wakáranaku nâru desyoo. 'S/he probably will no longer understand (will become non-comprehending) because it's become difficult.'

Drills

A 1. **Apâato, karírù desyoo?**
'You're going to rent an apartment—right?'

Ie, yáppàri karínai kotò ni simasita.
'No, after all, I decided not to rent one.'

2. **Kimono, kinâi desyoo?**
'You aren't going to wear a kimono—right?'

Ie, yáppàri kirú kotò ni simasita.
'No, after all, I decided to wear one.'

3. **arúbàito/yamenai**; 4. **Oota-kuñ/okôsu**; 5. **demae/tyuumoñ-suru**; 6. **gakkoo/akíramènai**; 7. **kore/haráwànai**; 8. **sore/kiḡàeru**

B 1. **Huyû made 'koko ni nokôru ñ da tte?**
'Did they say that you are going to stay on here until winter?'

Ñ, nokôru kotô ni nâtte nêe.
'Yeah, it's been decided that I'll stay, and . . .' (you know what that means).

2. **Atárasìi zimûsyo o saḡásù ñ da tte?**
'Did they say that you are going to look for a new office?'

Ñ, saḡásu kotô ni nâtte nêe.
'Yeah, it's been decided that I'll look for one, and . . .' (you know what that means).

3. **anó heñ ni sùmu**; 4. **hañbuñ nokôsu**; 5. **h(u)ôomaru na huku 'kiru**; 6. **siḡoto 'kaeru**; 7. **butyoo ni zêñbu mawasu**

C 1. **Kotíra dè wa, utí o karirù ñ desu ka⁄—apâato o karírù ñ desu ka⁄**
'Here—(is it that) you are going to rent a house, or an apartment?'

Apâato o karíru kotò ni narimasita.
'It's been decided that we are going to rent an apartment.'

2. **Demae wa, zyôo o tanômu ñ desu ka⁄—tokúzyoo o tanòmu ñ desu ka⁄**
'About home delivery (of food)—(is it that) you are going to order deluxe, or super-deluxe?'

Tokúzyoo o tanòmu kotô ni narimasita.
'It's been decided that we are going to order super-deluxe.'

3. **hukû/h(u)ôomaru na monô o kiru/rakû na monô o kiru**; 4. **hâru/koko de 'siḡoto o suru/ryokoo o suru**; 5. **kono teeburu/mukôo ni 'motte (i)ku/koko ni 'oit(e) oku**

D 1. **Nâni ka saḡásite (i)rù ñ desu ka⁄**
'(Is it that) you are looking for something?'

Ie, betu ni naní mo saḡásite (i)masèñ kedo . .
'No, I'm not specially looking for anything, but . . .' (why do you think I am?)

2. **Dâre ka mâtte (i)ru ñ desu ka**⤴
   '(Is it that) you are waiting for someone?'

   Ie, betu ni daré mo màtte (i)másèñ kedo . .
   'No, I'm not specially waiting for anyone, but . . .' (why do you think I am?)

3. **dôtira ka 'hituyoo na**; 4. **dôre ka nokôtte (i)ru**; 5. **nâni ka 'ki ni site (i)ru**; 6. **dôko ka e 'dekakeru**; 7. **dâre ka komâru**

E 1. **Sonó tamè ni wa, nihóñḡo no zyoozù na hitô ḡa irímasèñ ka**⤴
   'For that, don't you need a person who is competent in Japanese?'

   Êe, îma dâre ka nihóñḡo no zyoozù na hitô o saḡásite (i)rù ñ desu ḡa nêe.
   'Yes, (the fact is) we are now looking for someone who is competent in Japanese, but . . .' (it's not easy, you know!)

2. **Sonó tamè ni wa, mâdo no ôoki na zimûsyo ḡa irímasèñ ka**⤴
   'For that, don't you need an office where the windows are big?'

   Êe, îma dôko ka mâdo no ôoki na zimûsyo o saḡásite (i)rù ñ desu ḡa nêe.
   'Yes, (the fact is) we are now looking for some office where the windows are big, but . . .' (it's not easy, you know!)

3. **naíyoo no omosiròi bañḡumi**; 4. **miñnà no 'hima na zikañ**; 5. **kimóno no niàu zyosee**; 6. **kaímono no bènri na apâato**

F 1. **Anó misè aíte (i)rù ñ desu ka nêe.**
   'I wonder—(is it that) that shop is open?'

   Êe. Hoñtoo wa soñna hazu nài ñ desu kedo, aíte (i)ru-mìtai desu nêe.
   'Yes. Actually, you wouldn't expect that kind of thing, but it seems to be open, doesn't it!'

2. **Koñtakuto-rèñzu iréte (i)ru ñ desu ka nêe.**
   'I wonder—(is it that) s/he is wearing (*lit.* has put in) contact lenses?'

   Êe. Hoñtoo wa soñna hazu nài ñ desu kedo, iréte (i)ru-mìtai desu nêe.
   'Yes. Actually, you wouldn't expect that kind of thing, but it seems as if s/he is wearing [them] (*lit.* has put [them] in), doesn't it!'

3. **dâre ka 'iru**; 4. **miñnà ni syabêttyatta**; 5. **kono sakana 'yaku**; 6. **Yamâḡuti-kuñ 'dekakete (i)ru**; 7. **yukí hùtte kita**

G 1. **Kânozyo, kañḡòhu ka nâa.** /blunt/
   'Is she a nurse, I wonder!'

   Ñ, kañḡòhu-mitai nêe. /gentle/
   'Yeah, it seems as if she's a nurse, doesn't it.'

2. **Anô hito, siḡoto akíràmeta ka nâa.** /blunt/
   'Did s/he give up on the work, I wonder!'

   Ñ, akíràmeta-mitai nêe. /gentle/
   'Yeah, it seems as if s/he's given it up, doesn't it.'

3. **anó sèetaa/buátùi**; 4. **okâasañ/siñpai-site (i)ru**; 5. **kabañ/karui**; 6. **siḡoto/rakû (da)**; 7. **ano heñ/hûbeñ (da)**; 8. **anô ko/zyóobu (dà)**

H 1. **Ototoi no kooeñ wa, yôkatta soo desu nêe.**
'I hear that the lecture the day before yesterday was good, wasn't it!'

Âa, yôkatta yoo desu nêe. Watási wa itte (i)nài ñ desu ḡa . .
'Yes, it seems to have been good, doesn't it! (The fact is) I didn't go, but . . .' (I heard the same thing).

2. **Señsyuu no sibai wa, hîdôkatta soo desu nêe.**
'I hear that the play last week was awful, wasn't it!'

Âa, hîdôkatta yoo desu nêe. Watási wa itte (i)nài ñ desu ḡa . .
'Yes, it seems to have been awful, doesn't it! (The fact is) I didn't go, but . . .' (I heard the same thing).

3. **kon(ó) aida no pàat(e)ii/h(u)ôomaru datta**; 4. **getúyoo no zyùḡyoo/oózee kîta**; 5. **kyôneñ no tûaa/damê datta**

I 1. **Sono zisiñ, hîdôkatta?**
'Was that earthquake really awful?'

Îya, hidôi yoo datta kedo, hoñtoo wa hîdôku nâkatta ñ da tte.
'No, it seemed awful, but (the fact is) it actually was not awful, they say.'

2. **Anó hanasikàta, hâyâkatta?**
'Was that (way of) talking fast?'

Îya, hayâi yoo datta kedo, hoñtoo wa hâyâku nâkatta ñ da tte.
'No, it seemed fast, but (the fact is) it actually was not fast, they say.'

3. **sono siḡoto/mûri datta**; 4. **anó señsèe/tumárànakatta**; 5. **anô hito/ki ó tukète (i)ta**; 6. **yasai/nokôtte (i)ta**; 7. **anô hito/kuwâsìkatta**; 8. **kâre/awátetè (i)ta**

J 1. **Kono tokee, naôsita hoo ḡa îi ñ zya arímaseñ ka**↗
'Shouldn't you repair this watch?'

Sôo desu nêe. Zyâa, dâre ka himá na hitò ni naôsu yoo ni tanómimasyòo.
'You are right. Well then, I'll ask someone who's free to repair it.'

2. **Kono teḡami, îma kâita hoo ḡa îi ñ zya arímaseñ ka**↗
'Shouldn't you write this letter now?'

Sôo desu nêe. Zyâa, dâre ka himá na hitò ni kâku yoo ni tanómimasyòo.
'You are right. Well then, I'll ask someone who's free to write it.'

3. **konó kotobà/osieta**; 4. **koko/katázùket(e) oita**; 5. **kawári no hitò/saḡasita**; 6. **konó kimono to òbi/hâyâku todôketa**; 7. **sûmu tokoro/mitúket(e) òita**

K 1. **Konó kaisya no deñwabàñḡoo o saḡásite moraitài ñ desu ḡa . .**
'(It's that) I would like to have [someone] look for the telephone number of this company, but . . .' (is it possible?)

Âa, zyâa, hîsyo ni saḡásu yòo ni iímàsu kara . .
'Oh, then I'll tell the secretary to look for it, so . . .' (don't worry).

2. **Rêe no dañti è no 'ikikata o kâite móraitài ñ desu ḡa . .**

Âa, zyâa, hîsyo ni kâku yoo ni iímàsu kara . .

'(It's that) I would like to have [someone] write [out] the way (of going) to that apartment complex (we know about), but . . .' (is it possible?)

'Oh, then I'll tell the secretary to write it out, so . . .' (don't worry).

3. **dâre ka ni sibâraku ′koko ni nokôtte (i)te**; 4. **âsa hâyaku okôsite**; 5. **kâigi no koto o ′reñraku-site**; 6. **rêe no mâñsyoñ no ′nedañ o ′kiite**

L 1. **Nihoñgo, yôku tukáimàsu?**
'Do you use Japanese a lot?'

Sôo desu nêe. Mâa, narubeku tukáu yòo ni sité (i)rù ñ desu kedo . .
'Hmm. Well, (it's that) I'm trying (*lit.* acting in such a way) to use it as much as I can, but . . .' (it's not always possible).

2. **Tênisu, yôku reńsyuu-simàsu?**
'Do you practice tennis a lot?'

Sôo desu nêe. Mâa, narubeku reńsyuu-suru yòo ni sité (i)rù ñ desu kedo . .
'Hmm. Well, (it's that) I'm trying (*lit.* acting in such a way) to practice as much as I can, but . . .' (it's not always possible).

3. **tosyôkañ/yorímàsu**; 4. **kôñpa/demâsu**; 5. **tokkyuu/norímàsu**; 6. **koko/katázuke-màsu**; 7. **yasai/tabémàsu**

M 1. **Tokidoki okúreru-mìtai desu ne!**[2]
'It seems that you are sometimes late, aren't you.'

Êe, narubeku okúrenai yòo ni sité (i)rù ñ desu kedo, yáppàri nêe.
'Yes. (It's that) I'm trying (*lit.* acting in such a way) as much as possible not to be late, but after all, you know . . .' (it's difficult).

2. **Tokidoki matígaèru-mitai desu ne!**
'It seems that you sometimes make mistakes, don't you.'

Êe, narubeku matígaènai yoo ni sité (i)rù ñ desu kedo, yáppàri nêe.
'Yes. (It's that) I'm trying (*lit.* acting in such a way) as much as possible not to make mistakes, but after all, you know . . .' (it's difficult).

3. **gakkàri-suru**; 4. **wasureru**; 5. **syabérisugìru**; 6. **tabésugìru**

N 1. **Matá reńsyuu-site (i)rù ñ desu ka⟋**
'(Is it that) you are practicing again?'

Êe, hâyâku zyoózù ni nâru yoo ni, mâiniti reńsyuu-site (i)rù ñ desu.
'Yes. (It's that) I'm practicing every day so that (*lit.* in a way that) I get to be good quickly.'

2. **Matá tèepu o kiíte (i)rù ñ desu ka⟋**
'(Is it that) you are listening to tapes

Êe, hâyâku zyoózù ni nâru yoo ni, mâiniti kiíte (i)rù ñ desu.

2. Most of the stimulus statements of this drill would ordinarily be used only by a supervisor speaking to an employee.

again?' | 'Yes. (It's that) I'm listening every day so that (*lit.* in a way that) I get to be good quickly.'

3. **osiete moratte**; 4. **hôñ o mîte**; 5. **zyûĝyoo ni dête**; 6. **kyoókàsyo o yôñde**

O 1. **Ano gakusee, yôku wakárimàsu nêe.**
'That student understands well, doesn't s/he!'

Êe, sukôsi wa wakâru yoo ni narímàsita nêe. Mâe wa, zeńzeñ wakarànakatta ñ desu kedo nêe.
'Yes, s/he has reached the point where s/he understands a little (at least), hasn't s/he! (It's that) s/he didn't understand at all before, but . . .' (s/he has changed).

2. **Kânozyo, yôku syabérimàsu nêe.**
'She talks a lot, doesn't she!'

Êe, sukôsi wa syabêru yoo ni narímàsita nêe. Mâe wa, zeńzeñ syaberànakatta ñ desu kedo nêe.
'Yes, she has reached the point where she talks a little (at least), hasn't she! (It's that) she didn't talk at all before, but . . .' (she has changed).

3. **tyairo/niáimàsu**; 4. **kâre/yakû ni tatímàsu**; 5. **gosyûziñ/tasúkète kuremasu**; 6. **koñpyùutaa/tukáimàsu**

Application Exercises

A1. Conduct conversations similar to CC1 and 2 involving the following situations:

a. A (a student) is looking for an **arúbàito** job, and B (the sponsor) informs A of an opening at **Oríeñtaru-bòoeki,** only to have to explain later that the job has been filled.

b. A (a bank employee) wants to buy a car, and B (a colleague) tells A about a friend who wants to sell one. Later B must apologize because the car has already been sold.

c. A (a visiting professor) is looking for an apartment, and B (a graduate student) tells A about a vacancy in a building very near the university. The next day B must explain that the apartment has already been rented.

Develop your conversations along the lines of CC1 and 2, *not* as translations of original English creations. Utilize the newly introduced patterns as much as possible.

2. Using CC3 as a model, develop conversations that center about a compliment and a polite dismissal of it. Possible areas for compliments are driving, golf, use of the word processor, cooking (**ryôori**).

3. Practice relaying requests for activities that can easily be carried out in the classroom (opening and closing windows and doors, turning lights on and off, throwing away old newspapers, putting objects into—and taking them out of—desk drawers, etc.) Follow this sequence:

A to B: **C-sañ ni, mâdo o akéru yòo ni itte kuremaseñ ka**   'Would you tell C to open the window?'

B to C:	**Mâdo o akéte kuremasèñ ka** A-sañ ḡa akéte moraitài tte itta kara . .
	'Would you open the window? Because A says s/he wants it opened.'
C:	**Hâi.** (opens window) 'All right.'
D to C:	**Dôo site mâdo o akétà no?** 'Why is it you opened the window?'
C to D:	**A-sañ ḡa akéru yòo ni ittà kara . .** 'Because A said to open it.'

Assign new identities to the participants that result in changes in relative levels and speech style.

B. Core Conversations: Substitution

Practice the Core Conversations, making only minor changes through the substitution of individual vocabulary items and patterns which have similar meaning. For example: CC1(J)a. **Apâato o saḡásite irassyàru tte kikímàsita kedo . .** Next, make changes in style that become appropriate on the basis of variation in the participants and their relative levels.

SECTION B

Core Conversations

1(N)a. **Hîrosa wa kânari âru neʔ**

　　b. **Are. Konó màdo, kowáresòo ni nâtte (i)ru yo.**

　　c. **Môo nâñ-niñ ka mî ni kitá-rasìi kedo, daré mo kimaranàkatta yoo da si . .**

2(N)a. **Konáida mìta ití-d(e)iikèe, hudóosañya no hanasì de wa, mâda aíte (i)ru-rasìi yo.**

　　b. **Hiátari wa dòo daroo.**

　　c. **Mâa, anó yàtiñ no yâsusa da kara neʔ**

3(J)a. **Âa, kutábìreta. Kuttakuta dà yo. Tyôtto yasúmòo.**

(J)a. **Ñ. Wañrùumu da kara hirósòo ni miêru kedo, dôo daroo nêe.**

　　b. **Hoñtoo da. Yânusi wa hâyâku kimétasòo na kaó site (i)tà kedo, moó sukòsi kañḡàeta hoo ḡa yosásòo da nêe.**

(J)a. **Ano heñ wa, koótuu no bèñ ḡa îi si, bukka mo yasui-rasìi si ne!**

　　b. **Âa, hiatari ḡa moñdai da nêe. Nisí-muki dà kara . .**

(N)a. **Sikâsi, komâtta nêe. Ití-niti-zyuu arùite mîte mo, nañni mo nài ñ da kara . .**

b. **Kítto mitukarù yo—tekítoo nà no ḡa.**

c. **Kimí-ràsìku nâi yo—sońna koto iù no wa.**

b. **Môo doó de mo yòku nâttyatta.**

English Equivalents

(It is increasingly difficult to provide natural English equivalents which reflect the original Japanese structure. Be sure to study the Breakdowns and Miscellaneous Notes carefully, in order to check on how the Japanese is constructed.)

1(N)a. It's pretty big, isn't it?

b. Hey! This window looks as if it's going to fall apart!

c. Apparently a number of people already came to look at it, but there was no decision on anyone, it seems, and . . . (there are other reasons for thinking it over).

2(N)a. You know, the 1-DK you saw the other day, according to what the broker says, is apparently still vacant.

b. How about the exposure?

c. Well, since the rent is so cheap, (it's not surprising).

3(J)a. Oh, I'm exhausted. I'm bushed! Let's rest a little.

b. You'll surely find [an apartment]—one that's right for you.

c. That's not like you—saying something like that.

(J)a. Yeah. It's one room, so it looks big, but I wonder.

b. You're right. The landlord was looking as if he wanted to settle things quickly, but it looks as if it would be better to think about it a little more, doesn't it!

(J)a. That area has convenient transportation, and besides, the prices are apparently cheap, too.

b. Oh, it's the exposure that's a problem, isn't it! It faces west, so . . . (what can you expect?)

(N)a. But it's upsetting, isn't it! Because (it's that) even having wandered around and looked all day long, there's nothing.

b. It's already reached the point where anything will do.

BREAKDOWNS
(AND SUPPLEMENTARY VOCABULARY)

1. hírosa (SP1)   area, size (of area)
   + hirôi /-katta/   is spacious, wide, big (of area)
   + semâi /-katta/   is cramped, narrow, small (of area)
       kânari aru   there is quite a bit
       wañrùumu   one-room unit, studio apartment
   + señmeñzyo   washroom
       hirósòo /na/ (SP2)   spacious-looking
       hirósòo ni mîeru   appear spacious-looking
       kowárèru /-ru; kowâreta/   become broken, damaged, destroyed; fall apart

   + kowâsu /-u; kowasita/   break [something]; demolish, destroy
       kowáresòo /na/   looking as if it would break
       kowáresòo ni nâru   get to look as if it would break
       yânusi   landlord
       kimétasòo /na/   looking as if wanting to decide
       kao o suru   assume an expression
       kimétasòo na 'kao o site (i)ru   have an expression described as looking as if wanting to decide

       yosásòo /na/   looking good
       kañgàeta hoo ḡa yosásòo da   look as if it would be better to think
       nâñ-niñ ka   some number of people
       kitá-rasìi /-katta/ (SP3)   apparently has come
       dare mo kimaranakatta   no one was decided upon
2.ití-d(e)iikèe *or* wañ-d(e)iikèe   1-DK (i.e., one room + dining area/kitchen)

       hudoosañya   real estate broker
       X no hanásì de wa   according to what X says
       aite (i)ru   be vacant, available
       aíte (i)ru-rasìi   is apparently vacant
       kootuu   transportation
       bêñ   facilities; convenience
       bêñ ḡa îi   is convenient
       koótuu no bèñ ḡa îi   transportation facilities are good
       bukka   (commodity) prices
       yasúi-rasìi   is apparently cheap
       hiatari   exposure to the sun
       moñdai   problem

nisi-muki	facing west
yâtiñ	rent
yâsusa	cheapness
ano yatiñ no yasusa da	is (described in terms of) that cheapness of the rent
3. **kutábirèru /-ru; kutábìreta/**	become fatigued
kut(t)akuta	worn out, exhausted, dog-tired
sikâsi	but, however
iti-niti-zyuu	all day long
nañni mo	/emphatic equivalent of **nani mo**/
kitto	surely, certainly, undoubtedly
tekitoo /na/	suitable
doo de mo	however it is
doó de mo yòku naru	get to be all right no matter how it is
kimí-rasìi	is typical of you; seems to be you
kimí-ràsìku nâi	isn't typical of you; doesn't seem to be you

-zyoo: *Classifier for counting units of area covered by one tatami mat (jo) and naming the room of that size*

ití-zyòo	'1-mat area'	**rokú-zyòo**	'6-mat area/room'
ni-zyôo	'2-mat area'	**hatí-zyòo**	'8-mat area/room'
sañ-zyoo	'3-mat area' *or* '3-mat room'	**zyuú-zyòo**	'10-mat area/room'
yo-zyôo-hañ	'4½-mat area' *or* '4½-mat room'		

        nâñ-zyoo   'area/room of how many mats?'

-tubo: *Classifier for counting area covered by two tatami mats (tsubo)*

hitô-tubo	**rokû-tubo**
hutâ-tubo	**nanâ-tubo**
mî-tubo	**hât-tubo**
yô-tubo	**kyûu-tubo**
itû-tubo *or*	**tô-tubo**
gô-tubo	

nâñ-tubo 'area of how many 2-mat units?'

MISCELLANEOUS NOTES

1. In CC1, Smith (N) and his fellow graduate student, Kato (J), are checking out a vacant one-room unit as possible quarters for Smith, but there are problems. The style is casual and blunt, with direct-style predicates.

   (J)a. **Señmeñzyo** is a small room with a basin for washing the hands and face. Japanese homes regularly have **señmeñzyo** and **tôire** as two separate rooms.

(N)b. **Are** occurs frequently as an exclamation of surprise that attracts the attention of the addressee(s).

Kowáreru, an affective verbal, is the intransitive partner of **kowâsu**, an operational verbal. Note: **kowáreyasùi** 'is breakable, fragile' (stamped on packages); **kowaremono** 'fragile article'; **karáda o kowàsu** 'ruin one's health;' **onáka** (or **harâ**) **o kowàsu** 'develop stomach trouble.'

(J)b. **Kao** refers not only to the face but also to facial expression. Examples: **hêñ na kao** 'a strange expression'; **iyâ na kao** 'expression of displeasure'; **muzukasii kao** 'a grave expression.' Combined with **suru**, such sequences refer to having a particular kind of expression (cf. English 'make a face').

(N)c. **Môo** 'already' hooks up with the predicate **kitá-rasìi**. Note the use of /**dare mo** + intransitive **kimáranàkatta**/: 'no one was decided upon.' In careful style, we would expect **dare ni mo**.

Si, in final position ending a minor sentence, indicates that other things supporting the same theme are understood without being explicitly stated. Clearly, Smith and Kato are not enthusiastic about the room and are concerned about the overanxious landlord.

2. In CC2, Smith and Kato discuss further an apartment they looked at recently. Again, the style is casual and blunt, with direct-style predicates.

(N)a. In discussions of real estate, **-d(e)iikee** (written DK) combines with numerals of the Chinese series (written with Arabic numbers but with '1' representing **iti-** or **wañ-**) to indicate the size of an apartment—the number of rooms plus a dining area/kitchen combination: 1-DK, 2-DK. More spacious apartments may be /numeral + -LDK/, signifying the number of rooms plus a living room with a dining area/kitchen. Before these classifiers **ni** 'two' is lengthened to **nii**, and **go** 'five' to **goo**.

X no hanásì de wa: The **de** here indicates that what follows comes about through (i.e., by the medium of) 'X's talk.' Note also: **râzio, siñbuñ, têrebi, teńki-yòhoo**, etc. + **dè wa**. When responsibility for the information that follows is thus specifically assigned to someone or something other than the speaker, remember that the following predicate is appropriately qualified, with **sôo desu, tte**, or the like, or, as here, **yôo da**.

Aite (i)ru 'be open' extends to 'being open (= available) for use.' It may refer to seats, rooms, apartments, houses, people, etc.

(J)a. Here, two sequences, the first ending in **si**, provide supporting material regarding a single theme, without an overt expression of the result.

(J)b. **Muki** is derived from a verbal **muku** 'be(come) turned toward,' 'face.' Compounds consisting of /nominal X + **muki**/ imply literal 'facing toward X' or derived 'aimed at X' in the sense of 'suitable for X.' Thus, **minámi-muki no heyà** 'a room facing south'; **gaiziñ-muki no, hêñ na nihoñḡo** 'strange Japanese, aimed at foreigners'; **huyú-muki no òobaa** 'a coat suitable for winter.'

(N)c. Here, (N) relates the problem of the exposure of the apartment to the cheapness of the rent. Remember that **X da** covers not only equivalence ('[it] is X'), but also some kind of connection ('[it] is described in terms of X').

3. In CC3, Kato and Smith have become exhausted and discouraged after an unsuccessful day of apartment-hunting. Again, the style is casual and blunt, with direct-style predicates.

(J)a. **Kutábìreta** 'I became exhausted.' This intransitive, affective vowel verbal indicates a more intense degree of tiredness than **tukáreru**, which often occurs in ritualistic expressions that simply convey polite concern for effort expended (cf. **otúkaresama** [**dèsita**]). **Kutakuta** (or more emphatic **kuttakuta**) belongs to the category of Japanese onomatopoeia—words which are supposed to suggest their meaning by their sound. Such words are definitely culture-specific and must be acquired in the same way as other vocabulary items (cf. 19B-SP3).

(N)a. **Arûite mîte mo: arûku** here refers to wandering around. One can **arûku** through entire regions, countries, and even the world. Note **arûite mîru** 'wander around and see what develops.'

(J)b. **Kitto**, like 'undoubtedly' in English, does in fact allow for the possibility of some doubt. Accordingly it often occurs with tentative predicates: **Kitto kùru desyoo**. Note also **Kitto kùru to omoimasu**. While Kato and Smith are doing the searching, the finding of an apartment is *not* regarded as a volitional, operational act: it comes about—hence **mitukaru**, the affective intransitive 'be(come) found.'

(J)c. **Sońna koto iù no wa** '(the act of) saying things like that.'

Classifiers

-Zyoo is a classifier used in measuring room size. It equals the area covered by one tatami, approximately 18 square feet (6′ × 3′). Only the combinations listed above occur with any frequency. A /numeral + **-zyoo**/, besides indicating an area, may also be used as the name for a room having that area, reflecting the fact that rooms in Japanese dwellings are often multipurpose, not specifically 'dining rooms,' 'bedrooms,' 'studies,' and so on.

-Tubo is a classifier used in measuring the size of building lots, houses, gardens, etc. One tsubo is exactly two jo, the area covered by two tatami, or approximately 36 square feet. Notice the mixture of numerals from both the Japanese and Chinese series of numerals. From eleven on, only numerals of the Chinese series occur: **zyuúìt-tubo**, **zyuúnì-tubo**, etc.

Structural Patterns

1. **-sa**

The suffix **-sa** is attached to the root of adjectivals—the **-i** form minus **-i**—to form nominals that indicate the quantity of the adjectival quality. In most cases the accent corresponds to that of the **-ku** form of the adjectival (on the earlier mora when the **-ku** form has two alternatives). Thus:

âtusa	'heat'
hâyasa	'speed'
hîrosa	'size' (of an area)
kôsa	'strength' (of tea, coffee, etc.); 'depth' (of a color)
muzúkàsisa	'difficulty'
omósìrosa	'interest,' 'enjoyment'
ookisa	'size' (bulk)
sâmusa	'cold'
tûyosa	'strength'
yâsusa	'cheapness'

2. -soo

The nominal **sôo** combines with the stem of verbals (the **-masu** form minus **-masu**), the root of adjectivals (the **-i** form minus **-i**), and some **na-** nominals to form a nominal compound meaning 'looking as if ——,' 'appearing as if ——.' In some contexts, other senses may be involved: 'sounding as if ——,' 'smelling as if ——.' The compound is usually accented on the **so** of **-soo**, but there is an unaccented alternate when the preceding member of the compound is unaccented. Examples:

wakárisòo	'looking as if [s/he] understands'
dekísòo	'looking as if [s/he] can do it'
yamésòo/yamesoo	'looking as if [s/he] will quit'
nâni ka iísòo/iisoo	'looking as if [s/he] will say something'
oísisòo/oisisoo	'looking as if [it] is delicious'
muzúkasisòo/muzukasisoo	'looking as if [it] is difficult'
haíritasòo	'looking as if [s/he] wants to enter'
geńkisòo	'looking as if [s/he] is peppy'
zyoóbusòo/zyoobusoo	'looking as if [s/he] is sturdy'

The root **yo-** 'good' and negatives in **-nai** have special forms that include **-sa-** before **-soo**:

yosásòo	'looking as if [it] is good'
nasásòo	'looking as if there isn't any'
dekínasasòo	'looking as if [s/he] can't do it'

These compound nominals are all **na**-nominals.

zyoóbusòo na âkatyañ	'a sturdy-looking baby'
oísisòo na 'teñpura	'delicious-looking tempura'
âme ḡa hurísòo na hî	'days when it looks as if it will rain'

-Soo nominals occur before various forms of **dà**, as well as before the **ni** of manner:

Kowáresòo desu nêe. 'It looks as if it's going to break down, doesn't it!'

Naórisòo zya nâi desyoo? 'It doesn't look as if it will get fixed, does it?'

Atárasisòo ni miêru kedo, hoñtoo wa hurûi desu yo. 'It looks as if it's new (*lit.* appears in a new-looking manner), but actually it's old.'

Âme ni narísòo ni wa miémaseñ ḡa, neń no tamè ni, kâsa o moíte ikimasyòo. 'It doesn't look as if it will (get to be) rain, but let's take an umbrella, to be on the safe side.'

The last two examples, with both **-soo** and **miêru**, may seem redundant, but **miêru** refers to general 'seeming,' whereas **-soo** emphasizes the evidence of the senses.

☠ WARNING: Be sure to distinguish

Oísii-mìtai desu. *or* **Oísii yòo desu.** 'It's as if delicious'; 'It seems to be delicious' (on the basis of various kinds of evidence) *from*

Oísii sòo desu. 'I hear it's delicious'; 'They say it's delicious'; 'I'm told it's delicious' *and*

Oísisòo desu. 'It's delicious-looking.'

3. **-rasìi**

The adjectival **-rasìi** is a unique member of its class. While its various forms follow the regular adjectival pattern (**-rasìi, -ràsìku, -ràsìkatta, -ràsìkute**) and while it relates to what follows in an utterance in a perfectly predictable way, what precedes it is unique for an adjectival.

1. It may combine accentually with the preceding word with a dominant accent that eliminates any accent normally occurring on that word, or it may lose its accent following an accented word:

    kûru, *but* **kurú-rasìi** *or* **kûru-rasii**

    takâi, *but* **takái-rasìi** *or* **takâi-rasii**

The choice depends on which part of the meaning is focused. While the phenomenon of dominant accent has occurred in connection with some *nominal* add-ons (**-ḡùrai** and **-ḡòro**, for example), it does not occur with any other *adjectivals*.

2. Given this accent pattern, we would expect normal compounding (i.e., combining with verbal stems, adjectival roots, and nominals). Instead, we find that **-rasìi** is preceded by sentences consisting of or ending in the perfective or imperfective, but with those sentences that end in **dà** losing the **dà**. This particular distribution we have seen preceding **-mìtai** and the particle **ka** (as in **kâ mo sirenai**), but never before hooking up with a following adjectival. Examples:

    (a) **Wakáru-rasìi desu nêe.**

    (b) **Môo tuíta-rasìi desu kedo . .**

    (c) **Bukka wa takái-ràsìkatta desu yo**↗

    (d) **Anó apàato, môo aíte inàkatta-rasii desu ḡa . .**

    (e) **Nihóñḡo-ràsìku nâi desyoo?**

    (f) **Watási no-rasìi desu nêe.**

    (g) **Byoóki dàtta-rasii kedo . .**

Now what does **X-rasìi** mean? Unlike **yôo**, which indicates manner, resemblance, seeming in a rather imprecise sense, **X-rasìi** suggests that something apparently actually *is* X. The distinction is particularly clear when X is a nominal. Compare:

    Nihóñziñ no yoo desu. 'S/he's like a Japanese' (but isn't one).

    Nihóñziñ-rasìi desu. 'S/he's just like a Japanese' (and is one) *or* 'Apparently s/he's Japanese.'

    Oñna no yòo desu. 'He's like a woman.'

    Oñna-rasìi desu. 'S/he's just like a woman' (and is one) *or* 'Apparently that's a woman.'

Note also:

    harú-rasìi têñki 'weather typical of when it actually is spring'

    daíḡaku-rasìi daiḡaku 'a university worthy of the name' (i.e., that seems to be a university)

    otóna-ràsiku suru 'act as if actually an adult'

Now we add to the examples at the end of the preceding note:

Oísii-rasìi desu. 'Apparently it is delicious' (based on any kind of evidence; more assertive and positive than **yôo-** combinations)

And now we can provide glosses for the examples in (2) above:
(a) 'Apparently s/he understands, doesn't s/he!'
(b) 'S/he apparently has already arrived, but . . .' (do you know?)
(c) 'Prices were apparently high.'
(d) 'Apparently that apartment wasn't available any more, but . . .' (did you know?)
(e) 'That doesn't seem to be Japanese, does it?'
(f) 'That seems to be mine, doesn't it!' (I believe it is.)
(g) 'Apparently s/he was sick, but . . .' (I didn't know).

Drills

A 1. **Señsèe no otaku wa, kânari hirôi desu yo**   **Anoo, donó-g̃urai no hìrosa na ñ desu ka**
'The professor's house is quite large, you know.'   'Uhh, what is the approximate size (*lit.* largeness)?'

2. **Kyôneñ no taíhùu wa, hîdôkatta desu yo**   **Anoo, donó-g̃urai no hìdosa datta ñ desu ka**
'The typhoon last year was severe, you know.'   'Uhh, what was the approximate strength (*lit.* severity)?'

3. **Yamâmori-sañ no kaisya/oókìi**; 4. **konó heñ no natù/atûi**; 5. **asoko no dañti/sêmâkatta**; 6. **konó tìzu/kuwásìi**; 7. **konó suutukèesu/omoi**

B 1. **Sono kuruma, takâi ñ̃ zya nai?**   **Ñ, takásòo nêe.**[3]
'Isn't (it the case that) that car (is) expensive?'   'Yes, it looks expensive, doesn't it!'

2. **Kâre, wakâi ñ zya nai?**   **Ñ, wakásòo nêe.**[3]
'Isn't (it the case that) he (is) young?'   'Yes, he looks young, doesn't he!'

3. **rêe no mâñsyoñ/aite (i)ru**; 4. **asoko no niwa/semâi**; 5. **Tâkasi-tyañ/geñki na**; 6. **ohûro/atûi**; 7. **konó kèeki/damê na**; 8. **ano ryokañ/sîzuka na**; 9. **kyôo/yakeru**

C 1. **Sonó pài, oísìi desyoo.**   **Oísisòo ni miêru kedo, dôo desyoo nêe.**
'That pie is probably tasty.'   'It looks tasty, but I wonder how it is.'

2. **Kono sakana, daízyòobu desyoo.**   **Daízyoobusòo ni miêru kedo, dôo desyoo nêe.**
'This fish is probably all right.'   'It looks all right, but I wonder how it is.'

3. **atárasìi arúbàito no ko/dekíru**; 4. **âme/hûru**; 5. **anó òobaa/aítakài**; 6. **tokkyuu no kippu/mûri**; 7. **konó kutù/hakíyasùi**

D 1. **A, kowárèru.**   **E? A, hoñtoo da. Kowáresòo ni natte (i)masu nêe.**
'Look, it's going to break!'

---

3. The **-soo nêe.** pattern is gentle. The blunt equivalent ends in **-soo da nee.**

2. **A, yakeru.**
'Look, it's going to burn!'

'What? Oh, you're right. It looks (*lit.* has come to look) as if it's going to break, doesn't it!'

E? A, hoñtoo da. Yakésoo ni nàtte (i)masu nêe.
'What? Oh, you're right. It looks (*lit.* has come to look) as if it's going to burn, doesn't it!'

3. **dêru**; 4. **mitukaru**; 5. **miêru**; 6. **tûku**; 7. **simâru**

E 1. **Kimura-sañ wa, ano sigòto o yamétai to omòtte (i)ru-mitai desu nêe.**
'Mr/s. Kimura seems to be thinking s/he'd like to quit, doesn't s/he.'

Êe, yamétasòo na kao o site (i)masu nêe.
'Yes, s/he has an expression on her/his face that looks as if s/he wants to quit, doesn't s/he.'

2. **Sâtoo-sañ wa, anó mànsyoñ o kaítai to omòtte (i)ru-mitai desu nêe.**
'Mr/s. Sato seems to be thinking s/he'd like to buy that apartment, doesn't s/he.'

Êe, kaítasòo na kao o site (i)masu nêe.
'Yes, s/he has an expression on her/his face that looks as if s/he wants to buy [it], doesn't s/he.'

3. **Nôguti-sañ/anó wañrùumu o ′karitai**; 4. **Nakada-sañ/yânusi ni aítài**;
5. **hudoosañya/hâyàku ′uritai**; 6. **kodomo/niwá e detài**; 7. **Oota-kuñ/sibâraku yasúmitài**

F 1. **Zañnèñ?**
'Is it regrettable?'

Zañnèñ daroo?⁴
'It is regrettable, isn't it?'

2. **Semâi?**
'Is it small (in area)?'

Semâi daroo?⁴
'It is small (in area), isn't it?'

3. **ki ni suru**; 4. **kuwásii**; 5. **kigáèru**; 6. **soozi-suru**; 7. **hutuu (da)**; 8. **îi**; 9. **zyoobu (da)**

G 1. **Anô hito, yânusi desu ka⤴**
'Is that person over there the landlord?'

Yânusi darôo to omóimàsu.
'I think s/he probably is (the landlord).'

2. **Anó wañrùumu, hirôi desu ka⤴**
'Is that studio apartment large?'

Hirôi darôo to omóimàsu.
'I think it probably is (large).'

3. **kyoókàsyo/kimárimàsita**; 4. **koótuu no bèñ/yôkatta desu**; 5. **asoko/hudóosañya dèsu**; 6. **soko/wañ-d(e)ii-kèe desita**; 7. **kânozyo/syabérimàsu**

H 1. **Anô hito, nihóñzìñ desyoo?**
'That person over there is Japanese,

Êe, nihóñziñ-rasìi desu nêe. Nihóñgo hanàsite (i)ru si . .

---

4. In sentence-final position, **daroo** is blunt and more typical of male speech. Women are more apt to use **desyoo** except in markedly casual speech.

isn't s/he?'

'Yes, s/he apparently is Japanese, isn't s/he. S/he's speaking Japanese, and . . .' (there is other evidence).

2. **Anô hito, supéìnziñ desyoo?**
'That person over there is Spanish, isn't s/he?'

Êe, supéiñziñ-rasìi desu nêe. Supéiñgo hanàsite (i)ru si . . .
'Yes, s/he apparently is Spanish, isn't s/he. S/he's speaking Spanish, and . . .' (there is other evidence).

3. **doítùziñ**; 4. **tyuúgokùziñ**; 5. **huráñsùziñ**

I 1. **Môo nañ-niñ ka kitâ ñ desu ka⤴**
'(Is it that) some number of people came already?'

Kitá-rasìi ñ desu yo.
'(The fact is) they apparently did (come).'

2. **Zeñzeñ naorànai ñ desu ka⤴**
'(Is it that) it can't be fixed at all?'

Naóranai-rasìi desu yo.
'(The fact is) it apparently can't be (fixed).'

3. **hitô-ri de daízyòobu na**; 4. **hiátari mo wàrùkatta**; 5. **yâtiñ ga 'agaru**; 6. **koótuu ga moñdai dàtta**; 7. **nedañ ga tekítoo zya nài**; 8. **kânari arûita**; 9. **hutúu no ookisa nò na**

J 1. **Kâre-mitai na hito, nihóñzìñ ni wa oôi desu nêe.**
'People like him are numerous among Japanese, aren't they!'

Mâa, kâre wa, hoñtoo ni nihoñziñ-rasìi hito desu kara nêe.
'Well, he really is a typical Japanese, so—you know' (it's not surprising).

2. **Kokó-mìtai na tokoro, Sañhurañ-sìsuko ni wa oôi desu nêe.**
'Places like this place are numerous in San Francisco, aren't they!'

Maa, koko wa, hoñtoo ni Sañhurañsisuko-rasìi tokoro desu kara nêe.
'Well, this place really is a typical San Francisco place, so—you know' (it's not surprising).

3. **Tâkasi-mitai na kodomo/otókò no ko**; 4. **kokó-mìtai na dañti/Nihôñ**; 5. **asóko-mìtai na syokudoo/daígaku**; 6. **kinóo nò-mitai na hirôoeñ/kono heñ**

K 1. **Yosida-kuñ, kaisya o yamétài ñ da tte.**
'I hear (it's that) Yoshida wants to quit his job (lit. the company).'

Hee⤴ Sikâsi, Yosída-kuñ-ràsìku nâi nêe—kaísya o yametài to iû no wa.
'Really? But that isn't like Yoshida, is it—to want to quit.'

2. **Kêe-tyañ, rikóñ-sisòo na ñ da tte.**
'I hear (it's that) it looks as if Kei will get divorced.'

Hee⤴ Sikâsi, Keé-tyañ ràsìku nâi nêe—rikóñ-sisòo da to iû no wa.
'Really? But that isn't like Kei, is it—to (look as if she'll) get divorced.'

3. **Morimoto-sañ/gaíkoku ni sumitàku nâi**; 4. **katyoo/syabéritàku nâi**; 5. **Ôono-señ-see/zutto oyasumi ni nàru**; 6. **Suzuki-sañ/zyûgyoo ga wakáranakatta**; 7. **Mîyazi-sañ/dôñdoñ 'sutetyatta**

L 1. **Yâtiñ wa dôo daroo.**[5]   **Âa, yâtiñ ğa moñdai da nêe.**
'How do you suppose the rent is?'   'Oh, it's the rent that's the problem!'
2. **Koótuu wa dòo daroo.**   **Âa, kootuu ğa moñdai da nêe.**
'How do you suppose the transportation is?'   'Oh, it's the transportation that's the problem!'
3. **nedañ**; 4. **hîrosa**; 5. **señmeñzyo**; 6. **hiatari**; 7. **niwa**

M 1. **Ikímasyòo ka.**   **Ñ, îi yo**↗ **Ikôo.**[6]
'Shall we go?'   'Uh-huh, fine. Let's go.'
2. **Kaémasyòo ka.**   **Ñ, îi yo**↗ **Kaéyòo.**
'Shall we change [them]?'   'Uh-huh, fine. Let's change [them].'
3. **arúkimasyòo**; 4. **yasúmimasyòo**; 5. **kañğaemasyòo**; 6. **yakímasyòo**;
7. **dekákemasyòo**

N 1. **Zêñbu yarôo yo.**[7]   **Îi wa yo**↗[8] **Zyâa, zêñbu yarímasyòo.**
'Let's do the whole thing.'   'Fine. (Then) let's do it all.'
2. **Moó sukòsi sağásòo yo.**   **Îi wa yo**↗ **Zyâa, moó sukòsi sağásimasỳoo.**
'Let's search a little more.'   'Fine. (Then) let's search a little more.'
3. **sukôsi nokôsit(e) okoo**; 4. **môo kowâsityaoo**; 5. **zêñbu haráòo**; 6. **môo akírameyòo**

O 1. **Wañ-d(e)iikèe o karímasu ka**↗   **Êe, wañ-d(e)iikèe o karíyòo to omôtte (i)ru ñ desu.**
'Are you going to rent a 1-DK?'   'Yes, (it's that) I'm thinking of renting a 1-DK.'
2. **Syosái ni imàsu ka**↗   **Êe, syosái ni iyòo to omôtte (i)ru ñ desu.**
'Are you going to be in the study?'   'Yes, (it's that) I'm thinking of staying in the study.'
3. **dâburu o yoyáku-simàsu**; 4. **raísyuu màde yasúmimàsu**; 5. **anó iè ni sumímàsu**;
6. **kimóno o tukùtte moraimasu**; 7. **rokû-zi ni okímàsu**

P 1. **Ôono-sañ wa, nií-d(e)iikèe o karíru-rasìi desu nêe.**   **Êe, soó-rasìi kedo, watási wa nii-d(e)iikèe o karíyòo to wa omóimasèñ nêe.**
'Mr/s. Ono is apparently going to rent a 2-DK, isn't s/he.'   'Yes, that's apparently right, but I (at least) don't think I'd rent a 2-DK (as I think about it).'
2. **Suğîura-sañ wa, tônai ni sumú-rasìi desu nêe.**   **Êe, soó-rasìi kedo, watási wa tònai ni sumôo to wa omóimasèñ nêe.**

---

5. In sentence-final position, **daroo** is blunt and more typical of male speech. Women are more apt to use **desyoo** except in markedly casual speech. The responses here are also blunt.
6. These responses are blunt-style.
7. These stimuli are blunt-style.
8. These responses are feminine.

'Mr/s. Sugiura is apparently going to live in central Tokyo, isn't s/he.'

'Yes, that's apparently right, but I (at least) don't think I'd live in central Tokyo (as I think about it).'

3. **Watanabe-kuñ/taḱkyuubiñ o tanòmu**; 4. **Nakáda Kèeko-sañ/yâtiñ o 'ki ni site (i)ru**; 5. **Tâkano-sañ/kâzoku de 'ryokoo-suru**; 6. **Nisîzaka-sañ/h(u)ôomaru na monô o 'kite iku**; 7. **Itoo-sañ/zêñbu koṕpyùutaa de yaru**

Q 1. **Asítà mo apâato o mîru tumori desu ka⤴**
'Do you intend to look at apartments tomorrow, too?'

Êe, ití-niti-zyuu mìru tumori desu.
'Yes, I intend to look at [them] all day long.'

2. **Raíneñ mo Kùbota-señsee no syakâiḡaku ni dêru tumori desu ka⤴**
'Do you intend to attend Professor Kubota's sociology [lectures] next year, too?'

Êe, ití-neñ-zyuu dèru tumori desu.
'Yes, I intend to attend all year long.'

3. **raisyuu/tosyôkañ ni 'kayou**; 4. **râiḡetu/kokó de arubàito o suru**; 5. **nitíyòobi/gôruhu o suru**

R 1. **Kyôo kimárù ñ desu neʕ**
'(It's that) it's going to be decided today, isn't it?'

Êe, kyoó-zyuu ni kimàru daroo to omóimàsu yo⤴
'Yes, I think that it will probably be decided (within) today.'

2. **Kotósi dekìru ñ desu neʕ**
'(It's that) it's going to be completed this year, isn't it?'

Êe, kotósi-zyuu ni dekìru daroo to omóimàsu yo⤴
'Yes, I think that it will probably be completed (within) this year.'

3. **koñsyuu reñraku-site kureru**; 4. **koñḡetu mièru**; 5. **kinóo katazùketa**

Application Exercises

A1. Using an assortment of pictures as the basis, make **-rasii** statements, with a justification for your assumption. Examples:

Konó apàato, takái-rasìi desu. Nyuúyòoku ni âru si, hîrosa ḡa kânari âru kara . .
Konô hito, nihóñziñ-rasìi desu. Kimóno o kite (i)rù si, osûsi o tâbete (i)ru kara . .

2. Now practice making comments about how things and people—in the classroom and in pictures—look, using the **-soo** pattern. Examples: (of food) **Oísisòo desu nêe**; (of a child) **Zyoóbusòo na kodómo dèsu nêe**; (of a book) **Omósirosòo desyoo?** (of the weather) **Tyôtto âme ḡa hûtte (i)ru kedo, harésòo ni miémàsu nêe.**

3. Have several members of the class play the part of newcomers to the area. Have them ask other class members about local rental units: availability, size of typical apartments,

rents, transportation facilities, commodity prices, location of closest schools, churches, shops, etc.

B. Core Conversations: Substitution

Practice the Core Conversations, making stylistic changes appropriate to other kinds of participants, such as female students using gentle direct-style and business colleagues using plain distal-style. Next, practice asking and answering content questions on the conversations.

SECTION C

Eavesdropping

(Answer the following on the basis of the accompanying audiotape. In each conversation, A = the first speaker, and B = the second.)
 1a. What information does A give B?
  b. What does B think must be done?
  c. Why does A tell B to wait?
  d. What eventually proves to be true?
 2a. What does A note about the third floor? In what kind of building?
  b. What is B's explanation?
 3a. What does A note about the foreigner over there?
  b. What is B's reaction? Why?
 4a. According to A, how are the two Sugiuras related?
  b. What does B want to know?
  c. What is A's explanation?
 5a. What has A become aware of?
  b. What does B want to know?
  c. What explanation for it does A offer?
  d. What comment does B make about A, and why does B think that?
 6a. What is the topic of discussion?
  b. What in particular does A want to know?
  c. What information is B able to provide?
  d. What does A say about quitting?
  e. What is said to be Ota's attitude?
 7a. Who is B?
  b. What request does A make of B? Why?
  c. What is B going to do?
 8a. What is B doing at this time?
  b. What specifically has B not located?
  c. What two types that would be acceptable are mentioned?
  d. What location is B interested in?
  e. What is the problem with that location?
 9a. What is A wondering about?
  b. What is B's first reply? And then?
  c. What is the eventual answer to A's question?
  d. What happens in the end?
10a. Why is A apologizing?

b. What is B's reaction?
   c. What was A's intention before the event under discussion?
   d. How does B try to reduce A's regret over what happened?
   e. What does B request of A?
11a. Who is being discussed?
   b. What is that person's profession?
   c. What does B say about that person's activities yesterday? How were they accounted for?
   d. How does A react to this?
   e. What do A and B have to say about Sundays?
12a. In what room does this conversation take place?
   b. How does A describe the room? Mention three points.
   c. Toward what direction does the room face?
   d. How large is the room?
   e. What other rooms are mentioned?
   f. Where are they in reference to the room where A and B are at present?
13a. What compliment does A pay B?
   b. How does B respond to the compliment?
   c. What does A mention as being of great help?
   d. What concern does A have in regard to B?
   e. How does B dispel the concern?
14a. Where is B going, for what purpose, and for how long?
   b. What will happen to B's family? Why?
   c. What comment does B make about this planned lifestyle?
   d. In what connection does B use **betubetu**?
15a. What news does A give B?
   b. Why is B surprised?
   c. What does B want to do?
   d. What does A suggest? Why?
   e. How does B respond to the suggestion?
16a. What kind of invitation does A extend to B?
   b. What apology does A add?
   c. What are the positive points about the place under discussion?
17a. Who is the topic of discussion?
   b. Where is that person at present, in what general condition?
   c. Why is this surprising?
   d. What is the exact problem, and what is being done?
18a. Why is A disappointed?
   b. Why are A and B surprised at what happened?
   c. What does B assume is the explanation for what happened?
   d. What seems to be the actual explanation?
   e. In what terms does B describe the situation?
19a. What place is the topic of discussion?
   b. Why is it being discussed?
   c. Who has offered some explanation, and what is that explanation?
   d. Who is being looked for, and with what success?
   e. What does B confess to not knowing?
20a. Who is A?
   b. When does A play tennis?
   c. What does B assume about A's playing?
   d. What does A claim is actually true?

    e. What plans are made for the future?
21a. What has B decided to do? Why?
  b. What is the location of the topic of discussion?
  c. What is its size?
  d. What is one disadvantage of it?
22a. Where does B live? Since when?
  b. How long does it take from the station? Give details.
  c. How does A regard the distance?
23a. Who is B?
  b. What is the profession of B's spouse?
  c. What kind of person is A looking for?
  d. What encouraging information does B offer?
  e. In what connection is television mentioned?
  f. What is A's problem, and when did it start?
  g. What is B's advice?
  h. What does B offer to do?
24a. Who are A and B?
  b. How are A and B feeling at the moment? Why? Give details.
  c. What two hopeful comments are made in reference to the future?
  d. What general comment does A make about their work?
  e. How does it all seem to B?
25a. Who is B?
  b. Where is B going? When? By what means? Give details.
  c. For what purpose is B making the trip?
  d. What is B's ultimate professional goal?
  e. On what basis did B choose the place that has been decided upon?
  f. How often has B been to that place?
  g. What information about that place does A provide?

Utilization

(In addition to a Japanese equivalent for each of the following, provide at least an appropriate stimulus or response.)

　1. Tell your colleague that the housing development where you are living now is very inconvenient, so you've decided to rent an apartment that is nearer the office (*lit.* company).
　2. Tell the division chief that there are some things you'd like to talk over with him at some time that is convenient for him.
　3. Tell your colleague that it has been decided that Suzuki will go to Europe for six months, but his wife will stay on in Japan with their children.
　4. Someone is looking for the secretary. Tell him that she seems to have gone somewhere, but you don't know where she went.
　5. Ask a friend what she's looking for.
　6. You're making plans for an extended period of time away from your home. Ask a colleague if she knows anyone who will house-sit for you.
　7. You have been asked about an acquaintance of yours. Explain that you don't know the details, but apparently she is going to stay on in England for a while longer.
　8. Tell a colleague that that apartment (that you both know about) seems to be available until July.
　9. You're shorthanded in the office. Offer to keep watching out [to see if] there isn't some student who will help.

10. You've been asked about a colleague's Chinese ability. Explain that he speaks well, like a Chinese.

11. Complain to your colleague that you told the part-timer to bring some coffee, but she apparently forgot.

12. Compliment a new Japanese acquaintance on his English: tell him that there are few people who are (as) skilled in English as he is.

13. Tell a friend that you didn't understand Japanese at all last year, but now you've reached the point where you understand a little.

14. Tell a new acquaintance that you are trying to use Japanese as much as possible, but you aren't yet proficient.

15. Inquire as to how long it ordinarily takes to reach the point where you use a word processor with skill.

16. A friend is apologizing for something he did. Tell him not to be concerned; it doesn't matter.

17. Tell your colleague that by all means you want to reach the point where you can handle Japanese well, but you forget it quickly, and (you know!).

18. You are discussing a mutual friend with a colleague. Point out that she seems concerned at not understanding Japanese.

19. Comment that this morning it looked as if it would rain, but that apparently it isn't going to (rain).

20. Comment (a) on a spring day; (b) on a winter day on how springlike it is.

21. You are commenting on an apartment you are considering. Point out that the transportation facilities are good, it has southern exposure, the rent is reasonable—but it's a small 1-DK, so it probably won't be suitable.

22. A guest has commented on how spacious your home is. Explain that it looks large from the outside, but actually it is small.

23. A helper is about to move a box in your office. Tell him to be careful because there are fragile things in it.

24. A helper is moving a large, breakable object. Tell him to be careful (so as) not to break it.

25. In response to a question as to whether something is good, explain that it looks good, but you're not sure whether it actually is good or not.

26. Comment to a friend that she looks pale. Ask if she's all right.

27. You are preparing to move to a different city. Tell a friend that both rents and prices there are terribly high.

28. Someone is about to show you a rental apartment. Quietly ask your companion if he's the landlord or the real estate broker.

29. Reassure a discouraged apartment-seeker by telling him that he will undoubtedly find a suitable apartment soon.

30. Tell your colleague that you are renting (a) an 8-mat room; (b) a 20-tsubo house; (c) a furnished ('furniture attached') apartment.

31. Comment that that little girl looks Japanese: (a) you think she *is* Japanese; (b) you think she *isn't* Japanese.

32. Exclaim on your exhaustion!

Check-up

1. Compare the use of /—— **kotô ni suru**/ and /—— **kotô ni nâru**/. How does the difference relate to the basic difference in meaning between **suru** and **nâru**? (A-SP1)

2. What is the meaning of an /interrogative + **ka**/? Describe the usual occurrence of phrase-particles following this pattern. Under what circumstances are examples of this pattern more apt to be followed by **ḡa** or **o**? (A-SP2)

3. What is the meaning of /**X-mìtai**/? Identify X in terms of the different forms it may take. Why is **-mìtai** called an enclitic (an add-on) rather than an independent nominal? An /**X-mìtai**/ sequence functions within a sentence as a member of what word-class? What may follow an /**X -mìtai**/ sequence within a sentence? (A-SP3)

4. What is the basic meaning of **yôo**? To what word-class does it belong? How does it differ from **-mìtai**? Compare the use of **yôo** in **tukáu yòo ni 'iu, tukáu yòo ni 'suru, tukáu yòo ni nâru**. (A-SP4)

5. Compare the Japanese equivalents for 'I want to do' and 'I want to be able [to do].' What is the significant feature that accounts for the difference? (A-SP4)

6. Describe the nominal formation that indicates the degree of the quality of an adjectival, i.e., 'coldness,' 'heat,' 'size,' etc. (B-SP1)

7. The nominal **sôo** occurs as the second member of nominal compounds: what constitutes the first member of such compounds? What is special about negatives and **yôi** in combination with **-soo**? What is the meaning of **-soo** compounds? Within sentences, what occurs following **-soo** compounds? (B-SP2)

8. To what word-class does **-rasìi** belong? What is the meaning of **X-rasìi**, and what may constitute X in this combination? Why is **-rasìi** said to be a unique member of its class? (B-SP3)

9. Distinguish among the members of each of the following sets:

   (a) **Nihóñzìñ no yoo desu.**
   Nihóñzìñ-mitai desu.
   Nihóñzìñ-rasìi desu.

   (b) **Takásòo desu.**
   Takâi soo desu.
   Takâi yoo desu.

   (c) **Wakárisòo desu.**
   Wakâru soo desu.
   Wakáru-rasìi desu.

   (d) **Hâru no yoo na têñki desu.**
   Harú-rasìi têñki desu.
   Hâru-mitai na têñki desu.   (A-SP3, SP4) (B-SP2, SP3)

Japanese–English Glossary

The following list contains all the vocabulary introduced in Part 1 and Part 2 of this text—words occurring in the Miscellaneous Notes and Structural Patterns as well as those appearing in the Core Conversations. Only personal names are omitted. Numbers plus A or B following the entries refer to lesson and section; a number plus A or B alone means that the entry first occurs in the Core Conversations of that lesson and section; with a following plus sign it refers to a later part of that lesson. CI and GUP refer to Classroom Instructions[1] and Greetings and Useful Phrases, respectively.

Except in special cases, verbals and adjectivals are listed in their citation form only. Every verbal is assigned to the appropriate subclass;[2] its perfective form is also given. For example, **tabêru /-ru; tâbeta/** identifies **tabêru** as a verbal belonging to the **-ru** subclass (i.e., the vowel-verbal subclass), with perfective **tâbeta.**

Every adjectival is identified by /**-katta**/, the perfective ending, after the citation form. Thus, the adjectival meaning 'is big' appears as: **oókìi /-katta/**.

All forms of the copula which occur in the text are listed and identified.

Nominals occur with no special designation, except that the members of the subclass of **na**-nominals[3] are identified by a following /**na**/.

Particles and the quotative are identified as /ptc/ and /quotative/, respectively.

Pre-nominals are identified by the designation /+ nom/.

Classifiers are so identified and are listed with a preceding hyphen.

Except in a few special cases, words having a polite alternate that differs from the plain alternate only in the addition of the polite prefix **o-** or **go-** are listed only in the plain form.

For purposes of alphabetizing, hyphens and the macron of **ḡ** and **ñ** are ignored.

In most cases, combinations occurring as indented sublistings match the first occurrence of the pattern in the lessons; but a simpler, more generally occurring example of the pattern is cited in cases where the combination which occurs first seems less desirable as the model for a pattern of wide general use.

â(a) oh! 2A
abunai /-katta/ is dangerous 7B
aḡaru /-u; aḡatta/ go/come up; rise 18A
aḡeru /-ru; aḡeta/ give (to you/him/her/them) 17A

   kasite aḡeru lend (to you/him/her/them) 17A
aḡeru /-ru; aḡeta/ raise 18A+
   tê o aḡeru raise one's hand 18A+
   atámà o aḡeru lift up one's head 18A+

---

1. Words designated as CI are those which occur only in the Classroom Instructions.
2. For a description of verbal subclasses, see Lesson 9A, Structural Pattern 1, in Part 1.
3. See Lesson 5B, Structural Pattern 1, in Part 1.

aida interval; between-space 6A
   baiteñ to dêguti no aida between the stand and the exit 6A
âidea idea 11A
ainiku unfortunate; unfortunately 12A
aísukurìimu ice cream 3A+
akai /-katta/ is red 4A+
âkatyañ baby 10A+
akeru /-ru; aketa/ open [something] 16A
âki fall, autumn 19A+
akíramèru /-ru; akíràmeta/ give up, forego; resign oneself to 23A
aku /-u; aita/ become open; [something] opens 16A
   aite (i)ru be vacant, available 24B
amâdo storm door 16A+
amágàsa (rain) umbrella 23B+
amai /-katta/ is sweet; is bland 15B+
âme rain 4A
   âme ni nâru get to be rain, start to rain 22A
Amerika America 5B+
Amérika-giñkoo Bank of America 16A
amérikàziñ an American 10B+
amî net 16A+
amîdo screen door 16A+
anâta you 2B+
ane older sister; my older sister 11A+
âni older brother; my older brother 11A+
a(ñ)mari /+ negative/ not much; not very 1B
añna that kind (of) 4B+
   añna ni to that extent; like that 9B+
ano /+ nom/ that —— over there; that —— (known to both of us) 3A
   anô hitò he; she 10A+
   anó kàta he; she /polite/ 10A+
|**anoo**| uh 4B
aôi /-katta/ is blue; is green 4A
apâato apartment; apartment house 14B
   Itóo-apàato the Ito Apartments 14B
arau /-u; aratta/ wash 17B+
are that thing over there; that thing (known to both of us) 2B
arígatài /-katta/ is grateful; is obliged 18A
   arígàtàku tyoodai-suru ↓ accept gratefully /humble-polite/ 18A
Arîgatoo (gozaimasu). + Thank you. GUP
Arîgatoo (gozaimasita). + Thank you (for what you did). GUP
âru /-u; âtta/ be located (of inanimate existence); have 4A
   kesíte àru [it] has been turned off 16A

arúbàito part-time work, usually performed by students 10A
arûku /-u; arûita/ walk 7B
   arûite iku go on foot 7B
âsa morning 8B+
aságòhañ breakfast 14A+
asâtte day after tomorrow 3B
asî leg, foot 17A+
asítà tomorrow 1A
asoko that place over there; that place (known to both of us) 6B+
asû tomorrow 1A+
asuko /casual alternate of **asoko**/ 9A
atámà head 17A+
atárasìi /-katta/ is new; is fresh 1B+
at(á)takài /-katta/ is warm 11A
atira that side; that way; thereabouts; there; that alternative (of two) 6A+
âto later; remaining 8A
   dête simatta âto de (being) after having left 19B
   âto de (being) later on 11A
   âto ití-zìkañ one hour left 8A
attì /casual alternate of **atira**/ 7B+
atui /-katta/ is thick 23B+
atûi /-katta/ is hot 11A+
atúmàru /-u; atúmàtta/ come together 19B
atúmèru /-ru; atûmeta/ bring together 19B+
âtusa heat 24B+
âu /-u; âtta/ meet; see (a person) 11A
   X ni âu meet person X; see person X 11A
   X to âu meet (with) person X; see person X 11A+
âu /-u; âtta/ match up with 18A
   kutí ni àu suit one's taste 18A
   ma ní àu be on time 20B
awateru /-ru; awateta/ become confused, disconcerted, disorganized 19B
azi taste 22B
   azi ga suru have a taste 22B+
azúkàru /-u; azúkàtta/ accept for temporary keeping 19A+
azúkèru /-ru; azúketa/ hand over for temporary keeping; check 19A

baai case, circumstance 23B
   koo iu baai cases like this 23B
   baai ni yotte depending on circumstances 23B+
baiteñ stand; concession; kiosk 6A
bañ night 8B+

-bañ /classifier for counting nights/ 21A+
-bañ /classifier for serial numbers/ 3A
bañgòhañ dinner 14A+
bañgòo (assigned) number 12A
bañgumi program 18B
bâsu bus 7B+
basu-tuki with bath 21A+
bâta butter 14A+
Beekoku U.S.A. 5B+
bêekoñ bacon 14A+
bêñ facilities; convenience 24B
   bêñ ga îi is convenient 24B
beñgòsi lawyer 16B+
beñkyoo study 9B+
beñkyoo-suru study 9B
bêñri /na/ convenient 4A
beñtòo box lunch 14A+
Bêruriñ Berlin 12B+
bêtto/bêddo bed 17B+
betubetu separate 21A+
betu ni /+ negative/ not especially 9A
bîiru beer 5B+
biî-sètto the "B" meal 15B+
bikkùri-suru become surprised 11A
biñseñ stationery 4B+
bîru office building 6A
   Paáku-bìru the Park building 6A
bôku/boku I; me /M/ 2B+
booeki foreign trade 10A
   Oríeñtaru-bòoeki the Oriental Trading (Company) 10A
booeki-suru conduct foreign trade 10A+
boóekìsyoo foreign trader, importer-exporter 16B+
boorupeñ ballpoint pen 4B
boosi hat 23A
bôttyañ son; your son; young man /polite/ 10A+
bu division within a company 13B+
buatui /-katta/ is thick 23B
bukka (commodity) prices 24B
buñbòogu stationery; office supplies 7A+
buñboòguya stationery store; stationery dealer 7A+
bûñgaku literature 18B+
burâusu blouse 23A+
butyoo division manager 13B+
byooiñ hospital 6B+
byooki sick; sickness 9B

dà /copula: direct imperfective/ 9A

odekake da ↑ [someone] is going out /honorific-polite/ 23A
dâbúru(-rùumu) double room 21A+
-dai /classifier for counting vehicles and machines/ 7B+
daidokoro kitchen 17B
daídokoro-dòogu kitchen utensils 17B
daigaku university; college 7A+
daigakuiñ graduate school 7A+
dâiku carpenter 16B+
daitai for the most part 15B
daízì /na/ valuable, important 16A
daízyòobu /na/ all right; safe 2A
dakê just; only 5A
   soré dakè just that 5A
   kañgàeta dakê de just having thought about it 23B
   oókìi dakê da it's just big 23B+
   dekiru dake as much as possible 23B+
damê /na/ no good 2A
dañsee man; male 19B+
dañseego men's language 19B+
dañti apartment complex; housing development 24A+
dâre who? 2B
   dâre ka someone, somebody 24A
   dâre ka wakâi hito some young person 24A
   dâre mo /+ negative/ nobody 13A
darôo /copula: direct tentative/ 11A
dâsu /-u; dâsita/ put out; take out 17B+; serve 21A
   hôñ o dâsu publish a book 17B+
   tegámi o dàsu mail a letter 17B+
   sotó ni/e dàsu put [something] outside 17B+
dàtta /copula: direct perfective/ 9B
dè /copula: gerund/ 8A
   de gozaimàsu + /neutral-polite equivalent of dèsu/ 10A
   de (i)rassyàru ↑ /honorific-polite equivalent of dà/ 10A
   dê mo even so 8B
   dotíra dè mo whichever (of two) it is; wherever it is 21B
   pâat(e)ii de mo a party or something 23A
   matânai de without waiting; instead of waiting 23B
   matânai de kudasai please don't wait 23B
de /ptc/ in; at 7A; by means of 7B; because of 9B

kiśsateñ de tabèru eat at a coffee shop 7A
tâkusii de iku go by cab 7B
zìko de okureru become late because of an accident 9B
dêğuti exit 6A
-d(e)iikee /classifier for identifying apartments in terms of number of rooms + dining room and kitchen/ 24B
dekakeru /-ru; dekaketa/ go out; set out 23A
dekîru /-ru; dêkita/ become completed; can do; be possible 1A
demae home delivery of prepared food 14B
demúkaèru /-ru; demúkàeta/ meet; greet 19A
de nài: bôku de nâi it's not me 22B
dêñki electricity; electric lights 16A+
deñsya/dêñsya electric train 7B+
deñwa telephone (call) 2A
  deñwa ğa tooi sound far away (on the telephone) 13A
  deńwa ni dèru answer the telephone 13A
  deńwa o ireru put in a call 18B
  deńwa o kakèru make a telephone call 9B
deńwabañğoo telephone number 12A
deñwa-suru telephone 11A
deñwatyoo telephone book 19A
depâato department store 7A+
dèru /-ru; dêta/ go out; come out; leave; attend 9B
  deńwa ni dèru answer the telephone 13A
  tèrebi ni dêru appear on television 18B
  namáe ğa dète (i)ru names are carried, published, printed, etc. 20B
  syokúzi ğa dèru meals are served 21A
dèsita /copula: distal perfective/ 2A
dèsu /copula: distal imperfective/ 1B, 2A
|**desu nê(e)**| /filler/ 13B
desyòo /copula: distal tentative/ 6B
dê wa well then 13B+
-do /classifier for counting occurrences/ GUP; 12A
dôa door 16A
Dôitu Germany 5B+
doituğo German language 2A+
doítùziñ a German 10A+
dôko what place? where? 6B
  dôko ka someplace, somewhere 24A
  Toránomoñ no dòko where in Toranomon? what part of Toranomon? 6B
  dôko no Toránomoñ the Toranomon which is where? 6B

dônata who? /polite/ 2B+
dôñdoñ in rapid succession 24A
dôñna what kind (of)? 4B
  dôñna ni to what extent? in what manner? 9B+
dôno /+ nom/ which ——? 3A
  dono-ğurai about how much? 8A
dô(o) /abbreviation for **doyôo(bi)**/ 8A
  dô(o)·nîti Sat–Sun 8A
dôo what way? how? 2A
  Dôo itasimasite. Don't mention it. GUP
  dôo mo in every way; in many ways GUP; somehow or other 13A
  dôo de mo however it is 24B
  dôo iu hito a person described how? what kind of person? 18B
  dôo suru how will [you] act? what will [you] do? 11A
  dôo site how come? how? why? 11A
  âu ka dôo ka wakáràanai can't tell whether it matches or not 18A
doóğù tools, implements 17B
dôoka /alternate of **dôozo**/ 24A
Dôozo. Please (speaker offering something). GUP
Dôozo goyúkkùri. Take it easy! 12A+
Dôozo yorosiku. Please [treat me] favorably. 11B
dôre which thing (usually of three or more)? 2B
dôresu dress 23A+
-doru /classifier for counting dollars/ 3A+
dôtira which side? which way? whereabouts? where? which alternative (of two)? 6A
  dôtira mo both 12A
  dotíra dè mo whichever (of two) it is; wherever it is 21B
  dôtira no hoo which alternative? which direction? 6A
dôtira-sama who? /polite/ 12B
dôtti /casual equivalent of **dôtira**/ 7B+
doyôo(bi) Saturday 8A

e /ptc/ to; into; onto 7A
  hôñya e to the bookstore 7A
êe /affirmation/ GUP, 1A
êeğa/eeğa movie 18B+
eéğàkañ movie theater 6B+
eeğo English language 2A+
Eehuku-tyoo Eifuku-cho (section of Tokyo) 16B

Eekoku   England   5B+
Eékokùziñ   English person   10B+
eé-kòosu   the "A" meal   14A
eé-sètto   the "A" meal   15B
|eeto| uh   7B
eewa   English–Japanese   2B
eéwa-zìteñ   English–Japanese dictionary   2B
êggu   egg   14A+
êki   station   6A
-eñ   /classifier for counting yen/   2B
eñkai   dinner party (Japanese-style)   21B
eñpitu   pencil   4B+
eñryo   reserve; holding back   18A
   Goéñryo nàku.   Don't hold back.   18A
eñryo-suru   hold back; stand on ceremony   18A+
   eñryo-site oku   hold back for now; take a rain check   18A+

ḡa   /ptc/   4A, 4B, 5A
gaikoku   foreign country   11B+
gaikokuḡo   foreign language   11B
gaíkokùziñ   foreigner   10A+
gaikoo   diplomacy   16B+
gaíkòokañ   diplomat   16B+
gaímùsyoo   Foreign Ministry   11B+
gaisyutu-suru   go out   13B+
gaisyutu-tyuu da   be out   13B
gaiziñ   foreigner (particularly Westerner)   10A
gakkai   learned society, academic organization   20B
gaḱkàri-suru   become discouraged; become disappointed   20B
gakkoo   school   7A+
gakusee   student   2B+
gakutyoo   academic president   13B+
gâñ-neñ   initial year of an era   8B+
-ḡatu   /classifier for naming months/   8B
gekizyoo   theater   6B+
geñḡo   language   18B+
gêñkañ   entry hall   17B+
gêñki   /na/   pep, vim, high spirits; peppy, vigorous   14B
   gêñki ḡa dêru   perk up, become energetic   14B
   gêñki ḡa îi   is in good spirits   14B+
   Ogêñki desu ka⤴   Are you well?   14B+
gês·sûi·kîñ   Mon–Wed–Fri   8A
geta   wooden clogs (for outdoors)   23A+
gêtu/gêk-/gês-   /abbreviation for getúyòo(bi)/   8A

getúyòo(bi)   Monday   8A
giñkoo   bank   7A
gińkòoiñ   banker   16B+
gîsi   engineer   16B+
gô   five   2B
Gobúsata-simàsita.   I've neglected to be in touch.   11B+
goeñdama   ¥5 coin   19A+
Goéñryo nàku.   Don't hold back.   18A
gôḡo   afternoon; P.M.   8B
gôhañ   cooked rice; food   14A+
   Gôhañ ḡa dekímàsita.   Dinner is ready.   14A+
gohyakueñdama   ¥500 coin   19A+
gohyakueñsatu   ¥500 bill   19A+
Gokûroosama.   It's been trouble for you; Thanks for your trouble.   17B
Goméñ-kudasài.   Excuse me; Pardon me.   12B
gomî   trash; dust   17A
goórudeñ-uìiku   Golden Week (April 29–May 5)   20A
-ḡoositu   /classifier for naming room numbers/   14B
-ḡòro   about (approximate point in time)   8A
   kono-ḡoro   these days, nowadays   8A+
gôruhu   golf   4A
goseñeñsatu   ¥5000 bill   19A+
Gotísoosama (dèsita).   It was delicious.   5B
gozáimàsu⁺   /neutral-polite equivalent of âru/   5A
   de gozaimàsu⁺   /neutral-polite equivalent of dà/   10A
gôzeñ   A.M.   8B+
gozôñzi↑ da   /honorific-polite/ know   10B+
gozyuueñdama   ¥50 coin   19A+
guai   condition   14B
-ḡùrai   about, approximately   8A
   dono-ḡurai   about how much?   8A
gurêe   gray   5B
gurîiñ   green   5B+
guríiñsya   "green car"   19A+
gûuguu   /onomatopoeia/
   gûuguu netyau   fall sound asleep   19B

hâ   tooth   16B+
hâa   /polite affirmation/   GUP, 13B
hâai   ye-es!   18A
hâha   mother; my mother   11B+
hahaoya   mother   11B+

-hai /classifier for counting glassfuls and cupfuls/ 14B
hâi /affirmation/; here you are GUP, 1A
haiiro gray 5B+
hâiru /-u; hâitta/ go in, enter 16A
  hurô ni hâiru take a bath 21B
hâisya dentist 16B+
hâiyaa limousine available for hire 20A+
hakkìri clear(ly), precise(ly), exact(ly) 19A
hakkiri-suru become exact 19A
  hakkìri-sita zikañ exact time 19A
hako box 20A
hakobu /-u; hakoñda/ transport, carry 20A
-haku /classifier for counting nights of a stay/ 21A
  ippaku-suru stay one night 21A+
haku /-u; haita/ put (or wear) on the feet or legs 23A
  haite (i)ru be wearing (on the feet or legs) 23A
  haite iku wear (on the feet or legs) to a place 23A+
hâmu ham 14A+
hamú-sàndo ham sandwich 14A+
-hàñ one-half 8B
  hañ-zìkañ a half-hour 8B+
  yo-zí-hàñ 4:30 8B
  yo-zíkañ-hàñ four hours and a half 8B+
hana nose 17A+
hanâ flower 7A+
hanásì talk 13A
  X no hanásì de wa according to what X says 24B
hanasi-tyuu [in] the midst of talk; 'the line is busy' 13A
hanâsu /-u; hanâsita/ talk; speak 10B
hanâya flower shop; florist 7A+
hañbùñ half portion; half part 14B
hañdobàggu handbag 5A+
Haneda (name of airport) 20A+
hañtai opposite 20B
  hañtai ni conversely 20B+
hañtai-suru oppose 20B+
  X ni hañtai-suru oppose X 20B+
harâ belly, abdomen 22B
  harâ ga tâtu become angry 22B
  harâ ga oókìi be big-hearted 22B+
  harâ o kimeru make up one's mind 22B+
  hitó no harâ o yômu read a person's mind 22B+

harağee the art of reading the thoughts of others without resorting to language 22B+
harákìri ritual suicide 22B+
harâu /-u; harâtta/ pay 22B
harêru /-ru; hâreta/ become clear (of weather) 22A
  hârete (i)ru be clear 22A
hâru spring (season) 19A+
hâsi chopsticks 15A
hâtati twenty years of age 10A+
hatî eight 2B
hatto with a start; in surprise /onomatopoeia/ 19B
  hatto ki ğá tùku become aware with a start 19B
-hatu departure 19B
  Tookyoo-hatu departing Tokyo 19B+
  itî-zi hatu departing at one o'clock 19B
hatu-ka twenty days; twentieth of the month 8A
hayâi /-katta/ is early; is fast 9A+
hayámè ni early; in good time 10A
hâyasa speed 24B+
Hazímemàsite. How do you do? 11B
hazimeru /-ru; hazimeta/ begin [something] 11B+
hazîmete the first time 11B
hazu general expectation 20B
  sitte (i)ru hazu dà it is expected that [s/he] knows; [s/he] should know 20B
  âtta hazu da it is expected that there was; there should have been 20B
hazúkasìi /-katta/ is shy; is embarrassed 19B
hazusu /-u; hazusita/ take off; let go; unfasten 12B
  sêki o hazusu leave one's seat 12B
hêe/ /exclamation of surprise/ 3B
heñ area; vicinity 6A
hêñ /na/ strange 13A
hetâ /na/ unskillful; poor at 9B+
heyâ room 17B
-heya /classifier for counting rooms/ 21A
hî/hi day; sun 10A+, 22A
hiatari exposure to the sun 24B
hidari left 6B
  hidári no hòo the left side; the left direction 6B
hidáridònari next door on the left 6B
hidôi /-katta/ is severe 22A
  hidôku hûru rain (or snow) hard 22A
hiğásì east 19B

Japanese–English Glossary

higasiguti east entrance 19B
hikidasi drawer 17B+
hikôoki airplane 7B+
hiku /-u; hiita/ pull 16B
  kaze o hiku catch a cold 16B
hima /na/ free time 13A
hirôi /-katta/ is spacious, wide, big (of area) 24B+
hirôoeñ (wedding) reception (Japanese-style) 21B+
hîrosa area, size (of an area) 24B
hirû noon; daytime 14A+
hirúgòhañ lunch 14A
hisasiburi after a long interval 11B
hisyô/hîsyo secretary 13B
hitô/hito person 10A
  oñna no hitò woman 10A
  otóko no hitò man 10A
hitô-ri one person; alone; single (person) 11A
  hitô-ri de iku go alone (*lit.*, being one person) 11A
hitô-tu one unit 5A+
hituyoo /na/ necessary; necessity 22A
  hitúyoo ḡa nài there's no necessity 22A
hizyoo /na/ emergency; extraordinary, extreme 17B
  hizyoo ni extremely 17B
hizyóoburèeki emergency brake 17B+
hizyooguti emergency exit 17B+
-hodo about as much as 5B
  itû-tu-hodo about five (units) 5B
hodo extent 15A
  sore hodo to that extent 15A
  sore hodo yôku nâi isn't that good 15A
  koré o yòmu hodo omósìroku nâi isn't as interesting as reading this 20A+
hoka other, another, other than 5A, 15B
  Hoká ni nàni ka? Anything else? 5A
Hokkàidoo Hokkaido (northernmost main island of Japan) 11A
Hokudai Hokkaido University 11B+
hôñ book 2B+
-hoñ /classifier for counting long, cylindrical objects/ 4B
hoñ: hoñ no kimoti only feeling; no more than feeling 18A
hôñdana bookshelf 16A
Hôñsyuu Honshu (a main island of Japan) 11A+
hoñtoo true; truth 2B
hôñya bookstore; book dealer 7A

hôo direction; way; side; alternative 6A
  hidári no hòo left side; toward the left 6A
  miḡí no hòo right side; toward the right 6A
  hâsi no hoo the alternative of chopsticks 15A
  hâsi no hoo ḡa tabéyasùi chopsticks are easier to eat with 15A
  sonó hòo ḡa îi that alternative is better 15A
  itta hòo ḡa îi [you]'d better go 20A
  kurúma de iku hòo ḡa hayâi going by car is faster 20A+
hoómudòrama soap opera 18B+
hôra look! hey! 22A
hôteru hotel 6B
  Oókura-hòteru Hotel Okura 6B
hotôñdo almost; nearly; all but 3B
hudoosañya real estate broker 24B
huku /-u; huita/ wipe 17B+
hûku /-u; hûita/ blow 22A
hukû clothing 23A
Hukûoka Fukuoka 8A+
-huñ /classifier for counting and naming minutes/ 8A
hûne boat, ship 8B+
-huñkañ /classifier for counting minutes/ 8A+
h(u)ôoku fork 15A
h(u)ôomaru /na/ formal 23B
Hurañsu France 5B+
hurañsuḡo French language 2A+
huráñsùziñ French person 10B+
hurô bath 21B
  hurô ni hâiru take a bath 21B
huróba bathroom 17B+
hurosiki square wrapping cloth 4A
hûru /-u; hûtta/ fall (of rain, snow, etc.) 22A
hurûi /-katta/ is old (i.e., not new) 1B+
husúmà sliding door (opaque) 16A+
hutá-tù two units 5A
hutoñ futon (Japanese-style quilt for sleeping) 21B
  sikíbùtoñ bottom quilt 21B+
  kakébùtoñ top quilt 21B+
hutuu ordinary, regular, usual 19A
  /+ predicate/ ordinarily, regularly, usually 24A
  hutuu ni suru do in the usual way 19A+
  hutuu wa suru usually (at least) do [it] 19A
hutúu(rèssya) regular train (a local) 19A+
huyû winter 19A+
hyakû one hundred 2B

-hyaku /counter for hundreds/ 2B
hyakueñdama ¥100 coin 19A+

i stomach 17A+
iê house, home; household 7B+
iêie /negation/ 1B
Iĝirisu England 5B+
iĝírisùziñ English person 10B+
îi /yôkatta/ is good, fine, all right; never mind 1B
   yôku dekîru can do well 1B
   yôku suru do often 1B
i(i)e /negation/ GUP, 1A
iíkaèru /-ru; iíkàeta/ rephrase, say again in a different way 20B+
ikâĝa how? /polite/ 4A
ikê pond 18A+
ikenai /-katta/ it won't do; it's too bad 14B
   sitê wa 'ikenai [one] must not do 22B
iku /-u; itta/ go 1A
   kikâete iku go having changed; change and go; change before going 23B
îkura how much? 2B
îku-tu how many units? 5B; how old (of people)? 10A
îma now 7A
imâ (Western-style) living room 17B+
îmi meaning 18B
imôoto younger sister 11A
Îñdo India 5B+
iñ́dòziñ an Indian (from India) 10B+
iñ́tabyuu-bàñĝumi interview program, talk show 18B
îñtyoo hospital director 13B+
inû dog 17B+
ippai full 15A
ippaku-suru stay one night 21A+
irássyàru ↑ /-aru; irássyàtta ~ irâsita/ be located (of animate existence) 7A; come 4B; go 8B /honorific-polite/
   de (i)rassyàru ↑ /honorific-polite equivalent of dà/ 10A
   Irássyài(màse). ↑ Welcome! 4B
ireru /-ru; ireta/ put into; insert 16A
   otya o ireru make tea 17B
   deñwa o ireru put in a call 18B
iriĝuti entrance 6A+
irô color 5B
iroiro /no ~ na/ various 20B
   iroiro beñkyoo-suru study about all kinds of things 20B

iroñ /na/ various 20B+
iru /-ru; ita/ be located (of animate existence) 7A
   Tookyoo ni iru be in Tokyo 7A
   kekkoñ-site (i)ru be married 10B
   hanâsite (i)ru be talking 10B
iru /-u; itta/ need; be required 5A
iru /-u; itta/ enter 23A
   ki ni iru appeal 23A
isóĝasìi /-katta/ is busy 9A
isôĝu /-u; isôida/ be in a hurry, make haste 20B
   isôide iku go hurriedly 20B
îs-see first generation (used in reference to Japanese who have moved abroad) 10B+
issyo togetherness 11A
   issyo ni suru do together 11A
   tomodati to issyo together with a friend 11A
isu chair 17B+
isya medical doctor 16B
   isyá no tokorò the doctor's (place) 16B
itadaku /-u; itadaita/ ↓ drink; eat; accept; receive /humble-polite/ 1A, 17B
   tetúdàtte itadaku ↓ receive help, be helped 17B
itâi /-katta/ is painful; hurts 17A
Itaria Italy 5B+
itariaĝo Italian language 2A+
itáriàziñ an Italian 10B+
itasu /-u; itasita/ ↓ do /humble-polite/ 12B
itî one 2B
itibañ most, to the greatest degree 15B
   itíbañ sukì da is most pleasing; likes best 15B
iti-d(e)iikee 1-DK (i.e., one room + dining area/kitchen) 24B
itieñdama ¥1 coin 19A+
itímañèñsatu ¥10,000 bill 19A+
iti-niti-zyuu all day long 24B
itôko cousin 11B+
Itte (i)rassyài(màse). ↑ Goodbye (said to person leaving home). 7A
Itte kimàsu. Goodbye (said by person leaving home). 7A
Itte mairimàsu. ↓ Goodbye (said by person leaving home). /humble-polite/ 7A+
îtu when? 3B
îtu mo always 11A
itû-tu five units 5A

iu /-u; itta/ be called, be named 12A; say 18B
   X to iu be called or named X 12A
   X to/(t)te iu be named X 12A; say, "X" 18B
   X to/(t)te iu Y a Y named or called X 18B
   Soó itte kudasài. Please say that. 12A
   surú yòo ni iu tell [someone] to do 24A
iya /negation/ 1A
iyâ /na/ unpleasant, disagreeable 11A
izure someday, sometime 12A

ka /question particle/ 1A
   dôko ka someplace, somewhere 24A
   dôko ka îi tokoro some good place 24A
   kosyoo kâ mo sirenai maybe it's out of order 13A
   âu ka dôo ka wakáràṅai can't tell whether it matches or not 18A
   dâre ḡa dêru ka 'kiku ask (or hear) who will attend 18B
kâ section within a company 13B+
-ka/-niti /classifier for naming and counting days/ 8A
kâ(a) /abbreviation for **kayôo(bi)**/ 8A
   kâa·môku Tues–Thurs 8A
kabañ bag, suitcase 5A
kabûru /-u; kabûtta/ put (or wear) on the head 23A
kâdo street corner 7B
kaérì a return 8A
kaeru /-ru; kaeta/ change [something] 20B+
   noríkaèru transfer to another vehicle 20B+
   atárasìi no ni kaeru change to new ones 23B
kâeru /-u; kâetta/ return (home) 7A
   kâette kuru come back; come home 23A
   Okáeri-nasái(màse). Welcome back! 7A
-kaḡetu /classifier for counting months/ 8B
kaḡî key 16A
   kaḡî o kakêru lock [something] 16A
   kaḡî ḡa kakâru be(come) locked 16A
kâḡu furniture 17B+
kaḡûya furniture store 17B+
-kai /classifier for naming and counting floors/ 7A
-kai /classifier for counting number of times/ 19A
kâiḡi conference, meeting 3B
kaíḡìsitu conference room 10B

kaimono shopping 14A+
kaisatu ticket checking 19B+
kaísatùḡuti ticket-checking gate, wicket 19B
kaisya a company, a firm 11A
kaísyàiñ company employee 16B+
-kakañ/-kaniti /classifier for counting days/ 8A+
kâkari (no hito) person in charge 21A
kakâru /-u; kakâtta/ be required 8B
   zikâñ ḡa kakàru it takes time 8B+
kakâru /-u; kakâtta/ become suspended 16A
   kaḡî ḡa kakaru be(come) locked 16A
   omé ni kakàru ↓ meet, see [a person] /humble-polite/ 13B+
kakébùtoñ top quilt 21B+
kakénaòsu /-u; kakénaòsita/ suspend again 13A
   deńwa o kakenaòsu telephone again 13A
-kakeru /-ru; -kaketa/ set about ——ing 23A
   dekakeru go out; set out 23A
   ikikakeru be about to go 23A+
kakêru /-ru; kâketa/ suspend (something) 9B; sit down 19B+
   deńwa o kakêru make a telephone call 9B
   kaḡî o kakêru lock [something] 16A
kakíkaèru /-ru; kakíkaèta/ rewrite 20B+
kâku /-u; kâita/ write; draw 7A
kamâu /-u; kamâtta/ mind; care; concern oneself about 10A
   Okámai nàku. Don't bother; Don't go to any trouble. 18A
kamáwànai /-katta/ it doesn't matter 10A
kâmera camera 16A
kamî paper 4B
kamínarì thunder 22A+
Kânada Canada 5B+
kânai my wife 10B+
kânari fairly, rather, quite 19B
kańḡaeru /-ru; kańḡaèta/ think over, consider, ponder 23B
   kańḡaete simau think twice about a matter 23B+
kańḡohu nurse 16B+
kâńḡo-suru nurse, care for 16B+
kańkee connection 18B
   keézai-kàńkee a connection with economics 18B
Kâńkoku South Korea 5B+
kańkokùziñ a South Korean 10B+
kânozyo she 10A
kańzyoo the check 15A+

kao face 14B+; expression 24B
  kao o suru assume an expression 24B
  iyâ na kao o site (i)ru have a disagreeable expression 24B+
kaoiro (facial) color 14B
kâppu (coffee) cup 15B+
kara /ptc/ from 8B; because 11A; after 16B
  gôḡo kara from the afternoon 8B
  koko kara from here 8B
  iyâ da kara because it's displeasing 11A
  tûite kara after arriving 16B
karada body 17A+
karâi /-katta/ is spicy; is salty 15B+
kâre he 10A+
kariru /-ru; karita/ borrow; rent (from someone) 10B
  tomodati ni (or kara) kariru borrow or rent from a friend 10B
karui /-katta/ is light (of weight) 20A+
kâsa umbrella 4A
Kasíkomarimàsita. Certainly. I'll do as you asked. 4B
kasu /-u; kasita/ lend; rent (to someone) 10B+
-kata way of ——ing 22B+
  sikata way of doing 22B+
  hanasikata way of talking 22B+
kâta shoulder 17A+
katâ person /polite/ 10A+
katai /-katta/ is hard; is stiff; is tough 15B+
katázukèru /-ru; katázùketa/ make tidy; put in order 17A+
katázùku /-u; katázùita/ become tidy; be(come) put in order 17A
katyoo section manager 13B+
kau /-u; katta/ buy 1B
kawâ river 18A+
kawáìi /-katta/ is cute 10A
kawâku /-u; kawâita/ become dry 14A+
  nôdo ga kawâku become thirsty 14A+
kawari a change 11B; substitute, replacement 24A
  kawari ni as a substitute, instead 24A
  kawári ni sùmu reside as a substitute, house-sit 24A
kawaru /-u; kawatta/ undergo change 11B+; change places 13B
  X ni kawaru change into X 13B+
  X to kawaru (ex)change with X 13B+

  deñwa o kawaru make a replacement on the telephone 13B+
kayôo(bi) Tuesday 8A
kayou /-u; kayotta/ commute 20A+
kaze a cold 16B
  kaze o hiku catch a cold 16B
kaze wind 22A
kâzi a fire 9B+
kâzoku family; my family 11A
kedo /ptc/ 4B
keekeñ experience 21A
  bôku no keékeñ dè wa in my experience (at least) 21A
keekeñ-suru experience, go through 21A+
kêeki cake 3A
Keeoo Keio University 12B+
keésàñki calculator 17B
keesañ-suru calculate 17B+
kêezai economics 18B+
kekka result 22B
kekkòñsiki wedding ceremony 23A
kekkoñ-suru get married 10B
  kekkon-site (i)ru be married 10B
kêkkoo /na/ fine, great 13B
-keñ /classifier for counting buildings and shops/ 7B
keñkoo /na/ health; healthy 14B
  keñkoo ni ìi is good for one's health 14B
keñkyuu research 13B+
keñkyùusitu laboratory 13B+
keñkyuu-suru do research 13B+
keñkyuuzyo research institute 13B
keñtiku architecture 16B+
keñtikuka architect 16B+
kêsa this morning 9A+
kêsiki scenery 18A+
kesu /-u; kesita/ turn off; extinguish; erase 16A
ki mind, spirit; feelings; attention 19B+
  ki ḡá tùku notice; become aware 19B
  ki ó tukèru pay attention; be careful 19B+
  ki ni iru appeal 23A
  ki ni suru mind; worry about, concern oneself about 24A
  ki ní nàru weigh on one's mind; become a cause for concern 24A+
kî tree 17B+
kieru /-ru; kieta/ go out; be(come) turned off; be(come) extinguished 16A
kiiroi /-katta/ is yellow 4A+

kikáèru ~ kiĝáèru /-ru; kikâeta ~ kiĝâeta/ change clothing (worn on the body) 23B
kikâi machine 19A
kikóenikùi /-katta/ is difficult to hear 13A
kikoeru /-ru; kikoeta/ can hear; be audible 13A
kikóeyasùi /-katta/ is easy to hear 13A+
kiku /-u; kiita/ ask 7B; hear; listen 10B
kimaru /-u; kimatta/ become decided 17B+
  kimatta mono things that have been decided 21A
kimeru /-ru; kimeta/ decide [something] 17B
kimi you /familiar/ 9A+
kimono kimono 23B
kimoti feeling, mood 18A
  hoñ no kimoti only feeling; no more than feeling 18A
  kimóti ĝa ìi is pleasant; feels well 21B
  kimóti ĝa warùi is unpleasant; doesn't feel well 21B+
kiñ /abbreviation for **kiñyòo(bi)**/ 8A
  ĝes·sûi·kiñ Mon–Wed–Fri 8A
kinôo yesterday 1A
kiñyòo(bi) Friday 8A+
kîñzyo neighborhood 17A
kippu ticket 19A
kippu-ùriba ticket counter 19A+
kirai /na/ displeasing; dislike 15B
kirâsu /-u; kirâsita/ exhaust the supply 12A
  meési o kirâsite (i)ru be out of business cards 12A
kîree /na/ pretty; clean 2A
kiru /-ru; kita/ put (or wear) on the body 23A
  kite (i)ru be wearing 23A
  kite iku wear (to a place) 23A
kîru /-u; kîtta/ cut, cut off; hang up (the telephone) 13A
kissateñ/kissàteñ coffee shop; tearoom 7A
kisyâ (steam) train 7B+
kitâ north 19B+
kitto surely, certainly, undoubtedly 24B
kizûkai concern 18A
-ko /classifier for counting pieces/ 20A
ko child 10A
  okosañ child /polite/ 10A+
  oñnà no ko little girl; young girl 10A+
  otókò no ko little boy; young boy 10A+
kodomo child 10A+
kôe voice 13A
  ôoki na kôe loud voice 13A
  tîisa na kôe low voice 13A+

kôi /-katta/ is thick (of liquids); is strong (of coffee, tea, etc.); is dark (of colors) 15B+
koko this place, here 6B
  kokó no tosyòkañ the library here 6B
kokôno-tu nine units 5A+
kokuĝo the mother-tongue of the Japanese 2A+
kokutetu national railway (until 1987) 19A
komákài /-katta/ occurs in small units; is small, is detailed 17B
  komákài âme drizzle 17B+
komâru /-u; komâtta/ become upset; become a problem 1B
komê uncooked rice 14A+
koméya rice shop 14A+
kômu /-u; kôñda/ become crowded, congested, filled up 20A
konaida the other day 18A+
kôñbañ this evening, tonight 9A+
Koñbañ wa. Good evening. GUP
koñĝetu this month 9A+
koñna this kind (of) 4B
  koñna ni to this extent, like this 9B+
Koñniti wa. Good afternoon. GUP
kono /+ nom/ this —— 3A
  konó màe (in) front of this 6A+
kono-ĝoro these days, nowadays 8A+
kôñpa (student) party (Japanese-style) 21B+
koñpyùutaa computer 3A
koñsàrutañto consultant 16B+
koñsyuu this week 9A+
koñtakuto(-rèñzu) contact lens(es) 23B
  koñtakuto(-rèñzu) o suru put in contact lenses 23B
kôñya this evening, tonight 10A+
koobañ police box 6A+
Kôobe Kobe 8A+
kooeñ park 6B+
kooeñ speech, lecture 18B+
kôoĝi lecture 18B+
koóhìi coffee 3A+
koóhiikàppu (coffee) cup 15B+
kookoo high school 7A+
koómùiñ government employee 16B+
koori ice 14A+
koósàteñ intersection 7B
kôosu meal with fixed menu 14A
koósyuudèñwa public telephone 6A
kootuu transportation 24B
  koótuu no bèñ ĝa îi transportation facilities are good 24B

kootya black tea 5B+
kôppu drinking glass 15B+
kore this thing 2B
  kore kara from this point, after this 8A
kôru /-u; kôtta/ become stiff 17B
kôsa strength (of tea, coffee, etc.); depth (of a color) 24B+
kosî lower back 17A+
(kosí)kakèru /-ru; (kosí)kàketa/ sit down 19B+
kòso /ptc/ 11B
  Kotíra kòso. *I'm* the one. 11B
kosyôo pepper 14A+
kosyoo out of order 13A
kosyoo-suru break down 13A+
kotáèru /-ru; kotâeta/ answer CI
kotira this side; this way; hereabouts; here; this alternative (of two) 6A
  kotíra no hòo this direction; this alternative 6A
kotô fact; act 21A
  mińsyuku no kotò facts concerning tourist homes 21A
  nokôru koto ni suru decide on remaining 24A
  ikú kotò ni nâru be(come) decided that [someone] will go 24A
kotóbà (spoken) language; utterance; phrase; word 22B
kotosi this year 8B
kotti /casual alternate of **kotira**/ 7B
kowárèru /-ru; kowâreta/ become broken, damaged, destroyed; fall apart 24B
  kowáreyasùi is breakable, fragile 24B+
  kowaremono fragile article 24B+
kowâsu /-u; kowâsita/ break [something]; demolish, destroy 24B+
  karada o kowasu ruin one's health 24B+
  onaka o kowasu develop stomach trouble 24B+
kû nine 2B
kubi neck 17A+
kudâmono fruit 15A+
kudásài /imperative of **kudásàru**/ give me 4A
  Koré o kudasài. Please give me this one. 4A
  Kitê kudasai. Please come. 4A
  oágari-kudasài please go/come up 18A
kudásàru ↑ /-aru; kudásàtta ~ kudásùtta/ give me /honorific-polite/ 4A
  tetúdàtte kudasaru give help (to me/us/you) 17A

Kâite kudásaimasèñ ka Would (*lit.* won't) you be kind enough to write for me? 7A
kumôru /-u; kumôtta/ become cloudy 22A
  kumôtte (i)ru be cloudy 22A
-kuñ /suffix attached to male names; familiar/ 9A
kuni a country; one's native land or area 15A+
kureru /-ru; kureta/ give (to me/us/you) 17A
  tetúdàtte kureru give help (to me/us/you) 17A
  mîte kureru? will you look at (for me/us/you)? will he/she/they look at (for me/us/you)? 17A
kurôi /-katta/ is black 4A
kûroo toil, hardship 17B+
kûru /irreg; kîtâ/ come 1A
  hârete kuru come to be clear; begin to clear 22A
  itte kùru come, having gone (i.e., go and then come) 7A
  Itte kimàsu. 'So long!' (said leaving one's own quarters) 7A
  kâette kuru come back; come home 23A
kuruma car 5B
kusuri medicine 14B
  kusúri o nòmu take medicine 14B+
kusuriya drugstore 14B+
kutábirèru /-ru; kutábìreta/ become fatigued 24B
kuti mouth 17A+
  kutí ni àu suit one's tasate 18A
kut(t)akuta worn out, exhausted, dog-tired 24B
kutû shoes 23A
kutûsita socks; stockings 23B
kuukoo airport 7B
kuwásìi /-katta/ is detailed 24A
  kuwásìi koto details, particulars 24A
  X ni kuwásìi is well versed in X; has detailed knowledge of X 24A+
kyaku guest; visitor; customer 10B
kyôneñ last year 10A+
kyôo today 1A
Kyoodai Kyoto University 11B+
kyôodai brothers and sisters, siblings 11A+
kyookai church 6B+
kyoókàsyo textbook 10B
kyôosi instructor 13B+
kyoositu classroom 10B
Kyôoto Kyoto 2A+

kyoozyu professor 13B+
kyûu nine 3A
Kyuudai Kyushu University 11B+
kyuukoo express 19A+
kyuúkòokeñ express ticket 19A+
Kyûusyuu Kyushu (a main island of Japan) 11A+

ma ní àu be on time 20B
mâa /expression of qualified agreement/ 1B
mâa /expression of persuasion/ 15B+
mâa oh, my! /exclamation of surprise; F/ 18A
mâa·mâa so-so 1A
mâda /+ negative predicate/ not yet 14A
  /+ affirmative predicate/ still 14B
  mâda da not yet (*lit.* it is yet [to happen]) 14A
màde /ptc/ as far as; up to and including 7A; until 8B
  giñkoo màde as far as the bank 7A
  nâñ-zi made until what time? 8B
  sâñ-zi made ni by 3 o'clock 9A
  koko made ûmâku syabêru speak well as far as this level 24A
mâdo window 16A
madôğuti ticket window 20B
  mîdori no madôğuti ticket window for green-car tickets 20B
mâe front 6A; time before; past time 8A+
  toó-ka màe ten days ago 10B
  go-hûñ-mae five minutes before the hour 8A
  dêru mâe before going out 19A
mağaru /-u; mağatta/ make a turn 7B
-mai /classifier for thin, flat units/ 4B
mâiasa every morning 8B+
mâibañ every evening; every night 8B+
maido every time 4B
  Maido arîğatoo gozaimasu. Thank you again and again. 4B
maiğetu every month 8B+
maineñ every year 8B+
mâiniti every day 8B
mâiru↓ /-u; mâitta/ come 7A; go 8B /humble-polite/
maisyuu every week 8B+
maitosi every year 8B+
maituki every month 8B+
maiyo every evening; every night 10A+
-mañ /counter for ten thousands/ 3B
mâñsyoñ apartment; apartment house 24A

maru circle; zero 12A
maśsùğu straight 7B
mata again 4B
  matâ wa or on the other hand 12A
matî town, small city 20A+
matíğaèru /-ru; matíğaeta/ make a mistake 20B
  mití o matiğaèru mistake the road 20B+
  X o Y ni/to matíğaèru mistake X for Y 20B+
matíğàu /-u; matíğàtta/ be(come) wrong, get to be in error 20B+
mattaku precisely, totally, entirely 22B
mâtu /-u; mâtta/ wait 8A
mâtu pine 14B+
Matuzusi /name of sushi shop/ 14B+
mawaru /-u; mawatta/ go around; be(come) passed around; be(come) transferred 21A+
  Nihôñ omawaru go around Japan 21A+
mawasu /-u; mawasita/ send around; pass around; transfer 21A
mazûi /-katta/ tastes bad 7A+
mê eye 16B+
-mee(sama) /classifier for counting people/ 15A
meesi calling card; business card 12A
  meesi no motiawase cards on hand 12A
Mêezi the Meiji era (1868–1912) 8B+
mêğane eyeglasses 23B
  mêğane o kakêru put on eyeglasses 23B
mêisya eye doctor 16B+
mesiağaru↑ /-u; mesiağatta/ eat; drink; smoke /honorific-polite/ 15B
mêsseezi message 12B
Mêziro (section of Tokyo) 7B
mezúrasìi /-katta/ is amazing, surprising, unexpected 19B
mîdori green 5B+
  mîdori no madôğuti ticket window for green-car tickets 20B
mièru /-ru; mîeta/ be visible; can see 18A; appear, seem 23A
  tiğáu hitò ni mièru appear as if a different person 23A
miğí right 6B
  miğí no hòo right side, right direction 6B
miğídònari next door on the right 6B
mimî ear 17A+
minami south 19B+
minâsañ everyone /polite/ 5B+, 11B

minato harbor 18A+
miníkùi /-katta/ is hard to see with or look at 23B
mi(ń)nà all; everyone; everything 5B
miñsyuku tourist home 21A
miokuru /-u; miokutta/ see off 19A
mîru /-ru; mîta/ look at; see 5B
    kiíte mìru try asking, ask and see 19A
mîruku milk 5B+
misê store, shop 6A+
misêru /-ru; mîseta/ show 4A
-mìtai /na/ as if ——; ——like 24A
    kimátta-mìtai da it seems as if it was decided 24A
    anâta-mitai ni nihóñḡo ḡa zyoozù da is good in Japanese the way you are 24A
miti street; road 6A+
mít-tù three units 5A
mitukaru /-u; mitukatta/ be(come) found; be(come) discovered 23A
mitukeru /-ru; mituketa/ find, locate, turn up [something] 23A+
miyaḡe souvenir 15A
miyaḡeya souvenir shop 15A+
mizíkài /-katta/ is short 9B+
mizu cold water 14A+
mizúùmi lake 18A+
mo /ptc/ also, too 4B
    dôo mo in every way; in many ways GUP; somehow or other 13A
    dôtira mo both 12A
    îtu mo always 11A
    kore mo this one too 4B
    kore mo sore mo both this one and that one 5B
    mâe ni mo in the front too 6A
    sitê mo also (or even) having done 21B
    sinâkute mo also (or even) not having done 22A
    sitê mo îi? may [I] do [it]? will it be all right even/also if [I] do [it]? 21B
    sinâkute mo îi? will it be all right even/also if [I] don't do it? 22A
    dotíra dè mo whichever it is 21B
    nâni o sitê mo whatever [someone] has done 21B
    dôko e ittê mo wherever [someone] has gone 21B
    pâat(e)ii de mo a party or something 23A
modôru /-u; modôtta/ return; go/come back; back up 13B

môku/môk- /abbreviation for **mokúyòo(bi)**/ 8A+
môku·dôo Thurs–Sat 8A+
mokuteki purpose 22B
mokúyòo(bi) Thursday 8A+
mońbùsyoo Ministry of Education 11B
moñdai problem 24B
monô thing 14A+
monórèeru monorail 20A+
monósuḡòi /-katta/ is dreadful, awful 20A
    monósùḡòku omoi is awfully heavy 20A
moo /+ quantity expression/ more; additional 5A
    moó mit-tù three more units 5A
    moó sukòsi a little more; a few more 5A+
môo /+ affirmative predicate/ already, yet 14A
    /+ negative predicate/ no more 14B
moosiwake excuse 12A
    Moósiwake arimasèñ. I'm very sorry. (lit. There is no excuse.) GUP
môosu↓ /-u; môosita/ be called, be named 12A; say 18B /humble-polite/
    X to moósimàsu↓ my name is X 12A
    X to/(t)te môosu↓ be named X 12A; say, "X" 18B
morau /-u; moratta/ receive 17B
    naôsite morau have something fixed 17B
môsimosi hello (on the telephone); say there! 12A
Mosukuwa Moscow 8A
motiawase things on hand 12A
    meésí no motiawase ḡa nài have no business cards on hand 12A
motiawaseru /-ru; motiawaseta/ have on hand 12A+
motîroñ of course, certainly 15A
motte iku take (to a place) (said of things) 15A+
motte kùru bring (said of things) 15A+
môtto more; a larger amount 5A
    môtto yasûi no one that is cheaper 5A
mukae a meeting; a greeting; a welcoming 16B
mukaeru /-ru; mukaeta/ meet; greet; welcome 16B
-muki facing toward; aimed at; suitable for 24B
    nisi-muki facing west 24B
    gaiziñ-muki aimed at foreigners 24B+
    huyu-muki suitable for winter 24B+

mukôo/mukoo over there 6A; abroad 9B
mukoōgawa opposite side, the other side 6B+
muku /-u; muita/ be(come) turned toward; face 24B+
munê chest 17A+
murâ village 20A+
mûri /na/ unreasonable, excessive, forced, impossible 21B
  mûri o suru strain; lean over backward 21B+
mûsiro rather; more than that 20B
  mûsiro X no hôo ḡa hayâi rather, X is faster 20B
musuko son 10A+
musúmè daughter 10A+
mut́-tù six units 5A
muzukasii /-katta/ is difficult 3B
  muzúkasii hitò a person hard to get on with 11A+
muzukasisa difficulty 24B+
myôobañ tomorrow night 12B+
myoógòniti day after tomorrow 12B+
myôoniti tomorrow 12B
myootyoo tomorrow morning 12B+

ñ /casual-style affirmation/ 8A
ñ /contraction of nominal **no**/ 7B
  abúnài ñ da it's that it's dangerous 7B
na /pre-nominal alternate of **dà**/ 5B
nâa /sentence-particle of confirmation, agreement, or deliberation/ 13A
naḡâi /-katta/ is long 9B
Nâḡoya Nagoya 8A
nâihu knife 15A+
naiseñ extension 12A
naiyoo contents; subject matter, substance 22B
nâka inside, within 15B
  A to B to C no nâka de (being) among A and B and C 15B
  konó mit-tù no nâka de (being) among these three things 15B
nakanaka quite; rather; more than one might expect 4A
namae name 7A
nami regular 14B+
nâñ what? 2A
nâna seven 3A
nanâ-tu seven units 5A
nâni what? 4A

nâni ka something 5A
nani mo /+ negative/ nothing 13A+
naniḡo what language? 2A+
naniiro what color? 5B
naniziñ what nationality? 10B+
nañni mo /emphatic equivalent of **nani mo**/ 24B
naôru /-u; naôtta/ become repaired; recover 17B
naôsu /-u; naôsita/ fix, repair; correct 13A
naraberu /-ru; narabeta/ place in line 19A+
narabu /-u; narañda/ form a line; get in line 19A
narânai [it] won't come to anything 22B+
  sitê wa narânai [one] mustn't do 22B+
narêru /-ru; nâreta/ become accustomed 23A
  zîipañ ni narêru become accustomed to blue jeans 23A
Nârita (name of airport) 20A
naru /-u; natta/ sound 22A+
  kamínarì ḡa naru it thunders 22A+
nâru /-u; nâtta/ become; get to be 9A
  onári ni nàru↑ /honorific-polite equivalent of **nâru**/ 10A
  osóku nàru become late 9A
  rokú-syùukañ ni nâru get to be six weeks 9B
  ki ní nàru weigh on one's mind; become a cause for concern 24A+
  ikú kotò ni nâru be(come) decided that [someone] will go 24A
  syabêru yoo ni nâru reach the point of speaking 24A
narubeku as much as possible 15B
  narúbeku hàyàku as fast as possible 15B
naruhodo to be sure! of course! indeed! 9A
nasâru↑ /-aru; nasâtta/ /honorific-polite equivalent of **suru**/ do 12B
natû summer 19A+
nâze why? 11A+
nedañ price 21A
nê(e) /sentence-particle of confirmation, agreement, or deliberation/ 1A, 1B, 2A
nekasu /-u; nekasita/ put to sleep; put to bed; lay [something] on its side 19B+
nêko cat 17B+
nêkutai necktie 23A+
  nêkutai o simêru/suru put on a necktie 23A+
nemui /-katta/ is sleepy 19B+

-neñ /classifier for naming and counting years/ 8B

neñ care, caution 23B
  neñ no tame for the sake of caution; to be on the safe side 23B
  neñ o ireru use care; use caution 23B+

-neñkañ /classifier for counting years/ 8B+

neru /-ru; neta/ go to sleep; go to bed 19B

nî two 2B

ni /ptc/ in; on; at 6A; into; onto; to 7A; from 10B
  usíro ni àru be located in back 6A
  zyûu-zi ni kûru come at ten o'clock 8B
  hôñya ni iku go to the bookstore 7A
  Kimura-sañ ni deñwa o kakèru telephone Mr/s. Kimura 9B
  rokú-syùukañ ni nâru get to be six weeks 9B
  tomodati ni kariru borrow from a friend 10B
  soñna ni to that extent; like that 9B
  hayámè ni kûru come early 10A
  keñkoo ni ìi is good for the health 14B
  miyagè ni kau buy as a souvenir 15A
  mukae ni iku go to meet 16B
  tanósimì ni suru consider to be a pleasure 16B
  ikú no ni wa in the process of going 20A
  matâzu ni without waiting; instead of waiting 23B

niâu suit, become [someone] 23B
  X ni niâu suit X, be becoming to X 23B+

nigìyaka /na/ lively; bustling; prosperous 21B

nihaku-suru stay two nights 21A+

Nihôñ/Nippòñ Japan 5B+

nihoñgo/nippoñgo Japanese language 2A

nihoñma Japanese-style room 21A+

nihoñsyoku Japanese-style food 15A+

nihóñzìñ/nippóñzìñ Japanese person 10B+

nikkèezìñ person of Japanese ancestry 10B

nikû meat 15A+

-nikui /-katta/ is marked by difficulty 13A
  siníkùi is hard to do 13A

nîmotu luggage; things to be carried 19A

-niñ/-ri /classifier for counting people/ 11A

-niñmae /classifier for counting portions/ 14B

niôi smell 22B+
  niôi ga suru have a smell 22B+

ni-see second generation (used in reference to offspring of native Japanese who have moved abroad) 10B+

nisi west 19B+

-niti/-ka /classifier for counting days and naming dates/ 8A

nitíyòo(bi) Sunday 8A

niwa garden 17B

ññ /casual-style negation/ 9A

no /nom/ 3B
  oókìi no a big one 3B
  kawárù no de being the case that [I]'ll change; [I]'ll change so . . . 13B
  ikú no ni wa in the process of going 20A
  atúmàru no the gathering 19B

no /ptc/ 5B
  tomodati no kuruma a friend's car 5B
  kinoo no siñbuñ yesterday's newspaper 5B
  kokó no tosyòkañ the library here 6B

nò /ptc **no** + nominal **no**/ 5B
  kyôo no da it's today's (one) 5B

no ~ ga /ptc/
  Tanáka-sañ no mottè kita nîmotu luggage that Mr/s. Tanaka brought 19A

no /pre-nominal form of **dà**/
  uñteñsyu ga zyosée no tàkusii a taxi whose driver is a woman 19B

nôdo throat 14A+
  nôdo ga kawâku become thirsty 14A+

nokorimono leftovers 24A+

nokôru /-u; nokôtta/ be(come) left behind; remain, stay on 24A

nokôsu /-u; nokôsita/ leave behind; hold in reserve; save 24A+

nomîmono drink, beverage 14A

nômu /-u; nôñda/ drink 1A; take (of medicine) 14B

nôoka farmer 16B+

Noósuèsuto Northwest (airline) 19A

nôoto notebook 4B

noótobùkku notebook 4B+

norikae a transfer to another vehicle 20B

noríkaèru /-ru; noríkàeta/ transfer to another vehicle 20B+

noru /-u; notta/ get on; board a vehicle; ride 19B
  tâkusii ni noru take a taxi 19B

noseru /-ru; noseta/ place on [something]; take on board; give a ride 19B+

notihodo later 12B

nûgu /-u; nûida/ take off (of clothing) 23A+

nyûusu news 16A
Nyuúyòoku New York 8A

o /ptc/ 4A
   kore o iku go along this one (e.g., street) 7B
   kore o kau buy this one 4A
oba aunt; my aunt 11B+
obâasañ grandmother; your grandmother; old woman /polite/ 11B
obasañ aunt; your aunt; woman /polite/ 11B
ôbi kimono sash 14A+
   ôbi o simêru/suru put on an obi 23B+
obóeru /-ru; obôeta/ commit to memory; learn by heart 12B+
Odaizi ni. Take care of yourself. 16B
Oháyoo (gozaimàsu). + Good morning. GUP
ohîru noon; noon meal 14A; daytime 18B
oíde ni nàru ↑ go; come; be located (animate) /honorific-polite/ 10A+
oisii /-katta/ is delicious 5B
oitokosañ cousin /polite/ 11B+
oka hill 18A+
okâasañ mother; your mother /polite/ 11B+
Okáeri-nasài(màse). Welcome back! 7A
okaḡesama de thanks to you; thanks for asking 11B
Okámai nàku. Don't bother; Don't go to any trouble. 18A
okane money 19A+
okâsi cake; candy; sweets 15A+
okásìi /-katta/ is funny; is strange 13A
okâsi na /+ nom/ funny; strange 13A+
okîru /-ru; ôkita/ wake up; get up 21B+
okôru /-u; okôtta/ become angry 22B+
okosañ child /polite/ 10A+
okôsu /-u; okôsita/ wake [someone] up 21B
oku /-u; oita/ put, place 16A
   iret(e) oku put in for future use, put in and leave 16A
   tótt(e) oku put aside, set aside 21A
   oite (i)ku leave behind 16A
okureru /-ru; okureta/ become late or delayed 9B
   okúrete kùru come late 9B
okuru /-u; okutta/ send; send off, see off 16B
ôkusañ wife; your wife /polite/ 10B
Omátase-itasimàsita. ↓ I've caused you to wait /humble-polite/ 12B
omáti-kudasài please wait 4B
omâwarisañ policeman 7B+

omé ni kakàru ↓ **/-u; kakâtta/** meet, see (a person) /humble-polite/ 13B
   Hazîmete omé ni kakarimàsu. How do you do. 13B+
omoi /-katta/ is heavy 20A
omósiròi /-katta/ is interesting; is amusing; is fun 1B
omósirosa interest, enjoyment 24B+
omótè front side 7B+
omôu /-u; omôtta/ think 11A
   kâette (i)ru to omôu think [someone] is or will be back 11A
   deyôo to omôu [I] think [I]'ll leave 20A
onaka stomach 14A
   onaka ga suku become hungry 14A
onazi same 5B
   onazi zassi same magazine 5B
   koré to onazi tàipu a type the same as this 17B
(o)nêesañ older sister; your older sister /polite/ 11A+
Onéḡai-simàsu. ↓ I make a request of you. /humble-polite/ GUP
(o)nîisañ older brother; your older brother /polite/ 11A
oñnà female 10A
   oñna no hitò woman 10A
   oñna no katà woman /polite/ 10A+
   oñnà no ko little girl; young girl 10A+
ôobaa (over)coat, topcoat 23B
oôi /-katta/ are many; are frequent 20A
   nîmotu ga oôi there is lots of luggage 20A
oókìi /-katta/ is big 1B+
ôoki na /+ nom/ big, large; loud (of voice) 13A
ôokisa size (bulk) 24B+
Oókura-hòteru Hotel Okura 6B
oókuràsyoo Finance Ministry 11B+
oómìzu flood 22A+
Oosaka Osaka 8A+
Oósutorària Australia 5B+
oósutorariàziñ an Australian 10B+
oózèe large numbers of people; crowd 19A
oree reward; thanks, expression of appreciation 17A *See* **rêe**.
orîru /-ru; ôrita/ descend; get off (a vehicle) 19B
orôsu /-u; orôsita/ lower; unload; let off (a vehicle) 19B+
ôru ↓ **/-u; ôtta/** be located (of animate existence) /humble-polite/ 7A

Toókyoo ni òru ↓ be in Tokyo (animate) 7A
kekkoñ-sit(e) òru ↓ be married 10B
hanâsit(e) oru ↓ be talking 10B
kotíra ni nàtte orimasu + [it] has come to be here /neutral-polite/ 15B
Osaki ni. (Excuse me for going) ahead of you. /polite/ 9B
  Dôozo, osaki ni. Please go ahead. /polite/ 9B
Osewasama. (Thank you for) your helpful assistance. 6B
osieru /-ru; osieta/ teach; give instruction or information 7A
osiire closet 17B+
osoi /-katta/ is late; is slow 9A
  osóku nàru become late; become slow 9A+
  osókute mo even/also if it's late; at the latest 21B
osókù late (time) 11A
  osókù made until late 11A
Osôre-irimasu. I'm sorry; Thank you. 12B
ossyàru ↑ **/-aru; ossyàtta/** be called 12A; say 18B /honorific-polite/
  X to/(t)te ossyàru ↑ be named X 12B; say, "X" /honorific-polite/ 18B
otaku home; household /polite/ 7B
otókò male 10A
  otóko no hitò man 10A
  otóko no katà man /polite/ 10A+
  otókò no ko little boy; young boy 10A+
otona adult 10A+
otôosañ father; your father /polite/ 11B+
otóotò younger brother 11A+
otótòi the day before yesterday 3A
otôtosi the year before last 10A+
ôtto husband; my husband 10B+
Otúkaresama (dèsita). (You must be tired!) GUP
oturi change (money returned) 4B
otya tea 3A+
  otya o ireru make tea 17B
oyâ parent 11B+
oyagosañ parent; your parent /polite/ 11B+
Oyásumi-nasài. Goodnight. GUP
oyu hot water 14A+
ozi uncle; my uncle 11B+
ozîisañ grandfather; your grandfather; old man /polite/ 11B+
ozisañ uncle; your uncle; man /polite/ 11B+

ozyôosañ daughter; your daughter; young woman /polite/ 10A

Paáku-bìru the Park building 6A
pâat(e)ii party 21B+
pâi pie 3A+
pâñ bread 14A
pâñtaroñ slacks 23A+
pâñtu slacks 23A+
Pâri Paris 8A
Pâruko Parco (name of department store) 7B
peñ pen 4B+
pikunikku picnic 22A
pûriñ custard pudding 3A+
purógùramu program 20B

râigetu next month 9A+
raineñ next year 9A+
râisu cooked rice 14A
raisyuu next week 9A
rakû /na/ relaxed; comfortable; easy 8A
  rakû ni suru make comfortable 18A
rañti-sàabisu special lunch 14A
-rasìi /-katta/ apparently is; seems to be 24B
  kitá-rasìi apparently has come 24B
  yasúi-rasìi is apparently cheap 24B
  kimí-rasìi is typical of you; seems to be you 24B
rassyu-àwaa rush hour 11A
râzio radio 16A+
rêe zero 12A
  rêe-zi zero o'clock, midnight 19A+
rêe reward; thanks, expression of appreciation 17A
  rêe o siranai rude, ill-mannered 17A+
  oree o iu express thanks 17A+
  oree o suru reward 17A+
  omiyage no oree ni in return for a souvenir received 17A+
rêe no X that very X; that X known to both of us 24A
reñraku-suru get in touch; make contact 12B
reñsyuu-suru practice 22B
ressya a train 19A+
rêsutorañ restaurant (Western-style) 14B+
-ri/-niñ /classifier for counting people/ 11A
rikoñ-suru get divorced 10B+
rimúziñ-bàsu limousine bus 20A
rippa /na/ splendid, magnificent, great, eminent 20B
rokû six 2B+

Rôndoñ London 8A
roodoo-suru labor 16B+
roódòosya laborer 16B+
rooka corridor, hall 17B+
rosiaḡo Russian language 2A+
rosíaziñ Russian person 10A+
rûsu absence from home 9B
rusubañ a caretaker 13A
   rusubañ o suru act as a caretaker 13A+
rusúbañ-dèñwa telephone answering machine 13A
ryokañ Japanese-style inn 6B
ryokoo trip; travel 20A
   ryokóo ni dèru leave on a trip 20A
ryokoo-suru take a trip 20A+
   Amerika o ryokoo-suru travel through America 20A+
ryoóḡàeki money-changing machine 19A
ryôoḡae-suru make change; exchange money 19A
ryôori cooking 15B
ryôori-suru prepare food 15B+
ryoórìya restaurant (Japanese-style) 15B+
ryôosiñ both parents 11B+
ryôozi consul 13B+
ryoózìkañ consulate 6B
   Amérika-ryoozìkañ American consulate 6B

sâa hmmm! 6A
sâa here, now! come, now! /exclamation of urging/ 18A
sâabisu service; item or service offered "on the house" 15A
saḡasu /-u; saḡasita/ look for; locate; track down 24A
-sai /classifier for counting years of human age/ 10A+
sakana fish 13B
sakaya liquor store 14B+
saki ahead (of time or place) 6A, 21B
sakihodo a while ago /formal/ 18B
sâkki a while ago 16A
sakura cherry 18A+
-sama Mr.; Mrs.; Miss; Ms. /polite suffix/
samêru /-ru; sâmeta/ get cold 18A
samûi /-katta/ is cold (of atmosphere only) 11A+
sâmusa cold(ness) 24B+
sañ three 2B+
-sañ Mr.; Mrs.; Miss; Ms. /polite suffix/ 2A

sañdo/sañdoìtti sandwich 14A+
Sañhurānsìsuko San Francisco 8A
sâñkyuu thank you 17A
sâñ-see third generation (used in reference to grandchildren of native Japanese who have moved abroad) 10B+
Sapporo Sapporo 8A+
sara plate 15B+
saraiḡetu month after next 10A+
saraineñ year after next 10A+
saraisyuu week after next 10A+
sarárìimañ salaried employee 16B+
sasiaḡeru ↓ /-ru; sasiaḡeta/ give (to you/him/her/them) /humble-polite/ 17A+
   kasite sasiaḡeru ↓ lend (to you/him/her/them) 17A+
sasímì raw fish dish 14A+
satôo sugar 5B
-satu /classifier for counting books, magazines, etc./ 4B
satu a bill (currency) 19A+
sayoo /formal equivalent of **sôo**/ 13B
Sayo(o)nara. Goodbye. GUP
sebiro man's suit 23A
seereki Christian era; A.D. 8B
sêetaa sweater 23B
seezi politics 16B+
seezika politician 16B+
sêki seat; assigned place 12B
   sêki o hazusite (i)ru be away from one's seat 12B
seḱkakù with special trouble or effort 15A
   Seḱkakù desu ḡa .. It's especially [kind of you] but ... 15A+
   seḱkaku no pìkkunikku a picnic involving special effort 22A
semâi /-katta/ is cramped, narrow, small (of area) 24+
sêñ one thousand 2B
-señ /counter for thousands/ 2B
senaka back (part of the body) 17A+
seńeñsatu ¥1000 bill 19A
sêñḡetu last month 10A
seńkyòosi missionary 16B+
señmeñzyo washroom 24B+
seńsèe teacher; doctor 2B
seńsèñḡetu month before last 10A+
seńsèñsyuu week before last 10A+
señsyuu last week 10A
-señto /classifier for counting cents/ 3A+
señzitu the other day 18A

sétto-mènyuu set menu 15B
setumee-suru explain 18B+
sewâ helpful assistance 11B
  sewâ ni nâru become obliged for assistance 11B
si /ptc/ and (what is more) 23A
  mitúkaranài si it isn't found, and (what is more) 23A
sî four 2B+
sî city 20A+
Siâtoru Seattle 19A
sibai a show, a play 18B+
sibâraku a while (of indeterminate length) 11B+, 18A+
  Sibâraku desu. It's been a while (since our last meeting). 18A+
sî-go-niti four or five days 20A
sig̃oto work 8B
sîizuñ the season 21B
sika /ptc/ except for 21A
  âsa sika dasânai not serve except in the morning, serve only in the morning 21A
  miñsyuku nì sika tomáranai not stay except in tourist homes, stay only in tourist homes 21A
sikasi but 24B
sikata way of doing 22B+
  sikáta g̃a nài nothing can be done; it can't be helped 22B+
sikî ceremony, rite 23A+
sikíbùtoñ bottom quilt 21B+
Sikôku Shikoku (a main island of Japan) 11A+
siku /-u; siita/ spread out 21B
simâ island 18A+
simâru /-u; simâtta/ become closed; [something] closes 16A
simâtta damn! oh, dear! 21A
simau /-u; simatta/ put away; store 16A
  wasurete simau/wasuretyau forget completely; end up forgetting 16B
simêru /-ru; sîmeta/ close [something] 16A
sînai within a city (a **sî**) 20A+
siñbuñ newspaper 2B+
siñbuñkìsya journalist 16B+
sing̃oo traffic light 7B
sîñguru(-rùumu) single room 21A
siñkàñseñ bullet train 7B+
siñpai worry, concern 20B
  siñpai o kakèru cause [someone] to worry 20B+

siñpai-suru worry 20B+
siñsitu bedroom 17B+
siñzoo heart 17A+
Siñzyuku Shinjuku (section of Tokyo) 8B
siô salt 14A+
sirábèru /-ru; sirábeta/ look into, investigate, check 14B
siroi /-katta/ is white 4A+
siru /-u; sitta/ get to know 10B
  sitte (i)ru know 10B
sita bottom; down; below, under 17B+
sitag̃i underwear 23A+
sitêeseki reserved seat 19A+
sitî seven 2B+
situree /na/ rude; rudeness 12B
Sitúree-simasita. Excuse me (for what I have done). GUP
Sitúree-simasu. Excuse me (for what I am about to do). GUP
siyoo way of doing 22B+
  siyóo g̃a nài nothing can be done; it can't be helped 22B+
sôba nearby 6B
  êki no sôba near the station 6B
sôba buckwheat noodles 14A+
sobâya noodle shop 14B+
Sobíèto /see **Sôreñ**/ 5B+
sôbo (my) grandmother 11B+
sôhu (my) grandfather 11B+
soko that place (near you or just mentioned) 6B+
-soku /classifier for counting pairs of footwear/ 23A+
soñna that kind (of) 4B+
  soñna ni to that extent; like that 9B
sono /+ nom/ that —— near you; that —— just mentioned 3A
-soo /na/ looking as if 24B
  kowáresòo /na/ looking as if it would break 24B
  hirósòo ni mieru appear spacious-looking 24B
sôo that way; like that 2A
  âru soo da I hear that there are, it is said that there are 21A
soodañ-suru consult; talk over 11A
Sôoru Seoul 8A+
soozi-suru clean 17A+
sore that thing (near you or just mentioned) 2B
  sore kara after that; and then 4B

sore ni onto that; on top of that; in addition 11A
soré dè wa that being the case 13B
Sôreñ Soviet Union 5B+
soréñziñ Soviet citizen 10B+
sôrosoro slowly; gradually 18A
sorya /contraction of **sore wa**/ 14B
sotira that side; that way; thereabouts; there; that alternative (of two) 6A+
sôto outside 17B
sottí /casual equivalent of **sotira**/ 7B+
-suḡî past; after 8A
　go-hûñ-suḡi five minutes after the hour 8A
suḡîru /-ru; **sûḡita**/ go to excess 15A
　tabesuḡiru overeat 15A
suḡôi /-katta/ is awful, wonderful, weird, terrific 11A
　suḡôku zyoózù da is awfully skilled/skillful 11A
sûḡu soon; immediate 5B
　sûḡu kûru will come soon 5B
　sûḡu sôba immediate vicinity 6B
sûi /abbreviation for **suíyòo(bi)**/ 8A
　gês·sûi·kîñ Mon–Wed–Fri 8A
suíyòo(bi) Wednesday 8A
sukâato skirt 23A+
sukî /na/ pleasing; like 15B
sukiyaki sukiyaki (description in 14A) 14A+
sukkàri completely, utterly 17A
sukôsi a little; a few 5A
suku /-u; **suita**/ become empty 14A
　onaka ḡa suku become hungry 14A
sukúnài /-katta/ are few; is rare; is infrequent 20A+
　kâzi ḡa sukúnài there are few fires 20A+
sumáseru /-ru; **sumâseta**/ bring to an end, finish 21B
Su(m)ímaseñ. I'm sorry; Thank you. GUP
Su(m)ímaseñ desita. I'm sorry (for what I did); Thank you (for the trouble you took). GUP
sûmu /-u; **sûñda**/ come to an end 21B+
sûmu /-u; **sûñda**/ take up residence, reside 24A
Supêiñ Spain 5B+
supeiñḡo Spanish language 2A+
supéiñziñ Spaniard 10B+
supóotu-bàñḡumi sports program 18B+
supóotùkàa sportscar 5B
suppài /-katta/ is sour 15+
supûuñ spoon 15A+
surâkkusu slacks 23A+

surîppa slippers 23A+
suru /irreg; **sita**/ do; play (of games) 1A
　eé-kòosu ni suru make [it] (to be) the "A" meal; decide on the "A" meal 14A
　ki ni suru mind; worry about; concern oneself about 24A
　tukau yoo ni suru try to use 24A
　nokôru koto ni suru decide on remaining 24A
susî sushi (description in 14A) 14A+
susiya sushi shop 14B+
sutañdo lamp 17B+
suteru /-ru; **suteta**/ throw away 17A
suu /-u; **sutta**/ smoke (cigarettes, cigars, etc.) 14B
sûúpaa(màaketto) supermarket 7B+
sûutu man's or woman's suit 23A
suútukèesu suitcase 5A+
suuzi number(s) 12A
suwaru /-u; **suwatta**/ sit down 19B+
suzúsìi /-katta/ is cool 11A+
syabêru /-u; **syabêtta**/ speak, talk, chat 24A
syâiñ staff member 16B+
syakâiḡaku sociology 18B+
syasiñ photograph 16A
　syasíñ o tòru take a picture 16A
syâtu shirt 23A+
syatyoo company president 13B
-syoku /classifier for counting meals/ 21A
　ni-syoku-tuki with two meals, two meals included 21A
syokudoo dining room; restaurant 14A+
syokuzi dining; meal 16B
　syokúzi ḡa dèru meals are served 21A
　syokuzi ni suru make it dinner; have dinner 21B
syokuzi-suru dine, have a meal 16B+
syoo way of doing 22B
　syoó ḡa nài nothing can be done; it can't be helped 22B+
syooḡo noon 18B
　syoóḡo-suḡì after noon 18B
syookai-suru introduce 11B
syôosyoo a little 4B
syooti-suru agree to; consent to 21B
Syoowa the Showa Era (1926–) 8B+
syooyu soy sauce 14A+
syoozi sliding door (translucent) 16A+
syoppiñḡubàggu shopping bag 5A+
syosai study (room) 17B+
syotyoo institute director 12B
syukkiñ attendance at the office 22A+

zisá-syùkkiñ staggered work hours; flextime 22A
syuttyoo business trip 9B
syuttyoo-suru go away on a business trip 9B+
syuu week 10A+
-syuukañ /classifier for counting weeks/ 8B+
syuumatu weekend 21A+
syûziñ husband; my husband 10B+

tabako cigarette 14B
tabakoya cigarette shop, tobacconist 14B+
tabémòno food 14A+
tabéru /-ru; tâbeta/ eat 1A
tabésu ̄gìru /-ru; tabésùg ̄ita/ overeat 15A
tâbi bifurcated socks (Japanese-style) 23B+
tâbuñ probably 21A
Tadaima. Hello, I'm back. 7A
taiheñ /na/ awful; terrible; a problem 9B
taíhùu typhoon 22A
tâipu type, style, variety; typing 17B
taípuràitaa typewriter 3A
taisetu /na/ important 13A
tâisi ambassador 13B+
taísìkañ embassy 6B
 Amérika-taisìkañ American embassy 6B
Taisyoo the Taisho Era (1912–26) 8B
taitee usually 8B+
Taíwàñ Taiwan 5B+
takâi /-katta/ is expensive; is high 1B
take bamboo 18A+
takkyuubiñ (special baggage service) 20A
takúsàñ much; many 5A
tâkusii taxi 7B
tamâg ̄o egg 14A+
tamê reason, sake; benefit 23A
 tamê ni nâru mono a thing which is beneficial 23A+
 kyôosi ni nâru tamê (ni) in order to become a teacher 23A
 byoóki ni nàtta tamê (ni) because of having become sick 23A+
 neñ no tame for the sake of caution; to be on the safe side 23B
tana shelf 16A+
tanî valley 18A+
tanômu /-u; tanôñda/ request, ask for 14A+
tanósìmì a joy; a pleasure 8B
tanósìmu /-u; tanósìñda/ take pleasure in 8B+
tañsu chest (furniture) 17B+

tâsika /na/ certain, positive, reliable 20A
 tâsika ni /+ predicate/ certainly, positively, surely 20A+
 tâsika /+ predicate/ if I'm correct, if I remember correctly, most likely 20A+
tasúkàru /-u; tasúkàtta/ be(come) rescued, saved 17B
tasúkèru /-ru; tasûketa/ rescue, save 17B+
 Tasuketeeee. Help!!! 17B+
tatami (Japanese-style floor mat) 17B
 tatámi no heyà room with mats 17B
tatêmòno building 6B
tatêru /-ru; tâteta/ stand [something] up; erect [something] 19B+
 yakû ni tatêru put to use 20B+
 X o yakû ni tatêru put X to use 20B+
tâtu /-u; tâtta/ stand up; get built 19B
 yakû ni tâtu be of use 20B
 hará g ̄a tàtu become angry 22B
tâtu /-u; tâtta/ depart 19B+
tê hand 17A+
teârai toilet 6A
teeburu table 17B
têepu tape 3A
teesyoku meal with a fixed menu 14A
teg ̄ami letter 2A
Tekísasu-òiru Texas Oil 15A
tekitoo /na/ suitable 24B
temae this side (of) 7B
Teñhana (name of tempura restaurant) 15A
teñiñ salesperson 16B+
tênisu tennis 4A
têñki weather; good weather 22A
 (ìi) têñki ni nâru get to be good weather 22A
teńki-yòhoo weather forecast 18B+
teñpura batter-fried fish and vegetables 14A+
teñpuraya tempura shop 14B+
terâ Buddhist temple 6B+
têrebi television 16A
 têrebi ni dêru appear on television 18B
tetúdàu /-u; tetúdàtta/ help, lend a hand 17A
tig ̄au /-u; tig ̄atta/ be different; be wrong 1A
 ítu mo to tig ̄au be different from [what is] always [normal] 23A
tiísài /-katta/ is small 1B+
tîisa na /+ nom/ small, little; low, soft (of voice) 13A+
tikâ underground 7A

tikâi /-katta/ is near 13B
tikâku vicinity 13B+
tikatetu subway 7B+
tikázukèru /-ru; tikázùketa/ bring close; associate with 22A+
tikázùku /-u; tikázùita/ approach, draw near; become acquainted 22A
titî father; my father 11B+
titioya father 11B+
tîzu map 7B
tô the city of Tokyo 20A+
to /ptc/ and; with 3B
   kore to sore this and that 3B
   tomódati to hanàsu talk with a friend 10B
   tomodati to issyo together with a friend 11A+
   A to B to, dôtira ḡa îi? which is better, A or B? 15A
   îtu mo to tiḡau be different from [what is] always [normal] 23A
   X ni yoru to according to X 22A
to /quotative/ 11A
   îi to omôu think that it's good 11A
   deyôo to omôu [I] think [I] will leave 20A
   Tanaka to iu be named Tanaka 12A
   X to iu ~ ossyàru ~ môosu be named X 12A; say, "X" 18B
   to iu kotò wa that is to say 21B
   to iù yori more than saying what was just said; that is to say, rather 22B
to door 16A+
todana cupboard 17B
todókèru /-ru; todôketa/ deliver; report, notify 20A+
todôku /-u; todôita/ be delivered; reach; extend 20A+
tôire toilet 6A+
tokee clock; watch 8A
tokî occasion, time 13A
   himá na tokì ni at a time when [someone] is free 13A
   kodómo no tokì the time when [I] was a child 13A+
tokídokì sometimes 19A
Tokíwa-hòteru Tokiwa Hotel 21A
tokkyuu special express 19A+
tokkyùukeñ special express ticket 19A+
tokonoma alcove 21B
tokórò place; location 10B
tokubetu special 19A+

tokúbetu-kyùukoo/tokkyuu special express 19A+
tokuzyoo super-deluxe 14B+
tomaru /-u; tomatta/ come to a halt; stop over 8A
   miñsyuku ni tomaru stay in a tourist home 21A
tomeru /-ru; tometa/ stop (something); bring to a halt 7B
tomodati friend 2B+
tônai within the city of Tokyo 20A
tonari next door; adjoining place 6B
Toǹde mo nài. Heavens, no! 8B
tôo ten units 5A+
Toodai Tokyo University 11B
tooi /-katta/ is far 13A
   deñwa ḡa tooi sound far away (on the telephone) 13A
toókù the faraway 13A+
Tookyoo Tokyo 2A
toozitu the very day, the day in question 19B
toráñku trunk 16A
Toranomoñ (section of Tokyo) 6B
tori chicken 15A+
torikaeru /-ru; torikaeta/ exchange 20B+
tôru /-u; tôtta/ take up; take away 16A
   syasiñ o tòru take a picture 16A
   huráñsuḡo o tòru take French 16A+
   satôo o tòru pass the sugar 16A+
   tótt(e) oku put aside, set aside 21A
tosî year 8B+
tosíyòrì old person 10A+
tosyôkañ library (a building) 6B
tosyôsitu library (a room) 8B
tot(t)emo very, extremely 1B
(t)te /quotative/ 18B
   X (t)te iu ~ ossyàru ~ môosu be named X; say, "X" 18B
   X (t)te. Someone says, "X." 18B
-tu /classifier for counting units and years of human age/ 5A, 10A
tûaa tour 19B
-tubo /classifier for counting tsubo (= the area covered by two tatami mats)/ 24B+
tuḡî next 7B
tuḡoo convenience 13B
   tuḡóo ḡa ìi is convenient 13B+
   tuḡóo ḡa warùi is inconvenient 13B+
tuíñ(-rùumu) twin room 21A+
tuítatì first day of the month 8A
tukárèru /-ru; tukâreta/ become tired 17B

tukau /-u; tukatta/ use 3A
tukéru /-ru; tukéta/ attach [something]; turn on 16A
   ki ó tukèru pay attention; be careful 19B+
  -tuki attached 21A
   ni-syoku-tuki with two meals, two meals included 21A
tukî month; moon 8B+
tukiatari end of the street, corridor, etc. 7B+
tûku /-u; tûita/ arrive 16B
tûku /-u; tûita/ become attached; become turned on 16A
  ki ğá tùku notice; become aware 19B
Tukuba Tsukuba University 12B+
tukue desk 17B+
tukûru /-u; tukûtta/ make, construct 1A
  komê o tukûru grow rice 14A+
tûma wife; my wife 10B+
tumáranai /-katta/ is boring; is trifling 1B
tumetai /-katta/ is cold 14A
tumori plan, intention 20A
  ikú tumori dà I plan to go 20A
  minámiğuti no tumori dàtta I expected it to be the south entrance 20B
  kâre ğa mâtte kureru tumori de ita I was of the intention that he would wait for me 20B+
tuná-sàndo tuna fish sandwich 14A+
tureru /-ru; tureta/ take along (of people) 15A
  turete iku take (a person to a place) 15A+
tuukiñ commuting to work 19B
tuukiñ-suru commute to work 19B+
tuúkiñ-zìkañ commuting time 19B
tuuziru /-ru; tuuzita/ make oneself understood, get through 13A
tuyôi /-katta/ is strong 12A+
tûyosa strength 24B+
tuyu rainy season 22A
tya tea 5B+
tyairo brown 5B+
-tyaku arriving 19A
  Tookyoo-tyaku arriving in Tokyo 19A+
  itî-zi-tyaku arriving at one o'clock 19A
-tyaku /classifier for counting suits/ 23A+
-tyañ /polite suffix added to children's and young people's names/ 10A
tyanoma (Japanese-style) living room, sitting room 17B+
tyañto properly; exactly; neatly 17A
tyawañ bowl (for rice) 15B+

tyoodai-suru ↓ accept /humble-polite/ 18A
  aríğàtàku tyoodai-suru ↓ accept gratefully /humble-polite/ 18A
tyoodo exactly 4B
-tyoome /classifier for naming chome/ 14B
tyôtto a bit; a little 1A
  Tyotto . . I'm afraid not . . . /polite refusal/ 1A
-tyuu [in] the middle of 13A; throughout 24B
  hanasi-tyuu [in] the middle of talk; 'the line is busy' 13A
  gozeñ-tyuu all morning long 24B
  gozeñ-tyuu ni within the morning
Tyûuğoku China 5B+
tyuuğokugo Chinese language 2A
tyuúğokùziñ a Chinese 10B+
tyuúka-ryòori Chinese cooking 15B
tyuumoñ an order (for something) 14A+
tyuumoñ-suru place an order 14A

udê arm 17A+
uê/ue top; up; over 17B
ueki plant 17B+
uekiya gardener 17B+
ueru /-ru; ueta/ plant 17B+
ukağau /-u; ukağatta/ ↓ inquire, ask 6A; visit 13B /humble-polite/
uketuke receptionist 10B
umâi /-katta/ is skilled; is delicious 24A
ume plum 15A+
Umeteñ (name of tempura restaurant) 15A
ûmi ocean, sea 15A
uñteñ-suru drive a vehicle 16B+
uñtèñsyu driver, chauffeur 16B+
urâ reverse side; rear 7B
uru /-u; utta/ sell 19A
usiro back; rear 6A
usui /-katta/ is thin (of liquids); is weak (of coffee, tea, etc.); is pale (of colors) 15B+; is thin (of flat objects) 23B+
uti interval 13B; among 15B
  tikâi uti ni in the near future 13B
  A to B to C no uti de (being) among A and B and C 15B
  konó mit-tù no uti de (being) among these three things 15B
utî house, home; household; in-group 7B
  uti no /+ nominal/ our household's, our 7B
uwaği jacket 23B

Japanese–English Glossary • 373

wa /assertive sentence-particle/ 9A
wa /ptc/ in regard to; at least; comparatively speaking 4A
   Tanáka-san wa wakarimàsu. Mr/s. Tanaka (at least) understands. 4A
   Sinbun wa kaimasèn desita. A paper (in contrast) I didn't buy. 4A
   Konó hen nì wa arímasèn. It's not around here (at least). 6A
   sitê wa having done 22B
   sitê wa 'ikenai/naranai [one] must not do 22B
   sinâkute wa 'ikenai/naranai [one] must do 22B
   hoká no hitò de wa dekînai being (i.e., if it is) another person, it can't be done 22B
waapuro word processor 3A+
waee Japanese–English 2B
waée-zìten Japanese–English dictionary 2B
wahuku Japanese-style clothing 23A+
wâin wine 5B+
waisyatu man's dress shirt 23A+
wakâi /-katta/ is young 10A+
wakâru /-u; wakâtta/ be(come) comprehensible; understand 1A
wan bowl (for soup) 15B+
wanrùumu one-room unit; studio apartment 24B
warûi /-katta/ is bad; is wrong 7A
Wâseda Waseda University 12B+
Wasînton Washington 8A
wasitu Japanese-style room 21A+
wasuremono thing forgotten and left behind 14A+
wasureru /-ru; wasureta/ forget 12B
wasyoku Japanese-style food
wata(ku)si I; me 2B
wataru /-u; watatta/ go over, go across 19B+
watasu /-u; watasita/ hand over 19B
wâzawaza purposely, specially 18A

ya /particle/
   susî ya sasímì things like sushi and sashimi 15A
yahâri /see **yappàri**/
yakeru /-ru; yaketa/ get burned, baked, roasted 23A
   hi ni yakeru get sunburned 23A+
yakû duty, role, office 20B+
   yakû ni tâtu be of use 20B
   yakû ni tatêru put to use 20B+

   X o yakû ni tatêru put X to use 20B+
yaku /-u; yaita/ burn [something]; bake; roast 23A+
yakusoku appointment; promise 10A
yakusoku-suru make an appointment; promise 10A+
yamâ mountain 15A
yameru /-ru; yameta/ quit; give up 8B
yamu /-u; yanda/ stop (of rain, snow, etc.) 22A+
yânusi landlord 24B
yaoya vegetable store 7B+
yappàri after all 3B
yarínaòsu /-u; yarínaòsita/ redo 16B+
yaru /-u; yatta/ do 16B
yaru /-u; yatta/ give (to you/him/her/them) 17A+
   kasite yaru lend (to you/him/her/them) 17A+
yasai vegetable 15A+
yasasii /-katta/ is easy 3B+
   yasásii hitò a person who is gentle, kind, nice 11A
yasûi /-katta/ is cheap 1A
-yasui /-katta/ is marked by ease 13A+
   siyásùi is easy to do 13A+
yasúmì vacation; holiday; time off 8A
yasûmu /-u; yasûnde/ rest; take time off 8A+
yâsusa cheapness 24B
yâtin rent 24B
yat́-tù eight units 5A+
yawárakài /-katta/ is soft; is tender 15B+
yo /informative sentence particle/ 1A
yobu /-u; yonda/ summon, call 9A
yôi /-katta/ is good 1B+
yoko side 17B+
   yoko ni oku place on its side or at the side of 17B+
Yokohama Yokohama 8A+
yôku /see **îi**/
Yôku irássyaimàsita. Welcome! 18A
yômu /-u; yônda/ read 12A+
yon four 2B
yoo way of ——ing 22B
   siyoo/syoo way of doing 22B+
yôo /na/ manner; resemblance; seeming 24A
   aíte (i)ru yòo seeming to be open or available 24A+
   anâta no yoo na hito a person like you 24A+

anâta no yoo ni nihóñgo ga zyoozù da   is good in Japanese the way you are   24A+
surú yòo ni iu   tell [someone] to do   24A
tukáu yòo ni suru   try to use   24A
syabêru yoo ni nâru   reach the point of speaking   24A
yoohuku   Western-style clothing   23A+
yooma   Western-style room   21A+
Yoóròppa   Europe   8B
yoosyoku   Western-style food   15A+
yoozi   matters to attend to   9B
  yoozi de iku   go on business   12B
yori /ptc/   more than   15A
  sasímì yori   more than sashimi; compared to sashimi   15A
  sasímì yori ii   is better than sashimi   15A
  koré o yòmu yori omósiròi   is more interesting than reading this   20A+
yorókobu /-u; yorókòñda/   take pleasure in   16B
  yorókòñde ukağau ↓   visit with pleasure   16B
yorosii /-katta/   is good, fine, all right; never mind   5B
  Yorosiku.   (May things go well.)   11B+
  Ôkusañ ni yorosiku.   Regards to your wife.   11B+
yoru /-u; yotta/   stop in   16B
yoru /-u; yotta/   rely, depend; lean   22A
  X ni yoru to   according to X   22A
  X ni yotte   depending on X   22A
yôru   evening; night   8B+
yoť-tù   four units   5A+
yowâi /-katta/   is weak   12A
  suúzi ni yowài   is poor at numbers   12A
yoyaku   reservation   21A
yoyaku-suru   make a reservation   21A+
yu   hot water   14A+
yubî   finger   17A+
yukata   light cotton kimono   23B+
yukî   snow   4A+
yuḱkùri   slowly; leisurely   12A
  Dôozo, goyúkkùri.   Take it easy!   12A+
yunómì   teacup (Japanese-style)   15B+
yuúbè   last night   10A+
yuúbìñkyoku   post office   6B
yuumee /na/   famous; notorious   20B
yuútàañ   U-turn   7B
yuútàañ-suru   make a U-turn   7B

zadâñkai   round-table discussion; symposium   18B+
zañnèñ /na/   regrettable; too bad; a pity   2A
zassi   magazine   2B+
zêhi   by all means   24A
zêmi   seminar   10A
zêñbu   all; the whole thing   3B
zeñzeñ /+ negative/   not at all   3B
zêro   zero   12A+
zettai ni   absolutely   22B
-zi   /classifier for naming the o'clocks/   8A
zibuñ   oneself   17A+
  zibuñ de yaru   do by oneself   17A+
  zibuñ no kuruma   one's own car   17A+
z(i)eé-àaru   Japan Railway   19A+
ziipañ   blue jeans   23A
zikañ   time   8A+
  zikáñ ga àru   have time   8A+
  zikáñ ga kakàru   take time   15B
-zikañ   /classifier for counting hours/   8A+
zîko   accident   9B
zikokuhyoo   timetable   19A
zimûsyo   office   11A+
zîñzya   Shinto shrine   6B+
zîsa   time difference   22A+
zisá-syùkkiñ   staggered work hours; flextime   22A
zisiñ   earthquake   9B+
zisyo   dictionary   2B
zitêñsya   bicycle   7B+
zitû   truth, reality   13B
  zitû o iu   speak the truth   13B+
  zitû wa   in reality, the fact is   13B
ziyûu /na/   free, unrestricted   16B+
ziyûuğyoo   freelance worker   16B+
ziyûuseki   free (unreserved) seat   19A+
zoñziru ↓ **/-ru; zôñzita/**   get to know /humble-polite/   10B+
  zôñzite (i)ru ↓   [I] know /humble-polite/   10B+
  gozôñzi da ↑   [you] know /honorific-polite/   10B+
zoori   sandals (for outdoors)   23A+
zûibuñ   awfully; very   8B
zutto   by far   10B
  zutto màe   way before; long ago   10B
-zutu   of each; for each; at a time   5B
zyâ(a): sôo zya nâi   it's not so   2A
zyâ(a)   well then; that being the case   2B
zyama   nuisance, bother; interruption   17B
  Ozyáma desyòo ğa . .   Excuse me for interrupting you.   17B+

Ozyáma-(ita)simàsita. Excuse me for having interrupted you. 17B+

zyâñpaa windbreaker; jacket 23A

-zyoo /classifier for counting jo (= the area covered by one tatami mat)/ 24B+

zyôo deluxe 14B

zyoobu /na/ strong; rugged; sturdy 12A+

zyoósyàkeñ passenger ticket 19A+

zyoózù /na/ skillful; skilled 9B

   zyoózù ni nâru become skillful; become skilled 9B

zyosee woman, female 19B

zyoseeḡo women's language 19B+

zyûḡyoo schooltime; classtime 8A

zyuḡyoo-suru teach classes; give lessons 9B+

-zyuu throughout

   iti-neñ-zyuu all year long

   kotosi-zyuu ni within this year

zyûu ten 2B

zyuueñdama ¥10 coin 19A+

English–Japanese Glossary

This glossary, which includes only vocabulary introduced in Part 1 and Part 2 of this text, is intended as a reminder list for use when vocabulary items have been temporarily forgotten. It is not intended as a means of acquiring new vocabulary. On those occasions when both an item and the patterns in which it occurs have been forgotten, the Japanese equivalent should be located in this glossary and then further checked by using the Japanese–English glossary and the index.

Verbals are identified by a hyphen, the location of which identifies the verbal class: **X-u** = consonant verbal; **X-ru** = vowel verbal; **X-aru** = special polite verbal (cf. Lesson 9A-SP1 in Part 1).

Adjectivals are identified by a hyphen separating the root from **-i**, the imperfective ending: **X-i**.

Na-nominals are identified by /**na**/ immediately following the item: **X /na/**.

Polite alternates are included in cases where their use is particularly common and/or is in some way unusual or unpredictable in form.

A.M. **gôzeñ**
abdomen **harâ**
about (approximate amount) **-g̃ùrai**
about (approximate point in time) **-g̃òro**
about as much as **-hodo**
about how much? **dono-g̃urai**
absence from home **rûsu**
absolutely **zettai ni**
academic organization **gakkai**
accept **mora-u; itadak-u** ↓ **; tyoodai-suru** ↓
accept for temporary keeping **azúkàr-u**
accident **zîko**
according to X **X ni yoru to**
accustomed: become ~ **narê-ru**
acquainted: become ~ **tikázùk-u**
act **kotô**
adjoining place **tonari**
after **kara** /ptc/
~ that; and then **sore kara**
after (past) **-sug̃i**
ten ~ one **itî-zi zíṕpùñ-sug̃i**
after all **yahâri/yaṕpàri**

after a long interval **hisasiburi**
afternoon **gôg̃o**
again **matâ**
ago **mâe**
a while ~ **sakihodo; sâkki**
agree to **syooti-suru**
ahead **saki**
(Excuse me for going) ahead of you. **Osaki ni.**
aimed at **-muki**
airplane **hikôoki**
airport **kuukoo**
alcove **tokonoma**
all **miñnà; zêñbu**
all day long **iti-niti-zyuu**
all right **daízyòobu /na/**
is ~ **îi/yô-i; yorosi-i**
almost **hotôñdo**
alone **hitô-ri (de)**
already **môo**
also **mo** /particle/
alternative **hôo**

always   îtu mo
amazing: is ~   mezúrasì-i
ambassador   tâisi
America   Amerika
American (person)   amérikàziñ
American Consulate   Amérika-ryoozìkañ
American Embassy   Amérika-taisìkañ
among ——   —— no nâka/uti
angry: become ~   okôr-u; harâ ḡa tât-u
another   hoka
answer   kotáè-ru
answer the telephone   deńwa ni dè-ru
any time   itú dè mo
apartment (house)   apâato; mâñsyoñ
apparently is X   X-rasì-i
appeal   ki ni ir-u
appear   miê-ru
appear on television   têrebi ni dê-ru
appointment   yakusoku
  make an ~   yakusoku-suru
appreciation: expression of ~   (o)ree
approach   tikázùk-u
architect   keñtikuka
architecture   keñtiku
area (vicinity)   heñ; (size) hîrosa
arm   ude
around: go ~, be passed ~   mawar-u
  send ~, pass ~   mawas-u
arrive   tuk-u
arriving (at a time or place)   -tyaku
as if X   X-mìtai /na/
as much as possible   narubeku; dekiru dake
ask   kik-u; ukaḡa-u ↓
ask for   tanôm-u
associate with   tikázukè-ru
attach   tukê-ru; be(come) attached   tûk-u
attached   -tuki
attend   dê-ru
attendance at the office   syukkiñ
attention   ki
  pay ~   ki ó tukè-ru
aunt   oba; obasañ /polite/
Australia   Oósutorària
Australian (person)   oósutorariàziñ
autumn   aki
available: be ~   aite (i)-ru
aware: become ~   ki ḡá tùk-u
awful: is ~   taíhèn /na/; monósuḡò-i; suḡô-i
awfully   zûibuñ; taiheñ

baby   âkatyañ

back   usiro; urâ
back (body part)   senaka
  lower ~   kosî
back up   modôr-u
bacon   bêekoñ
bad: is ~   damê /na/; warû-i
bag   kabañ
baggage service   takkyuubiñ
bake [something]   yak-u; get baked   yake-ru
ballpoint pen   boorupeñ
bamboo   take
bank   giñkoo
Bank of America   Amérika-giñkoo
banker   gińkòoiñ
bath   hurô
  with ~   basu-tuki
bathroom   huróbà
be called   i-u; ośsy-àru ↑; môos-u ↓
be in a hurry   isôḡ-u
be located (of animate existence)   i-ru; irássy-àru ↑; ôr-u ↓
be located (of inanimate existence)   âr-u; goz-aru +
be named   i-u; ośsy-àru ↑; môos-u ↓
be on time   ma ní à-u
be possible   dekî-ru
because   kara /ptc/
become   nâr-u
bed   bêtto/bêddo
  put to ~   nekas-u
  go to ~   ne-ru
bedroom   siñsitu
beer   bîiru
before   mâe
begin [something]   hazime-ru
begin to clear   hârete ku-ru
belly   harâ
below   sita
benefit   tamê
between   aida
beverage   nomîmono
beyond   mukôo/mukoo
bicycle   ziteñsya
big: is ~   oókì-i; ôoki na /+ nom/; (of area)   hirô-i
bill (currency)   satu
  ¥500 ~   gohyákuèñsatu
  ¥10,000 ~   itímañèñsatu
black: is ~   kurô-i
bland: is ~   ama-i
blouse   burâusu

blow **hûk-u**
blue: is ~ **aô-i**
blue jeans **ziipañ**
board (a vehicle) **nor-u**
boat **hûne**
body **karada**
book **hôñ**
bookshelf **hôñdana**
bookstore; book dealer **hôñya**
boring: is ~ **tumáràna-i**
borrow **kari-ru**
both **dôtira mo**
~ parents **ryôosiñ; goryôosiñ** /polite/
~ this one and that one **kore mo sore mo**
bother **zyama**
bottom **sita**
bowl (for rice) **tyawañ**; (for soup) **(o)wañ**
box **hako**
box lunch **beńtòo**
boy **otókò no ko**
bread **páñ**
break [something] **kowâs-u**; [something] breaks **kowárè-ru**
break down **kosyoo-suru**
breakable: is ~ **kowáre-yasù-i**
breakfast **aságòhañ**
bring together **atúmè-ru**
broken: become ~ **kowárè-ru**
brother: older ~ **âni; (o)nîisañ** /polite/
younger ~ **otóotò; otootosañ** /polite/
brown **tyairo**
Buddhist temple **terâ**
build **tatê-ru**; get built **tât-u**
building **tatêmòno; bîru**
bullet train **sińkàñseñ**
burn [something] **yak-u**; get burned **yake-ru**
bus **bâsu**
business card **meesi**
cards on hand **meesi no motiawase**
business trip **syuttyoo**
bustling **niḡiyaka** /na/
busy: is ~ **isógasì-i**
but **sikasi**
butter **bâta**
buy **ka-u**
by all means **zêhi**
by far **zutto**

cake **kêeki; okâsi**
calculate **keesañ-suru**
calculator **keésàñki**

call (summon) **yob-u**
call on the telephone **deńwa o kakè-ru; deñwa-suru**
be called **i-u; ośsy-àru** ↑ ; **môos-u** ↓
camera **kâmera**
candy **okâsi**
car **kuruma**
care **nêñ**
use ~ **nêñ o ire-ru**
Take ~ of yourself. **Odaizi ni.**
careful: be ~ **ki ó tukè-ru**
caretaker **rusubañ**
act as a ~ **rusubañ o suru**
carpenter **dâiku**
carry **hakob-u**
case, circumstance **baai**
cat **nêko**
catch a cold **kaze o hik-u**
certain, positive **tâsika** /na/
certainly **kitto; tâsika ni**
Certainly. I'll do as you asked. **Kasí-komarimàsita.**
chair **isu**
change **kawari**
change: make ~ **ryôoḡae-suru**
change (= money) **oturi**
change [something] **kae-ru**; [something] changes **kawar-u**
change clothing **kikáè-ru/kiḡáè-ru**
change places **kawar-u**
chat **syabêr-u**
chauffeur **uńtèñsyu**
cheap: is ~ **yasû-i**
cheapness **yâsusa**
check, look into **sirábè-ru**
check, the bill **kañzyoo**
cherry **sakura**
chest (body part) **munê**
chest (furniture) **tañsu**
chicken **tori**
child **kodomo; ko; okosañ** /polite/
China **Tyuuḡoku**
Chinese (person) **tyuúḡokùziñ**
Chinese language **tyuuḡokuḡo**
chopsticks **hâsi**
Christian era, A.D. **seereki**
church **kyookai**
cigarette **tabako**
cigarette shop **tabakoya**
circle **maru**
circumstance **baai**

city: small ~ **matî**
   large ~ **sî**
classifiers *See list at end of glossary*
classroom **kyoositu**
classtime **zyúgyoo**
clean (verb) **soozi-suru**
clean **kîree** /**na**/
clear: become ~ (of weather) **harê-ru**
clear(ly) **hakkìri**
clock **tokee**
clogs **geta**
close: bring ~ **tikázukè-ru**
close [something] **simê-ru**; become closed
   simâr-u
closet **osiire**
clothing **hukû**
   Western-style ~ **yoohuku**
cloudy: become ~ **kumôr-u**
coat **ôobaa**
coffee **koóhìi**
coffee shop **kissàteñ/kissateñ**
coin: ¥5 ~ **goeñdama**
   ¥100 ~ **hyakueñdama**
cold: get ~ **samê-ru**
cold: is ~ **tumeta-i**; (of atmosphere only)
   samû-i
cold: a ~ **kaze**
cold(ness) **sâmusa**
collect (bring together) **atúmè-ru**; (come together) **atúmàr-u**
college **daigaku**
color **irô**
   facial ~ **kaoiro**
   what ~? **naniiro; dôñna irô**
come **kû-ru** /irreg/; **irássy-àru** ↑ ; **mâir-u** ↓
come back; come home **kâette ku-ru**
come out **dê-ru**
come together **atúmàr-u**
come up **agar-u**
comfortable **rakû** /**na**/
communicate **tuuzi-ru**
commute **kayo-u**
commute to work **tuukiñ-suru**
commuting time **tuúkiñ-zìkañ**
commuting to work **tuukiñ**
company **kaisya**
company employee **kaísyàiñ**
company president **syatyoo**
completed: become ~ **dekî-ru**
completely **sukkàri**
comprehensible: become ~ **wakâr-u**

computer **koñpyùutaa**
concern **kizûkai**
   become a cause for ~ **ki ní nàr-u**
   ~ oneself about **ki ni suru**
condition **guai**
conference **kâigi**
conference room **kaígìsitu**
confused: become ~ **awate-ru**
connection **kañkee**
consent to **syooti-suru**
consider **kañgaè-ru**
consul **ryôozi**
consulate **ryoózìkañ**
consult **soodañ-suru**
consultant **koñsàrutañto**
contact **reñraku-suru**
contact lens(es) **kôñtakuto(-rèñzu)**
contents **naiyoo**
convenience **tugoo; bêñ**
convenient **bêñri** /**na**/
   is ~ **tugóo ga ì-i; bêñ ga î-i**
conversely **hañtai ni**
cook, prepare food **ryôori-suru**
cooking **ryôori**
cool: is ~ **suzúsì-i**
corner: street ~ **kâdo**
correct **naôs-u**
corridor **rooka**
country **kuni**
cousin **itôko; oitokosañ** /polite/
cramped: is ~ **semâ-i**
crowd: a ~ **oózèe**
crowded: be(come) ~ **kôm-u**
cup: coffee ~ **kâppu**
cupboard **todana**
custard pudding **pûriñ**
cut, cut off **kîr-u**
cute: is ~ **kawáì-i**

damaged: become ~ **kowárè-ru**
damn! **simâtta**
dangerous: is ~ **abuna-i**
dark: is ~ (of colors) **kô-i**
daughter **musúmè; musumesañ, ozyôosañ**
   /polite/
day **hî/hi**
   ~ after tomorrow **asâtte; myoógòniti**
   ~ before yesterday **otótòi**
   the other ~ **konaida; señzitu**
   the very ~, the ~ in question **toozitu**
daytime **hirû**

decide **kime-ru**; be(come) decided **kimar-u**
  decide on X   **X ni suru/kime-ru**
  decide to X   **X kotô ni suru/kime-ru**
  be(come) decided that [someone] will X   **X kotô ni nâr-u/kimar-u**
delicious: is ~   **oisi-i; umâ-i**
  It was ~.   **Gotísoosama (dèsita).**
deliver **todókè-ru**; be delivered **todôk-u**
delivery (of prepared food) **demae**
deluxe (of food orders) **zyôo**
dentist **hâisya**
depart **tât-u; dê-ru**
departing **-hatu**
department store **depâato**
depend **yor-u**
depending on X   **X ni yotte**
depth (of color) **kôsa**
descend **orî-ru**
desk **tukue**
detailed: is ~   **kuwásì-i; komákà-i**
details **kuwásìi koto**
dictionary **zîsyo**
  English–Japanese ~   **eéwa-zìteñ**
different: be ~   **tiḡa-u**
difficult: is ~   **muzukasi-i**
difficulty **muzúkasìsa**
  is marked by ~   **-nikù-i**
dine **syokuzi-suru**
dining **syokuzi**
dining room **syokudoo**
dinner **bañgòhañ**
dinner party (Japanese-style) **eñkai**
diplomacy **gaikoo**
diplomat **gaíkòokañ**
direction **hôo**
disagreeable **iyâ /na/**
disappointed: become ~   **gaḱkàri-suru**
disconcerted: become ~   **awate-ru**
discouraged: become ~   **gaḱkàri-suru**
dislike **kirai /na/**
disorganized: become ~   **awate-ru**
displeasing **kirai /na/**
division (of a company) **bû/bu**
division manager **bûtyoo/butyoo**
divorced: get ~   **rikoñ-suru**
do **suru /irreg/; nas-âru↑; itas-u↓; yar-u**
  can ~   **dekî-ru**
doctor **señsèe**
doctor (medical) **isya; señsèe**
doesn't have to do **sinâkute mo îi**
dog **inû**

Don't bother. **Okámai nàku.**
Don't mention it. **Dôo itasimasite.**
door **dôa**; to
  sliding, opaque ~   **husúmà**
  sliding, translucent ~   **syoozi**
  screen ~   **amîdo**
  storm ~   **amâdo**
double room **dâbúru(-rùumu)**
down **sita**
draw **kâk-u**
drawer **hikidasi**
dreadful: is ~   **suḡô-i; monósuḡò-i**
dress **dôresu**
drink **nôm-u; mesiaḡar-u↑; itadak-u↓**
drink, beverage **nomîmono**
drive (a vehicle) **uñteñ-suru**
driver **uñteñsyu**
drugstore **kusuriya**
dry: become ~   **kawâk-u**
dust **gomî**

each: of ~; for ~   **-zutu**
ear **mimî**
early, in good time **hayámè ni**
early: is ~   **hayâ-i**
earthquake **zisiñ**
ease: is marked by ~   **-yasù-i**
east **hiḡásì**
east entrance **hiḡasiguti**
easy: is ~   **yasasi-i**
eat **tabê-ru; mesiaḡar-u↑; itadak-u↓**
economics **kêezai**
effort: with special ~   **seḱkakù**
egg **tamâḡo; êggu**
eight **hatî**
  ~ days; eighth of the month **yoo-ka**
  ~ units **yaṫtù**
either one **dotíra dè mo**
electric train **deñsya/dêñsya**
electricity; electric lights **dêñki**
embarrassed: is ~   **hazúkasì-i**
embassy **taísìkañ**
emergency **hizyoo /na/**
eminent **rippa /na/**
empty: become ~   **suk-u**
end: bring to an ~   **sumásè-ru**; come to an ~   **sûm-u**
end of the street, corridor, etc. **tukiatari**
energetic **geñki /na/**
engineer **gîsi**
England **Eekoku; Iḡirisu**

English–Japanese **eewa**
~ dictionary **eéwa-zìteñ**
English (person) **iḡírisùziñ; eékokùziñ**
English language **eeḡo**
enjoyment **omósìrosa**
enter **hâir-u**
entirely **mattaku**
entrance **iriḡuti**
entry hall **geñkañ**
erase **kes-u**; be(come) erased **kie-ru**
erect [something] **tatê-ru**
Europe **Yoóròppa**
even so **dê mo**
evening **bañ; yôru**
every day **mâiniti**
every month **maituki; maiḡetu**
every morning **mâiasa**
every night **mâibañ; maiyo**
every time **maido**
every week **maisyuu**
every year **maitosi; maineñ**
everyone **mińnà; minâsañ** /polite/
everything **mińnà; zeñbu**
exactly **tyoodo; haḱkìri; tyañto**
    exact time **haḱkìri-sita zikañ**
excess: go to ~ **suḡîru**
exchange **torikae-ru**
exchange money **ryôoḡae-suru**
excuse **moosiwake**
exhaust a supply **kirâs-u**
exhausted, tired out **kut(t)akuta**
exit **deḡuti**
expectation: general ~ **hazu**
expensive: is ~ **takâ-i**
experience (verb) **keekeñ-suru**
experience **keekeñ**
explain **setumee-suru**
exposure to the sun **hiatari**
express **kyuukoo**
    special ~ **tokúbetu-kyùukoo; tokkyuu**
    ~ ticket **kyuúkòokeñ**
expression **kao**
extend **todôk-u**
extension **naiseñ**
extent **hodo**
    to that ~; that much **sore hodo; soñna ni**
extinguish **kes-u**; be(come) extinguished **kie-ru**
extraordinary **hizyoo** /na/
extreme **hizyoo** /na/
extremely **hizyoo ni**

eye **mê**
eye doctor **mêisya**
eyeglasses **mêḡane**
    put on ~ **mêḡane o kakê-ru**

face (verb) **muk-u**
face **kao**
facilities; convenience **beñ**
facing toward **-muki**
fact **kotô**
fairly **kânari**
fall (of rain, snow, etc.) **hûr-u**
fall (season) **âki**
fall apart **kowárè-ru**
fall sound asleep **ĝuuguu netyau**
family **kâzoku; gokâzoku** /polite/
famous **yuumee** /na/
far: as ~ as **made** /ptc/
    is ~ **too-i**
    the ~ away **toókù**
    sound ~ away on the telephone **deñwa ḡa tooi**
farmer **nôoka**
father **titî; titioya; otôosañ** /polite/
fatigued: become ~ **kutábirè-ru**
feel unwell **kimóti ḡa warù-i**
feel well **kimóti ḡa ì-i**
feeling **kimoti**
female **ońnà**
few: are ~ **sukúnà-i**
Finance Ministry **oókuràsyoo**
find **mituke-ru**; be(come) found **mitukar-u**
find out **sir-u; gozôñzi da ↑ ; zoñzì-ru ↓**
fine **kêkkoo** /na/
    is ~ **îi/yô-i; yorosi-i**
finger **yubî**
finish [something] **sumásè-ru**; [something] finishes **sûm-u**
fire (conflagration) **kâzi**
first day of the month **tuítatì**
first generation **îs-see**
first time **hazîmete**
fish **sakana**
five **gô**
    ~ units **itû-tu**
    ~ days; fifth of the month **itu-ka**
fix **naôs-u**; be(come) fixed **naôr-u**
flex-time **zisá-syùkkiñ**
flood **oómìzu**
floor mat (Japanese-style) **tatami**
flower **hanâ**

flower shop; florist **hanâya**
food **tabémòno; gôhañ**
   Japanese-style ~ **nihoñsyoku; wasyoku**
foot **asî**
for the most part **daitai**
foreign country **gaikoku**
foreign language **gaikokuḡo**
Foreign Ministry **gaímùsyoo**
foreign trade **booeki**
foreign trader **boóekìsyoo**
foreigner **gaiziñ, gaíkokùziñ**
forget **wasure-ru**
fork **h(u)ôoku**
formal **h(u)ôomaru /na/**
four **sî; yôñ**
   ~ units **yot́-tù**
   ~ days; fourth of the month **yok-ka**
fragile: is ~ **kowáre-yasù-i**
fragile article **kowaremono**
France **Hurañsu**
free (unrestricted) **ziyûu /na/**
free time **hima /na/**
freelance work(er) **ziyûuḡyoo**
French (person) **huráñsùziñ**
French language **hurañsuḡo**
frequent: are ~ **oô-i**
fresh: is ~ **atárasì-i**
Friday **kiń̄yòo(bi)**
friend **tomodati**
from **kara /ptc/**
front **mâe; omótè**
fruit **kudâmono**
full **ippai**
funny: is ~ **okásì-i; okâsi na /+ nom/**; **omósirò-i**; (= strange) **okásì-i; okâsi /na/; hêñ /na/**
furniture **kâḡu**
furniture store **kaḡûya**

garden **niwa**
gardener **uekiya**
German (person) **doítùziñ**
German language **doituḡo**
Germany **Dôitu**
get **mora-u; itadak-u** ↓
get off (a vehicle) **orî-ru**
get on **nor-u**
get through, make oneself understood **tuuzi-ru**
get up **okî-ru**; get [someone] up **okôs-u**
girl **oń̄nà no ko**
give: ~ (to the in-group) **kure-ru, kudás-àru** ↑

   ~ (to the out-group) **aḡe-ru; sasiaḡe-ru** ↓ ; **yar-u**
give a ride **nose-ru**
give up, forego; resign oneself to **akíramè-ru**
give up, quit **yame-ru**
glass (for drinking) **kôppu**
go **ik-u; irássy-àru** ↑ ; **mâir-u** ↓
   ~ on foot **arûite iku**
go across **watar-u**
go in **hâir-u**
go out; leave **dê-ru**
go out (of the office or home) **gaisyutu-suru**
   be out **gaisyutu-tyuu da**
go out; set out **dekake-ru**
go over **watar-u**
go up **aḡar-u**
Golden Week **goórudeñ-uìiku**
golf **gôruhu**
good **kêkkoo /na/**
   is ~ **îi/yô-i; yorosi-i**
Good afternoon. **Koñniti wa.**
Good evening. **Koñbañ wa.**
Good morning. **Ohâyoo (gozaimàsu).**
Goodnight. **Oyasumi-nasai.**
Goodbye. **Sayo(o)nara.**
Goodbye. (said by person leaving home) **Ít́te kimàsu; Ít́te mairimàsu.** ↓
Goodbye. (said to person leaving home) **Ít́te (i)rassyài(màse).**
government employee **koómùiñ**
gradually **sôrosoro**
grandfather **sôhu; ozîisañ** /polite/
grandmother **sôbo; obâasañ** /polite/
grateful: is ~ **arígatà-i**
gray **gurêe; haiiro**
great **kêkkoo /na/; rippa /na/**
green **gurîiñ; mîdori**
green car **guríìñsya**
greet **mukae-ru; demukae-ru**
grow [something] **tukûr-u**
guest **kyaku; okyakusañ** /polite/

half **-hañ**
half part, half portion **hańbùñ**
hall **rooka**
ham **hâmu**
ham sandwich **hamú-sàñdo**
hand **tê**
   lend a ~ **tetúdà-u**
hand over **watas-u**
   ~ for temporary keeping **azúkè-ru**

handbag **hańdobàggu**
Haneda (airport) **Haneda**
hang (something) **kakê-ru**
hang up (on the telephone) **kîr-u**
harbor **minato**
hard: is ~ (= difficult) **muzukasi-i**; (= stiff) **katâ-i**
hardship **kûroo**
hat **boosi**
have **âr-u; môtte (i)-ru**
he **kâre; anô hitò; anó kàtà** /polite/
head **atámà**
health(y) **keñkoo** /na/
hear **kik-u**
heart **siñzoo**
heat **âtusa**
Heavens, no! **Tońde mo nài.**
heavy: is ~ **omo-i**
hello (on the telephone) **môsimosi**
  Hello, I'm back. **Tadaima.**
help **tetúdà-u**
  Help!!! **Tasuketeeee.**
helpful assistance **sewâ**
  Thank you for your ~. **Oséwasama (dèsita).**
here **koko; kotira; kóttì**
hereabouts **kotira; kóttì**
hey! **hôra**
high school **kookoo**
hill **oka**
hmmm! **sâa**
hold back, stand on ceremony **eñryo-suru**
hold in reserve **nokôs-u**
holiday **yasúmì**
home **utî; iê; otaku** /polite/
home delivery (of prepared food) **demae**
hospital **byooiñ**
hospital director **îñtyoo**
hot: is ~ **atû-i**; (= spicy) **karâ-i**
hotel **hôteru**
house; household **utî; iê; otaku** /polite/
house-sit **kawári ni sùm-u**
housing development **dañti**
how? **dôo; ikâḡa** /polite/
  How do you do? **Hazímemàsite.**
how many ——? **nañ-/iku-** + classifier
how many units? **îku-tu**
how much? **îkura**
how old? (of people) **îku-tu; nâñ-sai**
hundred **hyakû**
hungry: become ~ **onaka ḡa suk-u**
hurts; is painful **itâ-i**

husband **syûziñ, otto; gosyûziñ** /polite/

I; me **wata(ku)si; bôku**
ice **koori**
ice cream **aísukurìimu**
idea **âidea**
immediately **sûḡu**
implements **doóḡù**
important **taisetu** /na/; **daízì** /na/
importer-exporter **boóekìsyoo**
included: X ~ **X-tuki**
inconvenient: is ~ **hûbeñ** /na/; **tuḡóo ḡa warù-i**
India **Îñdo**
Indian (person from India) **iñdòziñ**
infrequent: is ~ **sukúnà-i**
inn (Japanese-style) **ryokañ**
inquire **kik-u; ukaḡa-u** ↓
insert **ire-ru**
inside **nâka**
instead of ——ing ——**(à)nài de;** ——**(a)zu ni**
institute director **syotyoo**
instructor **kyôosi**
intention **tumori**
interest **omósìrosa**
interesting: is ~ **omósirò-i**
interruption **zyama**
intersection **koósàteñ**
interval **aida**
introduce **syookai-suru**
investigate **sirábè-ru**
island **simâ**
it won't do; it's too bad **ikena-i**
Italian (person) **itáriàziñ**
Italian language **itariaḡo**
Italy **Itaria**

jacket **uwaḡi**; (windbreaker) **zyâñpaa**
Japan **Nihôñ/Níppòñ**
Japan Railway **z(i)eé-àaru**
Japanese–English **waee**
Japanese (person) **nihóñziñ/nippoñziñ**
Japanese language **nihoñgo/nippoñgo**
jeans **ziipañ**
journalist **siñbuñkìsya**
joy: a ~ **tanósìmì**
just; exactly **tyoodo**
just (no more than) **dakê**
  ~ having thought about it **kañḡàeta dakê de**
  it's ~ big **oókìi dakê da**

That's all (= It's ~ that.) **Soré dakè desu.**
just now **tadâima**

Keio [University] **Keeoo**
key **kaḡî**
kimono **kimono**
  cotton ~ **yukata**
kimono sash **ôbi**
  put on a ~ **ôbi o simê-ru/suru**
kiosk **baiteñ**
kitchen **daidokoro**
kitchen utensils **daídokoro-dòoḡu**
knife **nâihu**
know **sitte (i)-ru; gozôñzi da↑; zôñzite (i)-ru↓**
  come to ~ **sir-u**
Kyoto **Kyôoto**
Kyoto University **Kyoodai**

labor **roodoo-suru**
laboratory **keńkyùusitu**
laborer **roódòosya**
lake **mizúùmi**
lamp **sutañdo**
landlord **yânusi**
language **geñḡo**
  spoken ~ **kotóbà**
large: is ~ **oókì-i; ôoki na** /+ nom/; (of area) **hirô-i**
last month **señḡetu**
last night **yuúbè**
last week **señsyuu**
last year **kyôneñ**
late: is ~ **oso-i**
  get to be ~ **osóku nàru**
  ~ (= behind) **okure-ru**
  until ~ **osókù made**
later **âto de; notihodo** /formal/
latest: at the ~ **osôkute mo**
lawyer **beńḡòsi**
lay [something] on its side **nekas-u**
lean **yor-u**
learned society **gakkai**
leave **dê-ru; tât-u**
leave behind **oite ik-u; nokôs-u**; be(come) left behind **nokôr-u**
leave one's seat **sêki o hazus-u**
lecture **kôoḡi; kooeñ**
left (direction) **hidari**
  ~ side **hidári no hòo**
left (remaining) **âto**

one hour ~ **âto ití-zìkañ**
leg **asî**
leisurely **yukkùri**
lend **kas-u**
let [someone] off (a vehicle) **orôs-u**
letter **teḡami**
library (a building) **tosyôkañ**
library (a room) **tosyôsitu**
light: is ~ (of weight) **karu-i**
like, love **sukî** /na/
like X, X-like **X-mìtai** /na/
limousine available for hire **hâiyaa**
limousine bus **rimúziñ-bàsu**
line is busy **hanasi-tyuu da**
line up, form a line **narab-u**; place in line **narabe-ru**
liquor store **sakaya**
listen **kik-u**
literature **buñḡaku**
little: is ~ **tiísà-i; tîisa na** /+ nom/
  a ~ **sukôsi; tyôtto**
live (reside) **sûm-u**
lively **niḡiyaka** /na/
living room (Japanese-style) **tyanoma**; (Western-style) **imâ**
locate [something] **mituke-ru; saḡas-u**
located: be ~ (of inanimate existence) **âr-u; goz-âru+**
  (of animate existence) **i-ru; irássy-àru↑; ôr-u↓**
lock [something] **kaḡî o kakê-ru**; [something] locks **kaḡî ḡa kakâr-u**
long: is ~ **naḡâ-i**
look! **hôra**
look, seem **miê-ru; yôo** /na/; **-mitài** /na/
look at **mî-ru**
look for **saḡas-u**
look into **sirábè-ru**
looking as if **-soo** /na/
loud voice **ôoki na kôe**
low voice **tîisa na kôe**
lower (verb) **orôs-u**
lower back **kosî**
luggage **nîmotu**
lunch **hirúḡòhañ; ohîru**
  box ~ **beñtòo**

machine **kikâi**
magazine **zassi**
magnificent **rippa** /na/
mail a letter **teḡámi o dàs-u**

make　**tukûr-u**
make a turn　**maḡar-u**
make an appointment　**yakusoku-suru**
make haste　**isôḡ-u**
make tea　**otya o ire-ru**
male　**dañsee; otókò**
male language　**dañseeḡo**
man　**otóko no hitò; otóko no katà** /polite/;
　　ozisañ; dañsee
many　**takúsàñ**
　are ~　**oô-i**
　~ people　**oózèe**
map　**tîzu**
marry　**kekkoñ-suru**
match up with　**â-u**
matter (verb)　**kamâ-u**
　it doesn't ~　**kamáwàna-i**
matters to attend to　**yoozi**
may do (= permission)　**sitê mo îi**
maybe X　**X ka mo sirena-i**
meal　**syokuzi**
　fixed ~　**teesyoku; kôosu; seẗto-mèñyuu**
　the "A" ~　**eé-kòosu; eé-sètto**
　meals are served　**syokúzi ḡa dè-ru**
meaning　**îmi**
meat　**nikû**
medicine　**kusuri**
meet　**â-u; omé ni kakàr-u** ↓
meet; greet　**mukae-ru; demukae-ru**
Meiji Era (1868–1912)　**Mêezi**
message　**mêsseezi**
midnight　**rêe-zi**
midst of talk　**hanasi-tyuu**
milk　**mîruku**
mind　**ki**
Ministry of Education　**moñbùsyoo**
missionary　**seńkyòosi**
mistake: make a ~　**matíḡaè-ru**
Monday　**getúyòo(bi)**
money　**okane**
money-changing machine　**ryoóḡàeki**
monorail　**monórèeru**
month　**tukî**
　last ~　**sêñḡetu**
　~ before last　**señsèñḡetu**
　this ~　**koñḡetu**
　next ~　**râiḡetu**
　~ after next　**saraiḡetu**
mood　**kimoti**
moon　**tukî**
more　**môtto**

/+ quantity expression/　**moo**
　a little ~　**moó sukòsi**
　~ than that　**mûsiro**
morning　**âsa**
　this ~　**kêsa**
　tomorrow ~　**asíta no àsa; myootyoo**
most　**itibañ**
mother　**hâha, hahaoya; okâasañ** /polite/
mountain　**yamâ**
mouth　**kuti**
movie　**eeḡa**
movie theater　**eéḡàkañ**
Mr.; Mrs.; Miss; Ms.　**-sañ** /polite suffix/
much　**takúsàñ**
must do　**sinâkute wa 'ikena-i**
must not do　**sitê wa 'ikena-i**

Nagoya　**Nâḡoya**
name　**namae**
　be named　**i-u; ośsy-àru** ↑ **; môos-u** ↓
narrow: is ~　**semâ-i**
national railway (until 1987)　**kokutetu**
native land　**kuni**
near: is ~　**tikâ-i**
nearby　**sôba**
neatly　**tyańto**
necessary　**hituyoo /na/**
necessity　**hituyoo /na/**
neck　**kubi**
necktie　**nêkutai**
　put on a ~　**nêkutai o simê-ru/suru**
need　**ir-u**
neighborhood　**kîñzyo**
net　**amî**
never mind　**îi/yô-i; yorosi-i; kêkkoo da**
new: is ~　**atárasì-i**
news　**nyûusu**
newspaper　**siñbuñ**
next　**tuḡî**
next door　**tonari**
　~ on the left　**hidáridònari**
　~ on the right　**miḡídònari**
next month　**râiḡetu**
next week　**raisyuu**
next year　**raineñ**
night　**bañ; yôru**
　last ~　**yuúbè**
　tonight　**kôñbañ**
　tomorrow ~　**asita no bañ; myoobañ**
nine　**kû; kyûu**
　~ units　**kokôno-tu**

~ days; ninth of the month **kokóno-kà**
no   **i(i)e; iya; iêie; n̂n̂**
no good   **damê /na/**
no more   **môo** /+ negative/
nobody   **dâre mo** /+ negative/
noodle shop   **sobâya**
noodles: buckwheat ~   **sôba**
noon   **hirû/ohîru; syoôgo**
north   **kitâ**
Northwest (airline)   **noósuèsuto**
nose   **hana**
not at all   **zeñzeñ** /+ negative/
not especially   **betu ni** /+ negative/
not much; not very   **a(ñ)mari** /+ negative/
not yet   **mâda** /+ negative/
notebook   **nôoto**
notice   **ki ḡá tùk-u**
notify   **todókè-ru**
now   **îma**
nowadays   **kono-ḡoro**
nuisance   **zyama**
number(s)   **suuzi**
  assigned ~   **bañ́ḡòo**
nurse   **kañ́ḡòhu**
nurse, care for   **kâñḡo-suru**

obliged: be(come) ~ for assistance   **sewâ ni nâr-u**
  is ~   **aríḡatà-i**
occasion   **tokî**
ocean   **ûmi**
of course; to be sure   **naruhodo; motîroñ**
office   **zimûsyo**
office building   **bîru**
oh!   **â(a)**
old: is ~ (not new)   **hurû-i**
old man   **ozîisañ** /polite/
old person   **tosíyòri**
old woman   **obâasañ** /polite/
older brother   **âni; (o)nîisañ** /polite/
older sister   **ane; (o)nêesañ** /polite/
on time: be ~   **ma ní à-u**
one   **itî**
  ~ day   **ití-nitì**
  ~ person   **hitô-ri**
  ~ unit   **hitô-tu**
one hundred   **hyakû**
oneself   **zibuñ**
  do by ~   **zibuñ de suru**
only X; no more than X   **hoñ no X**

open [something]   **ake-ru**; [something] opens   **ak-u**
oppose   **hañtai-suru**
opposite   **hañtai**
opposite side   **mukooḡawa**
or on the other hand   **matâ wa**
order: an ~ for something   **tyuumoñ**
  place an ~   **tyuumoñ-suru**
ordinary   **hutuu**
other   **hoka**
  Anything else?   **Hoka ni nâni ka?**
  ~ than X   **X no hoka**
  ~ X   **hoka no X**
our household's; our   **uti no** /+ nom/
out: be(come) ~ of   **kirâs-u**
out of order   **kosyoo**
over   **uê**
over there   **asoko; atira; atti; mukoo**
overcoat   **ôobaa**
overeat   **tabésuḡì-ru**
own: one's ~ X   **X zibuñ no X**

P.M.   **gôḡo**
painful: is ~   **itâ-i**
pale: is ~   **aô-i**; (of colors)   **usu-i**
paper   **kamî**
parent   **oya; oyaḡosañ** /polite/
  both parents   **ryôosiñ; goryôosiñ** /polite/
park   **kooeñ**
part-time work(er)   **arúbàito**
party   **pâat(e)ii**
  student ~   **kôñpa**
pass [something to someone]   **tôr-u**
past   **-suḡi**
  ten (minutes) ~   **zíp-pùñ-suḡi**
pay   **harâ-u**
pay attention   **ki ó tukè-ru**
pen   **pêñ**
pencil   **eñpitu**
pep; peppy   **gêñki /na/**
pepper   **kosyôo**
perk up   **gêñki ḡa dê-ru**
person   **hitô; katâ** /polite/
person in charge   **kâkari (no hito)**
person of Japanese ancestry   **nikkèeziñ**
photograph   **syasiñ**
phrase   **kotóbà**
picnic   **pîkkunikku**
picture (photograph)   **syasiñ**
  take a ~   **syasíñ o tòr-u**
pie   **pâi**

pine **matu**
pity: a ~ **zańneń** /na/
place (verb) **ok-u**
place **tokórò**
place on [something] **nose-ru**
plan **tumori**
plant (verb) **ue-ru**
plant **ueki**
plate **sara**
play (= a show) **sibai**
pleasant: is ~ **kimóti ḡa ìi**
Please (speaker offering something) **Dôozo.**
  (speaker requesting something) **Onéḡai-simàsu.**
pleasing **sukî** /na/
pleasure: a ~ **tanósìmì**
  take ~ in **yorókòb-u**
  do with ~ **yorókònde suru**
plum **ume**
police box **koobań**
policeman **omâwarisań** /polite/
politician **seezika**
politics **seezi**
pond **ikê**
ponder **kańḡaè-ru**
positive **tâsika** /na/
post office **yuúbìńkyoku**
practice **reńsyuu-suru**
precise(ly) **hakkìri; tyańto; mattaku**
president of a company **syatyoo**
pretty **kîree** /na/
price **nedań**
  commodity prices **bukka**
probably **tâbuń**
problem **mońdai**
professor **kyoozyu**
program **bańḡumi; puróḡùramu**
promise **yakusoku**
  make a ~ **yakusoku-suru**
properly **tyańto**
public telephone **koósyuudèńwa**
publish books **hoń o dâs-u**; books are published **hoń ḡa dê-ru**
pull **hik-u**
purpose **mokuteki**
purposely **wâzawaza**
put **ok-u**
put aside **oite ok-u**
put away **sima-u**
put in order **katázukè-ru**; be(come) put in order **katázùk-u**

put into **ire-ru**
put on: ~ the body **ki-ru**
  ~ the head **kabûr-u**
  ~ the feet or legs **hak-u**
put out **dâs-u**

quilt (for sleeping) **hutoń**
  bottom ~ **sikíbùtoń**
  top ~ **kakébùtoń**
quit **yame-ru**
quite **nakanaka; kânari**

radio **râzio**
rain **âme**
rain check: take a ~, hold back for now **eńryo-site ok-u**
rainy season **tuyu**
raise **aḡe-ru**
rapid: in ~ succession **dôńdoń**
rare: is ~ **sukúnà-i**
rather **nakanaka; kânari; mûsiro**
reach **todôk-u**
real estate broker **hudoosańya**
reality: in ~ **zitû wa**
rear **usiro; urâ**
reason **tamê**
receive **mora-u; itadak-u↓; tyoodai-suru↓**
reception **hirôoeń**
receptionist **uketuke**
recover **naôr-u**
red: is ~ **aka-i**
redo **yarínaòs-u**
regrettable **zańneń** /na/
regular **hutuu**
  ~ train **hutuu(ressya)**
  ~ (order of food) **nami**
reliable **tâsika** /na/
rely **yor-u**
remain behind **nokôr-u**
rent **yâtiń**
rent (from someone) **kari-ru**; (to someone) **kas-u**
repair **naôs-u**; be(come) repaired **naôr-u**
rephrase **iíkaè-ru**
replacement **kawari**
report **todókè-ru**
request **tanôm-u**
required: be ~ (of time and money) **kakâr-u**
  (need) **ir-u**
rescue **tasúkè-ru**; be(come) rescued **tasúkàr-u**

research　keñkyuu
　～ institute　keñkyuuzyo
　do ～　keñkyuu-suru
reservation　yoyaku
reserve, holding back　eñryo
reside　sûm-u
resign oneself to　akírame-ru
restaurant (Western-style)　rêsutorañ;
　(Japanese-style)　ryoórìya
result　kekka
return: a ～　kaérì
return, go back　modôr-u
　～ (home)　kâer-u
reverse side　urâ
reward　rêe/oree
rewrite　kakíkae-ru
rice: cooked ～　gôhañ
　uncooked ～　komê
rice shop　komêya
ride　nor-u
right　miği
　～ side　miği no hòo
rise　ağar-u
river　kawâ
road　miti
roast [something]　yak-u; get roasted　yake-ru
room　heyâ
　Japanese-style ～　nihoñma, wasitu
　Western-style ～　yooma
round-table discussion　zadañkai
rude　sitûree /na/; rêe o 'sirana-i
rush hour　raśsyu-àwaa
Russian (person)　rośiàziñ; soréñziñ
Russian language　rosiağo

safe　daízyòobu /na/
safe side: to be on the ～　nêñ no tame
sake　tamê
saké (rice wine)　sake
salaried employee　saráriimañ
salesperson　teñiñ
salt　siô
salty: is ～　karâ-i
same　onazi
sandals (for outdoors)　zoori; geta
sandwich　sâńdo(ìtti)
Saturday　doyôo(bi)
save, hold back　nokôs-u
save, rescue　tasúke-ru; be(come) saved, rescued　tasúkar-u
say　i-u; ośsy-àru ↑; môos-u ↓

scenery　kêsiki
school　gakkoo
schooltime; classtime　zyûğyoo
sea　ûmi
season: the ～ (for something)　sîizuñ
seat (assigned place)　sêki
　reserved ～　sitêeseki
　leave one's ～　sêki o hazus-u
Seattle　Siâtoru
second generation　nî-see
secretary　hîsyô
section (within a company)　kâ
section manager　katyoo
see (a person); meet (with a person)　â-u; omé ni kakàr-u ↓
see: can ～　miê-ru
see (look at)　mî-ru
see off　okur-u; miokur-u
seem　miê-ru
seems to be X　X-rasì-i
sell　ur-u
seminar　zêmi
send, send off　okur-u
separate　betubetu
serve (a meal)　dâs-u
　meals are served　syokúzi ğa dè-ru
service　sâabisu
set aside　tôtt(e) ok-u
set out　dekake-ru
seven　nâna; sitî
　～ units　nanâ-tu
　～ days; seventh of the month　nano-ka
severe: is ～　hidô-i
she　kânozyo; anô hitò; anó kàtà /polite/
shelf　tana
ship　hûne
shirt　syâtu
　dress ～　waisyatu
shoes　kutû
shop　misê
shopping　kaimono
shopping bag　syoṕpiñğubàggu
short: is ～　mizíkà-i
shoulder　kâta
show　misê-ru
show (= a play)　sibai
Showa Era (1926–)　Syoowa
shy: is ～　hazúkasì-i
sick; sickness　byooki; gobyooki /polite/
side　hôo; yoko
single (unmarried)　hitô-ri

single room sîńguru(-rùumu)
sister: older ~ ane; (o)nêesañ /polite/
    younger ~ imôoto; imootosañ /polite/
sit down suwar-u; (kosí)kakè-ru
sitting room tyanoma
six rokû
    ~ units muť-tù
    ~ days; sixth of the month mui-ka
size (bulk) ookisa; (of an area) hîrosa
skillful; skilled zyoózù /na/; ozyoozu /polite/
    is ~ umâ-i
skirt sukâato
slacks surâkkusu; pâñtu; pâñtaroñ
sleep: put to ~ nekas-u; go to ~ ne-ru
sleepy: is ~ nemu-i
slippers surîppa
slowly yuḱkùri; sôrosoro
small: is ~ tiísà-i; tîisa na /+ nom/
    is ~ (occurs in small units) komákà-i
    is ~ (of area) semâ-i
smell, odor niôi
    have a ~ niôi ḡa suru
smoke (verb) su-u; (tabáko o) nòm-u/
    mesiaḡaru ↑
soap opera hoómudòrama
sociology syakâiḡaku
socks kutûsita
    bifurcated ~ tâbi
soft: is ~ yawárakà-i
somebody dâre ka
someday îtu ka; izure /formal/
somehow or other dôo mo
someplace dôko ka
something nâni ka
sometime îtu ka; izure /formal/
sometimes tokídokì
somewhere dôko ka
son musuko; musukosañ, bôttyañ /polite/
soon sûḡu
sorry: I'm ~ su(m)ímasèñ; moósiwake ari-
    masèñ
so-so mâa·mâa
sound, make a noise nar-u
sound far away (on the telephone) deñwa ḡa
    too-i
sour: is ~ suṕpà-i
south minami
South Korea Kâñkoku
South Korean (person) kańkokùziñ
souvenir miyaḡe
souvenir shop miyaḡeya

Soviet Union Sôreñ; Sobíèto
soy sauce syooyu
spacious: is ~ hirô-i
Spain Supêiñ
speak hanâs-u; syabêr-u
special tokubetu
special lunch rańti-sàabisu
specially, purposely wâzawaza
speech kooeñ
speed hâyasa
spicy: is ~ karâ-i
spirit ki
splendid rippa /na/
spoon supûuñ
sports program supóotu-bàñḡumi
sportscar supóotùkàa
spread out sik-u
spring (season) hâru
staff member syâiñ
staggered work hours zisá-syùkkiñ
stand (= concession) baiteñ
stand up tât-u; stand [something] up tatê-ru
start: with a ~ hatto
station êki
stationery (writing paper) biñseñ
    writing supplies buńbòoḡu
stationery store; stationery dealer buñbooḡuya
stay on nokôr-u
stay one night ippaku-suru
stiff: become ~ kôr-u
    is ~ katâ-i
still mâda
stockings kutûsita
stomach onaka; i
stop; bring to a halt tome-ru; come to a halt;
    stop over tomar-u
stop (of rain, snow, etc.) yam-u
stop in yor-u
store (verb) simâ-u
store misê
storm door amâdo
straight maśsùgu
strain mûri o suru
strange: is ~ okásì-i; okâsi na /+ nom/; hêñ
    /na/
street miti
street corner kâdo
strength tûyosa; (of coffee, tea, etc.) kôsa
strong: is ~ tuyô-i; (of coffee, tea, etc.) kô-i;
    (sturdy) zyoobu /na/
student gakusee
studio apartment wańrùumu

study (verb) **beñkyoo-suru**
study (a room) **syosai**
sturdy **zyoobu /na/**
substitute **kawari**
subway **tikatetu**
sugar **satôo**
suit **sûutu**
  (man's) ~ **sebiro**
suit, become [someone] **niâ-u**
suit, match up with **â-u**
  ~ one's taste **kutí ni à-u**
suitable **tekitoo /na/**
  ~ for **-muki**
suitcase **suútukèesu**
summer **natû**
summon **yob-u**
sun **hî/hi**
sunburned: get ~ **hi ni yake-ru**
Sunday **nitíyòo(bi)**
super-deluxe (order of food) **tokuzyoo**
supermarket **sûupaa**
surely **kitto**
surprise: become surprised **bikkùri-suru**
surprising: is ~ **mezúrasì-i**
sushi **susî**
sushi shop **susîya**
suspend (something) **kakê-ru**
sweater **sêetaa**
sweet: is ~ **ama-i**
sweets **okâsi**
symposium **zadâñkai**

table **teeburu**
Taisho Era (1912–26) **Taisyoo**
take (a train, taxi, etc.) **nor-u**
take (of medicine) **nôm-u**
take (require) **kakâr-u**
take, take up, take away **tôr-u**
take a bath **hurô ni hâir-u**
take off (of clothing) **nûḡ-u**
take on board **nose-ru**
take out **dâs-u**
take to a place (of things) **motte ik-u**; (of people) **turete ik-u**
talk (verb) **hanâs-u; syabêr-u**
talk **hanásì**
talk show **iñtabyuu-bàñgumi**
tape **têepu**
taste **azi**
  have a ~ **azi ḡa suru**
taxi **tâkusii**

tea **otya**
  black ~ **kootya**
teach **osie-ru**
teacher **señsèe**
teacup (Japanese-style) **yunómì**
telephone (verb) **deñwa-suru; deñwa o kakè-ru**
telephone: ~ call **deñwa**
  ~ answering machine **rusúbañ-dèñwa**
  ~ book **deñwatyoo**
  ~ number **deñwabàñḡoo**
television **têrebi**
  appear on ~ **têrebi ni dê-ru**
tempura **teñpura**
tempura shop **teñpuraya**
ten **zyûu**
  ~ units **tôo**
  ~ days; tenth of the month **too-ka**
tender: is ~ **yawárakà-i**
tennis **têenisu**
terrible: is ~ **suḡô-i; taíhèñ /na/**
terrific: is ~ **suḡô-i**
textbook **kyoókàsyo**
Thank you **Ariḡatoo (gozaimasu)⁺; Su(m)ímasèñ**
  Thanks for your trouble. **Gokûroosama desita.**
  thanks to you; thanks for asking **okaḡesama de**
that —— near you; that —— just mentioned **sono** /+ nom/
that —— over there; that —— (known to both of us) **ano** /+ nom/
that being the case **(soré) dè wa; (soré) zyà(a)**
that is to say **to iu kotò wa**
that kind of —— **soñna, añna** /+ nom/
that place **soko; asoko, asuko**
that side **sotira, sottì; atira, attì**
that thing (near you or just mentioned) **sore**
that thing over there (or known to both of us) **are**
that way; like that **sôo**
theater **gekizyoo**
  movie ~ **eéḡakàñ**
there **soko; asoko, asuko; sotira, sottì; atira, attì**
thereabouts **sotira, sottì; atira, attì**
thick: is ~ **atu-i, buatu-i**; (of liquids) **kô-i**
thin: is ~ (of liquids) **usu-i**
thing **monô; kotô**
things on hand **motiawase**

have no business cards on hand **meési no motiawase g̃a nài**
think **omô-u**
think over **kan̄g̃aè-ru**
third generation **sân̄-see**
thirsty: become ~ **nôdo g̃a kawâk-u**
this —— **kono** /+ nom/
this kind of —— **kon̄na** /+ nom/
this place **koko**
this side **kotira, kot́tì**
this side of **temae**
this thing **kore**
thousand **sên̄**
three **san̄**
~ units **mit́-tù**
~ days; third of the month **mik-ka**
throat **nôdo**
throughout **-tyuu, -zyuu**
~ the morning **gozen̄-tyuu**
~ Japan **Nihon̄-zyuu**
all day long **iti-niti-zyuu**
throw away **sute-ru**
thunder **kamínarì**
it thunders **kamínarì g̃a nar-u**
Thursday **mokúyòo(bi)**
ticket **kippu**
express ~ **kyuúkòokeǹ**
special express ~ **toḱkyùuken̄**
passenger ~ **zyoósyàken̄**
ticket checking **kaisatu**
~ gate **kaísatùg̃uti**
ticket counter **kíppu-ùriba**
tidy: make ~ **katázukè-ru**; be(come) ~ **katázùk-u**
time **zikan̄**
have ~ **zikán̄ g̃a àru**
take ~ **zikán̄ g̃a kakàr-u**
—— at a ~ **-zutu**
time: be on ~ **ma ní à-u**
time: free ~ **hima** /na/
time, occasion **tokî**
time difference **zîsa**
timetable **zikokuhyoo**
tired: become tired **tukárè-ru**
to be sure! **naruhodo**
today **kyôo**
together **issyo**
~ with a friend **tomodati to issyo**
do ~ **issyo ni suru**
toil **kurôo**
toilet **tôire; teârai**

tomorrow **asítà, asû; myôoniti**
tools **doóg̃ù**
tooth **hâ**
top **uê**
totally **mattaku**
touch: get in ~ **ren̄raku-suru**
tough: is ~ **katâ-i**
tour **tûaa**
tourist home **min̄syuku**
town **matî**
trader: foreign ~ **boóekìsyoo**
traffic light **sin̄g̃oo**
train: (electric) ~ **den̄sya/dên̄sya**
(steam) ~ **kisyâ**
a ~ **rêssya/ressya**
transfer (to another vehicle) **noríkaè-ru**
transport **hakob-u**
transportation **kootuu**
trash **gomî**
travel **ryokoo-suru**
tree **kî**
trip **ryokoo**
true; truth **hon̄too**
trunk **torân̄ku**
truth, reality **zitû**
try: ~ going **it́te mì-ru**
~ to go **ikú yòo ni suru**
Tuesday **kayôo(bi)**
tuna fish sandwich **tuná-sàn̄do**
turn: make a ~ **mag̃ar-u**
turn off **kes-u**; be(come) turned off **kie-ru**
turn on **tukê-ru**; be(come) turned on **tûk-u**
twenty days; twentieth of the month **hatu-ka**
twenty years of age **hâtati**
twin room **tuín̄(-rùumu)**
two **nî**
~ units **hutá-tù**
~ days; second of the month **hutu-ka**
type **tâipu**
typewriter **taípuràitaa**
typhoon **taíhùu**
typing **tâipu**

U-turn **yuútàan̄**
make a ~ **yuútàan̄-suru**
uh |anoo|; |eeto|
umbrella **kâsa; amág̃asa**
uncle **ozi; ozisan̄** /polite/
under **sita**
underground **tikâ**
underwear **sitag̃i**

undoubtedly **kitto**
unexpected: is ~ **mezúrasì-i**
unfasten **hazus-u**
unfortunate; unfortunately **ainiku**
university **daiḡaku**
unload **orôs-u**
unpleasant **iyâ** /na/
 is ~ **kimóti ḡa warù-i**
unreasonable **mûri** /na/
unreserved seat **ziyûuseki**
unrestricted **ziyûu** /na/
unskillful **hetâ** /na/
up **uê**
upset: become ~ **komâr-u**
use (verb) **tuka-u**
use: be of ~ **yakû ni tât-u**; put to ~ **yakû ni tatê-ru**
usual **hutuu**
usually **taitee**
utterance **kotóbà**
utterly **suḱkàri**

vacant: be ~ **aite (i)-ru**
vacation **yasúmì**
valley **tanî**
valuable **daízì** /na/
variety **tâipu**
various **iroiro** /no or na/; **iroñ** /na/
vegetable **yasai**
vegetable store **yaoya**
very **tot(t)emo; taiheñ; zûibuñ**
 that ~ X **rêe no X**
vicinity **heñ; sôba; tikâku**
village **murâ**
visible: be ~ **miê-ru**
visit **ukaḡa-u** ↓
visitor **kyaku; okyakusañ** /polite/
voice **kôe**

wait **mât-u**
wake up **okî-ru**; wake [someone] up **okôs-u**
walk **arûk-u**
warm: is ~ **at(á)takà-i**
wash **ara-u**
washroom **señmeñzyo**
watch; clock **tokee**
water: cold ~ **mizu**; hot ~ **(o)yu**
way (direction) **hôo**
way before; long ago **zuttó màe**
way of ——ing ——**kata**
 way of doing **sikata**

weak: is ~ **yowâ-i**; (of coffee, tea, etc.) **usu-i**
wear: on the body **ki-ru**
 ~ on the head **kabûr-u**
 ~ on the feet or legs **hak-u**
weather: good ~ **teñki**
weather forecast **teñki-yòhoo**
wedding ceremony **keḱkòñsiki**
wedding reception **hirôoeñ**
Wednesday **suíyòo(bi)**
week **syuu**
 this ~ **koñsyuu**
 last ~ **señsyuu**
 ~ before last **señsèñsyuu**
 next ~ **raisyuu**
 ~ after next **saraisyuu**
welcome (verb) **mukae-ru; demukae-ru**
Welcome! **Irássyài(màse); Yôku irás-syaimàsita.**
Welcome back! **Okáeri-nasài.**
welcoming: a ~ **mukae**
well, healthy **geñki** /na/
well then **dê wa; zyâ(a)**
west **nisi**
what? **nâñ, nâni**
what ——? **dôno** /+ nom/
what color? **naniiro; dôñna irô**
what kind of ——? **dôñna** /+ nom/
what language? **naniḡo**
what nationality? **naniziñ**
when? **îtu**
where? **dôko; dôtira, dôtti**
whether
 can't tell ~ there is any or not **âru ka dôo ka wakárànai**
 doesn't matter ~ there is any or not **âtte mo nâkute mo kamáwànai**
which ——? **dôno** /+ nom/
which side? **dôtira (no hoo); dôtti (no hoo)**
which thing? (usually of three or more) **dôre**
 (of two alternatives) **dôtira (no hoo), dôtti (no hoo)**
while: a ~ (of indeterminate length) **sibâraku**
white: is ~ **sirô-i**
who? **dâre; dônata, dôtira-sama** /polite/
whoever it is **daré dè mo**
whole: the ~ thing **zêñbu**
why? **dôo site; nâze**
wicket **kaísatùḡuti**
wide: is ~ **hirô-i**
wife **kânai, tûma; ôkusañ** /polite/
windbreaker **zyâñpaa**

window **mâdo**
  ticket ~ **madôguti**
wine **wâiñ**
  rice ~ **sake**
winter **huyû**
wipe **huk-u**
within: ~ a city **sînai**
  ~ Tokyo **tônai**
  ~ this year **kotosi-zyuu ni**
without ——ing ——(à)nài de; ——(a)zu ni
woman **ońna no hitò; ońna no katà, obasañ** /polite/
women's language **zyoseego**
wonderful **sugô-i**
work **sigoto**
worry **siñpai**
  cause worry **sińpai o kakè-ru**
worry about **siñpai-suru; ki ni suru**
wrapping cloth **hurosiki**
write **kâk-u**

wrong: be ~ **tiga-u; matiga-u**

yeah **ñ**
year **tosi**
  this ~ **kotosi**
  next ~ **raineñ**
  last ~ **kyôneñ**
  ~ before last **otôtosi**
  initial ~ of an era **gâñ-neñ**
yellow: is ~ **kiiro-i**
yes **hâi, êe; hâa** /polite/
yesterday **kinôo**
yet **môo** /+ affirmative/
  not ~ **mâda** /+ negative/
you **anâta; kimi** /familiar/
young: is ~ **wakâ-i**
younger brother **otóotò; otootosañ** /polite/
younger sister **imôoto; imootosañ** /polite/

zero **rêe, zêro, maru**
zero o'clock (midnight) **rêe-zi**

Classifiers

Counting

bound volumes	-satu
buildings and shops	-keñ
cents	-señto
dollars	-doru
glassfuls and cupfuls	-hai
hours	-zikañ
long, cylindrical objects	-hoñ
meals	-syoku
minutes	-huñkañ
months	-kağetu
nights of a stay	-haku
occurrences	-do; -kai
pairs of footwear	-soku
people	-ri/-niñ, -mee(sama)
pieces	-ko
portions	-niñmae
suits of clothing	-tyaku
thin, flat objects	-mai
tsubo (area covered by two tatami)	-tubo
vehicles and machines	-dai
weeks	-syuukañ
years	-neñkañ
years of age	-tu/-sai
yen	-eñ

Naming

chome	-tyoome
DK	-d(e)iikee
months	-ğatu
o'clocks	-zi
room numbers	-ğoositu
serial numbers	-bañ

Counting and Naming

days and dates	-ka/-niti
floors	-kai
jo (area covered by one tatami/corresponding room names)	-zyoo
minutes	-huñ
years	-neñ

Index

References are to Lesson, Section, and Structural Pattern: for example, 11B-3 refers to Lesson 11, Section B, Structural Pattern 3. MN refers to Miscellaneous Notes; GUP refers to Greetings and Useful Phrases in the Introduction.
Items designated simply as particles (ptc) are phrase-particles. /Ḡ/ and /ñ/ are alphabetized as /g/ and /n/.

Adjectivals, 1B-1,2; special polite forms, 17B-3, 18A-2; /+ nominal/, 3B-1; sentence modifiers ending in, 19A-1; ending in **-tai** 'want to ——,' 7B-4; /+ **nâru**/, 9A-5. *See also under individual forms*
Affective predicates, 5A-1, 15A-2, 16A-1, 19B-2, 24A-4
Affects: primary and secondary, 5A-1
Affirmative: distal-style: verbal, 1A-1; adjectival, 1B-1; /nominal + copula/, 2A-1; direct-style: verbal, 9A-1, 9B-1; adjectival, 1B-1; /nominal + copula/, 9A-2, 9B-2
Affirming, 1A-4
Age, counting, 10A-1
aḡeru 'give (to out-group),' 17A-1; /gerund +/, 17A-2
Alternate negative stem in **-(a)zu**, 23B-1; use of, 23B-2
Alternate questions, 12A-4; embedded, 18A-3
-(à)nài de, 23B-2
anâta 'you,' 2B-2
añna 'that kind of ——,' 4B-3; /+ **ni**/, 9B-5
ano 'that ——,' 3A-2
|**anoo**| 'uh,' 4B-5
Anticipatory **no**, 19A-2
Approximate numbers, 20A-5
Approximation: **-hodo**, 5B-3; **-ḡòro** and **-ḡùrai**, 8A-3
are 'that thing,' 2B-1
âru 'be located (inanimate),' 'have,' 4A-5, 5A-1; /transitive gerund +/, 16A-2
asoko 'that place,' 6B-1
atira 'that direction,' 'that alternative,' 6A-2
âto: /sentence-modifier +/, 19B-4

Blunt-style, 9A-3
bôku 'I,' 'me,' 3B-2

Careful-style, 8A-4, 9A-3
Casual-style, 8A-4, 9A-3

Chinese series of numerals, 2B-3
Classifiers, 2B-3; time, 8A-1, 8B-4. *See also list at end of English–Japanese glossary and individual listings in Japanese–English glossary*
Clause-particles, 4B-4
Comparison: of two items, 15A-1; of three or more items, 15B-2; of activities, 20A-2
Compounds, 6A-1, 13A-4; verbal compounds in **-suru**, 9B-6; in **-suḡìru**, 15A-3; nominal compounds in **-kata** and **-yoo**, 22B-3; in **-sa**, 24B-1; in **-soo**, 24B-2
Consonant verbals, 9A-1
Consultative: distal-style, 7B-1; direct-style, 20A-6
Copula, 2A-1; following a particle, 8B-2, 11A-2; polite equivalents, 10A-2. *See also under individual forms*
Counting: digits, 2B-3; hundreds, 2B-3; thousands, 2B-3; ten thousands, 3B-2

dà /copula/, 9A-2
dakê 'just,' 5A-2, 23B-3
daròo /copula/, 11A-5
Dates, 8B-4
dàtta /copula/, 9B-2
dè /copula/, 8A-5
de /ptc/ 'by means of,' 7B-2
de /ptc/ 'at,' 7A-1
de gozaimàsu⁺, 10A-2
de (i)rassyaimàsu↑, 10A-2
dekìru 'be possible,' 'can do,' 12B-2
dè mo: /interrogative +/, 21B-3; /nominal +/, 23A-4
dèsita /copula/, 1A-1, 1B-2, 2A-1
dèsu /copula/, 1B-1,2, 2A-1, 4A-5
dèsu nê(e), 13B-3
desyòo /copula/, 6B-2, 9A-6
Direct-style: 7A-5, 9A-3; verbals, 9A-1, 9B-1; adjectivals, 1B-1,2, 10A-6; /nominal + copula/, 9A-2, 9B-2; consultative verbal in **-(y)oo**, 20A-6; tentative copula (**daròo**), 11A-5

395

Distal-style: 7A-5, 9A-3; verbals, 1A-1, 9A-6, 9B-1; adjectivals, 1B-1, 2, 6B-2; /nominal + **desu**/, 2A-1; gerunds, 12A-3; consultative, 7B-1; tentative, 6B-2, 9A-6
dôko 'what place?' 6B-1
dôñna 'what kind of ——?' 4B-3; /+ **ni**/, 9B-5
dôno 'which ——?' 3A-2
dôre 'which thing?' 2B-1
dôtira 'which direction?' 'which alternative?' 6A-2, 15A-1
Double-**ḡa** predicates, 5A-1, 15A-2
Drink, 14A-4
Drinking, verbals of, 15B-1

e /ptc/ 'to,' 7A-1
Eating, verbals of, 15B-1
Embedded questions: alternate, 18A-3; information, 18B-2
Extended predicates, 7B-4, 9B-3; gerund of, 13B-1
Extent, 4B-2

Family, 10A-1, 11A-1, 11B-2
Feminine language, 9A-3
Fillers, 13B-3
Food, 14A-4
Fragments, Introduction

ḡa /ptc/, 4A-3, 11A-2; double-**ḡa** predicates, 5A-1, 15A-2
ḡa /ptc/ ~ **no**, 19A-1
ḡa /clause-particle/, 4B-4
Gentle-style, 9A-3
Gerunds: verbal: 4A-6; /+ **kudasài**/, 4A-6; /+ **kudásaimasèñ ka**/, 7A-3; /+ **kurémasèñ ka**/, 17A-2; /+ **kûru**/, 7A-2, 22A-3; /+ **(i)ru**/, 10B-1; /+ **ôru**/, 15B-3; /transitive + **âru**/, 16A-2; /+ **oku**/, 16A-3; /+ **simau**/, 16B-1; /+ **mîru**/, 19A-4; /+ verbal of giving/, 17A-2; /+ verbal of receiving/, 17B-1; /+ **kara**/, 16B-2; sentence-final in informal requests, 14B-3; adjectival: 13A-3; copula: 8A-5; /affirmative gerund + **mo**/, 21B-1; /negative gerund + **mo**/, 22A-1; /gerund + **wa**/, 22B-1; ending nonfinal clauses, 7B-5; ending minor sentences, 12A-3
giseeḡo, 19B-3
gitaiḡo, 19B-3
Giving, verbals of, 17A-1; /gerund +/, 17A-2
-**ḡòro** 'approximate point in time,' 8A-3
gozáimàsu+ 'be located (inanimate),' 'have,' 5A-3
-**ḡùrai** 'approximate amount,' 8A-3

hazu, 20B-1
Hesitation noises, 4B-5
hodo 'extent'; 'to the extent of,' 'as much as,' 15A-1; 20A-2
-**hodo** 'about as much as,' 5B-3
Honorific-politeness, 7A-5, 9A-3; of **dà**, 10A-2; verbal patterns in /**o-** + verbal stem + **ni** + **nâru**/, 10A-3; /**o-** + verbal stem + **dà**/, 23A-1

hôo 'alternative,' 15A-1, 20A-2
Humble-politeness, 7A-5, 9A-3; verbals in /**o-** + verbal stem + -**suru**/, 7B-3; /**o-** + verbal stem + **dekîru**/, 12B-2
-**hyaku** 'hundreds,' 2B-3

Imperfective: distal-style: verbal, 1A-1; adjectival, 1B-1,2; /nominal + copula/, 2A-1; direct-style: verbal, 9A-1, 10A-6; adjectival, 1B-1,2; /nominal + copula/, 9A-2
Informal requests, sentence-final gerunds in, 14B-3
In-group/out-group, 7A-5
Interrogative: /+ **mo**/, 13A-1; with /gerund + **mo**/ sequences, 21B-3; /+ **ka**/, 24A-2
Intransitive verbals, 16A-1
Introductions, 11B-1
Inverted sentences, 5B-2
Invitations, 1A-3
irássyàru ↑ 'come,' 'be (animate),' 7A-4; 'go,' 8B-3
Irregular verbals, 9A-1
iru 'be located (animate),' 7A-4; following a verbal gerund, 10B-1
itadaku ↓ 'receive (by in-group),' 17B-2; /gerund +/, 17B-2
itâi 'is painful,' 17A-MN
itasu ↓ 'do,' 12B-3
itibañ 'most,' in comparisons, 15B-2
iu 'say,' 'be called,' 12A-1, 18B-1; /—— **yòo ni** +/, 24A-4

Japanese series of numerals, 5A-4

ka /interrogative sentence-particle/, 1A-2; /+ **nê(e)**/, 6B-3
ka, following interrogatives, 24A-2
ka mo sirenai, 13A-2
kara /ptc/ 'from': following nominals, 8B-1, 10B-4; following imperfective and perfective predicates, 11A-2; following verbal gerunds, 16B-2
-**kata** 'way of ——ing,' 22B-3
ke(re)do(mo) /clause-particle/, 4B-4
kimaru/kimeru 'be decided/decide,' 17B-4, 24A-1
koko 'this place,' 6B-1
koñna 'this kind of ——,' 4B-3; /+ **ni**/, 9B-5
kono 'this ——,' 3A-2
kore 'this thing,' 2B-1
kotira 'this direction,' 'this alternative,' 6A-2
kotô 'act,' 'fact,' 21A-4; /—— **kotô ni suru**/, /—— **kotô ni nâru**/, 24A-1
kudásài ↑ 'give me,' 4A-6
kudásaimasèñ ↑ **ka** 'would(n't) you give me?' 7A-3
kudásàru ↑ 'give (to in-group),' 17A-1; /gerund +/, 17A-2; in request patterns, 4A-6, 7A-3, 17A-3
kureru 'give (to in-group),' 17A-1; /gerund +/, 17A-2

Loanwords, 3A-1

mâda 'still,' 'yet': /+ negative predicate/, 14A-1; /+ affirmative predicate/, 14B-2
màde /ptc/ 'as far as,' 7A-1; 'until,' 8B-1; /+ ni/ 'by (a time),' 9A-7
mâe 'before': /verbal +/, 19A-3
mâiru ↓ 'come,' 'go,' 8B-3
Major sentences, Introduction
-mañ 'ten thousands,' 3B-2
Manner, 4A-1, 11A-3
Masculine language, 9A-3
-masyòo, 7B-1
mesiaḡaru ↑ 'eat,' 'drink,' 15B-1
Minor sentences, Introduction
mîru: /verbal gerund +/, 19A-4
-mìtai '——like,' 'as if,' 24A-3
mo /ptc/ 'also,' 'even,' 4B-6, 6A-6; /interrogative +/, 13A-1; /—— mo —— mo/, 5B-4, 21B-1, 22A-1; /affirmative gerund +/, 21B-1; /negative gerund +/, 22A-1
moo /+ quantity/, 5A-5
môo: /+ affirmative predicate/, 14A-1; /+ negative predicate/, 14B-2
môosu ↓ 'say,' 'be called,' 12A-1, 18B-1
morau 'receive (by in-group),' 17B-1; /gerund +/, 17B-2
Multiple particles, 6A-6

ñ /contraction of no/, 7B-4, 9B-3
na /pre-nominal form of dà/, 19B-1; in extended predicates, 9B-3
na-nominals, 5B-1; in patterns of manner, 11A-3
nâ(a) /sentence-particle/, 13A-MN
nâka 'inside,' in comparisons, 15B-2
Narrative style, 19B-5
nâru: /adjectival +/, 9A-5; /nominal + ni +/, 9B-4; /o- + verbal stem +/, 10A-3; /—— kotô ni nâru/, 24A-1; /—— yòo ni nâru/, 24A-4
narubeku 'to the greatest extent possible,' 15B-4
nasâru ↑ 'do,' 12B-3
Necessity, 22B-2
nê(e) /sentence-particle/, 1A-2, 1B-3
Negating, 1A-4
Negative: distal-style: verbal, 1A-1; adjectival, 1B-2; /nominal + copula/, 2A-1; direct-style: verbal, 10A-6; adjectival, 1B-2; /nominal + copula/, 2A-1; questions, 1A-3
Negative permission, 22A-1
Neutral-politeness, 7A-5
ni /ptc/: /place +/, 6A-5, 7A-1; /time +/, 8B-1; /person + ni + kariru/, 10B-4; /nominal + ni + nâru/, 9B-4; /nominal + ni + suru/, 14A-3; /miyaḡe ni kau/, 15A-4; keñkoo ni ìi, 14B-1; in patterns of manner, 4A-1, 11A-3; in patterns of purpose, 16B-3, 20A-1; with verbals of giving, 17A-1,2; with verbals of receiving, 17B-1,2
no ~ ñ /nominal/, 3B-4; in extended predicates, 7B-4, 9B-3, 13B-1; anticipatory no, 19A-2
no /ptc/, 5B-1, 19B-1
no ~ ga /ptc/, 19A-1
no /pre-nominal alternate of the copula/, 5B-1, 9A-4, 19B-1

nò /contraction/, 5B-1
no de, 13B-1
no ni wa, 20A-1
Nominal, 2A-1; na-nominals, 5B-1; /adjectival +/, 3B-1; nominal modifying nominal, 5B-1; /nominal + particle +/, 9A-4; /sentence modifier +/, 19A-1, 19B-1
Nonvolition, 5A-1
Numbers, 2B-3; /nominal + number + particle/, 20A-3; approximate, 20A-5
Numerical nominals: Chinese series, 2B-3; Japanese series, 5A-4

o /ptc/, 4A-6, 7B-2
Okámai nàku. 18A-4
oku: /verbal gerund +/, 16A-3
omôu 'think,' 11A-4
onéḡai-simàsu 'I request,' GUP, 4A-6, 7B-3
Onomatopoeia, 19B-3
Operand, 5A-1
Operational predicates, 5A-1
Operational verbals, 5A-1
Operator, 5A-1
ôru ↓ 'be located (animate),' 7A-4; following a verbal gerund, 10B-1; as neutral-polite (+), 10B-1, 15B-3
ossyàru ↑ 'say,' 'be called,' 12A-1, 18B-1

Particles: sentence-particles, 1A-2; phrase-particles, 3B-3; clause-particles, 4B-4; multiple particles, 6A-6. *See also under individual particles*
Perfective: verbal, 1A-1, 9B-1; /+ nominal/, 21A-1; adjectival, 1B-1; copula, 2A-1, 9B-2; tentative, 9B-2, 11A-5
Permission, 21B-2; negative, 22A-1
Personal referents, 2B-2
Phrase-particles, 3B-3
Phrases, 6A-1
Place-words, 6A-3
Plain-style, 9A-3
Polite adjectivals, 17B-3, 18A-2
Politeness: honorific, humble, and neutral, 7A-5, 9A-3
Polite-style, 9A-3
Polite verbals, special, 9A-1
Predicates: verbal, 1A-1; adjectival, 1B-1; /nominal + copula/, 2A-1; /nominal + particle + copula/, 8B-2; /predicate + particle + copula/, 11A-2; double-ḡa, 5A-1; operational, 5A-1; affective, 5A-1; extended, 7B-4, 9B-3
Pre-nominals, 3A-2
Process: ikû no ni wa, 20A-1
Prohibition, 22B-2
Purpose, 16B-3

Questions: in ka and ne, 1A-2; without question-particle, 6B-2, 8B-5, 14A-2; negative, 1A-3; alternate, 12A-4; embedded alternate, 18A-3; embedded information, 18B-2
Quotation, 18B-1
Quotative particle to ~ (t)te, 11A-4, 12A-1, 18B-1

-rasìi 'apparently is,' 'seems to be,' 24B-3
Recall, perfective in, 8A-2
Receiving, verbals of, 17B-1; /gerund +/, 17B-2
Relationals, 6A-4
Relative time, nominals of, 10A-4
Requests, 4A-6, 7A-3, 14B-3, 17A-3, 18A-1, 18A-4
Ritual, 11B-1

-sa, 24B-1
-sama, 10A-1, 11A-1
-sañ, GUP, 2B-2
sasiağeru ↓ 'give (to out-group),' 17A-1; /gerund +/, 17A-2
sekkakù, 15A-MN
Self-correction, 22B-4
-señ, 'thousands,' 2B-3
señsèe, 2B-2
Sentence modifiers: with verbal and adjectival final predicates, 19A-1; with /nominal + copula/ final predicates, 19B-1; as partitive descriptors, 19B-2
si /clause-particle/ 'and,' 23A-3
sika /ptc/ 'except for,' 21A-2
simau: /verbal gerund +/, 16B-1
siru 'get to know,' 10B-2
soko 'that place,' 6B-1
soñna 'that kind of ——,' 4B-3; /+ **ni**/, 9B-5
sono 'that ——,' 3A-2
-soo /na/ 'looking as if,' 24B-2
sôo da 'that's right,' 2A-2; /predicate +/, 21A-3
sore 'that thing,' 2B-1
sotira 'that direction,' 'that alternative,' 6A-2
Special polite verbals, 9A-1
Spoken narrative style, 19B-5
Stem: verbal, 1A-1, 9A-1, 16B-3; adjectival, 1B-2; adjectival stem in sentence-final position, 18A-4
Style, 1A-1, 8A-4, 9A-3
-suğìru, compounds in, 15A-3
suru: humble verbals in /**o-** + verbal stem +/, 7B-3; verbal compounds in, 9B-6; /nominal + **ni** +/, 14A-3; /adjectival in **-ku** +/, 1B-2, 14A-3; /—— **kotò ni** +/, 24A-1; /—— **yòo ni** +/, 24A-4

-tai 'want to,' 7B-4
tamê 'reason,' 23A-2
Telephone conversations, 12B-1

Telephone numbers, 12A-2
Tentative: **desyòo**, 6B-2, 9A-6; **daròo**, 11A-5
Time when, 4A-1, 8B-1
to /ptc/ 'with': /nominal + **to** + nominal/, 3B-3; nominal + **to** + predicate/, 10B-3; /nominal + **to** + nominal + **to**/, 15A-1; /nominal + **to** + nominal + **to** + nominal **to**/, 15B-2; /—— **ni yoru to**/, 22A-2
to ~ **(t)te** /quotative particle/: /+ **omôu**/, 11A-4; /+ **iu**/, 12A-1, 18B-1
tokî 'time,' 'occasion,' 13A-MN
Transitive verbals, 16A-1
tumori, 20A-4, 20B-2
-tyañ, 11A-1

uti 'interval,' 13B-2; in comparisons, 15B-2

Verbal pairs: transitive and intransitive, 16A-1
Verbals: 1A-1; affective, 5A-1; operational, 5A-1; stem, 7B-3, 16B-3; root, 9A-1. *See also* Affirmative; Consultative; Direct-style; Distal-style; Honorific-politeness; Humble-politeness; Neutral-politeness; Perfective; Imperfective; Negative; Gerund
Volition, 5A-1
Vowel verbals, 9A-1

wa /ptc/, 4A-2; /gerund +/, 22B-1
wa /sentence-particle/, 9A-3
wata(ku)si 'I,' 'me,' 2B-2
Word order, 6A-7

ya /ptc/ 'and,' 15A-5
yaru 'give (to out-group),' 17A-1; /gerund +/, 17A-2
yo /sentence-particle/, 1A-2
yôo /na/ 'manner,' 'resemblance,' 'seeming,' 24A-4
-yoo 'way of ——ing,' 22B-3
yòri /ptc/ 'more than,' 'compared to,' 15A-1, 20A-2
yoru 'depend': X **ni yoru to** 'according to X'; X **ni yotte** 'depending on X,' 22A-2

zibuñ 'oneself,' 17A-MN
zoñziru 'get to know,' 10B-2
-zutu 'each,' 5B-MN
zya, 2A-1, 22B-1
-zyuu 'tens,' 3A-3